The Complete c3 Sicilian [B22]

To Nimet

American Batsford Chess Library

The Complete c3 Sicilian

Murray Chandler

An ICE Book
International Chess Enterprises, Seattle

International Chess Enterprises, Inc.
2005 Fifth Avenue, Suite 402
Seattle, Washington 98121-2850

P.O. Box 19457
Seattle, Washington 98109-1457

First published 1996
Copyright © 1996 by Murray Chandler

Typeset by Petra Nunn
and printed in Great Britain by
Redwood Books, Trowbridge, Wilts
for the publishers,
B. T. Batsford Ltd, 4 Fitzhardinge Street, London W1H 0AH

British Library Cataloging-in-Publication Data.
A catalog record for this book is
available from the British Library.

First published in the United States in 1996 by
International Chess Enterprises, Inc.
Originally published in Great Britain in 1996 by
B. T. Batsford.

ISBN 1-879479-50-8 (An ICE Book: pbk.)

First American edition – 1996

Printed in the United Kingdom
All first editions are printed on acid-free paper

A BATSFORD CHESS BOOK
Editorial Panel: Mark Dvoretsky, Jon Speelman
General Adviser: Raymond Keene OBE
Specialist Adviser: Dr John Nunn
Commissioning Editor: Graham Burgess

Contents

to.. gl see chap-23

Symbols

+	Check
++	Double Check
#	Mate
!	Good move
!!	Excellent move
?	Bad move
??	Serious blunder
!?	Interesting move
?!	Dubious move
±	Small advantage to White
∓	Small advantage to Black
±	Large advantage to White
∓	Large advantage to Black
+−	Decisive advantage to White
−+	Decisive advantage to Black
∞	Unclear position
=	Equal position
1-0	White wins
0-1	Black wins
½-½	Draw
Ch	Championship
Echt	European team championship
Wch	World championship
Wcht	World team championship
OL	Olympiad
Z	Zonal
IZ	Interzonal
Ct	Candidates event
corr	Correspondence game
(n)	nth match game
(D)	Diagram follows

Preface

"It is not easy to play against this line, partly because many people do not consider it a strong move and underestimate it" – Judit Polgar

Since my original book on this subject in 1981, the c3 Sicilian has gone through a remarkable transformation. Of course grandmasters like Sveshnikov and Rozentalis have always played it, and no doubt they always will, but this little second move has also gained a niche in the repertoires of GMs such as Kramnik, Adams, Nunn and J.Polgar, not to mention Anatoly Karpov. Its unexpected blossoming has probably been assisted by the advent of databases – which encourage top players to vary their openings – and faster time limits, which make surprises in the opening harder to deal with.

As the title suggests, this book aims to provide an in-depth reference work. I felt this was needed, as there has been an explosion of games played, and there is simply no modern work of any substance on the variation. Which variations should be classified as main lines were not even clear to me when I started my research this time, as the majority of variations have changed beyond recognition since my first book. I apologise in advance if some of the material is quite heavy. However as you work your way through a line, you

console himself with the pleasant thought that your efforts will certainly be rewarded soon over the board. Unlike many specialised variations, the chances of actually getting the c3 Sicilian are extremely high because it requires such minimal co-operation from the opponent. If Black plays the Sicilian, you get it!

Acknowledgements

Andrew Harley for providing many original ideas from his files, Michael Adams for explaining the entire opening on a flight from Dusseldorf, Graham Burgess for infinite patience through my disgraceful series of missed deadlines, John Nunn for ice-cream and technical assistance over the years, Petra Nunn for typesetting and fabulous meals, and finally John Wareing and Najet Needham for so competently managing the *BCM* Chess Shop in London during my six months of hibernation.

This book was prepared with the aid of the ChessBase program, and, on occasion, the Fritz analysis module (however, errors are entirely my own responsibility). For readers interested in further study a catalogue of top chess software, including ChessBase, can be obtained from the *BCM* Chess Shop, 69 Masbro Rd, Kensington, London W14 OLS, England (phone 0171-603 2877).

1 2...d5: Lines with ...e5

1	e4	c5
2	c3	d5
3	exd5	♕xd5
4	d4 (D)	

The main ...e5 break (4...♘c6 5 ♘f3 cxd4 6 cxd4 e5) received attention from Joe Gallagher when he made it one of his recommendations for Black in his 1994 book *Beating the Anti-Sicilians*. Gallagher contends that the main variation 7 ♘c3 ♗b4 8 ♗d2 ♗xc3 9 ♗xc3 e4 does not deserve its reputation as a poor line for Black, and this view is reasonable. In the principal continuation, 10 ♘e5 ♘xe5 11 dxe5 ♘e7, White has a wide choice, but against exact defence the route to an advantage remains problematic. Yet giving up the bishop pair so early simply does not seem to appeal to top players; the ...e5 defences continue to be used infrequently by Black at grandmaster level.

Game 1
Ubilava – Zaichik
USSR 1976

1 e4 c5 2 c3 d5 3 exd5 ♕xd5

For surprise value Black can try 3...♘f6?!, intending the pawn sacrifice 4 c4 e6 5 dxe6 ♗xe6 with play against White's backward d-pawn. However, after 4 d4 he has nothing better than 4...♕xd5 transposing into standard lines, as 4...cxd4 5 ♗b5+!? ♗d7 (for 5...♘bd7 6 ♕xd4 see Sermek-Nemet below) 6 ♗c4 dxc3 7 ♘xc3 ♘a6 8 ♘f3 ♕a5 9 ♘e5!? b5 10 ♘xd7 bxc4 11 ♘e5 ♘b4 12 0-0 ♖d8 13 ♕f3 gave White a substantial lead in development in the game Chandler-Van der Wiel, Wijk aan Zee 1982.

Black must also contend with 4 ♗b5+ ♘bd7 5 c4 (5 d4 cxd4 6 ♕xd4 g6 7 d6 a6 8 dxe7 ♕xe7+ 9 ♗e2 ♗g7 10 ♘f3 0-0 11 ♕e3 ♖e8 12 0-0 ♕xe3 13 fxe3 ♘b6 14 ♘d4 ♘bd5 15 ♗f3 was ± in Sermek-Nemet, Lucerne 1994, or 5...♕b6 6 c4 cxd4 7 ♘e2 e5 8 dxe6 fxe6 9 ♘xd4 ♗c5 10 ♗e3 0-0 11 0-0 ♘e5 12 ♘c3 ± Blatny-Plachetka, Trnava 1986) 5...a6 6 ♗xd7+!? (6 ♗a4 b5 ∞ Lane-Koch, Geneva 1988) 6...♗xd7 7 ♘f3 e6 8 ♕e2 ♗e7 9 dxe6 ♗xe6 10 0-0 ♗f5 11 ♖e1 ♗d3 12 ♕e5 ♔f8 (12...♗xc4 13 ♕xc5) 13 ♘c3 ♗d6 14 ♕e3! ♗xc4 (14...♘g4 15 ♕xd3! ♗xh2+

16 ♘xh2 ♕xd3 17 ♘xg4) 15 d4 ♕b6 16 ♘e5! ♗b5 17 ♕f3 is clearly better for White, Smagin-Sveshnikov, Amantea 1995.

4 d4 *(D)*

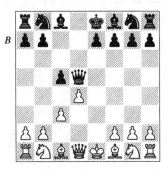

4...♘c6

For 4...g6 see the lines with 2...g6 in Chapter 23.

There are two variations where Black plays an early ...e5 without first developing his queen's knight. After 4...e5 5 dxe5 (5 ♘f3 is also playable, for example 5...e4?! 6 ♘e5 ♗e6 7 ♗c4 ♕d6 8 ♕b3 ± Matanović-Udovčić, Yugoslavia 1953; normally Black continues 5...♘c6 or 5...cxd4 6 cxd4 ♘c6 transposing into lines covered later) Black has:

a) 5...♕xd1+ 6 ♔xd1 ♘c6 7 f4 ♗f5 8 ♘f3 (8 ♗e3 0-0-0+ 9 ♘d2 f6 10 ♘gf3 fxe5 11 ♘xe5 ♘xe5 12 fxe5 ♘h6 13 ♗e2 ♘f7 14 ♖f1 ♗e6 15 ♗f4 g5 16 ♗g3 ♗g7 17 ♖xf7! ♖xd2+ 18 ♔xd2 ♗xf7 19 ♗g4+ ± Afek-Tyomkin, Amsterdam 1994) 8...0-0-0+ 9 ♔e1 f6 10 ♗b5 ♗d7 11 ♘bd2 ♖e8 (11...♘xe5 12 ♘xe5 ♗xb5 13 ♘f7; 11...fxe5!? 12 ♗xc6 ♗xc6 13 ♘xe5 ♗xg2 14 ♖g1 ♗d5 15 c4 ♗e6 16 f5! ± Ftačnik) 12 ♗xc6

♗xc6 13 ♔f2 ♘h6 14 h3 with a slight advantage for White, Rozentalis-Ftačnik, Germany 1994.

b) 5...♕xe5+ 6 ♗e3 (better are 6 ♗e2 ♘c6 7 ♘f3 ♕d6 8 ♕a4 ♗d7 9 ♗f4 ± Perlis-Tartakower, Vienna 1908, or 6 ♘e2!? ♘f6 7 ♘a3 ♗d7 8 ♕b3 ♕d5 9 c4 ♘c6 10 ♘f4 ♘a6 11 ♗e2 0-0-0 12 0-0 ♗f5 13 ♘b5 ♔b8 14 ♘d5! ± Lepeshkin-A.Ivanov, USSR 1981) 6...♘f6 7 ♘f3 ♕c7 8 ♗e2 ♗e7 9 0-0 0-0 = Harley-Mortazavi, British Ch 1994.

The other break is 4...cxd4 5 exd4 e5 6 ♘f3 (6 dxe5 is less effective now) 6...exd4 7 ♕xd4 (7 ♘xd4 ♗c5 8 ♗e3 ♘f6 9 ♘c3 ♕e5 10 ♗b5+ ♗d7 Makropoulos-Armas, Baile Herculane 1984, and now best is 11 0-0 ±) 7 ♕xd4 ♕xd4 8 ♘xd4 a6 (in Cvetković-Sokolov, Belgrade 1954, Black omitted this move but after 8...♘f6?! 9 ♗b5+ ♗d7 10 0-0 ♘c6 11 ♖e1+ ♗e7 12 ♗xc6 bxc6 13 ♘c3 ♘d5 14 ♘xd5 cxd5 15 ♗f4 was unable to get castled) 9 ♘c3 ♘f6 10 ♗g5!. After this old recommendation of Gligorić and Sokolov, White stands better.

5 ♘f3 cxd4

For 5...♘f6 6 ♗e3 e5!? see Chapter 3, Game 5. Instead 5...e5 allows White a safe plus with 6 ♘xe5 ♘xe5 7 dxe5 ♕xe5+ 8 ♗e3, for example 8...♘f6 9 ♗b5+ ♗d7 10 ♗xd7+ ♘xd7 11 ♘a3 ♘b6 12 ♘c4 ♕c7 13 ♘xb6 ± Gipslis-Tal, Riga Ch 1954 or 8...♗d7 9 ♕b3 ♘f6 10 ♘a3 ♗e7 11 ♗b5 ♕c7 12 0-0-0 a6 13 ♕a4 ♖d8 14 ♗xd7+ ♖xd7 15 ♗f4 ♕c8 16 ♖he1 b5 17 ♖xd7 bxa4 18 ♖exe7+ ♔f8 19 ♖xf7+ ♔g8 20 ♖xg7+ ♔f8

21 ♗d6+ 1-0 Okhotnik-Berg Hansen, Lyngby 1990.

Additionally White has 6 dxe5!? ♕xd1+ 7 ♔xd1 ♗g4 8 ♗f4 ♘ge7 9 ♗e2, e.g. 9...♘g6 10 ♗g3 0-0-0+ 11 ♘bd2 ♗xf3 12 ♗xf3 ♘gxe5 13 ♗e2 f5 14 ♔c2 ♗d6 15 ♖ad1 ♖he8 16 ♖he1 g5 17 f4 gxf4 18 ♗xf4 ♘f3 19 ♘xf3 ♗xf4 20 ♗d3 ♖f8 21 g3 ♗b8 22 ♗b5 ♖xd1 23 ♔xd1 ♘d8 24 ♗d3 ♗d6 25 ♘h4 f4 26 ♘f5 ♗c7 27 g4 ± Smagin-Nikac, Yugoslav Ch 1994. A good example of how White maintains a persistent endgame edge after Black regains his pawn.

6 cxd4 e5 *(D)*

The most widely played of the ...e5 breaks. It is unwise for White to continue 7 dxe5?! ♕xd1+ 8 ♔xd1 ♗g4 as Black has the f8-a3 diagonal available to his bishop, e.g. 9 ♘bd2 0-0-0 10 ♗e2 ♗c5 11 ♘g5 ♘h6 12 ♔e1 ♘xe5 13 ♘b3 ♗b4+ 14 ♔f1 ♖he8 ∓ Vollin-Conquest, Brest 1979. However as Black has exchanged pawns on d4, the c3-square is cleared for White's knight.

7 ♘c3 ♗b4 8 ♗d2

An interesting offshoot is the late Sir Stuart Milner-Barry's idea of 8

♗e2!?, when 8...e4 9 0-0! ♗xc3 10 bxc3 exf3 11 ♗xf3 is a dangerous piece sacrifice which Sir Stuart analysed as a win for White. Instead Black gets an unclear game with 8...♘xd4 9 ♗d2 (9 ♘xd4 ♕xd4 10 ♗b5+ ♗d7 alternatively 9 ♕a4+ ♕d7!) 9...♗xc3 (9...♕d6?! 10 ♘xd4 ♕xd4 11 0-0 with good play for the pawn, Finkel-Teplitsky, Israel 1993) 10 ♗xc3 ♘xf3+ 11 ♗xf3 ♕xd1+ 12 ♖xd1 f6 13 ♗a5! (Finkel) 13...♗e6! (Gallagher) and now after 14 ♗xb7 ♖b8 15 ♗c6+ ♔f7 and Black has adequate compensation due to his better development: ...♘e7 is coming with tempo.

Unconvincing is the continuation 8 ♕d2!? ♗xc3 9 bxc3 exd4 10 cxd4 ♘ge7 11 ♗e2 (Rozentalis-Witkowski, Poland 1985) when the suggested 11...♗e6 12 0-0 0-0 13 ♖d1 '±' looks more like '∞' to me.

8...♗xc3 9 ♗xc3 e4

After 9...exd4?! 10 ♘xd4 the position is opened up for White's bishop pair: 10...♘ge7 (10...♘f6 11 ♘xc6 ♕xc6 12 ♗xf6 ♕xf6 13 ♗b5+ ♔f8 14 0-0 ± Van Wijgerden-Glienke, Plovdiv 1983) 11 ♘xc6 ♕xc6 12 ♗e2!? (12 ♗xg7 ♖g8 13 ♗d4 ♗h3 14 ♖c1 ♕e4+ 15 ♗e3 ♗xg2 16 ♖g1 ♗xf1 17 ♖xg8+ ♘xg8 18 ♔xf1 ± Matulović-Cirić, Yugoslav Ch 1956) 12...0-0 13 0-0 ♗e6 14 ♕d4 f6 15 ♖fd1 ± Kavalek-Hermann, Bochum 1981.

10 ♘e5 ♘xe5

10...♘h6 11 ♗c4 ♕d6 12 ♕e2 ♗f5 13 ♖d1 ♖d8 14 0-0 0-0 15 h3 (the problem with Black's 10th is now clear; his h6-knight is badly decentralised) 15...♘xe5 16 dxe5 ♕g6 17 ♖xd8 ♖xd8 18 ♖d1 ♖c8 19 ♖d6 ♗e6 20 ♗d5 ± Ostermeyer-Kaiser, Germany 1987.

11 dxe5 ♘e7 12 ♕e2!? *(D)*

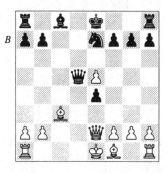

The major alternatives 12 ♕a4+!? and 12 ♕c2 are covered in Game 2. Worthy of serious examination is the underrated 12 ♗e2!, e.g. 12...0-0 13 0-0 ♗d7 (13...♕e6 14 ♕d4 ♕g6 15 ♖fe1 ♘c6 16 ♕e3 ♗f5 17 ♖ad1 ♖ad8 18 h4! ± Smagin-Yagupov, Moscow 1995) 14 ♕c1! (14 ♖e1 ♗c6 15 ♗f1 ♖fe8 16 ♕h5 ♕e6 17 g3 ♕g6 ∓ O'Shaughnessy-Chandler, Newcastle 1996) 14...♗c6 15 ♖d1 ♕e6 16 ♖d6 ♕f5 17 g4!? ♕c8 18 ♕g5 ♕c7?! (18...♘g6 is less clear) 19 ♖ad1 with a powerful bind, Van der Brink-Bezemer, Dutch Ch 1993.

12...0-0 13 ♖d1 ♕c6

13...♕xa2 14 ♗b4! ♕e6 15 ♕xe4 ♖e8 16 ♗b5 ♘c6 17 0-0! ♕g6 (17...♗d7 18 ♖fe1 ♖ad8 19 ♗d6 ♘xe5 20 ♗c7 ♗c6 21 ♖xd8 1-0 Kuijf-Wiersma, Leeuwarden 1995) 18 ♕xg6 hxg6 19 ♗c3 ♗e6 20 ♖d6 ± Anbuhl-Akermann, W.Germany 1982.

14 ♖d6

14 ♗b4 ♖e8 15 ♗xe7 ♖xe7 16 ♖d8+ ♖e8 17 ♖xe8+ ♕xe8 18 ♕xe4 ♗e6 ∞.

14...♕a4 15 ♕c4

15 b3!? ♕a3 16 ♕d2 ♕c5! 17 ♗c4 ♗e6! ∞ Schmittdiel-Hodgson, Bad Wörishofen 1994.

15...♕xc4

15...♕c2!? Hodgson.

16 ♗xc4 ♘f5! 17 ♖d1 ♗e6 18 ♗xe6 fxe6 19 ♔e2 (± according to Ubilava) **19...♖ac8?** (19...♖f7 or 19...♖ad8) **20 ♖d7 ♖f7 21 ♖hd1 ♖c7 22 ♖d8+ ♖f8 23 g4! ♘h6** (23...♘e7 24 ♗b4) **24 h3 ♘f7 25 ♖1d7! +− ♖xd8 26 ♖xc7 ♘g5 27 ♖xb7 ♘xh3 28 ♖xa7 ♖d3 29 ♖a4 ♘g1+ 30 ♔f1 ♘f3 31 ♔g2 ♘h4+ 32 ♔h1 ♖d1+ 33 ♔h2 ♘f3+ 34 ♔g3 ♘g5 35 ♔g2 ♖d3 36 ♖d4 ♖f3 37 ♗d2** (37 ♖xe4? ♖xc3) **37...♘h3 38 ♗e3 ♘f4+ 39 ♔f1 ♘d3 40 ♖xe4 ♘xb2 41 ♔e2 1-0**

Game 2
R.Marić – Rossolimo
Novi Sad 1972

1 e4 c5 2 c3 d5 3 exd5 ♕xd5 4 d4 ♘c6 5 ♘f3 cxd4 6 cxd4 e5 7 ♘c3 ♗b4 8 ♗d2 ♗xc3 9 ♗xc3 e4 10 ♘e5 ♘xe5 11 dxe5 ♘e7 *(D)*
12 ♕a4+

The white queen heads for the a3-f8 diagonal, though it is debatable whether the manoeuvre is worth the two tempi spent. For 12 ♕e2 see Game 1, while the other major try is 12 ♕c2 0-0 (12...♕c6!? intending 13 ♖d1 ♘f5!? ∞, however 13 0-0-0!? ± looks a promising deviation) 13 ♖d1 ♕xa2 when:

a) 14 ♕xe4 ♗f5:

a1) 15 ♗c4 ♗xe4 16 ♗xa2 ♗xg2 leads to exciting tactics: 17 ♖g1 ♗c6 18 e6 f6 19 ♗b4 ♖fe8 20 ♖d7 ♘g6 21 ♖f7 ♖ad8 22 ♖xg6 hxg6 23 e7 ♔h7 24 f3 ♗d5 25 ♔f2 ♗xa2 26 exd8♕ ♖xd8 27 ♖xb7 a6 28 ♗e7 ♗d5 29 ♖c7 ♖b8 30 ♗xf6 ♖b7 ½-½ Nun-Witkowski, Hradec Kralove 1975.

a2) Alternatively 15 ♕c4 ♕xc4 16 ♗xc4 ♖ac8 17 ♗b3 ♗e6 18 ♗xe6 fxe6 19 ♗b4 ♖fe8 20 0-0 ♘d5 with a better endgame for Black in J.Polgar-Kramnik, Monaco rpd 1995.

a3) 15 ♕d4!? ♖ac8 16 ♗e2 ♗c2 17 ♖d2 ♕b1+ 18 ♗d1 ♘c6 19 ♕g4 ♗xd1 20 ♖xd1 ♕g6 21 ♕f3 ♖cd8 22 0-0 h6 with equality, Sveshnikov-Ageichenko, Moscow 1987.

a4) 15 ♕xb7 ♖ad8! (15...♘g6?! 16 ♕a6! ± Chekhov-Novikov, USSR 1976) 16 ♗e2 (16 ♖xd8 ♖xd8 17 ♕xe7 ♕b1+ with perpetual check) 16...♘d5 17 ♗d2 ♖b8 18 ♕a6 ♕xb2 19 0-0 ♕xe5 20 ♗f3 ♘b4 21 ♕xa7 = Daniliuk-V.Ivanov, St Petersburg 1992.

b) 14 ♗b4 ♗g4! (a significant improvement; 14...♕e6 15 ♕xe4 ± transposes to a position examined

via the move-order with 12 ♕e2 in Game 1) 15 ♗xe7:

b1) 15...♗xd1 16 ♕xd1 ♕xb2 17 ♗xf8 and now 17...♖xf8 18 ♗e2 a5 19 ♕d2 ♕b1+ 20 ♗d1 ♕b5 21 ♕d4 ♖e8 22 ♗a4 ♕xe5 23 ♕xe5 ♖xe5 24 ♔e2 b5 25 ♖b1! ± was the game Sveshnikov-Tunik, Moscow 1994, but 17...♕c3+!? 18 ♕d2 ♕a1+ 19 ♔e2 ♕a6+ 20 ♔e3 ♕h6+ 21 ♔e2 ♕a6+ is a draw by perpetual check.

b2) 15...♖fc8! 16 ♕xe4 (after 16 ♕b1 ♕a5+, 17 b4? ♕xe5 18 ♗c5 ♕c3+ 19 ♖d2 ♖xc5! 20 bxc5 ♖d8 21 ♕b2 ♖xd2! -+ and 17 ♖d2 e3! 18 fxe3 ♕xe5 19 ♗h4 ♕xe3+ 20 ♗e2 ♗xe2 21 ♗f2 ♗d3+, winning, are two nice variations given by Afek) 16...♗xd1 17 ♗d3 g6 (Afek-Peretz, Israel Ch 1990) 18 0-0 ♕a4! 19 ♕e3 ♗c2! 20 ♗f6 ♕b4! ∓, as Black's queen can retreat to f8 to cover mate threats.

12...♗d7 13 ♕a3

13 ♕b4! may be the most accurate move-order if White wishes to transpose to the note given after White's 14th move; this occurs after 13...♘c6. Instead 13...a5 14 ♕b6 ♗c6 (14...♕c6 is answered by 15 ♗xa5: 15...♕d5 16 ♗c3 ♖xa2 17 ♖d1 ♕c6 18 ♕xc6 bxc6 19 ♗c4 with an attack; 15...♘d5!? 16 ♕xc6 ♗xc6 17 ♗d2 ± Harley-Gormally, London 1995) 15 ♖d1 ♕xa2 16 ♕c5 gives White a huge initiative for the pawn sacrificed.

13...♕e6! *(D)*

If 13...♗b5!? then 14 ♖d1 ♗d3 15 ♗xd3 exd3 16 0-0 ♘c6 (Mart-Kapungut, Ybbs 1968) 17 ♖fe1 0-0-0 18 ♖e3 ± Boleslavsky, while 13...♗g4

14 h3 ♗h5 15 g4! e3 (15...♗g6 16 ♖d1 ±) 16 ♖h2 ♗g6 17 fxe3 ♕f3 18 ♕a4+ ♘c6 19 ♕f4 ♕d5 20 ♖d2 ♕c5 21 h4 h5 22 0-0-0 ♖c8 23 ♖d5 ♕b6 24 e6 0-0 25 ♖b5 ♕a6 26 ♖xh5 1-0 was Kramnik-Piket, Monaco rpd 1995.

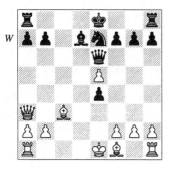

14 ♖d1

In the first editions of *Sicilian 2 c3* I recommended 14 ♕b4 as giving White the advantage. Joe Gallagher disagreed and gave some interesting analysis claiming that Black could equalise:

a) 14...♗c6 15 ♗b5 e3!? (alternatively 15...♘d5!? 16 ♗xc6+ ♕xc6 17 ♕xe4 ♘xc3 18 ♕xc6+ bxc6 19 bxc3 0-0-0 with active play in the rook ending) 16 fxe3 ♘d5 17 ♕c5 ♘xc3 18 bxc3 ♖c8 and White's extra doubled pawn is insignificant.

b) 14...♕c6 15 ♖d1 e3 16 fxe3 ♘d5 17 ♕d4 ♘xc3 18 ♕xc3 ♕xc3 19 bxc3 ♗e6 "and if anyone is better it is Black". While I will agree with Gallagher's analysis in 'a', but I believe 'b' is very murky, e.g. 16 ♖d6!? exf2+ 17 ♔xf2 ♕c7 with a position rich in possibilities for White, for example 18 ♗d3 or 18 ♗b5. This line with 14...♕c6 is particularly significant, since it appears that White can force it by choosing ♕b4 at move 13.

14...0-0 15 ♖d6?

This position has been reached several times. It is obviously tempting to attack the queen, as this mistake is often repeated; the problem is that Black now gains a strong kingside attack. 15 ♗e2 is about equal.

15...♕f5 16 ♗e2 (16 ♗c4 ♘g6 17 0-0 ♘h4 ∓ Luer-Thorsteinsson, Tel Aviv 1964) **16...♗e6! 17 0-0 ♘g6 18 ♗d4 ♘f4 ∓ 19 ♖e1 ♖ac8 20 ♗f1 ♗c4 21 ♕e3 ♗xf1 22 ♔xf1 ♘d3! 23 ♖d1** (23 ♕xe4 ♖c1!! is a nice touch) **23...♕h5 24 ♕e2 ♕xh2 25 ♕xe4 ♖c2! 0-1**

2 4...cxd4

1	e4	c5
2	c3	d5
3	exd5	♛xd5
4	d4	cxd4 *(D)*

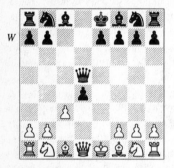

This move-order is usually used if Black is intending to play some line with ...e5 (for example 5 cxd4 ♘c6 6 ♘f3 e5) as already examined in the first chapter. However, if this is not the intention, then 4...cxd4 must be considered a gratuitously premature exchange of pawns by Black. He does not necessarily gain a disadvantage by force, but the move definitely gives White more possibilities about where to put his pieces.

The point is that 4...cxd4 5 cxd4 has freed the c3-square for White's knight very early. It has been accepted wisdom that then Black will have serious tactical problems if he tries any ...♗g4 systems: on 5...♘c6 6 ♘f3 ♗g4, the energetic 7 ♘c3 has long been considered to be a very

strong riposte. However, as can be seen from Game 4, things can no longer be considered so straightforward. But even if this previously discredited line does prove playable for Black, the significance is not enormous, as with the safe alternative 7 ♗e2 White brings the game back into the standard lines covered in Chapter 5. The one case where this move-order could conceivably be to Black's advantage is in avoiding some ♘a3 lines where White usually meets ...cxd4 by ♘b5, followed by capturing on d4 with the knight. Food for thought.

The most prudent follow-up for Black (after 5 cxd4 ♘c6 6 ♘f3) is 6...e6. With the ...♗g4 pin is no longer a worry, White can then seek more active squares for his king's bishop than the e2-square. The bishop can, of course, take up its traditional post on d3, contentedly controlling the b1-h7 diagonal, but White can also be more ambitious. In the variation 7 ♘c3 ♛d8, the bishop can also develop to the c4-square – giving an excellent IQP position by analogy with some other openings.

It should be noted that the position after 4...cxd4 can also arise via a Morra Gambit Declined move order: 1 e4 c5 2 d4 cxd4 3 c3 d5 4 exd5 ♛xd5.

Game 3
Harley – Dixon
England 1986

1 e4 c5 2 c3 ♘c6 3 d4 cxd4 4 cxd4 d5 5 exd5 ♕xd5

Via an unusual move-order (2...d5 3 exd5 ♕xd5 4 d4 cxd4 5 cxd4 ♘c6 is standard) we reach the normal position after Black's early pawn swap on d4. Now 6 ♘c3 ♕xd4 7 ♗d2 or 7 ♗e3 would actually be a transposition, with colours reversed, to the speculative Hennig-Schara Gambit (1 d4 d5 2 c4 e6 3 ♘c3 c5 4 cxd5 cxd4 5 ♕xd4 ♘c6 6 ♕d1 exd5 7 ♕xd5). I'm sure readers want more with White from the c3 Sicilian than this theoretically challenged pawn sacrifice; however if you want more information look under D32 in volume D of *ECO*, the Encyclopaedia of Chess Openings.

6 ♘f3 ♗g4

The most prudent move is 6...e6, when transposition to later chapters is highly likely if White chooses to develop his bishop to d3 (or e2). But he can also try for more. After 7 ♘c3 there is:

a) 7...♗b4?! 8 ♗d3 ♘f6 9 0-0 ♕d8 (9...♗xc3 10 bxc3 is very pleasant for White) 10 a3 ♗e7 11 ♖e1 0-0 12 ♗c2 (Tal-Arbouche, Seville 1989) and White is a tempo ahead of a main-line position. Not surprisingly this proved to be swiftly terminal for the lowly-ranked player of the black pieces.

b) 7...♕d8 8 ♗c4! (there is nothing wrong with 8 ♗d3, but this is stronger) 8...♘f6 9 0-0 ♗e7. Here we

have a position which can arise from a myriad of openings (Queen's Gambit Semi-Tarrasch, Queen's Gambit Accepted, Caro-Kann...), with one major difference being that, compared to some of these transpositions, here White is already a tempo ahead! For example, Sveshnikov-Tal, Riga 1973, opened 1 e4 c6 2 d4 d5 3 exd5 cxd5 4 c4 ♘f6 5 ♘c3 e6 6 ♘f3 ♗e7 7 ♗d3 dxc4 8 ♗xc4 ♘c6 9 0-0 with exactly the same position, except it is Black's move instead of White's. This gained tempo for White (via our c3 Sicilian move-order) gives Black an unpleasant defensive task, for example 10 ♖e1 (10 a3!? 0-0 gives a direct transposition to yet another opening, an E57 Nimzo-Indian) 10...0-0 11 ♗g5 b6 12 a3 ♗b7 13 ♕d3 ♘d5 14 ♗xd5 ♗xg5 15 ♗e4 h6 16 ♖ad1 ♖e8 17 d5 exd5 18 ♘xd5 ♔f8 19 ♕b5 ♕c8 20 h4 ♗d8 21 ♘b4 ♖e6 22 ♖c1 a6 23 ♕f5 ♗e7 24 ♕h7 ♗xb4 25 axb4 1-0 Andersson-Morović, Lucerne OL 1982. Actually the game lasted only 24 moves, as the opening move-order was different – if you are confused you should imagine what it is like for the author! For further study the Queen's Gambit Accepted, *ECO* code D26, gives coverage of the exact position arising after White's ninth move, assessed by Ribli as ±.

c) 7...♕d6!? cannot be refuted directly:

c1) 8 ♘b5 and after 8...♕d8, one outright attempt, 9 ♗f4, can be met by 9...♗b4+ 10 ♘d2 ♗a5! 11 ♘d6+ ♔e7; also possible is 8...♕b8 9 g3 ♗b4+ 10 ♗d2 ♗xd2+ 11 ♕xd2 ♘f6

12 ♗g2 0-0 B.Stein-Marxen, Germany 1981.

c2) 8 ♗c4 ♘f6 9 0-0 ♗e7 10 ♘b5 ♕d8 11 ♗f4 0-0 12 ♗c7 ♕d7 13 ♘e5 ♘xe5 14 dxe5 ♘e8 15 ♗a5 b6 16 ♗c3 a6 17 ♘d4 (or 17 ♕xd7 ♗xd7 18 ♘d4 ♘c7 with equality, Striković-Dlugy, New York Open 1988) 17...♘c7 18 ♕g4 b5 19 ♗b3 ♘d5 20 ♗d2 ♖d8 ∞ Nun-Haba, Prague Ch 1986.

c3) 8 ♗d3 and 8 ♗e3 are of course standard, and will inevitably transpose to later chapters.

7 ♘c3 *(D)*

7...♕a5?

7...♗xf3 8 gxf3 ♕xd4 9 ♕xd4 ♘xd5 10 ♘b5 is the subject of the next game.

8 d5 ± ♘e5

On 8...0-0-0, 9 ♗d2 followed by ♘b5 is very strong. 8...♖d8 fails likewise: 9 ♗d2 ♘d4 10 ♘b5 ♗xf3 11 ♗xa5 ♗xd1 12 ♖xd1 ♘c2+ 13 ♔d2 b6 14 ♗c3 a6 15 ♘c7+ ♔d7 16 ♘xa6 1-0 B.Stein-Kjeld, Gausdal 1992 alternatively 9...♘b4 10 a3 ♘a6 (10...♘xd5 11 ♗b5+ ♗d7 12 ♘xd5) 11 ♘b5 ♕b6 12 ♕a4 ♗d7 13 ♗a5 ♘c5? 14 ♗xb6 ♘xa4 15 ♘c7#!

was the abrupt finish of R.G.Lee-Clements, Hastings 1966/7.

9 ♘xe5

The queen 'sacrifice' has been played several times with success. Also promising is 9 ♗b5+ ♗d7 10 ♘xe5!? (10 ♗e2) 10...♗xb5 11 ♕f3 ♘f6 12 d6 ♖b8 13 b4 ♕b6 14 ♘xb5 exd6? (14...♕xb5 15 d7+ ♘xd7 16 ♕xf7+ ♔d8 17 ♘xd7 ♕xb4+ 18 ♗d2 ♕e4+ 19 ♗e3 ♕b4+ 20 ♔e2 ±) 15 ♕e2! ♗e7 16 ♘c4 and White had won a piece, Risino-Jyanter, Venice 1963.

9...♗xd1 10 ♗b5+ ♔d8 11 ♘xf7+ ♔c8 12 ♔xd1 g6

12...♘h6 13 ♘xh8 e5 14 dxe6 ♗b4 15 ♗d7+ ♔c7 16 ♘b5+ ♔b6 17 ♗e3+ ♔a6 18 a3 and White has more than enough material for the queen, Kirillov-Skuja, Latvian Ch 1965.

13 d6 exd6 14 ♖e1 b6 15 ♗d2 ♕b4 16 ♖e4 ♕c5 17 ♖c4 1-0

Game 4
Mes – Van der Meiden
Corr 1991

This obscure Dutch correspondence game, which I stumbled across in my research, threatened to become that nightmare all chess authors dread: a tiny sideline which may just alter the evaluation of a much bigger variation.

1 e4 c5 2 ♘f3

Yet another move-order to reach a c3 Sicilian. The normal route to the position at move 6 would be 2 c3 d5 3 exd5 ♕xd5 4 d4 cxd4 5 cxd4 ♘c6 6 ♘f3 ♗g4.

2...♘c6 3 d4 cxd4 4 c3 d5 5 exd5 ♕xd5 6 cxd4 ♗g4 7 ♘c3

Of course 7 ♗e2 in possible, when the game should soon transpose into lines covered in Chapter 5.

7...♗xf3 8 gxf3 ♕xd4 9 ♕xd4 ♘xd4 10 ♘b5! *(D)*

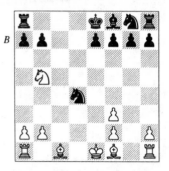

Theory's verdict on this dangerous sacrificial idea of Kirillov's had hitherto been unequivocal: that Black is in big trouble due to his lagging development.

10...♘c2+

ECO (the Encyclopaedia of Chess Openings) doesn't even bother to mention this knight fork! Alternatives have long been known to favour White:

a) 10...♘e6 11 f4! a6 (11...g6 12 ♗g2 0-0-0 13 ♗e3 a6 14 ♖c1+ ♔b8 15 ♗a7+ ♔a8 16 ♗b6 axb5 17 ♗xd8 ♘xd8 18 ♖c8+ ± The King-Amy II, 13th World Microcomputer Ch 1995) 12 f5 axb5 13 ♗xb5+ ♔d8 14 fxe6 fxe6 15 ♗e3 (Black's king is caught in the crossfire of the white bishops) 15...♘f6 16 ♗b6+ ♔c8 17 ♖c1+ and wins, Kirillov-Salati, Riga 1964.

b) 10...e5 11 ♘c7+ ♔d7 12 ♘xa8 ♗b4+ 13 ♔d1 (clearer than 13 ♗d2 ♘xf3+ 14 ♔e2 ♘d4+ 15 ♔d3 ♗xd2 16 ♔xd2 ♘e7 17 f4 Afek-Sobrecases, Montpellier 1985, when if 17...♖xa8 18 ♖d1 Afek assesses the position as ±) 13...♘e7 14 ♗h3+ f5 15 f4 ♗d6 16 fxe5 ♗xe5 17 ♗e3 ♘ec6 18 ♗xd4 ♘xd4 19 ♖e1 ♗f6 20 ♖c1 ♖xa8 21 ♖c4 and White remains the exchange up for a pawn, Hermann-Jacob, Esbjerg 1978.

c) 10...0-0-0 11 ♘xd4 ♖xd4 12 ♗e3 ♖d7 13 ♗b5 ♖c7 14 ♗xa7 e6 (14...e5 doesn't help: 15 ♗b6 ♗b4+ 16 ♔d1 ♖e7 17 ♖c1+ ♔b8 18 ♗d8! as in Zaitsev-Menkov, Leningrad 1966 as 18...♖e6 fails to 19 ♖c4) 15 ♗b6 ♖c2!? (Black's rook was trapped after 15...♗b4+ 16 ♔d1! +– Hennings-Bindrich, East Germany 1969: if 16...♖e7, 17 ♗d8) 16 0-0 ♘e7 17 ♖ac1 ♖xc1 18 ♖xc1+ ♘c6 19 a4 ♔b8 20 a5 ± Rohde-Seltzer, Los Angeles 1991.

11 ♔d1 ♖c8!?

Apart from this game there is only one known example with this move. More common has been 11...♘xa1 12 ♘c7+ ♔d7 13 ♘xa8 when, whilst in spite of a few quick white victories, Black's position can prove irritatingly resilient:

a) 13...e6 14 ♗e3 b6 15 ♗a6 ♘f6 16 ♗b7 ♗d6 17 ♔d2 ♖b8! 18 ♗a6 ♖xa8 19 ♖xa1 ♗xh2 Lund-Lampe, RLNS 1988-9, and Black went on to win. White must try another approach: 15 ♗b5+! ♔c8 16 ♔e2 ♔b7 17 ♖xa1 ♔xa8 18 ♖d1 and Black's kingside pieces are still spectators.

b) 13...g6 14 ♗e3 (14 ♗b5+ ♔c8 15 ♗e3 ♔b8 16 ♔e2 was my old recommendation, but 16...♗g7! looks unclear) 14...♗h6 (14...b6 15 ♗b5+

♔c8 16 ♗f4 ♗h6 17 ♗a6+ ♔d7 18
♗g3 ♘f6 19 ♘c7 e6 20 ♔e2 ♘c2 21
♖d1+ ♔c6 22 ♗e5 ♖f8 23 ♗xf6
♔xc7 24 ♗b5 ♗f4 25 ♖d7+ ♔b8 26
♖e7 ♖c8 27 ♗a6 e5 1-0 Wuhrmann-
Guiot, Paris 1993) 15 ♗b5+ (15
♗xa7 ♘f6 16 ♘b6+ ♔c7 17 ♗d3
♖d8 18 ♔e2 ♘c2! and the black
knight emerged in Geyer-Schafra-
nietz, Germany 1994) 15...♔d6 16
♗xa7 ♘f6 17 ♘b6 ♖d8 18 ♔e2 ♘c2
19 ♖d1+ ♔c7 20 ♖xd8 ♔xd8 21
♘c4 ♗f4 Crouch-Balinas, London
Lloyds Bank 1979. This endgame is
not clear, but interesting is Patrick
Wolff's suggestion in *Chess Life* of
22 a3, e.g. 22...♗xh2 23 ♗a4 ♘a1
24 ♗d4 ♘d5 25 b4 b5 26 ♗xb5 ♘b3
27 ♗b2 when White retains the better chances.

12 ♘xa7 ♖c5 13 b4

Of course White is no longer material down, and can always bail out
at this stage with 13 ♗e3 ♘xe3+ 14
fxe3 when the endgame is level.
However the pawn sacrifice 13 b4
has always been assumed to refute
Black's choice of defence.

13...♘xb4 14 ♗b5+ ♔d8!

With a neat defensive idea in
mind. Instead 14...♘c6 15 ♗e3 ♖d5+
16 ♔e2 gave White an unpleasant
lead in development in Smart-Nord-
ström, Student Teams 1963.

15 ♗e3 e6! *(D)*

This fine move could conceivably
make this whole variation playable

for Black. Now after 16 ♗xc5 ♗xc5
White's a7-knight would be doomed.

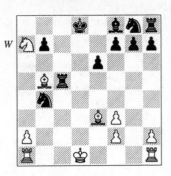

16 ♗a4 ♘f6!

16...♖d5+?! 17 ♔e2 still looks
dangerous for Black, but now White
has nothing better than to accept the
proffered exchange sacrifice. Black's
compensation is at least sufficient: a
pawn plus the far superior pawn
structure, plus excellent outposts for
his pieces.

**17 ♗xc5 ♗xc5 18 ♘b5 ♔e7 19
♔e2 ♘fd5 20 ♖hd1 h5 21 ♖ac1 b6
22 a3 ♘f4+ 23 ♔f1 ♘bd5 24 ♗b3
h4 25 a4 ♖a8 26 ♘c3 ♘xc3 27 ♖xc3
g5 28 ♖c2 ♖a7 29 ♖cd2 ½-½**

It may be that improvements are
found for White in this double-edged
line; certainly Black's total lack of
kingside development requires defensive nerves of steel from the second player. Nevertheless we can
certainly say that, in the past, Black's
defensive resources in the position
after 10 ♘b5 have been under-rated.

3 4...♘f6 (including 5 ♘f3 ♘c6!?)

1	e4	c5
2	c3	d5
3	exd5	♕xd5
4	d4	♘f6
5	♘f3	♘c6 (D)

Even in the second (1987) edition of *Sicilian 2 c3* there were scarcely any examples of players using this astute move-order. Since then, however, it has become highly popular. I recommended it at the time for attempting to cancel out White's entire ♗d3 systems (6 ♗d3 ♗g4!), since Black's idea is that White must develop his bishop at the less active e2-square. After 6 ♗e2 Black then plays 6...e6, reaching the less critical lines examined in Chapter 6.

But White has not been idle. In this section we examine interesting alternatives that aim to exploit Black's move-order. A principled challenge is 6 dxc5!? (Game 5). Some very strong grandmasters indeed (Ljubojević, Judit Polgar...) have been comprehensively wiped out as Black by this deceptively dangerous pawn capture. However, with accurate play White has only a minimal plus.

Therefore 6 ♗e3 has also emerged as a sound response, as it commonly brings Black back into standard lines examined in later chapters. After 6...cxd4 7 cxd4 e6 8 ♘c3 ♕d6, for example, White can continue 9 a3! ♗e7 10 ♗d3 and the king's bishop has, after all, occupied its rightful diagonal. True, White has committed his other bishop quite early to the e3-square, but this move-order has resulted in this system becoming the modern main line of the 2...d5 defence (see Chapter 10). If Black should try to cut across this plan with the esoteric 6...♘g4!? remains unclear.

The third try for White, 6 ♘a3, just doesn't work in this particular position – a quick ...♗g4 and ...0-0-0 by Black gives easy equality.

Game 5
Blatny – Bönsch
Brno 1993

1 e4 c5 2 c3 d5 3 exd5 ♕xd5 4 d4 ♘f6 5 ♘f3

Alternatives:

a) 5 ♘a3!? cxd4 6 ♘b5 ♘a6 7 ♕xd4 e5! 8 ♕a4 ♗d7 (8...♕e4+!?) 9 ♗e3 ♕c6 10 0-0-0 (10 ♘f3 ♘c5 11 ♕c4 ♘g4 12 ♕d5 ♘e6 13 0-0-0 ♕xd5 14 ♖xd5 ½-½ Svveshnikov-Petursson, Belgrade 1988) 10...♗c5 11 ♘f3 ♗xe3+ 12 fxe3 ♕c5 13 ♕a3 ♕xa3 14 ♘xa3 ♘g4! 15 ♗xa6 bxa6 16 ♖d6 f6 = Vorotnikov-Kholmov, Moscow 1995.

b) 5 ♗e3 ♗g4!? (avoiding normal lines with 5...cxd4 or 5...e6) 6 f3 (6 ♘e2 cxd4 7 cxd4 e5?! 8 ♘bc3 ♕a5 9 dxe5 ♕xe5 10 ♕b3 b6 11 ♗d4 ± Van Mil-Stangl, Reykjavik 1993) 6...cxd4 7 ♕xd4 ♘c6 8 ♕xd5 ♘xd5 9 ♗f2 (9 ♗xa7 ♘xa7 10 fxg4 ♘e3) 9...♗f5 10 ♘d2 g6 with a fine game for Black, Handoko-Magomedov, Bangladesh 1995.

5...♘c6 *(D)*

6 dxc5!?

Giving Black a difficult decision. Recapturing with 6...♕xc5 leads to a position where White can later gain time attacking the black queen (with moves like ♗e3). However 6...♕xd1+ 7 ♔xd1 is a murky gambit of the c5-pawn.

Instead of 6 dxc5 White can also try 6 ♘a3, but Black has no problems after 6...♗g4 7 ♗e2 (7 ♘b5 ♗xf3) 7...cxd4 (the plan of queenside castling is suddenly very logical here for Black; 7...e6 is reasonable, though after 8 h3 ♗h5 9 ♗e3 cxd4 10 ♘b5 ♖c8 11 ♘bxd4 Black erred in Pirrot-Ftačnik, Lugano 1987, with 11...♗c5?! 12 ♘xe6! ♕xe6 13 ♗xc5 ♗xf3 14 gxf3 ♘e5 15 ♗a3 and White has the initiative) 8 ♘b5 0-0-0! (8...♖c8) 9 ♘bxd4 e5 10 ♘xc6 ♕xc6 11 ♕c2!? (11 ♕b3 can be answered by 11...♗e6 12 c4 ♗c5 13 h3 ♕e4 ∓ Schmittdiel-Andersson, Dortmund 1987, while 11...♗c5 ∓ is also good, Petronić-Cvetković, Yugoslavia 1995) 11...♗c5! 12 0-0 ♖he8! 13 ♘g5! ♗xe2 14 ♕xe2 ♖d7 15 ♗e3 h6 = Haba-Stoica, Eforie Nord 1988.

6 ♗e3!? is the fashionable response, when Black usually transposes back into standard channels with 6...cxd4 7 cxd4 e6, a commonly used move-order to reach positions dealt with in Chapter 10. Black can also try to mix things up:

a) 6...e5!? (this recent try may soon receive more attention; compared with the ...e5 breaks in Chapter 1, here the white bishop on e3 can be targeted by Black's knight) 7 dxe5 (7 c4 ♕d6 8 d5 ♘d4 ∞ Demarre-Duncan, Paris-London 1994 or 7 ♘xe5 ♘xe5 8 dxe5 ♕xd1+ 9 ♔xd1 ♘g4 10 ♘a3 ♘xe3+ 11 fxe3 ♗g4+ 12 ♗e2 0-0-0+ 13 ♔e1 ♗e6 14 ♗c4 ♗e7 15 ♖f1 ♗xc4 16 ♘xc4 ♖hf8 17 a4 ♔d7 18 ♔e2 ♔e6 19 ♖f4 ± A.Sokolov-Duncan, Gausdal 1996, but this latter example does not look too convincing for White) 7...♕xd1+ 8 ♔xd1 ♘g4 9 ♘bd2 (9 ♗b5 ♘xe3+ 10 fxe3 ♗d7 11 ♗xc6 ♗xc6 12 c4 g6 13 ♘c3 ♗g7 = Saint Amand-Donaldson, Bermuda 1995) 9...♘xe3+ 10 fxe3 ♗e7 11 ♗c4 ♗g4 12 h3 ♗h5 13 g4 ♗g6 14 e4 0-0-0 15 ♗d5 ♔c7 16 ♔e2 ♖he8 17 e6 fxe6 18 ♗xc6 (18 ♗xe6!? ±) 18...♔xc6 19 ♘e5+ ♔c7 20 ♘xg6 hxg6 21 ♖af1 ♖f8 22 ♖xf8 ♖xf8 23 ♘f3 g5 24 ♖d1 ♖f4 25 ♘d2 ½-½ Motwani-Ward, British Ch 1994.

b) 6...♘g4 and here:

b1) 7 ♗g5?! h6 8 ♗h4 g5 9 ♗g3 f5! 10 h3 f4 ∓ Striković-N.Nikolić, Yugoslavia 1991.

b2) 7 ♗d3 ♘xe3 (Black can also try for an ...e5 break: 7...cxd4?! 8 cxd4 e5 9 ♘c3 ♗b4 10 0-0 ♗xc3 11 bxc3 e4 12 c4 ♕f5 13 ♗c2 0-0 14 ♘d2 favoured White in B.Filipović-Smolović, Kladovo 1992 while 7...e5 8 0-0! c4!? 9 ♗e2 ♘xe3 10 fxe3 e4 11 ♘fd2 ♕g5 12 ♘xe4 ♕xe3+ 13 ♘f2 ♗d6 14 ♗xc4 0-0 15 ♘d2 ♗f5 was a plausible pawn sacrifice that ultimately fell short in B.Filipović-Zakić, Kladovo 1992) 8 fxe3 e6 9 0-0 ♗e7 10 ♕c2 ♕h5! 11 ♘bd2 0-0 12 ♗e4!? ♗d7 13 ♘c4 ♖ad8 14 ♘fe5?! (in his notes Serper suggests the improvement 14 ♖f2!?, intending 15 ♖af1, without giving an assessment) 14...♘xe5 15 ♘xe5 ♗c8 16 ♖f3 f5! ∓ Lautier-Serper, Dortmund 1993.

b3) 7 ♘bd2!? (the threat of 8 ♗c4 discourages ...e5 and also other black possibilities) 7...cxd4 (7...♘xe3 8 fxe3 e6 9 ♗c4 ♕d8 Finkel-Sermek, Groningen 1994, and now Finkel gives 10 ♘e4! cxd4 11 exd4 ♗e7 12 0-0 0-0

13 ♕c2!? b6 14 ♖ad1! ♗b7 15 d5 exd5 16 ♗xd5 ♕c7 17 ♘eg5! ♗c5+ 18 ♔h1 ±; 7...e6 8 ♗c4 ♕d8 9 ♗g5!? ♘f6 10 ♘b3 cxd4 11 ♘bxd4 also gave White a tiny edge in the game Finkel-A.Shneider, Groningen 1993) 8 cxd4 ♘xe3 9 fxe3 e6 10 ♗d3 ♗e7 11 0-0 0-0 and now 12 ♗e4 ♕d8 (12...♕h5 13 ♘c4 ♗d7 14 ♘fe5 ♕xd1 15 ♖fxd1! ♗e8 16 ♖ac1 with unpleasant pressure against c6) 13 ♕c2 g6 14 ♘c4! (14 ♗xc6 bxc6 15 ♕xc6 ♖b8 16 ♕c2 ♗b7) 14...♗d7 15 ♘fe5 ♘xe5 16 ♘xe5 ♖b8 17 ♖f3! ± Finkel.

6...♕xc5

Or 6...♕xd1+!? 7 ♔xd1 and now:

a) 7...e5 8 b4 ♗f5 9 ♗c4! (9 ♗b5 transposes to positions covered in the following note while the line 9 ♗e3 ♘d5 10 ♔c1!? a5 11 b5 ♘d8 12 ♘xe5 ♘xe3 13 fxe3 ♗xc5 14 ♗c4 ♗xe3+ 15 ♔b2 0-0 16 ♖f1 ∞ was Rausis-Wirthensohn, Switzerland 1990) 9...0-0-0+ 10 ♔e2 ♗e7 11 ♘g5 ♖hf8 12 ♘xf7 ♖d7 13 ♗e3 ♘d5 14 ♘d6+ ♗xd6 15 ♗xd5 ♗e7 16 ♗c4 e4 17 h3 ♗f6 18 g4 ♗g6 19 b5 ± Schmittdiel-Donaldson, Liechtenstein 1994.

b) 7...♗f5 and then:

b1) 8 ♗c4!? is still interesting, by analogy with the line above, though Black can now blunt the bishop's diagonal with 8...e6. Treffert-Schuh, Germany 1989 continued 9 b4 a5 10 b5 ♘b8 11 c6 bxc6 12 bxc6 ♘xc6 13 ♗b5 0-0-0+ 14 ♔e2 ♘b8 15 ♘d4 ♗e4 16 f3 ♗b7 17 ♘b3 ∞.

b2) Instead 8 ♗e3 0-0-0+ 9 ♔e1 is Sveshnikov-Ugoltsev, USSR 1970 when *ECO* gives 9...♘d5! 10 ♗b5

e5 11 ♗xc6 bxc6 12 ♘xe5 ♖e8 ∞.
See also the 6...♗f5 reference in
Game 10.

b3) 8 ♗b5 e5 9 b4 0-0-0+ 10
♔e2 ♗e7!? (10...♘d5 11 ♗xc6 bxc6
12 ♗d2 f6 ∞ Blatny-Gross, Czechoslovak Ch 1988) 11 ♗e3 ♘d5 12
♗xc6 (as this pawn grabbing spectacularly backfires, 12 ♖c1 intending ♘a3-c4 was to be considered
according to Blatny) 12...bxc6 13
♘xe5 ♖he8! ∓ 14 ♘xf7?! (14 ♘xc6
♗g4+ 15 f3 ♖d7 16 fxg4 ♗g5 gives
Black a raging attack) 14...♘xe3 15
♘xd8 ♘c4 16 ♘xc6 ♗f6+ 17 ♔d1
♘b2+! 18 ♔c1 ♘d3+ 19 ♔c2 ♘xb4+
20 ♔b3 ♘xc6 21 ♘a3 ♖e7! 22 ♘b5
♖b7 23 a4 a6 24 c4 ♘d4+ 0-1 Ser-
mek-Wirthensohn, Mitropa Cup
1993. For information it should be
noted that this game used the move-
order 7...e5 8 b4 ♗f5 9 ♗b5.

The reader should also refer to
Chapter 5, Game 10, for similar
lines.

7 ♘a3! (D)

With irritating ideas of ♘b5 or
♘c4 followed by ♗e3. The immediate 7 ♗e3!? allows Black's queen access to the a5-square, but can still be
dangerous: 7...♕a5 8 ♘a3 ♗g4
(8...♘d5!? Bönsch; 8...e6!? 9 ♘b5
♘d5 10 ♗d2 ♕b6 11 c4 ♘f6 12 ♗d3
a6 13 ♘c3 ♗e7 14 a3 ∞ Schmittdiel-
Berg, Gausdal 1987) 9 ♕b3! 0-0-0 10
♘g5 ♘d4 11 ♕c4+ ♔b8 12 ♗xd4
♕xg5 13 ♘b5 +– was Schmittdiel-
J.Polgar, Dortmund 1990.

7...e5

Alternatives:

a) 7...e6 8 ♘b5 ♕e7 9 b3 a6 10
♗a3 ♕d8 11 ♘d6+ ♗xd6 12 ♕xd6

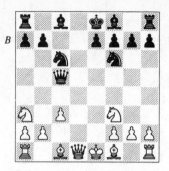

♕xd6 13 ♗xd6 ♘e4 14 ♗a3 ♘xc3
15 ♗b2 ♘d5 16 ♗xg7 ♖g8 17 ♗b2
b5 ∞ Kharlov-Tolnai, Budapest 1992;
by analogy with the main line White
should play 11 ♗xf8 ±.

b) 7...♕a5 8 ♗f4 ♗g4 (8...♕f5?!
9 ♗g3 a6 10 ♗d3 ♕e6+ 11 ♗e2! g6
12 0-0 ♗h6 13 ♖e1 ♕d5 14 ♘c4
♗e6 15 ♘b6 ± Blatny-Basin, Trnava
1989) 9 ♗e2 ♘d5 10 ♗d2 ♖d8 11 c4
♘db4 12 0-0 a6 ∞ Mukhametov-
Mikhalets, Yalta 1995.

c) 7...♗d7 8 ♗e3 ♕a5 9 ♕b3 e6
10 ♘c4 ♕c7 11 ♘d4 ♘xd4 12 ♗xd4
♗c5 13 ♗xc5 ♕xc5 14 ♕xb7 0-0 15
♕f3 ♗b5 16 ♕e3 ♕e7 17 ♗e2 ♖ac8
18 ♘e5 ♘d5 19 ♕f3 ♕g5 20 ♕g3
♕xg3 21 hxg3 with an extra pawn
for White in the endgame, Sermek-
Zso.Polgar, Vienna 1991.

d) 7...♘g4!? (a major branch) 8
♕e2 ♗f5 (8...a6?! proved disastrous
for the super-GM playing Black in
Blatny-Ljubojević, Antwerp 1994:
after 9 h3 ♘ge5 10 ♗e3 ♘xf3+ 11
♕xf3 ♕f5 12 ♕g3!? ♕e5?! 13 f4!
♕c7 14 ♘c4 ♗e6 15 ♗b6 ♕c8 16
♕e3! ♗xc4 17 ♗xc4 e6?! 18 f5!
♘e7 19 ♗b3 ♘xf5 White merci-
lessly hunted down the opposing
king with 20 ♗a4+ ♔e7 21 ♕d3!

♕b8 22 ♕d7+ ♔f6 23 0-0 ♔g6 24 ♗c2 ♕e5 25 ♖ae1 ♗c5+ 26 ♔h1 ♔h6 27 ♗xf5 1-0) 9 h3 ♗d3 (9...♘ge5 10 ♗e3 ♕a5 11 ♘xe5 ♘xe5 12 ♕b5+ ♕xb5 13 ♘xb5 ♖d8 14 ♗xa7 ± was Sermek-Estrada, Ljubljana 1994) 10 ♕xd3!? (giving up the queen for rook and two minor pieces looks far more promising than the 10 ♕d2 10 ♗xf1 11 ♖xf1 of Hraček-I.Sokolov, Pardubice 1994) 10...♕xf2+ 11 ♔d1 ♖d8 12 ♕xd8+ ♔xd8 13 hxg4 e6 14 ♘c4 ♗e7 15 ♗e3 ♕g3 16 g5 h5 17 ♔e2! e5? 18 ♖h4 +− ♗xg5 19 ♗xg5+ f6 20 ♖d1+ ♔c7 21 ♘e3 fxg5 22 ♖h3 1-0 Blatny-Wang Zili, Thessaloniki OL 1988.

8 ♘b5

8 ♗e3!? ♕a5 (8...♕e7 9 ♗b5! ♘g4 10 ♘c4 ♘xe3 11 fxe3 f6 12 ♕a4 ♕c7 13 0-0-0 ± Sveshnikov-A.Shneider, Podolsk 1993) 9 ♘c4 ♕c7 10 ♕a4 ♗d7 and despite the inventive continuation 11 ♘b6!? ♖d8 12 ♘xd7 ♘xd7, Sermek-Riegler, Maribor Pirc 1993, White is probably not better. Also worth exploring is 8 ♘c4!? with ♗e3 to follow.

8...♕e7 9 b3 ♗g4

9...a6!? 10 ♗a3 ♕d8 11 ♕xd8+ (11 ♘d6+ ♗xd6 12 ♗xd6 ♗g4 13 ♗e2 e4 with counterplay – Blatny) 11...♔xd8 12 0-0-0+ ♗d7 13 ♗xf8 ♖xf8 14 ♘d6 ♔c7 15 ♘g5 h6 16 ♘ge4! (16 ♘gxf7?! ♗e6 17 ♗c4 ♗xf7 18 ♘xf7 b5! 19 ♗e6 ♖ae8 ∓) 16...♘xe4 17 ♘xe4 Blatny-Tolnai, Kecskemet 1992. Blatny assesses this ending as ±, though White's advantage looks rather minimal to me.

10 ♗a3 ♕d8 (D)
11 ♗d6!?

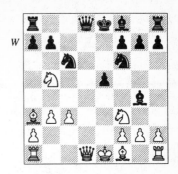

A subtle idea to lure Black's rook on to the c8-square, when White hopes that a later ♘d6 will gain time. Insufficient for advantage is the alternative 11 ♗xf8 ♔xf8 (also 11...♕xd1+ 12 ♖xd1 ♔xf8 13 ♗e2 ♔e7 S.Arkell-Thipsay, Kuala Lumpur 1992) 12 ♕d6+ ♕e7 13 ♘d2 ♖d8 14 ♕xe7+ ♔xe7 15 h3 ♗e6 16 0-0-0 ♖d7 17 ♗c4 ½-½ Sveshnikov-Tunik, Anapa 1991.

11...♗xd6?

Nevertheless 11...♖c8!? was preferable, when Blatny gives 12 ♗xf8 ♔xf8 13 ♗e2 ±. White can try the sharp 12 ♗c4?! when 12...e4 13 ♘g5! ♗xd1 14 ♗xf7+ ♔d7 15 ♗e6+ gives a draw by perpetual check. Black can play for more with 12...a6 13 ♘g5 axb5 14 ♗xf7+ ♔d7 (e.g. 15 ♗xf8+ ♗xd1 16 ♖xd1+ ♘d4 −+ Palkovi-V.Gurevich, Siofok Hungaroil 1990) but there follows the remarkable, and totally unclear, tactical shot 15 ♗e6+! ♗xe6 16 ♗c7+ ♔xc7 17 ♘xe6+ netting the black queen for three minor pieces.

12 ♕xd6 ♕xd6

Black has no way to avoid losing a pawn: on 12...♖c8 comes the capture 13 ♘xe5.

13 ♘xd6+ ♚e7 14 ♘xb7 ♖ab8 15 ♘c5 ♖hd8 (crippling the white pawns with 15...♗xf3!? 16 gxf3 ♖hd8 was probably more resilient; now Blatny gradually untangles, whereupon the extra material proves decisive in the endgame) **16 ♘d2! ♖d5 17 ♘ce4 ♘xe4 18 ♘xe4 ♗f5 19 ♘d2 ♖bd8 20 0-0-0 e4 21 ♗e2 ♘e5 22 ♘c4 ♘d3+ 23 ♗xd3 exd3 24 ♖he1+ ♚f6 25 ♘d2 g5 26 ♚b2 h5 27 ♖e3 h4 28 c4 ♖d4 29 ♚c3 ♖f4 30 f3 ♖fd4 31 ♘e4+ ♗xe4 32 ♖xe4 ♖xe4 33 fxe4 ♚e5 34 ♖xd3 ♖h8 35 ♖f3 f6 36 ♖f5+ ♚xe4 37 ♖xf6 h3 38 ♖f2! g4 39 gxh3 ♖xh3+ 40 ♚b4 1-0**

4 4...♘f6 5 ♘f3 ♗g4

1	e4	c5
2	c3	d5
3	exd5	♕xd5
4	d4	♘f6
5	♘f3	♗g4 *(D)*

The attraction of this sound and increasingly popular defence is obvious. The queen's bishop immediately takes up an active post, and Black's pieces will develop very naturally: ...e6, ...♘c6, ...♗e7 and ...0-0.

A key point about the circumspect move-order 4...♘f6 (as opposed to the less accurate 4...♘c6, covered in the next chapter) is that Black can usually delay swapping on d4. To precipitate this pawn exchange White is more or less forced into ♗e3 at some stage in the main line; not a bad developing move, of course, but also not as active a square for the bishop as g5, for instance. As soon as the white bishop comes to e3 (threatening dxc5)

Black must exchange pawns on d4, whereupon a subsequent ♘c3 for White gains the traditional tempo against the black queen on d5.

The most notable current adherent of 5...♗g4 is Garry Kasparov. Indeed he lost one of the most famous games of 1996 using it – to Deep Blue, in the first game of their man v computer match in Philadelphia. Despite this, the main variations are looking extremely solid for Black, and can be recommended as an excellent choice, especially if Black is content with a draw.

There are, naturally, slight downsides to the 5...♗g4 defence. On g4 the bishop can be something of a target; h3 invariably gains time for White, and just occasionally a later g4 follows. Black may also notice the absence of the bishop from his queenside when White plays moves like ♕b3, attacking the pawn on b7. Also, in developing a queenside piece like this, Black remains several tempi away from kingside castling. Whilst attempts to capitalise on this lagging development with 6 ♕a4+ have largely backfired on White, a startling new idea is 6 ♘bd2!?. See Michael Adams's fantastic demolition of Hübner (Game 9) as an example of just how effective the c3 Sicilian can be, even at the highest levels.

Game 6
Zakharov – Shipov
Moscow Open Ch 1995

1 e4 c5 2 c3 d5 3 exd5 ♕xd5 4 d4 ♘f6 5 ♘f3 ♗g4 6 ♕a4+?! *(D)*

This check has scored badly in tournament play.

6...♗d7

6...♘bd7!? contains a trap that has brought Hraček several easy points: 7 ♗c4 (7 ♗e2 e6 promises White little, while 7 ♗e3 ♗xf3 8 gxf3 cxd4 9 cxd4 as in the game Sveshnikov-Madsen, Gausdal 1992, would have left White little to show for his pawn after 9...♕xf3 10 ♖g1 ♕c6 11 ♗b5 ♕d6) 7...♕e4+ 8 ♗e3 ♗xf3 9 ♘d2? (better but ultimately insufficient was the pawn sacrifice 9 gxf3 ♕xf3 10 ♖g1 cxd4 11 cxd4 ♕c6 12 ♕b3 e6 13 ♘c3 ♖c8 14 ♗b5 ♕d6 15 d5 a6 16 ♗xd7+ ♕xd7 17 ♖d1 g6 18 ♗d4 ♗g7 19 ♘e4 ♘xe4 20 ♗xg7 ♖g8 21 ♗h6 exd5 22 ♖xd5 ♕e6 ∓ Vogt-Hraček, Altensteig 1995) 9...♕c6 10 ♗b5 ♗xg2! (the point) 11 ♗xc6 ♗xc6 12 ♕b3 ♗xh1 13 f3 cxd4 14 cxd4 ♗g2 and Black's rook and two pieces quickly proved too much for

the white queen in both Bräuning-Hraček, Kecskemet 1992 and Rabiega-Hraček, Bundesliga 1992/3.

6...♘c6?! is probably dubious: 7 ♗c4 ♕e4+ (7...♕d7 8 dxc5 ♗xf3 9 gxf3 and then 9...e6 10 ♗e3 ♘d5 11 ♗xd5 ♕xd5 12 ♕e4 ± was Sveshnikov-Neverov, Moscow 1989, but 9...g6 10 ♗e3 ♗g7 11 ♘d2 0-0 12 0-0-0 ♕h3 is less clear, Teitsson-Petursson, Icelandic Cht 1995/6) 8 ♗e3 ♗xf3 9 ♘d2 (9 gxf3 ♕xf3 10 ♖g1 cxd4 11 cxd4 e6 12 ♗b5 ♗e7 13 ♘d2 ♕d5 14 ♖xg7 h5 15 ♖g1 ♔f8 16 ♖c1 ♘d8 17 ♗e2 ♕d6 18 ♘f3 ♕b4+ = Vogt-Reeh, Bundesliga 1994/5) 9...♗d1! (wow! 9...♕g4 10 ♘xf3 ♕xg2 11 ♔e2 ± Sveshnikov) 10 ♖xd1 ♕xg2 11 ♔e2 cxd4 12 cxd4 e6 13 ♘f3 ♕g4 14 ♗b5 ♘d7 15 ♗xc6 bxc6 16 ♕xc6 ♖d8 (16...♖b8 17 b3 intending ♖g1 and ♘e5) 17 ♖hg1 ♕f5 18 ♖g5 ♕h3 19 ♖dg1 h6 20 ♖b5! ± Stević-Kurajica, Vinkovci 1995.

7 ♕b3 cxd4

In theory White claims a marginally better endgame after 7...♕xb3 8 axb3 cxd4 (8...e6 9 ♘a3 ♘c6 10 ♘b5 ♖c8 11 dxc5 ♗xc5 12 b4 ♗e7 13 ♗f4 ± Vogt-Bichsel, Swiss Ch 1995) 9 ♘xd4 ♘c6 10 ♘xc6 ♗xc6 11 ♘a3 a6 12 ♘c4. In practice this edge can evaporate, e.g.: 12...e6 13 ♘a5 ♗d5 14 c4 ♗e4 15 f3 ♗b4+ 16 ♗d2 ♗xd2+ 17 ♔xd2 0-0-0+ 18 ♔e3 ♗g6 = B.Filipović-Szekely, Budapest 1990.

Alternatively 7...e6 8 ♗c4 ♕e4+ (after 8...♕c6, Daniliuk-Petrosian, St Petersburg 1993, simplest is 9 0-0 ±) 9 ♗e3 ♘c6 10 ♘bd2 ♕f5 11 ♕xb7

Ξb8 12 ♕c7 Ξxb2 13 0-0 cxd4?! 14 ♗xd4 ♗e7 15 ♗b3 ± Sveshnikov-Goriachkin, Riga 1995; Sveshnikov's suggested improvement 14...♗e7 (intending 15 ♗b3 ♘d5) still looks ±.

8 ♗c4

8 ♘xd4 ♘c6!? (8...e6 is also reasonable: 9 ♘b5 ♘a6 10 ♕xd5 ♘xd5 = Schmittdiel-Kuczynski, Bundesliga 1994/5 alternatively 9 ♘d2 ♘c6 10 ♕xd5 ♘xd5 11 ♘2f3 ♘xd4 12 ♘xd4 ♗c5 13 ♗d3 ♗xd4 14 cxd4 ♘b4 15 ♗e4 ♗c6 ∓ Schmittdiel-Petursson, Gausdal 1996) 9 ♗c4 (9 ♗e3 ♘a5 10 ♕c2 ♘g4 11 ♘d2 ♘xe3 12 fxe3 g6 ∓ Smagin-Atalik, Iraklio 1993) 9...♕xg2 10 ♗xf7+ ♔d8 11 Ξf1 ♘xd4 12 cxd4 e6 13 d5 ♕xd5 ∓ An.Schmitt-A Sokolov, French Cht 1994.

8...♕e4+ 9 ♔f1 e6 *(D)*

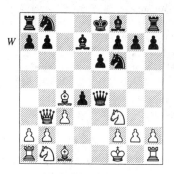

10 cxd4

10 ♘xd4 (10 ♘bd2 ♕c6 11 ♘xd4 ♕c7 12 ♘2f3 a6 13 ♗g5 ♗d6 14 Ξd1 ♘c6 15 ♘xc6 ♗xc6 16 ♘d4 ♗d7 17 ♗h4 0-0-0 ∓ Daniliuk-Dragomaretsky, Minsk 1994) 10...♘c6 11 ♘d2 ♕g6! (11...♘xd4 12 ♘xe4 ♘xb3 13 ♘xf6+ gxf6 14 axb3 ♗c5 = Kharlov-Tukmakov, Biel 1992) 12

♕xb7 Ξb8 13 ♕c7 Ξc8 14 ♕g3 ♘xd4 15 ♕xg6 hxg6 16 cxd4 ♗b4 17 b3 ♗c3 18 Ξb1 ♗xd4 19 ♘f3 ♗b6 20 ♗b2 ♘e4 ∓ de la Villa-Topalov, Pamplona 1995.

10...♘c6!? 11 ♘c3 ♕f5

11...♕g6 12 ♘e5?! ♕xe5 13 dxe5 ♗c6! ∓ Zakharov-Tregubov, St Petersburg 1995.

12 ♕xb7 Ξb8 13 ♕c7 ♗e7!

13...Ξc8?! 14 ♕f4 ♕xf4?! (or 14...♕a5 ∞ Kharlov) 15 ♗xf4 ♘xd4 16 ♘e5 ± ♘h5? (16...♗d6! Kharlov) 17 Ξd1 ♘c6 18 ♘xd7 ♘xf4 19 ♗b5 ± Kharlov-Hoffman, Cologne 1993.

14 b3! 0-0 (14...♗b4!? 15 ♗d2 0-0 ∞ Shipov) **15 ♕f4 ♕a5 16 ♗d2 ♗b4 17 ♘e2! Ξfd8** (17...Ξbd8!? Shipov) **18 ♗xb4 ♘xb4 19 ♘e5 ♗b5 20 g4 ♘c6 21 ♘xc6!** (if 21 g5? ♘xe5 22 gxf6 ♘xc4! 23 bxc4 – 23 ♕g5? ♘d2+ – 23...♗xc4 and White's king is too exposed) **21...♗xc6 22 f3 ♘d5 23 ♕c1?** (23 ♗xd5! ♗xd5 24 ♔f2 is ± according to Shipov; now White's airy king compels him to liquidate into a worse endgame) **23...Ξbc8 24 ♕e1 ♘e3+ 25 ♔f2 ♘xc4 26 bxc4 ♕a3 27 ♕c3 ♕xc3 28 ♘xc3 Ξxd4 ∓** (having regained his pawn, Black is better, though both sides make subsequent inaccuracies in the endgame) **29 ♘b5! Ξd2+ 30 ♔g3 Ξd7 31 Ξhd1 Ξcd8 32 Ξxd7 Ξxd7 33 Ξb1 ♔f8! 34 Ξb3 a6 35 ♘c3?** (35 ♘a3) **35...Ξd3?** (35...Ξd4 36 c5 Ξc4) **36 ♘b1 Ξxb3 37 axb3 a5! 38 ♔f4 ♔e7 39 c5?** (39 ♘c3! intending 39...♔d6 40 ♘e4+! =) **39...♔d5! 40 ♘d2 ♔d7 41 ♔e5 ♔c6 42 ♔d4 f6! 43 f4 e5+ 44 fxe5 fxe5+ 45 ♔c3 ♔xc5 -+ 46 h4 e4 47 ♘f1 ♔d6! 48 ♘e3** (48 b4 a4! −+) **48...♔e5 49 b4 axb4+ 50 ♔xb4 ♗e6 51 ♔c5 ♔f4 52 ♔d4 ♗xg4 53 ♘d5+ ♔f3 0-1**

In February 1996 the most powerful chess computer in the world used the c3 Sicilian to decimate Garry Kasparov in round one of a six-game game match. Kasparov's new opening idea, 10...♗b4!?, looks bizarre, but the PCA World Champion had enough faith in the plan to try to repeat it two games later in the match.

Game 7
Deep Blue – Kasparov
Philadelphia (1) 1996

1 e4 c5 2 c3 d5 3 exd5 ♕xd5 4 d4 ♘f6 5 ♘f3 ♗g4 6 ♗e2 (D)

6...e6

6...♘c6?! 7 h3 ♗h5 8 c4 ♕d6 9 d5 ♗xf3 10 ♗xf3 ♘d4:

a) 11 0-0 0-0-0!? (11...g6 12 ♗e3 ♘f5 ∞) 12 ♘c3 e5 13 ♗e3 ♔b8 14 a3 ♕a6 15 ♗e2 ♘d7 16 b4 ♗e7 17 ♖b1 ♘f5 18 ♘e4 ♘d4 19 bxc5 ♘xc5 20 ♗xd4 exd4 21 ♕xd4 ♘xe4 22 ♕xe4 ♗c5 23 d6 ♖he8 24 ♕f3 ♖xd6 25 ♖b5 ♕c6 26 ♕xc6 ♖xc6 27 ♗f3

♖c7 28 ♗xb7 ♖xb7 29 ♖xc5 won a pawn for White in the game Rozentalis-Savchenko, Tbilisi 1989.

b) 11 ♘c3 (the most accurate move-order according to Adams) 11...g6? (better is 11...e5!? 12 0-0 {12 dxe6 ♕xe6+ 13 ♗e3 0-0-0 14 0-0 ♕xc4 ∞ Adams} 12...0-0-0 transposing to the above Rozentalis game) 12 ♗e3 ♘xf3+ (now if 12...♘f5, 13 ♕a4+) 13 ♕xf3 ♗g7 14 0-0 0-0 15 ♖fe1 ♖fe8 16 ♖ad1 a6 17 ♗f4 ♕d7 18 ♗e5 ± Adams-Lutz, Dortmund 1994.

7 h3

In the third game Deep Blue-Kasparov, Philadelphia 1996, the computer varied here with 7 0-0. After 7...♘c6 8 ♗e3 cxd4 9 cxd4 ♗b4!? 10 a3 ♗a5 11 ♘c3 ♕d6 the same position was reached as in game one, excluding the moves 7 h3 ♗h5. Joel Benjamin, the American grandmaster advising on Deep Blue's opening book, had prepared a new idea, but had mis-assessed the resulting position: 12 ♘e5 ♗xe2 13 ♕xe2 ♗xc3 14 bxc3 ♘xe5 15 ♗f4 ♘f3+! (this desperado, underestimated by Benjamin, gives Black a comfortable game) 16 ♕xf3 ♕d5 17 ♕d3 ♖c8 18 ♖fc1 ♕c4 19 ♕xc4 ♖xc4 (now ...b5 and ...♘d5 threatens to give Black a strategically won game, but Deep Blue finds a very nice manoeuvre to disrupt this plan) 20 ♖cb1! b6 21 ♗b8 ♖a4 22 ♖b4! ♖a5 23 ♖c4!? (an intriguing decision, though not a bad one; most humans would play 23 c4 to control the d5-square) 23...0-0 24 ♗d6 ♖a8 25 ♖c6 b5 26 ♔f1 ♖a4 27 ♖b1 a6 28 ♔e2 h5 29 ♔d3 ♖d8 30

♗e7 ♖d7 31 ♗xf6 gxf6 32 ♖b3 with equality.

A different tack is 7 ♘a3, e.g. 7...a6 8 ♘c2 (intending ♘e3; 8 ♘c4 ♗xf3!) 8...cxd4 9 ♘cxd4 e5 10 ♘c2 ♕xd1+ 11 ♗xd1 ♘c6 12 ♘e3 ♗h5 13 ♗b3 ♗c5 14 ♘f5 0-0 15 0-0 ♖fe8 16 h3 ♗xf3 17 gxf3 e4 ∞ Adams-Romero, Leon 1995.

7...♗h5 8 0-0

Castling quickly is a logical way of cutting down Black's options, but amongst the alternatives the 8 ♗e3 move-order is also common:

a) 8 ♗e3 cxd4 (8...♗e7 9 c4 ♕d6 10 ♘c3 0-0 11 dxc5 ♕xc5 12 ♗e3 ♕c8 13 ♘d4 ♗xe2 14 ♕xe2 ± Rozentalis-Gavrikov, USSR 1988) 9 cxd4 ♘c6 (after 9...♗b4+!? 10 ♘c3 0-0 11 0-0 ♕a5!? 12 ♕b3 ♘c6, 13 a3 ♗xc3 14 bxc3 ♘d5 ∞ was Kramnik-Kasparov, Paris PCA rpd 1994 while 13 ♖fd1 ♖fd8 14 g4!? ♗g6 15 ♗g5 ♗xc3 16 bxc3 ♗e4 17 ♗xf6 gxf6 18 ♘d2 ♗d5, as in V.Ivanov-Belikov, Moscow 1995, is assessed by Belikov as equal) 10 ♘c3 ♕d6. Here White has an ambitious try with 11 g4 (surely 11 0-0 ♗e7 12 g4 ♗g6 13 ♘e5 is the more prudent move-order?) 11...♗g6 12 ♘e5 ♗e7 13 0-0 0-0 14 ♗f4! ♕b4!? (14...♕d8 15 ♗f3 ♖c8 16 ♘xg6 hxg6 17 ♗e3 ♗d6 18 g5 ♘d7 19 d5 exd5 20 ♕xd5 ± Adams-Topalov, Las Palmas 1994 while V.L.Ivanov suggests 14...♘d5! offering a promising exchange sacrifice with 15 ♘xg6 ♘xf4, or if 15 ♗g3 ♕b4 ∓) 15 a3 ♕xb2 16 ♘a4 ♕c2 17 ♘xg6 ♕xg6 18 ♗d3 ♘e4 19 f3 ♕f6 20 fxe4 ♖xd4+ 21 ♔h2 ♖ad8 22 ♗b5 ♕xe4 23 ♘c3 ♕g6 24 ♕b1 f5 ∞ Waitzkin-Nunn, San Francisco 1995.

b) 8 ♘a3 (to avoid an IQP) 8...♘c6 9 ♗e3 cxd4 10 ♘b5 0-0-0! 11 ♘bxd4 (11 cxd4 ♗xf3! 12 gxf3 ♗b4+) 11...♗c5 (11...e5 12 ♘xc6 ♕xc6 13 ♕b3 ♗c5 = Blauert-Mikhalchishin, Dortmund 1995) 12 0-0 e5 = Mufić-Stohl, Croatia 1995.

c) 8 c4 (the Lithuanian grandmaster Rozentalis has had some highly complex struggles with this) 8...♕d8 (8...♕d6!? 9 ♘c3 cxd4 10 ♘b5 ♕d8 11 ♗f4 ♗b4+ 12 ♔f1 ♘a6 13 ♘c7+ ♘xc7 14 ♕a4+ b5 15 ♕xb4 bxc4 16 ♕xc4 ♘cd5 17 ♕c6+ ♔f8 18 ♗d6+ ♔g8 ∓ Rozentalis-Szekely, Odessa 1989 but not 8...♕d7 9 d5 exd5 10 g4 ♗g6 11 ♘e5 ♕e6 12 ♘xg6 hxg6 13 g5 ♘e4 14 cxd5 ♕f5 15 ♗e3 ♘d6 16 ♘c3 ♖xh3 17 ♕a4+ ♔d8 18 ♖xh3 ♕xh3 19 0-0-0 ± Rozentalis-Loginov, Manila OL 1992) 9 ♕b3 cxd4 (9...♕b6 10 ♕xb6 axb6 11 ♘c3 ♘c6 12 ♘b5 0-0-0 13 ♘e5! cxd4 14 ♗f4 ♗b4+ 15 ♔f1 ♗xe2+ 16 ♔xe2 ♘h5 17 ♗h2 ♘xe5 18 ♗xe5 d3+ 19 ♔f3 ∞ B.Filipović-Cvetković, Yugoslavia 1995) 10 ♕xb7 ♘bd7 11 ♘xd4 ♖b8 12 ♕a6 ♗b4+ (12...♗xe2 13 ♘xe2 V.Ivanov-Kalinen, Moscow 1993, and now 13...♗b4+ 14 ♘bc3 0-0 15 0-0 ♘c5! 16 ♕c6 ♕d3! = Ivanov) 13 ♘c3 0-0 14 ♘c6 ♖b6 15 ♘xd8 ♖xa6 16 g4 ♖xd8 17 gxh5 ♘e4 18 ♗d2 ♖xd2 19 ♔xd2 ♘e5+ 20 ♔c1 ♖c6 ∓ Rozentalis-Heissler, Bundesliga 1992.

8...♘c6 9 ♗e3

In the game Short-Topalov, Novgorod 1995, the British grandmaster played one of his deceptive quiet moves, 9 a3!?. He made some progress too: 9...♗e7 10 c4 ♕d8 11 dxc5 ♕xd1 12 ♖xd1 a5 13 ♗e3 ♘e4 14 ♘c3 ♘xc3 15 bxc3 ♗g6 16 ♘d4 0-0-0 17 ♘xc6 bxc6 18 ♗f3 ♗f6 19 ♖ac1 ♖xd1+ 20 ♖xd1 ♖d8 21 ♖xd8+ ♔xd8 22 ♗xc6 ♗xc3 though White's extra doubled c-pawn proved insufficient to win.

9...cxd4

After 9...♖d8!?, 10 ♘bd2?! ♗e7 11 c4 ♕f5! worked out well for Black in the game Men-Yermolinsky, King's Island 1993. Instead 10 dxc5 ♕xd1 (but of course not 10...♗xc5?? 11 ♕xd5 ♖xd5 12 c4 +−) 11 ♖xd1 ♖xd1+ 12 ♗xd1 ♘d5 13 b4 ♗e7 14 a3 ♗f6 15 ♗d2 0-0 16 ♖a2 ♖d8 17 ♔f1 e5 is a variation given by Yermolinsky without assessment, but now 18 c4 followed by 19 ♘c3 looks better for White.

10 cxd4

Very safe is 10 ♘xd4!? ♗xe2 11 ♕xe2 ♘xd4 12 ♗xd4 ♗e7 13 ♖d1 ♕c6 14 ♘d2 0-0 15 ♘f3 ♖fd8 16 c4 ♕e4 17 ♔f1 b6 18 b3 ♖ac8 19 ♖d3, giving White a queenside pawn majority in the endgame, Tiviakov-Lautier, Linares 1995.

10...♗b4!? (D)

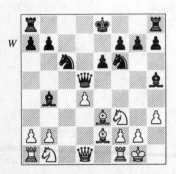

"I was quite proud of my move ...♗b4" said Kasparov afterwards, although it looks strange to develop the bishop here when White's knight has not yet come to c3. The solid alternative 10...♗e7 is covered in Game 8.

11 a3 ♗a5 12 ♘c3 ♕d6 13 ♘b5 ♕e7?!

After this White is better, so critical is 13...♕d5!, the improvement Kasparov had planned when he repeated this line in game three of his match with Deep Blue. Indeed it appears that White has nothing better than to repeat with 14 ♘c3, because both 14 b4 and 14 ♗c4 (intending 14...♗xc4?? 15 ♘d6+) are met by the surprising 14...♗xf3! capture.

14 ♘e5 ♗xe2 15 ♕xe2 0-0 16 ♖ac1 ♖ac8 17 ♗g5! ♗b6 18 ♗xf6

Crippling the black pawn structure, as on 18...♕xf6?, 19 ♘d7.

18...gxf6 19 ♘c4! ♖fd8

Now Black's queenside pawns will be doubled as well, but 19...♘xd4 is impossible on account of the piece-winning fork 20 ♘xd4 ♗xd4 21 ♕g4+.

20 ♘xb6 axb6 21 ♖fd1 f5 22 ♕e3 ♕f6 23 d5!? ♖xd5 24 ♖xd5 exd5 25 b3! (the immediate 24 ♕xb6 allows 25...♕xb2, attacking the rook on c1) **25...♔h8?** (preparing a whirlwind kingside assault, but with hindsight the decisive error; Kasparov could have still simplified to a draw with the surprising piece sacrifice 25...♘e7! 26 ♖xc8+ ♘xc8 27 ♕e8+ ♔g7 28 ♕xc8 ♕a1+ 29 ♔h2 ♕e5+ 30 g3 ♕e2, attacking b5 and f2) **26 ♕xb6 ♖g8 27 ♕c5** (27 ♕xb7? ♕g5 hitting g2 and c1) **27...d4 28 ♘d6 f4 29 ♘xb7 ♘e5 30 ♕d5 f3 31 g3 ♘d3** (the critical moment; after 31...♕f4 32 ♔h2?? comes 32...♖xg3! 33 fxg3 ♕d2+, but the winning alternative 32 ♖c8! had clearly been foreseen by Deep Blue) **32 ♖c7 ♖e8! 33 ♘d6! ♖e1+ 34 ♔h2 ♘xf2** (threatening mate in one with ...♖h1, but there is a forced tactical win for White) **35 ♘xf7+ ♔g7** (35...♔xf7 36 ♕d8+) **36 ♘g5+ ♔h6 37 ♖xh7+ 1-0**

After 37...♔g6 38 ♕g8+ ♔f5 39 ♘xf3 Black's mating net has vanished.

This brilliant tactical victory created a little history; it was the first time ever a computer had beaten a human World Champion in a normal time limit game.

Game 8
Nunn – Lutz
Germany 1994

1 e4 c5 2 c3 d5 3 exd5 ♕xd5 4 d4 ♘f6 5 ♘f3 ♗g4 6 ♗e2 e6 7 0-0

Usually White inserts 7 h3 ♗h5 here, but the move-order can simply be a matter of preference.

7...♘c6 8 ♗e3 cxd4 9 cxd4 ♗e7

A recent idea is to spend a tempo putting pressure on the white d-pawn with 9...♖d8!? 10 h3 ♗h5 11 ♘c3 ♕a5. Then 12 a3 (12 ♕b3 ♕b4 13 ♖fd1 a6 14 g4 ♗g6 15 ♘e5 ♕xb3 16 axb3 ♘b4 17 ♗f3 ♘fd5 with equality, Palkovi-Zsu.Polgar, Stara Zagora 1990) 12...♗e7 13 ♕b3 (13 b4 ♕c7 14 ♖c1 a6 15 ♕b3 0-0 16 ♖fd1 ♕d6 17 ♘a4 b5 18 ♘c5 ♖a8 ∞ Kiselev-A.Sokolov, Russian Ch 1994)

13...♕c7 14 ♖fd1 0-0 15 d5 exd5 16 ♘xd5 ♘xd5 17 ♖xd5 ♗g6 18 ♖c1 ♖xd5 19 ♕xd5 ♗f6, Acs-Palkovi, Budapest 1995, and here perhaps 20 b4!? would give a tiny pull for White as 20...♗b2?! 21 ♖c5 ♗xa3? fails to 22 ♕b3! ♗xb4 23 ♕xb4.

10 ♘c3 ♕d6

The most common retreat, though the queen can also stay active with 10...♕a5 11 h3 ♗h5 when for 12 ♕b3 ♕b4 see the note after Black's 12th move in this game, and for others see Game 13, Chapter 5.

11 h3 ♗h5 *(D)*

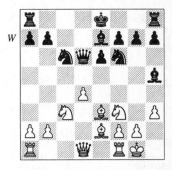

12 ♕b3

White has a substantial choice:

a) 12 a3!? (maybe the best move-order) 12...0-0 13 ♕b3 with a transposition to the note to White's 13th move, and possibly the main game, whilst avoiding the irritating 12 ♕b3 ♕b4.

b) 12 ♕d2 0-0 13 ♖fd1 (13 ♗f4 ♕d8 14 a3 ♗xf3 15 ♗xf3 ♘xd4!? 16 ♗xb7 ♖b8! and then 17 ♗a6 e5 ∞ was the game Marković-Atalik, Heraklio 1993; instead 17 ♗xb8? fails to 17...♘f3+ 18 ♗xf3 ♕xd2) 13...♖fd8 14 ♖ac1 ♖ac8 15 a3 ♘d5 16 b4 ♘xe3

17 ♕xe3 ♗xf3 18 ♗xf3 ♘xd4 19 ♗xb7 ♖xc3 20 ♖xc3 ♘e2+ 21 ♕xe2 ♕xd1+ 22 ♕xd1 ♖xd1+ 23 ♔h2 g5 24 g3 ♖d2 = Afek-Andrianov, Rishon le Zion 1993.

c) 12 ♖c1 0-0 13 ♘b5 ♕d8 14 ♘e5 ♗xe2 15 ♕xe2 ♘b4 16 ♘c3 a6 17 ♖fd1 ♖c8 18 ♗g5 ♘fd5 19 ♗xe7 ♘xe7 20 ♕f3 ♘bd5 ∓ Handoko-Petursson, Dubai OL 1986.

d) 12 ♘b5 ♕d8 (12...♕b8 13 ♘e5 ♗xe2 14 ♕xe2 0-0 15 ♘xc6 bxc6 16 ♘c3 ♘d5 17 ♘xd5 cxd5 18 ♖ac1 ♕b6 and a draw was soon agreed in Ljubojević-Kasparov, Moscow OL 1994) 13 ♘e5 ♗xe2 14 ♕xe2 ♘b4 15 d5 ♘fxd5 16 ♗xa7 0-0 17 ♖fd1 ♕a5 18 a3 ♘c6 19 ♗d4 ♘f4 20 ♕f1 ♘xd4 21 ♖xd4 ♗f6 ∓ A.Ivanov-Petursson, Saint Martin 1991.

e) 12 g4 ♗g6 13 ♘e5 0-0 (or 13...♘d5 14 ♘xd5 exd5 15 ♗f4 0-0 16 ♖c1 ♕b4 17 ♘xc6 bxc6 18 ♕d2 ♕b6 19 a3 a5 20 ♖c3 ♗f6 ∞ Blatny-Fominykh, Stary Smokovec 1990) 14 f4 ♖ad8 15 ♘xc6 bxc6 16 ♗f3 h6 17 ♖c1 ♘d5 18 ♘xd5 cxd5 19 ♕a4 ♕b8 ∞ Kharlov-Loginov, USSR Cht 1991.

12...0-0 *(D)*

Although the b-pawn is not yet a problem (13 ♕xb7?! ♖fb8 14 ♕a6 ♖xb2), it was possible to offer the immediate exchange of queens with 12...♕b4. This position has added importance, because it can also be arrived at via the move-order 1 e4 c5 2 c3 d5 3 exd5 ♕xd5 4 d4 ♘c6 5 ♘f3 ♗g4 6 ♗e2 cxd4 7 cxd4 e6 8 ♘c3 ♕a5 9 0-0 ♘f6 10 h3 ♗h5 11 ♗e3 ♗e7 12 ♕b3 (now the threat to the b-pawn is real) 12...♕b4. See

Game 13, Chapter 5, for detailed coverage: the crucial continuation starts 13 g4 ♗g6 14 ♘e5.

13 ♖fd1

13 a3!? and then:

a) 13...a6?! (depriving White use of the b5-square and cancelling out any ideas of capturing the pawn on b7, due to 14 ♕xb7? ♖fb8; nevertheless, this dual-purpose move proves time consuming, as White can advance in the centre) 14 ♖fd1 ♖fd8 15 ♖ac1 b5 16 d5! (16 ♕a2 b4 17 d5 exd5 18 ♘a4? ♗xf3! 19 ♗xf3 ♘e5 20 ♗xd5?! ♘xd5 21 ♘b6 ♘f3+! 0-1 Cherniaev-B.Lalić, Hastings 1994) 16...♘a5 (after 16...exd5, 17 ♘xd5 ♘xd5 18 ♖c5 ♕e6 19 ♖cxd5 ♖xd5 20 ♕xd5 ♕xd5 21 ♖xd5 ♗g6 22 ♘d4 ♘xd4 ½-½ was Cherniaev-Rausis, Gausdal 1995, but 17 g4!? ♘a5 18 ♕a2 ♗g6 19 g5 is a transposition back to Harley-Roberts; 16...♘xd5 17 ♘xd5 exd5 18 ♖xc6! ♕xc6 19 ♘d4 ♕g6 20 g4 Harley) 17 ♕a2 exd5 (17...♘xd5 18 ♘xd5 exd5 19 ♗c5 ±) 18 g4 ♗g6 19 g5! ♘e4 20 ♘xd5 ♕e6 21 ♗b6 ♗xg5 22 ♗xd8 (22 ♘xg5! ♕xg5 23 ♗g4 +−) 22...♗xd8 23 ♗f1 ♕f5 24 ♗g2 ♗h5 25 ♘e3

♕f4 26 ♕d5 1-0 Harley-Roberts, British Ch 1993.

b) Passive but possible is the line 13...♖ad8 14 ♖ad1 ♖d7, e.g. 15 ♘e5 ♗xe2 16 ♘xd7 ♗xf1 17 ♘xf6+ ♗xf6 18 ♘e4 ♘a5 19 ♘xd6 ♘xb3 20 ♔xf1 ♖d8 21 ♘e4 ♗e7 22 ♘c3 ♗f6 23 ♘e4 ♗e7 ½-½ Ivanović-Miles, Nikšić 1983.

c) Instead 13...♖fd8 14 ♖fd1 will transpose into the main game.

13...♖fd8

13...♕b4 14 d5!? transposes to a variation analysed in Game 13, Chapter 5.

14 a3

Now 14 ♖ac1 ♕b4!? looks equal: 15 ♕xb4 (15 g4 ♕xb3 16 axb3 ♗g6 17 g5 ♘d5 18 ♘xd5 ♖xd5 19 ♗c4 ♖f5! ∓ Vorotnikov-Bazhin, Podolsk 1993) 15...♘xb4 16 g4 ♗g6 17 ♘e5 ♘fd5, Estrada Gonsalez-Ljubojević, France 1995.

14...♖ac8

14...♘d5!? 15 ♘xd5 (15 ♖ac1 ♖ab8 16 ♘b5 ♘a5! 17 ♕c2 ♗g6! 18 ♘xd6 ♗xc2 19 ♖xc2 ♗xd6 is equal, Kindermann-Babula, Moscow OL 1994) 15...♕xd5 (15...exd5 16 ♖ac1 ♖ab8 17 ♕c3 ♖bc8 18 ♕d2 ♗f6 19 ♗f4 ½-½ Harley-P.Nunn, London 1996) 16 ♕xd5 (note that here 16 ♕xb7 is answered by 16...♖ab8 17 ♕a6 ♖xb2, not 16...♘xd4 17 ♕xe7 ♘xe2+ 18 ♔h2 ♕xd1 19 ♖xd1 ♖xd1 20 ♘e5 ±) 16...♖xd5 17 g4 ♗g6 18 ♗c4 ♖dd8 19 ♘e5 ♗e4 ∓, as in the game Bashkov-Schlosser, European Cup 1992.

15 ♖ac1 ♕b8?!

John Nunn gives the improvement 15...♘d5 16 ♘xd5 ♕xd5 so

that 17 ♕xb7? can be countered with 17...♘xd4 ∓.

16 d5! ± ♘xd5 17 ♘xd5 exd5 18 ♖xd5 ♗g6 (18...♖xd5 19 ♕xd5 ♗g6 20 b4 ±) **19 ♖b5! b6 20 ♖d5** (having probed for the weakness, White now has the idea of ♗a6) **20...♗f6?** (20...♕b7! 21 ♖xd8+ ♘xd8 22 ♖xc8 ♕xc8 23 ♕a4 ♘c6 24 ♗a6 ±) **21 ♗a6 ± ♘e7 22 ♖xc8 ♖xc8 23 ♖d7 ♖e8?! 24 ♕a4! ♗f5 25 ♖b7 ♕d8 26 ♖xa7 ♘d5 27 ♗d4 h6 28 ♗xf6 ♘xf6 29 ♗c4 ♗g6 30 ♕b3?! ♘d7 31 ♕d1?** (giving Black a fighting chance; 31 ♗d5! retains control of the position) **31...♘e5! 32 ♕xd8 ♘xf3+ 33 gxf3 ♖xd8 34 ♖b7 ♖d6 35 b4 ♖f6 36 a4 ♖f4 37 ♖c7 ♖xf3 38 ♖c6 ♖f4??** (allowing a neat simplification leading to a winning rook endgame; after 38...♗e4 39 ♖xb6 ♖xh3 40 f4 White's queenside pawns should be fastest, but there is a lot of play remaining) **39 ♖xg6! ♖xc4 40 ♖xb6 ♖c1+ 41 ♔g2 1-0**

Game 9
Adams – Hübner
Wijk aan Zee 1996

1 e4 c5 2 c3 d5 3 exd5 ♕xd5 4 d4 ♘f6 5 ♘f3 ♗g4 6 ♘bd2!? *(D)*

A remarkable new attempt. According to the Russian international master Vladimir Belikov, this eccentric-looking move was dreamt up by Vladimir Kramnik in 1995 (though in fact there follow here several game references from earlier). White's idea is to play ♗c4, followed by a lightning ♕b3 or ♕a4, depending on Black's response. Black's f7- and/or b7-pawns come under immediate pressure, and whatever the objective merits ultimately turn out to be, 6 ♘bd2 has already chalked up some quick victories.

6...♘c6

a) 6...cxd4 7 ♗c4 ♕h5 (7...♕d7 is proposed as best by Adams; instead 7...♕d8 8 ♕b3 hits f7 and b7) 8 ♕b3 ♘bd7 9 cxd4 (9 ♕xb7 ♖b8 10 ♕xa7 dxc3 11 bxc3 is assessed ± by Shipov and Vlassov) and then:

a1) 9...♘b6 10 ♗b5+ ♗d7 11 ♘e5 e6 12 g4 ♘xg4 13 ♘xd7 0-0-0 14 ♕c3+ 1-0 Knazovcik-Voboril, Czech Cht 1993/4.

a2) 9...♖b8 10 0-0 b5 11 ♗d3 ♕d5 12 ♖e1 ♗e6 13 ♕d1 ♗f5 14 ♗xf5 ♕xf5 15 ♘e5 ♘xe5 16 dxe5 ♘d5 17 ♘f3 ♕d7 18 e6 fxe6 19 ♘e5 ♕d6 20 ♕h5+ +− Lindgren-Cvetković, Eger 1987. This latter reference appears to be the earliest known game with 6 ♘bd2.

a3) 9...e6 10 ♕xb7 ♖b8 11 ♕c6! ♗b4 12 ♘e5! 0-0 13 ♘xd7 ♘xd7 14 ♕xd7 e5? (Belikov gives best play as 14...♕a5! 15 ♕c6! ♖fc8 16 ♕a6! ♕c7 17 0-0 ♗xd2 18 ♗xd2 ♕xc4 19 ♕xc4 ♖xc4 20 ♗c3 and White is a

pawn ahead) 15 ♕xa7 ♕g6 16 0-0 ♖bd8 17 f3 ♗h3 18 ♖f2 ♖xd4 19 ♗f1 ♖c8 20 ♘b3 ♗e1 21 ♘xd4 exd4 22 ♕xd4 ♗xf2+ 23 ♔xf2 ♖c2+ 24 ♗d2 ♕g5 25 f4 ♕a5 26 b4 1-0 Sveshnikov-Belikov, Russian Ch 1995.

b) 6...♗xf3 7 ♘xf3 e6 was a radical solution to the problem of ♗c4 in Bojković-Lukin, Groningen 1991, but White must be better with the two bishops.

c) 6...e6 7 ♗c4 (7 ♗b5+ ♘c6 8 ♕a4 is promising for White – Adams) 7...♕c6 (after 7...♕d8, 8 ♕a4+ ♘bd7 9 ♘e5 ♗f5 10 ♘df3 a6 11 ♘xd7 ♕xd7 12 ♕xd7+ ♘xd7 13 ♗e2 ♗e4 = was Knazovcik-Walek, Czech Ch 1993 but moves like 8 ♕b3!? are possible too) 8 ♕e2 ♘bd7 9 h3 ♗h5 10 g4 ♗g6 11 g5 ♘d5 12 ♗b5 ♕c7 13 ♘e5 0-0-0 14 ♘xd7 ♖xd7 15 ♗xd7+ ♕xd7 16 ♘b3 cxd4 17 ♘xd4 ♗c5 18 ♘b3 ♗b6 19 ♗d2 ♕c6 20 ♖g1 e5 ½-½ Dolmatov-Szekely, Calcutta 1996. White is an exchange up in the final position, but 21 0-0-0 could be risky. Whilst the immediate 21...♘b4? fails to the fork 22 ♕g4+, Black could prepare this (or ...♕a4) for later.

7 ♗c4 ♗xf3

As 7...♕d7 8 ♕b3 e6 9 ♘e5 favours White.

8 gxf3

Here Adams gives some thought-provoking analysis: 8 ♕b3 ♘a5 (8...♗xg2!?) 9 ♕b5+ ♕d7 10 ♘xf3 ♘xc4 11 ♕xc4 = or 8 ♕a4 ♕g5 9 ♘xf3 ♕xg2 10 ♔e2! ("a move which I noticed at the board but didn't have the guts to play" – Adams) and now, in this totally unclear position, 10...♕xh1 11 d5, 10...0-0-0 11 ♗xf7 and 10...♕g4 11 ♖g1 could all be dangerous for Black.

But there is a flaw in the 8 ♕a4 line; the fantastic riposte 8...♗d1!! (Fritz) is ∓, as on 9 ♕xd1 or 9 ♔xd1 comes 9...♕xg2.

8...♕g5?

8...♕d7 (8...♕d6 9 ♕b3 e6 10 dxc5 ♕c7 11 ♗b5 ½-½ Sveshnikov-M.Makarov, Novgorod 1995; 10 ♕xb7 is stronger) 9 dxc5 e6 10 b4 (10 ♘b3 gives White a solid edge according to Adams) 10...a5 and now instead of the unclear 11 ♖b1 ♘d5 12 ♗xd5 ♕xd5 13 a3 ♗e7 of Vlassov-Atalik, Rethymnon 1995, 11 ♕b3!? ± (Shipov and Vlassov) looks promising.

9 ♘e4 ♕f5

As 9...♕g2 10 ♘g3 threatens ♗f1, trapping the queen.

10 ♕e2 e6

On 10...0-0-0, 11 ♘g5! is strong.

11 ♘g3 ♕h3 12 d5 ♘d8 13 ♗b5+ ♘d7 14 ♗f4!

After just 14 moves it is apparent that Black's position is a disaster. His queen is offside, and his king is caught in the centre, about to lose the right to castle.

14...a6 15 ♗xd7+ ♔xd7 16 0-0-0 ♔e8 17 ♖he1 ♗e7 18 d6 ♗f6 19 d7+ ♔f8 20 ♖d5 g6 21 ♗d6+ ♔g8 22 ♘h5! *(D)*

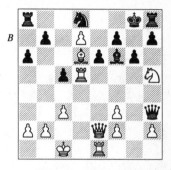

Wrecking whatever hopes Hübner may have had of co-ordinating his pieces. 22...gxh5 23 ♖g1+ ♗g7 24 ♖dg5 is terminal.

22...♗g7 23 ♖xc5 ♘c6 (the threat was 24 ♖c8) **24 ♖xc6 bxc6 25 ♕xa6! ♗h6+ 26 f4 ♖d8 27 ♕c8 ♕h4 28 ♗c7 ♖f8 29 d8♕ ♕xh5 30 ♕xf8+ ♗xf8 31 ♗d6 1-0**

If 31...♔g7, 32 ♗e5+ f6 33 ♕d7+ while on 31...♕h6, 32 ♖xe6! is quickest.

5 4...♘c6

1	e4	c5
2	c3	d5
3	exd5	♕xd5
4	d4	♘c6 (D)

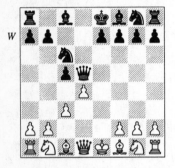

This move-order is inaccurate for Black. After 5 ♘f3 ♗g4 6 ♗e2 it can be risky for him not to exchange pawns with 6...cxd4 – on the alternative 6...e6 White has the option of 7 h3 ♗h5 8 c4! followed by advancing his d-pawn to d5. Whilst exchanging pawns on d4 early is not necessarily catastrophic for Black, it does mean that White has many more options than in the related lines examined in Chapter 4 (with the cautious 4...♘f6 5 ♘f3 ♗g4 move-order). The most significant variation (after 5 ♘f3 ♗g4 6 ♗e2) runs 6...cxd4 7 cxd4 e6 8 ♘c3 ♕a5!? (Game 13). The assessment of the endgame that can arise after the continuation 9 0-0 ♘f6 10 h3 ♗h5 11 ♗e3 ♗e7 12 ♕b3 ♕b4 is important, but it seems that with

energetic play White can gain reasonable winning chances.

Finally 5 dxc5 (Game 10) is nothing special for White after either 5...♕xc5 or 5...♕xd1+.

Game 10
Sveshnikov – Paoli
Plovdiv 1973

1 e4 c5 2 c3 d5 3 exd5 ♕xd5 4 d4 ♘c6 5 dxc5 ♕xc5

The positions arising after this recapture, and 5...♕xd1+, are similar to those covered in Chapter 3 (see Game 5, Blatny-Bönsch). Indeed if Black plays ...♘f6 and White ♘f3 over the next few moves, there will likely be a direct transposition. A definitive evaluation of the ending arising after 5...♕xd1+ 6 ♔xd1 is rather difficult, as Sveshnikov is the only top grandmaster who has regularly played the position. However the omission here of ♘f3 and ...♘f6 would appear to favour Black: 6...e5 (6...♘f6 7 ♘f3 transposes to the aforementioned Chapter 3; 6...♗f5 7 ♗e3 ♘f6 8 ♘f3 0-0-0+ 9 ♘bd2 e6 10 ♗b5 ♘d5 11 ♗xc6 bxc6 12 ♘e5 ♘xe3+ 13 fxe3 ♗xc5 = Sveshnikov-Martynov, Val Maubuee 1990 – see Chapter 3 for another reference) 6...e5 7 ♗e3 (7 b4 a5 8 ♗b5 ♗d7 9 ♘f3 f6 10 ♗d2 ♘ge7 11 ♖e1 axb4 12 cxb4 ♘d5 13 ♗xc6 ♗xc6 14 ♔c1 ♔f7 15

a3 b6! ∓ Sveshnikov-Rashkovsky,
Moscow is a reminder of how the
white queenside pawns can be badly
undermined: if 16 cxb6 ♘xb4)
7...♘f6 8 f3 ♗f5 9 ♘d2 ♘d5 10 ♗f2
0-0-0 11 g3 was Izvozchikov-Gudi-
meako, Rostov-on-Don 1977, and
now 11...e4! would have been good
– if 12 fxe4 then 12...♘xc3+! 13
bxc3 ♗xe4.

6 ♘a3

6 ♗e3 ♕a5 gives White a choice:

a) 7 b4 ♕c7 8 ♘a3 ♘f6 9 ♘b5
♕b8 10 ♘f3 e5? (Euwe suggested
10...♘g4 = intending ...g6) 11 ♗c4
♗e7 12 ♕b3 0-0 13 ♘g5 ♘d8 14
♖d1 ± Canal-Euwe, Zurich 1954.

b) 7 ♘a3!? ♘f6 (7...e5?! 8 ♘c4
♕c7 9 ♕a4 ♗e6 10 ♘f3 f6 11 b4!
♖c8 12 b5 ± Markus-Bebchuk, Moscow 1962) 8 ♘b5? (instead 8 ♘f3!?
gives a transposition to Chapter 3)
8...a6 9 b4 ♘xb4 10 cxb4 ♕xb4+ 11
♕d2 ♕xd2+ ∓, etc. was Bronstein-
Vasiukov, USSR 1968.

6...e5

A risky line. Safer is 6...♕a5 7
♘b5 ♗d7 8 ♘f3 (8 b4 ♕d8 9 ♘f3 a6
10 ♘bd4 ♘f6 11 ♘xc6 ♗xc6 12
♕xd8+ ♖xd8 13 ♘e5 ♗a4 with the
somewhat better endgame for Black,
Sveshnikov-Kuindzhi, Daugavpils
1974) 8...a6 9 ♘bd4 e5 10 ♘xc6
♗xc6 11 ♗c4 ♖d8 12 ♕e2 ♗d6 13
0-0 ♘f6 14 ♘d4 with active piece
play for White, Bannik-Shaskov,
Kiev 1978.

7 ♘b5 ♕e7 8 ♗e3 (D)

8 b3!? gives a safe if modest
endgame plus to White; the threat is
9 ♗a3, so Black might have to continue 8...♕d8 9 ♕xd8+ ♔xd8.

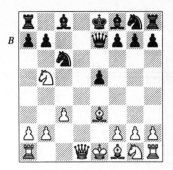

8...b6?

Black had to allow White's threat:
in fact 8...a6 9 ♗c5 ♕xc5 10 ♘c7+
♔e7 11 ♘xa8 ♘f6 12 ♕b3 b5 13 a4
♗e6 14 ♕d1 b4 15 ♘c7 (15 ♕d3!?)
15...bxc3 gave a very unclear position in the game Chekhov-Evans, Al-
garve 1975.

**9 ♕f3! ♗b7 10 0-0-0 ♖d8 11
♖xd8+ ♘xd8 12 ♕d1 ♗c6**

Or 12...♘c6 13 ♕a4 a6 14 ♘f3 f6
15 ♗xb6! axb5 16 ♗xb5 ♕e6 17
♖e1 ♘ge7 18 ♗c4 ♘d5 19 ♕b5 +−
Sveshnikov-Taimanov, USSR 1972.

**13 ♕a4 ♕d7 14 ♘f3 ♗xf3 15
gxf3 ♘c6 16 ♗c4 1-0**

Game 11
Alekhine – Podgorny
Prague 1943

**1 e4 c5 2 c3 d5 3 exd5 ♕xd5 4 d4
♘c6 5 ♘f3 ♗g4 6 ♗e2 (D)**
6...cxd4

This leads to the usual problems
Black has when he exchanges pawns
on d4 very early in the 2...d5 variation. White's knight comes to c3
quickly, and Black's inferior development starts to show. However, as
Black has played 4...♘c6 (rather than

the circumspect 4...♘f6 of Chapter 4) delaying this pawn exchange is also not ideal:

a) 6...0-0-0?!. You can well understand why this has been shunned by most strong players – the black king is visibly less safe on the queenside – yet there has been no demonstrable refutation:

a1) 7 ♗e3 e5 and then 8 dxc5 ♕xd1+ 9 ♗xd1 f5! 10 h3 ♗xf3! 11 ♗xf3 f4 12 ♗c1 ♗xc5 gave Black a fine game in Barlov-Krnić, Vrnjačka Banja 1983, while the continuation 8 c4 ♕d7 9 d5 ♗xf3 10 ♗xf3 ♘d4 is not so clear.

a2) Perhaps 7 0-0!? is the most accurate:

a21) 7...cxd4 8 cxd4 ♘xd4 9 ♘xd4 ♗xe2 10 ♕xe2 ♕xd4 11 ♗e3 ♕f6 12 ♗xa7 ± Lane-Vratonjić, Sweden 1984.

a22) 7...e5 8 ♘xe5! ♗xe2 9 ♕xe2 cxd4 10 ♘xc6 ♕xc6 11 cxd4 ± A.Cohen-P.Tomesanyi, Balatonbereny 1992 is, like the previous line, clearly horrendous for Black.

a23) 7...♘f6 8 h3! ♗h5 9 ♗e3 e5 10 c4 ♕d7 11 d5 ♗xf3 12 ♗xf3 ♘d4 13 b4 ♕f5 14 bxc5 ♗xc5 15 ♘d2! ♔b8 16 ♖b1 ♖c8 17 ♗xd4 ♗xd4 18

a4 ♖hd8 19 a5 and the semi-open b-file gives White a strong attack, E.Vancini-J.Ježek, Corr 1990-2.

b) 6...e6?! 7 h3 (7 c4 immediately followed by 8 d5 is also possible, but White might as well insert the useful h3) 7...♗h5 8 c4 ♕d6 (8...♕d7 9 g4 {9 d5 is a safe plus for White} 9...♗g6 10 d5 exd5 11 cxd5 ♘b4 12 ♘e5 ♕xd5 13 ♗b5+ ♔d8 14 0-0 ± Adamski-Schneider, Warsaw 1981) and here:

b1) 9 g4 ♗g6 10 d5 ♘b4 11 0-0 exd5! (11...f6? 12 ♘c3 ♘c2 13 ♘b5 ♕b6 14 ♗f4 e5 15 ♘xe5! fxe5 16 ♗xe5 0-0-0 17 g5 h5 18 ♖c1 ♘b4 19 ♗c7 ♕xb5 20 cxb5 ♔xc7 21 ♗c4 +– was the spectacular game Nunn-Sher, Vejle 1994, while Nunn also analyses 11...♘c2? 12 ♘a3! ♘xa1 13 ♘b5 ♕b6 14 ♗f4 ♖c8 15 ♕a4! as good for White; however, Judit Polgar's over-the-board improvement looks, with hindsight, very natural) 12 cxd5 0-0-0! 13 ♘c3 ♘f6! 14 ♕a4?! a6 15 a3 ♗c2! (did Short overlook this shot?) 16 b3 ♘bxd5 17 ♘xd5 ♕xd5 18 ♗f4 ♕xb3 19 ♕a5 ♘d5 20 ♗e5 f6 21 ♗g3 ♕c3 22 ♕xc3 ♘xc3 23 ♗c4 ♗a4 and Black wins, Short-J.Polgar, Stornoway rpd 1995.

b2) 9 d5 ♗xf3 10 ♗xf3 ♘d4 and here:

b21) 11 0-0 e5 12 ♘c3 0-0-0?! (12...f5!? is an untested suggestion by Vlassov) 13 ♗e3 f5 14 b4! cxb4 15 ♗xd4 bxc3 was Vlassov-Landa, Polanica Zdroj 1993 when 16 c5! ♕c7 17 d6 ♗xd6! 18 ♖b1!! would have been winning for White.

b22) 11 ♘c3 ♘f6 12 ♗e3 e5 13 0-0 ♗e7 14 ♗xd4 exd4 15 ♘b5 ♕d7

16 d6 ♗xd6 17 ♗xb7 ♖b8 and now
the tempting 18 ♘xd6+ ♕xd6 19
♕a4+ ♔f8 did not achieve much in
Vlassov-Obodchuk, Moscow 1995.
However 18 ♖e1+! ♗e7 19 ♕f3! 0-0
20 ♗c6 ± is the way to play.

7 cxd4 e6

Of course not 7...♗xf3? 8 ♗xf3
♕xd4? as 9 ♗xc6+ removes the defender of the queen.

8 ♘c3

8 h3 ♗h5 is commonly inserted at
this point. Play will generally transpose, and in some lines (for example
the 8...♕d7 variation of Game 12) it
can be argued that 8 h3 is the more
accurate move-order. The routine 8
0-0!? of course is also possible.

8...♗b4

The least meritorious of Black's
alternatives. 8...♕d7 and 8...♕d6 are
covered in Game 12, and 8...♕a5 in
Game 13. The 'undeveloping' 8...♕d8
loses time – Black will have to rede-
velop the queen soon anyway.

9 0-0 ♕a5 10 a3! *(D)*

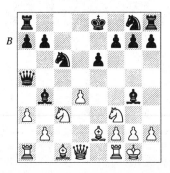

Putting pressure on Black to relinquish the bishop pair with 10...♗xc3
11 bxc3. It is risky for Black then to
win a pawn with 11...♕xc3 due to 12

♖b1 ♘ge7 (12...0-0-0 13 ♕a4 ♗xf3
14 ♗xf3 ♘ge7 15 ♕b5 ♖d7 16 ♗f4
and if 16...♕xd4, 17 ♗xc6 ♘xc6 18
♕xc6+!) 13 ♖xb7 0-0 14 ♕a4 ±.

10...♘f6 11 d5! exd5

On 11...♖d8 White continues 12
♕b3 with the idea of 13 axb4 ♕xa1
14 ♗e3 trapping the queen.

12 axb4! ♕xa1 13 ♘d2! ♗xe2
(Black has no choice, since White
threatens to trap his queen with
♘b3) **14 ♕xe2+ ♘e7** (after 14...♔f8
15 ♘b3 ♕a6 16 b5 ♕b6 17 ♘a4
♘d4 18 ♕d1! White wins a second
minor piece for his rook) **15 ♖e1 0-0
16 ♘b3 ♕a6 17 ♕xa6 bxa6 18
♖xe7 ♖ab8 19 b5 axb5 20 ♖xa7 b4
21 ♘e2 ♖fc8 22 f3 ♖a8 23 ♖xa8
♖xa8 24 ♔f2 ♘d7 25 ♘f4 ♘b6 26
♔e3 ♖c8 27 ♔d3 g5 28 ♘h5 1-0**

Game 12
Chandler – Jacoby
Hamburg 1980

**1 e4 c5 2 c3 d5 3 exd5 ♕xd5 4 d4
♘c6 5 ♘f3 ♗g4 6 ♗e2 cxd4 7 cxd4
e6 8 ♘c3 ♕d7?!**

The move 8...♕a5 is examined in
Game 13. The other plausible queen
retreat is 8...♕d6, when if White
continues unambitiously with 9 0-0
♘f6 10 ♗e3, we will reach a position already examined in Chapter 4.
However the temptation is to try to
exploit the queen on d6 with a quick
♘b5 whilst Black's knight is not yet
on f6. Indeed there have been some
marvellously imaginative (and successful) attempts:

a) 9 ♘b5 ♕d8 10 ♗f4 ♗b4+ 11
♘d2 ♗xe2 12 ♕xe2 ♘xd4 (12...♖c8

13 d5 ♕xd5 14 ♘c7+ ♖xc7 15 ♗xc7 ♕xg2 is a more critical test) 13 ♘xd4 ♕xd4 14 ♕b5+ ♔f8 15 ♗e3 ♗xd2+ 16 ♗xd2 ♕e4+ 17 ♗e3 ♕xg2 18 ♗c5+ ♘e7 19 0-0-0 ♕g5+ 20 ♔b1 b6 21 ♕d7 ♖e8 22 ♗a3 with a dangerous bind for the two sacrificed pawns, Hajkova-Kubikova, Pardubice 1991.

b) 9 d5!? exd5 10 0-0 ♘f6 11 ♘b5 ♕d7 12 ♗f4 ♖c8 13 ♘e5 ♗xe2 14 ♘xd7 ♗xd1 15 ♘xf6+ gxf6 16 ♖axd1 ♖d8 17 ♖fe1+ ♘e5 18 ♗xe5 fxe5 19 ♖xe5+ ♗e7 20 ♖de1 ♖d7 21 ♘c3 ± Adams-McDonald, Hastings 1995.

c) 9 h3 ♗h5 10 ♘b5 ♕d8 11 ♗f4 ♖c8 12 ♕a4 ♗b4+ 13 ♔f1 ♘ge7 14 ♘xa7 ♘d5 15 ♘xc8 ♘xf4 16 ♘a7 +− 1-0 B.Filipović-Zakić, Yugoslavia 1995.

No doubt Black has improvements, but these examples give an idea of the risks to which Black has gratuitously exposed himself by adopting the 4...♘c6 move-order.

9 0-0 ♘f6 (D)

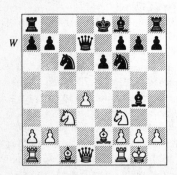

10 h3

The direct 10 ♘e5! could be more accurate in this particular position, as it cuts out some Black options. 10...♗xe2 (10...♘xe5 11 dxe5 is similar variations examined in the main game) 11 ♘xd7 ♗xd1 12 ♘xf6+ gxf6 13 ♖xd1 0-0-0 14 ♗e3 ♗b4 15 d5! ♗xc3 16 dxc6 ♗xb2 17 cxb7+ ♔b8 18 ♖ab1 ♗e5 19 g3 ♗c7 20 ♖dc1 Matulović-Trifunović, Yugoslav Ch 1958, with good prospects due to the dangerous passed pawn on the seventh.

10...♗h5?!

After this we soon see the defect with the position of the black queen, when the white knight leaps to e5. Necessary was 10...♗xf3!? 11 ♗xf3 ♘xd4 12 ♗xb7 ♕xb7 13 ♕xd4 ♗e7 14 ♕a4+ ♕d7 restricting White's advantage to a modest endgame edge. However, it is worth bearing in mind that if White had chosen to insert h3 ♗h5 earlier (at move 8), Black would not have this possibility.

11 ♘e5! ♘xe5

11...♗xe2 12 ♘xd7 ♗xd1 13 ♘xf6+ gxf6 14 ♖xd1 gives White a superior version of the Matulović endgame in the note to White's move 10.

12 dxe5 ♗xe2 (12...♕xd1? 13 ♗xd1! ♗xd1 14 ♖xd1 ♘d7 15 ♘b5 is very unpleasant) **13 ♕xe2 ♘d5 14 ♘xd5 ♕xd5 15 ♖d1 ♕a5 16 ♗g5!** ♗e7 (or 16...h6 17 ♕d3! ♕d5 18 ♕xd5 exd5 19 ♗e3, but now Black's centralised king suffers the attentions of the white heavy artillery) **17 ♗xe7 ♔xe7 18 ♕g4! ♕xe5 19 ♕b4+ ♔f6 20 ♖d7 ♖hf8 21 ♖e1 ♕b8 22 ♕h4+! ♔g6 23 ♕g4+ ♔f6 24 ♖xf7+! 1-0**

After 24...♖xf7, 25 ♖xe6 is mate.

Game 13
Smagin – Armas
Germany 1991

1 e4 c5 2 c3 d5 3 exd5 ♕xd5 4 d4 ♘c6 5 ♘f3 ♗g4 6 ♗e2 cxd4 7 cxd4 e6 8 ♘c3 ♕a5 *(D)*

Soundest; now, in response to ♕b3 at any stage, Black has the possibility of ...♕b4. It requires accurate and energetic white play to maintain the advantage once queens are exchanged.

9 0-0

9 h3 ♗h5 10 d5! is a very interesting and aggressive plan discovered by Benjamin, involving a pawn sacrifice for White: 10...exd5 (10...0-0-0 11 ♘d2! ♗xe2 12 ♕xe2 exd5 13 0-0 ♘f6 14 ♘b3 ♕c7 15 ♗g5 ♗e7 16 ♖ac1 ∞, Benjamin; if 10...♖d8 then 11 ♕b3 with an attack) 11 ♘d4 ♘xd4 (if 11...♗g6, then 12 ♗b5 ±; after 11...♗xe2 12 ♕xe2+ ♗e7 13 ♘xc6 bxc6 14 0-0 ♔f8 15 ♖e1 ♕d8!, 16 b3?! ♗b4! 17 ♗b2 h5 18 ♕d3 ♖h6 ∓ was the game Marković-Maksimenko, Vrnjačka Banja 1992, but Maksimenko suggests the improvement 16 ♗f4 with an unclear

position, and certainly White has compensation for the pawn) 12 ♗xh5 ♘e6 13 0-0 ♘f6 14 ♖e1 g6 15 ♗g4 ♗g7 16 ♗xe6 fxe6 17 ♕b3 0-0 18 ♖xe6 ♔h8 19 ♗e3 ± Benjamin-Zsu.Polgar, New York 1985.

9...♘f6 10 h3 ♗h5 11 ♗e3

After this the variation can often transpose into lines examined in Chapter 4, Game 8. A flexible alternative worth further study is 11 ♕b3 ♕b4 12 ♖d1!?, delaying the queen's bishop's development a little longer. The move-order 11 a3 is also normal: 11...♖d8?! provoked sharp play in Capablanca-Czerniak, Buenos Aires OL 1939 after 12 g4 ♗g6 13 b4 ♗xb4(?) 14 axb4 ♕xa1 15 ♕b3 ♖xd4 16 ♗a3 ♗c2 17 ♕xc2 ♕xa3 18 ♘b5 and White won easily. More natural is 11...♗e7 12 ♕b3 ♕c7! (12...♗xf3 13 ♗xf3 ♘xd4 14 ♕xb7 ♘xf3+ 15 ♕xf3 0-0 16 ♗e3 ± Salov) 13 d5 ♘xd5 14 ♘xd5 exd5 15 ♕xd5 ♗g6 16 ♗e3 0-0 17 ♖ac1 ♖ad8 18 ♕b3 ♕b8 with a satisfactory position for Black, Salov-Gelfand, Wijk aan Zee 1992.

11...♗e7 12 ♕b3

Attacking b7. The other main continuation is 12 a3 0-0 (12...♘d5 13 ♕b3 ♘xc3 14 bxc3 ♕c7 15 c4 ± Istratescu-Vl.Georgiev, Halle 1995) 13 b4 (13 ♕b3 ♕c7 14 ♖fd1 ♖fd8 15 d5 exd5 16 ♘xd5 ♘xd5 17 ♖xd5 ♖xd5 18 ♕xd5 ♗g6 with equality, Schmittdiel-Zsu.Polgar, Dortmund 1990) 13...♕d8 and now:

a) 14 ♕b3 ♖c8!? (14...♗xf3 15 ♗xf3 ♘xd4 16 ♗xd4 ♕xd4 17 ♗xb7 ♖ad8) 15 ♖ad1 ♘d5 16 ♘e4 ♔h8 17 ♗c1?! ♕b6 18 ♕b2 ♕c7 19

♞c5 b6 20 ♞d3 ♝f6 21 ♞de5?!
♞xd4! 22 ♛xd4 ♝xe5! 23 ♛h4
♝xf3 24 ♝xf3 ♞f6 ∓ Zo.Varga-
Zsu.Polgar, Lillafüred 1989.

b) 14 b5 ♞a5 15 ♛a4 (this was
good enough for a small advantage
after 15...b6?! 16 ♜fc1 in Vasiukov-
Toprover, USSR 1954, but a later
game shows that White has over-ex-
tended) 15...♝xf3! 16 ♝xf3 ♜c8 17
♞e2 ♜c4 18 ♛d1 ♛d7 19 a4 ♞d5 20
♝d2 ♝d8 ∓ Gutop-Kuindzhi, Moscow 1976.

c) 14 ♜c1 ♜c8 15 ♛d2!? (Grosz-
peter-Zapata, Innsbruck 1977 went
15 ♞a4 ♛d6 16 ♞b2!? ♜fd8 17 ♞c4
∞) 15...♞d5 16 ♜fd1 with a position
that needs practical tests.

12...♛b4 (D)

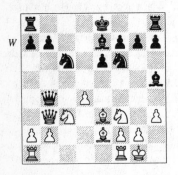

13 g4!?

Some typical variations run 13
♜fd1 (13 ♛xb4!? ♝xb4 14 g4 ♝g6
15 ♞e5 0-0 16 ♞xc6 bxc6 17 ♜ac1
and White might claim a modest
plus, Sveshnikov-Hansen, Copenhagen 1984) 13...♜d8 (13...0-0 14 d5
♛xb3 15 axb3 exd5 16 ♞xd5 ♞xd5
17 ♜xd5 ♝xf3 18 ♝xf3 ♝f6 19 ♜d7
± Okhotnik-F.Lengyel, Hajdubosz-
ormeny 1995) 14 ♛xb4 ♝xb4 15 g4
♝g6 16 ♞e5 0-0 17 ♞xg6 hxg6 18
♝f3 ♝xc3 (18...♞a5 19 ♜ac1 ♜c8 ∞
Okhotnik-Van Wely, Lyngby 1990)
19 bxc3 ♞a5 ∞ Van Mil-Zsu.Polgar,
Lillafüred 1989.

**13...♝g6 14 ♞e5 0-0 15 g5 ♛xb3
16 axb3 ♞d5 17 ♞xd5 exd5 18
♜fc1 ♝f5 19 ♞xc6 bxc6 20 ♝g4?!**

White will still win a pawn with
this, but the resulting endgame looks
drawn. However 20 ♜xc6!? a5 21
♝f3 gives White excellent winning
chances: 21...♜fd8 22 ♝d2 ♝e6 23
♜xa5 ♜ab8 24 ♝g4 ♝xg4 25 hxg4
♜xb3 26 ♜a7 ♝f8 27 ♝c3 ± Sermek-Sher, Bled 1993.

**20...♝xg4 21 hxg4 f6 22 ♜xc6
fxg5 23 ♜c7 ♝f6 24 ♜axa7 ♜xa7 25
♜xa7 ♜b8 26 ♜a3 ♚f7 27 ♚f1 ♝e7
28 ♜a5 ♚e6 29 ♜a6+ ♚f7 30 ♜a7
h6 31 ♜a5 ♚e6 32 ♜a6+ ♚f7 33
♜a5 ♚e6 ½-½**

6 4...e6 (including 5 ♘f3 ♘c6)

1	e4	c5
2	c3	d5
3	exd5	♕xd5
4	d4	e6 (D)

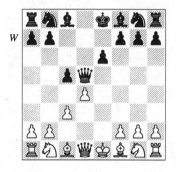

Here we examine lines where Black plays an early ...e6, and generally ...♘c6 also, and White avoids the main-line variations (with ♗d3) of later chapters. There are several reasons why developing the queen's knight so quickly with ...♘c6 can cause some small extra worries for Black. Also bear in mind that as the position can be reached via the move-order 1 e4 c5 2 ♘f3 ♘c6 3 c3 d5 4 cxd5 ♕xd5 5 d4, these positions cannot necessarily be avoided if Black wishes to always play the ...d5 lines of the c3 Sicilian.

In Game 14 we see one of those niggling problems for Black. After 6 ♘a3!?, 6...cxd4?! 7 ♘b5 ♕d8? is powerfully answered by 8 ♗f4! ±. In contrast, had Black played 5...♘f6

instead of 5...♘c6 (Chapter 7), he would have the defence 8...♘d5 against this plan. There are also several variations where Black would like to have the useful option of ...♘a6 or ...♘bd7, as can be seen in the following chapter which deals with lines where ...♘c6 is delayed. Therefore 6 ♘a3, against this particular move-order, is a promising continuation. White has real chances of an endgame edge in the main lines that arise after 6...♘f6 7 ♘b5 ♕d8 8 dxc5.

In Games 15, 16 and 17 we examine (after 5 ♘f3 ♘c6) the deceptively ambitious move 6 ♗e2. If Black then tries to delay exchanging pawns on d4 for too long (6...♘f6 7 0-0 ♗e7), White has the thematic plan of 8 c4! ♕d8 9 dxc5 ♕xd1 10 ♖xd1 (Game 15). Again a typical c3 Sicilian formation is reached, where White has that slight but nagging endgame edge on account of his queenside pawn majority. Therefore Black usually exchanges pawns in the centre, and after 7...cxd4 8 cxd4 ♗e7 9 ♘c3 must decide where to retreat his queen. 9...♕d8 10 ♗e3 0-0 11 ♘e5!? is the subject of Game 16. Against the crucial test, 9...♕d6, some world-class players have had success with the enterprising manoeuvre 10 ♘b5!? ♕d8 11 ♗f4 ♘d5 12 ♗g3 which must now be considered the main branch of this variation (Game 17).

Game 14
Sermek – Andersson
Tilburg 1994

1 e4 c5 2 c3 d5 3 exd5 ♕xd5 4 d4 e6 5 ♘f3

It is worth mentioning here that Smagin occasionally plays a system with 5 ♗e3. After 5...cxd4 play will transpose into lines examined in Chapter 10; instead one unique continuation was 5...♘f6 6 ♘a3!? cxd4 7 ♘b5 ♕d8 8 ♕xd4! ♘c6 (8...♕d5 9 ♘xa7; 8...♘bd7!? 9 ♘d6+ ♗xd6 10 ♕xd6 ♘g4 Smagin) 9 ♕xd8+ ♔xd8 10 ♘f3! ♘d5 11 0-0-0 ♔e7 12 ♗c5+ ♔f6 13 ♘d6! ♗xd6 14 ♗xd6 ♖d8 15 ♗g3 ± Smagin-Jovičić, Yugoslavia 1995.

Another annoying line (for Black) is 5 ♘a3!?, as there are some differences with the related variation 5 ♘f3 ♘f6 6 ♘a3 covered in Chapter 7:

a) 5...a6 6 ♘c4 ♘d7 7 ♘f3 b5?! (for 7...♘f6 see Chapter 7) 8 ♘e3 ♕c6 9 a4 ♗b7 10 axb5 axb5 11 ♖xa8+ ♗xa8 12 dxc5 ♗xc5 13 ♘d4 ♗xd4 14 ♕xd4 ♘gf6 15 ♕b4 ♘d5 16 ♕xb5 ± Kharlov-Sanchez, Ibercaja 1994.

b) 5...♕d8 6 ♗f4 ♘f6 (6...cxd4 7 ♘b5 ♘a6 8 ♕a4! ♗d7 9 ♕xd4 ± Glavina-Pogorelov, Ceuta 1995) 7 dxc5 (7 ♘b5 ♘d5 8 ♗xb8 ♖xb8 9 ♘xa7 ♗d7 10 ♘b5 ♗e7 11 ♘f3 0-0 12 ♗e2 ♘f4 13 0-0 ♕b6 14 a4 cxd4 15 cxd4 ♖fd8 ∞ Mukhametov-Kiselev, Russia 1994) 7...♘d5 8 ♗d6 ♗xd6 9 cxd6 ♕xd6 10 g3 0-0 11 ♗g2 ♕a6 12 ♕e2 wasn't much for White in the game Vorotnikov-Stepanov, Moscow 1992.

c) 5...cxd4 6 ♘b5 ♘a6 7 ♕xd4 ♕xd4 (for 7...♘f6 8 ♗e3 see the next note) 8 ♘xd4 with a better endgame for White, e.g. 8...♘c7 9 ♗f4!? ♘d5 10 ♗b5+ ♗d7 11 ♗xd7+ ♔xd7 12 ♗g3 ♗d6 13 c4 ♗xg3?! 14 cxd5! ♗e5 15 dxe6+ fxe6 16 ♘gf3 ± Kharlov-Tunik, USSR 1990.

d) 5...♘f6 6 ♘b5 (or 6 ♗e3 cxd4 7 ♘b5) 6...♘a6 7 ♗e3 (7 ♘f3 ♘f6 transposes to Chapter 7, Game 19) 7...cxd4 8 ♕xd4 ♕xd4 (8...♗c5? is a blunder: 9 ♕xc5!! ♕xc5 10 ♗xc5 ♘xc5 11 ♘c7+, winning, was Sveshnikov-Osnos, Rostov 1993, while 8...b6?! 9 ♕a4! is also unpleasant) 9 ♗xd4 b6 10 ♗e2 (10 a4!? ♘d7 11 a5 ± Sermek-Bukić, Bled 1992) 10...♗b7 11 ♗f3 ♗xf3 12 ♘xf3 ± Sveshnikov-Novikov, Tallinn Cup rpd 1988 and Kharlov-Zilberman, Leeuwarden 1994.

Some of the sting could be removed from the above line by adopting the move-order 4...♘f6 – see Chapter 3, Game 5.

5...♘c6

In fact the game used the move-order 5...♘f6 6 ♘a3 ♘c6, but I have reversed moves in order to give some variations *en route*.

6 ♘a3

For 6 ♗e2 see Games 15, 16 and 17. Instead 6 ♗e3 cxd4 7 cxd4 ♘f6 8 ♘c3 ♕d6 transposes to the main line of Chapter 10.

6...♘f6

The fishy 6...cxd4?! 7 ♘b5 ♗d6 has been played a few times (but not 7...♕d8? 8 ♗f4). One route to an advantage is 8 ♗c4 ♕e4+ 9 ♗e3! (threatening ♘xd6+) 9...♗b8 10

♘bxd4 ♘xd4 11 ♕xd4 ♕xd4 12 ♗xd4 f6 12 0-0-0.

Instead, the prophylactic 6...♕d8 (to prevent ♘b5 with tempo) gives White a pleasant game after 7 ♘c2! (for 7 ♗f4 ♘f6 see Chapter 7) 7...♘f6 8 ♗d3 (8 ♗e2 is also covered by transposition in Chapter 7; after 8 ♗f4!?, 8...cxd4 9 ♘cxd4 ♘xd4 10 ♕xd4!? ♕xd4 11 ♘xd4 a6 12 ♗e2 ♗d7 13 0-0 ♗c5 14 ♘b3 ± was Sveshnikov-M.Makarov, Russia 1994; 8...♕b6!? ∞ Platunov-Kondyba, Podolsk 1993) and now *(D)*:

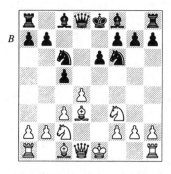

a) 8...♕c7 9 ♕e2 a6 10 ♗g5 cxd4 11 ♘cxd4 ♘xd4 12 ♘xd4 ♗e7 13 0-0 ♘d5 14 ♗xe7 ♕xe7 15 ♗e4 ♘f4 16 ♕f3 ± Vorotnikov-Vladimirov, USSR 1974.

b) 8...♗e7 9 0-0 0-0 10 ♕e2 b6 11 dxc5 ♗xc5 12 ♗g5 ♗b7 13 ♖ad1 ♕c7 (13...♕e7 14 b4) 14 ♗xf6 gxf6 15 ♕e4 ± Braun-Postler, West Germany 1977.

c) 8...cxd4 9 ♘cxd4 ♗d7 10 ♕e2 ♘xd4 11 ♘xd4 ♗e7 12 ♗f4 ♘d5 13 ♗g3 ♗f6 14 ♘b5 0-0 15 0-0 ♗xb5 16 ♗xb5 ♕b6 17 ♗d3 ± Vorotnikov-Pukshanskia, Leningrad 1981.

7 ♘b5 ♕d8

After 7...♕d7, 8 dxc5 ♗xc5 9 ♕xd7+ ♔xd7 10 ♗f4 ♘d5 11 0-0-0 ♔e7 is a known transposition to the main game, but White also has 8 ♘e5! ♘xe5 9 dxe5 ♘d5 10 c4 ♘b4 11 ♗e3 ♗e7 12 a3 ♕xd1+ 13 ♔xd1 ♘a6 14 ♗e2 ♗d7 15 ♗f3 0-0-0 16 ♔e2 ♗xb5 17 cxb5 ± Blatny-Bönsch, Leipzig 1988.

8 dxc5 ♗xc5 9 ♕xd8+ ♔xd8 10 ♗f4!

10 ♗g5 offers little, e.g. 10...♔e7 11 ♖d1 a6 12 ♘bd4 ♘xd4 13 ♘xd4 ♖d8 = S.Arkell-Carlier, Guernsey 1987.

10...♘d5

Alternatives:

a) 10...♘e4 11 ♘bd4 f6 12 ♖d1 ♘xd4 13 ♘xd4 ♔e7 14 ♗d3 ♘d6 (14...♗g5 15 ♗xg5 {15 ♗e3!?} 15...fxg5 16 ♘f3 h6 17 h4 gxh4 18 ♖xh4 ♖d8 19 ♔e2 ♗d7 20 ♖g4 with a very small initiative to White, Barlov-Sosonko, Haninge 1988) 15 ♗e3 ♗b6 16 f4 h6 17 0-0 g5 18 ♖de1 ♗d7 19 ♘xe6! ♗xe6 20 f5 ± Dončević-Kiefer, Germany 1986.

b) 10...♗d7 11 ♘d6 ♗xd6 12 ♗xd6 gaining the two bishops is simply better for White, Howell-Murugan, Calcutta 1996.

c) 10...a6!? has proved solid in practice: 11 ♖d1+ (11 ♘d6 ♔e7) 11...♔e7 12 ♘bd4 ♘xd4 13 ♘xd4 ♖d8! (intending ...♗xd4) 14 ♗e3 ♗a7 ½-½ Lutz-Cladouras, Budapest 1989 is a typical example where White achieved nothing. However, there is an unexplored, if rather maniacal, possibility: 11 0-0-0+ ♔e7 (11...♗d7 12 ♘bd4) 12 ♘c7!? ♖a7 13 b4! ♗b6 (13...♗xf2? 14 ♗d6+

♔d7 15 ♗g3+) 14 ♗d6+ ♔d7 15 b5! and White is the aggressor in the crazy complications.

11 0-0-0

11 ♗g3 a6?! (11...♔e7) 12 ♘d6 ♔e7 13 ♘e4 ♗a7 14 ♗d6+ ♔e8 15 ♗a3 ± was Rodriguez Talavera-Veingold, Seville 1993 and Smagin-Worsfold, London 1990.

11...♔e7 12 ♗g3 a6 13 ♘bd4 ♘xd4 14 ♘xd4 ♖d8 15 ♗e2 ♗d7

Or 15...♘f6!? 16 ♘b3 ♗d6 17 ♗xd6+ ♖xd6 18 ♗f3 ♖b8 19 ♘a5 ♖d7 20 ♖he1 with the usual modest endgame plus for White, Striković-Franco, San Sebastian 1994.

16 ♗f3 ♗a4

16...♗xd4 17 ♖xd4 ♗c6 as in Wöber-Titz, Austria 1995, is a typical liquidation. White gets a small edge with the bishop pair, but converting the advantage will not be easy.

17 ♖d2! ± ♖d7?!

17...♖ac8? allows the combinational motif that also happened in the game: 18 ♗h4+ ♘f6 19 ♗xb7 ♖c7 20 ♘f5+! exf5 21 ♖e1+, winning. The best defence is 17...♔f8, but Andersson was actually following (albeit slowly) the first round game his opponent had had at the same tournament. This turned out to be a most unfortunate strategy for the unsuspecting Swedish super-grandmaster...

18 ♖e1 ♖ad8 *(D)*

Now on 18...♔f8 Sermek gives 19 ♖e4! and if 19...♘b6, 20 ♘xe6+! fxe6 21 ♖xa4! ♖xd2 22 ♖f4+ ♔e8 23 ♔xd2 ±. 19 ♖xe6? would be a mistake because of 19...♖xc3! 20 bxc3 ♗a3+ 21 ♔b1 fxe6.

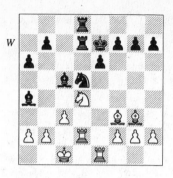

19 ♗h4+! ±

This fine combination was a prepared improvement on 19 ♖e4 ♘f6 20 ♘f5+ ♔f8 21 ♖xd7 ♗xd7 22 ♖c4 exf5 23 ♖xc5 ± Sermek-Magerramov, Tilburg 1994. White ends up with rook and three pawns vs two minor pieces.

19...♘f6 20 ♗xb7! ♖xb7

In his *Informator* notes Sermek analyses:

a) 20...♗xd4 21 ♖xd4 ♖xd4 (or 21...♖xb7 22 ♖xa4) 22 cxd4 ♖xd4 23 ♗xf6+ ♔xf6 24 ♗xa6 ±.

b) 20...a5 21 ♖e4! (21 ♗c6 ♖xd4! 22 cxd4 ♗b4! with an equal position) 21...♗xd4 (21...♖xb7 22 ♘f5+) 22 ♖exd4 ♖xd4 23 ♖xd4 ♖xd4 24 cxd4 ±.

21 ♘f5+ ♔e8 22 ♘xg7+ ♔f8 (22...♔e7 23 ♖xd8 ♔xd8 24 ♗xf6+) **23 ♘xe6+ fxe6 24 ♖xd8+ ♔f7 25 ♖c8 ♗d6 26 ♗g3 ♗e7 27 b3 ♗d7 28 ♖c7 ♖xc7 29 ♗xc7 ♗c6 30 f3 ♘d5 31 ♗e5 ♗g5+ 32 f4 ♗e7 33 g3 h5 34 ♔c2 ♗c5 35 ♔d3 ♘e7?! 36 b4! ♗f2 37 ♖e2 ♗b6 38 c4 ♘f5 39 a4! ♗g1 40 b5 ♗f3 41 ♖c2 ♔e7 42 bxa6 ♘d6 43 ♖b2 ♗e4+ 44 ♔c3 ♗c6 45 ♗d4 ♘e4+ 46 ♔d3 ♘c5+ 47 ♗xc5+ ♗xc5 48 ♖b8 1-0**

Game 15
Sveshnikov – A.Sokolov
Moscow 1991

1 e4 c5 2 c3 d5 3 exd5 ♕xd5 4 d4 ♘f6

Of course 4...♘c6 5 ♘f3 e6 6 ♗e2 ♘f6 is another move-order.

5 ♘f3 e6 6 ♗e2 ♘c6 7 0-0 ♗e7 8 c4! *(D)*

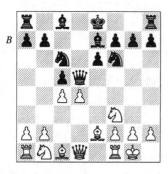

As Black is refusing to exchange on d4, White frees the c3-square himself for his queen's knight. The kind of ending that now results is typical of many c3 Sicilian lines; White has a useful queenside pawn majority to advance, and real prospects of a long-term endgame edge. On the plus side for Black, the open d-file means some major piece exchanges are almost inevitable, which helps ease the defence. Instead after 8 ♗e3 Black has a choice:

a) 8...0-0 (steadfastly refusing to swap on d4) 9 dxc5!? (9 c4 ♕d8 10 dxc5 is possible, when 10...♕xd1 11 ♖xd1 ♘g4!? 12 ♗f4 has led to some complicated encounters) 9...♕xd1 10 ♖xd1 ♘g4 11 ♗d2 ♗xc5 12 ♗e1! ♖d8 13 ♖xd8+ ♘xd8 14 a4 ♘c6 15 ♘bd2 ♗d7?! (15...a5!?) 16 a5! ♖d8 17 b4 ♗d6 18 ♘c4 ♗b8 19 b5 ♘ce5 20 ♘cxe5 ♘xe5 21 ♖d1 ♔f8 22 c4 ± Přibyl-Tarjan, Majdanpek 1976.

b) 8...cxd4 9 ♘xd4!? (9 cxd4 leads to positions examined in Games 16 and 17, but where White has committed his bishop to e3 rather prematurely, e.g. the most dangerous plan, involving ♘b5 and ♗f4, is no longer sensible because White would have lost a tempo compared to Game 17) 9...♘xd4 (9...e5 10 c4! followed by 11 ♘xc6 ±) 10 cxd4 (10 ♗xd4 =) 10...0-0 11 ♘c3 and now 11...♕d8?! 12 ♗f3 ♗d7 13 d5 exd5 14 ♘xd5 ♘xd5 15 ♕xd5 ♗c6 16 ♕xd8 ♖fxd8 17 ♗xc6 bxc6 18 ♖ac1 ± was Sydor-Drimer, Bath 1973, but 11...♕a5 12 ♗f3 ♗d7!? planning ....♗c6 with equality would have been better.

8...♕d8

a) 8...♕f5 9 ♘c3 cxd4 (9...0-0? 10 ♘h4 traps the black queen!) 10 ♘xd4 ♘xd4 11 ♕xd4 e5! (11...0-0 12 ♗f4 ♖d8 13 ♕e5 ±) 12 ♕d3 0-0 13 ♕xf5 ♗xf5 14 ♗e3 ♖fc8 15 ♖fd1 ± Sveshnikov-Sunye, Moscow 1989.

b) 8...♕d7 9 ♘e5!? (9 dxc5 ♗xc5 10 ♘c3 intending a3 and b4 gives positions similar to the main line) 9...♕xd4 10 ♘xc6 ♕xd1 11 ♖xd1 bxc6 12 ♗f3 ♗b7 13 ♘c3 0-0 14 ♗e3 ♖fd8 15 b3 e5 16 ♘a4 e4 17 ♗xc5! gave White a very good ending in Afek-Redon, Paris 1993.

9 dxc5 ♕xd1 10 ♖xd1 ♘e4

Black delays recapturing the c5-pawn to stop ♘c3 by White. Also common is the alternative 10...♗xc5, which leads to the same type of thematic endgame where White tries to make something of his queenside majority: 11 ♘c3 0-0 12 a3 b6 13 b4 ♗e7 14 ♗f4 ♗b7 15 ♘b5!? ♖ad8 16 ♗c7! (16 ♘e5 a5 17 ♘xc6 ♗xc6 18 bxa5 bxa5 19 ♗c7 ♖xd1+ 20 ♖xd1 ♖a8 21 ♗d6 ♔f8 = Sveshnikov-Serper, Minsk 1986) 16...♖xd1+ 17 ♖xd1 ♖c8 18 ♗d6 ♔f8 19 ♗xe7+ ♔xe7 20 ♘d6 ♖b8 21 b5! ± Kharlov-Istratescu, Metz 1993.

11 ♗e3 ♗xc5

11...♘b4 does not prevent White from expanding on the queenside: 12 ♘bd2 ♘xc5 13 ♘d4 a5 14 a3 ♘ba6 15 b4! ♘a4 16 ♖dc1 0-0 17 c5 e5 18 ♘4b3 ± Ivanchuk-Petursson, Lucerne Wcht 1993. Also 11...♘xc5 12 ♘c3 b6 13 ♖ab1 a5 14 ♘g5 ♗b7 15 ♘ge4 ♖c8 16 a3 ♘xe4 17 ♘xe4 ♘e5 18 ♘d6+ ♗xd6 19 ♖xd6 ♘xc4 20 ♗xc4 ♖xc4 21 ♖xb6 ♗e4 22 b3! ♖c8 23 ♖e1 gave White what should have been a winning endgame edge in Acs-Csom, Budapest 1995.

12 ♘d4! *(D)*

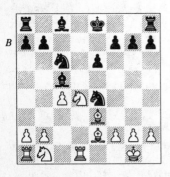

12...♗d7

After 12...♘xd4 13 ♗xd4 ♗d7 14 ♗f3 0-0-0 White gained a large positional advantage with the clever 15 ♗xe4! (15 ♗xg7 ♘xf2 16 ♖xd7

♔xd7 17 ♗xh8 ♘g4+ 18 ♔h1 ♘f2+ ½-½ Sveshnikov-M.Makarov, Moscow 1991) 15...♗c6 16 ♗d5! ♗xd4 17 ♖xd4 exd5 18 c5 ± in Malaniuk-Al Modiakhi, Calcutta 1995.

13 ♗f3 ♗xd4 14 ♗xd4 ♘xd4

On 14...♘g5 White continues 15 ♗xc6 ♗xc6 16 b4 ±.

15 ♖xd4 ♘f6 16 ♘c3 0-0-0 17 ♖ad1 ♗c6 *(D)*

Sveshnikov has pressure on the d-file and h1-a8 diagonal, and given a few moves will advance the queenside pawns. Sokolov understandably decides to simplify, but the cost is a weakening of his pawn structure.

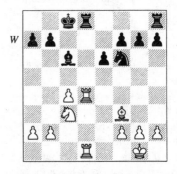

18 ♗xc6 bxc6 19 ♖xd8+ ♖xd8 20 ♖xd8+ ♔xd8 21 f3! (± according to Sveshnikov, who believes that this is a winning knight endgame for White, in spite of the material equality) **21...♘d7** (21...c5 22 ♘b5 a6 23 ♘d6 ♔e7 24 ♘b7 ♘d7 25 ♔f2 intending a3, b4 ± Sveshnikov) **22 ♔f2 f5 23 ♔e3 ♔e7 24 b4 e5 25 a4 ♔d6 26 ♔d3 ♘f6 27 c5+ ♔e6?** (27...♔c7 28 ♔c4 a6 would put up the most resistance; now watch that legendary Soviet grandmaster technique as White plays over the whole board whilst keeping everything under control) **28 b5! ♔d7 29 ♔c4 ♔c7 30 a5! a6 31 b6+ ♔b7 32 g3 h5 33 h4 +– ♘d7 34 f4 exf4 35 gxf4 ♘f8 36 ♘e2 ♘g6 37 ♘d4 ♘xh4 38 ♘e6 ♔c8 39 ♘xg7 ♘g6 40 ♘xh5 ♔d7 41 ♔d3 ♔c8 42 ♔e3 ♘e7 43 ♘g7 ♘d5+ 44 ♔f3 ♘e7 45 ♘e6 ♘d5 46 ♘d4 1-0**

Game 16
Sveshnikov – J.Polgar
Biel IZ 1993

1 e4 c5 2 c3 d5 3 exd5 ♕xd5 4 d4 ♘f6 5 ♘f3 ♘c6 6 ♗e2 cxd4 7 cxd4 e6 8 0-0

Also 8 ♘c3 first is quite routine, when Black should move his queen. 8...♗b4 is inadvisable: 9 0-0 ♕d6 10 a3 ♗a5 11 ♕a4 0-0 12 ♗g5! a6 (12...♗d8) 13 ♗xf6 gxf6 14 ♖ad1 b5 15 ♕b3 ♗c7 16 ♘e4 ♕e7 17 ♕c3! ♗b7 18 d5 ♗e5 19 ♘xe5 ♘xe5 20 f4 ♖ac8? 21 d6! and after Black's mistakes White has a completely won game, Em.Lasker-Bernstein, New York 1940.

8...♗e7 9 ♘c3 ♕d8

For 9...♕d6 see Game 17. 9...♕a5 is played rarely; in addition to 10 ♗e3 followed by a3 and b4, White also has 10 ♗b5 0-0 11 ♘e5 ♘b4 12 ♕e2 a6 13 ♗c4 ♕d8 14 a3 ♘bd5 15 ♖d1 ♗d7 16 ♗g5 ± Tartakower-Gligorić, Amsterdam 1950.

10 ♗e3

To facilitate ♘e5. Other squares for the bishop achieve little, e.g. 10 ♗f4 0-0 11 ♖c1 ♘b4 12 ♗e5 ♗d7 13 a3 ♘bd5 14 ♘xd5 ♘xd5 15 ♗d3 ♗c6 16 ♕c2 g6 17 ♕d2 ♖e8 18

♖fe1 ♘f6 19 ♕f4 ♘h5 20 ♕e3 ♖c8 = Tal-Ricardi, Buenos Aires 1991.

10...0-0

Alternatively, 10...♘d5 11 ♘xd5 ♕xd5 (11...exd5) 12 ♘e5!? ♘xe5 13 dxe5 ♕a5 14 ♕d4 0-0 15 ♖fd1 ♖d8 16 ♕e4 ♖d5 17 ♗d4 b5 18 a4 bxa4 19 ♗c3 ♕b6 20 ♖xd5 exd5 21 ♕xd5 ♗b7 22 ♕d7 ♕c6 23 ♕xc6 ♗xc6 24 ♗f3 ± Vaulin-Groszpeter, Kecskemet 1993.

11 ♘e5!? *(D)*

11...♘b4?!

Aiming to maintain a blockading knight on d5 looks tempting, but in the long-term White can bring too many pieces to bear on that square. From the alternatives, both 'b' and 'c' give good prospects for equality:

a) 11...♗d7?! (too passive) 12 ♗f3 ♗e8 13 ♖c1 ♖c8 14 ♖e1 ♘a5 15 d5 exd5 16 ♘xd5 ♘xd5 17 ♖xc8 ♕xc8 18 ♕xd5 ♘c6 19 ♖c1 ± Harley-Headlong, British Ch 1993.

b) 11...♗d6!? (interesting; Black thinks his active pieces will compensate for the defects in his pawn structure) 12 ♘xc6 bxc6 13 ♗g5 ♖b8 (also 13...♗e7) 14 ♕d2 h6 15 ♗e3 ♘d5 16 ♘xd5 cxd5 with equality,

Yagupov-Tiviakov, St Petersburg 1993.

c) 11...♘d5!?, for example 12 ♘xd5 exd5 13 ♕b3 ♘a5 14 ♕a4 f6 15 b4 fxe5 16 bxa5 e4 (16...exd4 17 ♗xd4 ♗d7 18 ♗b5 ♗xb5 19 ♕xb5 ± Sveshnikov-A.Sokolov, Moscow 1983) 17 a6 bxa6 18 ♗xa6 ♗xa6 19 ♕xa6 ♕b6 = Vaulin-Ruban, Smolensk 1991.

12 ♗f3

Another method of pressuring d5 is 12 ♗c4!?; then Smagin-Banas, Trnava 1987 continued 12...♘bd5 13 ♕f3 ♕d6 14 ♖ac1 a6 15 ♗g5 ♘xc3 16 bxc3 ♘d5 17 ♗xe7 ♘xe7 18 ♗d3 ♘c6 19 ♖fe1 g6 20 h4! ±.

12...♘bd5 13 ♕b3 a5 14 ♖ac1 ♘xc3

Or 14...h6 15 ♖fd1 ♖a6 16 ♗d2 ♘b6 17 ♕b5 a4 18 a3 ± Sveshnikov-Georgadze, Tashkent 1984.

15 bxc3 a4 16 ♕c2 ♘d5 17 c4 ♘b4

17...♘xe3 18 fxe3 ♗g5 19 ♖ce1 ± Sveshnikov.

18 ♕b1 a3 19 ♖fd1 ♕c7 20 ♗f4 ♗d6 21 ♗g3?!

Stronger was 21 c5 ♗xe5 22 ♗xe5 ♕a5 23 ♗e4 ±.

21...♘c6! 22 ♘xc6 ♗xg3! 23 hxg3 bxc6 24 ♖c3 e5! 25 ♕c1 exd4 26 ♖xd4 ♗e6 27 ♖xa3 ♖xa3 28 ♕xa3 c5 29 ♖d1 ♗xc4 30 ♖c1 ♗e6 31 ♖xc5 ♕b6 32 ♖a5! g6 33 ♖a8 ♖xa8 34 ♕xa8+ ♔g7 35 a4?

35 ♗d5! was still easily decisive according to Sveshnikov. The point is there is no immediate perpetual with 35...♕d4 36 ♗xe6 ♕d1+ 37 ♔h2 ♕h5+? on account of 38 ♗h3. Now, in the game, White, has to

work hard to shepherd his passed a-pawn through whilst shielding his king from checks.

35...♕b1+ 36 ♔h2 ♕b6! 37 a5 ♕xf2 38 a6 ♕e3 39 ♕e4 ♕h6+ 40 ♕h4 ♕e3 41 ♕f4 ♕a7 42 ♕e5+ ♔g8 43 ♕b5 ♕e3 44 ♕b8+ ♔g7 45 g4 ♕h6+ 46 ♔g3 ♕e3 47 ♕b2+ ♔g8 48 ♕a1 ♕a7 49 ♕a4 ♕c7+ 50 ♕f4 ♕a5 51 ♗b7 g5 52 ♕e3 h6 53 ♔h2 ♔g7 54 ♕d4+ f6 55 ♕d6 ♕e1 56 ♕g3 ♕a5 57 ♕e3 ♔f7 58 ♕h1! (to stop ...♕c7+; meanwhile 58...♕a1+ can be met by 59 ♕g1) **58...♕b5 59 ♕c1 ♕a5 60 ♕e3 ♕b5 61 ♕c1 ♕a5 62 ♕g1 ♗d5 63 ♗xd5+ ♕xd5 64 ♕b1 ♕a5 65 a7 ♔g7 66 ♕b7+ 1-0**

Game 17
Lautier – J.Polgar
Linares 1994

1 e4 c5 2 c3 d5 3 exd5 ♕xd5 4 d4 ♘c6 5 ♘f3 ♘f6 6 ♗e2 e6 7 0-0 cxd4 8 cxd4 ♗e7 9 ♘c3 ♕d6 10 ♘b5!?

Giving a different type of position to routine continuations, as the white queen's bishop will end up on the unusual square g3.

a) 10 ♗g5 0-0:

a1) 11 ♖c1!? inhibits Black's development: 11...b6 12 ♗xf6 ♗xf6 13 ♘e4 or 11...♖d8 12 ♘b5 ♕b8 13 ♗h4! or 12...♕d7 13 ♘e5!?. However Black solves all problems with the simplifying 11...♘d5 12 ♗xe7 ♘cxe7 13 ♘e5 b6 14 ♕d2 ♗b7 15 ♖fd1 ♘g6 as in Bjelajac-Jovičić, Stara Pazova 1984.

a2) 11 ♕d2 b6 12 ♖fd1 (12 ♖ad1 ♘d5 13 ♘xd5 ♕xd5 14 ♗xe7 ♘xe7 15 ♘e5 ♕d6 16 ♗f3 ♘d5 17 ♘c4

♕d8 ∓ Kurajica-Timman, Bugojno 1980) 12...♗b7 13 ♖ac1 ♖ac8 14 h3 ♖fd8 15 ♕e3 ♘d5 16 ♘xd5 ♕xd5 17 ♗c4 ♕a5? (after 17...♕d6 Black should be OK – 18 d5 ♘a5!) 18 ♗xe6 fxe6 19 ♕xe6+ ♔h8 20 d5 ♘d4 21 ♕xe7 ♘xf3+ 22 gxf3 ♗xd5 23 ♖xc8 ♖xc8 24 ♕d7 ♗e6 (a last hope – 25 ♕xe6 ♕xg5+) 25 ♕xc8+! 1-0 Ionescu-Chandler, Innsbruck 1977.

b) 10 a3 0-0 11 b4 b6 12 ♗e3 ♗b7 13 ♕b3 ♖ac8 14 h3 ♖fd8 15 ♖fd1 h6 16 ♖ac1 ∞ Rogers-Tarjan, Buenos Aires OL 1978.

c) 10 ♕b3 0-0 11 ♖d1 b6 12 ♘b5 ♕d8 13 ♘e5 ♗b7 14 ♕h3! (an ingenious transfer of the queen to the kingside; Black should reply 14...♘b4 ∞) 14...a6?! 15 ♘c3 ♘b4 (15...♘xd4 16 ♗d3) 16 a3 ♘bd5 17 ♗d3 ♖c8 18 ♘e2 ♕d6 19 ♗g5 g6 20 ♘g3 with an attack, Balshan-Speelman, Hastings 1978.

d) 10 ♗e3 0-0 11 ♖c1 and here Black has tried a variety of set-ups:

d1) 11...♘g4 12 ♗d3! b6?! was the game Brynell-Khenkin, Stockholm 1991, and now Khenkin analyses 13 ♗xh7+!! ♔xh7 14 ♘e4 ♕d5 15 ♘fg5+ ♗xg5 16 ♘xg5+ ♔g8 17 ♕xg4.

d2) 11...♖d8 12 ♕d2 b6? 13 ♗f4 ♕d7 14 ♗b5 ♗d6 15 d5 exd5 16 ♗g5 ♗b7 17 ♗xf6 gxf6 18 ♘xd5 ± Harley-Hennigan, Norwich 1994.

d3) 11...b6 12 ♕d2 (alternatively 12 ♘b5?! ♕d7 13 ♘e5 ♘xe5 14 ♖c7 ♕d8 15 dxe5 ♘d5 16 ♖xa7 ♖xa7 17 ♘xa7 ♗b7 18 ♗f3 ♕b8 19 ♕a4 ♕xe5 20 ♗d4 ♕f4 21 ♕d7 ♗a6 22 ♖d1 ♗d6 0-1 Přibyl-Tal,

Erevan 1982) 12...♗b7 13 ♗f4 ♕d8 14 ♖fd1 ♘b4 15 ♘e5 ♖c8 16 a3 ♘bd5 17 ♗f3 ♗a8 18 ♘xd5 ♗xd5 19 ♘c6 ♕d7 20 ♘xe7+ ♕xe7 = Sveshnikov-Tal, USSR Ch 1985.

Although these standard continuations are quite playable, Black can usually equalise with a well-timed ...♘d5 or ...b6. Hence the keenness of White to disturb the equilibrium with the swift 10 ♘b5!? followed by ♗f4, as in the main game we are following.

10...♕d8 *(D)*

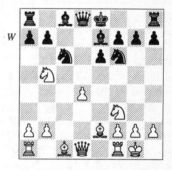

11 ♗f4

This aggressive plan has become very popular. Instead 11 ♘e5 0-0 12 ♘xc6 bxc6 13 ♘c3 and Black seeks active piece play to compensate for his weak c6-pawn:

a) 13...♘d5 14 ♘a4 ♗f6 15 ♗f3 ♖b8 16 b3! ♗a6 17 ♖e1 ♗b5 18 ♘c5 ♘c3 19 ♕c2 ♗xd4? (19...♕xd4!? 20 ♗e3 ♕d8 21 ♖ac1 intending 22 ♘e4 ∞ Blatny) 20 ♗b2! ♗xc5 21 ♕xc3 ♕f6 22 ♕xf6 gxf6 23 ♗xf6 ± Braga-Schlosser, Mitropa Cup 1993.

b) 13...♕a5 14 ♕a4 ♕b6 15 ♕c4 ♖d8 16 ♖d1 ♘d5 17 ♘a4 ♕c7 18 ♗f3 a5 19 ♘c5 ♕a7 20 b3 e5 21 ♗b2 f5!

22 g3 e4 23 ♗g2 ♔h8 Smyslov-Polgar, Monaco 1994, assessed by Smyslov as ∞.

c) 13...♖b8 14 ♘a4 ♘d5 15 ♕c2 ♖b4 16 ♗e3 ♘xe3 17 fxe3 ♗g5 18 ♖f3 ♗xe3+! 19 ♖xe3 ♕xd4 20 ♔f2 ♖xa4 21 ♖d1 ♕f6+ 22 ♖f3 ♖f4 ∓ Bannik-Korchnoi, Moscow 1961.

11...♘d5

On 11...0-0 a key position arises after 12 ♗c7 ♕d7 13 ♘e5 ♘xe5 14 dxe5 (14 ♗xe5 a6 15 ♘c7 ♖a7 has been seen a few times) 14...♘d5 15 ♗d6 a6 16 ♗xe7 ♕xe7 17 ♘d6 ♗d7. White's knight on d6 is certainly dominating, but in practice Black has held the draw by putting his bishop on c6, playing ...f6, and exchanging some rooks on the f-file, e.g. 18 ♕d4 ♗c6 19 f4 f6 20 ♗g4 ♖ad8 21 ♖ae1 (21 ♖ad1 fxe5 22 fxe5 ♘c7 23 ♕e3 ♘d5 24 ♕g3 h6 25 ♗h5 ♖xf1+ 26 ♖xf1 ♖f8 27 ♖xf8+ ♔xf8 28 ♕g6 ♘f4 29 ♕h7 ♕g5 30 ♕h8+ ♔e7 31 ♘c8+ ♔d7 32 ♘b6+ ♔e7 ½-½ Yagupov-Kiseliov, Russia 1994) 21...♘c7 22 ♕e3 fxe5 23 fxe5 ♘d5 24 ♕d2 ♘c7 25 ♕e3 ♘d5 26 ♕g3 ♘c7 27 h4 ♗d5 28 a4 ♗c6 29 ♗d1 ♖xf1+ 30 ♖xf1 ♖f8 31 ♖xf8+ ♕xf8 32 ♗b3 ♘d5 33 ♗xd5 ♗xd5 34 a5 h6 35 ♕f2 ♕e7 = Meister-Yagupov, Russia 1994.

12 ♗g3 0-0

Of course 12...a6!? 13 ♘c3 0-0 is possible, but then White has greater pressure on d5:

a) 14 ♖c1 ♘f6 15 h3 b6 16 a3 ♗b7 17 ♗d3 ♖c8 18 ♗b1 b5 19 ♕d3 ♘a5 20 ♘e5 ♘c4 ∞ J.Polgar-Tiviakov, Madrid 1994.

b) 14 ♕b3 and now:

b1) 14...♗d6 15 ♖ac1 ♘f4?! 16 ♖fd1 ♘xe2+ 17 ♘xe2 ♗xg3 18 hxg3 ♕d6 19 ♘f4 ♖d8 20 d5 ± Sveshnikov-Kaiumov, USSR 1983.

b2) 14...b6 15 ♘xd5 exd5 16 ♖ac1 ♗b7 17 ♖fd1 ♖c8 18 ♖c3 b5 19 ♘e5 ± Sveshnikov-Micić, Cheliabinsk 1990.

b3) 14...♘f6 15 ♖fd1 b5!? is interesting, e.g. 16 ♖ac1 ♗b7 17 a3 ♖c8 18 ♕a2 ♕b6 19 d5 exd5 20 ♘xd5 ♘xd5 21 ♕xd5 ♗f6 ∓ Daniliuk-Galkin, Briansky 1995.

b4) 14...♘xc3 15 bxc3 b5 (or 15...♗d6 16 ♗xd6 ♕xd6 17 ♕b6 with modest pressure for White, Stripunsky-Nedobora, Noiabrsk 1995) 16 ♖fd1 ♗b7 17 a4 b4 18 d5! exd5 19 cxb4 ♘xb4 (19...♗xb4!? Cherniaev) 20 a5! ♖e8 (20...♗c8!? Cherniaev) 21 ♗f1 ♗c5 22 ♖a4 ♕e7 23 ♖b1 ± Cherniaev-Khenkin, Biel 1994.

13 ♗c4 a6 14 ♗xd5 *(D)*

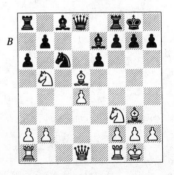

14...exd5?!

Safer is 14...axb5 15 ♗e4!? ♖a6 (15...♕b6 16 ♗f4 ♖d8 17 ♗e3 ♕a5 18 ♕c2 g6 19 ♗xc6 bxc6 20 ♕xc6 b4 21 ♘e5 f6 22 ♘c4 ♕a6 23 d5 ♗d7 24 ♕xa6 ♖xa6 25 d6 ± Kharlov-Badea, Berlin 1994) 16 ♕e2! f5

(16...♘xd4 17 ♘xd4 ♕xd4 18 ♖fd1
♕b6 19 ♗d3 ♖a5 20 ♕c2) and now
instead of 17 ♗d3 ∞ Sveshnikov-
Korchnoi, Biel IZ 1993, Sveshnikov
claims 17 ♗xc6 bxc6 18 ♗f4 is ±.

15 ♘c7 ♖a7

15...♖b8 16 ♘e5 ♗f6 17 ♖c1
♗xe5 18 ♗xe5 ♘xe5 19 dxe5 d4 20
♕d3 ♗g4 21 h3 ♗h5 22 e6 ♖c8 23
♕g3 favoured White in Sveshnikov-
Foisor, Sochi 1985.

16 ♕b3 ♗d6

16...♗g4!? (with the idea 16 ♘xd5
♗d6! ∞) has not yet been refuted.
17 ♖ad1 (17 ♕b6 ♗xf3 18 gxf3
♗b4 intending ...♗a5 was Bousfiha-
Lhagvasuren, Moscow OL 1994)
17...♗d6 18 ♘xd5 ♗xg3 19 hxg3
♗e6 20 ♘f6+ ♕xf6 21 d5 ♗g4 22
dxc6 ♕xc6 was nothing for White in
Sveshnikov-Gola, Moscow 1989. As
the game continuation is advanta-
geous for White, this looks the currently critical line.

17 ♗xd6 ♕xd6 18 ♕b6 f6

White threatened ♘e5.

19 ♖ac1 ♖f7

Alternatively 19...♗g4 20 ♖c5
♖f7 (20...♗xf3 21 gxf3 ♕f4 22 ♖xc6

bxc6 23 ♕xa7 ♕xf3 24 ♖c1 and
Black has no perpetual, Kharlov-
Röder, Torcy 1991) 21 ♘xd5 ♗xf3
22 gxf3 a5 Fomin-Shulman, St Petersburg 1994, and here Lautier gives
23 ♖e1! ±.

20 ♘e8! ♕d7

On 20...♕f4!? Lautier gives 21
♖xc6! (21 ♕c5 ± ♗g4!?) 21 bxc6 22
♕d8 ♖f8 23 ♕xc8 ♖e7 24 ♕xa6
♖fxe8 25 ♕xc6 with a clear advantage for White.

21 ♖fe1 a5! 22 ♘c7 h6 (of course
if 22...♕xc7, 23 ♖e8+) **23 ♘e6! a4
24 h3 ♖a6 25 ♕c5 ♘e7 26 ♘f4 ♖c6
27 ♕a5** (now that White's queen's
knight has settled on f4, after its remarkable journey via e8, White has
an edge; best now for Black is
27...♔h7 according to Joel Lautier)
27...♖xc1?! 28 ♖xc1 ♔h7 29 ♕c5!
± **♕f5** (the black pieces are too awkwardly placed to stop the threat;
29...♖f8 30 ♘xd5! doesn't help) **30
♘xd5! ♘xd5 31 ♕xc8 ♖d7 32 ♖e1
♘f4 33 ♖e8 ♘g6 34 ♕c4?! h5 35
♕e6 ♕b1+? 36 ♔h2 ♖c7 37 ♕d5!
♔h6 38 g4 hxg4 39 hxg4 f5 40 ♕d6
1-0**

7 4...e6 5 ♘f3 ♘f6 deferring ...♘c6

1	e4	c5
2	c3	d5
3	exd5	♕xd5
4	d4	e6
5	♘f3	♘f6 (D)

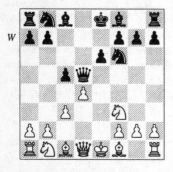

As the title of the chapter suggests, here we deal with lines where the move ...♘c6 is either long delayed or not played by Black. Naturally if Black does play ...♘c6, there are often transpositions to and from other chapters. There is also another important point to note: the move 6 ♗e3!? is commonly employed to seek a transposition to Chapter 10 (after 6...cxd4 7 cxd4 ♘c6 8 ♘c3 ♕d6 9 a3 ♗e7 10 ♗d3), and it is not clear that Black can avoid this.

Game 18 deals with the modest 6 ♗e2 systems. For once Black might regret not developing his queen's knight earlier, as 8 ♘e5!? is a direct

and logical exploitation. Games 19 and 20 cover the 6 ♘a3 lines, where postponing ...♘c6 definitely gives Black a wider choice of defences to counter ideas like ♘b5 and ♗f4. For example, the move ...♘a6 is available if required. However, these 6 ♘a3 systems are popular with White, and this is understandable when you see that the 'undeveloping' 6...♕d8 (Game 20) is the main line! After the continuation 7 ♘c2 (also 7 ♗f4!?) White very rarely gets an isolated d-pawn, as he can always recapture on d4 with either his queen or a knight. Whether to evaluate many of the resulting positions '=' or '±' is a matter of taste. White has, in many cases, only an exceedingly modest edge; but there again, he has no weaknesses and there are few losing chances. On the whole I have assessed these positions as equal, but if you are a higher-rated player wanting to win with Black, this is not the sort of equality you want! So if you favour the ♘a3 systems with White, don't necessarily be discouraged by the '=' assessments – many of these positions have play left in them.

Finally, Game 21 covers 6 ♗d3 lines where Black attempts to gain a tangible concession by delaying both the development of his queen's knight and the exchange ...cxd4. After 6...♗e7 7 0-0 0-0 White has a choice. He can concede that Black has played a clever move-order, and continue 8 ♗e3 or 8 ♕e2, when after ...cxd4 and/or ...♘c6 we reach positions examined in later chapters where White is now committed to certain systems. Or White can continue 8 c4!?, with unclear play. At present this move-order looks quite playable for Black.

In conclusion, as a general rule, it is sensible for Black to delay ...♘c6 for a while as it takes some of the sting out of White's early ♘a3 systems. However if White chooses the 6 ♗e2 ♗e7 7 0-0 line (with a view to a quick ♘e5!?), then 7...♘c6 or 7...cxd4 8 cxd4 ♘c6 should be considered, giving a transposition to other chapters.

Game 18
Kr.Georgiev – Lalev
Bulgaria 1983

1 e4 c5 2 c3 d5 3 exd5 ♕xd5 4 d4 e6 5 ♘f3 ♘f6 6 ♗e2 ♗e7 7 0-0

Instead 7 ♗e3 cxd4 8 cxd4 0-0 9 ♘c3 ♕d6 10 0-0 would transpose into a line from Chapter 6, Game 17, while 7...♘g4 8 ♗f4 0-0 9 0-0 is analysed in the note to White's eighth move in the present game. 7 c4 also transposes to the present game after 7...♕d8 8 0-0 0-0.

A flexible move is 7 ♘a3 when 7...♘c6?! 8 ♘b5 ♕d8 9 dxc5 ♗xc5 10 ♕xd8+ gives White an extra tempo (♗e2) on the endgame examined in Chapter 6, Game 14. White

also seems to retain a plus after 7...0-0 8 ♘b5, e.g. 8...♘a6 9 0-0 cxd4 10 ♘bxd4 ♘c5 11 c4! ♕d8 12 ♗f4 ♘h5 13 ♗e3 ♕c7 14 ♘b5 ♕b8 15 b4 ♘d7 16 c5 ± Radovici-Sveshnikov, Bucharest 1976. A good response is the prophylactic 7...♕d8!, when after 8 ♘c2 the white bishop is less aggressively posted at e2 (rather than d3) in comparison to some other ♘a3 lines. Nevertheless White is in no danger of becoming worse, as he can always recapture with a piece on d4 and avoid an isolated pawn.

Please note that the actual move-order of the illustrative game (1 e4 c5 2 ♘f3 e6 3 c3 d5 4 exd5 ♕xd5 5 ♗e2 ♘f6 6 0-0 ♗e7 7 d4) has been changed to accommodate the above note.

7...0-0 *(D)*

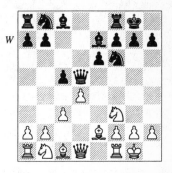

8 ♘e5

a) 8 c4!? (aiming to utilise that queenside majority again) 8...♕d8 (8...♕f5?! 9 ♘c3 ♖d8?? 10 ♘h4 1-0 trapping Black's queen was the brief game Lane-Flesch, London 1983) 9 ♘c3 (9 dxc5 ♗xc5 10 ♘c3 ♕xd1 11 ♖xd1 ♘c6 12 a3 b6 13 b4 ♗e7 14 ♗f4 ♗b7 15 ♗d6 ♗xd6 16 ♖xd6

♖fd8 17 ♖ad1 ♖xd6 18 ♖xd6 ♔f8 = is Stein-Fahnenschmidt, Germany 1989 while 9...♘bd7!? Vatter-Ribli, Germany 1986 is also possible) 9...cxd4 (9...b6!? ∞ of Sveshnikov-Georgiev, Athens 1983 is worth consideration; presumably the idea is 10 d5 exd5 11 cxd5 ♗b7 12 ♗c4 b5) 10 ♘xd4 a6 (10...e5 11 ♘db5 ♘c6 12 ♘d5 ± Mariotti-Soos, Rome 1982) 11 ♗f4 ♘bd7 12 ♗g3 ♘c5 (12...♗b4 13 ♕c2 ♕a5 14 ♖ac1 ♖e8 15 ♖fd1 ♕g5 16 ♘f3 ♕g6 17 ♘e5 ♘xe5 18 ♗xe5 ♘d7 19 ♗g3 ± Brynell-Kochiev, Leningrad 1989) 13 ♗f3 ♕b6 14 ♕c2 ♗d7 15 ♖ab1 a5 16 ♖fd1 ♖ac8 17 ♕e2 ♖fe8 18 ♘db5 and White went on to win with a masterly endgame demonstration in Hort-Nunn, BBC Mastergame 1979.

b) 8 ♗e3 ♘g4 (8...cxd4) 9 ♗f4:

b1) 9...♘c6 10 c4 ♕f5 11 ♗c7 cxd4 (Adorjan gives 11...♘f6 12 ♘c3 cxd4 13 ♘xd4 ♘xd4 14 ♕xd4 ♗d7 =) 12 ♘xd4 ♘xd4 13 ♕xd4 ♘f6 14 ♗f3 ± Sveshnikov-Adorjan, Sarajevo 1983.

b2) 9...♖d8?! 10 h3 (improving on 10 ♕c2 ♘c6 11 ♖d1 cxd4 12 cxd4 ♘b4 13 ♕d2 ♕f5 ∓ Hulak-Adorjan, Banja Luka 1983) 10...♘f6 11 ♗c7! ♖d7?! (11...♖e8 12 ♘e5 ±; alternatively 11...♖f8 12 ♘e5 ♘a6 13 ♗f3 ♘e4 14 ♕c2 f5 15 ♘d2 ♘xc7 16 ♘xe4 fxe4 17 ♗xe4 ♕d8 18 ♗xh7+ ♔h8 19 ♘g6+ ♔xh7 20 ♘xe7+ ♔h8 21 ♘g6+ ♔g8 22 ♘xf8 ♕xf8 23 dxc5 ♕xc5 24 ♖ad1 ± is analysis by Tsyn and Pechenkin) 12 c4! ♕f5 13 g4 ♘xg4 14 hxg4 ♕xg4+ 15 ♗g3 ± Pechenkin-Vershinin, Russia 1994.

8...cxd4

8...♖d8 9 ♗f3 ♕d6 10 ♗f4! ♕b6 11 ♘d2 ♕xb2 12 ♘dc4 ♕b5 13 ♖b1 ♕e8 14 ♗xb7 ♗xb7 15 ♖xb7 ± Sveshnikov-Novikov, Tashkent 1984.

9 cxd4 ♖d8

a) 9...♕d8 10 ♘c3 (10 ♗f3 is also reasonable: 10...♘d5 11 ♘c3 ♘xc3 12 bxc3 ♘d7 13 ♗f4 ♘xe5 14 ♗xe5 ♗d6 15 ♖e1 ♖b8 16 ♕d3 b6 17 a4 ♗b7 18 ♗e4 ♗xe4 19 ♕xe4 ♖c8 with equality, Dubrovolsky-Chekhov, Germany 1993, but White had more testing plans available) 10...♘bd7 (10...♘c6) 11 ♗f4 ♘b6 12 ♗f3 ♘bd5 13 ♗g3 ♕b6 14 ♘c4 ♕d8 15 ♕b3 b6 16 ♖fe1 ♖e8 17 ♖ac1 ♗a6 18 ♘e3 ♗b7 19 ♘b5 ♖c8 20 ♘c7! ♖f8 21 ♘cxd5 ± Sveshnikov-Inkiov, Sochi 1983.

b) 9...♘bd7!? 10 ♘c3 (10 ♗f3 ♕a5 11 ♘xd7!?) 10...♕a5 11 ♘c4 ♕c7 12 ♕b3 b6! 13 ♗f3 ♗b7 14 ♘b5 ♕b8 15 ♗xb7 (15 ♗f4? ♕xf4 16 ♗xb7 a6! 17 ♘c3 ♘g4 18 g3 ♕h6 19 h4 ♗xh4 −+ Petursson) 15...♕xb7 16 ♗f4 a6 17 ♘c3 ♖fc8 18 ♖fe1 b5 19 ♘e3 ♘h5 20 ♗g3 ♘xg3 21 hxg3 ♗f8 = Hjartarson-Petursson, Tilburg 1992, but again, White had many options earlier on.

10 ♘c3!

Stronger than 10 ♗e3, because Black cannot capture the d-pawn with impunity: 10...♕xd4 11 ♕xd4 ♖xd4 12 ♘b5 ♖e4 13 ♗f3 ♖xe5 14 ♘c7.

10...♕a5 11 ♗f3

Perhaps even more promising is 11 ♘c4!? ♕c7 12 ♘b5 ♕c6 13 ♘e5 ♕b6 14 a4! ♖f8 15 ♗f4 ♘d5 16 ♘c4 ♕d8 17 ♗xb8 ♖xb8 18 ♘xa7 ± Sveshnikov-Gostisa, Bled 1991.

11...♘bd7 12 ♕e2 ♘xe5 13 dxe5 ♘d7

Dubious according to Georgiev, but 13...♘d5 did not fare better in the game Kharlov-Franco, Ibercaja 1994: 14 ♘xd5 exd5 15 ♖d1 d4?! (perhaps 15...♗e6) 16 ♕e4 ♕b6 17 b3 a5 18 ♗b2 ♗c5 19 ♖ac1 a4 20 ♕c2 ♖a5 21 b4 ♗xb4 22 ♕xc8 ♗f8 23 ♕c7 1-0.

14 ♗f4 ♖b8?

Falling for a magnificient tactic. 14...♘c5!? intending 15...♗d7 needs a practical test.

15 ♘d5! ♗f8

Or 15...exd5 16 e6 ♖a8 (16...fxe6 17 ♕xe6+ ♔h8 18 ♕xe7 +−) 17 exd7 ♖xd7 18 ♗g4 ±.

16 ♗d2! ♕a6 17 ♗g5! ♕xe2 18 ♗xe2 ♘f6 (desperation, but after 18...♖e8 19 ♘c7 the rook is trapped) **19 ♘xf6+ gxf6 20 ♗xf6 ♖d2 21 ♗f3 ♗d7 22 ♖ad1 ♖xd1 23 ♖xd1 ♗c6 24 ♗xc6 bxc6 25 g4 ♗g7 26 b3 h6 27 ♖d7 a5 28 ♖d8+ ♖xd8 29 ♗xd8 1-0**

Game 19
Blatny – Chekhov
Leipzig 1988

1 e4 c5 2 c3 d5 3 exd5 ♕xd5 4 d4 ♘f6 5 ♘f3 e6 6 ♘a3 ♗e7

For the main line, 6...♕d8, see Game 20.

a) 6...a6 is an understandable reaction to White's last move. Denied b5, the white knight now nevertheless centralises with gain of time by threatening a fork on the freshly weakened b6-square. 7 ♘c4 ♘bd7 and here:

a1) 8 ♗e2 cxd4 (8...b5 9 ♘ce5 ∞ Dückstein-Zso.Polgar, Vienna 1993) 9 ♕xd4 (9 cxd4 ♗b4+) 9...♗c5 10 ♕xd5 ♘xd5 = as in Sermek-Skembris, Ljubljana Vidmar mem 1993.

a2) 8 a4!? b6 (8...cxd4 9 ♕xd4 ♗c5 10 ♕xd5 exd5 11 ♘e3 ± and for once Black has the isolated d-pawn, Hort-Kishnev, Bern 1992) 9 ♗e2 ♗b7 10 0-0 ♗e7 11 ♗f4 ♘e4 12 ♗d3 0-0 13 ♖e1 ♘ef6 14 ♘e3 ♕c6 15 ♘e5 ♕c8 16 ♗g5 ♖e8 17 ♘3g4 ♕d8 18 ♘xf6+ ♘xf6 19 ♗xf6 ♗xf6 20 ♗xh7+! +− Gluzman-Landa, Belgrade 1991.

a3) 8 ♗f4 (played repeatedly by Vorotnikov) 8...b5 9 ♘e3 ♕c6 (10...♕e4 10 ♗g3 ♗b7 11 a4 is riskier, Vorotnikov-Bönsch, Leipzig 1979 and Vorotnikov-Vasiukov, Beltsy 1979) 10 ♗e2 ♗b7 11 ♘e5 ♘xe5 12 ♗xe5 ♘d7!? 13 ♗f3 ♕b6 14 ♗xb7 ♕xb7 15 ♕g4 cxd4 16 cxd4 ♘xe5 17 dxe5 g6 18 0-0 ♗g7 19 ♕f4 h5 20 ♖fe1 ♕b8 21 ♘f1 0-0 = Vorotnikov-Baby, Vladivostok 1990.

a4) 8 ♗g5!?:

a41) 8...b5 9 ♗xf6! ♘xf6 10 ♘b6 ♕e4+ 11 ♗e2 ♖b8 12 ♘xc8 ♖xc8 13 0-0 ± illustrates White's idea.

a42) After 8...♗e7 9 ♗e2, 9...b5?! backfired spectacularly in the game Smagin-Stohl, Tallinn 1986, viz. 10 ♗xf6 ♗xf6 11 ♘fd2!! bxc4 12 ♗f3 ♕d6 13 ♗xa8 ±; safest was 9...cxd4 10 ♕xd4 ± Smagin.

a43) 8...cxd4 9 ♗xf6 gxf6 10 ♘xd4 ♗c5 (Black's pawns are doubled but he has active pieces) 11 ♘e3 ♕d6 12 ♗e2 ♘e5 13 0-0 ♗d7 14 ♕b3 ♕b6! 15 ♕xb6 ♗xb6 16 ♖ad1 0-0-0 = Kotliar-Yermolinsky, New

York Open 1992. However White's 14th looks suspicious; after 14 b4!? for example, it is not clear where Black's king will ultimately find sanctuary.

b) Another try is 6...cxd4 7 ♘b5 and now:

b1) 7...♘a6 8 ♕xd4 ♗c5 9 ♕xd5 ♘xd5 10 b4 ♗e7 11 a3 ♘ac7 (or 11...0-0 12 c4 ♗f6 13 ♖a2 ♘c3 14 ♘xc3 ♗xc3+ 15 ♗d2 ± Lombardy-Arnason, Iceland 1985) 12 ♗b2 f6 13 0-0-0 ♗d7 14 ♘xc7+ ♗xc7 15 ♗d3 e5 16 ♖he1 0-0-0 17 c4 a5!? ∞ Vorotnikov-Osnos, USSR 1986, although clearly Black is struggling to restrain the queenside pawns in this line.

b2) 7...♕d8:

b21) 8 ♘bxd4!? a6 9 ♗f4 ♘d5 10 ♗g3 ♗d6 11 ♕a4+?! (Striković suggests the improvement 11 ♗c4) 11...♗d7 12 ♕b3 ♗xg3 13 hxg3 ♕c7 14 ♕a3 ♘c6!, Striković-Andersson, San Sebastian 1994, is equal, as 15 ♘b5 can be answered by 15...♕a5 16 ♘d6+ ♔e7! 17 ♘f5+ ♔f6.

b22) 8 ♕xd4 a6 (8...♘d5 9 ♘xa7 costs a pawn and 8...♕xd4 9 ♘fxd4 ♘a6 10 ♗f4 is ±, for example 10...♘d5 11 ♘d6+ ♗xd6 12 ♗xd6 ♗d7 13 ♘b5 f6 14 ♗a3 Meštrović-Skembris, Cannes 1995) 9 ♕xd8+ ♔xd8 10 ♘bd4 (10 ♘e5!? axb5 11 ♘xf7+ ♔e8 12 ♘xh8 ♗c5?! 13 ♗xb5+ ♗d7 14 ♗d3 ± as in the game Gurieli-Ioseliani, Tbilisi 1991, is critical and possibly strong; White will probably be able to desperado his/her knight for two more pawns even after the superior 12...♗d7) 10...♗d6 11 ♗g5 ♗d7 12 0-0-0 ♔c7

13 ♗h4 ♘c6 = Rozentalis-Andersson, Tilburg 1993.

7 ♘b5 ♘a6 (D)

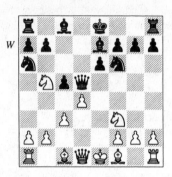

8 ♗e2

Preferable is 8 c4! (8 ♗e3 ♘g4 ∞ Chekhov-Yusupov, USSR 1979):

a) 8...♕e4+ 9 ♗e2 cxd4 10 0-0 0-0 11 ♗d3 ♕g4 12 ♖e1 ♘d7 and now tremendous complications resulted from 13 ♗e2 ♕g6 14 ♘fxd4 ♖d8 15 ♗h5 ♕f6 16 ♗g5 ♕xg5 17 ♗xf7+ ♔xf7 18 ♘xe6 ± in Svesh-nikov-A.Sokolov, Sochi 1983; in his notes Sveshnikov recommends an improvement: 13 a3 ♘ac5 14 ♗xh7+ ♔xh7 15 ♘g5+ ♕xg5 16 ♗xg5 ♗xg5 17 b4 ♘a6 18 ♕h5+ ±.

b) 8...♕d8 9 ♗e2 0-0 10 0-0 cxd4 (10...♘c7 11 ♘c3 cxd4 12 ♕xd4 ♕xd4 13 ♘xd4 e5 14 ♘f3 ± Vera-Remon, Cienfuegos 1984) 11 ♗f4! (11 ♘fxd4 e5) 11...♘e8 (11...♗d7 12 ♘bxd4 ♕b6 13 ♖b1 ♕a5 14 a3 ♖fc8 15 b4 ♕d8 16 ♘e5 ♗a4 17 ♕d3 ♗d6 18 ♕e3 ± Am.Rodriguez-Adorjan, Thessaloniki OL 1984) 12 ♕xd4 ♕xd4 13 ♘fxd4 ±. That White has real chances from this position is illustrated by two games: 13...♗f6 14 ♗e3 ♘ac7 15 ♖fd1 ♔h8

16 &f3 g6 17 &d2 &e7 18 &xc7 &xc7 19 &f4 &e8 20 &c6! ± C.Rinaldi-D.Hamilton, corr. 1985 and 13...f6 14 &b3 &b4 15 a3 &c6 16 &f3 g5 17 &e3 a6 18 &xc6 bxc6 19 &a7 c5 20 &c6 &d6 21 &xc5 ± Ree-Langeweg, Amsterdam 1980.

8...cxd4 9 &xd4

Very solid is 9 &bxd4 0-0 10 0-0 &d8 11 &f4 with an equal position, as in Vorotnikov-Chekhov, Moscow 1991 and Nadyrkhanov-Poluliakhov, Novorossisk 1995.

9...0-0 10 0-0 &d8!

After this Black even has chances of an advantage. Others:

a) 10...&d7 11 &xd5 (11 &e5 &xb5 12 &xd5 &xd5 13 &xb5 &c5 14 &d2 &e4 15 &ad1 ½-½ Benko-Petrosian, Lone Pine 1978) 11...&xd5 12 &d1?! (12 &bd4 &c5 13 &e5) 12...&fd8 13 &d2 &c5 14 &bd4 a5 15 c4?! &b4 ∓ Blatny-Vogt, Leipzig 1988.

b) 10...&xd4 11 &bxd4 &c5 12 &g5 (12 &e5 &fd7 13 &c4 &a4 14 &d2 &db6 15 &xb6 &xb6 16 &ad1 a6 17 &c1 e5 18 &f3 f6 = Benko-Sax, Aruba 1992) 12...h6 13 &h4 g5 14 &g3 &fe4 15 &fd1 &xg3 16 hxg3 &f6 17 &b3 &a4 = Bondoc-Gheorghiu, Romania 1978.

11 &g5

11 &d1 &d7 12 &f4 &e4 13 &xe4 &xe4 14 &e3 &c5 15 &xc5 &axc5 16 &e5 &xb5 17 &xb5 f6 18 &d3 a6 19 &xc5 &xc5 20 &c4 &f7 ∓ Lutovac-Smyslov, Bor 1980.

11...&xd4 12 &bxd4 &c5 13 &ad1 &d7 14 &e5?!

14 &c2 &a4 15 b3 &c6 16 &c1! intending &b2.

14...&a4 15 b3?

15 &c1 h6 ∓. Now substantial tactical complications begin which ultimately net Black the better endgame.

15...&ce4! 16 &f3!?

After 16 bxa4 &xg5 17 f3 &d5 18 h4 Black has 18...&xc3 19 hxg5 &c5! −+.

16...&xg5 17 &xb7 &ab8 18 &c6 &ge4! 19 &xa4 &xc3 20 &ec6 &xd1

Chekhov and Blatny give 20...&c5! 21 &xb8 &xd4 22 &xd4 &xd4 ∓ as more accurate. Clearly Black has acquired a sizeable advantage in any case, so the rest of the game is scarcely relevant to the opening.

21 &xe7+ &f8 22 &xd1 &xd4 23 &xd4 &xe7 24 f3?! &d5 25 &c6 &b4 26 &d7+ &f6 27 &e4 &xa2 28 &xa7 &c3 29 &b7 &d8 30 &f2 &d2+ 31 &e3 &xg2 32 h4 &xe4 33 fxe4 &h2 −+ 34 e5+ &g6 35 &b4 &h3+ 36 &d2 h5 37 &c2 &f5 38 &b7 &xe5 39 &xf7 g6 40 b4 &xh4 41 &c3 &d5 42 b5 &c5 43 &f6 &g4 44 &xe6 &xb5 45 &d3 &c5 46 &e5+ &d6 47 &a5 &e6 48 &e3 &f6 49 &f3 &g7 50 &a7+ &h6 51 &a5 &b4 52 &g3 &b3+ 53 &g2 h4 54 &h2 g5 55 &a6+ &h5 56 &a7 &b2+ 57 &h1 &d2 58 &b7 &e2 59 &a7 h3 60 &g1 g4 61 &h1 g3 62 &a1 &g4 63 &b1 &f3 64 &a1 &d2 65 &e1 &f2 66 &g1 g2+ 67 &h2 &e2 0-1

The conclusion must be that after 9 &xd4 Black has a fully satisfactory position, as it is difficult for White to get his queenside majority rolling in this particular line. Therefore the sideline with 8 c4! is the only realistic try for advantage.

Game 20
Vera – J.Horvath
Sochi 1985

**1 e4 c5 2 c3 d5 3 exd5 ♕xd5 4 d4 e6
5 ♘f3 ♘f6 6 ♘a3 ♕d8** *(D)*

7 ♘c2
Or:
a) 7 ♗f4!? (an interesting idea patronised by Blatny; White aims for dxc5 and a promising endgame) and now:

a1) 7...cxd4!? (logical and under-rated) 8 ♘xd4 (8 ♘b5 ♘d5 9 ♗xb8 ♖xb8 10 ♕xd4 a6 11 ♕e5 ♖a8) 8...♗c5 (8...♗xa3 9 ♕a4+ ♘bd7 10 ♕xa3 ±; alternatively 8...a6?! 9 ♕b3! ± Vera-Gheorghiu, Timisoara 1987 as 9...♘d5? would lose to 10 ♗xb8 ♖xb8 11 ♘c6) 9 ♘ab5 ♘d5 10 ♗g3 a6 (10...0-0 11 ♘b3 ♗e7 fails to 12 ♘xa7! ♖xa7 13 ♗xb8 winning a pawn, Blatny-Bönsch, Bad Wöris-hofen 1992) 11 ♘b3 ♗e7 12 ♘5d4 as in Marić-Cordes, Bad Wörishofen 1985 looks equal to me. *Informator*'s assessment of ± may have put people off this line, but after 12...0-0 13 ♗d3 Black has numerous alternatives to 13...f5?! as played by Cordes.

a2) 7...a6?! 8 dxc5 ♕xd1+ 9 ♖xd1 ± ♗xc5 10 ♘c4 ♘d5? (10...0-0) 11 ♘d6+ ♗e7 12 ♘f5+! ± (a neat ma-noeuvre; 12...♔f6 13 ♗g5+ ♔xf5 14 ♗d3+ leads to a swift mate) 12...♔f8 13 ♗c4! exf5 (now 13...♘xf4? 14 ♖d8 is mate) 14 ♗xd5 ± Blatny-Brustman, Warsaw 1987.

a3) 7...♘bd7 8 ♘c4 ♘d5 9 ♗g3 (trying to improve on 9 ♗d6 ♗e7 with equality, Blatny-Votava, Ger-many 1993) 9...♗e7 10 ♘e3 (10 ♘d6+?! ♗xd6 11 ♗xd6 ♕b6 Blatny) 10...0-0 11 ♘xd5 exd5 12 ♗e2 ♕b6 13 ♕c2 (± Blatny) and now instead of 13...f5?! as in Blatny-Votava, Lazne Bohdanec 1995, Ftačnik's sugges-tion 13...♘f6 looks unclear after 14 0-0 ♗g4.

a4) 7...♘c6 8 dxc5 ♘d5! 9 ♗d6 ♗xd6 10 cxd6 ♕xd6 11 ♗c4 (11 ♕d2!? ♗e7 12 ♗b5 0-0 13 ♖d1 ♗d7 14 0-0 was the game Blatny-Suba, Baden-Baden 1988; White can play but his edge is very small) 11...♕e7! 12 ♕d2 (12 0-0? ♘xc3! ∓ Hennings-Korchnoi, Siegen 1970) 12...0-0 13 0-0 ♖d8 14 ♖ad1 b6 (14...♘f6 is a more solid move) 15 ♕e2 ♘xc3? 16 bxc3 ♕xa3 17 ♕e4 ♗b7 18 ♘g5 ± 1-0 Striković-Zarković, Yugoslavia 1992.

b) Another possibility is 7 ♘c4 (heading for e5) 7...♘c6 (7...♗e7 8 ♗e3 cxd4 9 ♘xd4 ♘d5 10 ♗d2 0-0 11 ♗d3 ♗f6 12 ♘f3 ♕c7 13 0-0 ♘f4 14 ♗xf4 ♕xf4 15 ♘d6 g6 16 ♘xc8 ♖xc8 17 ♕e2 ♘d7 ½-½ Kholmov-Dolmatov, Klaipeda 1988) 8 ♘ce5 cxd4 (8...♘xe5!? 9 ♘xe5 a6 Hort-Dydyshko, Debrecen Echt 1992) 9 ♗b5 ♕d5 10 ♕a4 ♗d7 11 ♘xd7

♘xd7 12 ♗xc6 bxc6 13 ♕xd4 ♗c5
= Rozentalis-Yudasin, Lvov 1987.

c) Finally 7 ♗e2 ♘c6 8 ♘c2 (8 0-0 cxd4 9 ♘b5 and now 9...dxc3 looks risky, e.g. 10 ♕xd8+ ♔xd8 11 ♘g5 ♔e7 12 bxc3 Knobel-Daubenfeld, corr. 1988; instead 9...♗e7 10 ♘bxd4 ♘xd4 11 ♕xd4 is an acceptable ending for Black that has been played several times, while 9...a6!? 10 ♘bxd4 ♘xd4 11 ♕xd4 ♕xd4 12 ♘xd4 e5 13 ♘b3 ♗e6 is a reasonable alternative, Nun-A.Petrosian, Polanica Zdroj 1989) and now:

c1) 8...b6!? 9 ♗b5 (9 0-0 ♗b7 = Dorfman) 9...♗d7 10 ♕e2 cxd4 11 ♘cxd4 ♘xd4 12 ♘xd4 ♗c5 13 ♘c6? (13 ♗e3 =) 13...♕c7 14 ♘e5 ♗xf2+! 15 ♔f1 (15 ♔xf2 ♕xe5 ∓) 15...♗c5 16 ♗f4 0-0 17 ♘g6 ♗xb5 18 ♕xb5 e5! 19 ♗xe5 ♕c8 ∓ Sveshnikov-Dorfman, USSR 1979.

c2) 8...cxd4 9 ♘cxd4 ♘xd4 10 ♕xd4 ♕xd4 11 ♘xd4 a6 12 ♗f4 ♘d7 13 ♘b3 ♗e7 14 0-0-0 e5 15 ♗e3 0-0 = Minev-Honfi, Bucharest 1973.

c3) 8...♗e7 9 0-0 0-0:

c31) After 10 ♘e5, 10...cxd4 11 ♘xc6 bxc6 12 ♕xd4?! c5! 13 ♕xd8 ♖xd8 14 ♗f3 ♖b8 ∓ gave Black active pieces in M.Mihaljčišin-Bukić, Banja Luka 1974 and 10...♕c7!? was also to be considered.

c32) The developing 10 ♗g5 cxd4 11 ♘cxd4 = Hulak-Suba, Vinkovci 1977 is sensible.

c33) 10 dxc5 ♗xc5 11 ♗f4 b6 12 ♗d3 ♗b7 13 ♕e2 ♗d6 14 ♗g5 ♗e7 15 ♖ad1 ♕c7 16 ♘cd4 ♖ad8 = Kholmov-Ionescu, Baile Herculane 1984.

7...♗e7

Or 7...♘bd7 (for 7...♘c6 8 ♗d3 see Chapter 6 while 7...♕c7 8 ♗d3 ♘bd7 gives standard-type positions, e.g. 9 ♕e2 a6 10 a4 b6 11 0-0 ♗e7 12 ♗g5 ♗b7 13 ♗h4 0-0 14 ♗g3 ♗d6 15 ♗xd6 ♕xd6 16 ♘e5 ♖fd8 17 ♖fd1 cxd4 18 ♘xd7 ♖xd7 19 ♘xd4 ♖ad8 = Okhotnik-Mochalov, Ajka KC 1992) 8 g3!? (this fianchetto is a common theme in the ♘a3-c2 variation; 8 ♗e2 ♕c7 9 0-0 ♗e7 10 ♗g5 0-0 11 dxc5 ♘xc5 12 ♘cd4 a6 13 ♕c2 b6 14 ♗h4 ♗b7 15 ♗g3 ♕c8 16 ♘d2 ♘fe4 = Borgo-Portisch, Reggio Emilia 1993) 8...b6 9 ♗g2 ♗b7 10 0-0 ♖c8!? 11 ♕e2 ♗e7 12 ♖d1 0-0 13 dxc5 ♗xc5 14 ♘e5 ♗xg2 15 ♔xg2 ♖c7 16 ♘xd7 ♖xd7 17 ♗e3 ♗xe3 18 ♘xe3 h5 = Karaklajić-Averkin, Cetinje 1990.

8 ♗d3

Again 8 g3!? is a solid plan: 8...b6 (8...♗d7 9 ♗g2 0-0 10 0-0 ♗c6 11 ♕e2 ♘bd7 12 ♖d1 ♕c8 13 c4 ♖e8 14 b3 a5 15 ♗b2 b6 16 ♘e3 ± Sveshnikov-Romanishin, Moscow 1985) 9 ♗g2 ♗b7 10 0-0 ♘bd7 11 c4 0-0 12 ♗f4 ♕c8 13 ♕e2 ♗e4 14 ♘e5 ♗xg2 15 ♔xg2 cxd4 16 ♘xd4 ♘xe5 17 ♗xe5 ♘d7 18 ♘f3 ♘xe5 19 ♘xe5 ♗f6 = Lane-Sher, Hastings 1990.

8...0-0 9 ♕e2 ♘bd7 *(D)*
10 ♗f4

The standard 10 0-0 transposes to Dončević-Razuvaev, Palma 1991: 10...b6 11 ♗g5 h6 (11...♗b7 12 ♖ad1 ♕c7 13 ♗a6 ♗xa6 14 ♕xa6 ♖fe8 15 ♖fe1 ♗f8 16 ♗h4 ♕c8 17 ♕xc8 ♖axc8 18 ♘e5 ± Godena-Novikov, Forli 1991) 12 ♗h4 ♗b7 13 ♖ad1 ♘h5!? 14 ♗xe7 ♕xe7 15 ♗e4 ♘f4

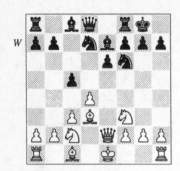

16 ♕e1 ♘f6 17 ♗xb7 ♕xb7 18 ♕e5 ♘g6 =. With the move 10 ♗f4, White is hinting he is gutsy enough to castle queenside depending on how Black reacts.

10...a6!?

10...b6 11 0-0-0 (11 0-0) 11...♗b7 12 ♘e5 ♕c8 13 ♖he1 a6 14 ♗g5 cxd4 15 ♘xd7 ♕xd7 16 ♘xd4 ♘d5 17 h4 ∞ Sveshnikov-Gavrikov, Riga 1985 while 10...♖e8 11 ♘e5 cxd4 12 ♘xd4 ♘xe5 13 ♗xe5 ♘d7 Vorotnikov-Yudasin, USSR 1984 is also possible.

11 ♘e5 b5!? 12 ♘c6 ♕e8 13 a4 c4 14 ♗e4 ♘xe4 15 ♕xe4 ♘b6 16 axb5 ♗b7 17 ♗e5! axb5

17...f6 18 ♗c7!.

18 ♖xa8 ♗xa8?

Vera points out that the surprising 18...♘xa8! is an improvement. After 19 ♕g4, in contrast to the game, Black has 19...f6! 20 ♕xe6+? (20 ♘xe7+ ♕xe7 21 ♗f4 is equal – Vera) 20...♖f7 21 ♘xe7+ ♕xe7 –+ as the black knight is no longer *en prise* on b6.

19 ♕g4 g6 20 ♘xe7+ ♕xe7 21 ♕g3 ± ♕b7 22 ♘e3 ♕e4 23 0-0 f5? (now the dark squares around the black king really start to suffer) **24**

♕g5 ♘d7?! 25 f3! ♕d3 26 ♗d6 ♖e8 27 h4 e5 28 ♖d1 ♕e2 29 dxe5 ♗c6 30 ♖f1 ♖xe5 31 ♘xf5 ♘f7 32 ♕g3 ♕e6 33 ♘d4 ♕xd6 34 ♕xd6 ♘xd6 35 ♘xc6 ♖e2 36 ♖f2 ♖e1+ 37 ♖f1 ♖e2 38 ♖f2 ♖e1+ 39 ♔h2 ♘f5 40 ♘a7 ♘xh4 41 ♘xb5 ♘f5 42 ♘a3 ♘e3 43 ♔g3 ♗f7 44 ♘c2 ♘f5+ 45 ♔f4 ♖e7 46 g4 ♘d6 47 ♖d2 1-0

Game 21
Halasz – Sax
Bagneux 1984

1 e4 c5 2 c3 d5 3 exd5 ♕xd5 4 d4 e6 5 ♘f3 ♘f6 6 ♗d3 ♗e7

Black's most significant independent idea in this variation involves waiting until White captures with dxc5, and then playing his queen's knight via d7 or a6 to recapture the pawn on c5. White as usual has the queenside majority, and the prospect of advancing b4 with tempo against the knight on c5.

7 0-0

Alternatives:

a) 7 dxc5:

a1) 7...♕xc5 8 0-0 0-0 9 ♕e2 ♘bd7 10 ♘bd2 ♖d8 11 ♖d1 ♕c7 12 ♘b3 b6 13 ♗g5 ♗b7 14 ♗h4 ♗xf3 15 ♕xf3 ♘e5 = Grzesik-Lobron, Germany 1987.

a2) 7...0-0 is complicated after 8 ♗e3!?, e.g. 8...♖d8 9 ♗c2 ♕h5 10 ♕e2 ♗xc5 11 ♗g5 ♘c6 12 ♘bd2 e5 13 ♗xf6 gxf6 14 ♘e4 ♗e7 15 ♘g3 ♕h6 16 ♗f5 ± Ghinda-Radev, Bankya 1977, although Black can try 8...♘c6!?, when 9 0-0 ♖d8! would be Chapter 8.

a3) 7...♗xc5 8 0-0 0-0 9 ♕c2 ♘bd7 10 ♘bd2 b6 11 ♘e4 ♗b7 12 ♖e1 h6 13 c4 ♕c6 14 ♗f4 ♖ad8 15 ♖ad1 ♘xe4 16 ♗xe4 ♕c8 17 a3 a5 18 ♘e5 ♘f6 19 ♗xb7 ♕xb7 20 ♘d3 ♗d4 = Novopashin-Mikhalchishin, Volgodonsk 1981.

b) 7 ♗e3!? usually transposes into later chapters. One unique response is 7...b6 8 0-0 ♗b7 9 c4 ♕d8 10 dxc5 bxc5 11 ♘c3 ♘bd7 12 ♕e2?! (12 ♗c2 looks ⩲) 12...♗xf3 13 gxf3 0-0 14 ♖ad1 ♕c7 ∓ Makropoulos-Csom, Banco di Roma 1981.

7...0-0 8 c4!? *(D)*

A logical counter to Black's refusal to exchange pawns on d4 is the plan c4 and dxc5. Instead 8 ♗e3 ♘c6 or 8...♖d8 9 ♕e2 ♘c6 transposes to positions examined next chapter, where Black plays ...♘c6 early on.

A major alternative is 8 ♕e2, when 8...cxd4! 9 cxd4 ♘c6 (e.g. Braga-Karpov, Mar del Plata 1982 among many examples) is a move-order that will reach positions examined in Chapters 8, 9 or 10 where White has already committed himself to ♕e2 lines. Neither is it forced for Black to exchange on d4: 8...♘c6 9 dxc5 (what else? 9 ♖d1 cxd4 10 cxd4 again gives White a poor version of Chapter 8 or 9 while on 9 c4, 9...♕h5!? is now viable, not to mention 9...♕d8 10 dxc5 ♘b4) transposes to Chapter 8, Game 23.

8...♕d8

The two main alternatives may be superior:

a) 8...♕h5!? 9 ♗e2 (Black has no problems after 9 dxc5, e.g. 9...♖d8

10 ♗f4 ♕xc5 11 ♕e2 ♘c6 12 ♘c3 ♘d4 13 ♘xd4 ♕xd4 14 ♗e4 ♘xe4 15 ♘xe4 b5 16 c5 ♗b7 17 ♗d6 with equality, Rozentalis-Novikov, USSR 1984 or 9...♗xc5 10 ♘c3 ♘c6 11 ♗g5 ♘d4!? 12 ♘xd4 ♕xg5 = Vogt-Stangl, Altensteig 1993) 9...♖d8 10 ♗e3 (White can force a draw with 10 ♘e5 ♕h4 11 ♘f3; also 10 ♘g5 ♕g6 11 ♗d3 ♕h5 12 ♗e2 has been played, drawing: 12 ♗xh7+!? ♔f8! is unclear as ...g6 and ...cxd4 are threatened) 10...cxd4 (10...♘g4 11 ♗f4 cxd4 12 h3 e5!? and then 13 ♘xe5! ♕f5 14 ♘d3 ± was Kiselov-Novikov, Belgrade 1991; note that instead if 13 hxg4 ♗xg4 14 ♗xe5 then 14...d3! 15 ♗xd3 ♘c6 works nicely for Black) 11 ♘xd4 ♕e5 12 ♘c3 ♗d7 13 ♗f3 ♘c6 14 ♘xc6 ♗xc6 15 ♕e2 ♖dc8 16 ♖ac1 a6 17 ♖fd1 ♕f5 18 ♗xc6 ♖xc6 19 b3 ♖ac8 20 a4 ♗a3 21 ♖a1 ♗b4 22 ♖ac1 ♗a3 23 ♖a1 ♗b4 ½-½ Dvoretsky-Polugaevsky, Leningrad 1974.

b) 8...♕d7!? 9 dxc5 ♖d8 10 ♘e5 (10 ♗c2 ♕xd1 followed by ...♗xc5) 10...♕d4 11 ♕e2 ♘bd7! (11...♕xc5 12 b4!? ♕c7 13 a3 a5 14 ♘c3 axb4 15 ♘b5 ♕a5 16 ♗b2 was an interesting pawn sacrifice in the game

P.David-R.Bernard, Poznan 1984)
12 ♘xd7 (12 ♘f3 ♕xc5 13 ♘c3 b6
14 ♘e4 ♕c7 with ...♗b7 to follow is
also OK for Black) 12...♗xd7 13 ♗e3
♕e5 14 ♘c3 (14 ♘d2 ♗c6 15 ♘b3?
♖xd3! 16 ♕xd3 ♘g4 17 ♗f4 ♕xf4
18 ♕g3 ♕xg3 ∓ Kharlov-M.Mak-
arov, Riabinsk 1991) 14...♗xc5 15
♗xc5 ♕xc5 16 ♘e4 ♘xe4 17 ♗xe4
♗c6 ½-½ Makarychev-Anikaev,
Frunze 1979.

9 dxc5 ♘bd7

a) 9...♗xc5:

a1) 10 ♗g5 ♗e7 11 ♕e2 ♘bd7
12 ♘c3 b6 13 ♖ad1 ♗b7 14 ♘e5
♕e8 15 ♘xd7 ♘xd7 16 ♗xe7 ♕xe7
17 ♗xh7+! +− Lehmann-Kiefer,
Germany 1986 illustrates White's
tactical chances; if 17...♔xh7 then
18 ♕d3+ and 19 ♕xd7.

a2) 10 ♘c3 ♘c6 11 ♗g5 h6 12
♗h4 ♗e7 13 ♕e2 ♘d4 14 ♘xd4
♕xd4 15 ♗g3 ± Zysk-Lobron, Dortmund 1984.

a3) 10 ♕e2 ♘bd7 11 ♘c3 b6 12
♗g5 ♗b7 13 ♖ad1 ♕c7 14 ♘e4
♘xe4 15 ♗xe4 ♗xe4 16 ♕xe4 ♘f6
17 ♗xf6 gxf6 18 ♕h4 ± Csom-
A.Schneider, Budapest 1977.

b) 9...♘a6 10 ♕e2 (10 c6!? bxc6
11 ♘c3 may also give a edge, Har-
dicsay-Sax, Hungary 1984, but not
10 ♘c3 ♘xc5 11 ♗c2 ♕xd1 =)
10...♘b4 11 ♖d1 ♕c7 12 ♘c3 ♘xd3
13 ♖xd3 ♕xc5 14 ♘e5 ♖d8 (14...b6
has been suggested as an improvement, but in the game Howell-Bator,
Groningen 1983, White replied aggressively with 15 b4! ♕c7 16 ♘b5
♕b7 and now best would have been

16 ♗g5 with an attack) 15 ♖g3 ±
Tseitlin-Lukin, USSR 1977.

10 ♕e2 ♘xc5 11 ♗c2 b6

11...♕c7 12 ♘c3 a6 13 b4 ♘cd7
14 a3 b6 15 ♗b2 ♗b7 16 ♘e4 ♖ac8
17 ♖ac1 ± Hort-Hartston, Hastings
1974.

12 ♘c3 ♗a6

12...♗b7 13 ♗g5 ♕c7 (13...♘fd7
14 ♗xe7 ♕xe7 15 b4 ♘a6 16 a3 ±)
14 ♘e5 (14 ♘b5 ♕c6) 14...♖ad8 15
♘b5 ♕b8 16 ♖ad1 a6 17 ♘c3 ♕c7
18 ♕e3 ± Sax/Hazai.

13 ♘e5 ♕c8 14 ♗g5 ♘cd7! 15 ♘xd7

Not 15 ♗xh7+? ♔xh7 16 ♕d3+
♔g8 17 ♘xd7 ♗xc4 −+.

15...♕xd7 16 ♖fd1?!

Sax and Hazai give 16 ♖ad1! ♕c7
17 b3 ♗b7 (17...♖fd8 18 ♘e4 ♘xe4
19 ♕xe4 g6 20 ♗f4 ♕c5 21 ♕f3 ±)
18 ♕d3 ♖fd8 (18...♖ad8? 19 ♘d5!
exd5 20 ♗xf6 g6 21 ♗b2 dxc4 22
♕c3) 19 ♕h3 h6 20 ♗c1 ±.

16...♕c7 17 b3 ♖fd8 18 ♘e4 ♘d5! = 19 ♖ac1 ♘f4 20 ♕f3 ♘g6 21 ♗xe7 ♕xe7 22 ♖xd8+ ♖xd8 23 ♖d1 f5 24 ♘c3 ♗b7 25 ♖xd8+ ♕xd8 26 ♕xb7 ♕d2 27 ♗d3 ♕xd3 28 ♕f3 ♕xf3 29 gxf3 ♘e5 30 ♘b5 ♘c6 31 ♔f1? (White would still be OK after 31 f4; now the knight ending turns nasty) 31...g5 32 ♔e2 ♔f7 33 ♔e3 e5 34 a3 h5 35 b4 ♔e7 36 ♔d3 ♔d7 37 c5 bxc5 38 bxc5 a6 39 ♘d6 ♘d4 40 ♔c4 ♔c6 41 ♘c8 ♘xf3 42 ♘e7+ ♔d7 43 ♘xf5 ♘xh2 44 ♔d5 ♘f3 45 c6+ ♔c7 46 ♘g7 h4 47 ♘e8+ ♔d8 48 c7+ ♔c8 49 ♔e6 ♘d2 0-1

8 6 ♗d3 ♘c6 7 0-0

1	e4	c5
2	c3	d5
3	exd5	♕xd5
4	d4	e6
5	♘f3	♘f6
6	♗d3	♘c6
7	0-0	*(D)*

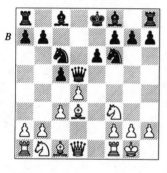

Black's reason for delaying the central pawn exchange (with ...cxd4) is a rather familiar one. He wishes to deny White's knight use of the c3-square, at least until White has made a small concession like playing ♗e3 or ♕e2. After either of these moves Black can safely exchange on d4, knowing that White can no longer opt for some of the very sharpest main lines of Chapters 9 and 10. This would be a near perfect strategy for Black were it not for 8 c4!? (Game 22). Whilst this pawn advance is virtually White's only try to punish Black for 'move-ordering' him, it remains a respectable option. However

there are surprisingly few top-level games in the line.

One explanation for this lack of games is that strong players (such as Michael Adams) are as White currently utilising a move-order involving a much earlier ♗e3, with the specific intention of forcing Black to exchange early on d4. After 6 ♗e3 cxd4 7 cxd4 ♘c6 8 ♘c3 White has avoided this whole chapter, and after 8...♕d6 or 8...♕d8 we reach thematic main line positions, albeit ones where the white bishop is committed to the e3-square.

Game 22
Sveshnikov – Averkin
USSR Ch 1973

1 e4 c5 2 ♘f3 e6 3 c3 d5 4 exd5 ♕xd5 5 d4 ♘f6 6 ♗d3 ♘c6 7 0-0 ♗e7

With 7...♗d7 Black bluffs that he might risk queenside castling, or hopes White will lose a tempo with 8 dxc5?! ♗xc5. *ECO* B (2nd edition) recommends 8 ♖e1 ♗e7 9 dxc5 ♗xc5 10 b4 ♗d6 11 ♘a3 ♖d8 12 ♘c4 ±. Also possible is 8 ♗e3 cxd4 9 cxd4 ♘b4 10 ♘c3 ♕a5 11 ♗c4!? ♖c8 12 ♘e5 ♗d6 13 ♘xd7 ♕xd7 14 ♗b3 ♕f5 15 h3 ♔e7?! (15...h5∞ Hort) 16 g4 ± Hort-Lobron, Bochum 1981.

8 c4!?

8 ♕e2 is Game 23. Alternatives:

a) 8 dxc5 (considered dubious because of a game of Adorjan's in which he refrained from immediately recapturing the pawn) 8...0-0! and now it is difficult to find a progressive continuation:

a1) 9 ♕e2 transposes to lines covered under 8 ♕e2.

a2) 9 b4 ♖d8 10 ♗c2 ♕xd1 11 ♖xd1 ♖xd1+ 12 ♗xd1 a5 will successfully undermine the white pawns.

a3) The original key game went 9 ♕c2 ♖d8 10 ♖d1 ♕xc5 11 ♗g5 h6 = 12 ♗xf6 ♗xf6 13 ♘bd2 ♗e7 14 ♗h7+ ♔h8 15 ♗e4 ♗d7 16 ♘b3 ♕b6 17 ♕e2 ♕c7 18 ♕e3 ♗f6 ∓ Hulak-Adorjan, Osijek 1978.

a4) 9 ♗e3 ♖d8 10 ♗e2 ♕xd1 (10...♕f5!? 11 ♕a4 ♗xc5 12 ♗xc5 ♕xc5 = Sveshnikov-Gufeld, USSR 1982) 11 ♖xd1 ♖xd1+ 12 ♗xd1 ♘g4 13 ♗f4 e5!? (even 13...♗xc5 14 ♗g3 is not much for White) 14 ♗g3 e4 15 ♘fd2 e3 16 ♘e4 exf2+ 17 ♗xf2 ♘xf2 18 ♔xf2 ♘e5 19 ♗e2 b6! ∓ Hebden-Al Modiakhi, Calcutta 1995, as after 20 cxb6 f5! 21 ♘g3 ♗c5+ the black bishops are dangerously active.

b) 8 ♗e3 0-0 (8...cxd4!? 9 cxd4 0-0 10 ♘c3 would transpose to Chapter 10) 9 c4 (for 9 dxc5 see above) 9...♕h5!? (9...♕d8 10 dxc5 ♘b4 ∞ Makropoulos-Inkiov, Pernik 1981; 10 ♘c3!? ±) 10 ♗e2 (10 h3 cxd4 11 ♘xd4 ♘xd4 12 ♗xd4 ♖d8 ∓ Ambrož-Adorjan, Riga 1981) 10...♘g4 11 ♗f4 cxd4 (11...♕f5 12 ♗c7! cxd4?! 13 ♘xd4 ♘xd4 14 ♕xd4 ♘f6 15 ♗f3! ± Sveshnikov-Adorjan,

Sarejevo 1983) 12 h3 ♕f5 13 ♗c7 ♘ge5 14 ♘xe5 ♘xe5 15 ♕xd4 ♘c6 16 ♕e3 ± Sveshnikov-Makarychev, Moscow 1983.

8...♕d8 *(D)*

8...♕h5!? 9 ♘c3? (9 ♗e2 – compare with the variations beginning 8 ♗e3 0-0 9 c4 ♕h5 10 ♗e2) 9...cxd4 10 ♘b5 0-0 11 ♘fxd4 ♘xd4 12 ♘xd4 ♖d8! ∓ Chandler-Sosonko, Wijk aan Zee 1982. Worth consideration is 8...♕d7 9 dxc5 0-0!? intending 10 a3 ♖d8 or 10 ♕e2 ♘b4.

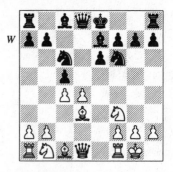

9 dxc5 ♘d7

Black's idea is to swap queens, something he doesn't do after 9...0-0 10 a3 a5 11 ♘c3 ♗xc5 12 ♗g5 ♗e7 13 ♕e2 h6 14 ♗f4 ♘d4 15 ♘xd4 ♕xd4 16 ♗e5 ♕h4 17 ♘e4 ♘xe4 18 ♗xe4 ♗c5 19 ♖ad1 ±, as in Sveshnikov-Onoprienko, USSR 1974.

The straightforward 9...♗xc5 is playable:

a) 10 ♘c3 0-0 11 ♗g5 h6 12 ♗h4 ♗e7 13 ♕e2 ♘d4 (or 13...♕h5 14 ♗xe7 ♕xe7 15 ♕e3 Hazai-Orso, Budapest 1977) 14 ♘xd4 ♕xd4 15 ♗g3 ♗d7 Lyell-Turner, Edinburgh 1989 and Zysk-Lobron, Dortmund 1984, and White doesn't have very much.

b) 10 a3!? 0-0 11 b4 ♗e7 12 ♗b2 (11 ♖a2 intending ♖d2 is another plan) 12...b6 13 ♕e2 ♗b7 14 ♘c3 a5. In this unclear position White became worse after the continuation 15 ♘e4 axb4 16 ♖fd1 ♘xe4 17 ♕xe4 g6 18 axb4 ♗f6 19 ♗c2 ♕e7 20 ♖xa8 ♗xa8 21 ♗xf6 ♕xf6 22 ♕e1 ♕b2 ∓ in Eriksson-L.Schneider, Rilton Cup 1980. However there are several other plans, e.g. 15 ♖ad1!? ♕c7 and then 16 ♘b5 or 16 b5!? ♘b8 17 ♘e4.

10 a3 ♘xc5 11 ♗c2 ♕xd1 12 ♖xd1 ♗f6 13 ♗e3 b6 14 ♖a2 ♗b7 15 ♘g5

In view of the next note, 15 b4!? might be more accurate. White has a little more space and a queenside pawn majority.

15...♘e5

15...♗xg5! 16 ♗xg5 e5 17 ♘c3 ♘d4 18 b4 ♘ce6 = gave Black sufficient central control to compensate for the bishop pair in C.Johansson-Thurnhuber, corr. 1991.

16 b4 ♘cd7 17 ♗a4 h6? 18 ♗xd7+

Perhaps Black had only considered 18 ♘xf7 ♔xf7 19 ♗xd7 ♖hd8 with counterplay. Now his position crumbles, as on 18...♘xd7 there comes 19 ♘xf7.

18...♔e7 19 ♘xf7 ♔xf7 20 ♗a4 ♖hd8 21 ♖ad2 ♖xd2 22 ♖xd2 a5 23 bxa5 ♖xa5 24 ♗b5 ♗e4 25 ♗xb6 ♖a8 26 ♖d1 ♗d3 27 ♗c5 ♗xc4 28 ♗xc4 ♘xc4 29 g3 ♗b2 30 ♖d3 e5 31 ♔g2 ♔e6 32 h4 g5 33 h5 e4 34 ♖b3 ♔d5 35 ♗b4 ♗d4 36 ♘c3+ ♔e5 37 ♘b5 ♗b6 38 ♘d6 ♘xd6 39 ♗xd6+ ♔xd6 40 ♖xb6+ ♔e5 41

♖xh6 ♖xa3 42 ♖h8 ♔f6 43 ♖g8 ♖a2 44 h6 ♖a7 45 ♔h3 ♖h7 46 ♔g4 ♖xh6 47 ♖xg5 ♖h1 48 ♖f5+ ♔g6 49 ♖a5 ♖e1 50 ♖a6+ ♔f7 51 ♖a2 ♔e6 52 ♔f4 ♔d5 53 ♖d2+ ♔c4 54 g4 ♔c3 55 ♖d8 ♖e2 56 g5 ♖xf2+ 57 ♔xe4 ♖g2 58 ♔f5 ♖f2+ 59 ♔e6 ♖e2+ 60 ♔f6 ♖f2+ 61 ♔g7 1-0

Game 23
Braga – Portisch
Mar del Plata 1982

1 e4 c5 2 c3 d5 3 exd5 ♕xd5 4 d4 e6 5 ♘f3 ♘f6 6 ♗d3 ♗e7 7 0-0 0-0 8 ♕e2

Having run out of 'waiting' moves (because of Black's refusal to exchange on d4) White sets up a formation with his queen on e2 and king's rook on d1. Whilst this will certainly encourage Black to exchange on d4, White's pieces will not be ideally posted in the resultant IQP position.

8...cxd4

8...♘c6 and now:

a) 9 ♖d1 ♕h5 (9...cxd4) 10 ♗f4 (10 dxc5!?) 10...cxd4 11 cxd4 ♘b4 12 ♘c3 b6 ∓ Hünerkopf-Hort, Germany 1987.

b) 9 dxc5 ♕xc5! 10 ♗g5 (10 ♘bd2 ♖d8 11 ♖d1 ♗d7 12 ♘f1 ♕b6 13 ♘g3 ♗e8 = Short-Andersson London 1980) 10...h6 11 ♗h4 ♗d7 12 ♘bd2 ♖ad8 13 ♖ad1 ♖fe8!? 14 ♗xf6 ♗xf6 15 ♘e4 ♕e7 16 ♘d6?! (16 ♘xf6+ ♕xf6 17 ♗e4 ♕e7 =) 16...♘d4! 17 ♘xd4 ♕xd6 ∓ Tompa-Ribli, Hungary 1975.

9 cxd4 ♘c6 10 ♖d1

10 ♗e3 ♘b4 11 ♘c3 ♕d8 gives similar positions to the text. 11...♕h5

in the game Speelman-Cu.Hansen, Munich 1992 ended in an amusing draw after 12 ♗c4 b6 13 a3 ♘bd5 14 ♘xd5 ♘xd5 15 ♖ac1 ♗b7 16 ♗a6 ♗d6 17 ♗xb7 ♗xh2+ 18 ♔h1 ♗g3+ 19 ♔g1 ♗h2+ ½-½ .

10...♘b4 11 ♘c3 ♕d8!? *(D)*

11...♕d6 is a good version of Chapter 9. However the situation after 11...♕d8 is quite important, and we should certainly note that the great Karpov has played it. We are now on the fringe of variations which start transposing into IQP (isolated queen pawn) positions that arise from completely different openings. By Chapter 10 these often surprising transpositions will be coming out of your ears, but, be warned, tempi can be both won and lost along the way!

12 ♗c4

After this bishop move, just as warned, we have transposed into a tempo-down version of a Queen's Gambit Accepted (D26): 1 d4 d5 2 c4 dxc4 3 ♘f3 ♘f6 4 e3 e6 5 ♗xc4 c5 6 0-0 ♘c6 7 ♕e2 cxd4 8 ♖d1 ♗e7 9 exd4 0-0 10 ♘c3 ♘b4. Arising from the QGA it is White to move; in the c3 Sicilian it is Black to move!

The c3 Sicilian practitioner could try to argue (assuming he is even aware of the transposition) that, as the QGA version is considered favourable for White anyway, so the loss of time is not life-threatening. Nevertheless for White to play a normal line a tempo down gives an odd feeling.

Unfortunately 12 ♗b1, the usual c3 Sicilian retreat square, also leaves White struggling to justify his IQP. After 12...b6 some typical examples go:

a) 13 ♘e5 ♗b7 14 a3 ♘bd5 15 ♘e4 ♘e8 16 ♕c2 g6 17 ♗h6 ♘g7 18 ♘c6 ♗xc6 19 ♕xc6 ♕c8 20 ♕b5 ♖d8 21 ♘g3 ♕b7 22 ♕e2 ♗h4 23 ♗e4 ♕e7 24 ♗xg7 ♔xg7 ∓ Braga-Karpov, Mar del Plata 1982.

b) 13 ♗g5 ♗b7 14 ♘e5 ♖c8 15 h4 (15 a3 ♘bd5 16 ♘xd5 ♕xd5 17 f3 = Panchenko) 15...♘bd5 16 ♘xd5 ♕xd5 17 f3 ♕d6 18 a3 ♖fd8 ∓ Nun-Panchenko, Hradec Kralove 1981.

c) 13 a3 ♗a6 14 ♕e1 ♘bd5 15 ♘xd5 ♘xd5 16 ♕e4 ♘f6 17 ♕h4 g6 18 ♗g5 ♖c8 19 ♗a2 ♗e2 ∓ Velimirović-Inkiov, Banja Luka 1983 (and this game actually arose via a 2 c4 Caro Kann...).

12...b6 13 ♘e5 ♗b7 14 a3 ♘bd5 15 ♘e4?!

15 ♖d3!? ♖c8 (tempo or no tempo Black must be careful: 15...a6 16 ♖h3 ♘xc3 17 bxc3 b5 18 ♗b3 ♖c8 19 ♗d2 ♗a8 20 ♖e1 ♖c7 21 ♕d3 ♗d5 22 ♗c2 g6 23 ♕g3 ♗d6 24 ♗g5 ♗e7 25 ♗h6 ♗d6 26 ♕h4 ♘h5 27 ♕xh5! 1-0 was the game R.Bernard-Nowak, Poznan 1983) 16 ♖h3 ♘xc3 17 bxc3 ♗e4 18 g4 (giving a

dangerous attack, but ultimately over-ambitious...) 18...♗g6 19 ♗d2 ♘d5 20 ♖f1 ♗xa3 21 f4 ♘e7 22 f5 exf5 23 gxf5 ♘xf5 24 ♘xg6 hxg6 25 ♖xf5 ♖xc4 26 ♖f4 ♕d5 27 ♖fh4 f6 28 ♖e3 ♗d6 ∓ Mariotti-Toth, Rome 1981. After 15 ♖d3!? the knowledge-able Portisch says ∞, an assessment with which we concur.

15...♘xe4 16 ♕xe4 ♖c8 17 ♗d3 f5 18 ♕e1 ♔h8 19 ♗d2 ♘f6 20 ♗b4 ♘d5 21 ♗d2 ♗g5 22 ♗xg5?

22 ♘f3 was required; now the black kingside attack quickly mounts before ending with a queen sacrifice finale.

22...♕xg5 23 ♘f3 ♕h6 24 ♖ac1 ♖xc1 25 ♖xc1 ♘f4 26 ♗f1 ♗xf3 27 gxf3 ♕g5+ 28 ♔h1 h6 29 ♕b4 ♖d8 30 ♕d2 e5 31 d5 ♖xd5 32 ♖c8+ ♔h7 33 ♕c2 b5 34 ♖f8 ♖d3 35 ♕c8 *(D)*

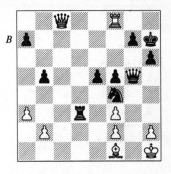

35...♕g2+! 0-1

9 9...♕d8 and 9...♕d6

1	e4	c5
2	c3	d5
3	exd5	♕xd5
4	d4	e6
5	♘f3	♘f6
6	♗d3	♘c6
7	0-0	cxd4
8	cxd4	♗e7
9	♘c3 (D)	

Here Black can choose between 9...♕d8 and 9...♕d6, with either queen retreat leading to a thematic IQP (isolated queen's pawn) position. It is extraordinary how some of these positions can arise via totally different openings (including the Centre Counter and Nimzo-Indian). For example, 9...♕d8 (Game 24) will shortly become a Semi-Tarrasch Defence (*ECO* code D42) by transposition, an opening which arises via 1 c4 or 1 d4. Technically, therefore, some of these lines are outside the scope of the present book, but, of course, your writer is not the kind of brutal, uncaring author who would refuse to cover them for such a pedantic reason. However due to the mass of older references, the material has had to be summarised, as these Semi-Tarrasch variations were quite popular a number of years ago. For further study, the Encyclopaedia of the Chess Openings (*ECO*), volume D, has reasonable coverage. If you do compare the move-orders, you will see that it is actually quite favourable for White to utilise the c3 Sicilian route – some of Black's best Semi-Tarrasch defensive options are unavailable, or can be easily sidestepped. It is fair to say that, after 9...♕d8, White's dynamic piece play and attacking chances clearly compensate for the IQP, and his chances are somewhat preferable.

Nowadays the active 9...♕d6 is more common, and here some of the game references have arisen via the Caro-Kann Defence (*ECO* code B10): 1 e4 c6 2 c4 d5 3 exd5 cxd5 4 cxd5 ♕xd5 5 ♘c3 ♕d6 6 d4 ♘f6 7 ♘f3 e6 8 ♗d3 ♘c6 9 0-0 ♗e7. If White now plays a quick a3 and ♗e3, play will transpose to the Modern Main Line (6 ♗e3) examined in the next chapter. Instead Game 25 covers several perfectly playable alternatives for White. The most troublesome of these for Black to effectively counter are 10 ♘b5!? and 10 ♗e3 0-0 11 ♖c1!?.

Game 24
Christiansen – Gheorghiu
Torremolinos 1977

1 e4 c5 2 c3 d5 3 exd5 ♕xd5 4 d4 e6 5 ♘f3 ♘f6 6 ♗d3 ♘c6 7 0-0 cxd4 8 cxd4 ♗e7 9 ♘c3 ♕d8

Please note that actual opening moves of this illustrative game were very different: 1 c4 c5 2 ♘f3 ♘f6 3 ♘c3 e6 4 e3 d5 5 cxd5 ♘xd5 6 d4 cxd4 7 exd4 ♗e7 8 ♗d3 ♘c6 9 0-0 0-0 10 ♖e1 ♘f6 11 a3 b6 12 ♗c2 ♗b7 13 ♕d3, reaching the position after White's 13th move. I have used the c3 Sicilian move-order (which gives Black fewer options) in order to insert various alternatives along the way.

10 a3

White's idea is to create mating threats against h7 by setting up the formation ♗c2 and ♕d3. Then if Black responds with the defensive ...g6, the white queen's bishop will be able to develop from c1 to the h6-square in one hop. Therefore this move-order is more forcing than 10 ♖e1 0-0 11 a3 b6 12 ♗c2 which gives Black the option of 12...♗a6!? (stopping White's ♕d3), and now White can play:

a) 13 ♗g5 ♖c8 14 ♕d2 (after 14 ♖c1 ♘d5 15 ♘e4 Black achieves a solid position with the continuation 15...♗xg5 16 ♘fxg5 h6 17 ♘f3 ♕e7, as in Balashov-Hübner, Tilburg 1977 alternatively 15...h6 16 ♗xe7 ♕xe7 Berg-Adianto, Gausdal 1992 and

Kindermann-Fahnenschmidt, Bundesliga 1990) and now:

a1) 14...♗c4 15 ♖ad1 ♘d5 16 ♘e4 ♗xg5 17 ♘exg5 ♘f6 lost a pawn to 18 ♘xh7! ♘xh7 19 ♗xh7+ ♔xh7 20 ♕c2+ ♔g8 21 ♕xc4 in Gobet-Campora, Bern 1988.

a2) 14...♕d6 15 ♖ad1 ♖fd8 16 ♗b1 ♕b8 17 ♕c2 g6 18 ♗a2 h6 19 ♗xe6 hxg5 20 ♕xg6+ ♔h8 21 ♕h6+ ♔g8 22 ♘xg5 ♖f8 23 ♖e4 1-0 Tal-Chikovani, Gori 1968 is a graphic illustration of White's attacking possibilities in this line.

a3) 14...♘a5 15 ♖ad1 (15 ♕f4 ♖e8 16 d5 ♘xd5 17 ♘xd5 ♕xd5 18 ♗xh7+ ♔xh7 19 ♗xe7 ∞ Chekhov-Psakhis, Vladivostok 1978) 15...♘c4 16 ♕c1 ♕c7 17 d5 ♘xb2 18 d6! ♕xc3 19 dxe7 ♘xd1 was Novik-Vasiukov, Leningrad 1991. Here Novik suggests 20 ♗xf6! ♕xc2 21 ♕g5 ♕g6 22 exf8♕+ ♖xf8 23 ♕xg6 hxg6 24 ♗e7 ♘c3 25 ♗xf8 ♔xf8 26 ♘d4 ±, as 24...♖e8 would have failed to 25 ♖xd1 ♖xe7 26 ♖d8+ ♔h7 27 ♘g5+ ♔h6 28 f4 and the black king is in a mating net.

b) 13 b4!? with a further split:

b1) 13...♗c4 14 b5 ♘a5 15 ♘e5 ♖c8 16 ♖e3 (16 ♗g5 g6 17 ♕f3 ♗d5 ∞ Franco-Short, Arnhem/Amsterdam 1983) 16...g6 (16...♖c7 17 ♖g3 ♖e8 18 ♗h6 ♗f8 19 ♗g5 ♗e7 20 ♗xf6 ♗xf6 21 ♗xh7+ ♔xh7 22 ♕h5+ ♔g8 23 ♘e4 ♗d5 24 ♖h3 ♔f8 25 ♕xf7+!! 1-0 was a lovely queen sacrifice in Kaidanov-Anand, Moscow 1987) 17 ♖h3 (17 ♖g3 ♘d5 18 ♘xg6 fxg6 19 ♗xg6 hxg6 20 ♕h5 ♗d3 21 ♖xg6+ ♗xg6 22 ♕xg6+ ♔h8 23 ♕h6+ ♔g8 24 ♕g6+ ♔h8

25 ♕h6+ ♔g8 26 ♕g6+ ½-½ Howell-Machulsky, Dublin Telecom 1991) 17...♗d5 and now instead of 18 ♕d2 ♗b3! Savon recommends 18 ♗h6 ♖e8 19 ♕d2 ± intending ♕f4.

b2) 13...♖c8!? and here *(D)*:

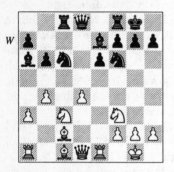

b21) 14 ♖e3!? ♗c4 15 b5 ♘a5 16 ♘e5 as in B.Filipović-N.Lalić, Banja Vrucica 1987, transposed into the 13...♗c4 line above.

b22) After 14 b5 ♘a5 15 ♕d3, 15...♗b7 was fine for Black in both Hmadi-De Boer, Cannes 1990 and Pyhälä-Østenstad, Slupsk 1987. Black tried to be too clever with 15...♕c7 16 ♗d2 ♘c4 in Pyhälä-Christiansen, Reykjavik 1986 and paid the price after 17 ♘e4 ♘xe4 18 ♕xe4 g6 19 ♗f4 ±.

b23) 14 ♗b2 ♗c4 (of course not 14...♘d5?? 15 b5 ♘xc3 16 ♕d3! g6 17 ♗xc3 ♕c7 18 bxa6 ♘a5 19 ♗xa5 1-0, which was the brevity Anand-Adams, London Lloyds Bank 1987) 15 ♕d2 (15 b5 ♘a5 16 ♘e5 is no longer dangerous, as White's bishop on b2 can be blocked out of the attack, e.g. 16...♘d5 17 ♘xd5 ♗xd5 18 ♗xh7+ ♔xh7 19 ♕h5+ ♔g8 20 ♖e3 ♗h4 21 f4 ♖c2 22 ♖h3 ♖xg2+

23 ♔f1 ♖f2+ 24 ♔g1 ♖xf4 0-1 Lanka-Østenstad, 1989) 15...♘d5 16 ♘e4 a5 ∓ Mortensen-Østenstad, Nordic Ch 1987, though White later won with a scandalous swindle.

Another line is 10 ♖e1 0-0 11 ♗g5, not bothering with a3. After 11...b6 (the immediate 11...♘b4 12 ♗b1 b6 allows 13 ♘e5 ♗b7 14 ♖e3 g6 15 ♖g3 ± with attacking chances, Keene-Miles, Hastings 1975) 12 ♕e2 ♗b7 13 ♖ad1 ♘b4 14 ♗b1 ♖c8 15 ♘e5 ♘bd5 (15...♘fd5 16 ♗d2 ♘f6 17 ♕e3 ♘fd5 18 ♕h3 f5 19 a3 ♘a6 20 ♗a2 ± Petrosian-Najdorf, Moscow 1967) 16 ♕d3 (but not 16 ♖d3? ♗a6 17 ♘xd5 and now instead of 17...♘xd5 18 ♗xe7 ♕xe7 19 ♖h3 = Bobotsov-Petrosian, Moscow 1967 Black should play 17...exd5! ∓, as 18 ♗xf6 ♗xf6 19 ♖h3 ♗xe2 20 ♗xh7+ ♔h8 21 ♗d3+ ♗h4 is −+) 16...♘xc3 (16...g6 17 ♗h6 ♖e8 18 ♕h3 ± Kottnauer-Donner, Leysin 1967) 17 bxc3 ♕d5 18 ♕h3 ♖xc3 19 f3 h6 20 ♗xf6 ♗xf6 21 ♗e4 ♕xe4 22 ♖xe4 ♗xe4 23 ♘d7 ± Polugaevsky-Khasin, USSR Ch 1961.

10...0-0 *(D)*

11 ♗c2

For 11 ♗e3 see Chapter 10, while 11 ♗g5 b6 (11...h6? 12 ♗h4 ♔h8 13 ♗c2 g5 14 ♗g3 g4 15 ♗e5! ± Kavalek-Grefe, USA Ch 1973) 12 ♕e2 ♗b7 13 ♖ad1 ♖e8 (13...♖c8 14 ♗xf6 ♗xf6 15 d5 exd5 16 ♗f5 ± Lein-Yaroslavtsev, USSR 1965, or 13...g6 14 ♗c4 ♘d5 15 ♗h6 ± Ghitescu-Donner, Beverwijk 1967) 14 ♖fe1 g6 15 ♗c4 ♘d5 16 ♗xd5! ♗xg5 (16...exd5 17 ♗xe7 ♖xe7 18 ♕d2 ±) 17 ♗e4 ♗f6 18 ♘e5 ± was the game Korchnoi-Tal, Moscow Ct (8) 1968.

11 ♖e1 is a major alternative:

a) 11...a6 12 ♗c2 b5 13 ♕d3 ♗b7? (a more refined version of the blunder is 13...♖a7?! 14 d5! ♖d7 15 ♘e4 g6 16 ♗h6 ♘xd5 17 ♗xf8 ± Makarychev-Ageichenko, Moscow Ch 1987; necessary is 13...g6 14 b4 ♖a7 15 ♗h6 ♖e8 16 ♖ad1 ♖d7 17 h3 ♗b7 18 ♕e3 ♕a8 19 ♗b3 ♘d8 20 ♘e5 ±, as in the game Cramling-Hort, London 1982) 14 d5! exd5 15 ♗g5 g6 16 ♖xe7! ♕xe7 (16...♘xe7 17 ♗xf6 ±) 17 ♘xd5 ♘xd5 18 ♗xe7 ± Ligterink-Donner, Leeuwarden 1977, is a familiar trap that has claimed several subsequent victims. The theme is simple but effective – White prises open the c-file and captures on e7.

b) 11...b6 12 ♗g5 (for 12 ♗c2 see the main game; 12 ♘e5 has led to several boring draws after 12...♗b7 13 ♗a6 ♕c8 14 ♗xb7 ♕xb7 15 ♘xc6 ♕xc6 16 d5 ♕c4, e.g. 17 ♕e2 ♕xe2 18 ♖xe2 ♗c5 19 dxe6 fxe6 20 ♗e3 ♗xe3 21 ♖xe3 ♘d5 22 ♖xe6 ♘xc3 23 bxc3 ♖ac8 24 ♖e3 ♖f4 25 h3 ♖fc4 26 ♖c1 ♖8c7 27 ♔f1 ♖a4

28 ♖a1 ♖ac4 29 ♖c1 h6 ½-½ Ribli-Kavalek, Tilburg 1980) 12...♗b7 13 ♗c2 (13 ♗b1!? ♖e8 14 ♕d3 g6 15 ♗a2 ± is another interesting plan, Suba-Velikov, Lucerne OL 1982) 13...♖c8 14 ♕d3 g6 15 ♖ad1 ♘d5 (15...♖e8 16 h4 would transpose to the game Kavalek-Larsen, Solingen 1970, which went 16...a6 17 ♗b3 ♘a5 18 ♗a2 b5 19 ♘e5 ♘d5 20 ♗xd5 ♗xd5 21 ♗xe7 ♖xe7 22 ♘xd5 ♕xd5 23 ♘g4 ±) 16 ♗h6 ♖e8 17 ♗a4 a6 18 ♘xd5 ♕xd5 19 ♗e3 ♗f6 20 ♗b3. Here 20...♕h5? 21 d5 ♘d8 22 d6 ± ♖c5 23 d7 ♖e7 24 ♕f4 ♗g7 25 ♕b8 ♕xh6 26 ♕xd8+ ♗f8 27 ♖e3 ♗c6 28 ♕xf8+ ♕xf8 29 d8♕ 1-0 was Smyslov-Karpov, Leningrad 1971 and Karpov's attempt to improve for Black many years later was only partially successful: 20...♕d7 21 d5 exd5 22 ♕xb6 ♖xe1+ 23 ♖xe1 ♗xb2 24 ♗xd5 ± Beliavsky-Karpov, Trud-CSKA 1986.

11...b6 12 ♕d3 ♗b7 13 ♖e1 *(D)*

Setting up a highly disguised and deadly trap. Instead 13 ♗g5 g6 14 ♖fe1 ♘d5 15 ♗h6 ♖e8 16 ♘e4 ♖c8 17 ♖ac1 ♖c7 18 h4 ♘f6 19 ♘g3 ♖d7 20 ♗a4 ♘xd4 21 ♗xd7 ♘xf3+ 22

gxf3 ♘xd7 ∞ was Gallagher-Brunner, Switzerland 1994.

13...g6

This defensive move, blocking the potential threat against h7, is now essentially forced, but many players (including Anatoly Karpov and Vassily Smyslov) have not appreciated just how dangerous the position is for Black, and the blunders 13...♖e8 and 13...♖c8 have been seen on many occasions:

a) 13...♖e8 14 d5!! exd5 15 ♗g5! (the trap is sprung! Now White threatens ♗xf6 followed by ♕xh7+, but 15...g6 loses to 16 ♖xe7! ♕xe7 17 ♘xd5 – so Black must return the pawn and suffer an onslaught against his king) 15...♘e4 16 ♘xe4 dxe4 17 ♕xe4 g6 18 ♕h4 ♕c7 19 ♗b3 h5 20 ♗f6 (also 20 ♖ac1 ♗f8 21 ♗f6 ♗g7 22 ♗xg7 ♔xg7 23 ♘g5 ± Makarychev-Velikov, Frunze 1985) 20...♗c5 21 ♕g5 ♔h7 22 ♗c2 1-0 Borik-Werner, Germany 1981 – and Dizdar-Dizdarević, Sarajevo 1988!

b) 13...♖c8 14 d5!! (in the game Smyslov-Karpov, USSR Ch 1971, White missed 14 d5, but still won a fine game after 14 ♗g5 g6 – see the note beginning 11 ♖e1) 14...exd5 (14...♘a5 15 ♗g5! and Black had to give up an exchange with 15...♖xc3 16 ♕xc3 ♘xd5 17 ♕d3 ♘f6 in Barbulescu-Campora, Lucerne 1985) 15 ♗g5! ♘e4 (again if 15...g6, 16 ♖xe7) 16 ♘xe4 dxe4 17 ♕xe4 g6 (with the saving defence 18 ♗xe7 ♘xe7 19 ♕xe7 ♗xf3 20 gxf3 ♖xc2 in mind) 18 ♗h6 ♖e8 19 ♖ad1 ♕c7 20 ♗b3 ♘d8 21 ♕d4 1-0 Wl.Schmidt-Imanaliev, Moscow OL 1994.

14 ♗h6 ♖e8 15 ♖ad1 ♖c8

15...♗f8 16 ♗g5 ♗e7 17 ♗a4 (17 ♗b3 ♘d5 18 ♗xd5 ♗xg5 19 ♗xc6 ♗xc6 20 d5 exd5 21 ♖xe8+ ♗xe8 22 ♘xg5 ♕xg5 23 ♕d4 ♗c6 24 h4 ♕e7 25 ♘xd5 ♗xd5 26 ♕xd5 ♖e8 27 h5 is only slightly favourable, Velimirović-Böhm, Amsterdam 1976) 17...♖c8 18 ♘e5 ♘d5 19 ♗xe7 ♖xe7 20 ♘xd5 ♕xd5 21 ♕g3 ♘xe5 22 dxe5 ♕c4 23 ♕g5 ♕c7 24 h4 h5 25 ♖c1 ± Sigurjonsson-Böhm, Amsterdam 1976.

16 ♗b3

Probably stronger is 16 h4!? ♘d5 17 ♘xd5 ♕xd5 18 ♕d2 ♕d6 (not 18...♘xd4 19 ♕xd4 ♖xc2 20 ♕g7#) 19 ♗e4 ± Ribli-Gheorghiu, Warsaw Z 1979. Take heed, however, that GM Florin Gheorghiu still consistently patronises these systems for Black, even though most sources agree White holds an initiative. The point is that one inaccuracy can turn the tables – if Black neutralises his opponent's active piece play then the IQP becomes a weakness.

16...♘a5 17 ♗a2 ♘d5 18 ♘e4 ♖c7 (better is 18...♘f6, with a tacit offer of a draw by repetition, because 19 ♘eg5 ♗d5 20 ♘xf7? ♔xf7 21 ♘e5+ ♔g8 22 ♘xg6 ♗d6 proved an unsound sacrifice for White in Lehtivaara-Gheorghiu, Lenk 1992) **19 ♘e5 ♗f8 20 ♗g5 ♗e7 21 ♗xe7 ♖exe7 22 ♗xd5! exd5 23 ♘f6+ ♔g7 24 ♕h3 h5** (now White has a strong piece sacrifice, but 24...♔xf6 loses to 25 ♘g4+ ♔g7 26 ♕h6+ followed by 27 ♘f6) **25 ♘xh5+ gxh5 26 ♖d3 ♕h8 27 ♖g3+ ♔f8 28 ♖g5 ♖e6 29 ♕xe6 fxe6 30 ♘g6+ ♔g7 31 ♘xh8+**

♔xh8 32 ♖xh5+ ♔g7 33 h4 ♘c6 34 ♖xe6 ♘xd4 35 ♖g5+ ♔h7 36 ♖d6 ♖f7 37 f3 ♘f5 38 ♖xf5 ♖xf5 39 ♖d7+ ♔g6 40 ♖xb7 ♖f4 41 ♖xa7 1-0

Game 25
Dorfman – Razuvaev
USSR 1979

1 e4 c5 2 c3 d5 3 exd5 ♕xd5 4 d4 e6 5 ♘f3 ♘f6 6 ♗d3 ♗e7 7 0-0 cxd4 8 cxd4 ♘c6 9 ♘c3 ♕d6 (D)

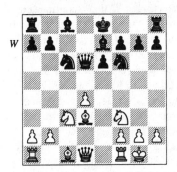

10 ♘b5!?

The most unstereotyped of several sidelines. Instead a common move-order to reach the ...♕d6 main line (covered next chapter) runs 10 a3 0-0 11 ♗e3. Other sensible alternatives:

a) 10 ♗e3 0-0 11 ♖c1!? (specifically to discourage Black's immediate ...b6 plan) 11...♘b4 (11...b6?! 12 ♘e4! ♘xe4 13 ♗xe4 ♗b7 14 ♘e5 ♖ac8 15 ♗f4 ± ♘xe5 16 ♖xc8 ♗xc8 17 ♗xe5 ♕b4 18 ♕c2 f5 19 a3 ♕b5 20 ♗c6 ♕a5 21 ♖d1 h6 22 h3 ♔h7 23 ♗f3 ♕b5 24 ♕c7 ♕d7 25 ♖c1 1-0 Hort-Mišta, Czech Cht 1977/8; 11...♖d8 12 ♖e1 ♗d7 13 a3 ♖ac8 14 b4 ♗e8 15 ♕e2 ♗f8 16 ♗b1 a5 17 b5 ♘e7 18 a4 ∞ Chandler-Matera, Lone Pine 1979) 12 ♗b1 b6 (12...♗d7 13 ♘e5 is more passive) 13 ♘e5 (worth attention is the line 13 ♘b5 ♕d8 14 ♘c7 ♖b8 15 ♗f4 ♗d6 16 ♗e5!? Ra.Müller-Schlosser, Germany 1995) 13...♗b7 14 ♗f4 ♕d8 15 ♖e1 ♖c8 16 ♗g5 ♕d6 17 a3 ♘bd5 18 ♕d3 g6 with equality, Gorelov-Panchenko, Moscow 1981.

b) 10 ♖e1 0-0 11 ♗g5 (leaving the d-pawn insufficiently bolstered) 11...♖d8 12 ♘b5 ♕d7 13 ♕a4 h6 14 ♗h4 ♘d5 15 ♗xe7 ♕xe7 ∓ Sanz-Sosonko, Amsterdam 1978.

c) 10 ♕e2 0-0 11 ♖d1 can commonly arise via move-orders where Black has delayed exchanging on d4. Black has a good game after 11...♘b4 12 ♗b1 b6 13 ♗g5 (or 13 ♘e4 ♗a6 14 ♕xa6 ♘xa6 15 ♘xd6 ♗xd6) 13...♗b7 14 a3 ♘bd5 15 ♘e4 ♘f4 16 ♕e3 ♘xe4 17 ♗xe7 ♕xe7 18 ♕xf4 ♘f6 ∓ Sanz-Stean, Amsterdam 1978.

d) 10 ♗g5 0-0 11 ♖c1 ♖d8 (not 11...b6? 12 ♗xf6 ♗xf6 13 ♘e4) 12 ♘b5 ♕d7 13 ♘e5!? is interesting and forcing. After 13...♘xe5 14 ♖c7! (14 dxe5 ♕xd3) 14...♘d5 15 dxe5 ♕xe5! (the only move! 15...♕xd3 16 ♕xd3 ♖xd3 17 ♖xe7 ♗d7 18 ♘d6, a line given in the first edition of this book, duly won for White in Hermann-Seibold, Germany 1991) 16 ♖xe7 ♕xg5 17 ♗xh7+ ♔xh7 18 ♕xd8 ♗d7 19 ♕xa8 ♗xb5 20 g3! (not 20 ♕xb7? ♗xf1 21 ♔xf1 ♕c1+ 22 ♔e2 ♕c2+ ∓ Suskov-Loginov, Leningrad 1979) 20...♗xf1 21 ♔xf1 ♕c1+ 22 ♔g2 ♕c6+ draws, Malaniuk-Gorelov, Sarato 1981.

10...♕d8

After 10...♛d7, 11 ♘e5 ♛d8 12 ♕f3 ♘b4! (12...♘xd4?! 13 ♕g3! gives White a strong attack) 13 ♖d1 ♘xd3 14 ♖xd3 0-0 with equality, was Smyslov-Espig, Berlin 1979, but White has many other tries. For example, after 11 ♗f4 ♘d5 12 ♗g3 the queen on d7 is more of a target than in the analogous lines of the main game.

11 ♗f4 ♘d5 12 ♗g3 *(D)*

Manoeuvring the bishop to the h2-b8 diagonal was the idea behind White's 10th move.

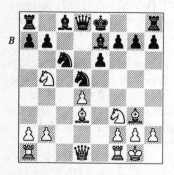

12...0-0

Or 12...a6 13 ♘c3 and now:

a) 13...♘cb4 14 ♗b1 ♘f6 15 ♘e5 0-0 16 ♖e1 ♗d7 17 ♗h4 ♗c6 18 ♖e3 g6 19 ♖h3 and while White had some kingside attacking chances in Henley-Kuligowski, New York 1981, Black defended satisfactorily with 19...♘d7 20 ♗xe7 ♕xe7 21 ♘xc6 ♘xc6 22 ♗e4 ♖ac8 23 ♕d2 ♖fd8 24 d5 exd5 25 ♕h6 ♘f8 26 ♗xd5 ♘d4.

b) 13...♘xc3 (this capture generally gives White a pleasant game) 14 bxc3 0-0 15 ♕e2 g6 16 ♖ad1 ♗f6 17 ♘e5 ♗d7 18 ♗e4 ♗g7 19 ♘c4 b5

20 ♘d6 ♖a7 21 d5 ± Stripunsky-Kushch, Ukrainian Ch 1990.

c) 13...0-0 14 ♖c1 ♘xc3 15 bxc3 ♗f6 16 a4 ♗d7 17 ♕c2 g6 18 ♗d6 ♖e8 19 ♕b1 e5 20 d5 ♘a7 21 ♖fe1 ♗xa4 22 ♗xe5 ♗xe5 23 ♘xe5 ♕c7 24 d6 ♕xd6 25 ♕xb7 ± Brodsky-Vehi Bach, Groningen 1994.

13 ♕e2

13 ♗c4!? looks strange, but actually it transposes to Game 17, Chapter 6. Instead 13 ♖c1 ♗d7 14 ♗e4 ♘cb4 forced White to continue combinatively in Grefe-Dzindzihashvili, Lone Pine 1980. The continuation 15 ♗xd5! ♘xd5 16 ♘c7 ♘xc7 17 ♗xc7 ♕e8 18 ♘e5 ♗b5 19 ♖e1 ♖c8 20 d5 exd5 21 ♕xd5 looked promising, but after accurate defence by Black the game petered out to a draw: 21...♗g5! 22 ♖c3 ♗c6 23 ♕d1 ♖xc7 24 ♘xc6 ♕d7 25 ♕xd7 ♖xd7 26 ♘xa7 g6 27 a3 ♖a8 28 ♘b5 ♗d2 29 ♖d1 ♗xc3 30 ♖xd7 ♗xb2 31 ♖xb7 ♗xa3 ½-½.

Also possible is 13 ♖e1, when the continuation 13...a6 14 ♘c3 ♘f6 15 ♖c1 ♘b4 16 ♗b1 b5 17 ♘e4 ♘xe4 was punished by a strong *zwischenzug* in Jamieson-Hase, Lucerne OL 1982: 18 ♗c7! ♕e8 19 ♗xe4 ♘d5 20 ♗xd5 exd5 21 ♗d6 ±.

13...♘cb4 14 ♗b1 a6 15 ♘c3 b5?!

15...♗d7 – Razuvaev.

16 ♘e4! ±

A natural move, but to play it Dorfman had to calculate the consequences of 16...f5. The tactics will favour White: 17 ♘c5! f4 (17...♗xc5 18 dxc5 f4 19 ♗h4) 18 ♘xe6 ♗xe6 19 ♕xe6+ ♔h8 20 ♕h3 h6 21 ♘e5 fxg3 22 ♘g6+ ♚g8 23 ♛e6+ ♖f7 24 ♘e5.

16...g6 17 ♖c1 ♝d7 18 a3 ♘c6 19 ♛d2 ♘f6 20 ♛h6?!

Razuvaev gives 20 h3 ±. Now Black is able to mount an inspired defence.

20...♘g4 21 ♛f4 *(D)*

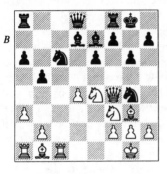

21...♖c8!!

An amazing move, just leaving the g4-knight *en prise*, but the point is simple enough: on 22 ♛xg4? e5! White will have to give up his queen (23 ♘f6+ ♝xf6 24 ♛e4 ♝f5). Instead the immediate 21...♘xd4 is bad after the continuation 22 ♘xd4 e5 23 ♛d2 exd4 24 ♝c7 ♛e8 25 ♘d6.

22 ♝a2 ♘xd4! 23 ♘xd4 e5 24 ♛d2 exd4 25 ♛xd4 ♖xc1+ 26 ♖xc1 ♝e6 27 ♛xd8 ♖xd8 28 ♝xe6 fxe6 29 ♚f1 ♘f6 (White still has a slight edge, but insufficient to win; now if 30 ♘g5, then 30...♘h5 31 ♘xe6 ♘xg3+ 32 hxg3 ♖d2) **30 ♘c5 ♖c8 31 ♘d3 ♖xc1+ 32 ♘xc1 ♘e4 33 ♝e5 ♘d2+ 34 ♚e2 ♘c4 35 ♝c3 ♚f7 36 ♚d3 e5 37 a4 e4+ 38 ♚xe4 bxa4 39 ♚d5 ♘b6+ 40 ♚c6 ♘c4 41 ♚d5 ♘b6+ ½-½**

10 Modern Main Line: 6 ♗e3

1	e4	c5
2	c3	d5
3	exd5	♕xd5
4	d4	e6
5	♘f3	♘f6
6	♗e3 (D)	

One of the reasons 6 ♗e3 is so popular is that it can also be played against the popular move-order 4...♘f6 5 ♘f3 ♘c6 first seen back in Chapter 3. The most likely result is a transposition into the lines examined in this chapter. With 6 ♗e3 (against either move-order) White aims to force early clarification in the centre, by getting Black to exchange pawns on d4.

In Game 26, Rozentalis-Andersson, we see an enterprising attempt to inhibit Black's routine development with 11 ♕c2!?. In Game 27, Adams-Tiviakov, we explore what is now the main variation of the 2...d5 defence against the c3 Sicilian, the

position arising after 13 ♖ad1. This is a deeply complex variation, where White often has to manoeuvre positionally in order to create threats, rather than just point his pieces at the kingside and lurch in. If you insist on an assessment I am afraid I am going to hide behind that classic author's phrase 'An unclear position with chances for both sides!' The last word is nowhere near being said on these strategically rich positions.

Game 26
Rozentalis – Andersson
Tilburg 1993

1 e4 c5 2 c3 d5 3 exd5 ♕xd5 4 d4 e6 5 ♘f3 ♘f6 6 ♗e3 cxd4

White's idea with 6 ♗e3 is to resolve the situation in the centre, but occasionally Black refuses to swap pawns on d4. After 6...♘c6 two logical continuations have been played (though the untried 7 a3!? is worth a thought, since after 7...cxd4 8 cxd4 play will inevitably transpose to the main line):

a) 7 dxc5 ♕xd1+ 8 ♔xd1 ♘g4 9 b4 a5 10 ♗b5 ♗d7 11 a3 (11 h3 ♘xe3+ 12 fxe3 axb4 13 ♗xc6 ♗xc6 14 cxb4 b6 15 ♘c3 bxc5 16 b5 ♗xf3+ 17 gxf3 ♖a3 18 ♔c2 c4 ∞ Handoko-Bancod, Jakarta 1993) 11...axb4 12 ♗xc6 ♗xc6 13 cxb4 ♘xe3+ 14 fxe3 b6 15 ♘c3 bxc5 16 b5 ♗b7 17 a4 g5

18 ♔c2 g4 19 ♘d2 f5 20 a5 and the two connected passed pawns ultimately won for White in Varavin-Serper, Novosibirsk 1989.

b) 7 ♘a3 cxd4 8 ♘b5 ♕d8 (the alternative 8...♕d7 9 ♘bxd4 ♘d5 10 ♗b5 looked dangerous for Black in the game Makarychev-Dzindzihashvili, Tbilisi 1973) 9 ♘bxd4 ♘d5 10 ♗g5 (10 ♗b5 ♗d7 11 0-0 ♘xe3 12 fxe3 ♗c5 13 ♗xc6 ♗xc6 14 ♘e5 = Prins-Ståhlberg, Trenčianske Teplice 1949 or 10 ♗d2 ♘xd4 11 ♘xd4 ♗c5 = Meulders-Sosonko, Amsterdam 1978) 10...f6 (10...♕b6!?) 11 ♗d2 ♗e7 12 ♗c4 0-0 13 ♕e2 ♕d6 14 0-0 ♗d8 15 ♖ad1 ± Vorotnikov-Petrushin, USSR 1985.

Also possible is 6...♘g4 7 ♗d3 (7 ♗g5!? Smagin; 7 c4 ♘xe3 8 fxe3 ♕d8 9 ♘c3 ♗e7 10 d5 is another plan, Handoko-Adianto, Beijing 1992) 7...♗e7?! (7...♘xe3 8 fxe3 ♘c6 transposes to Chapter 3, Game 5, note to White's 6th move) 8 ♗f4! 0-0 9 0-0 ♖d8?! 10 ♕c2 ♘f6 11 ♗c7! ♖d7 12 ♗e5 cxd4 13 cxd4 ♘c6 14 ♘c3 ♕a5 15 ♗xf6 ♗xf6 16 ♗xh7+ ± Smagin-Maksimenko, Yugoslavia 1994.

A third sideline is 6...♗e7, for example. 7 dxc5 ♕xd1+ 8 ♔xd1 0-0 9 ♘bd2 ♘g4 10 b4 a5 11 ♘d4 axb4 12 cxb4 ♖d8 13 ♔c2 ♗f6 14 ♘2b3 e5 15 ♘b5 ♘c6 16 a3 ♗f5+ 17 ♔c3 e4+ 18 ♘3d4 with very unclear play, Seret-Adorjan, Lucerne 1985, although the onus is on Black to justify his pawn sacrifice.

7 cxd4 ♘c6 8 ♘c3 ♕d6

After 8...♕d8 9 ♗c4! White has a sort of Semi-Tarrasch type position with accelerated development:

9...♗e7 10 0-0 0-0 (10...♘d5? 11 ♗xd5 exd5 12 ♕b3 0-0 13 ♕xd5 ± Lautier-I.Sokolov, Corrèze 1992) 11 ♘e5! ± ♘a5 (11...♗d7 Polak-Rogers, Biel 1992, and here 12 a3!? ♖c8 13 ♗a2) 12 ♗e2 ♘d5 (12...b6 13 ♗f3 ♗b7 14 ♗xb7 ♘xb7 15 ♘c6 ♕d7 16 ♕f3 ± Smagin) 13 ♘xd5 exd5 14 ♗d3 ± Smagin-Olafsson, Erevan 1988.

Less effective, after 8...♕d8, is the same ♕c2 plan of the main game: 9 ♗d3 ♗e7 10 a3 0-0 11 ♕c2 ♗d7 (11...h6 12 0-0 b6 also looks reasonable by analogy with other variations) 12 0-0 ♖c8 13 ♖ad1 ♕a5 14 ♕e2 ♖fd8 15 h3 ♗e8 16 ♖fe1 Dolmatov-Sosonko, Cannes 1994, and here Dolmatov suggests 16...a6!? as 17 ♗c1? is met by 17...♗xa3.

However we should also examine the more standard positions (which may also be reached via other move-orders) arising after 8...♕d8 9 ♗d3 ♗e7 10 0-0 0-0 and now:

a) 11 ♖c1 b6 (11...♘b4 12 ♗b1 b6 13 a3 ♘bd5 14 ♕d3 ♘xc3 15 bxc3 ♗b7 16 ♘g5 g6 17 c4 ♘g4 ∓ Karlsson-Hjartarson, Iceland 1995) 12 ♘e4 ♘b4 13 ♘xf6+ ♗xf6 14 ♗b1 ♗b7 15 a3 ♘d5 16 ♕d3 g6 17 ♗h6 ♗g7 18 ♗xg7 ♔xg7 19 ♕d2 ♕e7 = Chandler-Gheorghiu, USA 1979.

b) 11 a3 b6 12 ♕e2 (12 ♖c1 ♗b7 13 ♗b1 ♖c8 14 ♕e2 ♖e8 15 ♖fd1 ♘d5 16 ♕d3 g6 17 ♗a2 ♘xc3 18 ♖xc3 ♗f6 19 ♖dc1 ♗g7 20 h4 ♘e7 21 ♖xc8 ½-½ Fedorowicz-De Firmian, USA Ch (Estes Park) 1987) 12...♗b7 13 ♖ad1 ♖c8 14 ♖fe1 (in Game 27, note to Black's 13th, you will find a reference where Black has played first ...♕d6 and then ...♕d8; so by analogy Black should be OK here with an extra tempo, but no one told Motwani...) 14...♘a5?! (14...♖e8) 15 ♗g5 ♘d5 16 ♕e4!? ♘f6 (16...g6) 17 ♕h4 g6 18 d5 ♗xd5 19 ♘xd5 ♘xd5 20 ♗a6! ± Motwani-Tiviakov, Gausdal 1992, as White threatens 21 ♗xc8 and 21 ♖xd5.

Returning to the position after 8...♕d6 (D):

9 a3

Less clear but still possible is 9 ♗c4!? ♗e7 10 0-0 0-0 11 ♕e2 (11 a3!? a6 transposes to the game Mikhalchishin-Vukić, Yugoslavia 1994, which continued 12 ♗a2 ♖d8?! 13 ♕e2 b5 14 b4!? ♗b7 15 ♖fd1 ♘b8 16 d5 e5 17 ♗c5 ♕c7 18 ♕xe5 ±) 11...a6 (if 11...b6 White's bishop looks well placed on c4; compare many ♗d3 lines of Game 27 where White often spends a tempo re-deploying his bishop to the a2-g8 diagonal) 12 a3 (12 ♖ad1 b5 13 ♗b3 ♘b4 14 ♗g5 ♗b7 15 ♘e5 ♖ac8 16 ♖fe1 ♘bd5 17 ♖d3 ∞ Rozentalis-Serper, Vilnius 1988) 12...b5 13 ♗a2 b4 14 ♘a4 bxa3 15 bxa3 ♖b8 16 ♘c5 ♘d5 17 ♖ac1 ♖d8 18 ♕c2 ♕c7

19 ♘e4 ♗b7 20 ♘eg5 g6 21 ♕e4 ∞ Vlassov-Kharitonov, St Petersburg 1994.

9...♗e7 10 ♗d3

If White intends to play the ♕c2!? plan examined in this game, then in fact 10 ♕c2! is more accurate – see the note after Black's next move.

10...0-0

With the prudent 10...b6 (!), delaying castling by one move, Black can side-step the whole 11 ♕c2 line (as happened, for example, in the game Short-Tiviakov, Wijk aan Zee 1995 and in several games where Rozentalis was White). After 10...b6 there is nothing better than 11 0-0, transposing to Game 27, because 11 ♕c2 has lost its point: 11...♗b7 12 ♘e4 ♘xe4 13 ♗xe4 and White has no threats. Therefore White should prefer the less common move-order 10 ♕c2! 0-0 11 ♗d3 if he wishes to ensure he reaches this main game variation.

11 ♕c2!? (D)

For the main line 11 0-0 see the next game. At first glance c2 appears an odd square for the queen, since Black will shortly place a rook on the open c-file. Indeed White almost invariably subsequently moves the queen to e2, but this is not a straight-forward loss of a tempo. White's subtle idea is to prevent Black from achieving the fianchetto with ...b6 and ...♗b7; the immediate 11...b6? now can be strongly met by 12 ♘e4 ♘xe4 13 ♗xe4 attacking both h7 and c6. Therefore Black often responds by developing his bishop to the less active square d7.

11...♗d7

Alternatives:

a) 11...g6 (a concession, but it does allow Black to fianchetto) 12 0-0 b6 (as now after 13 ♘e4 ♘xe4 14 ♗xe4 ♗b7 the h-pawn is no longer *en prise*) 13 ♖ad1 ♗b7 14 ♖fe1 ♖ac8 15 ♕e2 ♖fe8 16 ♗c4 ♘d5 17 ♗xd5 exd5 18 ♗h6 f6 19 h4 ♘d8 20 ♘b5 ♕b8 21 ♕d2 ♗c6 22 ♗f4 Rozentalis-Hellers, Stockholm 1990; ± due to Black's slightly airy kingside.

b) 11...h6 is another possibility, when I cannot see a reason why after 12 0-0 (or 12 ♖d1) nobody has now tried the fianchetto with 12...b6!? (instead 12...♗d7 gives positions similar to the main game).

12 0-0 ♖ac8 13 ♖ad1 ♖fd8

Or 13...g6 14 ♖fe1 ♖fd8 15 ♕e2 ♗e8 16 ♘g5 ♕c7 17 ♗c4 ♘d5 18 ♗xd5 exd5 19 ♕f3 ♕d7 20 ♘h3 f6 21 ♗h6 ♗f7 22 ♘f4 b6 23 ♖e3 ± Vogt-Vatter, Germany 1995.

14 ♖fe1 ♗e8 15 ♗c1

Other examples:

a) 15 ♕e2 ♘d5!? (15...♕b8 16 ♗b1 a6 17 ♗a2 b5 18 ♗g5 h6 19 ♗h4 b4 20 axb4 ♘xb4 21 ♗b1 ♘bd5 22 ♘xd5 ♘xd5 23 ♕e4 ♘f6

24 ♗xf6 ♗xf6 25 ♕h7+ ♔f8 26 d5 ± Rozentalis-Novikov, Leningrad 1990) 16 ♘e4 ♕c7 17 ♗b1 ♕b6 18 h3 ♘xe3 19 fxe3 ♘a5 20 ♗d3 ♕b3 ∞ Yanovsky-Dolmatov, Dortmund 1992.

b) 15 h3!? ♕b8 16 ♕e2 a6 17 ♗b1 b5 18 ♗g5 h6 19 ♗h4 ♕a7 20 d5 ♘xd5 21 ♘xd5 ♗xh4 22 ♘xh4 exd5 23 ♘f5 with good play for White, Smagin-Jukić, Pula 1991.

15...h6 16 ♕e2 ♗f8 17 ♗b1 g6 18 ♗a2 ♗g7 19 h3

White's patient opening manoeuvres are a good illustration of how White may try to improve his position in this line. Instead the alternative 19 d5 exd5 20 ♘xd5 ♘xd5 21 ♖xd5 ♕f6 achieves nothing, while after 19 ♘b5 ♕f8 20 ♘c3 ♕d6 21 ♘e4 ♕e7 22 ♘g3 ♘d5 23 h4 ♘a5! (intending ...♗a4) 24 ♗d2 b6 25 b4 ♘c6 Black was already better in Sermek-Zagrebelny, Ljubljana 1994.

19...♘e7 20 ♘e5 ♘f5 21 ♗f4 ♕a6

After this Black has a worse ending, but could Black have captured the pawn on d4? In his *Informator* notes Rozentalis gives the variation "21...♘xd4? 22 ♕e3 g5 23 ♗h2 ♕b6 24 ♘c4 +–", perhaps being unaware of the spectacular defence 24...♘c2! with completely unclear complications.

22 ♕xa6 bxa6 23 d5 exd5 24 ♘xd5 g5 25 ♗h2 ♔f8 26 ♘c3 ♖xd1 27 ♖xd1 ♔g8! 28 ♔f1 ♗f8 29 ♖d3 ♔g7 30 ♘g4 ♘xg4 31 hxg4 ♘e7 32 ♔e1 ♘g6 33 ♔d2 ♘f4 34 ♗xf4 gxf4 35 ♗d5 ♗e7 36 ♖d4 ♗f6 37 ♖e4 ♖d8 38 ♔c2! ♔f8? (and not

38...&xc3 39 &xc3 &xd5 40 &xe8,
but Rozentalis gives 38...&b5 =) **39
&c4** (with both f4 and a6 attacked
Black must lose a pawn) **39...&d4 40
&xa6 &c6 41 &xd4 &xd4 42 f3
&e7 43 &d3 &e5 44 b4 f6 45 &c8
&e8 46 &b7 h5 47 gxh5 &xh5 48
&b5 &b8 49 &c4 &f7+ 50 &c5
&e8 51 &c8 &d8 52 &f5 &e7 53
&d4 &d6+ 54 &d5 &e5 55 &c6+
&xc6+ 56 &xc6 &b2 57 a4 &c3 58
b5 &a5 59 &b7 &b6 60 &a6 &d6
61 a5 &c5 62 &b7 1-0**

Black cannot stop 63 b6 axb6 64
a6.

Game 27
Adams – Tiviakov
New York Ct (6) 1994

**1 e4 c5 2 c3 d5 3 exd5 &xd5 4 d4
&f6 5 &f3 &c6 6 &e3 cxd4**

6...&g4 and 6...e5!? are covered
in Chapter 3, Game 5.

**7 cxd4 e6 8 &c3 &d6 9 a3! &e7
10 &d3 0-0 11 0-0 b6 12 &e2**

12 &e4 &xe4 13 &xe4 &b7 14
&e5 &ad8 is fine for Black, as in the
game Makropoulos-Gufeld, Athens
1985, while 12 &c2 gives the possibility of 12...&a6!?, as in Vorotni-
kov-Dolmatov, USSR 1978.

12...&b7 13 &ad1 *(D)*

This (by whatever move-order)
has become the key position in the
8...&d6 variation. There are many
ways for both White and Black to develop their pieces, together with a
bewildering mixture of move-orders.
Black can put his rooks on c8 and d8,
or d8 and e8 for example. He might
retreat his queen to b8, or play ...&f8

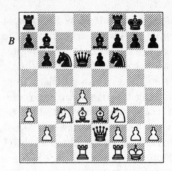

and ...&e7. Even the plan ...&d8 followed by ...&e7 and ...&ed5 has been
seen. White meanwhile can build up
the pressure with moves like &fe1,
&b1, &g5 or &g5 in almost any order. There are simply so many ways
to play, that I have decided to choose
the examples to illustrate as many of
the different relevant themes as possible.

13...&ad8

Typical alternatives:

a) 13...&d8!? (a very original
plan) 14 &b1 (14 &g5!?) 14...&e7
(the point: White has taken away the
b4-square so the knight takes another route to d5) 15 &e5 &ed5 16
&c1 &c8 17 &e4 &xe4 18 &xe4 f5
19 &e2 &xc1!? 20 &xc1 &f4 21
&e3 &g5 with unpleasant threats,
Yanovsky-C.Horvath, Budapest 1991.

b) 13...h6!? 14 &fe1 &fd8 15 &c1
(15 &b1) 15...&f8 (this formation
with ...h6 and ....&f8 is similar to An-
dersson-Rozentalis from the note below with 13...&ac8) 16 &e4 &e7 17
&b1 g6 18 &xf6+?! &xf6 19 &e4
&g7 20 &b5 &d6! 21 &e5 &c8 ∓
Vi.Ivanov-Zagrebelny, Moscow 1995.

c) 13...&fd8 14 &g5 (14 &fe1
&ac8 would transpose to 13...&ac8)

14...g6 15 ♗b1 ♖ac8 16 ♖fe1 ♘d5 17 ♘e4 ♕c7 18 ♗a2 ♗xg5 19 ♘exg5 ♕e7 20 ♕d2 ♕f6 21 ♖e4 ♖c7 22 ♖h4 h5 23 ♘e4 ♕g7 24 ♕g5 f6 25 ♘xf6+! ♕xf6 26 ♗xd5 ♕xg5 27 ♗xe6+ ♔g7 28 ♘xg5 ♘xd4 29 ♗b3 ± Tal-Yurtaev, USSR 1979.

d) 13...♖ac8 (also a standard square for the queen's rook) 14 ♖fe1:

d1) 14...♘d5?! 15 ♘xd5 exd5 (15...♕xd5 16 ♗c4 ♕h5 17 d5 ♘a5 18 ♗a2 ♗xd5 19 ♗xd5 exd5 20 ♗xb6 axb6 21 ♕xe7 ± Rozentalis) 16 ♘e5 ♘xe5 17 ♗f4 ± Rozentalis-Mikhalchishin, Trnava 1988.

d2) 14...♕d8 (Gheorghiu has experimented a bit with this retreat) 15 h3!? g6 16 ♗h6 ♖e8 17 ♗c4 ♘a5 18 ♗a2 ♘d5 19 ♘e4 ♘c6 20 h4! ± Yanovsky-Gheorghiu, Biel 1991.

d3) 14...♖fd8 (the most solid) 15 ♗g5 (15 ♗c1!? h6!? 16 ♗b1 ♗f8 ∞ was Rozentalis-Andersson, Tilburg 1993; after the game continuation of 17 ♘e4 ♘xe4 18 ♕xe4 g6 19 ♕h4 ♕e7 20 ♕h3 ♕f6 21 d5 ♖xd5 22 ♖xd5 exd5 23 ♗xh6 all sources assess '±', but why not then 23...♕xb2 in reply?) 15...g6 (15...♘d5? 16 ♘xd5 ♕xd5 17 ♗e4 ♕d6 18 d5 ♘a5 19 b4! with a winning position was Palkovi-Danner, Budapest 1995, as 19...♘c4 loses a piece to 20 dxe6; however, the most testing may be 15...h6!, as if 16 ♗c1 White would be a tempo down on Rozentalis-Andersson above) 16 ♗c4 ♘a5 17 ♘b5!? (bold; 17 ♗a2 is routine) 17...♗xf3 18 ♕xf3 ♕c6 19 d5 ♕xc4 20 ♗xf6 ♗xf6 21 ♕xf6 ♕xb5 22 dxe6 ♖f8 23 ♖d7! gave White a dangerous attack in return for the sacrificed piece,

Jonkman-Wojtkiewicz, Wijk aan Zee 1994.

Returning to the position after 13... ♖ad8 *(D)*:

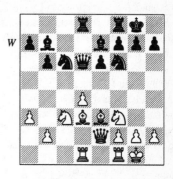

14 ♗g5!?

The openings of the Scottish GM Paul Motwani are always interesting, so also worth study is 14 ♗b1!? ♖fe8 (15...♕b8 and 15...♘d5 are alternatives) 15 ♖fe1 ♕b8 16 ♘g5!?. In Motwani-J.Bellin, Walsall 1992, White won incisively after 16...♗d6 17 ♘ce4 ♘xe4 (17...♗xh2+ 18 ♔h1 ♘xe4 19 ♗xe4 h6 20 ♘xf7 ♔xf7 21 ♕h5+ ♔g8 22 ♕xh2 ±) 18 ♗xe4 h6 19 ♘xf7!? ♔xf7 20 ♕h5+ ♔g8 21 ♗xh6! ♘xd4 22 ♗xg7 ♔xg7? (but 22...♘e2+ 23 ♔f1 ♗xe4 24 ♗f6! is still unpleasant for Black) 23 ♕h7+ ♔f8 24 ♕h6+ ♔g8 25 ♗h7+ 1-0.

Another possibility is 14 ♖fe1 ♕b8 (14...♘d5 15 ♘e4 ♕d7 16 ♗b1 ♕c8 17 h4 ♗a6 18 ♕c2 g6 19 ♗h6 ♖fe8 20 ♖c1 ♗b7 21 ♘eg5 with typical play, Van Mil-Tiviakov, Tilburg 1992) 15 ♗b1 when an interesting defensive plan was 15...♖d7 16 ♗g5 ♕d8 17 ♗xf6 ♗xf6 18 d5 exd5 19 ♘xd5 ♘d4 20 ♘xf6+ ♕xf6 21 ♘xd4 ♖xd4 22 ♖xd4 ♕xd4 23 ♗a2

½-½ Van Mil-A.Sokolov, Wijk aan Zee 1993.

14...g6

Or 14...♖fe8 (14...♕b8!? 15 ♗b1 ♖fe8 16 ♖fe1 transposes) 15 ♖fe1 ♕b8 (15...♘d5 16 ♘xd5 ♕xd5 17 ♗e4 ♕d7 18 d5 exd5 19 ♖xd5 ♕e6 20 ♕d3 with an attack – V.Ivanov) 16 ♗b1 g6! (16...♘d5?! 17 ♕e4 g6 18 ♕h4 ♘xc3 19 bxc3 ± V.Ivanov-Yarkovich, Russian Ch 1994) 17 ♗a2 ♘h5 18 ♗h6 ♗f6 19 ♕e3 ♗g7 20 ♗xg7 ♔xg7 21 ♘e5 ♘f6 22 h3 ♘e7! was Adams-Hulak, Wijk aan Zee 1995, when the continuation 23 ♘g4 ♘f5! 24 ♕e5 ♕xe5 25 dxe5 ♘xg4 26 hxg4 ♘h4! was good for Black. Instead 23 ♕f4!? ∞ is one plausible deviation.

15 ♗c4 ♖fe8 16 ♖fe1 ♘d5

On 16...♘h5 comes 17 d5! (Tiviakov).

17 ♗xd5?

Both players later criticised this capture in their annotations, but suggested different improvements.

Tiviakov gives 17 ♘e4 ±, while Adams assesses 17 ♘xd5 exd5 18 ♗b5 as ±.

17...exd5 18 ♕d2 f6! 19 ♗f4 ♕d7 20 b4 g5 21 ♗g3 ♗f8 22 h4 h6 23 hxg5 hxg5 24 ♖xe8 ♖xe8 25 ♕a2 ♘e7? (missing White's following excellent manoeuvre; 25...♘d8! followed by ...♘f7 is fine for Black) **26 ♘e4! ± ♗g7 27 ♘d6 ♖d8 28 ♖c1 ♗c6 29 ♕e2 ♗a8 30 ♕d3! ♗f8 31 b5 ♗h6 32 ♖e1 ♖f8 33 ♘h2** (heading for f1, e3 and f5; meanwhile Black's pieces are dreadfully disco-ordinated, and his kingside weakened) **33...♗g7 34 ♘f1 f5 35 ♗e5 ♘g6 36 ♘g3 +− ♗xe5 37 dxe5 ♘h4 38 ♘dxf5! ♘xf5 39 e6 ♕h7 40 ♘xf5 ♗b7** (40...♕xf5 41 ♕xf5 ♖xf5 42 e7 wins) **41 e7 ♖e8 42 ♖e6 ♗c8 43 ♕xd5 1-0**

The conclusion is that this main line variation leads into a complex and genuinely unclear middlegame, where there is a rich variety of plans for both White and Black.

11 2...♘f6: Early Deviations

In this chapter we cover lines that do not fit in easily anywhere else, but this does not mean they are insignificant! Game 28, for example, features a crucially important recent idea for White to side-step the main-line positions (Ivanchuk, Adams, Nunn and Dolmatov have all been seen on the white side). With 1 e4 c5 2 c3 ♘f6 3 e5 ♘d5 4 ♘f3!? ♘c6 5 ♗c4 ♘b6 6 ♗b3 White intends to postpone (or omit) the central pawn advance d4 in favour of faster piece development. For the present Black has manoeuvred his way to a reasonable game, but there is still scope for new discoveries.

In Game 29 the main subject is the brilliant 8 e6! pawn thrust invented by Eduardas Rozentalis (after 1 e4 c5 2 c3 ♘f6 3 e5 ♘d5 4 d4 cxd4 5 cxd4 d6 6 ♗c4!? ♘b6 7 ♗b5+ ♗d7). Several of the dapper Lithuanian grandmaster's most creative 2 c3 ideas are to be found in this chapter. Fortunately for Black, the bark of 8 e6 is worse than its bite, and there are a number of subsequent continuations to reach an unclear position. Game 30 covers the related system 1 e4 c5 2 c3 ♘f6 3 e5 ♘d5 4 d4 cxd4 5 ♗c4 (which club-players seem fond of using) where Black plays the well-known 5...♕c7! antidote.

Finally, Game 31 covers the variation where White fianchettoes with 4 g3, another line to which Rozentalis has made an enormous contribution. Whilst playable it does not give White any advantage against sensible play.

Game 28
Lutz – Khalifman
Wijk aan Zee 1995

1 e4 c5 2 c3 ♘f6 3 e5 ♘d5 4 ♘f3!?

Preparing a new and interesting plan, made better-known by an Ivanchuk-Kasparov encounter. White intends to get positions similar to the main-line variations of Chapters 18-20, but with d4 delayed or even omitted. The same idea can be used via the move-order 4...d6 5 ♗c4 ♘b6 6 ♗b3 when 6...♘c6 transposes.

4...♘c6 5 ♗c4

5 ♘a3 (an old Heidenfeld speciality of no real merit) 5...g6! (5...d6 6 exd6 ♗g4 7 ♗b5 ♕xd6 8 0-0 e6 9 ♘c4 ♕c7 10 ♘ce5 ♗xf3 11 ♘xf3 ♗d6 = Heidenfeld-Penrose, Madrid Z 1960; 5...e6 is also satisfactory) 6 g3 ♗g7 7 ♗g2 ♘c7! (7...d6 8 exd6 ♕xd6 9 0-0 0-0 10 d4 cxd4 11 ♘b5 ♕c5 12 ♘bxd4 ♖d8 13 ♘xc6 bxc6 14 ♕a4 ♖b8 15 ♘d4 ♗d7 16 ♘b3 ♕b6 17 ♕h4 ♗f5 = Heidenfeld-Portisch, Madrid 1960) 8 ♕e2 0-0 9 0-0 d6 10 d4 cxd4 11 cxd4 ♗g4 12 ♖d1 ♘e6 with an excellent game for Black, Bisguier-Fischer, Stockholm 1962.

5...♘b6 (D)

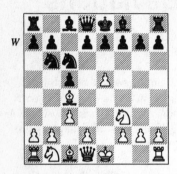

6 ♗b3

Instead 6 ♗e2!? saw some high-level usage in 1994/5 – for example Adams employed it in his PCA Candidates Match against Tiviakov. After 6...d6 (6...g6 7 d4 cxd4 8 cxd4 ♗g7 9 ♘c3 0-0 10 ♗f4 d5 11 exd6 exd6 12 h3!? a6 13 0-0 d5 14 ♕d2 ♗e6 15 ♖ad1 ♘d7 16 ♖fe1 ♖e8 17 ♗h6 ± Keitlinghaus-Videki, Budapest 1996) 7 exd6 Black has:

a) 7...e6 8 d4 ♗xd6 9 0-0 (9 dxc5 ♗xc5 10 ♕xd8+ ♘xd8 = Adams-Tiviakov, New York PCA Ct (8) 1994) 9...0-0 10 ♗d3 (threatening ♗xh7+) 10...g6 11 dxc5 ♗xc5 12 ♕e2 ♗e7 13 ♘bd2 ♘d5?! (13...♗f6 followed by ...♗g7 – Tiviakov) 14 ♘c4 ♕c7 15 ♗e4 ♘f4 16 ♕e3 ♘h5 17 ♕h6 ± Adams-Tiviakov, New York PCA Ct (14) 1994.

b) 7...♕xd6 and then:

b1) 8 d4 cxd4 9 cxd4 is a rather innocuous IQP.

b2) 8 ♘a3!? e5 (8...a6 9 d3 g6 10 ♗e3 ♗g7 11 ♘d2 ♘e5 12 d4 ± Godena Bacrot, Cannes 1995) and now 9 d3 ♗e7 10 ♘bd2 f5 was Adams-Vaïsser, New York rpd 1994 while 9

d4 cxd4 10 cxd4 e4 11 ♘b5 ♕e7 12 ♘g5 h6 13 ♘xe4 ♕xe4 14 0-0 ♔d8 15 ♗d3 was a completely unclear piece sacrifice in M.Bönisch-Enders, Germany 1995.

b3) 8 0-0:

b31) 8...g6 9 d3 (9 ♘a3 ♗g7 10 d3 0-0 11 ♘b5 ♕d8 12 ♗e3 a6 13 ♘a3 ♘d7 14 d4 ± Kharlov-Ernst, Haninge 1992) 9...♗f5 10 ♘a3 ♗g7 11 ♗e3 ♘d5 12 ♘c4 ♕d7 13 ♗xc5 b6 14 ♗a3 0-0 15 ♘e3 ♘f4 16 ♘xf5 ♕xf5 17 g3 ♘xe2+ 18 ♕xe2 ♖fd8 19 d4 ± Sveshnikov-King, Bern 1992.

b32) 8...♗f5 9 ♘a3 a6 10 d4 cxd4 11 ♘xd4 ♘xd4 12 cxd4 ♗e6 13 b3 ♖c8 14 ♗b2 ♘d5 15 ♖c1 ♖xc1 16 ♕xc1 g6 17 ♕c5!? (17 ♘c4 ♕d8 18 ♗f3 ♗g7 = Sveshnikov-Ragozin, Russian Ch 1994) 17...♖h6 18 ♘c4 ♕d8 19 ♗f3 with chances of an edge, Daniliuk-Nadyrkhanov, Moscow 1995.

c) 7...e5! 8 d4 (8 d3 ♗xd6 9 0-0 0-0 10 a4 ♘d5 = Hjartarson-H.Olafsson, Icelandic Ch 1994) 8...cxd4 9 cxd4 e4!? (9...exd4 10 ♘xd4 ♗xd6 11 ♘xc6 bxc6 12 ♘c3 0-0 13 0-0 ♘d5 14 ♘xd5 cxd5 15 ♗f3 favours White, Kharlov-Visier, Canete 1994 and Sveshnikov-A.Ivanov, Vladivostok 1994, but the ending with 9...♗xd6 10 dxe5 ♘xe5 11 ♘xe5 ♗xe5 12 ♕xd8+ ♔xd8 is playable, as in Hraček-Jirovsky, Czech Ch 1995) 10 ♘g5 ♗xd6 11 ♘xe4 ♗b4+ 12 ♘bc3 ♕xd4 13 0-0 ½-½ Adams-Khalifman, Wijk aan Zee 1995.

6...d5

6...d6 7 exd6 comes to the same thing, while 6...g6 7 d4 is a transposition to Chapter 17. This leaves the forcing move 6...c4!, when after 7 ♗c2 (D) Black has:

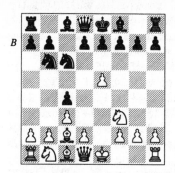

a) 7...d5 (or 7...d6) 8 exd6 ♕xd6 9 0-0 reaches the position examined in the note to move nine in the main game, and is in fact a more reliable way to get there, while 9 ♘a3 ♕e6+ 10 ♕e2 ♕xe2+ 11 ♔xe2 ♗g4 12 b3 cxb3 13 axb3 ♖c8 ∞ 14 h3 ½-½ was the game Sveshnikov-Yudasin, Kemerovo 1995.

b) 7...g6 8 b3 (8 ♘a3 d6?! {8...d5} 9 ♕e2! d5 10 h3 ♗g7 11 0-0 ± ♘d7?! 12 e6 fxe6 13 ♘g5 ♘f8 14 f4 ± was Adams-Gelfand, Wijk aan Zee Ct (7) 1994) 8...d5 9 exd6 ♕xd6 10 0-0 with a transposition to the main game, as in the later reference Dolmatov-Yudasin for example.

As the 6...c4 move-order cuts out some of White's options it seems preferable.

7 exd6 ♕xd6

a) 7...♗f5 8 d4 exd6 9 0-0 ♗e7 10 ♗f4 0-0 11 ♖e1 d5 Afek-Nijboer, Groningen 1994 and now 12 dxc5 ♗xc5 13 ♗e3 ± would have been logical.

b) 7...exd6 8 d4 ♗g4!? 9 h3 (9 dxc5! dxc5 10 0-0 ♗e7 11 ♘a3 0-0

12 ♗f4! ± Ivanchuk) 9...♗h5 10 ♗e3!? ♗e7 (10...c4!?) 11 dxc5 dxc5 12 ♘a3 0-0 13 0-0 ♕c8!? 14 ♗f4 ♖d8 (14...♕f5!?) 15 ♕e2 ♗f8?! (15...♕f5!? 16 ♗g3!?) 16 ♖fe1 ♕f5 17 ♗g3 ♗xf3 18 ♕xf3 ♕xf3 19 gxf3 ± Ivanchuk-Kasparov, Dortmund 1992.

8 0-0

8 ♘a3!? (stopping ...c4) is a valid idea, and was the move-order of Sveshnikov-Filipov (note to Black's eighth move in the main game) which transposed after 8...♗e6 9 0-0 ♗xb3, etc. Therefore Black might prefer 6...c4 to prevent this possibility.

8...c4

8...♗e6 9 ♘a3 ♗xb3 (9...c4 10 ♗c2 g6 11 d4!? cxd3 12 ♘b5 ♕d7 ♕xd3 ♕xd3 14 ♗xd3 0-0-0 15 ♗e2 a6 16 ♘bd4 ♘xd4 17 cxd4 f6 18 ♗d2 Benjamin-Gavrikov, Horgen 1994 and here Benjamin gives 18...♔b8 19 ♗a5 ♔a7 20 ♖fe1 ♗d5 =) 10 axb3 (10 ♕xb3 e6 11 d4 cxd4 12 ♘b5 and now instead of 12...♕d8?! 13 ♖d1 ± Dolmatov-Grünfeld, Haifa 1995, Dolmatov gives 12...♕d7 13 ♘xa7 ♖xa7 14 ♕xb6 dxc3 15 bxc3 =) 10...e6 11 ♘c4 ♕d8 12 d4 cxd4 13 ♘xd4 ♘xd4 14 ♘xb6 ♕xb6 15 ♗e3! ♖d8 16 ♗xd4 ♗c5 17 ♗xc5 ♕xc5 18 b4! ♕c6 19 ♕g4 0-0 20 ♖xa7 ♖d2 21 ♕f3 ♕xf3 22 gxf3 ♖b8 23 ♖fa1 ♔f8 24 ♖a8 ± Sveshnikov-Filipov, Russian Ch 1995.

9 ♗c2 g6

9...♗g4!? is also interesting:

a) 10 ♕e2 ♕e6!? (10...g6 11 ♘a3 ♕e6 12 ♕e3 ♕xe3 13 fxe3 ♗g7 14 b3 ♘a5 15 ♖b1 cxb3 16 axb3 ♖c8 17 b4 ± Hellers-Kuczynski, Leeuwarden 1994) 11 ♕xe6 ♗xe6 12 ♘a3 ♗d5 13 ♘g5 g6 14 b3 ♗g7 15 ♖b1 h6 16 ♘e4 0-0-0 17 ♖e1 ♖he8 18 ♘c5 ♘e5 19 f4 ♘d3 20 ♘xd3 cxd3 21 ♗xd3 ♗xg2 22 ♗xg6 ½-½ Daniliuk-Fomichenko, Russia 1995.

b) 10 ♖e1 ♘e5 (10...e6 11 h3 ♗h5 12 b3!? Nunn-Anand, Monaco rpd 1994) 11 ♖xe5 ♗xf3 12 ♕e1 ♗d5 13 b3 e6 14 ♗a3 ♘c6 15 ♗xf8 ♔xf8 16 ♘g5 f6! 17 ♖g3 h5 18 ♘a3! h4 19 ♖g4 h3 20 bxc4 ♗xg2 21 ♘b5 ♘xc4? (21...e5 22 ♕b1 a5 23 ♕b3 ∞ Adams) 22 ♘d4 ♘e5 23 ♖g3 ♕d5 24 ♗b3 ± Adams-Miladinović, Belgrade 1995.

10 b3 ♗g7 (D)

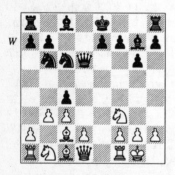

10...cxb3 11 axb3 ♗g7 12 d4 0-0 13 ♘bd2 ♘d5 14 ♘c4 ♕d8 15 ♗d2 b6 16 ♘fe5 ♘xe5 17 ♘xe5 ♗b7 18 c4 ♘c7 19 ♗c3 e6 20 ♕e2 ± Afek-Grünfeld, Israeli Ch 1992.

11 ♘a3!? cxb3

11...♗e6 12 ♕e2 cxb3 13 axb3 0-0 14 d4 ♘d5 15 ♗d2 ♕d7 16 ♖ad1 ♗g4 17 h3 ♗xf3 18 ♕xf3 ± Rozentalis-W.Watson, Germany 1995.

12 axb3 0-0 13 d4 ♗g4! 14 h3 ♗xf3 15 ♕xf3 e5 16 ♘b5 ♕d5

Also 16...♕d7 17 ♗a3 ♖fd8 18 dxe5 ♘xe5 19 ♕e2 a6 20 ♘d6 and now instead of 20...♕c7?! 21 ♖ad1 ± Dolmatov-Yudasin, Haifa 1995, Dolmatov analyses 20...♘d5! 21 c4 ♘c3 22 ♕e3 ♘c6 with counterplay.

17 ♕xd5 ♘xd5 18 ♗e4 a6! = 19 ♗xd5 axb5 20 ♖xa8 ♖xa8 21 dxe5 ♗xe5 22 c4 bxc4 23 bxc4 ♖a1 24 g3 ♗d4 25 ♗f4 ♖xf1+?! (Lutz gives 25...♖a2 26 g4 ♔g7 27 ♗g3 ♗e5 28 ♗xc6 ♗xg3 29 ♗xb7 ♗d6 followed by ...♗c5 with an easy draw despite the pawn minus) **26 ♔xf1 ± ♘e5 27 ♔e2 b6 28 ♗h6 ♘d7 29 g4 ♗g7 30 ♗f4 ♗e5 31 ♗e3 ♔f8 32 f4 ♗d6 33 ♔f3 ♔e7 34 g5 ♗c5 35 ♗d2 ♗d4 36 h4 ♗g7 37 ♗b4+ ♘c5 38 ♔g4 h6 39 gxh6 ♗xh6 40 f5 ♗e3 41 ♗e4 ♗d2 42 ♗a3 ♗c1 43 ♗xc1 ♘xe4 44 ♔f4 gxf5 45 h5 ♔f8 46 ♔e5 ♔g7 47 ♗e3 ♘f6 48 ♔xf5 ♘xh5 49 ♗xb6 ♔f8 50 ♗d4 ½-½**

Game 29
Rozentalis – Aseev
Klaipeda 1988

1 e4 c5 2 c3 ♘f6 3 e5 ♘d5 4 d4 cxd4 5 cxd4 d6 6 ♗c4!? ♘b6 7 ♗b5+

With a spectacular idea in mind. The old line was 7 ♗b3 and here 7...♘c6 8 ♘f3 would transpose to Chapter 16, though White could consider the sharp 8 e6!? fxe6 9 ♘f3 g6, which is unclear, e.g. 10 ♘g5 ♗g7!? or 10 h4 ♗g7 11 ♘c3 e5 12 d5 ♘d4 13 ♘xd4 exd4 14 ♘b5 ♘xd5! 15 ♘xd4 ♘f6 16 0-0 d5 Van Wijgerden-Ki.Georgiev, Plovdiv Echt 1983. However (after 7 ♗b3) Black can enter the forcing variation 7...dxe5!? 8

♕h5 e6 9 dxe5 ♘c6 and here White has two possibilities:

a) 10 ♘f3 ♕d3! 11 ♘c3 ♗b4 (12...♘c4 13 ♕h4!? ∞ R.Marić-Honfi, Monte Carlo 1968) 12 ♗d2 ♗xc3 (12...♘c4 13 0-0-0 ∞ but 12...♘a5!? is good: 13 0-0-0?! ♘xb3+ 14 axb3 ♗d7 15 ♕h4 ♗xc3 16 ♗xc3 ∓ Tong-Alterman, Beijing 1995) 13 ♗xc3 ♘d5 14 ♖d1 ♕e4+ 15 ♔f1 0-0! 16 ♘g5 ♕f5! 17 ♗xd5 exd5 18 g4 ♕g6 19 ♖xd5 h6 ∓ R.Marić-Radulov, Novi Sad 1974.

b) 10 ♘c3!? ♗c5 (10...♕d3!? 11 ♘f3 would be the previous note; 10...♘b4 11 ♗g5 ♘d3+ 12 ♔e2 ♕d4 13 ♘f3 ♘f4+ 14 ♗xf4 ♕xf4 15 g3 ♕b4 16 ♘g5 ♕e7 17 ♘ce4 ± was Papp-Cserna, Hungary 1981, while 10...g6 11 ♕g5 ♕xg5 12 ♗xg5 ♗g7 13 f4 h6 14 ♗f6 has been seen) 11 ♘f3 ♕d3 12 ♗g5 ♗b4 13 ♖d1 ♗xc3+ 14 bxc3 ♕xc3+ 15 ♗d2 ♕d3 16 ♕h4 ∞ Hort-Ballmann, Swiss Cht 1994.

7...♗d7

Surprisingly the natural 7...♘c6! has barely been played, even though 8 ♘f3 in reply would lead to Chapter 16, which is fine for Black. Instead after 8 ♘c3, 8...dxe5 9 d5 a6 was the game Rozentalis-Tukmakov, Lvov 1990, which ended in a draw after 10 ♗a4 ♘xa4 11 ♕xa4 b5 12 ♘xb5 ♗d7 13 ♘c3 ♘d4 14 ♕d1 g6 15 ♘ge2 ♗g7 16 ♗e3 ♕b6 17 ♕d2 ♖b8 18 b3 0-0 19 0-0 ♖fc8 20 ♖ac1 ♕b4 21 ♖fd1 ½-½. That leaves the variation 8...a6 ∞ completely untested, but if Black is OK there too, then the whole 7 ♗b5+ line rather loses its point.

8 e6!? (D)

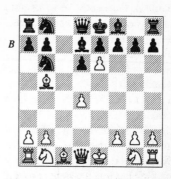

A wonderful shock move, but the bishop sacrifice is only temporary. Now if 8...fxe6 9 ♗d3 ♗c6 White has at least enough compensation for the pawn by bringing pressure to bear on e6. Some examples: 10 ♕g4 (10 ♘f3 ♘8d7 11 ♘g5 ♘f6 12 0-0 e5 13 ♘c3 exd4 14 ♘b5 e5 15 ♖e1 ♗e7 16 ♘e6 ♕d7 17 ♘bc7+ ♔f7 18 ♗f5! ± Carlier-Rajković, Brussels 1987) 10...♕c8 (10...♕d7 11 ♘h3 ♘a6 12 a3 g6 13 ♘g5 e5 14 ♘e6 e4 15 ♗xe4 ♗xe4 16 ♕xe4 ♕c6 17 ♕xc6+ bxc6 = Rozentalis-Vitoliņš, USSR 1989) 11 ♘e2 (11 ♘c3 ♘8d7 12 ♘h3 ♘f6 13 ♕g3 ♕d7 14 ♘g5 g6 15 0-0 ♘h5 16 ♕e3 ♗h6 17 ♕xe6 ♗xg5 18 ♕xd7+ ♔xd7 19 ♗xg5 ∞ Rozentalis-Domont, Geneva 1987) 11...g6 12 0-0 e5 13 ♕h4 ♗g7 14 dxe5 dxe5 (if 14...♗xe5, 15 f4!) 15 ♘bc3 ♘8d7 16 ♗h6 ♗f6 17 ♕g3 ♘c5 18 ♗c2 ♘e6 19 ♖ac1 ♘g7 20 ♗xg7 ♗xg7 21 ♘e4 ± Meszaros-Janošević, Harkany 1987.

8...♗xb5 9 ♕h5 ♕c8!

In response to White's double attack (against f7 and b5) Black defends with a neat double attack of his own against e6 and c1. Black's king remains in the centre in some subsequent variations, but he is not necessarily worse.

10 ♕xb5+ ♔d8

Solid is 10...♕c6!? 11 exf7+ and now:

a) 11...♔xf7 12 ♕f5+! (to keep queens on; 12 ♕h5+ g6 13 ♕f3+ ♕xf3 14 ♘xf3 h6 with equality, Antonio-Xu, Shenzhen 1992) 12...♔e8 13 ♕g5 defending c1 and g2, and the black king has lost the right to castle.

b) 11...♔d8 (to get queens off) 12 ♘c3 ♕xb5 13 ♘xb5 ♔d7 (13...♘8d7 14 ♘e2 ♘f6 15 0-0 ♔d7 16 f4 ♘bd5 17 f5 g6 18 ♘bc3 ± Rozentalis-Tunik, Podolsk 1989) 14 ♘f3 ♘c6 15 ♗e3 e6 16 0-0 ♗e7 17 ♖fe1 ♖hf8 18 ♖e2 ♖xf7 = Rozentalis-Arbakov, USSR 1988.

11 ♗e3! ♕xe6

The position is also highly unclear after:

a) 11...♕c4 12 ♕xc4 ♘xc4 13 exf7 g6 (if 13...♘xb2 then 14 ♘c3 ♘c4 15 ♘f3 intending d5 and ♘d4) 14 ♘f3 ♔d7 15 ♘c3 ♗g7 16 h4 ♘c6 17 h5 ♖af8 18 b3 ♘b6 19 ♔d2 ♖xf7 20 hxg6 hxg6 21 ♖xh8 ♗xh8 22 ♖h1 with a good endgame for White, Rozentalis-A.Shneider, USSR 1987 – the original game where Rozentalis unveiled his inspired 8 e6 move for the first time.

b) 11...fxe6!? 12 ♘c3 ♕c4 13 ♕g5 ♘d5 14 ♘ge2 ♘xc3 15 ♘xc3 ♘c6 16 0-0-0 g6 and so far Black has done well from this position: 17 h4 ♗g7 18 h5 ♗f6 19 ♕g3 ♔d7! ∓ Mirchev-Shmuter, Sofia 1989, 17 ♖d2 ♗g7 18 ♖hd1 ♖c8 19 ♔b1 ♗f6

20 ♕g3 ♘b4 ∓ Ekström-Ballmann, Swiss Cht 1995 or 17 d5 ♘b4 18 dxe6 ♘xa2+ 19 ♔c2 ♘xc3 20 ♕a5+ ♕c7 ∓ Pirrot-Gyimesi, St Ingbert 1995.

12 d5! ♕d7 *(D)*

Clearly not 12...♕xd5 13 ♗xb6+ while if 12...♘xd5 13 ♕xb7 ♘c7 14 ♘c3 d5, rather than 15 ♘f3 ♕a6 16 ♕b3 e6 ∞ Preissmann-Adler, Swiss Cht 1995, White can try 15 ♘xd5!? ♕c6 16 ♕xc7+ ±.

13 ♗xb6+ axb6 14 ♕xb6+ ♕c7 15 ♕e3 ♕c5 16 ♕d2 g6 17 ♘e2 ♗g7 18 0-0 ♘a6

18...♘d7 19 ♘bc3 ♘b6 20 ♖ac1 h5 21 ♕d3 ♘d7 22 ♘b5 ♕b6 23 ♘ec3 h4 24 b4 ♖h5 25 a4 ± Rosenthal-Schneider, Budapest 1990.

19 ♘bc3 h5 20 a3!? ∞

20 ♔h1 h4! ∓ 21 ♖ac1 ♖h5 22 ♕f4 ♔e8 23 ♕g4 ♕c8 24 ♕a4+ ♕d7 25 ♕xd7+ ♔xd7 ∓ Viksnin-Polovodin, USSR 1988.

20...♕c7 21 ♕d3 h4 22 b4 ♕b6 23 h3 ♖h5 24 a4!? ♕xb4 25 ♖ab1 ♕a5 26 ♖fc1? (26 ♖xb7 ∞) 26...♘xd5?! (26...♕a6! ∓) **27 ♖b5 ♘xc3 28 ♖xa5 ♘xe2+ 29 ♕xe2 ♖hxa5 ∓ 30 ♕a2! ♔e8 31 ♕b3 ♖xa4 32 ♕b5+ ♔f8??**

(falling into a bank-rank mate;
32...♔d8 33 ♕b6+ ♔e8 34 ♕b5+ =)
33 ♕xa4 1-0

Game 30
Braga – Gutman
Ostend 1984

**1 e4 c5 2 c3 ♘f6 3 e5 ♘d5 4 d4 cxd4
5 ♗c4** *(D)*

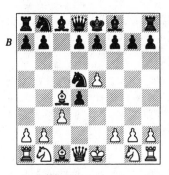

5...♕c7!

A dynamic reply. Both White's
bishop and e5-pawn are threatened;
on 6 ♗xd5? comes 6...♕xe5+ while
6 ♕b3 ♕xe5+ 7 ♘e2 d3 8 ♗xd3 e6
is also fine.

The alternative 5...♘b6 6 ♗b3 has
many transpositional possibilities:

a) 6...e6 7 cxd4 d6 8 ♘f3 with a
transposition to Chapter 17, Game
47, note to Black's fifth.

b) 6...♘c6 7 cxd4 (7 ♘f3) 7...d5
– see the 6...d5 lines below.

c) 6...d6 7 exd6 (7 cxd4!? dxe5 8
♕h5 is covered via Game 29; 7 ♘f3
would transpose to various main
lines after 7...♘c6) 7...♕xd6 8 cxd4
and the IQP position should be satisfactory for Black. One immediate try
to alleviate any pressure is 8...♗e6!?

9 ♘c3 ♗xb3 10 ♕xb3 e6, e.g. 11
♘f3 ♗e7 12 0-0 0-0 13 ♖d1 ♘c6 14
d5 exd5 15 ♗e3 ♕b4 16 ♕xb4 ♗xb4
17 ♗xb6 axb6 18 ♘xd5 ♗c5 19 a3
♖fd8 20 ♘c7 ♖ac8 = Kurajica-San
Segundo, Ibercaja 1994 or 11 ♘ge2
♘c6 12 0-0 ♗e7 13 ♗f4 ♕b4 =
Hedke-Bruk, Groningen 1992.

d) 6...d5!? (if Black later puts his
bishop on f5 White has the automatic attacking plan of ♘e2, ♘g3,
f4-f5, but Black's position may still
be viable if he gets his defensive
timing right) 7 cxd4 (for 7 exd6,
see 6...d6 above) 7...♘c6 (7...♗f5
8 ♘c3 e6 9 ♘ge2 h5!? 10 ♘g3
♗g6 11 f4 h4 12 f5 ♗h7 13 fxe6
fxe6 14 ♘h5 ♘c6 15 0-0 ♗f5 =
Braga-Kochiev, Mexico 1980) 8
♘c3 (8 ♘e2 ♗g4 9 f3 ♗f5 10 0-0
e6 11 ♘bc3 ♖c8 12 ♗e3 ♕d7 13
♘g3 ♗g6 14 f4 ♘a5 15 f5 ♗xf5 16
♘xf5 exf5 17 ♕f3 ♘xb3 18 axb3
a6 19 ♗d2 ♖c6 20 ♕h3 ♗e7 21
♖xf5 ½-½ Matulović-Durašević,
Sombor 1957) 8...♗f5 (8...g6?! 9
♘ge2 ♘a5 10 ♗c2 ♗g7 11 0-0 0-0
12 ♘f4 ± Braga-Browne, Buenos
Aires 1981) 9 ♘ge2 e6 10 0-0 ♖c8
11 ♗e3 ♗e7 (11...♕d7!? 12 ♘g3
♗g6 13 f4 ♘a5!? as per the above
Matulović game) 12 ♘g3 ♗g6 13
f4 ♕d7 14 f5 exf5 15 ♕f3 f4 16
♕xf4 0-0 17 ♘f3 ± M.Mihaljčišin-
Ankerst, Vrnjačka Banja 1962.

6 ♕e2 ♘b6 7 ♗d3

7 ♗b3?! fails to 7...d3 (also
7...♘c6 8 ♘f3 d3) 8 ♕e4 ♕c6 (or
8...♘a6 ∓, for example 9 ♘f3 ♘c5 10
♕f4 ♘xb3 11 axb3 d6 12 ♘a3 a6 13
exd6 ♕xd6 14 ♕xd6 exd6 15 0-0 ♗f5
Okhotnik-Ikonnikov, Le Touquet

1993) 9 ♕f4 (9 ♘d2 ♕xe4+ 10 ♘xe4 ♘c6 11 ♘f3 f6 ∓ Papapostolous-Geller, Varna OL 1962) 9...d5 10 ♘f3 (10 exd6 e6 ∓ Janošević-Rabar, Yugoslavia 1954) 10...♕g6 11 0-0 ♘c6 12 ♘a3 ♗g4 with advantage to Black, Lukin-Rabar, Novi Sad 1955.

7...♘c6

Keeping the pawn with 7...dxc3? is especially bad here because the black queen on c7 becomes a target when White's pieces develop: 8 ♘xc3 ♘c6 9 ♘f3 a6 10 0-0 g6 11 a4 ♘b4 12 ♗e4 ♗g7 13 ♗f4 e6 14 ♖ac1 ♕d8 15 ♗g5 f6 16 exf6 ♗xf6 17 ♗xf6 ♕xf6 18 a5 d5 19 axb6 dxe4 20 ♘xe4 ♕e7 21 ♖c7 ♗d7 22 ♖d1 ♖d8 23 ♘d6+ 1-0 Pinho-Dubao, Lisbon Ch 1992.

7...d6!? 8 ♗f4 (8 exd6 ♕xd6 – see 7...d5 next) 8...e6 9 ♘f3 ♘d5 10 exd6 ♗xd6 11 ♗xd6 ♕xd6 12 ♘xd4 0-0 = was Mikhalchishin-Ornstein, Pamporovo 1976.

It is also a good question why 7...d5!? is not played more: 8 ♗f4 is nothing special and 8 exd6 ♕xd6 9 cxd4 ♘c6 10 ♘f3 ♗g4 11 ♗e3 e6 12 0-0 ♗e7 13 ♘c3 0-0 14 ♖ad1 ♘d5 ∓ gave Black a superb anti-IQP position in the game Braga-Semkov, Forli 1988.

8 ♘f3 d5

Or:

a) 8...♘b4!? 9 0-0 ♘xd3 10 ♕xd3 ♕c4 = Taylor-De Fotis, USA 1971 and Novak-Blecha, Plzen 1995.

b) 8...d6 9 ♗f4 (best is 9 exd6 transposing into the main game) 9...♘d5 10 ♗g3 dxc3 11 ♘xc3?! (11 bxc3 e6 ∓ Zimmermann-Bellon, Bern 1996) 11...♘xc3 12 bxc3 ♘d4!

∓ 13 ♘xd4 ♕xc3+ 14 ♕d2 ♕xa1+ 15 ♔e2 ♗g4+ 16 f3 ♕xh1, etc. Neminovski-J.R.Koch, Cannes 1989.

c) 8...g6 (formerly popular, but White has an initiative for his pawn) 9 0-0 (9 cxd4? ♘xd4 or 9 ♗f4?! ♘d5 10 ♗g3 ♗h6 11 ♕e4 dxc3 12 bxc3 ♕a5 13 0-0 f5 14 ♕h4 ♗g7 ∓ Pasman-Gutman, Israeli Ch 1984) 9...dxc3 10 ♘xc3 ♗g7 11 ♗f4 (11 ♖e1 0-0 12 ♗g5 d5 13 exd6 ♕xd6 14 ♖ad1 ♕b4 Miles-Sax, Bath Echt 1973, and now best is 15 ♗xe7 ♘xe7 16 ♕xe7 ♗xc3 17 bxc3 ♕xc3 18 ♗b5 ∞) 11...0-0 12 ♖ac1 f6 13 ♘b5 ♕b8 14 ♗g3 fxe5 15 ♘g5 ♘d5 16 ♗c4 e6 17 ♗xd5 exd5 18 ♕d3 d4 19 ♕c4+± San Marco-Leontxo Garcia, Ales 1984.

9 exd6

9 h3 is slow, and 9 0-0 ♗g4 10 ♗f4 e6 11 ♖c1, Pasman-A.Martin, London 1984, looks like insufficient compensation for the pawn.

9...♕xd6 10 ♘xd4 g6!?

To deny White the easy development obtained after 10...♘xd4 11 cxd4 e6 (grabbing the pawn with 11...♕xd4 would be asking for trouble) 12 0-0 ♗e7 13 ♘c3 ± Braga-Larsen, Mar del Plata 1982.

11 ♘b5

White could look for improvements with 11 ♘xc6!? bxc6 12 0-0 ♗g7 and now:

a) 13 ♘d2 0-0 14 ♘e4 ♕c7 (15 c4 ♗f5 16 ♖b1 ♖ad8 17 b3 ♘d7 ∞ Buisman-C.Shephard, Corr. 1989) 15 ♘c5 ♕e5 16 ♕xe5 ♗xe5 17 ♗e4 ♗d6 18 ♘b3 ♗a6 19 ♖e1 ♖ac8 with equality, D.Graham-W.Taylor, Corr. 1989.

b) 13 ♗g5!? is a suggestion by Gary Lane; logically White should have a nice game (better development and pawn structure) but somehow Black's pieces also seem quite active. Maybe 13...♘d5 ∞ is the best reply.

11...♕b8 12 0-0 ♗g7 13 ♗g5 ♘d5?!

In his notes Gutman later gave 13...0-0!, e.g. 14 ♗xe7 ♖e8 15 ♗d6 ♖xe2 16 ♗xb8 (16 ♗xe2 ♗g4! 17 ♗xb8 ♗xe2) 16...♖xb2 17 ♗d6 ♘e5 18 ♖e1 ♗d7 ∓.

14 ♗c4 (14 ♗e4!?) **14...h6 15 ♗h4 ♘f4 16 ♕e3 g5 17 ♗g3 a6 18 ♘5a3 h5** (the position is unclear, but White shortly goes astray) **19 h4 ♗h6 20 hxg5 ♗xg5 21 ♘d2 ♘h3+ 22 gxh3 ♗xe3 23 ♗xb8 ♖xd2 24 ♗c7 ♗xh3** (with an extra pawn, which is ultimately converted after some erratic technique) **25 ♖fd1 ♖c8 26 ♗g3 ♗g5 27 ♗d5 h4 28 ♗h2 ♗g4 29 f3 ♗h3 30 ♔f2 e6 31 ♗e4 ♗e7 32 ♗d6 ♗d8 33 ♘c4 b5 34 ♖h1 bxc4 35 ♖xh3 f5 36 ♗xc6+ ♖xc6 37 ♗e5 ♖g8 38 ♖d1 ♖c5 39 ♗d4 ♖d5 40 f4 ♖g4 41 ♔f3 ♗c7 0-1**

Game 31
Rozentalis – Gelfand
Tilburg 1992

1 e4 c5 2 c3 ♘f6 3 e5 ♘d5 4 g3 *(D)* **4...d6**

4...♘c6 5 ♗g2 and now:

a) 5...e6 6 ♕e2 (or 6 ♘f3 d6 with a transposition to the illustrative game after 7 exd6) 6...♗e7 7 f4 (more solid is the transposition 7 ♘f3 d6 8 exd6 ♕xd6 9 0-0 0-0 10 ♘a3 b6 11

♘c4 ♕c7 12 a4 ♗b7 13 d3, the move-order of the game Rozentalis-Ljubojević found in the note to Black's ninth move in the illustrative game) 7...0-0 8 ♘f3 d6 9 0-0 dxe5 10 ♘xe5 ♘xe5 11 fxe5 ♖b8 12 d3 b6 13 ♘d2 ♗a6 14 ♘e4 ♖b7 15 a3 ♖d7 16 c4 ♘c7 17 ♘f2 ♕b8 18 ♗f4 ♗b7 19 ♘e4 ∞ Rozentalis-Panzalović, Biel 1990.

b) 5...♕c7!? (forcing White's committal response; on 6 ♕e2 comes the trick 6...♕xe5! 7 ♕xe5 ♘xe5 8 ♗xd5 ♘d3+, e.g. 9 ♔e2 ♘xc1+ 10 ♔e3 e6 11 ♗c4 b5 12 ♗xb5 ♖b8 13 ♘a3 c4! 14 ♗xc4 ♖xb2 15 ♘b5 d5 16 ♗f1 ♘xa2 ∓ Onoprienko-Kjeldsen, Budapest 1995) 6 f4 e6 7 ♕e2 ♗e7 (7...a6!? 8 d3 b5 9 ♘f3 d6 and now 10 0-0?! dxe5 11 fxe5 ♗e7 12 a4 ♗b7 13 axb5 axb5 14 ♖xa8+ ♗xa8 15 ♘a3 ♕b8 16 c4 bxc4 17 dxc4 ♘c7! ∓ was Rozentalis-Shirov, Manila OL 1992, but Shirov claims White could improve with 10 c4! bxc4 11 dxc4 ♘b6 12 exd6 ♗xd6 13 0-0 ±) 8 ♘f3 d6 (8...a6 9 0-0 b5 10 a4 bxa4 11 ♖xa4 ♘b6 12 ♖a1 c4! ∞ Rozentalis-Kotronias, Manila OL 1992) 9 d3 0-0 10 0-0 a6 11 ♘bd2 dxe5 12 fxe5 b5 13 a4 ♗b7 14 axb5 axb5 15 ♖xa8 ♗xa8 16 ♔h1 b4 17 c4 ♘b6 and White's backward d-pawn is a potential target, Rozentalis-Dvoirys, Leningrad 1990. Forcing White to play f4 so early seems an interesting plan.

5 exd6 e6

Black can also keep the c8-h3 diagonal open to develop his bishop with 5...♕xd6!?, which gives a more open struggle compared to the illustrative game. 6 ♗g2 ♘c6 (6...g6!? needs more tests) 7 ♘e2 (on 7 ♘f3 White must contend with both 7...♗f5 8 0-0 ♗d3 9 ♖e1 h6 ∞ Wang Wenhao-Zhang Weida, Beijing Lee Cup 1995 and 7...♗g4) and here:

a) 7...♗g4 8 h3 ♗h5 9 0-0 e6 10 d4 ♖d8 11 g4 ♗g6 12 ♘a3 ♕d7 13 c4 ♘b6 14 d5 exd5 15 cxd5 ♘b4 16 ♘f4 ♗e7 ∞ Finkel-Portisch, Biel 1995. Play proceeded increasingly wildly: 17 h4 ♗xh4 18 ♖e1+ ♗e7 19 ♘xg6 hxg6 20 ♗g5 f6 21 ♗f4 ♔f8 with an ultimate draw.

b) 7...♗f5 8 d4 cxd4 (8...e6 9 ♘a3 ♕d7 10 ♘c4 ♗g4 11 dxc5 ♗xc5 = Hoffman-De Firmian, Buenos Aires 1995) 9 ♘xd4 ♘xd4 10 ♕xd4 ♕e6+ 11 ♗e3 ♘xe3 12 fxe3 ♕a6 13 ♕d5! and now rather than 13...e6?! 14 ♕xb7 ♕xb7 15 ♗xb7 ♖b8 16 ♗c6+ ♔d8 17 b4 ± Rozentalis-Gelfand, Tilburg rpd 1992, Blatny's suggestion of 13...♗g4 14 ♗f1 ♕d6 15 ♗b5+ ♔d8 looks OK for Black.

c) 7...g6 and now:

c1) 8 d4 cxd4 9 ♘xd4 should not be met by 9...♘xd4?! 10 ♕xd4 ♕e6+ 11 ♕e4 ♗g7 12 0-0 ♕xe4 13 ♗xe4 ♘c7 14 ♘a3 ± McDonald-Enders, Budapest 1995 but rather 9...♗g7!

10 ♘xc6 ♕e6+ 11 ♘e5 ♕xe5+ 12 ♕e2 ♕xe2+ 13 ♔xe2 ♗g4+ 14 f3 ♗e6, which was excellent for Black in Mufić-Palac, Pula 1994.

c2) 8 ♘a3 ♘c7 9 0-0 (9 d3 ♗f5 10 ♕b3 0-0-0 with a good game for Black, Seul-Enders, Budapest 1995) 9...♗g7 10 d3 0-0 11 ♘c4 ♕d7 12 ♗e3 ♘e6 13 ♖e1 ♖e8 = Rozentalis-Hellers, Malmö 1993.

6 ♗g2 ♗xd6 7 ♘f3

7 ♘e2 ♘c6 8 0-0 0-0 9 d4 ♘de7?! (9...cxd4 10 ♘xd4 transposes to the note to 9 ♘a3 in the main game) 10 ♘a3 cxd4 11 ♘b5 ♗b8 12 ♘bxd4 e5 13 ♘xc6 ♘xc6 14 ♗e3 ♗g4 15 ♖e1 with perhaps a little edge for White due to the queenside majority, Rozentalis-Rogers, Biel 1990.

7...0-0

7...♘c6 8 0-0 0-0 is the common move-order, but it is simply a transposition.

8 0-0 ♘c6 *(D)*

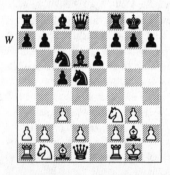

9 ♘a3

This leads to structures reminiscent of the King's Indian Attack, whilst a similar position arises after 9 d3, for example 9...b6 10 ♘bd2 ♗b7 11 ♕e2 ♗c7 12 ♘c4 ♖e8!? 13

a4 h6 14 ♗d2 ♕d7 15 ♖ad1 ♖ad8 16
♗c1 e5 with a good game for Black,
Short-Kasparov, London rpd 1993.
In *Beating the Anti-Sicilians* Gallagher makes the claim that "White
is in fact playing a King's Indian Attack but with a tempo less than normal. For example, take the moves 1
e4 c5 2 ♘f3 e6 3 d3 ♘c6 4 g3 d5 5
♘bd2 ♗d6 6 ♗g2 ♘ge7 7 0-0 0-0 8
exd5 ♘xd5 9 c3 and you will notice
that we have the same position as in
Short-Kasparov, apart from the fact
that White has an extra ♘bd2 – and
this is Short's next move!" Joe con-
cludes: "If this is the best White can
do I don't predict a very bright future
for the Rozentalis variation."

Whilst the comparison is well-
spotted, the logic is unconvincing.
True, if both sides played in a certain
way in the KIA you could reach that
position – but they don't. Black, for
example, would recapture on d5 with
the pawn on move eight, not the
knight. A database sweep did not re-
veal any King's Indian Attack games
that used the moves or reached the
position given by Gallagher, so the
claim of a transposition is unrea-
sonable. The c3 Sicilian player could
as easily argue that, by investing a
mere tempo, he has forced *Black* into
an unfavourable line of the KIA!
However, I won't argue with Joe's
overall assessment, since Black does
reach comfortable equality.

The other way to play is 9 d4 and
now:

a) 9...♘de7 10 dxc5 ♗xc5 11 ♕e2
♘g6 12 h4 ± M.Makarov-Filipov,
Moscow 1994.

b) 9...b6 (risky) 10 c4 ♘de7 11
♘c3 ♗b7 12 d5!? (the sacrificial
course; 12 dxc5 ♗xc5 13 ♘e4 ±)
12...exd5 13 cxd5 ♘b4 14 ♘g5 h6
15 ♘ge4 ♘bxd5 16 ♗xh6!? ♗e5?!
(in his notes White later gave the best
defence as 16...gxh6 17 ♘xd5 ♘xd5
18 ♕g4+ ♔h7! 19 ♕f5+ ♔g7 20
♖ad1 ♗e7 21 ♘c3 ♕c8 22 ♕xc8
♖axc8 23 ♗xd5 ♗xd5 24 ♘xd5 ♗f6
=) 17 ♗d2 ♘xc3 18 bxc3 ♘g6 19 f4!
± Magem-Tiviakov, Madrid 1994.

c) 9...♗d7 10 ♘a3!? (10 c4 ♘f6
11 ♘c3 ♘xd4 12 ♘xd4 cxd4 13
♕xd4 ♕c7 14 b3 ♖fd8 15 ♗b2 ♗c6
= Ochoa-Ubilava, Las Palmas 1994
or 10 dxc5 ♗xc5 11 ♘bd2 ♗e7 12
♕e2 ♕c7 13 ♘e4 ♖fe8 14 c4 ♘f6 15
♘c3 a6 16 b3 e5 17 ♗b2 ♗g4 18
♘d5 ½-½ Rozentalis-Khalifman,
Rakvere 1993) 10...cxd4 11 ♘b5
♗e7 12 ♘bxd4 ♗f6 13 c4 ♘de7 14
♗e3 a6 15 ♕d2 e5 16 ♘xc6 ♗xc6
17 ♖ad1 ♘f5 18 ♕xd8 ♖fxd8 19
♗b6 ♖xd1 20 ♖xd1 h5 21 ♘e1
(White has the better endgame due to
the queenside majority and control
of the d-file) 21...♖c8 22 b3 ♗e7 23
♗d5 ♔f8 24 ♘f3 f6? 25 ♘xe5!
♗xd5 (25...fxe5 26 ♗e6) 26 ♘g6+
♔f7 27 ♘xe7 ♔xe7 28 ♖xd5 ± Vor-
otnikov-Taimanov, Leningrad 1984.
Perhaps Black could have played
more actively earlier, but this game
illustrates how White can play these
quiet positions effectively.

d) 9...cxd4 10 ♘xd4 and now:

d1) After 10...♗c5 11 ♘xc6 bxc6
White should continue 12 ♕e2, rather
than 12 ♕a4?! ♕b6 13 ♕e4 ♗a6 14
c4 ♖ac8! 15 ♘d2 ♘f6 16 ♕c2 ♗d4
∓ Finkel-Alterman, Israel 1994.

d2) 10...♗d7!? is a significant idea, as 11 ♘xe6?! fails to 11...fxe6 12 ♗xd5 (12 c4 ♘f4!) 12...exd5 13 ♕xd5+ ♖f7 14 ♕xd6 ♗h3 ∓. Instead the game Rozentalis-Shirov, Tilburg 1993 went 11 c4 ♘de7 12 ♘b5?! (12 ♘c3 ♗e5! ∞ Shirov) 12...♗e5 13 ♘1c3 a6 14 ♘d6 ♕c7 15 c5 ♖ad8 16 ♖e1 ♗c8 17 ♕h5 ♗xd6 18 cxd6 ♕xd6 and White did not have enough compensation for the pawn.

d3) 10...♘xd4 11 ♕xd4 ♕c7 12 ♘d2 ♗d7!? (after 12...♗c5, 13 ♕e4 b5 14 a4 bxa4 15 ♕xa4 ♗d7 16 ♕c2 ♖ac8 = was Nunn-Tisdall, San Francisco 1995 but White managed to get an advantage after 13 ♕d3 ♗d7 14 ♘b3 ♗e7 15 ♕e2 ♗f6 16 ♖d1 ♖ac8 17 ♗xd5!? exd5 18 ♗f4 ♕c6 19 ♕h5 ♗e6 20 ♗g5 ♗xg5 21 ♕xg5 ± in Keitlinghaus-Rosandić, Vinkovci 1995) 13 ♘e4 ♗e5 14 ♕d3 and here 14...♖ad8 = Rozentalis-Akopian, Philadelphia 1994 or 14...a6 = Pedersen-Schandorff, Danish Ch 1994.

9...♗d7

a) 9...♖b8 10 ♘c4 ♗e7 11 d4 b6 12 ♘fe5 ♘xe5 13 ♘xe5 ♗b7 14 c4 ♘f6 15 ♗xb7 ♖xb7 16 ♕f3 ♕c7 17 ♗f4 ♗d6 18 dxc5! bxc5 19 b3 ♖bb8 20 ♖fe1 ± Rozentalis-Fossan, Oslo 1992.

b) 9...a6 10 ♘c4 ♗c7 11 a4 ♘b6 12 ♘xb6 ♗xb6 13 d3 ♕e7 14 ♗g5 f6 15 ♗e3 ♗c7 16 d4 ♖d8 17 ♕b3 ± Nunn-U.Nielsen, Vejle 1994.

c) 9...♘e5 10 d3! (10 ♘xe5 ♗xe5 11 d3 ♗d7 = Rozentalis-Khalifman, Germany 1991) 10...♗d7 11 ♘g5 ♗c6 12 ♘c4 ± Rozentalis-Gelfand, Tilburg 1992.

d) 9...b6!? 10 ♘c4 (10 ♖e1 ♗b7 11 d3 ♗e7 12 ♕e2 ♕d7 13 ♘c4 ♖ad8 14 ♗d2 ♗f6 15 ♖ad1 ♗a6 is unclear, Freckmann-Yakovich, Munich 1992) 10...♗c7 (for 10...♗e7 see the next note with 9...♗e7) 11 a4 ♗b7 12 d3 ♖b8 13 ♕b3 ♔h8 14 ♖e1 a6 15 ♗d2 ♗a8 16 ♖ad1 b5 17 axb5 axb5 18 ♘e3 ♘ce7 19 ♗c1 ♗d6 with equality, Wahls-Tischbierek, Biel 1993.

e) 9...♗e7 10 d3 b6 11 ♘c4 ♗b7 12 a4 ♕c7 (12...a6 13 ♕b3 ♖b8 14 ♖d1 ♕c7 15 ♗g5 ♗a8 16 ♗xe7 ♘dxe7 17 ♘e3 ♖fd8 18 d4 = A.Sokolov-Banas, Viernheim 1992) 13 ♕e2 ♖ad8 (13...h6 14 ♗d2 ♖ad8 = Rozentalis-Ljubojević, Moscow OL 1994) 14 ♗d2 ♖fe8 15 ♖ae1 ♗f8 16 ♗g5 f6 17 ♗c1 e5 18 ♘h4 ♕d7 19 ♕c2 g5? (19...♘ce7 = Rozentalis) 20 ♘f3 ♘c7 21 ♘fd2! ♕xd3 22 ♕xd3 ♖xd3 23 ♘e4 ♔g7 24 f4! with a dangerous attack, Rozentalis-Rogers, Malmö 1993.

10 ♘c4

For 10 d4!? cxd4 11 ♘b5 see the 9...♗d7 note at White's ninth move. After 10 ♘c4 we again reach a type of King's Indian Attack where Black has satisfactory play, but White often manages a slow build-up against the black kingside.

10...♗c7 11 d3 ♖c8 12 a4 b6 13 ♕e2 ♕e7 14 ♘h4?! (14 ♗d2 – Rozentalis) **14...♘f4! 15 ♗xf4 ♗xf4 16 ♖ae1** (or 16 ♗e4 f5!) **16...♖fd8?!** (16...♗g5) **17 ♗e4! ♗g5 18 ♘g2 ♗f6 19 f4 g6 20 g4 ♗g7 21 ♕f2 ♕f6 22 ♕g3 ♘a5 23 ♘d6 ♖b8 24 g5** (Rozentalis now believes 25 f5! was stronger) **24...♕e7 25 f5 ♗c6 26**

♘xf7! ♛xf7 27 fxg6 ♛e8 28 gxh7+ ♚h8 29 g6 ♖b7 30 h4 ♖bd7 31 h5 ♗xe4 32 ♖xe4 ♖xd3 33 ♛g4 ♖3d6 34 ♘f4 ♘b3 35 ♘xe6 ♘d2 36 ♘g5! (the sacrifice on move 26 was very unpleasant for Black; White's kingside pawns are horrendously cramping, and are worth far more than a piece) 36...♘xe4 37 ♛xe4 ♖6d7 38 ♛xe8+ ♖xe8 39 ♘f7+ ♖xf7 40 ♖xf7 ♗h6 41 ♖xa7 ♗c1 42 b3 c4 43 bxc4 b5 44 ♚g2 bxa4 45 ♖xa4 ♚g7 46 c5 ♗g5 47 c6 ♗f6 48 ♖a7+ ♚h6 49 c4 ♖e6 50 h8♛+ 1-0

12 3 e5 ♘d5 4 d4 cxd4 5 ♕xd4

1	e4	c5
2	c3	♘f6
3	e5	♘d5
4	d4	cxd4
5	♕xd4 *(D)*	

Remarkably little of interest has happened in these ♕xd4 lines recently, and there is no change to the old conclusion that these lines give White nothing. After 5...e6 the move 6 ♗c4 (Game 31) is easily parried, while in the main line, 6 ♘f3 ♘c6 7 ♕e4, Black has a very pleasant choice of defences: 7...d6 (Game 33) and 7...f5 (games 33 and 34). Black's extra central pawn even gives him good prospects on a medium-term edge. The old rule of thumb about not developing your queen too early does seem to apply here.

Nevertheless, I recommend a careful study of the lines in this chapter, since these lines are still popular at club level.

Game 31
Handoko – Martin Gonzalez
Lucerne OL 1982

1 e4 c5 2 c3 ♘f6 3 e5 ♘d5 4 d4 cxd4 5 ♕xd4 e6

Almost invariably played, but the alternatives are not completely out of the question:

a) 5...♘b6 6 ♗f4! (to discourage ...d5 for a while; after 6 ♘f3 ♘c6 7 ♕e4 d5 Black won a beautiful game in Sedor-Pelts, USSR 1974: 8 exd6 ♕xd6 9 ♗f4 ♕d5 10 ♘bd2 ♗f5 11 ♕xd5 ♘xd5 12 ♗g3 f6 13 ♗c4 ♘b6 14 ♗b3 e5 15 0-0-0 ♘b4! 16 ♘e1 ♖c8 17 f3 ♘xa2+! 18 ♗xa2 ♖xc3+ 19 bxc3 ♗a3#) 6...♘c6 7 ♕e4 g6 8 a4 a5 9 ♘f3 ♗g7 10 ♗b5 0-0 11 0-0 d5 12 ♕e3 ± Jacobs-Pavlovich, Hollywood 1973.

b) 5...♘c7 6 ♘f3 (or 6 ♗c4!?) 6...♘c6 7 ♕e4 d5!? (7...g6 8 ♗c4 ♗g7 9 0-0 b5 10 ♗b3 ♘a5 11 ♘bd2 ♗b7 12 ♕h4 ♘xb3 13 axb3 ♘e6 14 ♘e4 ± R.Marić-Deže, Yugoslavia 1969) 8 exd6 ♕xd6 9 ♗c4!? (9 ♗f4?! ♕e6 10 ♕xe6 ♘xe6 11 ♗e3 g6 = Vuličević-Waitzkin, ACC International 1993) 9...e5 10 ♗f4 f6 11 ♘a3 ±.

6 ♗c4

For the more usual 6 ♘f3 see Games 32, 33 and 34. White's idea in playing 6 ♗c4 is clear enough – he wants to force the centralised black knight to move, or enter the line 6...♘c6 7 ♕e4 f5?! 8 ♕e2 where his bishop is not hemmed in on f1 (as occurs in some similar variations after 6 ♘f3).

Unfortunately this plan is not effective for two reasons. The first is that the black knight can often decentralise itself rather effectively by ...♘de7 and ...♘g6, putting pressure on the white e-pawn. The second reason is that the bishop move does not threaten much in the line 6...♘c6 7 ♕e4 d6!?. White would simply get the worse endgame by capturing on d5, and his c4-bishop is often harassed by the opposing knights.

6...♘c6

If Black plays 6...d6 White can transpose to normal variations with 7 ♘f3 or 7 exd6, or try 7 ♗xd5 dxe5 8 ♕xe5 ♕xd5 9 ♕xd5 exd5 10 ♗e3 ±, as in Mokry-Skacel, Czechoslovakia 1976.

7 ♕e4 (D)

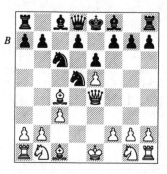

7...d6

7...f5?! is dubious after the continuation 8 ♕e2 ♕h4 9 ♘f3 ♕e4 10 ♗xd5 exd5 11 ♗e3 ♘xe5 12 ♘bd2

♘xf3+ 13 ♘xf3 ± Matulović-Bogdanović, Yugoslav Ch 1958, but Black has several alternatives:

a) 7...♘b6?! (as we shall see, this knight is needed on the kingside) 8 ♗b3 d6 9 exd6 ♗xd6 10 ♘f3 and now:

a1) 10...0-0 11 ♘g5 g6 12 ♕h4 gives White an attack.

a2) With that in mind, in Panchenko-Silseth, Gausdal 1991, Black tried 10...h6!?. After 11 0-0 0-0 12 ♖e1 ♕c7 13 ♘a3 ♗xa3 14 bxa3 ♘a5 White still won on the kingside with the dashing sacrifice 15 ♗xh6!? gxh6? 16 ♕g4+ ♔h8 17 ♕h5! +– attacking both a5 and h6. A relevant question is how much better White is after the improvement 15...♘xb3!? 16 ♗f4 f5! 17 ♕b4! ♘d5 18 ♕xf8+ ♔xf8 19 ♗xc7 ♘xa1 20 ♗d6+ ♔f7 21 ♖c1! intending ♗e5 followed by ♖xa1.

a3) 10...♘d7 11 0-0 (11 ♗c2 ♘f6 12 ♕e2 ♕e7 13 ♘bd2 e5 = Rakay-Peev, Stary Smokovec 1974) 11...♘c5 (11...0-0 12 ♗c2 ♘f6 13 ♕h4 ±) 12 ♕g4! ♘xb3 (12...0-0 13 ♗c2 f5 14 ♕h5 ♕e8 15 ♕xe8 ♖xe8 16 ♖d1 ♗f8 17 b4 ♘d7 18 ♗b3 ± was R.Marić-Huguet, Monte Carlo 1969, but some years later Marić indicated he preferred 13 ♗h6 ♕f6 14 ♗g5 ♕f5 15 ♕xf5 exf5 16 ♖d1 ±) 13 ♕xg7! ♘xa1 14 ♕xh8+ ♔d7 15 ♕xh7 ♕f6 16 ♖d1 ± ♔c7 17 ♘bd2 e5 18 ♘e4 ♕f5 19 ♕xf5 ♗xf5 20 ♘xd6 +– and White was two pawns up in R.Marić-Coulon, Strasbourg 1973.

b) 7...♘de7!? 8 ♘f3 ♘g6 9 ♗b5 (9 0-0 ♕c7 transposes to the next

note) 9...♕c7 10 ♗xc6 ♕xc6 11
♕xc6 bxc6 12 0-0 f6 13 ♖e1 ♗b7 ∓
Semeniuk-Yuferov, USSR 1977.

c) 7...♕c7!? 8 ᘔf3 ᘔde7 9 0-0
(or 9 ♗f4!? ᘔg6 10 ♗g3 b6 11 ᘔbd2
♗b7 12 ♕e2 d6 13 exd6 ♗xd6 14
♗a6 0-0-0 15 ♗xb7+ ♔xb7 16
♗xd6 ♖xd6 17 g3 ♖hd8 18 0-0-0
♖d5 ½-½ Mukhamedzhanov – Sideif-Zade, Naberezhnye Chelny 1993)
9...ᘔg6 10 ♖e1 b6 (though even
10...ᘔcxe5 11 ᘔxe5 ᘔxe5 12 ♕xe5
♕xc4 13 ᘔa3 ♕c6 ∓ did not give
White quite enough for the pawn in
the game Tseitlin-Timoshchenko,
USSR 1977) 11 ♗b3 ♗b7 12 ♕e2
f6! (also 12...d6 as in Röder-Cordes,
Bundesliga 1980/1) 13 exf6 gxf6 14
ᘔa3 ♗xa3 15 bxa3 0-0-0 ∓ Timosh-
chenko-Zaichik, USSR 1977. Transferring the knight to g6 does seem a
promising plan for Black.

8 ᘔf3

Or 8 exd6 ᘔf6 9 ♕e2 ♗xd6 10
♗g5 (10 ᘔf3 h6!? = Marić-Smailbe-
gović, Sarajevo 1958) and here:

a) 10...0-0 11 ᘔd2!? (11 ᘔf3
♗e7 12 0-0 b6 13 ᘔbd2 ♗b7 14
♖ad1 ♕c7 15 ♗xf6?! ♗xf6 16 ᘔe4
♗e7 17 ♗d3 ♕f4 18 ᘔg3 ♖fd8 was
∓ in Angelov-Spassky, USSR 1975)
11...♗e7 12 ᘔgf3 b6 13 0-0-0!?
♕c7 14 ᘔe4 ᘔxe4 15 ♕xe4 ♗b7 16
♗d3 g6 17 ♕h4 with kingside pressure.

b) 10...♕a5 11 ᘔf3 ᘔd4! (tricky!)
12 ᘔxd4 ♕xg5 13 ♗b5+ ♔e7 14 0-0
♕e5 ∓ Stein-L.D.Evans, Gausdal
1978.

c) 10...ᘔe5!? 11 ᘔd2 ᘔxc4 (or
11...♗d7?! 12 ᘔgf3 ♕c7 13 ᘔxe5
♗xe5 14 ᘔf3 ♗f4 15 ♗xf4 ♕xf4 16

ᘔe5 ♕e4 17 0-0-0 ± Marić-Parma,
Bled 1963) 12 ᘔxc4 ♗e7 13 ♖d1
♕c7 14 ᘔe5 0-0 15 ᘔgf3 b6 16 0-0
♗b7 ∓ Alexandrescu-Pavlov, Timisoara 1972.

8...dxe5

If Black is content to just to equalise there are other choices:

a) 8...ᘔb6 9 ♗b3 when Black
has both 9...ᘔd7 10 exd6 ᘔc5 = Ma-
tulović-Larsen, Sarajevo 1960 and
9...d5 10 ♕e2 ♗e7 11 0-0 ♗d7 12
♖e1 0-0 13 ♗f4 ♖c8 14 ᘔbd2 a6 15
♖ad1 ᘔa5 16 ♗c2 ♗b5 = Cirić-
Damjanović, Ljubljana 1960.

b) 8...♗e7 9 0-0 (9 exd6 ♕xd6!
10 0-0 0-0 11 ♗g5 ♗xg5 12 ᘔxg5
ᘔf6 13 ♕e3 ♕e5 14 ♕xe5 ᘔxe5 15
ᘔd2 ♖d8 16 ♖fd1 ♗d7 with an excellent endgame for Black, Matulo-
vić-Geller, Belgrade 1969) 9...dxe5
10 ᘔxe5 ᘔf6 (10...ᘔxe5 11 ♕xe5
0-0 12 ♗xd5 ♗f6 13 ♕e2 exd5 = Koz-
omara-Shamkovich, Sarajevo 1963)
11 ᘔxc6 ᘔxe4 12 ᘔxd8 ♗xd8 13
♗e3 ♗d7 14 ᘔa3 ᘔd6 15 ♗d3 ♗c7
= Kholmov-Andersson, Sochi 1973.

9 ᘔxe5 ♗d6 = (D)

Or:

a) 9...ᘔf6?! 10 ᘔxc6 ᘔxe4 11
ᘔxd8 ♔xd8 12 0-0 ♗d7 13 ♖d1 ♖c8
14 ♗b5 ♗d6 15 ᘔa3 a6 16 ♗xd7
♔xd7 17 ♖d4 f5 18 ᘔc4 with problems for Black in Striković-Vera, El-
goibar 1994.

b) 9...ᘔxe5 10 ♕xe5 ♕d6 with
an equal position in the game Macie-
jewski-Pietrusiak, Polish Ch 1973.

c) 9...♕c7! (similar to the main
game) 10 ᘔxc6 bxc6 11 ᘔd2 ♗d6
12 ᘔf3 0-0 13 0-0 e5! 14 ♖d1 h6 15
♗xd5?! cxd5 16 ♕xd5 ♗b7! 17

♕b5 c4 ∓ Nun-Kuligowski, Warsaw 1978.

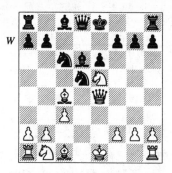

10 ♘xc6 bxc6 11 0-0 0-0 12 ♘d2 e5

Seeking to open the position for the two bishops, even at the cost of a pawn (13 ♗xd5 cxd5 14 ♕xd5 ♗e6 ∞). However both alternatives are maybe preferable: 12...♕c7!? 13 ♘f3 e5 would transpose to the previously mentioned Nun-Kuligowski game, while solid was 12...♗b7 13 ♘f3 h6 14 ♖e1 ♖b8 15 ♗d3 ♘f6 = Barle-Csom, Ljubljana 1973.

13 ♕e2 f5 14 ♘f3 ♕f6?! (14...e4 was still fine for Black, but now Handoko comes up with an inspired exploitation of the pin on the a2-g8 diagonal) **15 ♗g5 ♕g6?! 16 ♘xe5!! ♕xg5 17 ♘xc6 ♗xh2+ 18 ♔xh2 ♕h6+ 19 ♔g1 ♕xc6 20 ♖fd1 ♗e6** (it seems that Black saved himself, but...) **21 ♕xe6+! ♕xe6 22 ♗xd5 ♖fe8 23 c4 a5 24 ♖ac1 ♔f7 25 c5 ♖ad8 26 ♗xe6+ ♔xe6 27 ♖xd8 ♖xd8 28 ♖e1+ ♔f6 29 c6 ♖c8 30 ♖c1 ♔e6 31 ♖c5 a4 32 ♖c4 a3 33 b4 ♔d5 34 ♖c5+ ♔d6 35 ♖c3 ♖xc6 36 ♖xa3 ♖c1+ 37 ♔h2 ♖b1 38 ♖a6+ ♔e5 39 ♖a5+ ♔f4 40 b5 ♖b2 41 a3 g5 42**

♖a4+ ♔e5 43 ♖b4 ♖xb4 44 axb4 f4 45 ♔g1 ♔d6 46 ♔f1 f3 47 gxf3 ♔c7 48 ♔g2 ♔b6 49 ♔g3 ♔xb5 50 ♔g4 ♔xb4 51 ♔xg5 ♔c5 52 f4 ♔d6 53 ♔f6 h5 54 ♔g5 ♔e6 55 f5+ 1-0

Game 32
Rogers – Yudasin
Moscow OL 1994

1 e4 c5 2 c3 ♘f6 3 e5 ♘d5 4 d4 cxd4 5 ♕xd4 e6 6 ♘f3 ♘c6

6...b6 has not done badly in the handful of games it has been seen, but this may be due to the higher-rated players being on the black side:

a) 7 c4 ♘c6 8 ♕d1 ♘de7 9 ♗d3 ♘g6 10 ♗e4 ♗b7 11 ♘c3?! (11 0-0 looks fine; then 11...♕b8 12 ♖e1) 11...♕b8 12 ♕e2 ♘gxe5 13 0-0 ♘xf3+ 14 ♕xf3 ♗d6 ∓ Zurla-Jansa, Cattolica 1993.

b) 7 ♗d3 ♗a6 8 ♗xa6 ♘xa6 9 ♘bd2 ♘c5 10 ♘e4 f5 11 ♘xc5 bxc5 12 ♕d3 ♕c7 13 c4 ♘b4 14 ♕e2 ♗e7 15 0-0 0-0 16 ♗d2 ∞ Ekström-Taimanov, Wroclaw 1979.

c) 7 ♘bd2 ♗b7 8 ♘c4 ♘c6 9 ♕g4 ♕c7 10 ♘d6+ (why so early? 10 ♕g3 and 10 ♗d3 look promising) 10...♗xd6 11 exd6 ♕xd6 12 ♕xg7 0-0-0 ∞ Bajović-V.Nikolić, Yugoslav Cht 1990.

7 ♕e4 *(D)*

7...d6

7...f5 is examined in the following two games.

Instead 7...♘de7 is well met by 8 ♘a3! d5 9 exd6 ♘f5 10 ♗f4 ♗xd6 11 0-0-0 ♗xf4+ 12 ♕xf4 ♕f6 13 ♗b5 0-0 14 ♗xc6 bxc6 15 ♘e5 ± Vasiukov-Gufeld, USSR 1979, so

Black should preface this move with 7...♕c7!? (with the idea of ...♘de7 followed by ...♘g6, attacking the white e-pawn) and now:

a) 8 ♗c4 ♘de7 transposes to lines already examined in Game 31, note to Black's 7th.

b) 8 ♗b5 b6 (also 8...a6) 9 0-0 ♗b7 10 ♖e1 0-0-0 11 c4 ♘de7 12 ♕e2 f6 ∓ Lehmann-Beckemeyer, Bundesliga 1984/5.

c) 8 g3 ♘de7 9 ♘a3 ♘g6 10 ♘b5 ♕b8 11 ♗f4 a6 (11...b6 12 ♗g2 ♗b7 13 0-0 a6 14 ♘d6+ ♗xd6 15 exd6 0-0 16 ♖ad1 ♘ce5 ½-½ was Grzesik-Fleck, Bundesliga 1984/5) 12 ♘bd4 (12 ♘d6+!? ♗xd6 13 exd6 b5 14 ♗g2 ♗b7 15 0-0-0 0-0 16 ♕e2 looks unclear, though White won a complicated game in Rozentalis-Lanc, Trnava 1988) 12...♘xd4 13 ♕xd4 b6 14 ♗g2 ♗c5 15 ♕d2 ♗b7 (15...0-0 16 0-0 ♖a7 17 b4 ♗e7 18 ♗e3 ♗d8 ∞ Vorotnikov-Klaman, USSR 1979) 16 b4 ♗e7 17 0-0 0-0 18 ♖fd1 ♖a7 19 ♕d4 ♗d5 20 ♘d2 ♗xg2 21 ♔xg2 f6 ∓ Grzesik-Wahls, Bundesliga 1986/7.

d) 8 ♗d3!? f5 (8...♘de7 9 0-0 ♘g6 10 ♖e1 b6 11 h4 ♗b7 12 ♕e2 d6 13 exd6 ♗xd6 14 ♗a6! with a

small plus for White, Rogovskoy-Semeniuk, Podolsk 1993) 9 exf6 ♘xf6 10 ♕e2 (10 ♕h4 ♘e5! =) 10...d5 11 0-0 ♗d6 12 h3 (12 ♗g5) 12...0-0 13 ♘d4 ♕f7 14 f4 ♗d7 15 ♗e3 ♘h5! ∓ Marjanović-Barlov, Yugoslavia 1986.

e) 8 ♘bd2!? is a line patronised by Vorotnikov (D):

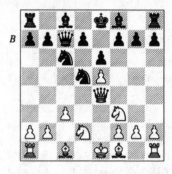

e1) 8...♘de7 9 ♘c4 ♘g6 10 h4!? (10 ♗f4 f6 11 0-0-0 b5! 12 ♘d6+ ♗xd6 13 exd6 ♕a5 ∞ Vasiukov – Sideif-Zade, USSR 1979) 10...f6 11 ♗f4 ♘xf4 12 ♕xf4 ♗e7 13 ♘d6+ ♗xd6 14 exd6 ♕b6 15 ♕d2 ♕c5 16 ♖h3 b6 17 ♖g3 ± Vorotnikov-Labunsky, Vladivostok 1990.

e2) White's position is also better after 8...f5 9 exf6 ♘xf6 10 ♕h4: 10...d5 11 ♗d3 ♘e5 12 ♗b5+ ♔f7 13 ♘xe5+ ♕xe5+ 14 ♗e2 ♕c7 15 g4 with an attack was Vorotnikov-A.Ivanov, USSR 1979, or 10...♗e7 11 ♗d3 ♘e5 12 ♗c2!? b6 13 ♕g3 ♘xf3+ 14 gxf3!? d6 (14...♕xg3 is better) 15 ♕xg7 ♖g8 16 ♕h6 ± Vorotnikov-Mukhutdinov, Moscow 1992.

e3) 8...b6 9 ♗d3 (9 g3 ♗b7 10 ♗g2 ♘de7 11 0-0 ♘g6 12 ♕e2 ♗e7

13 ♖e1 ∞ Vorotnikov-Ivanov, Beltsy 1979) 9...♘de7 10 ♘c4 ♘g6 11 a4 ♗b7 12 ♕e2 ♖c8 13 0-0 ♘a5 14 ♘xa5 ♗xf3 15 gxf3 bxa5 16 f4 ♗e7 ∞ Rogers-Velikov, Khania 1991.

8 ♘bd2

8 ♗b5 ♗d7 9 c4 is an interesting recent try:

a) 9...♘c7 10 exd6 ♗xd6 11 0-0 ♘xb5 (or 11...♕e7 12 ♖d1 0-0 ∞ B.Stein-Kovalev, Gausdal 1990) 12 cxb5 ♘e7 B.Stein-Plachetka, Copenhagen 1990, and now instead of 13 ♕xb7 ∞ as in the game, Plachetka gives 13 ♘c3! ♕c7 14 ♖d1 0-0 15 ♕d3 ♘d5! 16 ♘xd5 exd5 17 ♕xd5 ♗e6 ∞.

b) 9...♘b6 10 exd6 ♗xd6 11 0-0 a6 12 ♖d1 ♕c7 13 ♘c3! (Bernd Stein has reached this excellent position at least three times) 13...♘e5 (13...0-0 14 ♗e3! ♘c8 15 c5 ♗e7 16 ♗f4 ♕a5 17 ♖d7 axb5 18 ♖xb7 ± B.Stein-Bebchuk, Dortmund 1993 or 15...♗xh2+ 16 ♘xh2 axb5 17 ♘xb5 ♕a5 18 a4 ♗e8 19 ♘g4 ± de la Villa-Sion Castro, Zaragoza 1995) 13...♘e5 14 ♘xe5 ♗xe5 15 c5 axb5 (15...♗xb5 16 cxb6 ♗xh2+ 17 ♔h1 ♕e5 18 ♕h4 1-0 B.Stein-Birmingham, Hamburg 1986) 16 cxb6 ♕b8!? 17 ♕b4 (critical, but 17 h3!? or 17 g3!? may be better) 17...♗xh2+ 18 ♔h1 ♕e5 19 ♕h4 b4 20 ♘e4 ♗c6! 21 ♘d6+ ♕xd6 22 ♖xd6 ♗xd6 B.Stein-Skembris, Dortmund 1990, when with rook, bishop, pawn and a solid position Black should be OK.

8...dxe5

8...♗d7!? keeps more tension in the position. One idea is that 9 ♘c4 can be met by 9...♘xc3!? 10 bxc3 d5

11 ♕f4 dxc4 12 ♗xc4 ♗e7 13 0-0 (13 ♗d3 ♕a5 14 ♗d2 g5! 15 ♘xg5 ♘xe5 ∓ Buljovčić-Browne, Novi Sad 1979) 13...0-0. Now 14 ♗d3 ♕a5 15 ♕g3 ♖fd8! ∞ 16 ♘g5 g6 17 ♗f4 ♗e8 18 ♘e4 ♘xe5 19 ♗xe5 ♖xd3! 20 f3 (Black has good compensation for the exchange after 20 ♕xd3 ♕xe5) 20...♕d8 21 ♕f4 f5 ∓ was Sveshnikov-Beliavsky, USSR Ch 1978, but it seems to me that it is worth White questioning this old assessment, as the original *Informator* notes were not done by either of the players. For example 14 ♕g3!? ♔h8 15 ♖d1 ♕c7 16 ♗d3 is clearly superior to the game.

Instead the usual continuation runs 9 exd6 ♗xd6 10 ♘c4 ♗c7 and here:

a) 11 ♘ce5? ♘xc3!! (a fantastic concept) 12 ♕g4 (12 bxc3 ♗xe5 13 ♘xe5 ♕a5 with threats to e5 and c3) 12...♘xe5 13 ♕xg7 ♘xf3+ 14 gxf3 ♖f8 15 ♗h6 ♗d6 ∓ Govedarica-Plachetka, Trnava 1987.

b) 11 ♗d3 ♕e7 12 ♘ce5 0-0-0 13 ♗c2?! (or 13 ♘xc6 ♗xc6 14 ♘d4 ♗d7 15 ♗d2 e5 16 ♘f5 ♕f6 ∓ Plachetka-Tal, Nice OL 1974; perhaps interesting 13 0-0 ♘xe5 14 ♘xe5 ∞ is best, Buljovčić-Sigurjonsson, Novi Sad 1976) 13...♘xe5 14 ♘xe5 ♗e8 15 ♘f3 ♔b8 16 ♗d2 ♕c5 17 a3 e5 18 b4 ♕d6 19 0-0-0 ♕a6 ∓ Klemencić-Plachetka, Maribor 1977.

9 ♘xe5 ♘xe5 10 ♕xe5 ♕c7

10...♕d6 11 ♗b5+ ♗d7 12 ♗xd7+ ♕xd7 reaches the same position.

11 ♗b5+ ♗d7 12 ♗xd7+ ♕xd7 13 0-0 *(D)*

Keeping the options of the white knight open for one more move. White made no progress with 13 ♘f3 ♕c7 (the imaginative 13...0-0-0!? is also playable, as in Böllsteling-P.Fink, Porz 1991/2; with this kind of creativity it is no surprise that Black later became a superlative chef, famous for her Roehampton curries) 14 ♕xc7 ♘xc7 15 c4 ♗c5 16 ♔e2 a5!? 17 ♗f4 ♘a6 18 ♗d2 ♗b4 19 ♗e3 ♗c5 20 ♖hd1 ♗e7 ½-½ Bronstein-Hort, Monte Carlo 1969.

13...♕c7!

13...♘f6 14 ♘f3 ♗d6 15 ♕e2 0-0 16 ♖d1 ♕c7 17 ♗g5 gave White a viable edge in Rogers-Gallagher, Biel 1992, continuing 17...♘d5?! 18 c4 ♘f6 19 g3 ♖ad8 20 a3 ♗e7 21 ♗f4 ♖xd1+ 22 ♖xd1 ♕a5 23 ♖d3 ♖c8 24 ♘e5 ♖d8 25 b4 ♕a4 26 ♖xd8+ ♗xd8 27 ♕f3 ♕a6 28 b5 ♕b6 29 a4 (Gallagher's time-wasting has cost him dear) 29...h6 30 a5 ♕xa5 31 ♕xb7 ♗c7 32 ♔g2 ♕b6 33 ♕c8+ ♔h7 34 ♗e3 ♕d6 35 ♘f3 ♗b6 36 c5 ♕c7 37 ♕xc7 ♗xc7 38 c6 ♗b8 39 ♗xa7 1-0. A salutary lesson on what can happen if the queenside pawn majority is not kept under control.

14 ♕e2

14 ♕xc7 ♘xc7 15 ♘e4 ♗e7 16 ♗e3 ♘d5 17 ♗c5 ♗xc5 18 ♘xc5 b6 19 ♘d3 ♖c8 = Sveshnikov-Panchenko, Sochi 1980.

14...♗d6 15 ♘f3 ♖c8! =

Inhibiting White's hopes of queenside expansion with c4. The black pieces are active, and now easily keep the queenside majority under control.

16 g3 0-0 17 ♘d4 ♕c5 18 ♗e3?! (18 ♖d1 is equal) **18...♘xe3 19 ♕xe3 ♖fd8 20 ♖fd1 ♗e7 21 ♘b3?!** (21 ♕e2) **21...♕xe3 22 fxe3 h5** (better is 22...♔f8 ∓; now White gets some counterplay) **23 ♘a5! ♗g5 24 ♔f2 b6 25 ♘b3 ♔f8 26 ♘d4 ♗e7 27 ♔e2 ♗d6 28 ♘b5 ♗b8 29 ♖xd8+ ♖xd8 30 ♘d4 ♖c8 31 ♖d1 ♔e7 32 ♘f3 f6 33 ♖d4 g5** (34...e5!? ∓) **34 g4 f5 35 h3 ♔f6 36 ♔f2 ♖h8 37 ♔g1 ♖h7? 38 gxf5 exf5 39 ♖d8 ♗g3 40 ♖f8+ ♔g6 41 ♖g8+ ♔f6 42 ♖f8+** (on 42 ♘xg5 ♖e7 Black should hold the draw) **42...♔g6 43 ♖g8+ ♔f6 ½-½**

Game 33
Novopashin – Sveshnikov
USSR 1981

1 e4 c5 2 c3 ♘f6 3 e5 ♘d5 4 d4 cxd4 5 ♕xd4 e6 6 ♘f3 ♘c6 7 ♕e4 f5 8 exf6

The retreat 8 ♕e2 is examined next game.

9...♘xf6 9 ♕h4

After this White has a clear plan: ♗d3 will threaten ♗g6+. If Black castles early to avoid this, White can nevertheless often seize the initiative with ♗g5, threatening to remove the defender of the h7-square. Instead Black takes control of the centre after 9 ♕c2 d5 (also quite playable is 9...♕c7, e.g. 10 ♗g5 ♘e5!? 11 ♘bd2 b6 12 ♗e2 ♗b7 13 ♗h4 ♘g6 14 ♗g3 ♘f4 ∓ Hort-Hartston, Hastings 1975) 10 ♗g5 e5 11 ♗b5 ♗d6 ∓ Lechtynsky-Ungureanu, Moscow 1977 and Lendwai-Stanec, Gamlitz 1993.

9...d5!?

As we will see, Black can allow White his ♗d3 idea. Of the alternatives, 'c' and 'd' are very sound:

a) 9...♕a5 10 ♗g5 ♗e7 11 ♘bd2 ♘e5 12 ♕d4 ♘c6 13 ♕h4 ♘e5 14 0-0-0! ♘f7 (14...♘xf3 15 ♘xf3 ♕xa2 16 ♗d3 ± Becerra Rivero) 15 ♘b3! ♕c7 (15...♕xa2? 16 ♗c2 +−) 16 ♗d3 ± Becerra Rivero-Livshits, Moscow OL 1994.

b) 9...♗e7 (long thought inferior, but perhaps playable) 10 ♗d3 0-0 11 ♗g5 ♖f7!? 12 ♘bd2 d5 13 ♘d4 h6 14 ♘xc6 bxc6 15 ♗e3 ½-½ Mik.Horvath-Torok, Hungary 1994.

c) 9...♕c7 is solid:

c1) The point is 10 ♗d3? ♘b4! 11 ♗g6+ hxg6 12 ♕xh8 ♘c2+.

c2) 10 ♗e2 ♗e7 11 0-0 and now 11...0-0 is equal, but not 11...b6 12 ♗d3 ♗b7 13 ♗g6+ ♔f8 14 ♗f4 ± Peresypkin-Suetin, USSR 1976.

c3) 10 ♗g5 ♗e7 11 ♘bd2 is possible: 11...♘e5 12 ♘xe5 ♕xe5+ 13 ♗e2 0-0 14 ♕g3!? ♕xg3 15 hxg3 ♗c5 16 f3 d5 17 0-0-0 ± Kurajica-Popović, Vrbas 1980; Kurajica suggests 11...d5.

c4) 10 ♘bd2 ♘e5 (also 10...b6!? 11 ♘e4 ♘xe4 12 ♕xe4 ♗b7 13 ♗f4 ♗d6 14 ♗xd6 ♕xd6 with equality,

Padevsky-Sax, Vrnjačka Banja 1974 or 10...♗e7 11 ♗d3 ♘e5 12 ♘xe5 ♕xe5+ 13 ♘e4 ♕d5 14 ♘xf6+ ♗xf6 15 ♕h3 b6 16 0-0 ♗b7 ½-½ Padevsky-Taimanov, Vrnjačka Banja 1974) 11 ♘xe5 ♕xe5+ 12 ♗e2 b6 13 ♘f3 ♕e4 14 ♕xe4 ♘xe4 = Przewoznik-Vogt, Polanica Zdroj 1980.

d) 9...e5!? (to prevent White's ♗d3/♗g6+ plan, e.g. 10 ♗d3?! e4 11 ♗xe4 ♕e7 12 0-0 ♘xe4 13 ♖e1 ♕xh4 14 ♘xh4 d5 15 f3 ♗c5+ 16 ♗e3 ♗e7 ∓ Sauvetre-Yacob, Paris 1996) 10 ♗g5 (10 ♗b5!? e4!? 11 ♘g5 ♗c5 12 ♘d2 d5 13 c4 ♘g4 14 0-0 e3 15 cxd5 ♕xd5 16 ♗c4 ∞ C.Baker-Cafferty, England 1979) 10...d5 11 ♗b5 ♗d6 12 0-0 0-0! 13 c4 e4 14 cxd5 exf3 15 dxc6 fxg2 16 ♖e1 (16 ♔xg2 was the original game, Hort-Miles, BBC Mastergame 1979; after 16...bxc6 17 ♗c4+ ♔h8 18 ♘c3 ♕c7 ∓ White's king was the more exposed, though Black blundered with 19 ♖ad1 ♗b7?! 20 ♗d3! ♖ad8 21 ♗f5 ♗e5? allowing the killer 22 ♗xh7! ±) 16...♕c7 17 ♗xf6 gxf6 18 ♘c3 bxc6 19 ♗c4+ ♔h8 20 ♖e3 ♗e5 ∓ Wockenfuss-Hartston, EEC OL, Berlin 1980.

10 ♗d3 ♗d6 *(D)*

11 ♗g6+

So White achieves his objective of making Black's king move, but in fact he may already be worse. The bishop manoeuvre costs several tempi, and Black's control of the centre means his king is not that likely to run into trouble before later 'castling by hand' is achieved. Similar positions arise 11 ♗g5 ♔f7! (∓ Sveshnikov; instead after 11...e5 12 ♗g6+

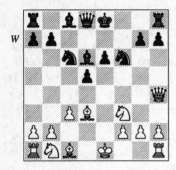

♔e7, 13 ♗h5 ♕b6 14 ♗xf6+ gxf6 15 ♕g3 ♔f8 16 ♘bd2 ♖g8 17 ♕h4 ♗e7 18 0-0-0 ♕a6 19 a3 f5 20 ♕h3 f4 21 g4 fxg3 22 ♕g2 ♗f5 23 ♘e1 ♘b4! 0-1 was a pretty finish in Mufić-Kožul, Pula 1994, but 13 ♗c2 is unclear) 12 ♘d4 h6 13 ♗e3 ♘e5 14 ♗c2 g5 15 ♕h3 ♘g6 ∓ Vorotnikov-Sveshnikov, Lvov 1983.

11...♔e7!?

After 11...♔d7 12 ♗c2, 12...♔c7 13 ♘d4 ± was Alburt-Smit, USSR 1970, but 12...h6 is not so clear; certainly 13 ♕a4 ♕a5 14 ♕xa5 ♘xa5 = Trabert-Rashkovsky, Kuopio 1992 was not the refutation.

12 ♗c2 h6 13 ♗g6 ♗d7

Riskier is 13...e5?! 14 0-0 e4 15 ♘d4 ♘e5 16 ♗f5 g5 17 ♕h3 ♗c5 18 ♗e3 and Black's king looks shaky, Barlov-Kožul, Yugoslav Ch 1989.

14 ♗f4 e5 15 ♗g3 ♗e8 16 ♗xe8 ♖xe8 17 ♕a4

The simple 17 0-0 is possible, but after 17...♔f8 Black has an excellent position: plenty of space in the centre and his king is nearly in safety.

17...♔f7 ∓ 18 0-0 e4 19 ♘d4 ♗xg3 20 hxg3 ♕b6 21 ♘a3 ♘xd4 22 cxd4 ♖ac8 23 ♖ae1 ♖e7 (now 24...♕xb2 is a threat) **24 ♖e2 ♖ec7**

25 ♖d2 ♔g8 26 ♕d1 e3! 27 fxe3 ♘e4 28 ♖c2 ♖xc2 29 ♘xc2 ♕xb2 ∓ 30 ♘e1 ♕c1 31 ♕xc1 ♖xc1 32 ♘d3 ♖xf1+ 33 ♔xf1 ♘xg3+ 34 ♔e1 ♘e4 35 ♘f4 ♘f6 36 ♘e6 b6 37 ♘c7 ♔f7 38 ♘b5 a6 39 ♘c7 a5 40 ♔e2 ♔e7 41 ♘b5 0-1

Game 34
Vorotnikov – Zilbershtein
USSR 1978

1 e4 c5 2 c3 ♘f6 3 e5 ♘d5 4 d4 cxd4 5 ♕xd4 e6 6 ♘f3 ♘c6 7 ♕e4 f5 8 ♕e2 ♕c7

a) 8...d6 9 g3 ♕c7 transposes to the game.

b) 8...♘de7 and now White should probably continue 9 h4!? ±, in view of 9 g3?! ♘g6 10 ♘bd2 (Black's move-order has cancelled out 10 ♘a3 due to 10...♗xa3; compare with the 9...♘de7 lines in the note to Black's 9th move) 10...♕c7 11 ♘c4 b5 12 ♘d6+ ♗xd6 13 exd6 ♕xd6 14 ♕xb5 0-0 ∓ Alexopoulos-Kelleher, New York 1993.

c) 8...♗e7 9 g3 ♕c7 (9...♖b8 10 c4 ♘c7 11 ♘c3 a6 12 a4 0-0 13 ♗g2 b6 14 h4 with a useful space advantage for White, Tan-Panno, Manila IZ 1976) and now best is 10 c4 ±, as 10 ♗g2 b5! 11 0-0 (11 ♕xb5? ♘cb4! threatening ...♗a6/...♘c2) 11...a5 12 ♘bd2 ♗a6 and Black stands well, Jamieson-Woodhams, Australian Ch 1976.

d) 8...b6 9 g3 (9 c4 ♗a6 10 b3 ♗b4+ 11 ♗d2 ♘f4 12 ♕e3 ♘g6 13 ♗xb4 ♘xb4 14 ♘d4 ♕h4! 15 ♔d2? f4 16 ♕e4 ♕xf2+ ± was a disastrous opening experiment for White in the game Vorotnikov-Semeniuk, Podolsk 1993) 9...a5!? (9...♕c7 transposes to the 9...b6 note in the main game) 10 ♗g2 ♗a6 11 c4 ♗b4+ (11...♗c5 12 0-0 0-0 13 b3 f4 14 ♗b2 a4 15 ♕d1 ♘de7 16 ♘c3 fxg3 17 hxg3 a3 18 ♗c1 ♕c7 19 ♘e4! ♗b7 20 ♘xc5 bxc5 21 ♕d6 ± Rogers-Shirov, Brno 1991) 12 ♗d2 0-0 13 0-0 ♕c7 14 b3 (±Lalić) 14...♗xd2 15 ♕xd2 ♘xe5!? 16 cxd5 ♗xf1 17 ♔xf1 f4! with complications, Magem-B.Lalić, Manresa 1995.

9 g3 *(D)*

9...d6

Although this leaves e6 temporarily weak, Black will later advance in the centre with ...e5 and ...e4.

a) 9...b6 and here:

a1) 10 ♘bd2 g5!? 11 ♘xg5 ♕xe5 was a novel idea for Black in Rogers – Har-Zvi, Biel 1992.

a2) The routine 10 ♗g2?! meets a dangerous reply: 10...♘cb4! and now 11 ♕d2? ♗a6 12 cxb4 ♗xb4 13 ♘c3 ♘xc3 14 a3 ♘b1! −+ Baker-Basman, London 1978, or 11 c4 b5 12 a3 ♘a6 13 ♘d4 ♕xc4 14 ♕xc4 bxc4 ∞ Kozhevin-Mololkin, Russia 1994.

a3) 10 c4 ♗a6 11 b3 ♗b4+ 12 ♗d2 ♗xd2+ 13 ♘bxd2 ♘db4 14 ♘b1 ♘xe5 (14...g5! Gallagher) and now instead of the tactical complications of 15 ♘xe5 ♘c2+ in Vorotnikov-Georgadze, USSR 1979, the line 15 ♕xe5 ♕xe5 16 ♘xe5 ♗b7 17 ♖g1 ♘c2+ 18 ♔d2 ♘xa1 19 ♘c3 (with ♗d3 to follow) was assessed ± by Vorotnikov.

b) 9...♘de7!? 10 ♘a3 (or 10 ♗f4 ♘g6 11 ♘bd2 ∞, e.g. 11...a6 12 ♗g2 ♗e7 13 0-0 0-0 14 ♖fd1 b5 B.Kristjansson-Cherniaev, Gausdal 1993 or 11...♘xf4 12 gxf4 ♘e7 13 0-0-0 ♘d5 14 ♘c4 b5 15 ♘d6+ ♗xd6 16 exd6 ♕xd6 17 ♘e5 0-0 Mellado-Tukmakov, Barcelona 1993) 10...♘g6 11 ♘b5 ♕b8 12 ♗f4 a6 13 ♘bd4 ♘xd4 14 ♘xd4 b5 15 ♗g2 ♗b7 16 0-0 (White's king is safest after short castling, but possible is 16 ♗xb7 ♕xb7 17 0-0-0 ♖c8 18 ♔b1 ♗c5 19 ♘b3 ♗e7 20 f3 0-0 21 ♖d3 ♖c7 22 ♖hd1 b4 23 ♗d2 with typical pressure against the d7-pawn, Rozentalis-Sturua, Vilnius 1984) 16...♗xg2 (16...♗e7 17 ♖fd1 0-0 18 ♖d3 again gives pressure against d7, Rozentalis-Yarkovich, USSR 1986) 17 ♔xg2 ♕b7+ 18 ♕f3 ♖b8 19 ♕xb7 ♖xb7 20 b4 ♗e7 21 a4 ♔f7 22 axb5 axb5 23 ♖a5 ♖hb8 24 ♖fa1 ♗d8 25 ♖a7 ♖xa7 26 ♖xa7 ♔e8 (threatening ...♗b6) 27 ♖a6 ♗c7 with an equal position, Rozentalis-Dvoirys, Kharkov 1985.

10 exd6 ♗xd6 11 ♗g2 0-0 12 0-0 ♘f6

12...♕f7 looks less natural, Sveshnikov-Ungureanu, Dubna 1979.

13 ♘bd2 *(D)*

Unclear is the line 13 c4!? e5 14 c5 ♗e7 15 ♘c3 a6 16 ♕c4+ ♔h8 17 b4 h6 18 ♘a4 ♗d7 19 ♘b6 ♖ad8 20 ♘xd7 ♕xd7 21 ♗b2 e4 22 ♘h4 ♔h7 23 f3, Vorotnikov-Gorbatov, Moscow 1992. The game concluded wildly: 23...♘d5 24 ♖ad1 ♗xh4 25 gxh4 e3 26 f4 e2 27 ♕xe2 ♘xf4 28 ♕f3 ♘d3 29 ♗h3 ♘e7 30 ♕g3 g5 31 hxg5 ♖g8 32 ♗f6 ♖g6 33 ♗xe7 ♕xe7 34 ♗xf5 ♘xb4 35 ♖xd8 1-0, but alternatives like 23...♕d2!? or 23...g5!? are critical.

13...e5 14 ♘c4 e4 15 ♘fd2

15 ♘g5 h6 16 ♘xd6 ♕xd6 17 ♘h3 g5 ∞ Vorotnikov-Tseitlin, Leningrad 1978.

15...♗e6

15...♗e7 16 ♘b3 ♗e6 17 ♗f4 ♕d7 18 ♖ad1 ♘d5 ∞ 19 ♗c1 ♕e8 20 ♘d4?! ♘xd4 21 cxd4 ♕b5! 22 ♖fe1 ♘f4! 23 ♗xf4 ♗xc4 24 ♕e3 ♗b4 and Black had won an exchange in B.Kristjansson-Kotronias, Gausdal 1994.

16 ♘xd6 ♕xd6 17 ♘b3

17 f3 ♗d5 18 fxe4 fxe4 19 ♘b3 ♘e5 20 ♗f4 ♕b6+ 21 ♗e3 ♘f3+! 22 ♔h1 ♕c6 23 ♘d2 ♖ae8 ∓ Novopashin-Rashkovsky, Volgodonsk 1981.

17...♗e7 18 ♗e3 ♕f7 19 ♘d2 ♘g4 20 f3 exf3 21 ♗xf3 ♘xe3 22 ♕xe3 ♖ad8 23 ♘b3 ♖fe8 24 ♕f4 ♗c4 25 ♖fe1 ♗xb3 26 axb3 ♕xb3 27 ♖xe8+ ♖xe8 28 ♕xf5 ♘e5 29 ♖f1 ♘xf3+ 30 ♕xf3 h6 31 ♖f2 ½-½

13 5 cxd4 e6 6 ♘f3 d6 including 7 a3

1	e4	c5
2	c3	♘f6
3	e5	♘d5
4	d4	cxd4
5	cxd4	e6
6	♘f3	d6 (D)

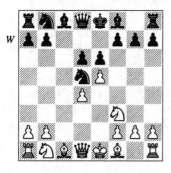

For some reason this line is not very fashionable for Black, even though he can also reach it via White's modern move-order (5 ♘f3 e6!? 6 cxd4 d6). Much of the time, when Black does utilise this defensive system, it is because he has been tricked into it – for example, 1 e4 c5 2 ♘f3 e6 3 c3 ♘f6 4 e5, and, as ...e6 has already been played, the main lines of later chapters are not an option any more. Speaking of tricky transpositions, here is one you probably haven't seen before: 1 e4 ♘f6 2 e5 ♘d5 3 c4 ♘b6 4 c5 ♘d5 5 ♗c4 e6 6 d4 d6 7 cxd6 cxd6 8 ♘f3. The

Chase variation of the Alekhine has metamorphosed into a c3 Sicilian! This position is covered in the ♗c4 note to White's seventh move in Chandler-Kasparov below. *[Editor's note: There are quite a lot of transpositions between the Alekhine and c3 Sicilian, e.g. 1 e4 ♘f6 2 e5 ♘d5 3 ♗c4 ♘b6 4 ♗b3 c5 5 c3 c4 6 ♗c2 ♘c6 7 ♘f3 (= 1 e4 c5 2 c3 ♘f6 3 e5 ♘d5 4 ♘f3 ♘c6 5 ♗c4 ♘b6 6 ♗b3 c4 7 ♗c2) and 1 e4 ♘f6 2 e5 ♘d5 3 c4 ♘b6 4 c5 ♘d5 5 ♘c3 c6 6 ♘xd5 cxd5 7 d4 d6 8 cxd6 exd6 9 ♘f3 ♘c6 (= 1 e4 c5 2 c3 ♘f6 3 e5 ♘d5 4 d4 cxd4 5 ♘f3 e6 6 cxd4 ♘c6 7 ♘c3 d6 8 ♘xd5 exd5) being two of the more obscure.]*

The most critical test of these ...e6/...d6 variations is White's little preparatory move 7 a3, preparing ♗d3, when White is all geared up for kingside pressure should Black castle short. After the routine 7...♘c6 (Game 35) it can indeed be difficult for Black to generate counterplay, and this may account for the general lack of popularity of this whole variation. However, Black should look again at the old system with 7...♗d7!? (Game 36), followed by easy development with ...♗c6, ...♘d7 and ...♗e7. True, the white bishop on d3 does remain visually impressive on the b1-h7 diagonal, but by postponing castling in favour of developing the queenside minor pieces, Black can take much of the venom out of White's potential kingside threats.

Game 35
Chandler – Kasparov
Wattignies 1976

1 e4 c5 2 c3 ᐁf6 3 e5 ᐁd5 4 d4 cxd4

The actual game had the more unusual move-order 4...ᐁc6 5 ᐁf3 cxd4 6 cxd4 e6 7 a3 d6. I have transposed it in order to present the alternatives more logically.

5 cxd4 e6 6 ᐁf3 d6 7 a3!?

This quiet but excellent pawn move simply prepares White to develop his bishop on d3, without fear of molestation from ...ᐁb4. Combined with the white pawn wedge on e5, and the general lack of black pieces on the kingside, the bishop will exert unpleasant pressure on the b1-h7 diagonal should Black castle short.

Instead 7 ᐁc3 will lead into a position examined in a later chapter (which one depends on how the game continues), while 7 exd6 ♗xd6 8 ᐁc3 followed by ♗d3 is quite a solid option for White if he wants. Against 7 ♗d3 ᐁb4 8 ♗e2 dxe5 9 a3 the *zwischenzug* 9...e4! was played with success for Black in Rauze-Lerner, Nîmes 1991 and de Haro-Toth, Mar del Plata 1996.

However 7 ♗c4 is a common continuation, when if Black continues with ...ᐁc6 either now or shortly, we transpose into lines examined in

Chapter 15. It is not apparent that Black can benefit especially from avoiding this transposition:

a) 7...ᐁb6 when 8 ♗d3 and 8 ♗b3 are examined in the course of Chapter 17, in the notes of games 48 and 49 respectively.

b) 7...dxe5 8 dxe5 ♗b4+ 9 ♗d2 (9 ᐁbd2 ᐁb6 10 0-0 ᐁxc4 11 ♕a4+ ᐁc6 12 ᐁxc4 ♕d3 13 ᐁd6+ ♗xd6 14 ♖d1 ♕a6 15 ♕xa6 bxa6 16 exd6 e5 17 ♗e3 ♗d7 18 ᐁd2 ± was Svidler-Taimanov, St Petersburg Ch 1995) 9...ᐁc6 (9...♗e7 10 0-0 ᐁc6 11 ♕e2 ♕b6 12 ᐁc3 ᐁxc3 13 bxc3 ♗d7 14 ♗d3 ♖d8 15 ♖ab1 ♕c7 16 ♖fe1 0-0 17 ᐁg5 g6 18 ᐁxh7! was a winning sacrifice for White in Yanovsky-Krasenkov, Voskresensk 1992) 10 0-0 ♗e7 11 ♕e2 0-0 12 ᐁc3 ᐁxc3 13 ♗xc3 b6 14 ᐁd2 ♗b7 15 ᐁe4 ᐁd4 16 ♕g4 h5 17 ♕xh5 ♗xe4 18 ♖ad1 ♗c5 19 b4 ♗g6 20 ♕g4 ♗f5 21 ♕f4 ♕c7 22 bxc5 bxc5 23 ♗xd4 cxd4 24 ♖xd4 ± Wolff-Rotshtein, Wijk aan Zee 1993.

c) 7...♗e7 8 0-0 0-0 9 ♕e2 (9 ᐁc3 ᐁxc3 10 bxc3 ᐁc6 11 ♗d3 dxe5 12 dxe5 ♕a5 13 ♕c2 g6 14 ♖e1 ♖d8 15 ♖b1 ♖b8 16 ♗f4 ♗d7 17 ᐁd2 ♗e8 18 ᐁc4 ∞ Sveshnikov-Saltaev, Vladivostok 1994) 9...♗d7 10 ᐁc3! ᐁxc3 11 bxc3 ♗c6 12 ♗f4!? (12 exd6 ♗xd6 13 ᐁe5 ± Sveshnikov-Vera, Sochi 1985) 12...♕c7 13 exd6 ♗xd6 14 ♗xd6 ♕xd6 15 ᐁe5 ᐁd7 16 f4! ± Sveshnikov-Goriachkin, Böblingen 1991.

7...ᐁc6

For other Black seventh moves, including 7...♗d7, see the following game.

8 ♗d3 *(D)*

8...♕a5+?!

This dubious check is an attempt to disrupt White's development which rebounds.

a) 8...♕b6? 9 0-0 ♗d7 10 ♗c2 ♖c8 11 b3 dxe5 12 dxe5 ♗c5 13 ♘bd2 ♕c7 14 ♗b2 ♘ce7 15 ♘e4 0-0 16 ♖c1 ♘e3 17 ♕d3! +− Balshan-Kirov, Amsterdam 1978.

b) 8...♗d7 9 0-0 ♕c7 10 ♖e1 g6 11 exd6 ♕xd6 12 ♘c3 ♗g7 13 ♘xd5 ♕xd5 14 ♗e4 ♕c4 15 d5 ± Okhotnik-Duponchel, Le Touquet 1992.

c) 8...g6!? 9 0-0 ♗g7 10 ♖e1 (10 ♕e2 0-0 can become sharp, for example 11 b4 ♕b6 12 ♕e4 f5 13 exf6 ♘xf6 14 ♕h4 ♘d5 15 ♗e3 ♖xf3 16 gxf3 ♗xd4 ∞ Rabiega-Kraut, Bundesliga 1991 and 11 h4?! ♕b6 12 ♕e4 f5! 13 exf6 ♘xf6 14 ♕f4 ♘d5 15 ♕xd6 ♖xf3 16 gxf3 ♕xd4 ∓ Lane-Kraut, Zug 1989. White must evidently watch out for ...f5 in this variation) 10...0-0 11 b4. This position has been reached several times, in all cases with an inconclusive outcome:

c1) 11...f6 12 exd6 ♕xd6 13 ♘bd2 b6 14 ♘c4 ♕d7 15 h4 ♗b7 16 h5 g5

17 ♕c2 h6 18 b5 ♘ce7 Finkel-Milov, Israeli Ch 1992.

c2) 11...b6 12 ♗b2 ♗b7 13 ♗f1 dxe5 14 dxe5 ♘f4 15 ♕b3 ∞ Godena-Kaenel, Switzerland 1991 or 11...dxe5 12 dxe5 ♕c7 Tringov-Filipowicz, and now 13 ♕e2!? intending ♕e4.

c3) 11...a6 12 ♗b2 ♘ce7 13 ♗f1 b6 14 ♘bd2 ♗b7 15 ♘e4 dxe5 16 dxe5 ♘f5 17 ♕b3 A.Cohen-Milov, Isle of Man 1994.

How you feel about these kinds of positions (for either side) is partly a matter of taste; I prefer White.

d) 8...♗e7 is rather passive. 9 0-0 and now:

d1) 9...♗d7 10 ♖e1 dxe5 11 dxe5 ♖c8 12 ♗e4 0-0 13 ♕d3 h6 14 ♗d2 ♕b6 15 ♗xd5 exd5 16 ♘c3 ♗e6 17 ♘xd5 ± Bronstein-Hartston, Hastings 1975.

d2) 9...b6 was met by 10 ♕c2 ♗b7 11 ♘c3 ♘xc3 12 bxc3 dxe5 13 dxe5 ♕c7 14 ♗e4 0-0-0 ∞ in the game Fatalibekova-Gaprindashvili, USSR 1979, but an improvement was 10 ♘bd2!? dxe5?! 11 ♘xe5 ♘xe5 12 dxe5 ♗b7 13 ♕a4+ ♔f8 14 ♗e4 ± S.Arkell-Lanc, Cappelle la Grande 1991.

d3) 9...0-0 and now:

d31) 10 ♘c3 immediately is possible, e.g. 10...♘xc3 11 bxc3 dxe5 12 dxe5 ♕c7 13 ♖e1 ♖d8 14 ♕c2 g6 15 h4 ± S.Arkell-Sigurpalsson, Reykjavik 1990.

d32) 10 ♖e1 scored a thematic white win in the game Okhotnik-Mukhin, USSR 1976 after the continuation 10...dxe5 11 dxe5 ♗d7 12 ♕c2 h6 13 ♕e2 ♖c8 14 ♗d2 ♘a5 15

♗xh6 gxh6 16 ♕e4 f5 17 exf6 ♖xf6 18 ♕h7+ ♔f8 19 ♕h8+ ♔f7 20 ♘e5#!

d33) 10 ♕e2!? ♗d7 11 ♘c3 ♘xc3 12 bxc3 dxe5 13 dxe5 ♕c7 14 ♖e1 ♖fd8 15 ♗f4 ♗e8 16 h4 ± Shirazi-Sherzer, New York 1987.

e) 8...dxe5 9 dxe5 ♗e7 (the e-pawn snatch 9...♕c7 10 0-0 ♘xe5 11 ♘xe5 ♕xe5 has been played a number of times, but Black is in great danger for example 12 ♗b5+ ♗d7 13 ♗xd7+ ♔xd7 14 ♖e1 ♕d6 15 ♕f3 ♗e7 16 ♘c3 ♘xc3 17 bxc3 ♕c6 18 ♕xf7 ♖ae8 19 ♗e3 ♖hf8 20 ♕xg7 ♖g8 21 ♕d4+ ♔c8 22 g3 ± 1-0 Vogt-Reich, Bundesliga 1994) 10 0-0 g5!? (a drastic bid for counterplay; 10...♕c7 11 ♖e1 ♗d7 12 ♘bd2 h6 13 b4 0-0 14 ♗b2 ♖fd8 15 ♖c1 a6 16 ♗b1 ♘f4 17 ♕c2 ♘g6 18 h4 ♖ac8 19 ♕e4 gave White the initiative in Vasiukov-Diaz, Cienfuegos 1975) and now:

e1) 11 ♕a4!? h5 12 ♖d1 ♗d7 13 ♕e4 ♕c7 14 ♗xg5 ♗xg5 15 ♘xg5 ♕xe5 16 ♕xe5 ♘xe5 17 ♗e4 ♘f6 18 ♘c3 ♘xe4 19 ♘cxe4 ♗c6 Kristensen-H.Olafsson, Groningen 1975/76, and instead of 20 ♘d6+ ♗e7 21 f4 ♖hg8! ∓ White could try 20 f4!? ±.

e2) 11 ♕e2 g4 12 ♘e1 ♕c7 13 ♗h6 ♗d7 14 ♘d2 ♕xe5 15 ♕xg4 ♕f6 16 ♗g7 ♖g8 17 ♗xf6 ♖xg4 18 h3 ♖a4 19 ♗xe7 ♔xe7 ∞ Lane-Dvoirys, Cappelle la Grande 1996.

e3) 11 ♖e1! g4 12 ♘fd2 ♘f4 13 ♗f1 h5 14 b4 ± was Golod-Kuzmin, Iraklion 1995.

9 ♗d2 ♕b6 10 ♘c3! ± ♘xc3

The pawn snatch 11...♘xd4 12 ♘xd5 ♘xf3+ 13 ♕xf3 exd5 has

never been tried, but Black is lagging dangerously in development.

11 ♗xc3

11 bxc3 dxe5 12 dxe5 g6 13 0-0 ♗g7 14 ♕e2 ♕c7 15 ♗f4 b6 16 h4 ♗b7 17 h5 0-0 18 ♖fe1 ♖ad8 is less clear, although White later won in the game Acs-Volzhin, Budapest 1995.

11...dxe5 12 dxe5 ♗e7

In Velimirović-Sax, Amsterdam 1976, Black tried keeping the e7-square free to re-deploy his knight, but his lack of development told after 12...♗d7 13 0-0 h6 14 ♕e2 ♘e7 15 ♗d4 ♕d8 16 b4 ♘d5 17 ♗e4 ♗a4 18 ♖fc1 ♗e7 19 ♗c5 ♗xc5 20 ♖xc5 b6 21 ♗xd5 bxc5 22 ♗xa8 ♕xa8 23 ♕c4 ♕d5 24 ♖c1 ♕xc4 25 ♖xc4 ± and White won a pawn.

13 0-0 ♗d7 14 ♘d2!? (14 ♕e2 is natural, to answer 14...0-0 with 15 ♕e4, but probably Kasparov has resigned himself to castling queenside anyhow) **14...♕c7 15 ♕g4 0-0-0 16 ♖fc1 ♔b8 17 ♕c4** (indirectly protecting the e-pawn; if 17 b4? then 17...♘xe5) **17...♖c8 18 b4 f6 19 ♘f3 ♕b6 20 ♕e4 f5 21 ♕e1 a6 22 ♖ab1 g5 23 ♘d2 ♘d4?** (the start of an unsound sacrificial attempt to gain counterplay; 23...♖hd8) **24 ♕e3 ♖xc3 25 ♖xc3 f4 26 ♕e1 g4 27 ♘e4 ♗c6 28 ♘c5 ♔a7 29 a4 ♗f3 30 a5 ♕d8 31 ♗c4 ♗xc5 32 bxc5 ♕h4 33 gxf3! gxf3** (33...♘xf3+ 34 ♖xf3 +−) **34 ♔h1 ♖g8 35 ♕e4 ♖g7 36 ♕xd4 ♕g5** *(D)*

37 c6+ ♔b8 38 c7+ ♖xc7 39 ♖g1 ♕h5 40 ♖g8+ ♖c8 41 ♕d6+ ♔a7 (having reached the time-control, Kasparov notices he is a rook and a

w

bishop down, and facing mate in four) **1-0**

Game 36
Ree – Langeweg
Amsterdam 1976

1 e4 c5 2 ♘f3 e6 3 c3 ♘f6 4 e5 ♘d5 5 d4 cxd4 6 cxd4 d6 7 a3 ♗d7!?

This straightforward and quite promising plan was originally patronised by the East German GM Malich. Black's bishop will take up an active post on c6, after which the queen's knight will come naturally to d7. Black is happy to develop his queenside minor pieces in advance of moving his bishop on f8, perhaps to avoid provoking White into a quick exd6. Others:

a) 7...♗e7 8 ♗d3 0-0 (8...♗d7 is a common move-order to transpose back to the main game) 9 0-0 ♘d7 10 ♖e1 dxe5 11 dxe5 ♘c5 12 ♗c2 a5 13 ♕d4 ♗d7 14 ♘bd2 ♗c6 15 ♕g4 ♖c8 16 ♘e4 ± Tringov-Taimanov, Vrnjačka Banja 1977.

b) 7...♘d7!? 8 ♗d3 dxe5 9 dxe5 (9 ♘xe5?! ♕a5+! 10 ♗d2 ♕b6 ∓ attacking d4 and b2, Votava-Rotshtein, Warsaw 1989) 9...♗e7 10 0-0 0-0 11

♕c2 g6 12 ♗h6 ♖e8 13 ♘c3 ♘xc3 14 ♕xc3 ♘b6 15 ♖ad1 ♘d5 16 ♕c4 ♗d7 17 ♕g4 ± Vatter-Vogt, Baden-Baden 1993.

8 ♗d3

8 ♘bd2 dxe5 9 ♘xe5 ♗e7 10 ♗c4 ♗c6 11 ♘df3 0-0 12 0-0 ♘f6 13 ♘xc6 ♘xc6 14 ♗e3 ♕d6 15 ♕e2 ♘d5 = was Vasiukov-Polugaevsky, Palma de Mallorca 1989.

8...♗c6 9 0-0 ♘d7 *(D)*

If 9...♗e7, 10 ♖e1 will probably transpose back to the game, although Hartston's idea of 10 b4!? has the merit of making ...♘d7 impossible (because of b5). Instead 10 ♘c3!? ♘d7 (10...♘xc3 11 bxc3 ♘d7 12 exd6! ♗xd6 13 c4 with an attack, Přibyl-Malich, Děčín 1976) 11 exd6 ♗xd6 12 ♘e4 ♘7f6! 13 ♘xd6+ ♕xd6 14 ♘e5 0-0 gave Black a solid position in Möhring-Malich, East Germany 1977.

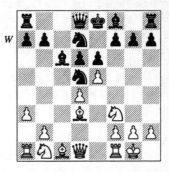

w

10 ♖e1

a) 10 ♗d2 ♗e7 (not surprisingly 10...dxe5 11 dxe5 ♕b6 12 ♘c3 ♘c5?! 13 ♘xd5 ♗xd5 14 ♗e3 ♕xb2 15 ♖b1 ♕xa3 16 ♗b5+ ♗c6 17 ♘d4 ± is dangerous for Black, Dončević-Martinović, Zurich 1984) 11 ♘c3

♘xc3 12 ♗xc3 0-0 (also 12...dxe5 13 dxe5 ♘c5 14 ♗e2 0-0 Dončević-Illescas, Las Palmas 1989)13 ♕e2 ♖c8 14 ♖fd1 ♗d5 = Sarközy-Lanc, Slovakian Cht 1994.

b) 10 b4!? a6 (10...b6 11 ♖e1 dxe5 12 ♘xe5 ♘xe5 13 dxe5 ♖c8 14 b5?! ♗b7 15 ♗e4 ♕c7 16 ♗b2 ♗c5 and Black's minor pieces are well posted, Nun-Ristić, Dortmund 1989) 11 ♖e1 (11 ♘bd2 ♘f4 12 ♗e4 ♗b5 13 ♖e1 d5 14 ♗c2 ♘d3 ∞ Bacetić-Mir.Marković, Yugoslav Cht 1993) 11...♗e7 12 ♘bd2 dxe5 13 dxe5 ♘f4 14 ♗e4 ♖c8 (perhaps 14...0-0!? 15 ♗xc6 bxc6 when 16 ♕c2 ♘g6 17 ♕xc6 ♘dxe5! ∞ worked well for Black in Pinter-Estevez, Kecskemet 1977, because 18 ♘xe5 ♘xe5 19 ♖xe5? loses to 19...♕d4) 15 ♘f1 ♗xe4 (15...♘g6 16 ♗b2 ± Brynell-Velikov, Haifa Echt 1989) 16 ♖xe4 ♘d5 17 ♖g4!? ♔f8 (17...h5 ½-½ Hermann-Tompa, Hamburg 1990, although White's position looks better after 18 ♖d4 ±) 18 ♖d4 ♘7b6 19 ♘g3 ± Onishchuk-Degraeve, Groningen 1995.

c) 10 ♕e2 ♗e7 11 exd6 ♗xd6 12 ♘c3 0-0 13 ♗e3 ♕b8 ∓ Manca-Portisch, Reggio Emilia 1992.

10...♗e7
A flexible idea, played several times by the Russian GM Alexander Vaulin, is 10...♖c8!?, delaying the development of the f8-bishop still further. The complications after 11 b4 a6 12 ♘bd2 ♘c3 13 ♕b3 dxe5! 14 ♗c4 e4 ½-½ Haba-Vaulin, Zlin 1995 were very unclear whilst 11 ♕e2 ♗e7 12 ♘d2 0-0 13 ♘c3 ♘xc3 14 ♗xc3 ♗d5 gave a solid position

in Jacek-Vaulin, Mlada Boleslav 1995.

Instead 10...dxe5 looks a premature exchange of pawns: 11 dxe5 (11 ♘xe5 ♘xe5 12 dxe5 g6!? 13 ♕g4 ♗g7 14 ♕g3 0-0 15 ♘d2 ♘e7 16 ♘c4 ♕d4! = Nun-Ruban, Sochi 1989) 11...♗e7 12 b4!? (as the bishop is now more effective on the a1-h8 diagonal) 12...♘5b6 13 ♘bd2 (Kholmov suggests 13 ♘c3! with the idea 13...a5 14 b5 ♗xf3 15 ♕xf3 ♘xe5?! 16 ♖xe5 ♕d4 17 ♖e2 ♕xc3 18 ♗b2 ±) 13...a5 14 b5 ♘c5 ∞ Kholmov-Polugaevsky, USSR 1980.

11 exd6?!
Although White wins this illustrative game quickly, it is better to maintain the pawn on e5; perhaps 11 b4!? is White's best – see the 10 b4 note after White's 10th move. Others:

a) 11 ♕c2 (to provoke 11...h6 12 ♕e2 and Black has weakened his kingside formation, but is White really going to be so cheeky as snatch the h-pawn?) 11...♖c8 (11...dxe5 12 ♘xe5 ♘xe5 13 dxe5 ♖c8 14 ♗d2 ♗g5 15 ♗e4 h6 16 ♗xg5 hxg5 17 ♘d2 g4 ∞ Haba-Martinović, Germany 1995) 12 ♗xh7 (yes!) 12...dxe5 13 dxe5 ♘c5 14 b4 ♗a4 15 ♕b2 ♖xh7 16 bxc5 ♗xc5 17 ♗g5 ♕b6 ∓ Ayas-Semkov, Sitges 1992.

b) 11 ♘bd2!? (this natural developing move is better than its current reputation) 11...dxe5 12 dxe5 (12 ♘xe5 ♘xe5 13 dxe5 ♘f4 14 ♗e4 ♘d3 15 ♗xc6+ bxc6 ∓ Vogt-Spiridonov, Brno 1975) 12...♘c5 (12...♘f4 13 ♗e4 ±) 13 ♗f1! (13 ♘e4 ♘c3 14 ♘xc3 ♘xd3 ∓ Van Dongen-Mirallès,

France 1989, while 13 ♗e4 ♘xe4 14 ♘xe4 ♘b6 15 ♕e2 ♕d5 16 ♘c3 ♕c4 was also satisfactory for Black in Makropoulos-Martinović, Dortmund 1988) 13...♘f4 14 ♖e3 0-0 (in his notes Grivas suggests 14...♘cd3, but 15 g3! seems a strong reply) 15 ♕c2 ♖c8 16 b4! ♗a4 (the line "16...♗xf3! 17 ♘xf3 ♘cd3 18 ♕d1 ♘xc1 19 ♖xc1 =" is given by Grivas in *Informator*, but in this line 18 ♖xd3! ± wins two pieces for a rook) 17 ♕b1 ♘d7 18 ♕e4! ♘d5 19 ♖e1 ♗c2!? 20 ♕g4 with a White initiative, Grivas-Velikov, Plovdiv 1988.

c) 11 ♗c2 ♕c7 (11...dxe5 12 dxe5 ♘f8 13 ♘d4 ♘g6 14 ♘xc6 bxc6 15 ♘d2 ± Vasiukov-Balashov, USSR 1975) 12 exd6 (12 ♘bd2!? *ECO*) 12...♗xd6 13 ♘bd2 ♘5f6 14 ♘c4 0-0 15 ♘fe5 ♖fd8 16 ♘xd6 ♕xd6 17 ♘xc6 ♕xc6 18 ♗g5 ♖ac8 = Dvoretsky-Polugaevsky, USSR 1975.

11...♗xd6 12 ♘bd2

Inferior is 12 ♘e5 ♘xe5 13 dxe5 ♗c5 14 ♕g4 ♕b6 15 ♕g3 h5 16 h4 0-0-0 17 ♗e4 f6 18 ♘d2 g5 with a powerful kingside attack imminent, Nun-Palac, Prague 1990. Instead 12 ♘c3 ♘xc3 13 bxc3 looks normal, but Black has two reasonable replies: 13...0-0!? has the point that 14 c4?!

♗xf3! 15 ♕xf3 ♕h4 attacks both h2 and d4, Russek-Velikov, Saint John 1988, while 13...♕a5!? 14 ♘g5!? (14 ♗d2 ♕h5) 14...♘f6 (14...♕xc3!? 15 ♘xe6 fxe6 16 ♖xe6+ ♔f7 17 ♖xd6 ♕xa1 18 ♗c4+ is given as +− by Vogt in his notes, but 18...♔f8 wins for Black. Instead White has compensation after 15 ♖b1, but is it enough?) 15 c4 0-0 16 ♗d2 ♕c7 ∓ was Sznapik-Vogt, Poznan 1976.

12...0-0 13 ♘c4 ♗e7 14 ♘fe5 ♖c8 15 ♗d2 ♗b5 16 ♕b3 ♗a6 17 ♗a5 ♕e8 (17...b6) **18 ♖ac1 f6??** *(D)*

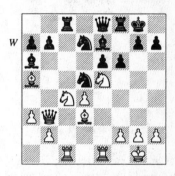

Black misses a devastating tactic; 18...♘f4 or 18...♘xe5 would have been fine for Black.

19 ♗xh7+! 1-0. After 19...♔xh7, 20 ♕h3+ ♔g8 21 ♕xe6+ followed by 22 ♘xd7 wins.

14 5 cxd4 e6 6 ♞f3 b6

1	e4	c5
2	c3	♞f6
3	e5	♞d5
4	d4	cxd4
5	cxd4	e6
6	♞f3	b6 (D)

It makes no difference if White plays 5 ♞f3, as after 5...e6 6 cxd4 b6 play has transposed. Therefore this counter-attacking system has the advantage, from Black's viewpoint, that it is not easy for White to avoid. Furthermore White already has to make a major decision on move seven, over whether to challenge the centralised black knight immediately. The less aggressive lines with 7 ♗d3 and 7 a3 (Game 37) allow Black to simplify by means of either ...♗b4+ or ...♗a6, or both, though White can usually maintain a solid position.

The main lines with 7 ♞c3 ♞xc3 8 bxc3 are complex and unclear. It is favourable for Black to slip in the important developing move 8...♛c7!, hitting the loose c3-pawn, as White invariably replies with the less useful 9 ♗d2. Then the continuation 9...d6 10 ♗d3 ♞d7 11 0-0 is one subtle move-order that gives both sides options (Game 38). However, the main line is usually reached via 9...♗b7 10 ♗d3 d6 11 0-0 ♞d7 and now 12 ♗f4 is covered in Game 38, and the critical 12 ♖e1 is the subject of Game 39. The pawn sacrifice 9 ♗e2 is an interesting way to enliven the game immediately.

In many of these lines visually the black kingside often looks a little shaky, due to a lack of defensive minor pieces. Black needs steady nerves, but objectively it is not that easy for White to whip up a really dangerous attack. Even in the lines where the white rook brazenly plonks itself on the h-file, a timely ...f5! by Black is often the key defensive move. And, potentially, the backward c-pawn is a target for Black, so White must be careful that his initiative doesn't peter out.

Note that some positions in this chapter can also be reached via different move-orders, e.g. 1 e4 c5 2 c3 ♞f6 3 e5 ♞d5 4 d4 cxd4 5 ♞f3 e6 6 cxd4 d6 7 ♞c3 ♞xc3 8 bxc3 ♛c7 and if/when Black plays a later ...b6 we will transpose.

Game 37
Blatny – Jansa
Czechoslovakia 1986

1 e4 c5 2 c3 ♘f6 3 e5 ♘d5 4 d4

One attempt to avoid the black queenside fianchetto was with the unusual 4 ♘f3 e6 5 ♗c4!? of the game Sveshnikov-Cvitan, Tilburg 1993, when the continuation 5...d6 6 0-0 ♗e7 7 d4 cxd4 8 cxd4 ♘c6 was a transposition to Chapter 15. If 5...b6 Sveshnikov gives 6 ♗xd5 exd5 7 d3 ±. In turn Black could try to cancel out this finesse with 4 ♘f3 b6!? 5 ♗c4 ♗b7.

4...cxd4 5 ♘f3 e6 6 cxd4 b6 7 ♗d3

For 7 ♘c3 see Games 37 and 38.

7 ♘bd2 ♗a6 (the waiting move 7...♗e7 is more prudent, when 8 ♘e4 0-0 9 a3 ♗e7 transposes to the 7 a3 line below) 8 ♗xa6 ♘xa6 9 ♘e4 ♗e7 10 0-0 0-0 11 ♗d2 ♘ac7 12 ♖c1 f5 13 exf6 gxf6 14 ♗h6 ♖f7 15 ♘fd2 ♗f8 16 ♕h5 ♗xh6 17 ♕xh6 ♖g7 18 ♘c4 ♖g4 19 f3 ♖g6 = Hort-Ftačnik, Germany 1995.

A more common idea is 7 a3, stopping any black pieces coming to b4 (and also avoiding having spent a tempo with the king's bishop should Black continue 7...♗a6). However Black can usually gain a good game by playing a timely ...f5 to take pressure off his king: 7...♗e7 (7...♗b7 8 ♗d3 d6 9 0-0 ♘d7 10 ♖e1 dxe5 11 ♘xe5 ♘xe5 12 dxe5 ♕c7 13 ♗b5+ ♗c6 14 ♕a4 ♖c8 15 ♗d2 ♕d7 16 ♗xc6 ♕xc6 17 ♕xc6+ ♖xc6 18 ♘c3 ½-½ Westerinen-Bellon, Alicante 1989) and now:

a) 8 ♗c4 ♗a6 9 ♗xa6 was the move-order of the game Rosandić-Stohl, quoted shortly – Stohl gives 9 ♗xd5 exd5 10 ♘c3 0-0! 11 ♘xd5 d6 as unclear.

b) 8 ♘bd2 doesn't lead to much after 8...0-0 9 ♘e4 f5 10 exf6 ♘xf6 11 ♗d3 ♗b7 12 ♘fg5 ♘xe4 13 ♘xe4 ♗a6 14 0-0 ♖f5 15 ♘c3 ♗xd3 16 ♕xd3 ♘c6 = Goldgewicht-Rotshtein, Cannes 1995 or 8...f5 9 exf6 ♘xf6 10 ♗d3 ♗a6 11 ♘c4 0-0 12 0-0 ♗b7 13 ♘e3 ♕e8 14 ♗c4 ♕h5 15 ♘e5 ♕xd1 16 ♖xd1 d5 = Goldgewicht-Razuvaev, Geneva 1996.

c) 8 ♗d3 is the main line:

c1) 8...♗b7 9 0-0 ♘a6 10 ♖e1 ♘ac7 11 ♘bd2 0-0 12 ♘e4 f5 13 exf6 gxf6? (13...♘xf6 = Miles) 14 ♕d2 ♖f7 15 ♕h6 ♖g7 16 ♕h3 f5 17 ♗h6 fxe4 18 ♖xe4 ♘f6 19 ♖h4?! (19 ♗xg7 ± Miles) 19...♗f8 20 ♗xg7 ♗xg7 21 ♖e1? (21 ♘e5!) 21...♗xf3 22 gxf3 ♕e7 ∓ Sanz-Miles, Amsterdam Z 1978.

c2) 8...♗a6 (exchanging White's bishop usually forestalls any potential kingside attack) 9 ♗xa6 (9 0-0 0-0 10 ♖e1 ♗xd3 11 ♕xd3 ♘c6 12 ♘bd2 f5 13 exf6 ♗xf6 ∓ Gaprindashvili-Kushnir, Riga 1972) 9...♘xa6 10 0-0 0-0 11 ♘bd2 f6! 12 exf6 gxf6!? 13 ♘e4 ♔h8! ∞ as in Wians-Kouatly, Budel Z 1987 and Rosandić-Stohl, Vinkovci 1995 – Black has ...♖g8 coming with pressure down the g-file.

7...♗b4+ *(D)*

Surprisingly, it does not seem especially good for Black to exchange light-squared bishops at this precise moment as White, about to castle, is just a little too well developed. The continuation 7...♗a6 (7...♗e7 8 0-0 ♗a6 is an alternative move-order) 8 0-0 (8 ♗xa6 ♘xa6 9 0-0 ♗e7 10 ♘bd2 0-0 11 ♘e4 ♘ac7 12 ♗g5 f6 13 exf6 ♘xf6 14 ♗xf6 gxf6?! 15 ♖c1 d5 16 ♘g3 ♕d7 17 ♘h4 ♗d6 18 f4 f5 19 ♘h5 ♕f7 20 ♖f3! ± Adams-Benjamin, New York 1996) 8...♗e7 (also 8...♕c8 9 a3 h6 10 ♖e1 ♗xd3 11 ♕xd3 ♘a6 12 ♘bd2 ♘ac7 13 ♘e4 ♕a6 14 ♕c2 ♖c8 15 ♗d2 ♗e7 16 ♘d6+ ♗xd6 17 exd6 ♘a8 18 ♕b3 0-0 19 ♘e5 ± Blatny-Mokry, Czechoslovakia 1986) 9 ♘c3 ♗xc3 10 bxc3 ♗xd3 11 ♕xd3 contains a nasty trap. After 11...d5 12 exd6 ♕xd6 White has shocked Black in at least four games with 13 ♗a3! ±, for example 13...♕c7 (13...♕xa3 14 ♕e4) 14 ♗xe7 ♔xe7 15 ♖ad1 ♘d7 16 d5 ♕d6 17 ♖fe1 with an attack, Fossan-Iskov, Gausdal 1988 and Godena-Cvitan, Reggio Emilia 1991 or 13...♕d8 14 ♗xe7 ♔xe7 15 ♖ad1 f6 16 ♖fe1 ♔f7 17 ♘g5+ 1-0 Braga-Priehoda, Catania 1993.

Another possible move is 7...♗b7 with transpositional possibilities after 8 ♘c3 or 8 a3: instead 8 0-0 ♘b4 9 ♗e2 ♗e7 10 ♘c3 0-0 11 a3 ♘d5 12 ♘e4 f6 13 exf6 ♘xf6 14 ♘xf6+ ♗xf6 15 ♗f4 ♘c6 16 ♗d6 ♗e7 17 ♗xe7 ♘xe7 18 ♘e5 ∞ was Turov-Zviagintsev, Rostov 1993.

8 ♗d2 ♗xd2+ 9 ♕xd2

9 ♘bxd2 ♗a6 gives Black an equal position, but 9 ♘fxd2!? has the point of allowing White's queen fast access to the kingside. Then 9...0-0 (9...♗a6 10 ♘e4 0-0 11 ♘bc3 ♗xd3 12 ♕xd3 ♘xc3 13 bxc3 ♘c6 14 0-0

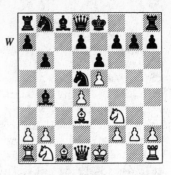

transposes) 10 ♘c3 (10 ♕h5 h6 11 ♕g4 ♗a6 12 ♗xa6 ♘xa6 13 0-0 ♖c8 14 ♘e4 f5 = Nun-Koch, Dortmund 1989) 10...♘xc3?! (Blatny gives 10...♗b7 with the idea 11 ♗e4 d6 12 ♕f3 ♘c6! or 11...♘xc3 12 bxc3 ♗xe4 13 ♘xe4 ♘c6 saving a tempo) 11 bxc3 ♗a6 12 ♘e4 ♗xd3 13 ♕xd3 ♘c6 14 0-0 ♘e7 15 f4 (± Blatny) 15...f5 16 exf6 gxf6 with a small edge for White in Blatny-Jansa, Namestovo 1987 and David-Plachetka, Bard Cup 1991.

9...♗a6

9...♘a6?! 10 ♘c3 ♘ac7 11 ♘g5 h6 12 ♘ge4 0-0 13 0-0 ♘xc3 14 bxc3 d5 15 ♘f6+! ♔h8 16 ♖ae1 ♘e8 17 ♘g4 ♕h4 18 ♕d1 h5 19 ♘e3 ± Sveshnikov-Bönsch, Cienfuegos 1979.

10 0-0

Or:

a) 10 ♘c3 ♘xc3 11 bxc3 ♗xd3 (11...0-0 12 0-0 ♗xd3 13 ♕xd3 ♘c6 14 ♖ad1 ♖c8 15 d5 ♘a5 16 ♖fe1 h6 ∞ Barlov-Rajković, Kragujevac 1977) 12 ♕xd3 d5 13 exd6 ♕xd6 14 0-0 ♘d7 = Vogt-Grosar, Altensteig 1995.

b) 10 ♗e4!? ♘c6 11 ♗xd5!? (11 ♘c3 ♘xc3 12 bxc3 ♖c8 13 h4 and following 13...♘e7 14 ♖c1 h6 15

♖h3 ♕c7 Marjanović-Cvitan, Yugoslav Ch 1986, Cvitan gives 16 ♖g3 ±; however Gallagher's suggestion of 13...f5 14 exf6 ♕xf6 is unclear) 11...exd5 12 ♘c3 ♘b4 (12...♘e7 13 0-0-0!? was Godena-Belotti, Reggio Emilia 1994) 13 a3! ♘d3+ 14 ♔d1 d6 15 ♘e1 ♘xe1 16 ♖xe1 ± Harley-Pigott, London 1994.

10...0-0 11 ♘a3?!

White is trying to keep the position complex, but sounder was 11 ♘c3 with similar play to the previous note (with 10 ♘c3). Instead after 11 ♖c1 ♗xd3 12 ♕xd3 ♘c6 13 a3 f6 14 ♘c3 ♘f4 15 ♕e4 fxe5 16 dxe5 ♕e8 17 ♖d1 ♕h5 White's king came under some pressure in Espinosa-Vera, Cuban Ch 1989, though he managed a draw after 18 ♘e2 ♘xe2+ 19 ♕xe2 ♖f5 20 ♕e4 ♕f7 21 ♖d3 ♖f8 22 ♖ad1 ♖f4 23 ♕e2 ♕h5 24 ♖e3 ♖8f7 ½-½.

11...♗xd3 12 ♕xd3 ♘c6 13 ♘c4 f6 14 ♖fe1 fxe5 15 dxe5?! (15 ♘cxe5 =; now Jansa heads towards the white king) **15...♕e8! 16 ♖ad1 ♕h5 17 ♕d2?** (provoking Black into an obviously powerful exchange sacrifice) **17...♖xf3 18 gxf3 ♖f8 19 ♖e4 ♖xf3 20 ♖de1 ♘f4! 21 ♔h1** (21 ♖xf4 ♕g5+) **21...♘d3 22 ♖1e2 b5 23 ♘e3 ♘cxe5 24 ♘f1 ♘g4 25 ♔g1 ♘gxf2 26 ♘g3 ♖xg3+ 0-1**

Game 38
Hmadi – Murugan
Novi Sad OL 1990

1 e4 c5 2 c3 ♘f6 3 e5 ♘d5 4 d4 cxd4 5 ♘f3 e6 6 cxd4 b6 7 ♘c3 *(D)*
7...♘xc3

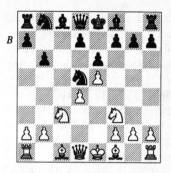

Black can also maintain the knight on d5 for a while with 7...♗b7. Then 8 ♗c4?! is a mistake on account of Basman's 8...♘xc3 9 bxc3 ♕c8! forcing 10 ♕d3. Black should not continue 10...♗a6? 11 ♗xa6 ♕xa6 12 ♕xa6 ♘xa6 13 a4 ♖c8 14 ♔d2 ♘b8 15 ♔d3 ± as in Markland-Basman, Woolacombe 1973, but should play 10...♘c6, for example 11 0-0 ♘a5 12 ♗b5 a6 13 ♗a4 ♗d5 with commanding control of the light squares.

Instead 7...♗b7 8 ♗d3 gives Black the problem that if he exchanges late on c3 he is likely to have an inferior version of the main line: 8...♗e7 9 0-0 0-0 and now *(D)*:

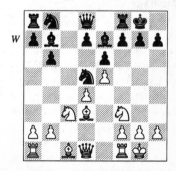

a) 10 ♗c2 f5 11 exf6 gxf6 12 ♗b3 ♘xc3 13 bxc3 d5 14 ♖e1 and the backward e6-pawn was an obvious target in Evans-Hail, London 1978, though Black's weakening of his kingside was self-inflicted in this case.

b) 10 ♕e2!? f5 11 ♗d2! is promising: 11...a6 12 ♗c4 ᐃxc3 13 bxc3 b5 14 ♗d3! ♗a3 15 ♖fb1 ♗xf3 16 ♕xf3 ± Illescas-J.Polgar, Linares 1994.

c) 10 ♖e1 ᐃxc3 11 bxc3 d6 12 exd6 ♕xd6 13 ᐃe5 ᐃc6 14 ♗f4 ᐃxe5 15 ♗xe5 ♕d8 when the black kingside looks vulnerable, but it is not clear that this can be exploited. For example 16 ♕h5 f5 17 ♖e3!? ♗f6 18 ♖h3 ♗xe5!? 19 ♕xh7+ ♔f7 20 dxe5 ♖h8 21 ♕xh8 ♕xh8 22 ♖xh8 ♖xh8 23 ♖d1 ♖c8 24 ♗b5 ♖c5 25 ♖d7+ ♔f8 26 c4 a6 27 ♖xb7 axb5 28 ♖xb6 bxc4 29 f4 c3 30 ♖b1 ♖c4 31 g3 ♖a4 32 ♖c1 ♖xa2 33 ♖xc3 ♖a1+ 34 ♔g2 ♖a2+ 35 ♔h3 ♔f7 36 ♖c7+ ♔f8 37 ♖c8+ ♔f7 38 ♖c7+ ♔f8 39 ♖c1 ♔f7 40 ♖g1 g5 41 fxg5 ♔g6 42 ♖g2 ♖a5 ½-½ Veingold-Hartston, Tallinn 1979. Imaginative defence from Black.

8 bxc3 ♕c7!

If 8...♗a6 9 ♗xa6 ᐃxa6 White has a comfortable space advantage after 10 h4 or 10 ♕d3. The reason Black usually develops with 8...♕c7 is to force White to play 9 ♗d2. Quite often this dark-square white bishop ends up on the f4-square anyway later, and if ...♕c7 is delayed, White can save a whole tempo by playing ♗f4 in one hop. Even so there have been a few games – even with grandmasters playing Black – where Black has delayed ...♕c7, and

ended up a tempo adrift of the current illustrative game.

Some sample references from routine (but less accurate) move-orders that did not transpose back to the main lines:

a) 8...♗e7 9 ♗d3 ♗b7 10 0-0 d6 11 ♗f4 ᐃc6 12 ♖e1 dxe5 13 ᐃxe5 ᐃxe5 14 ♗xe5 ♗f6 15 ♕h5 ♗xe5 16 ♗b5+ ♔f8 17 dxe5 ♕d5 18 ♗f1 ♗c6 19 ♖ad1 with a dangerous development advantage, Dončević-Tal, Germany 1992.

b) 8...♗b7 9 ♗d3 ♗e7 (9...ᐃc6 10 0-0 ♗e7 11 ᐃd2 d6 12 exd6 ♕xd6 13 ♕g4 g6 14 ᐃc4 ♕d5 15 ♗h6 ♕h5 16 ♕xh5 ± Smagin-Velikov, Naleczow 1985) 10 h4!? ♕c7 11 ♗d2 d6 12 h5 dxe5 13 ᐃxe5 ᐃc6 14 ♗b5 0-0 15 ♗xc6 ♗xc6 16 ♕g4 ♗f6 17 ♕g3 ♗xe5 18 dxe5 f5 19 0-0 ♖ad8 20 ♗g5 ♖d5 21 ♖fe1 ♕f7 22 h6 ♕g6 23 hxg7 ♔xg7 24 ♖e3 f4 25 ♗f6+ ♖xf6 26 exf6+ ♔f7 27 ♕xg6+ hxg6 28 ♖e4 ♖g5 29 ♖xf4 ♖xg2+ 30 ♔f1 with winning chances for White, Sepp-Lputian, Moscow OL 1994.

9 ♗d2

Alternatives are rarely seen: 9 c4 ♗a6 10 ♕a4? (10 ♕b3!? Sveshnikov) 10...b5! 11 cxb5 ♕c3+ 12 ♔d1 ♗b7! 13 ♕c2 (13 ♖b1 ♗xf3+ 14 gxf3 ♕xf3+ 15 ♔e1 ♕xh1) 13...♕xa1 14 ♗d3 ᐃc6! 15 bxc6 ♗xc6 ∓ was a disaster for White in Sveshnikov-Pugachev, St Petersburg 1994, although plausible is 9 ♕b3 ♗b7 10 ♗e2 d6 11 ♗f4 ᐃd7 12 0-0 ♗e7 13 ♗g3!? (tricky; now 13...0-0 14 ♕a3! ±) 13...♖c8 14 ♖fc1 dxe5 15 ᐃxe5 ᐃxe5 16 ♗xe5 ♕d7 17 a4 f6 18

♗b5 ♗c6 19 ♗g3 ♔f7 20 ♖e1 ♕d5 21 ♕xd5 exd5 = Nunez-P.Cramling, Oviedo rpd 1991.

However, White has an interesting if speculative attempt to cut corners with 9 ♗e2!?, not bothering with ♗d2. Then if Black spurns the pawn on c3, White develops quickly: 9...♗b7 10 0-0 d6 11 ♗f4 ♘d7. In Yrjölä-Jansa, West Berlin 1986, White now tried the enterprising 12 d5!? exd5 13 ♖e1 0-0-0 and now instead of 14 c4? dxe5 15 ♘xe5 ♘xe5 16 ♗xe5 ♗d6, Jansa gives 14 e6 fxe6 15 ♘g5 ♘c5 16 ♘xe6 ♘xe6 17 ♗g4 ± while 14 ♕a4 ± is also possible. So logically Black should continue (after 9 ♗e2!?) with 9...♕xc3+ 10 ♗d2 ♕a3 and now:

a) 11 0-0 ♗b7 (or 11...♘c6 12 ♗c1 ♕a5 13 ♘g5 ♗e7 14 ♕d3 ♗b7 15 ♖d1 ♘b4 16 ♕b1 ♖c8 17 a3 ♘d5 18 ♘e4 ♘c3 19 ♘xc3 ♖xc3 Polašek-Lanc, Prague 1989, for example 20 ♗d2 ♕d5) 12 ♕c2 ♘a6 13 ♖fc1 ♗e7 14 ♖ab1 0-0 15 ♖b3 ♖ac8! 16 ♕b1 ♖xc1+ 17 ♗xc1 ♕a5 ∓ Seifert-Pekarek, Porabka 1987.

b) 11 d5 (imaginative, but at the end of the day White is still a pawn down) 11...♗b4 12 0-0 0-0 13 ♘d4 ♗xd2 14 ♕xd2 ♗a6 15 ♖ac1 ♗xe2 16 ♕xe2 ♘a6 17 ♘b5 ♕a4 ∓ Polašek-Haba, Prague 1989.

c) 11 ♖c1! ♘c6 (perhaps best is 11...♗a6!? 12 0-0 ♘c6 13 d5 exd5 14 ♗xa6 ♕xa6 15 ♗g5 ♕xa2 16 ♘d4 ♘xd4 17 ♕xd4 h6 18 ♗h4 ♗c5 19 ♕g4 g5 20 ♗g3 ♖g8 21 ♔h1 ♖g6 22 f4 ♕a4 ∓ Van der Werf-Van Wely, Dutch Ch 1995) 12 ♗c3 ♕e7 13 ♘g5 (with superior development and the

black queen on e7, it is obvious that White has compensation for the pawn; in a later game White continued more simply with 13 0-0!? ♗b7 14 ♗g5 f6 15 ♗h4 0-0-0 16 exf6 gxf6 17 ♕c1!? ♖g8 18 ♗g3 and in Van Mil-Rechmann, Germany 1991, Black was so frightened by the prospect of ♕f4 that he played 18...♖xg3 19 hxg3 ♕d6 after which White was material up) 13...f5 (a mistake would be 13...♘xd4 14 ♗h5 g6 15 ♘e4! and if 15...gxh5 16 ♘d6+ ♔d8 17 ♗g5!; best may be Gallagher's suggestion of 13...h6 14 ♘e4 ♕h4 "with a double-edged position") 14 exf6 ♕xf6 15 ♘xe6 dxe6 16 ♗b5 ♗d7 17 ♗xc6 ♗xc6 18 ♖xc6 ♗e7 19 ♕e2 ♕xd4 Van Mil-Krasenkov, Budapest 1989, and now 20 ♗c3! would have favoured White.

In conclusion we can say this bold pawn sacrifice with 9 ♗e2!? ♕xc3+ deserves further tests.

9...d6!? *(D)*

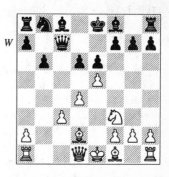

This move-order, whereby Black puts direct pressure on the white e-pawn, gives both sides more options than the straightforward 9...♗b7 10 ♗d3 d6 11 0-0 ♘d7 (Game 39).

Nevertheless a common outcome, as in this game, is that play stays in normal channels.

A completely different idea is 9...♗e7 (waiting!) 10 ♗d3 ♗a6, for example 11 ♗xa6 ♘xa6 12 ♕a4 (12 ♕e2!?) 12...♕b7 13 0-0 0-0 14 c4 ♖fd8 15 ♕b3 d5 16 exd6 ♗xd6 17 ♖fe1 ♖ac8 = Chikovani-Frias, London 1994 or 11 c4 ♗xc4 12 ♖c1 b5 13 ♗xc4 bxc4 14 ♕a4 0-0 15 ♖xc4 ♘c6 16 0-0 ♖ab8 17 ♕c2 f5 18 exf6 ♗xf6 ∞ Fragiadakis-Grivas, Iraklio 1994.

10 ♗d3

After 10 ♗b5+ safest is 10...♘d7 11 0-0 a6 12 exd6 ♗xd6 13 ♗d3 ♗b7 14 h3 0-0 15 ♖e1 ♗f4 16 ♗xf4 ½-½ Dolmatov-Tukmakov, Elenite 1995. Instead 10...♗d7 11 a4! (11 ♗d3 ♗c6!? is similar the main game, with Black's bishop on c7 instead of b7) 11...♘c6 12 exd6 ♗xd6 13 0-0 0-0 14 ♖e1 ♘e7 15 ♕e2 ♖ac8 16 ♗a6 ♖b8 17 h4 ♗f4?! (17...♘g6!?) 18 ♗xf4 ♕xf4 19 ♘e5! ± Smagin-Borriss, Germany 1992.

10...♘d7 11 0-0

After 11 exd6 ♗xd6 we reach a very comfortable position for Black which can also arise from other move-orders (1 e4 c5 2 c3 ♘f6 3 e5 ♘d5 4 d4 cxd4 5 ♘f3 e6 6 cxd4 d6 7 ♘c3 ♘xc3 8 bxc3 ♕c7 9 ♗d2 ♘d7 10 exd6 ♗xd6 11 ♗d3 b6 for example): 12 0-0 ♗b7 13 ♖e1 0-0 14 ♘e5 (14 h3 h6 15 ♕e2 ♗f4 16 ♘e5 ♗xe5 17 dxe5 ♖fd8 18 ♗f4 ♘c5 19 ♗c2 f5 20 ♖ad1 ♗e4 ∓ Vogelmann-Jansa, Eupen 1994) 14...♗xe5 15 dxe5 ♘c5 (15...f5 16 exf6 ♘xf6 17 ♕e2 ♖ad8 18 ♖ad1 e5 19 ♗g5 e4 20 ♗xf6

♖xd3 ½-½ Asmundsson-Lombardy, Grindavik 1984) 15...♘c5 16 ♗c2 ♖fd8 17 ♖e3 ♕c6 18 ♖g3 ♘e4 19 ♗xe4 ♕xe4 ∓ Brynell-Jansa, Næstved 1988.

The only other major deviation for White is 11 ♘g5 ♗b7 12 0-0 (12 f4 ♗e7 13 ♕g4 h5 14 ♕g3 h4 15 ♕g4 ♗xg5 16 ♕xg5 h3 17 ♗f1 g6 ∓ Lehtivaara-Murugan, London 1989), which transposes to the ♘g5 note to move 12 in the game.

11...♗b7

Now we are back in the main line. Because of the move-order he has chosen, Black had the possibility of 11...dxe5:

a) 12 dxe5 ♗b7 13 ♖e1 transposes to Game 39, note to White's 13th.

b) For 12 ♘g5 ♗b7 see the note to 12 ♗f4 in the current main game.

c) There is also 12 ♖e1, when no one has dared capture on d4, but several other moves have been tried:

c1) 12...♗b7 transposes to Game 39.

c2) 12...g6 and here 13 ♘xe5 ♘xe5 14 ♗f4 ♗g7 15 ♗xe5 ♗xe5 16 ♖xe5 0-0 17 ♕d2 ♗b7 18 h4 ♖ac8 19 ♖c1 ♖fd8 20 ♕e3 ♖d5 21 f4 ♕e7 was not much for White in the game Blatny-Plachetka, Austria Cht 1993, but 13 ♕a4 is also possible: 13...♗g7 14 ♘xe5 0-0 15 ♗e4 ♘xe5 16 ♗xa8 ♘g4 17 g3 ♗d7 18 ♕d1 ♘xf2 19 ♕f3 ± Majzlan-Timoshchenko, Sweden 1995.

c3) 12...♗d6 13 dxe5 (13 ♘xe5 ♗xe5 14 dxe5 can be answered by 14...♗b7 15 ♗g5! ♕c5 16 ♕a4 h6 17 ♗h4 g5 18 ♗e4 = Luther-Stohl,

Namestovo 1987 or 14...♘c5 15 ♗c2 ♗b7 16 ♗g5 h6 17 ♕h5 ♕c6 18 f3 ♖g8 19 ♗h4 g5 20 ♗f2 0-0-0 ∞ Iotov-Forgo, corr. 1991) 13...♗e7 14 ♘g5!? (14 ♗f4 ♘c5 15 ♗b5+ ♗d7 16 ♘d4 ♗xb5 17 ♘xb5 ♕c6 18 a4 0-0 ∞ Hmadi-Plachetka, Tunisia 1992) 14...♗b7 15 ♕h5 ♗xg5 16 ♕xg5 h6! 17 ♕h4! ± Blatny-Pekarek, Namestovo 1987.

Instead 12 ♘xe5 ♘xe5 is a sensible alternative:

a) 13 ♗f4!? ♗d6 14 dxe5 ♗e7 (Black has had to lose some time, and will shortly give up the right to castle, but White has not yet found the way to exploit this) 15 ♕f3 (15 ♕g4 ♔f8 16 ♗e4 ♗b7 17 ♗xb7 ♕xb7 18 ♖ad1 h5 19 ♕e2 g6 20 ♕e3 ♔g7 21 ♗g5 ♖hc8 = Dückstein-Arakhamia, Vienna 1993) 15...♗b7 16 ♗b5+ ♔f8 17 ♕g3 h6 18 ♖ad1 ♖d8 19 ♖xd8+ ♕xd8 20 ♗e2 g6 21 ♖d1 ♕c7 22 h4 ♔g7 23 h5 g5 24 ♗c1 ♖g8 ∞ Dobrovolsky-Jansa, Ceske Budejovice 1993.

b) 13 dxe5 ♗b7 (13...♗c5 14 ♕g4 ♗b7 15 ♗b5+ ♗c6 16 ♗xc6+ ♕xc6 17 ♕xg7 0-0-0 with a kingside attack for Black, Cigan-Slibar, Slovenia 1993) 14 ♗b5+ ♗c6 15 ♕f3 (15 ♕a4 ♗xb5 16 ♕xb5+ ♕d7 17 a4 ♗c5 18 ♖fd1 0-0-0!? ∞ G.Lee-Murugan, British Ch 1993) 15...♖c8 16 a4 a6 (16...♗e7 17 ♕g3 ♔f8 18 ♖fd1 h5 19 ♗xc6 ♕xc6 20 ♗g5 f6 ∞ Degraeve-Jansa, Royan 1989) 17 ♗xc6+ ♕xc6 18 ♕g3 g6 19 c4!? ∞ A.Marić-P.Cramling, Belgrade 1988.

12 ♗f4

For the more dangerous 12 ♖e1 see the next game, while 12 exd6 has

already been covered in the note to White's 11th move. Against 12 ♘g5 Black seems able to beat off the attack with careful defence: 12...dxe5 (12...♗e7!? 13 exd6 ♗xd6 14 ♕h5 ♘f6 15 ♗b5+ ♔f8 16 ♕h4 h6 17 f4 hxg5 18 ♕xh8+ ♔e7 19 ♕h3 gxf4 20 ♗e2 g5 21 ♗f3 ♖g8 22 ♗xb7 ♕xb7 23 ♕f3 ♕xf3 24 gxf3 ♖c8 25 a4 ♘d5 26 ♖fc1 ♖c4 27 ♔f2 e5 ½-½ Sermek-Landenbergue, Ptuj Z 1995) 13 ♕h5 g6 (not 13...♘f6? 14 ♗b5+ +-) 14 ♕h3 and here *(D)*:

a) 14...♗g7 15 ♖ae1 (15 ♖fe1 ♕d6 16 f4 – a typical theme in this line – 16...e4! 17 ♗xe4 ♗xe4 18 ♘xe4 ♕d5 19 ♘g5 h6 20 ♘f3 0-0 ∓ Basirov-Minasian, Kstovo 1994) 15...e4 (15...a6 16 f4 e4 17 ♗xe4 ♗xe4 18 ♖xe4 ♘f6 19 ♖xe6+ fxe6 20 ♕xe6+ 1-0 Sermek-David, Bled 1996) 16 ♗xe4 ♗xe4 17 ♖xe4 ♘f6 18 ♖xe6+ +- Sermek-Osterman, Ljubljana 1993.

b) 14...♗e7 15 ♖fe1 (15 ♖ae1 h6 16 f4 ♗xg5 17 fxg5 h5 ∓ Jonkman-Kjeldsen, Cannes 1995) 15...♖f8! (improving on the 15...a6 of V.L.Ivanov-Sobolev, Cherepovec 1993, while 15...h6 16 f4! e4? 17 ♘xe4 ± with an

attack was V.L.Ivanov-Doroshke-
vich, Moscow 1995) 16 dxe5 (16
♘xh7 ♖h8 ∓) 16...0-0-0 17 ♗f4 ♘c5
18 ♗c2 h6! ∓ Nadyrkhanov-Zvia-
gintsev, St Petersburg 1994.

Incidentally, it is worth noting
that Black has misplayed the opening, since the position after 12 ♗f4
can occur with White to move, e.g. 1
e4 c5 2 c3 ♘f6 3 e5 ♘d5 4 d4 cxd4 5
♘f3 e6 6 cxd4 b6 7 ♘c3 ♗b7 8 ♗d3
d6 9 0-0 ♘xc3 10 bxc3 ♘d7 11 ♗f4
♕c7 as in the game Claesen-Tuk-
makov, Antwerp 1993. Obviously
the extra tempo is a bonus for White;
nevertheless Black went on to score
a crushing victory in 31 moves!

12...♗e7 13 ♖e1 *(D)*

13...♖c8

A mistake is 13...g6? 14 d5 ♗xd5
15 exd6 ♗xd6 16 ♗xd6 ♕xd6 17
♗e4! ♘f6 18 c4 1-0 Keller-P.Cram-
ling, Zurich 1984, but 13...0-0 is
natural:

a) 14 ♖e3!? ♗xf3!? (14...g6 15
♖c1 dxe5 16 ♘xe5 ♘xe5 17 ♗xe5
♗d6 18 h4 ♗xe5 19 ♖xe5 ♖ad8 20
h5 ♖d5 21 f4 ± Ambrož-Jansa,
Czechoslovak Ch 1982 although of
course 15...♗xf3 could be played in

this line as well) 15 ♕xf3 g6 16
♖ae1 dxe5 17 dxe5 ♖fd8 18 ♗h6
♖ac8 19 ♕f4 ♘xe5! 20 ♗a6 ♘c4!
21 ♖e4! ♘d6! (21...♘d2? 22 ♖4e2)
22 ♗xc8 ♖xc8 23 ♕e5! ♕xc3! 24
♖c1 ♕xc1+! 25 ♖xc1 ♗f6!? 26 ♕f4
g5 27 ♕e3 ♘xe4 28 h3 ♖c4 and with
a dominating position and rook,
knight, and two pawns for the queen
Black had a large advantage in Sari-
ego-Estevez, Sagua la Grande 1987.
A model of defensive technique
from Black.

b) 14 ♖c1 ♖fd8 (14...♖c8 transposes back to the main game) 15
♘g5 g6 16 ♕g4 ♘f8 17 h4 ♕d7 18
h5 dxe5 19 hxg6 hxg6 20 ♗xe5 f6 21
♗xg6 ♘xg6 22 ♕h5 1-0 Striković-
Dimovski, Pula Cht 1990. For the record the move-order of this game
was 13 ♖c1 0-0 14 ♖e1.

14 ♖c1 0-0 15 ♘g5?!

15 ♗b1 ♗xf3 16 ♕xf3 dxe5 17
dxe5 (17 ♗xe5 ♘xe5 18 ♖xe5 g6 was
nothing for White in Dubois-Koch,
France 1992) 17...♖fe8 18 h4 ♕c6
19 ♕g3 ♕a4 20 h5 ♔h8 21 ♖ed1
♘f8 22 h6 ♘g6 23 hxg7+ ♔xg7 24
♗g5? (24 ♖d4 ∞) 24...♗xg5 25
♕xg5 ♕f4 26 ♕h5 ♖c5 ∓ M.Han-
sen-Benjamin, London 1987.

15...♗xg5 16 ♕h5 f5!

An effective defensive response.
If 16...♗h6, 17 ♗xh6 gxh6 18 ♕xh6
f5 19 ♕xe6+ gives White several
pawns and an attack for the sacrificed piece. Now, however, 17 exf6
can be well met by either 17...h6 18
♗xg5 ♘xf6 or 17...♘xf6 immediately.

**17 ♕xg5 dxe5 18 dxe5 ♘c5 ∓ 19
♖e3 ♖fd8 20 ♗f1 ♕f7 21 ♕h4 ♖d7**

**22 ♖h3 g6 23 ♗b5 ♗c6 24 ♗c4
♖cd8 25 ♖e3** (not surprisingly the
white attack has got nowhere, and
now the rook ignominiously retreats) **25...♖d1+ 26 ♖e1 ♖xe1+ 27
♖xe1 ♖d7 28 ♕g3 ♗d5 29 ♗b5
♖c7 30 ♕h4 ♖c8 31 ♖d1 a6 32 ♗f1
b5 33 ♗h6 ⚘e4 34 f3 ♕a7+ 35 ♖d4
⚘xc3 36 ♔h1 ♕b6 37 h3 ♕d8 38
♗g5 ♕e8 39 ♗f6 ♕f7 40 ♕h6
⚘xa2 41 ♔h2 ⚘c3 42 ♖h4 a5 43
♕e3 b4 44 ♕b6 ♕c7 45 ♕a6 ♖a8
46 ♕d3 b3 47 ♕e3 b2 48 ♗d3 b1♕
49 ♗xb1 ⚘xb1 0-1**

Game 39
Smagin – Plachetka
Trnava 1987

**1 e4 c5 2 c3 ⚘f6 3 e5 ⚘d5 4 d4 cxd4
5 ⚘f3 e6 6 cxd4 b6 7 ⚘c3 ⚘xc3 8
bxc3 ♕c7 9 ♗d2 ♗b7 10 ♗d3 d6
11 0-0 ⚘d7 12 ♖e1 dxe5**

12...♗e7 is possible:

a) **13 exd6!? ♗xd6** is best, putting White a tempo ahead of the line
covered in Game 38, note to White's
11th move. A couple of examples:

a1) **14 ⚘e5?** (not a wise use of
the extra move) **14...♗xe5 15 dxe5
0-0-0 ∓** Prié-Dizdarević, Cannes
Martinez 1995.

a2) **14 c4 0-0 15 h3 ♖ac8 16 ♗c3
♖fe8 17 ⚘g5 g6 18 ♕g4 e5 19 d5
♗f8 20 ♕h4 h6 21 ⚘e4 b5 22 ♖ab1
bxc4 23 ♗xc4 ♗g7 24 ♗b3 ±** Roz-
entalis-Lesiège, Montreal 1995.

b) **13 ⚘g5** is a sharp attempt:
13...dxe5 14 ♕g4 (14 ♕h5 ♗xg5 15
♕xg5 0-0 16 dxe5 ♖fd8 17 ♕h4
⚘f8 18 ♖e3 ∞** Acs-Fancsy, Budapest
1996) **14...h5 15 ♕h3 ♗xg5 16 ♗xg5**

f5!? 17 ♖ad1 0-0 18 dxe5 g6 ∞ Rau-
sis-Gallagher, Nîmes 1992.

c) The more positional **13 a4** has
been seen in a couple of games.

d) Instead the tactical **13 ♗g5** has
had a chequered career:

d1) **13...dxe5 14 ♗xe7 ♔xe7** (or
**14...♗xf3 15 ♕xf3 ♔xe7 16 ♕g3
♔f8 17 ♗b5 ±** Ostermeyer-Ramos,
Germany 1987) **15 ⚘xe5 ⚘xe5 16
♖xe5 ♕xc3!? 17 ♖c1 ♕xd4 18
♖c7+** now instead of **18...♔d6?** 19
♖d7+! ± Weiss-Siegler, Germany
1994, 18...♔f6 is toughest, though
the white attack still looks dangerous
after 19 ♖e3.

d2) **13...♕d8 14 ♗f4! ♗xf3** (if
14...dxe5, 15 ⚘xe5 ±) **15 ♕xf3 dxe5
16 dxe5 0-0 17 ♖ad1 ♕c7 18 ♗xh7+
♔xh7 19 ♕d3+ ♔g8 20 ♕xd7 ±**
Smagin-Dizdarević, Zenica 1987.

d3) **13...♗xg5 14 ⚘xg5 dxe5** (or
**14...h6 15 ♕h5 0-0 16 ♖e3 dxe5 17
♖g3 e4 18 ⚘xe4 ♗xe4 19 ♗xe4 ⚘f6
20 ♕f3 =** Smagin-Adamski, Budapest 1988) **15 ♕h5 ⚘f6 16 ♕h3**
(Smagin once published some analysis claiming 16 ⚘xe6? ♕c6 17 d5
won for White, missing the reply
17...♕xe6! −+ as later happened in
De Boer-Krockenberger, Germany
1992) **16...e4 17 ⚘xe4 ⚘xe4 18
♗xe4 ♗xe4 19 ♖xe4 0-0 =** Wach-
Landenbergue, Ptuj Z 1995.

13 ⚘xe5

13 dxe5 gives Black no problems:
13...♗e7 (13...g6 14 ♗f4?! ♗g7 15
⚘d4 0-0 16 ⚘b5 ♕c6 17 ♗e4 ♕xb5
18 ♗xb7 ♖ab8 ∓** S.Lalić-Stohl, Isle
of Man 1994) **14 ⚘d4** (14 ♕e2 0-0
15 ⚘d4 ♖fd8 16 h4 ⚘c5 17 ♗c2
♖d5 18 f4 ♖ad8 19 ♖ad1 ♗a6 20 ♕f3**

♗c4 ∓ M.S.Hansen-Jansa, Gausdal 1987) 14...a6 15 ♕g4 g6 16 ♕g3 ♘c5 17 ♗c2 ♗d5 18 a4 ∞ Ernst-Cramling, Gausdal 1987.

13...♘xe5 14 ♖xe5 ♗d6 15 ♖h5!? (D)

Transferring the rook to the king-side unbalances the game. Later on, after Black castles kingside, White usually manoeuvres his queen to the h-file as well, forcing Black into the defensive ...f5 (to protect h7 along his second rank). However, this is a double-edged strategy for White, as after he obtains the concession ...f5, it is usually difficult to make attacking progress on the kingside (the illustrative game is unrepresentative in this respect). If play switches to the queenside White's rook on the h-file can be misplaced. However, 15 ♗b5+ is insufficient for advantage: 15...♗c6 (after 15...♔f8 16 ♖h5, 16...♗e4 17 ♕e2 ♗g6 18 ♖h3 ± was the game Blatny Grosar, Debrecen 1992, while 16...g6 transposes to the note after White's 16th move in the main game) 16 ♕f3 ♖c8 (16...0-0-0 17 ♗xc6 ♗xe5 18 a4! ♖d6! 19 ♗b5 ♖d5 20 c4 ♖xd4 21 ♗c3 ♕b7 ∞ Seguera-Akopian, Mamaia jr Wch 1991) 17 ♗xc6+ ♕xc6 18 d5 ♕c7!? (18...♕b7 19 ♖h5 e5 20 ♖e1 f6 21 ♕h3 ♕d7 22 ♕h4 ♕f7 23 ♖xh7 ♖xh7 24 ♕xh7 ♕xd5 with an equal position, Lombardy-Panno, Buenos Aires 1994) 19 ♖g5?! (19 ♖h5 e5 20 ♖e1 f6 21 ♕h3 ♕d7 = Hmadi-Hughes, Moscow OL 1994) 19...g6 20 dxe6 0-0 21 ♕h3 ♖cd8 22 ♗e3 ♕xc3 23 ♖c1 ♗a3 24 ♖f1 ♕f6 25 exf7+ ♕xf7 26 ♗xb6? axb6 27

♕xa3 ♕xf2+! 0-1 Michalek-Orsag, Czech Ch 1995.

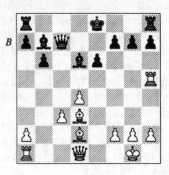

15...g6

For 15...0-0-0 16 a4 g6 17 ♖h3 see the note after Black's 17th.

16 ♖h3 (D)

On 16 ♗b5+ Black has a choice of the double-edged 16...♗c6 17 ♕f3! 0-0-0! 18 ♗xc6 gxh5 19 a4 a6 20 ♗e4 ♔b8 21 ♕xh5 ♗f4 22 ♗e1 ∞ Rizzitano-Miles, USA 1980, and the solid 16...♔f8 17 ♖h3 h5 (17...♖c8 18 ♗h6+ ♔g8 19 ♕d2 a6 20 ♗f1?! (20 ♗a4 ∞) 20...f6 21 ♗e3? ♕xc3 ∓ M.Hansen-P.Cramling, Gausdal 1987) 18 ♕e2 ♗f4 19 ♖e1 ♔g7 20 ♗xf4 ♕xf4 with a fine game for Black, Blatny-Akopian, Philadelphia 1994.

16...♕c6

a) 16...♗f4 17 ♕a4+!? ± Vysochin-Chernosvitov probably offers more than 17 ♗b5+ ♔f8 18 ♕c1 ♗xd2 19 ♕xd2 h5.

b) 16...0-0-0 (possible, but in the long term Black's king is more exposed on this wing) 17 a4 (17 ♗g5!? ♗e7 18 ♗xe7 ♕xe7 19 a4 has been seen, when Black's best is probably now 19...♕g5 20 ♖g3 ♕d5) 17...g5!? and now instead of 18 c4 h5, Pandavos-Gobet, Thessaloniki OL 1984, 18 a5 is more consistent.

c) 16...h5 and now:

c1) 17 c4 0-0-0!? ∞ de las Heras-Spangenberg, Buenos Aires 1995.

c2) 17 ♗b5+ ♗c6 18 ♕f3 ♖c8 19 ♗xc6+ ♕xc6 20 ♕f6 ♖h7 21 ♗g5 ♕d5 = H. de Greef-Hajkova Maskova, Manila OL 1992.

c3) 17 a4!? ± could be tried, waiting to Black to castle somewhere.

d) 16...0-0!? *(D)*:

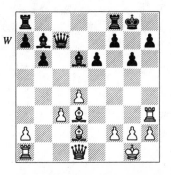

d1) 17 ♗h6 ♖fe8 18 ♕g4 e5 19 ♕h4 ♗e7 20 ♗g5 ♗xg5 21 ♕xg5 ♕xc3 22 ♖c1 ♕xd4 23 ♕h6 e4 24 ♕xh7+ ♔f8 25 ♖c7 ♗d5 26 ♗b5 ♕a1+ 27 ♗f1 ♕g7 = Grosar-Striković, Geneva 1991.

d2) 17 c4 ♖fe8 18 ♕g4 f5 19 ♕h4 ♕g7 20 ♗h6 ♕f7 21 ♖d1 ♖ac8 and White's hanging pawns are under pressure, as in Greger-P.Cramling, Valby 1991.

d3) The modest 17 ♕e2 ♕c6!? 18 f3 ♕c7 19 ♖e1 ♖ac8 20 ♕e3 ♖fe8 21 ♕h6 f5 left White's pieces uncoordinated in Zila-Medvegy, Hajduboszormeny 1995.

d4) 17 ♕g4 f5 18 ♕e2 (this makes sense now Black has weakened ...e6; 18 ♕h4 ♖f7 19 ♖c1 ♕c6 20 f3 b5 21 ♗g5 ♖e8 22 ♗f6 ♗e7 23 ♗xe7 ♖fxe7 24 ♕g5 ♕d5 ∓ Donguines-Kouatly, Manila OL 1992) 18...♖ae8 19 ♗b5 ♗c6. The situation is rather unclear; the black king position is marginally compromised, but his pieces are well-centralised. Sariego-Vera, Linares 1992 continued 20 ♗c4 ♗d5 21 ♗xd5 exd5 22 ♕d3 ♕c4 23 ♕xc4 dxc4 24 ♖e3 ♖xe3 25 fxe3 ♔f7 26 ♖e1 ♖e8 27 ♔f2 ♔e6 28 e4 fxe4 29 ♖xe4+ ♔d7 30 ♖xe8 ♔xe8 31 g3 ½-½; 20 ♖e1!? is a logical attempt to improve.

17 f3

17 ♕f1!? 0-0 18 ♖e1 aims to avoid the discoordinating move f3, when the game Rovid-Zila, Hungary 1995, showed White's dream strategy in this type of position: 18...♕c7 19 ♕e2 ♗f4 (19...♕c6!) 20 c4 ♗xd2 21 ♕xd2 ♖fe8 22 ♕h6 f5 23 ♖he3 (instantly targeting the new weakness on e6) 23...♕d7 24 ♕h4 ♖e7 25 d5 ♖ae8 26 ♕f6 ♗c8 27 h4 ♖f8 28 ♕e5 ♖d8 29 h5 ♕d6 30 hxg6 ♕xe5 31 gxh7+ ♖xh7 32 ♖xe5 exd5 33 ♖e8+ 1-0.

17...0-0 18 ♕e1 ♕d7?

Here the queen proves a target for a later *zwischenzug*; 18...♕c7 was an option. Alternatively 18...♗e7 (to stop ♕h4, but White's queen can still get to the h-file) 19 ♕e3 f5 20 ♗b5 ♕d6 21 ♕h6?! (21 ♖e1!?) 21...♖f7 22 ♗f4 (provoking tactics, but Black's defences are adequate) 22...♕d5 23 ♗a4 ♕a5 24 ♗e5 ♕xa4! 25 ♕xg6+ ♔f8 26 ♕h6+ ♔e8 27 ♕xe6 ♕c6 ∓

and Black defends, Fedorov-Fornari, Aosta 1989.

19 ♕h4 f5 20 ♗b5! ♕f7 21 ♖e1

Suddenly the position has turned nasty for Black. Although in principle his defensive set-up is solid, it is hard to counter the threat of ♖xe6.

21...h5 22 ♕g5 ♕f6 23 ♖xe6! 1-0

23...♕xe6 24 ♗c4! ♕xc4 25 ♕xg6+ is the point.

15 5 cxd4 d6 6 ♘f3 ♘c6

1	e4	c5
2	c3	♘f6
3	e5	♘d5
4	d4	cxd4
5	cxd4	d6
6	♘f3	♘c6 (D)

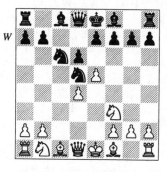

Here we examine possibilities (for both White and Black) to avoid the position reached after 7 ♗c4 ♘b6 (examined in Chapter 16). The first of these deviations is the insipid 7 ♘c3?! (Game 40), which typically leads to the endgame 7...dxe5 8 dxe5 ♘xc3 9 ♕xd8+ ♘xd8 10 bxc3. White's modest lead in development barely compensates for his weakened pawn structure. Furthermore Black could choose 7...♘xc3 8 bxc3 ♕c7 9 ♗d2 ♘d7 10 exd6 ♗xd6 11 ♗d3 b6, which is an excellent version of the ...b6 systems already covered in Chapter 14.

In Game 41 we see an interesting deviation for Black in 7 ♗c4 dxe5!?, when after 8 ♗xd5!? (8 dxe5 is also critical) 8...♕xd5 9 ♘c3 ♕d6 10 d5 ♘d4 11 ♘xd4 exd4 12 ♕xd4 e5 Black has usually come away quite well with his bishop pair. But actually the illustrative game shows there are little-appreciated dangers in the position for the second player, and any route to equality is much narrower than previously thought.

Finally the move 7...e6 is the subject of the remaining two illustrative games. 10 ♘c3!? (Game 43) is the most dynamic continuation, where White gains persistent pressure on the kingside in return for compromising his queenside pawn structure. Black has reasonable defensive resources and can certainly play the position, but – as is always the problem with defending your king – one inaccuracy can lead to severe problems.

Game 40
Razuvaev – Shamkovich
Moscow 1967

1 e4 c5 2 c3 ♘f6 3 e5 ♘d5 4 d4 cxd4 5 cxd4 d6 6 ♘f3 ♘c6 7 ♘c3?!
Minor alternatives:

a) 7 ♗e2 g6 (of course 7...e6 is possible while 7...dxe5 8 ♘xe5 e6 9 0-0 ♗e7 10 ♘xc6 bxc6 11 ♘d2 0-0 12 ♘c4 ♗a6 with equality, was Mukhitdinov-Smyslov, Moscow Cht

1959; alternatively 7...♗f5!? 8 0-0
e6 9 ♘c3 ♘xc3 10 bxc3 d5 = was
Bogdanović-Janošević, Yugoslav Ch
1963) 8 0-0 ♗g7 9 ♕b3 dxe5 10
dxe5 0-0 11 ♖d1 e6 12 ♘c3 ♘xe5 13
♘xd5 exd5 14 ♖xd5 ♘xf3+ 15 ♗xf3
♕c7 = Alburt-Sosonko, USSR Ch
1967 and 7 ♕b3 e6 8 ♗b5 ♗d7 9 ♘c3
♘xc3 (9...dxe5 10 ♘xd5 exd5 11
♗xc6 ♗xc6 12 ♘xe5 ♕b6 13 ♕xb6
axb6 = Minev-Geller, Zagreb 1955)
10 bxc3 dxe5 11 ♗xc6 ♗xc6 12
♘xe5 ♕d5 = Minev-Najdorf, Amsterdam 1954.

b) 7 exd6 is more common:

b1) 7...e6 8 ♘c3 and then:

b11) After 8...♗xd6, 9 ♗d3?! ♘f4
10 ♗xf4 ♗xf4 = was Przewoznik-
Binham, Graz 1981, but for 9 ♗c4
see Game 42, note to White's 8th
move.

b12) 8...♕xd6!? 9 ♗d3 ♗e7 10
0-0 0-0 11 ♕e2 ♘f6 = is an astute
idea, as in Moulton-Browne, USA
1991, which actually transposes to a
satisfactory position from Chapter 9!

b2) 7...♕xd6 8 ♘c3:

b21) Again 8...e6 9 ♗d3 ♗e7 10
0-0 0-0 11 ♕e2 ♘f6 would be a transposition to the 2...d5 lines, Chapter
9.

b22) 8...g6 also offers good play
for Black, e.g. 9 ♕b3 ♘xc3 10 bxc3
♗g7 11 ♗e2 0-0 12 0-0 ♘a5 13 ♕a4
b6 14 ♗a3 ♕c7 ∞ Galego-Rantanen,
Haifa Cht 1989 or 9 ♗e2 ♗g7 10 0-0
0-0 11 ♘b5 ♕d8 12 h3 ♗f5 ∓
Stukalov-Golubev, Yalta 1995.

b23) 8...♗g4 9 ♗e2 e6 10 0-0
♗e7 gives White a choice:

b231) 11 ♕b3 can be answered
by 11...♕b4 12 ♘xd5 ♕xb3 13 axb3

exd5 ∓ Smyslov-Hort, Amsterdam
1994 or 11...0-0 12 ♘xd5 exd5 13
♗e3 = Unzicker-Geller, Gothenburg
IZ 1955.

b232) A further unsuccessful try
was 11 ♘e4 ♕c7 12 h3 ♗h5 13 ♘g3
♗g6 14 ♘e5 ♘xe5 15 dxe5 0-0 16 f4
♘b4 ∓ Eilertsen-Savchenko, Gausdal 1993.

b233) 11 h3 ♗h5 12 ♘b5 (12
♕b3 0-0 13 ♘xd5 exd5 14 ♗e3 f5
15 ♖ac1 f4 with good play for Black,
Teschner-Tal, Riga 1959) 12...♕d8
13 ♘e5 ♗xe2 14 ♕xe2. Now the position would be roughly level after
14...0-0, but in the game Zhuravlev-
Abrosimov, Leipaja 1962 Black continued poorly with 14...♘xe5?! 15
dxe5 a6 16 ♘d4 0-0 17 ♖d1 ♕b6?
allowing 18 ♘f5! ♕c5 19 ♖xd5
exd5 20 ♗h6! with a powerful initiative for White.

7...dxe5

7...e6 gives a position examined
in Chapter 17, while 7...♘c7?! 8
exd6 exd6 9 d5 ♘b8 10 ♕d4! was
bad for Black in Csom-Quinteros,
Siegen OL 1970. Instead 7...♘xc3 8
bxc3 e6 also transposes to Chapter
17, though it should be noted that via
the present position Black also has
the move-order option of 8...♕a5 9
exd6 e6 10 ♗d2 (10 ♕b3 ♗xd6 11
♗e2 0-0 12 0-0 e5 = Mikhalchishin-
Minić, Zagreb 1961) 10...♗xd6 11
♗d3, which cuts out one or two sidelines for White.

However, 7...♘xc3 8 bxc3 dxe5?
is weak on account of 9 d5! e4
(9...♘a5 10 ♗b5+ ♗d7 11 ♕a4 b6
12 ♘xe5 wins outright) 10 ♘g5 ♘e5
11 ♘xe4 g6 (11...♕c7 12 ♕d4 ♗d7

13 ♗a3 ± Chiburdanidze-Andreeva, Tbilisi 1973) 12 d6 f5 13 ♕d5 ♗g7 14 ♗h6! ♗xh6 (14...e6 15 d7+ ± Withuis-Boven, Amsterdam 1957) 15 ♕xe5 ♖f8 16 d7+!! 1-0 Tamburro-Russett, corr. 1988.

8 dxe5 ②xc3

Or:

a) 8...♗e6:

a1) On 9 ♗d2 Black should not play 9...②db4 10 ②b5 ♗f5 11 ♗xb4 ②xb4 12 ②bd4 ♗d7 on account of 13 e6! fxe6 14 ♗c4 ♕a5 15 0-0 ±, as in Redolfi-Saidy, Varna 1958, but should continue 9...②xc3 10 ♗xc3 ♗d5 ∞.

a2) After 9 ②g5 Tal gives the line 9...②xc3 10 ♕xd8+ ♖xd8 11 bxc3 ♗f5 12 e6 fxe6 13 ♗c4 ♖d5 with sufficient compensation for the exchange.

a3) 9 ②d4 ②xd4 (9...②xc3!? 10 bxc3 ♗d5 e6 is unclear – Sveshnikov) 10 ♕xd4 ②xc3 11 ♕xc3 ± Sveshnikov-Tal, USSR Ch 1979.

b) 8...②db4 9 a3 ♕xd1+ 10 ♔xd1 ②a6 11 b4 ②c7 (or 11...♗g4 12 b5 0-0-0+ 13 ♗d2 ②xe5 14 bxa6 ②xf3 15 gxf3 ♗xf3+ 16 ♔c2 ♗xh1 17 ♗h3+ e6 18 ♖xh1 ± Kiik-Rõtsagov, USSR 1990) and the position is unclear according to Sveshnikov. Two examples:

b1) 12 h3?! ♗e6 13 ♗d3 g6 14 ♗b2 ♗g7 15 ②e4 ♗d5 ∓ Menvielle-Gheorghiu, Las Palmas 1972.

b2) 12 ②b5 ②xb5 13 ♗xb5 ♗d7 14 ♗c4 (14 ♖e1!? 0-0-0 15 ♗d2 intending 15...♗g4 16 ♖c1) 14...0-0-0 15 ♔e2 ♗g4 16 ♗b2 Babiarz-C.P.Mokrys, corr. 1988.

9 ♕xd8+ ②xd8

After 9...♔xd8 10 bxc3 Black's king is a little uncomfortable in the centre: 10...h6 (against the alternative 10...♗g4, 11 e6 is recommended, though 11...♗xe6 12 ②g5 g6 13 ②xe6+ fxe6 14 ♗c4 ♗g7 15 ♗d2 ♔c7 16 ♗xe6 ♖ad8 17 0-0-0 ♖hf8 18 f4 b5 was reasonable for Black in Torre-Jun, Shenzhen 1992) with the possibilities:

a) 11 ♗e3!? ♗g4 12 ♖b1 ♔c8 13 ②d4! led to sharp play in the game Sveshnikov-Ruban, Kemerovo 1995: 13...②xe5 14 f4 ②d7 15 h3 ♗h5 16 g4 e5 17 gxh5 exd4 18 ♗xd4 ♔c7 19 ♗c4 ±.

b) Another idea is 11 ♗f4 e6 12 ②d2 g5 13 ♗g3 ♗g7 14 ②c4 ♔e7 15 0-0-0 ± Milner-Barry – Benko, Moscow 1956.

c) 11 ♗b5 e6 12 ♗e3 ♗d7 13 0-0 (13 a4! b6? 14 a5! bxa5 15 0-0 ♔c7 16 ♖fd1 ± Csom-Hennings, Berlin 1968) 13...♔c7 14 a4 ♗e7 15 ♖fd1 ♖hd8 16 a5 ♗e8 17 ♖db1 g5 18 h3 ♗f8 19 h4!? gxh4 20 ♖a4! h3 21 ♖c4 ♖d5 22 ②d4 a6 23 ②xc6! axb5! 24 ♗b6+ ♔d7 25 ②b8+! ♖xb8 26 ♖c7+ ♔d8 27 ♖xf7+ ♔c8 28 ♖xf8 ± Csom-Matulović, Athens 1969.

10 bxc3 *(D)*

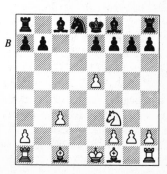

10...♗d7

White's only justification for liquidating to this endgame lies in a slight edge in development. However practice has proven that, with sensible play, Black can easily neutralise any initiative, whereupon the weak white c3-pawn invariably becomes a subsequent target. Along with the natural 10...♗d7 Black has other possibilities:

a) 10...a6?! 11 ♗e3 ♘c6 12 ♗c4 ♗f5 13 e6 fxe6 14 ♘d4 ♘d8 15 0-0 g6 16 ♘xf5 gxf5 17 ♗d4 ♖g8 18 ♖fe1 ♖g6 19 ♗e2 ♘f7 20 ♗f3 e5 21 ♗xe5 ♘xe5 22 ♖xe5 ♖b6 23 ♖xf5 ± Csom-Gerusel, Amsterdam 1969 – an example of how White hopes to exploit his better development in this line.

b) 10...e6 11 ♘d4 ♗c5 12 ♘b3 ♗e7 13 ♗b5+ ♗d7 14 a4 ♘c6 15 f4 a6 16 ♗e2 f6 17 exf6 ♗xf6 18 ♗d2 ♗e7 19 ♗e3 0-0-0 20 0-0 e5 21 f5 ♖df8 22 ♗d3 ± Bronstein-Lerner, Odessa 1976.

c) 10...♘c6!?:

c1) 11 ♗f4 e6 and then 12 ♘d4 ♘xd4 13 cxd4 ♗d7 14 ♖b1 0-0-0 ∓ Leban-Krogius, Sarajevo 1968 or 12 ♗d3 ♗e7 13 ♖b1 ♖b8 14 0-0 ♗d7 15 ♖fd1 h6 16 ♘d4 ♘xd4 17 cxd4 ♗c6 18 ♗b5 ♔d7 ∓ Sarapu-Krogius, Wildbad 1993.

c2) 11 ♖b1 e6 12 ♗e3 b6 13 ♗b5 ♗d7 14 0-0 ♗e7 15 ♖fd1 ♖c8 16 a4 ♘b8 17 a5 ♗xb5 18 ♖xb5 ½-½ Radovici-Krogius, Polanica Zdroj 1969.

d) 10...g6!? (similar to the game line) 11 ♘d4 (after 11 ♗f4, 11...♗g7 12 ♗b5+ ♗d7 13 ♗xd7+ ♔xd7 14 0-0-0+ ♔e8 15 ♘d4 ♖c8 16 ♔b2

♘c6 17 ♖he1 ♘xd4 18 cxd4 ♔d7 19 d5 ♖c4 ∞ was Nyström-Ernst, Stockholm 1994, but 11...♘e6 or 11...♗d7 seems simpler) 11...♗g7 12 f4 ♗d7 13 ♗a3 ♖c8 14 ♔d2 g5 15 fxg5 ♗xe5 ∓ Hresc-Ljubojević, Yugoslav Ch 1982.

11 ♘d4

11 ♗d3 ♖c8 12 ♗d2 g6 13 0-0 ♗g7 14 ♖fe1 0-0 15 ♘d4 ♘e6 16 f4 ♖fd8 17 ♗f1 f6! ∓ O'Donnell-Kožul, Toronto 1990.

11 ♗e3 g6! is again an excellent plan for Black:

a) 12 0-0-0 ♗g7 13 ♗c4 ♖c8 14 ♗d5 ♖xc3+ 15 ♔b2 ♖c8 16 ♗xa7 ♘c6 17 ♗b6 ♗g4 with a good game for Black, Afek-Grünfeld, Tel Aviv 1992.

b) 12 h4 h6 13 ♗e2 ♗g7 14 0-0 ♘c6 with a slight advantage for Black, Pomar-Polugaevsky, Palma de Mallorca 1972.

c) 12 ♗e2 ♗g7 13 0-0 0-0-0 14 ♖fe1 ♖c6 15 ♗c5 ♖e8 16 a4 ♘e6 17 ♗d4 ♖ed8 ∓ Redolfi-Taimanov, Cordoba 1960.

d) 12 ♖b1 ♗g7 13 ♗b5 ♗xb5 14 ♖xb5 was Sveshnikov-Gutman, Hastings 1984, and here Gutman gives 14...♖c8 15 ♔d2 b6 ∓.

11...♖c8 12 ♗e3 a6

On 12...♖xc3 comes 13 ♘b5, but again 12...g6 (or even 12...g5!?) looks promising.

13 ♔d2 e6 14 f4 ♗c5 15 ♗d3 0-0 16 ♖ab1 ♖c7 17 c4 f6 = 18 exf6 gxf6 19 ♖he1 ♗e8 20 g4 ♖d7 21 ♔c3 ♖c7 22 ♔d2 ♗f7 (22...♗d7) 23 f5 e5 24 ♘c2 ♗xe3+ 25 ♘xe3 ♘c6 26 ♘d5 ♗xd5 27 cxd5 ♘d4 28 ♖ec1 ♖d7 29 ♖b6 ♔g7 30 ♔e3 h5? 31

gxh5 ♔h6 32 ♖g1! ♔xh5 33 ♖g6 (now Black's king is in great danger, trapped on the h-file) 33...♖df7 34 ♔e4 ♔h4 35 a4 a5 36 ♖b1 ♖h8 37 ♖bg1 ♘b3 38 ♖6g4+ ♔h3 39 ♗f1+ 1-0

Game 41
K.Regan – Grünfeld
USA 1979

1 e4 c5 2 c3 ♘f6 3 e5 ♘d5 4 d4 cxd4 5 ♘f3 d6 6 cxd4 ♘c6 7 ♗c4 dxe5 *(D)*

For 7...♘b6 see Chapter 16, and for 7...e6 see the next two games. 7...dxe5 has been played less often than either of these alternatives. In fact in practice Black has scored quite well with it, but whether he can equalise may depend on a judicious offer to exchange queens on move 14.

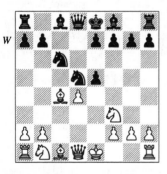

8 ♗xd5!?

Instead 8 ♘xe5 permits comfortable equality after the reply 8...e6, for example 9 0-0 ♗e7 10 ♖e1 0-0 11 ♘c3 ♘xc3 12 bxc3 ♘xe5 13 ♖xe5 ♗f6 14 ♖e3 ♗d7 15 ♗d3 g6 Walter-Donchev, Oberwart 1992.

However 8 dxe5 is far more complex:

a) 8...e6?! 9 0-0 ♘b6 (9...♗e7 10 ♕e2 0-0 11 ♖d1 ♕c7 12 ♗xd5 exd5 13 ♘c3 ♗g4 14 ♘xd5 ♗xf3 15 gxf3 ± Harabor-Vestergaard, corr. 1992) 10 ♕xd8+ (alternatively 10 ♗d3!? ♘b4 11 ♗e4 ♕xd1 12 ♖xd1 f5 13 exf6 gxf6 14 ♘c3 f5 15 ♗b1 ♘4d5 16 ♘xd5 ♘xd5 17 ♗xf5 exf5 18 ♖xd5 ± Blatny-Fernandez, Debrecen Echt 1992) 10...♘xd8 11 ♗b3 ♗d7 12 ♘c3 ♗c6 13 ♘d4 ♗b4 14 ♘cb5 0-0 15 ♗e3 ♘d7 16 ♘c7 ♖c8 17 ♘xc6 ♘xc6 18 ♘xe6 fxe6 19 ♗xe6+ ♖f7 20 ♖fd1! ♖c7 21 f4 ± Csom-Wedberg, Dortmund 1983.

b) 8...♘bd4 (the jury is still out on this one) 9 0-0 ♕xd1 10 ♖xd1 ♗g4!? (if 10...♘c2, 11 ♘c3 ♘xa1 12 ♘b5 with unpleasant threats, such as mate in one) 11 e6 fxe6 12 ♘c3 g6 13 ♘b5 ♖c8 14 ♗f4 ♗xf3 15 gxf3 ♘d5 16 ♖xd5 (16 ♗xd5 exd5 17 ♖xd5 ♗g7 18 ♘c7+ ♔f7 ∓ Möhring-Banas, Stary Smokovec 1979) 16...exd5 17 ♗xd5 e5 18 ♗e6 ♖b8 19 ♗g5 ♗e7 20 ♗e3. Here 20...♗f6 21 ♗c5 ♗e7 22 ♗e3 ♗f6 23 ♗c5 ♗e7 24 ♗e3 was a draw by repetition in the old game Sveshnikov-Hartston, Sochi 1979. However, in Jakubiec-Pokorny, Lazne Bohdanec 1996, 20...h6!? was played, and White could not justify his exchange sacrifice: 21 f4 exf4 22 ♗xf4 ♖d8 23 ♘c7+ ♔f8 24 ♗c4 ♖d7 25 ♘e6+ ♔e8 26 ♖e1 ♖h7 27 b3 ♘d4 ∓.

c) 8...♘b6!? (recently revived!) 9 ♕xd8+ ♘xd8:

c1) 10 ♗b5+ ♗d7 11 ♘c3 and now 11...a6 12 ♗xd7+ ♘xd7 13 0-0

e6 14 ♖d1 ᐱc6 15 ♗f4 h6 16 h4 ♗e7 17 ᐱe4 ½-½ Scetinin-Faibisovich, Pula 1990 or 11...e6 12 0-0 a6 13 ♗e3 ♗xb5 14 ᐱxb5 ᐱd5 15 ᐱbd4 h6 16 ♖ac1 g5 ∓ Eichhorn-Sveshnikov, Finkenstein 1994.

c2) 10 ♗b3!? (the most critical) 10...♗e6 (for 10...0-0 see 8...e6 below) 11 ♗e3 ᐱc4 12 ♗xc4 ♗xc4 13 ᐱa3 ♗a6 14 ᐱd4 ♖c8 15 ᐱdb5 ᐱc6 16 e6 fxe6 17 ᐱxa7 ᐱxa7 18 ♗xa7 g5 19 ♗d4 ♖g8 and Black's bishop pair compensated for his damaged pawn structure in Godena-Enders, Budapest 1995.

8...♕xd5 9 ᐱc3 ♕d6

The best square for the queen: 9...♕c4? 10 d5 ᐱb8 11 ᐱxe5 ± was Kaidanov-Kalinichev, USSR 1975 and similarly 9...♕a5 10 d5 ᐱb4 11 ᐱxe5 e6 12 0-0 ♗e7 13 d6 ♕xe5 14 dxe7 ᐱc6 15 ♖e1 ♕f6 16 ᐱe4 ♕xe7 17 ♗g5 gave White an enormous attack in Groszpeter-Barczay, Hungary 1978.

10 d5 ᐱd4 11 ᐱxd4 exd4 12 ♕xd4 e5 13 ♕d3

13 ♕e4 merely encourages Black: 13...♗e7 14 0-0 f5! 15 ♕e2 0-0 16 ᐱb5 ♕f6 17 f4 ♗d7! 18 a4 a6 19 ᐱa3 (19 fxe5? ♕b6+ 20 ♗e3 ♗c5) 19...♖fe8 20 ♕c4 ♗d6 ∓ Chikovani-G.Zaichik, USSR 1978.

13...♗d7 14 0-0

Or 14 ᐱe4 ♕g6!? (14...♕b4+ 15 ♗d2 ♗b5!? 16 ♗xb4 ♗xd3 17 ♗xf8 ∞ Negele-Olsson, corr. 1992) 15 0-0 f5 16 ᐱg3 ♗d6 ∓ Kuhnert-Vefling, corr. 1982.

14...f5

Double-edged and probably bad. 14...♕g6!? 15 ♕xg6!? (15 ♕e2 ♗d6

16 f4 0-0 17 fxe5 ♖fe8 18 ♗f4 ♗xe5! 19 ♗xe5 f6 = Cuartas-Sigurjonsson, Bogota 1978) 15...hxg6 16 f4 ♗c5+ 17 ♔h1 exf4 18 ♗xf4 ♗f5? (to free d7 for the king, but the idea does not work out; 18...0-0 looks a sensible bid for equality) 19 ᐱa4! b6 20 ᐱxc5 bxc5 21 ♖ac1 ♖c8 22 ♗e3 left Black was struggling to avoid permanent material loss in Kwiatkowski-Ward, British Ch 1988.

15 ♖e1

15 ᐱb5 was another Kwiatkowski-Ward encounter, this one from Lloyds Bank 1994: 15...♗xb5 16 ♕xb5+ ♕d7 17 ♕e2 ♗d6 18 ♗f4 0-0 19 ♗xe5 ♖ae8 20 f4 ♗xe5 21 fxe5 ♕xd5 22 ♖fe1 ♖e6 and the white pawn on e5 is a weakness.

15...♔f7 16 a4!?

Only this plan sets Black problems. After the passive 16 ♗d2 Black has an edge: 16...e4 17 ♕g3 ♕xg3 18 hxg3 ♖c8 ∓ Groszpeter-Szekely, Hungary 1978. If Black is given time to develop, then his two bishops almost certainly give him the initiative.

16...a6 17 b3! e4 18 ♕h3 ♖c8 19 ♗a3 *(D)*

Harassing the queen is stronger than 19 ♗b2 ♗e7 ∞ Rahls-Szekely, Berlin 1988.

The whole situation after 19 ♗a3 is very problematic for Black, since White has irritating tactical threats based on ᐱxe4. For example 19...♕h6 20 ᐱxe4! ♕xh3 (as 20...dxe4 21 ♕xd7+) 21 ᐱg5+ and 22 ᐱxh3. In the game White pursues the overcentralised black king with convincing determination.

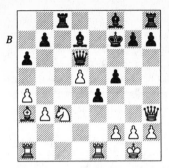

B

the bishop to d3, when Black will be forced to compromise his dark squares with the defensive ...g6.

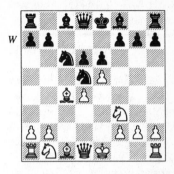

W

8 0-0

8 exd6 seems gratuitously early, but playable. For example 8...♗xd6 (for 8...♕xd6!? see the note to 9 ♕e2 in the illustrative game) 9 0-0 0-0 10 ♘c3 ♘xc3 (10...♘f6 11 ♗g5 ♗e7 as in Malevinsky-Yudasin, Kostroma 1985, has transposed to a reasonable IQP position for White that can also arise from many other openings including the Caro-Kann and Nimzo-Indian) 11 bxc3 ♕c7 12 ♗d3 (12 ♕d3!? is interesting) 12...e5 13 ♘g5 g6 14 ♘e4 exd4 15 ♘xd6 ♕xd6 16 cxd4 ♕xd4 17 ♗e3 ♕d6 18 ♗e4 ½-½ Bernard-Nun, Warsaw 1978.

An alternative move-order to the game is 8 ♕e2 when 8...♗e7 9 0-0 transposes. Instead 8...dxe5?! 9 dxe5 ♗b4+ 10 ♗d2 (10 ♘bd2!? ♘a5 11 ♗b5+ ♗d7 12 0-0 ♗xb5 13 ♕xb5+ ♕d7 14 ♕e2 ♖c8 15 ♘e4 0-0 16 ♘fg5 h6 17 ♕h5 with attacking chances for White, Gliksman-Bogdanović, Sarajevo 1976) 10...♗xd2+ 11 ♘bxd2 ♘a5 12 0-0 (12 ♗xd5!? is interesting, e.g. 12...exd5 13 ♘d4 ±

19...♕c7 20 ♗b2! (if 20 ♗xf8, 20...♕xc3!) **20...♗c5 21 d6! ♕d8** (21...♕xd6 22 ♖ad1 is very strong, but now White smashes through with a dashing e4 sacrifice anyway) **22 ♘xe4 fxe4 23 ♕h5+ g6** (23...♔f8 24 ♖xe4 ♗xd6 25 ♖e3 ♗c6 26 ♕f5+ ♔g8 27 ♕e6+ ♔f8 28 ♖d1 +−) **24 ♕d5+ ♗e6 25 ♕xe4 ♕xd6 26 ♖ad1 ♗xf2+** (26...♕c6 27 ♕e5) **27 ♔h1 ♕e7 28 ♕f4+ ♔e8 29 ♕xf2** (now material is level but stuck in the centre Black's king is obviously doomed) **29...♖f8 30 ♕g3 ♖c6 31 ♗a3 ♕xa3 32 ♕b8+ ♔f7 33 ♕xb7+ ♔g8 34 ♕xc6 ♗xb3 35 ♖a1 ♕b4 36 ♕xa6 ♗d5 37 ♕e2 ♖f4 38 ♖ab1 1-0**

Game 42
Berelovich – Obukhov
Sochi 1993

1 e4 c5 2 c3 ♘f6 3 e5 ♘d5 4 d4 cxd4 5 ♘f3 ♘c6 6 ♗c4 e6 7 cxd4 d6 *(D)*

Black maintains his knight in the centre, at the cost of shutting in his queen's bishop. The white strategy, after developing, involves a straightforward kingside assault, spearheaded by the pawn on e5. A typical manoeuvre is ♕e2-e4, followed by retreating

G.Schmid-Wachinger, Bavarian Ch 1986 or 12...♕xd5 13 0-0 0-0 14 ♘e4) 12...♘xc4 13 ♘xc4 0-0 14 ♘d6 ♕b6 15 ♖ad1 ♗d7 16 ♖d4 f5! = Enklaar-Najdorf, Wijk aan Zee 1973.

8...♗e7

8...♘c7!? 9 ♕e2 b6 10 ♘c3 d5 11 ♗d3 ♘b4 12 ♗g5 ♕d7 13 ♘b5 (better than 13 ♖fc1 ♘xd3 14 ♕xd3 h6 15 ♗h4 ♗a6 Novak-Cvetković, Stary Smokovec 1977) 13...♘xd3 14 ♘xc7+ ♕xc7 15 ♕xd3 ♕c4 16 ♕e3 h6 17 ♗h4 g5 18 ♗g3 ♗e7 19 h4? (19 ♖fc1 ±) 19...♗a6 20 ♖fd1 ♕e2 ∓ Preissmann-Ungureanu, Satu Mare 1979.

Also 8...dxe5 9 dxe5 ♗c5?! (for 9...♘b6 see Game 41, note to 8 ♗xd5) 10 ♕e2 ± a6?! 11 ♘bd2 ♘f4 12 ♕e4 ♘g6 13 b3 ♕c7 14 ♗b2 b5 15 ♖ac1! ♗b7 16 ♗xe6! ♘ce7 17 ♖xc5 ♕xc5 18 ♕xb7 +− Chekhov-Groszpeter, Tjentište 1975.

9 ♕e2

Or:

a) 9 ♘c3 ♘xc3 10 bxc3 dxe5 11 ♘xe5 ♘xe5 12 dxe5 ♕xd1 13 ♖xd1 ♗d7 is nothing for White, Müller-Möhring, Halle 1974.

b) 9 ♘bd2 dxe5 (9...0-0 10 ♘e4 ♘b6 11 ♗d3 dxe5 12 dxe5 ♘b4 13 ♗b1 ♕xd1 14 ♖xd1 ♗d7 = Gurgenidze-Petrosian, Gagra 1953) 10 dxe5 ♘b6 11 ♗b3 ♘d4 12 ♘xd4 ♕xd4 13 ♕e2 ♗d7 14 ♖d1 ♗c6 15 ♘c4 ♕e4 = Antoshin-Averbakh, Leningrad 1956.

c) 9 exd6!? is possible, when 9...♕xd6 10 ♘c3 0-0 gives an isolated queen pawn position that looks typical, but in fact this exact position does not arise from other openings:

c1) 11 ♖e1 ♘xc3 (11...♖d8 12 ♗b3!? ∞ Rausis-Lechtynsky, Osterskars 1995) 12 bxc3 b6 with two illustrative examples:

c11) 13 ♗d3 ♗b7 14 ♕e2 ♖ac8 15 ♗d2 ♖fe8 16 h4 ♕d5 17 ♗e4 ♕h5 ∞ Schandorff-Rausis, Copenhagen 1995.

c12) 13 h4 ♗b7 14 ♘g5 ♗xg5 15 ♗xg5 ♖fc8 16 ♗d3 ♘e7 17 ♖c1 h6 18 ♗d2 ♘d5 19 ♖e4 ♘f6 20 ♖e3 ♖d8 21 ♖g3 ♔f8 22 ♗e3 ± Dorfman-G.Zaichik, Beltsy 1979.

c2) 11 ♕e2!? transposes to the game Browne-Hort, Venice 1971 (a game which started life from the 'chase' variation of Alekhine's Defence): 11...♘xc3 12 bxc3 b6 13 ♗d3 ♗b7 14 ♕e4 and we are back in lines examined briefly in Game 43, albeit a slightly favourable version for White. Food for thought.

d) 9 a3:

d1) 9...b6!? 10 ♖e1 (10 ♕e2 ♗b7 11 ♖d1 a5!? 12 ♗xd5 exd5 13 ♘c3 ♗a6 14 ♕e1?! ♗c4 15 ♘d2 ♗d3 16 ♘f3 ♗c2 17 ♖d2 ♗b3 18 ♘e2 0-0 ∓ Herbert-Miles, Buenos Aires OL 1978) 10...dxe5 11 dxe5 (11 ♘xe5 ♘xe5 12 ♖xe5 ♗b7 13 ♘c3 ♗f6 14 ♗b5+ ♔f8 ∓ Angelov-Ničevski, Bulgaria 1975) 11...♗b7 12 ♗d2!? 0-0 13 ♗d3 ♖c8 14 ♕e2 ♘a5 ∞ Angelov-Cvetković, Bulgaria 1975.

d2) Interestingly 9...0-0 10 ♗d3 leaves White a tempo down on a position from Chapter 13. But in that chapter Black avoids that dubious line anyway, and here White still retains attacking chances: 10...♗d7 11 ♕e2 dxe5 12 dxe5 ♕c7 13 ♗d2 ♖fd8 14 h4 ♗e8 15 ♘c3 ♘xc3 16 ♗xc3

♖d7 17 ♖ad1 ♖ad8 18 h5 ± Kurajica-Robatsch, Tuzla 1981 or 10...dxe5 11 dxe5 ♕c7 12 ♕e2 b6 13 ♗d2 ♗b7 14 ♘c3 ♘xc3 15 ♗xc3 ♖ac8 16 ♖ac1 g6 17 h4 ♖fd8 18 h5 ± Cripe-Browne, Reno 1994.

9...0-0

a) 9...♕c7 10 ♗xd5 (10 ♕e4 dxe5 11 dxe5 ♗d7 12 ♗d2 0-0 13 ♗xd5 exd5 14 ♖xd5 ♗f5 15 ♕c4 ♖ad8 16 ♖e1 is slightly better for White, Sermek-Kožul, Portorož 1993) 10...exd5 11 ♘c3 ♗e6 12 ♘b5 (12 ♗f4 dxe5 13 ♘xe5 ♕b6 14 ♘xc6 bxc6 15 ♖fd1 0-0 16 ♖ac1 ♖fe8 17 ♘a4 ♕a5 18 b3 ♗a3 19 ♖c3 ♗d7 = Sermek-Kožul, Ljubljana 1993) 12...♕d7 13 ♗g5 dxe5 14 ♗xe7 ♕xe7 15 dxe5 0-0 16 ♖ad1 ♖fd8 17 h3 ♗f5 18 ♘fd4 ♗g6 19 f4 f6 20 f5 ♗f7 21 e6 ± Godena-Kožul, Reggio Emilia 1993.

b) 9...b6?! 10 ♘c3 (10 ♕e4 ♗b7 11 ♕g4 ♕d7!? 12 ♕xg7 0-0-0 gave Black a dangerous attack in the game Yagupov-Vulfson, Moscow 1989) 10...♘xc3 11 bxc3 ♗b7 12 d5 exd5 13 ♗xd5 0-0 14 ♕e4 ♖c8 (14...♕c7 15 exd6 ♕xd6, Vi.Ivanov-Umansky, Russia 1995, is a puzzling reference annotated in *Informator* 64; the unmentioned 16 ♘d4 +− wins out of hand) 15 ♘d4 ♕c7 16 ♘b5 ♕b8 17 ♗a3 ± Zakharov-Korneev, Moscow 1995.

c) 9...♘b6 (? – Dolmatov, but not so clear) 10 ♗b3 d5 11 ♘c3 ♗d7 (11...a5!? 12 a3 ♗d7 13 ♗c2 a4 14 ♗e3 ♘a5 15 ♘d2 ♘ac4 16 ♘xc4 ♘xc4 17 ♗d3 ♖c8 18 f4 ♕b6 Striković-Velikov, Kavala 1990) 12 ♗f4 (another plan is 12 ♕e3, e.g. 12...a5 13 ♕f4 a4 14 ♗d1 ♘a5 15 ♕g3 ±

Gliksman-Möhring, Stary Smokovec 1976 or 12 ♕e3 ♖c8 13 ♕f4 0-0 14 ♕g3 f5 15 ♗h6 ± Bergström-Kotronias, Gausdal 1993) 12...a6 13 ♖ac1 ♖c8 14 ♖fd1 ♘a5?! 15 ♗c2 g5?! 16 ♗e3 ± Dolmatov-Milov, Haifa 1995.

10 ♕e4 (D)

For the more critical 10 ♘c3 see the next illustrative game. White's idea (with 10 ♕e4) is to force a weakening of the black king position by playing ♗d3, not to capture twice on d5. Pawn grabbing would not compensate for the loss of the valuable light-squared bishop.

10 ♖d1 has been played a few times, but serves no real purpose at present.

Or 10 a3 ♕b6 (10...dxe5?! 11 dxe5 ♕c7 12 ♕e4 ♗d7 was followed by 13 ♗g5?! ♘xe5! 14 ♕xe5 ♕xc4 15 ♗xe7 ♘xe7 16 ♕d6 ♘g6! 17 ♕xd7 ♖fd8 18 ♕xb7 ♖db8 ½-½ in Chandler-Leontxo Garcia, Alicante 1979 but 13 ♗d3 would have been strong) 11 ♖d1 (11 ♕e4 ♘a5 and White has nothing after 12 ♗d3 f5 13 exf6 ♘xf6 14 ♕h4 ♘b3 15 ♖a2 ♘xc1 16 ♖xc1 h6 Grigorian-Sveshnikov, Moscow 1983 or 12 ♘bd2 ♘xc4 13 ♘xc4 ♕c7 Marjanović-Simić, Cetinje 1993) 11...♘a5 = Sveshnikov-Timoshchenko, USSR 1974.

10...b6?!

This is a mistake as it actively assists White's plan: now 11 ♗d3 cannot be met by 11...f5, due to 12 exf6 ♘xf6 13 ♕xc6. Therefore (along with 10...♘db4!? 11 exd6 ♕xd6 12 ♘c3 ♘a5!?) several 'waiting' moves could be seriously considered:

a) 10...♔h8 11 ♗d3 (11 a3!? ±) 11...f5 12 exf6 ᐂxf6 13 ♕e2 ♕b6 14 ♗e3 ᐂd5 15 ᐂc3 ᐂxc3 16 bxc3 ♗d7 = Chekhov-Dorfman, USSR 1975.

b) 10...♕b6 11 exd6 ♗xd6 12 ᐂc3 ᐂf6 13 ♕h4 ᐂe7 14 ᐂe4 ᐂxe4 15 ♕xe4 ♗d7 16 ♗d3 ᐂf5 17 d5 exd5 18 ♕xd5 ½-½ Ostojić-Vaulin, Belgrade 1993.

c) 10...♖e8 11 ♖e1 dxe5 12 dxe5 ᐂa5 13 ♗d3 g6 14 ♗h6 ♗d7 15 ᐂbd2 ♗c6 16 ♕g4 ᐂb4 17 ♗e4 ᐂd3 18 ♗xd3 ♕xd3 = Smagin-Kalegin, St Petersburg 1993.

d) 10...♗d7 11 a3 (11 ♗d3!? f5 12 exf6 ᐂxf6 13 ♕e2 ᐂd5 14 ᐂc3 ᐂcb4 15 ♗e4 ∞ Sermek-Kersten, Biel 1994) 11...ᐂa5 12 ♗d3 f5 13 exf6 ᐂxf6 14 ♕e2 (14 ♕e3 ᐂd5 15 ♕e2 ᐂb3 16 ♗xh7+ ♔h8 17 ♗g6 initiated crazy complications which favoured Black in Efimov-Azmaiparashvili, USSR 1979) 14...ᐂb3 ∓ Chekhov-Cvetković, USSR v Yugoslavia 1976.

e) 10...dxe5 11 dxe5 b6 12 ♗d3 g6 13 ♗h6 ♖e8 14 ᐂbd2 ᐂdb4 15 ♗c4 ♗b7 16 ♕f4 ᐂd3!? 17 ♗xd3 ♕xd3 18 ♗g5 ᐂd4 19 ᐂxd4 ♗xg5 20 ♕xg5 ♕xd4 21 ♖fe1 ∞ Cherniaev-Neverov, St Petersburg 1995.

f) 10...♕c7 11 ♗d3 (11 ♗g5? dxe5 12 ♗xe7 ᐂdxe7 13 dxe5 ᐂg6 14 ♖e1 ᐂcxe5! 15 ᐂxe5 ᐂxe5 16 ♕xe5 ♕xc4 ∓ Yanovsky-Kožul, Belgrade 1988) 11...g6 (after 11...f5 12 exf6 ᐂxf6 13 ♕e2 White will gain time when ᐂc3 comes) 12 ♗h6 ♖d8 13 ᐂbd2 dxe5 14 dxe5 ᐂb6 (in several games Black has gone passive with 14...♗d7 15 a3 ♗e8) 15 ♖fe1 (after 15 ♖ac1 ᐂd7 16 ♗b5 Black neatly tricked his way to equality in Striković-Kožul, Pula 1990: 16...ᐂdxe5 17 ᐂxe5 ♕xe5 18 ♗xc6 ♕h5! 19 ♗xb7 ♖xb7 20 ♕xb7 ♗d6 21 g3 ♕xh6 22 ᐂc4 ♕f8 23 ♖fd1 ½-½) 15...ᐂd7 16 ♗f1 ᐂc5 17 ♕f4 ± Sermek-Dimitrov, Velden 1993.

11 ♗d3

Now Black has to weaken his dark squares, which White must then seek to exploit – typically with moves like ♕f4 and ♗g5 if given time. Instead on 11 ♗xd5 exd5 12 ♕xd5 Black has excellent compensation for the pawn after either 12...♗b7 or 12...♗a6. A plausible alternative is 11 h4 ♗b7 12 ♕g4 ♔h8 13 ♗xd5 (13 ♗g5 ♗xg5 14 ᐂxg5! h6 15 ᐂf3 ± Sveshnikov) 13...exd5 14 ᐂc3 dxe5 15 dxe5 f6 (15...d4! =) 16 exf6 ♗xf6 17 ♗g5 ± Sveshnikov-Gufeld, Sochi 1979.

11...g6 12 ♗h6 ♖e8 13 ᐂc3

13 ᐂbd2 allowed Black to equalise with 13...ᐂdb4 14 ♗b1 ♗a6 15 ♖d1 dxe5 16 dxe5 ♕d5 = in Dvoretsky-Taimanov, Vilnius 1975.

White still has chances of an edge with 13 a3 ♗b7 14 ᐂbd2 ♖c8 15 ♖ad1 (15 ♖ac1 ♖c7 16 ♖fe1 dxe5 17 dxe5 ᐂb8 18 ♖xc7 ♕xc7 19 ♕g4 ᐂd7 20 h4 ᐂc5 21 ♗b1 ♗a6 22 h5

♗d3 ∓ Sermek-Kožul, Portorož 1996)
15...♘a5 16 ♕g4 dxe5 17 ♘xe5 ♘f6
18 ♕f4 ♘c6 19 ♘df3 ± Platonov-
Agzamov, USSR 1977.
   13...♘cb4 14 ♗e2
   Or 14 ♗b5 ♗d7 15 ♗xd7 ♕xd7
16 ♗g5!? (16 a3 ♘xc3 17 bxc3 ♘c6
18 ♖fe1 dxe5 19 dxe5 ♖ad8 ∓ Stri-
punsky-Mitenkov, Moscow 1991)
16...dxe5 17 dxe5 ♘xc3 18 bxc3
♘d5 19 c4 ♘b4 20 ♕h4 ♖ac8 21
♖ad1 ♕c7 22 ♖d4 ± Sanz-Martin,
Alicante 1978.
   14...♗b7 15 ♘xd5 ♗xd5
   If 15...♘xd5 White has 16 ♗b5
♘c3 17 ♕xb7 ♘xb5 18 ♖ac1 ±
Berelovich.
   **16 ♕f4 ♗xf3 17 ♗xf3 d5?! 18
♗e2! ± a6 19 ♖fc1 ♕d7 20 a3 ♘c6
21 ♖c3 ♖ec8 22 ♖h3 ♖c7 23 ♗d3
♕d8 24 ♖e1 b5 25 ♖ee3** (White's
pieces are all massed for the final
kingside assault) **25...♖ac8 26 ♖ef3
♗f8 27 g4!** (avoiding any back-rank
mate tricks, such as 27 ♗g5? ♘xd4!)
**27...♘b8 28 ♗g5 ♕e8 29 ♗f6 ♘d7
30 ♖xh7 ♔xh7** (or 30...♘xf6 31
♕xf6 ♔xh7 32 ♖h3+ ♗h6 33 g5) **31
♖h3+ 1-0**

Game 43
Sveshnikov – Am.Rodriguez
Cienfuegos 1979

**1 e4 c5 2 c3 ♘f6 3 e5 ♘d5 4 d4 cxd4
5 ♘f3 ♘c6 6 cxd4 d6 7 ♗c4 e6 8 0-0
♗e7 9 ♕e2 0-0 10 ♘c3!?** *(D)*
   With this move White aims for
fast development at the cost of giving himself a weak pawn on c3.
There invariably follows the well-
known manoeuvre ♕e4 and ♗d3 to

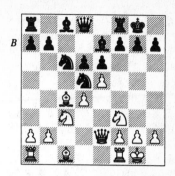

soften up the dark squares around
Black's king. Black is certainly not
without defensive resources (the deviations 13...♕c7 or 15...♘a5 in the
main line for example), and I suspect
the position is objectively rather unclear. However in practice White can
find it much easier to play, especially
as he has the automatic attacking
plan h4-h5.
   10...dxe5
   Of course 10...♘xc3 11 bxc3 is
another move-order, with the following possibilities if Black doesn't then
exchange on e5:
   a) 11...♗d7 12 ♗d3 d5 13 h4 ♖c8
14 ♘g5 g6 15 ♘xh7 (forcing a draw,
but of course White can continue
otherwise) 15...♔xh7 16 ♕h5+ ♔g8
17 ♗xg6 fxg6 18 ♕xg6+ ♔h8 19
♕h6+ ♔g8 ½-½ Grosar-Milov, Geneva 1996.
   b) 11...d5?! 12 ♗d3 ♘a5 (alternatively 12...f5 13 exf6 gxf6 14 ♖e1
♖f7 15 ♘h4 ♗d7 16 ♕h5 ♗d6 17
♗h6 ♘e7 18 ♖e3 ♖c8 19 f4 ♗e8 20
♖g3+ ♔h8 21 ♕g4 f5 22 ♕g5 1-0
Van der Sterren-Van der Vliet, Wijk
aan Zee 1977) 13 h4! (offering a
pawn to open the h-file) 13...♗xh4
14 g3 ♗e7 15 ♔g2 f6 16 exf6 ♗xf6

17 ♖h1 g6 18 ♘e5 ♗xe5 19 dxe5 ♖f7 20 ♕g4 ± ♘c6 21 ♗xg6! hxg6 22 ♕xg6+ ♔g7 23 ♕h5! ♕f8 24 ♖h4 ♘e7 25 ♗a3! 1-0 Sveshnikov-Rashkovsky, Sochi 1976.

c) 11...b6 12 ♗d3 ♗b7 13 ♕e4 (13 exd6!? ♕xd6 14 ♘g5 ♗xg5 15 ♗xg5 ♘e7 16 ♕g4 ♘g6 17 h4 f5 18 ♕h3 h6 19 ♗d2 ± Sveshnikov-Krogius, Sochi 1976) 13...g6 14 ♗h6 ♖e8 15 ♖ad1 ♘a5 (or 15...♖c8 16 ♕f4 f5 17 exf6 ♗xf6 18 ♖fe1 ± Nun-Mozny, Czechoslovakia 1978; 15...dxe5 is best, transposing back to the illustrative game) 16 ♕f4 ♗xf3 17 ♕xf3 ± Hermann-Miles, Bad Lauterberg 1977.

11 dxe5 ♘xc3 12 bxc3 b6

Or:

a) 12...♕a5!? is unclear:

a1) 13 ♖b1 ♖d8 14 ♕e4 ♕xc3 15 ♗g5 ♗xg5 16 ♘xg5 h6! 17 ♕h7+ ♔f8 18 ♗xe6 hxg5 19 ♗xc8 ♖axc8 20 ♕h8+ ♗e7 21 ♕xg7 ♘xe5 ∓ V.L.Ivanov-Saltaev, Moscow 1995.

a2) 13 ♕e4 ♕a4 14 ♗g5 ♗d7 15 ♖fd1 ♖ad8 16 ♗xe7 ♘xe7 17 ♕xb7 ♕xc4 ½-½ Pavasović-Sulava, Nova Gorica 1996.

a3) 13 ♖e1 ♖d8 (13...♕xc3!?) 14 ♗d2 b6 15 ♕e4 ♗b7 16 ♘g5 g6 17 ♕h4 h5 18 ♕f4 ♗xg5 19 ♕xg5 ± Rahls-Ostermeyer, Bundesliga 1986.

b) 12...♕c7 leads to similarly murky play:

b1) 13 ♗d3 b6 (13...♖d8 14 ♖e1 ♗d7 15 ♗g5 h6 16 ♗xh6! gxh6 17 ♕e4 f5 18 exf6 ♗xf6 19 ♕h7+ ♔f8 20 ♖e4 was a very dangerous sacrifice in Rausis-Piesina, Riga Z 1995) 14 ♖e1 (for 14 ♕e4 see the main game) 14...♗b7 15 ♘g5 ♗xg5 16

♗xg5 ♘e7 (16...♘xe5 17 ♕xe5 ♕xe5 18 ♖xe5 f6 19 ♖xe6 ±) 17 ♕h5 ♘g6 18 ♖e3 ♕xc3 19 ♖d1 ∞ Gorelov-Maiorov, USSR 1981.

b2) 13 ♕e4:

b21) 13...♗d7 14 ♗d3 (an improvement over 14 ♖e1 ♖ac8 15 ♗g5 ♘xe5!? 16 ♗xe7 ♘xf3+ 17 gxf3 ♕xc4 18 ♗xf8 ♕xe4 19 fxe4 ♔xf8 and the endgame should be a draw, Sveshnikov-Cvitan, Tilburg 1993) 14 ♗d3 g6 15 ♗h6 ♖fd8 16 ♖fe1 ♗e8 17 ♖ad1 ♖d5 18 c4 ♖c5 19 ♕f4 ♖d8 20 ♗g5 ♗xg5 21 ♕xg5 ♕e7 22 ♕f4 ♔g7 23 h4 ± with the usual play against Black's dark squares, Manca-Kožul, Reggio Emilia 1993.

b22) 13...♖d8 14 ♖e1 (14 ♗d3 g6 15 ♗h6 ♗d7 16 ♖ad1 ♗e8 17 ♕f4 ♕a5 18 ♗e4 ♕xc3 19 ♖c1 ♕a3 20 ♗xc6 bxc6 Machulsky-Ruban, Šibenik 1990 and now 21 ♗g5 ♖ab8 22 ♗xe7 ♕xe7 23 ♘g5 ∞ is given by Ruban) 14...♗d7 15 ♘g5 g6 16 ♕h4 h5 17 ♕f4 ♖f8 18 ♗d3 ♖ad8 19 ♘h7! ♗c8 (19...♖xh7 20 ♕h6+ ♔g8 21 ♗xg6) 20 ♕h6 ♘xe5 21 ♗f4 ♘g4 22 ♕xf8+ ♖xf8 23 ♗xc7 ♔xh7 24 h3 ± Motwani-Grosar, Moscow OL 1994. However I expressly disclaim responsibility if there is a flaw in this maniacal variation!

13 ♕e4 ♗b7

13...♕c7!? has the advantage of freeing the d8-square for Black's king's rook after 14 ♗d3 g6 15 ♗h6 ♖d8 ∞. A good example is Mukhametov-Blasek, Moscow 1990 which continued 16 ♖ad1 ♗b7 17 ♕f4 ♖d5 18 ♗e4 ♖xd1 19 ♖xd1 ♖d8 20 ♖xd8+ ♗xd8 (the wholesale exchanges should always ease Black's defensive task, but as we shall see he must still be vigilant) 21 h4 ♘a5 22 ♘g5 ♗d5? 23 ♗xd5 exd5 24 ♘e6! ♕e7 25 ♘xd8 ♕xd8 26 e6! f6 (Black is already lost: 26...fxe6 27 ♕e5 ♕e7 28 ♕b8+ ♔h7 29 ♕h8) 27 ♕d4 ♕e7 (27...♘c6 28 e7! +−) 28 ♕xd5 ♘b7 29 ♕c6 ♘d6 30 ♕a8+ ♘e8 31 ♕c8 1-0. In spite of this debacle 13...♕c7 is a valid plan, as Black has chances of gaining a tempo on the main line by getting his rook immediately to the d-file.

However White can consider varying with 14 ♗g5!? ♗b7 (14...♗xg5 15 ♘xg5 g6 16 ♖ae1 h6? 17 ♗xe6! ± was a nice combination in Howell-Ward, British Ch 1994 – 17...fxe6 18 ♘xe6 ♗xe6 19 ♕xg6+ ♔h8 20 ♕xh6+ ♔h7 21 ♕xe6 nets four pawns for the piece) 15 ♗d3 g6 16 ♕h4 ♗xg5 (16...♖fe8 17 ♖ae1 ♗f8 18 ♖e3 ♘e7 19 ♘d4 ♘f5 20 ♗xf5 exf5 Sax-Kagan, Hastings 1978, and now 21 f4 would have favoured White according to Sax) 17 ♘xg5 h5. Now White should continue 18 f4 or 18 ♖ae1 ∞, since 18 ♖fe1, as in Preissmann-Ghitescu, Buenos Aires 1978, would allow Black various defensive possibilities including the surprising 18...♘xe5! 19 ♕g3 ♕xc3! ∓.

14 ♗d3 g6 15 ♗h6 ♖e8

The *zwischenzug* 15...♘a5!? has the idea that White's queen cannot currently go the f4-square (the d3-bishop would *en prise*): 16 ♕e3 ♖e8 17 ♗b5 (17 ♘g5 ♕d5 18 ♕g3 ♖ac8 19 ♗e4 ♕c4 20 ♗xb7 ♘xb7 21 ♖ad1 ♕xc3 22 ♖d3 ♕c7 23 ♖f3 ♗xg5 24 ♕xg5 ♕e7 25 ♕f4 f5 26

exf6 ± Maksimenko-Neverov, Copenhagen 1994; White always had play for the pawn, but 23...♘d8 was an alternative) 17...♗c6 18 ♗xc6 (18 ♖fd1 ♕c7 19 ♘d4 ♖ed8 20 ♗f1 ♗a4 21 ♖e1 ∞ Zhuravlev-Gufeld, USSR 1979) 18...♘xc6 19 ♖ad1 ♕c7 20 ♕f4 ♖ad8 21 h4 ♖xd1 22 ♖xd1 ♖d8 23 ♖xd8+ ♗xd8 24 h5 ♕d7 25 ♗g5 ♗xg5 26 ♕xg5. This was the game Kharlov-Gallego, Canete 1994, where logically Black should have equality due to successful exchanges on the d-file, but actually White may still claim a lingering edge due to the plan of h6.

16 ♖ad1

16 ♕e3!? is an interesting idea, intending not to contest the d-file and thus avoiding later major piece exchanges. 16...♗c5 (dangerous is 16...♕d5? 17 ♖ad1 ♕c5 18 ♕f4! ♕xc3 19 ♗e4 ± Markun-Sale, Bled 1995 with threats of ♖c1 or ♖d7) 17 ♕e2 ♕c7 18 ♖fe1 ♘e7 19 ♖ac1 ♘f5 20 ♗g5 ♗e7 21 ♗e4 ♖ac8? (21...♗xe4 22 ♕xe4 ♖ac8 is better, e.g. 23 ♕f4 f6) 22 ♗xb7 ♕xb7 23 ♗f6 (planning g4) 23...h5 24 h3 b5 25 g4 ♘g7 26 ♘d2 ♖ed8 27 ♘e4 ♖c4 28 ♕e3 +− Westerinen-Hartston, Esbjerg 1979.

16...♕c7 17 ♕f4 ♖ad8 (D)
18 h4!?

The habitual plan for White: in addition to giving attacking possibilities this useful move also cancels out any potential bank-rank mate problems. Less direct are 18 ♗e4 ♖xd1 19 ♖xd1 ♖d8 20 ♖xd8+ ♘xd8 21 ♗xb7 ♘xb7 22 ♕a4 ♕d8 23 ♘d4 = Men-Wolff, USA Ch 1992

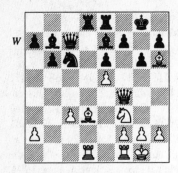

and 18 ♖fe1 ♖d5 19 ♗e4 ♖xd1 20 ♖xd1 ♖d8 21 ♖xd8+ ♘xd8 22 ♗xb7 ♘xb7 23 ♕a4 ♗f8 24 ♗xf8 ♔xf8 25 ♕xa7 ♕xc3 26 h4 ½-½ Barle-Jansa, Sombor 1976.

18...♘a5 19 ♘g5 f5!

A clever way of dealing with the attack on f7, based on the tactical point 20 ♘xe6? ♕c6 threatening mate on g2 and the knight on e6. Instead 19...♗xg5? 20 ♗xg5 ♕c6 21 f3 leaves Black's kingside dark squares fatally weak, while 19...f6? fails tactically to 20 ♘xh7! ♔xh7 21 ♗g7!!

(Sveshnikov) 21...♔g8 (21...♔xg7 22 exf6+ and 23 ♕xc7) 22 ♕h6 ♕c6 23 f3 with a decisive attack for White.

20 ♗b5! ♖xd1 21 ♗xe8! ♖xf1+ 22 ♔xf1 ♕xc3 23 ♗f7+ ♔h8 24 ♔g1 (heading back to safety; now if 24...♕c6, 25 ♕g3 ± Sveshnikov) **24...♗d5 25 h5 ♕c4 26 ♕g3 ♕g4 27 ♕xg4 fxg4 28 ♘xe6 ♗xe6 29 ♗xe6 ♘c6** (29...gxh5 30 f4) **30 hxg6 hxg6 31 ♗f4 ±** (White has the bishop pair and is about to win a pawn) **31...g5 32 ♗h2?!** (32 ♗g3 intending ♗xg4, followed by e6 and f4) **32...♗c5 33 ♗xg4 ♔g7 34 ♗d7 ♘b4 35 a4 ♘d3 36 ♔f1 ♗d4?!** (36...♔g6) **37 e6 ♗c5 38 ♗b8 a6 39 ♗c7 ♔f8 40 ♗d8 ♘xf2 41 ♗c8 ♘e4 42 ♗xa6 ♔e8 43 e7 ♗xe7 44 ♗xb6 ♗d8 45 ♗b5+ ♔e7 46 ♗xd8+ ♔xd8 47 ♔e2 ♔c7 48 ♔f3 ♘f6 49 a5 ♔b7 50 a6+ ♔b6 51 ♗c4 ♔a7 52 ♔e3 ♔b6 53 ♔d4 ♘h5 54 ♔e4 ♘f4 55 g3 ♘g2 56 ♔f3 1-0**

16 5 cxd4 d6 6 ♘f3 ♘c6
7 ♗c4 ♘b6

1	e4	c5
2	c3	♘f6
3	e5	♘d5
4	d4	cxd4
5	cxd4	d6
6	♘f3	♘c6
7	♗c4	♘b6 (D)

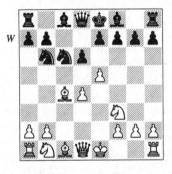

The former main-line position arising after 8 ♗b5 dxe5 9 ♘xe5 ♗d7 (games 45 and 46) gives White no advantage. This was established in some top-level Soviet Championship games in the 1970s, and the assessment has not changed since. This is hardly surprising, considering that the Soviet players involved in the original games were legends such as Tal, Petrosian, Polugaevsky and Kasparov (all playing Black against Sveshnikov of course!). This line is the principal reason that White has switched his move-orders over the years, and that most games now proceed with the move-order 5 ♘f3 (as per later chapters).

There have, however, been some recent developments with the more dynamic move 8 ♗b3 (which merited only two references in the previous edition, *Sicilian 2 c3*). White has been experimenting with a speculative pawn sacrifice (see Game 44), and further games are needed for evaluation – as yet the move has not been extensively tested at grandmaster level.

Game 44
Sermek – Sveshnikov
Bled 1996

1 e4 c5 2 c3 ♘f6 3 e5 ♘d5 4 ♘f3 ♘c6 5 d4 cxd4 6 cxd4 d6 7 ♗c4 ♘b6 8 ♗b3

This sideline (generally involving an unclear pawn sacrifice) has been the subject of some interesting attention in the 1990s (for 8 ♗c4 see games 45 and 46). Certainly if White could revive 8 ♗b3, the implications for the whole ...♘f6 defence would be very considerable.

8...dxe5

Or:

a) 8...g6 9 ♘g5 (9 e6 fxe6 10 h4 ♗g7 11 h5 e5 12 dxe5 ♗f5 13 hxg6 hxg6 14 ♖xh8+ ♗xh8 15 exd6 ♕xd6 16 ♕xd6 exd6 17 ♘h4 with equality, Yagupov-Eriksson, Minsk 1993) 9...d5 10 f4 ♗g7 11 ♘c3 f6 12 ♘f3 ♗e6 13 0-0 ± Karpatchev-Gunnarsson, Gausdal 1993.

b) 8...e6 (rather passive, but this position can be reached from other move-orders) 9 ♕e2 (for 9 exd6 see Chapter 17) 9...dxe5 (9...d5 10 ♘c3 a5 11 ♗g5 ♗e7 12 ♗xe7 ♕xe7 13 ♕b5!? ♕b4 14 a3 ♕xb5 15 ♘xb5 ♔e7 16 a4 ♗d7 17 ♔d2 h6 18 ♖ac1 ± Vlassov-Scherbakov, Russia 1995) 10 dxe5 ♘d4 11 ♘xd4 ♕xd4 12 0-0 ♗e7 13 ♖d1 ± Yagupov-Furman, Smolensk Alekhine 1992.

c) 8...d5!? 9 ♘h4!? (to stop ...♗f5 or ...♗g4, although after 9 ♗e3 ♗f5 10 ♘h4 ♗xb1 11 ♖xb1 e6 12 ♘f3 ♗b4+ Schandorff-Wang Zili, Copenhagen 1995, White would have kept an edge with 13 ♗d2) 9...a5 (9...e6 10 ♘f3 ♗d7 11 ♘c3 ♗e7 12 ♗c2 ♘c4 13 0-0 ♕a5 14 a3 0-0-0 15 ♕d3 g5 16 b3 g4 17 ♘g5 ± Har-Zvi – Shmuter, Rishon le Zion 1995) 10 ♘c3 a4 11 ♗c2 a3 12 bxa3 e6 13 g3 ♘c4 14 0-0 ♗e7 15 ♕g4 ♔f8 16 ♘f3 h6 17 h4 f5 18 exf6 ♗xf6 19 ♕f4 g5!? 20 hxg5 hxg5 with very unclear play in Yagupov-Ragozin, Russia 1992, though both sides have other possibilities *en route* of course.

9 d5 ♘a5

A valid alternative is 9...♘b4!? 10 ♘c3 e6 11 ♗g5 ♗e7 and now:

a) 12 dxe6 ♗xe6 13 ♗xe6 fxe6 14 ♗xe7 ♕xd1+ 15 ♖xd1 ♔xe7 16 ♘xe5 ♖hd8 17 ♔e2 ♘6d5 18 ♘xd5+ ♖xd5 19 ♖xd5 exd5 20 ♘d3 ½-½ Vl.Ivanov-Mi.Ivanov, Moscow 1995.

b) 12 ♗xe7 ♕xe7 13 d6 ♕f6 14 ♘e4?! (14 0-0!? 0-0 15 ♖e1 ♘c6 16 ♕d3 with interesting compensation) 14...♕g6 15 ♕e2 ♘c6 ∓ Pavasović-Volzhin, Budapest 1995. The game continued 16 0-0 f5 17 d7+ ♔xd7 18 ♘h4 ♕h6 19 ♘d6+ ♔f8 20 ♘hxf5 exf5 21 ♖ad1 ♘b6 22 ♘f7 ♕f6 23 ♘xh8 ♗e6 24 ♖d6 ♘d4 25 ♕h5 ♕xb3 26 axb3 ♔g8 ∓.

10 ♘c3 ♘xb3

10...f6, while obviously risky, is not out of the question, e.g. 11 ♗e3 g6 12 0-0 ♗g7 13 ♗c5 ♔f7 14 ♖e1 ♘bc4 15 ♘e4 ♗f5 16 d6 e6 ∞ Rausis-Müller, Germany 1995. Alternatively 10...g6 11 ♘xe5 ♗g7 12 ♗f4 ♘d7 13 ♕e2 0-0 14 0-0 ♘xe5 15 ♗xe5 ♗g4 16 ♕e3 ♘xb3 17 axb3 ♕b6 18 ♗xg7 ♕xe3 19 fxe3 ♔xg7 20 ♖f4 ♗d7 21 ♖c4 ♖fc8 and the ending should probably have been tenable for Black in Rausis-Sadler, Gausdal 1995, though in the game White gained a clear advantage after 22 e4 a6 23 e5 ♗f5 24 ♔f2 ♖xc4 25 bxc4 ♖c8 26 ♖a4 ♗d7 27 ♖b4 b5 28 cxb5 axb5 29 ♔e3 e6 30 dxe6 fxe6 31 h4.

11 ♕xb3 e6

11...g6 12 ♘xe5 ♗g7 13 ♗f4 0-0 14 ♖d1 ♘d7 15 ♘xd7 ♕xd7 16 0-0 ± Yagupov-Kozyrev, Podolsk 1992.

12 ♘xe5!?

Inferior are 12 ♗g5?! ♗e7 13 ♖d1 exd5 14 ♗xe7 ♕xe7 15 ♘xd5 ♘xd5 16 ♖xd5 f6 17 0-0 ♗e6 18 ♕a4+ ♔f7 ∓ Roos-Ligterink, Amsterdam 1978 and 12 dxe6?! ♗xe6 13 ♕b5+ ♕d7 14 ♘xe5 (14 ♕xe5 ♗b4 15 ♕xg7 0-0-0 16 0-0 ♖dg8 with an attack, Pachman-Mazel, corr.

1986) 14...♕xb5 15 ♘xb5 ♗b4+ 16
♗d2 ♗xd2+ 17 ♔xd2 0-0-0+ 18 ♔e2
♖d5 ∓ Kresoja-M.Makarov, Belgrade 1993.

12...exd5

12...♘xd5 13 ♕b5+ ♗d7 14 ♕xb7
± was Yagupov-Tratar, Groningen
1993.

13 ♗e3 ♗d6 14 ♕b5+ ♔f8 *(D)*

Or 14...♗d7 15 ♘xd7 ♕xd7 16
0-0-0 and now:

a) 16...0-0-0 17 ♕a5! ♕c6 (alternatively 17...♘c4 18 ♕xa7 ♘xe3 19
fxe3 ♕c6 20 ♖xd5 ♗b8 21 ♕d4 ±
was Sermek-Olivier, Cannes 1995)
18 ♕xa7 ♗c7 19 ♔b1 ♖he8 20
♗d4! ♖e6 21 ♖c1 ♘c4 (21...♔d7 22
♘a4! +− V.L.Ivanov) 22 b3 ♘d2+
23 ♔b2 ♕a6 24 ♕xa6 ♖xa6 25 f3! ±
V.L.Ivanov-Mirzoev, Moscow 1994
– Black's knight on d2 is trapped.

b) 16...♕xb5!? 17 ♘xb5 ♔d7 18
♗xb6 axb6 19 ♖xd5 ♔c6 20 ♖xd6+
(obviously White's position is a little
better, but rather than simplification
to a double-rook ending 20 ♖hd1!? ±
could be tried) 20...♔xb5 21 ♖e1
♖ac8+ 22 ♔d2 ♖hd8 23 ♖xd8
♖xd8+ 24 ♔c3 ♖c8+ 25 ♔b3 ♖c5
½-½ V.L.Ivanov-Kriventsov, Moscow 1994.

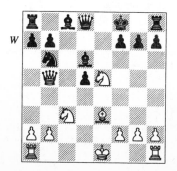

15 0-0-0!?

With very unclear compensation
for the pawn: if 15...♗xe5 White's
idea is 16 ♘xd5 ♗d7 17 ♕b4+ ♔e8
18 ♖he1 with a tremendous attack
for the piece.

15...♗e6 16 ♘f3

Supporting the knight with 16 f4
is also natural:

a) 16...g6 17 ♗d4 f6 18 ♘d3 ♖c8
19 ♔b1 ♖c4 20 ♘c5 ♗f5+ 21 ♔a1
♕c8 22 ♘b3 ♔g7 23 ♘xd5 ♘xd5 24
♕xd5 ♖d8 25 ♖he1 ♗c2 26 ♗xf6+
♔xf6 27 ♕g5+ ♔f7 28 ♖xd6 ♖xd6
29 ♕e7+ ♔g8 30 ♕xd6 ♗xb3 31
axb3 ♖c1+ 32 ♖xc1 ♕xc1+ 33 ♔a2
with an extra pawn in Rausis-Fos-
san, Gausdal 1993, although White
could hardly have expected to win
the queen ending so quickly: 33...♕c8
34 ♕d5+ ♔g7 35 ♕d4+ ♔h6 36 ♕e3
♕f5 37 ♕d2 a6 38 h3 ♕b5 39 g4
♔g7 40 ♕d4+ ♔h6 41 g5+ ♔h5 42
♕d1+ 1-0.

b) 16...♗xe5!? 17 fxe5 h6 (here
Informator assesses ∓, although 18
♔b1 still looks unclear) 18 h4? ♔g8
19 ♔b1 ♕c7 20 ♗xb6 ♕xb6 21 ♕xb6
axb6 22 ♘xd5 ♖a5 23 ♘c3 ♗xe5 24
♖d6 b5 25 ♖b6 ♗d7 26 ♖xb7 ♗c6
27 ♖b6 ♖e6 28 ♔c1 ♗xg2 ∓ Van der
Werf-Van Wely, Wijk aan Zee 1995.

16...♖c8

16...♕c7 17 ♔b1 ♖d8 18 ♕a5 with
an unclear game, V.L.Ivanov-Rogow-
ski, Dnepropetrovsk 1993.

17 ♔b1 ♖c6 18 ♘d4

18 ♖he1 is another possibility for
White. The whole position is rather
complex. Logically, having forced
the opposing king to f8, White
should have some compensation for

the pawn, and sometimes the material can be later regained with a ♗xb6/♘xd5 combination anyway, but an exact assessment will await more tests. In the game Sermek's idea of an ambitious piece sacrifice just falls short.

18...♖c4 19 ♘xe6+ fxe6 20 ♘xd5 exd5 21 ♗xb6 axb6 22 ♖xd5 ♖c6 23 ♖e1 h5 24 ♖d3 ♖h6! ∓

Black's second rook joins the defence, and it becomes clear that White's attack can be fended off.

25 ♖f3+ ♖f6 26 ♕xh5 ♗e7 27 ♖fe3 ♖ce6 28 ♖d1 ♖d6 29 ♖de1 ♖de6 30 ♖d1 ♕c7 31 ♖c3 ♖c6 32 ♖e3 ♖xf2 33 a3 ♖h6 34 ♖f3+ ♖xf3 35 ♕xf3+ ♖f6 36 ♕h5 ♕c5 37 ♕h8+ ♔f7 38 ♖c1 ♕d5 0-1

Game 45
Sveshnikov – Kasparov
USSR Ch 1979

1 e4 c5 2 c3 ♘f6 3 e5 ♘d5 4 d4 cxd4 5 ♘f3 ♘c6 6 cxd4 d6 7 ♗c4 ♘b6 8 ♗b5 dxe5

Here Black has several minor alternatives, and one more major:

a) 8...a6 9 ♗xc6+ bxc6 10 ♘c3 ♗g4 11 h3 ♗xf3 12 ♕xf3 d5 looks dubious after 13 e6! fxe6 (Karaklajić-Tesić, Yugoslav Ch 1991) and now 14 ♕h5+! ♔d7 (14...g6 15 ♕e5) 15 0-0. Black's king has insufficient long-term shelter on the queenside.

b) 8...d5 9 ♘c3 ♗g4 (9...♗f5 10 ♘h4 ♗d7 11 0-0 has also been seen) 10 h3 ♗xf3 (10...♗h5 would be a mistake: 11 g4 ♗g6 12 e6! fxe6 13 ♗f4 ±) 11 ♕xf3 e6 12 0-0 ♗e7 13 ♕g3 ♔f8 14 ♘e2 ♖c8 15 ♗f4 h5 16

♖fc1 ± Sveshnikov-Palatnik, USSR 1973.

c) White also has a modest edge after 8...e6 9 ♘c3 ♗e7 (9...♗d7 transposes to 8...♗d7 lines below) 10 0-0 0-0, e.g. 11 ♕e2 ♗d7 12 ♗f4 dxe5 13 dxe5 ♘b4 14 ♗xd7 ♕xd7 15 ♗g5 ♗xg5 16 ♘xg5 ♕d3 17 ♕g4 ♘c6 18 f4 ♘c4 19 ♘ce4 h6 20 ♖ad1 ♕c2 21 ♘xe6 fxe6 22 ♖d7 ♖f7 23 ♘f6+ ♔f8 24 ♕xe6 ♘e7 25 ♖xe7 ♘xe5 26 ♖e8+ 1-0 Groszpeter-Georgiev, Innsbruck 1977.

d) 8...♗d7 (the important, and sharper continuation) 9 ♘c3 (after 9 exd6 soundest is 9...e6 10 ♗g5 ♕b8 11 ♘c3 ♗xd6 12 0-0 0-0 13 ♖e1 a6 14 ♗d3 ♘b4 15 ♗e4 h6 16 a3 ♘4d5 17 ♗xd5 exd5 18 ♗h4 ♗e6 = Bannik-Polugaevsky, USSR Ch 1958) and now:

d1) 9...dxe5 10 dxe5 (10 ♘xe5 transposes to Game 46 while 10 d5 ♘b4 11 ♘xe5 ♗xb5 12 ♘xb5 g6 13 ♕b3 ♘4xd5 14 ♗e3 was unclear in Sveshnikov-Zaid, USSR 1976) 10...g6 11 0-0 (11 h3 ♗g7 12 ♕e2 ♕c7 13 ♗f4 a6 14 ♗d3 ♘b4 15 ♗e4 ♗e6 16 ♖c1 ♕c4 ∞ Gipslis-Semeniuk, USSR 1976) 11...♗g7 12 ♕e2 a6 13 ♗xc6 ♗xc6 14 e6 f5 15 ♘e5 0-0 16 ♘xc6 bxc6 17 ♗f4 (17 ♖d1!? ±) 17...♘d5 18 ♗e5 ♗xe5 19 ♕xe5 ♕b8 = Thipsay-Ljubojević, Lucerne OL 1982 as 20 ♕e2 ♘f4 21 ♕c4 ♕xb2! threatens ...♕xc3.

d2) 9...e6 10 0-0 (10 ♗g5 ♗e7 11 ♘e4 dxe5 12 ♘d6+ ♔f8 13 ♗xe7+ ♕xe7 14 dxe5 a6 15 ♗e2 ♘d5 16 ♕c2 ♖d8 17 0-0 ♘xe5 18 ♘xb7 ♘xf3+ 19 ♗xf3 ♖c8 20 ♕d2 ♗b5 21 ♗xd5 exd5 22 ♘a5 ♗xf1 ∓

Gulko-Tal, Tallinn 1977) and now Black must be careful *(D)*:

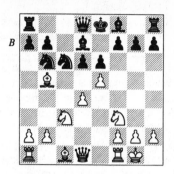

d21) 10...♗e7?! 11 d5! exd5 12 exd6 ♗xd6 13 ᐁxd5 ± as in Hermann-Ristoja, Malta OL 1980 is good for White.

d22) The complications after 10...ᐁb4?! 11 ♗g5! ♗e7 12 ᐁe4! are also in White's favour, for example 12...dxe5 (12...♗xb5 13 ᐁxd6+ ♚f8 14 ♗xe7+ ♛xe7 15 ᐁxb5 alternatively 12...♗xg5 13 ᐁfxg5 ♗xb5 14 ᐁxd6+) 13 ᐁd6+ ♚f8 14 ᐁxe5!? (also 14 ᐁxb7! ♛c7 15 ♗xe7+ ♚xe7 16 ♛b3 with advantage for White, Sveshnikov-Misuchkov, USSR 1972; 14 ♗xe7+ ♛xe7 15 dxe5 ♗xb5 16 ᐁxb5 g6 17 ♖c1 ½-½ was Rausis-Anand, France 1993 but even here White is doing well in the final position) 14...♗xb5! 15 ᐁdxf7 ♛d5 16 ♛h5 ♗xg5 17 ᐁxg5 ♗e8 18 ♛g4 ♚e7! 19 ♖ae1 h5 20 ♛h4 ♖h6 21 ᐁxe6+! ♚xe6 22 ᐁg4+ ♚f7 23 ♛e7+ ♚g8 24 ᐁxh6+ gxh6 25 ♖e3 h4! Sveshnikov-Yurtaev, USSR 1975, and here Sveshnikov gives 26 ♛xb4 ±.

d23) 10...a6 is therefore safest. For example, 11 ♗d3 ♗e7 (11...dxe5 12 dxe5 ᐁb4 13 ♗g5 ♗e7 14 ♗xe7 ♛xe7 15 ♗e4 ♗c6 16 a3 ᐁ4d5 17 ♛b3 0-0 18 ᐁd4 ♖ac8 19 ᐁxc6 ♖xc6 20 ♖ad1 ± Chekhov-Grigorian, 43rd USSR Ch or 11...ᐁb4 12 ♗b1 ♗c6 13 a3 ᐁ4d5 14 ᐁe4 ᐁc8 15 ♖e1 ♗e7 16 ᐁfg5 dxe5 17 ♛h5 g6 18 ♛f3 ᐁf4 19 dxe5 ♗xg5 20 ♗xf4 ± J.Cobb-A.Kogan, London 1994) and now White should prefer 12 a3 ± to 12 ♗f4 dxe5 13 dxe5 ᐁb4 14 ᐁd4 ᐁ6d5 15 ᐁxd5 ᐁxd5 16 ♗g3 ♛b6 ∞ O.Castro-Sunye Neto, Sao Paulo 1978.

9 ᐁxe5

Premature is 9 ♗xc6+, when after 9...bxc6 10 ᐁxe5 Black has a satisfactory game with either 10...♗e6 or 10...♗a6, for example 11 ᐁc3 e6 12 ♛f3 ♛c7 13 ♗f4 ᐁd5 14 ♗g3 ♛b7 15 0-0-0 ♗b4 Fedorov-Leonidov, USSR 1979.

9...♗d7 *(D)*

Overambitious is the alternative 9...♛d5 10 ♗xc6+ bxc6 11 0-0 c5 12 ᐁc3 ♛xd4 13 ᐁb5 ♛xe5 14 ♖e1 ♗g4 and now White has a choice between 15 ᐁd6+! ± Makropoulos-Ljubojević, Albufeira 1978 and 15 f3 ♖d8 16 ♛xd8+ ♚xd8 17 ♖xe5 ♗d7 18 ᐁc3 e6 19 ♖e2 ± Polak-Lipka, Pardubice 1991.

10 ᐁc3

For 10 ♗xc6 and 10 ᐁxd7 see the next game.

10...ᐁxe5

Or 10...e6!? and here:

a) 11 ♗xc6 ♗xc6 12 ᐁxc6 bxc6 see the note to White's 12th move in Game 45.

b) 11 ♛g4 ᐁxe5 (11...h5 12 ♛e4 ᐁxe5 13 dxe5 ♗xb5 14 ᐁxb5 ᐁd5

15 0-0 ♗e7 16 ♗d2 0-0 17 ♘c3 ♘xc3 18 ♗xc3 ♕b6 19 ♖ad1 ½-½ Sveshnikov-Petrosian, USSR Ch 1977) 12 dxe5 ♗xb5 13 ♘xb5 ♕d7 14 ♘c3 ♕d3 15 ♗d2 ♘c4 16 0-0-0 ♖c8 (16...h5 17 ♕f4 ♖c8 18 ♗e1 ♕g6 19 ♕d4 ♘b6 20 ♕d3 ♕xd3 21 ♖xd3 ♖c5 = Sveshnikov-Polugaevsky, Tbilisi 1978) 17 ♗f4 ♕g6 18 ♕xg6 hxg6 19 ♔b1 ♘a3+ 20 ♔a1 ♘c2+ 21 ♔b1 ♘a3+ ½-½ Sveshnikov-Tal, USSR Ch 1978.

c) 11 0-0 ♗e7 (11...♖c8 12 ♗xc6 ♗xc6 13 ♕g4 h5 and then 14 ♕e2?! ♗b4 15 ♘xc6 ♖xc6 16 ♘e4 ♕xd4 17 ♗g5 ♕c4 18 ♕f3 f5 19 ♖ad1 0-0 ∓ was the game Szabo-Marjanović, Vršac 1979 but Marjanović's 14 ♕f4!? suggestion improves; a simpler move is 11...♘xe5 – see the note to Black's 11th move in the main game) 12 ♕f3 (12 ♗e3 0-0 13 ♗d3 ♘xe5 14 dxe5 ♗c6 15 ♕c2 g6 16 ♗h6 ♖e8 17 ♗e4 ♘d5 18 ♖fd1 ♕a5 19 ♘xd5 exd5 20 ♗f3 ♗f8 21 ♗xf8 ♔xf8 with an equal position, Schweber-Browne, Buenos Aires 1979) 12 ♕f3 0-0 13 ♖d1 ♖c8 14 ♘xd7 (14 ♗e3 a6 15 ♗e2 f5?! 16 ♘xd7 ♕xd7 17 d5 ± Rausis-Browne, Saint Martin 1991) 14...♕xd7 15 d5 ♘d5 16

♘xd5 exd5 17 ♖xd5 ♕e6 = Palkovi-Stohl, Stara Zagora Z 1990.

11 dxe5 ♗xb5

A little-used route to equality is 11...e6 12 0-0 ♗xb5 13 ♘xb5 a6! = as in Zaitsev-Rashkovsky, Sochi 1979, when a few subsequent games have confirmed that Black has no problems. In contrast to the dangerous related line in the main game (11...♗xb5 12 ♘xb5 a6? 13 ♗e3!) the white move 14 ♗e3 is nothing to worry about here since Black has 14...♘d5.

12 ♘xb5 ♕xd1+

12...a6? 13 ♗e3! sets Black severe problems (13...♘d5 14 ♕xd5 or 13...axb5 14 ♕xd8+ ♖xd8 15 ♗xb6 or 13...♘c4 14 ♕a4 axb5 15 ♕xb5+ ♕d7 16 ♕xc4). 13...♘d7 14 e6! axb5 15 exd7+ ♕xd7 16 ♕xd7+ ♔xd7 17 0-0-0+ ± was first played in Sveshnikov-Govashelishvili, USSR 1979, and 12 years later another strong player fell into this trap: 17...♔c7 18 ♖d3 b6 19 ♔b1 f6 20 ♖c1+ ♔b7 21 ♖d7+ ♔a6 22 ♖c6 ♖b8 23 b4 e5 24 ♖cc7 ♖a8 25 a3 1-0 was the quick finish of Rausis-Mokry, Germany 1992 – White's ♖b7 is imminent and deadly.

13 ♔xd1 ♘d5 *(D)*

Very solid. If 13...♖d8+?! then 14 ♔e2 a6 15 ♘c7+ ♔d7 16 ♗e3!, but 13...0-0-0+!? is exciting 14 ♔e2 ♖d5 15 a4 ♖xe5+ (after 15...a6 16 ♗e3, 16...♖xe5? 17 ♖ac1+ ♔b8 18 ♖hd1 ♘d5 19 ♖xd5! 1-0 was Galyas-Dobos, Budapest 1995 though even 16...axb5 17 ♗xb6 ♖xe5+ 18 ♔f3 ♔d7 was unclear in Kolcak-Golod, Slovakian Cht 1994) 16 ♗e3 ♘d5 17

♖ac1+ ♔b8 18 ♖hd1 e6 19 ♔f3 (19 ♘c7 ♗e7 20 ♘xd5 exd5 21 ♔f1 ♗g5 22 ♗d4 ♖f5 23 ♖c3 ♗f6 24 ♗xf6 ½-½ Kristjansson-Tisdall, Vestmann Isles 1985) 19...♖f5+! (White threatens ♗xa7+ and 19...b6? 20 ♗f4! 1-0 Biro-Adler, Budapest 1990 is an evil trap as 20...♘xf4 21 ♖d8+ ♔b7 22 ♖c7+ ♔a6 23 ♖xa7 mates) 20 ♔e2 b6!? (20...♖e5 21 ♔f3 with a draw by repetition) 21 g4 ♖e5 22 ♘d4 ♔b7 23 ♘c6 ♗d6! 24 ♘xe5 ♗xe5 25 ♗d4 ♗xh2 ∓ Tiviakov-Kharlov, USSR 1991.

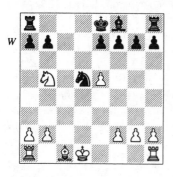

14 ♔e2

After 14 ♗d2 Black has 14...e6 15 ♔e2 ♗e7 16 ♖ac1 ♔d7 17 ♖hd1 ♖hc8 18 ♘c3 ♘xc3+ 19 ♗xc3+ ♔e8 20 ♗d4 b6 21 f4 ♖xc1 22 ♖xc1 ♔d7 23 ♔d3 ♖c8 24 ♖xc8 ♔xc8 ½-½ Sveshnikov-Andersson, Wijk aan Zee 1981 or 14...a6 15 ♘c3 ♖d8 16 ♔e2 e6 17 ♖hd1 ♗e7 18 ♖ac1 ♘b4 19 ♘e4 ♘c6 20 ♗c3 ♖d5 ½-½ Sveshnikov-Tal, USSR 1980.

14...a6 15 ♖d1 0-0-0 16 ♘a3

After the continuation 16 ♘d6+ exd6 17 ♖xd5 Black has both 17...♖e8 ∓ and 17...dxe5 18 ♖xd5 ♗d6 ∓. Perhaps 16 ♘d4 e6 is best,

with an equal position after 17 ♗d2 b6 18 ♖ac1+ ♔b7 19 ♖c4 ♗c5 20 ♘f3 ♖d7 21 ♘g5 ♖hd8 22 ♖dc1 h6 23 ♘e4 ♗e7, as in Tiviakov-Korsunsky, Frunze 1989 or 17 ♗g5 ♖d7 18 ♖ac1+ ♔b8 19 ♘b3 h6 20 ♗e3 ♗e7 Borg-Ki.Georgiev, Thessaloniki OL 1984.

16...e6 17 ♘c4 ♗e7 18 ♗d2 b6! ∓ Black has somewhat the better endgame, as the e5-pawn makes the white bishop bad.

19 g3 ♗b7 20 ♘e3 ♘c7 21 ♘c4 ♖d4 22 ♖ac1 ♘d5 23 f3 ♖c8 24 ♘e3 ♘xe3 25 ♗xe3 ♖xd1 26 ♖xd1 ♖c2+ 27 ♖d2 ♖xd2+ 28 ♔xd2 ♔c6 29 f4 b5 30 ♔d3 ♔d5 31 h4 h5 32 ♗f2 ♗b4 33 b3 g6? (33...♗a5 34 ♔e2 ♔e4 35 ♗c5 f6 36 exf6 gxf6 intending ♔f5, e5 ± Kasparov) **34 ♔e2 ♗c5 35 ♗xc5??** (35 ♗e1 is equal) **35...♔xc5 36 ♔d3 ♔b4 37 ♔c2 ♔a3 38 ♔b1 a5 39 ♔a1 a4 40 bxa4 ♔xa4 41 ♔b1 ♔a3 42 ♔a1 b4 43 ♔b1 b3 0-1**

Game 46
Dolmatov – Alterman
Pardubice 1993

1 e4 c5 2 c3 ♘f6 3 e5 ♘d5 4 d4 cxd4 5 ♘f3 ♘c6 6 cxd4 d6 7 ♗c4 ♘b6 8 ♗b5 dxe5 9 ♘xe5 ♗d7 10 ♗xc6

10 ♘c3 was covered in the previous game. 10 ♘xd7 gains White the bishop pair, but the weakness of the d-pawn soon forces him to relinquish it for an equal game: 10...♕xd7 11 ♘c3 e6 12 0-0 (12 ♕g4 h5 13 ♕f3 a6 14 ♗xc6 ♕xc6 15 ♕xc6+ bxc6 16 ♔e2 ♔d7 gives an equal endgame, as in Sveshnikov-Shirov,

Val Maubuee 1990 and Stripunsky-Dvoirys, Katowice 1992) and here:

a) 12...a6 13 ♗xc6 ♕xc6 14 ♕g4 (14 ♖e1 ♗e7 15 ♕g4 ♗f6 16 ♗g5 ♗xg5 17 ♕xg5 0-0 18 ♖e3 h6 19 ♕g4 ♔h8 20 ♖ae1 ♘d5 = Alexandria-Chiburdanidze, USSR 1981) 14...h5 (14...g6 is weakening, although 15 d5 ♘xd5 16 ♘xd5 ♕xd5 17 ♖d1 h5 18 ♕a4+ ♕b5 19 ♕d4 e5 20 ♕e4 ♗g7 21 ♖d5 as in Chekhov-Zilbershtein, Moscow 1976, may not be so clear, for example 21...♖d8!) 15 ♕e2 (15 ♕h4 ♗e7 16 ♕h3 ♖d8 17 ♗e3 ♘d5 18 ♖ac1 ♘xc3 19 bxc3 ♕c4 20 ♕g3 0-0 21 ♗h6 ♗f6 = Sveshnikov-Popov, Lvov 1973 or 15 ♕g5 ♖d8 16 f3 ♖h6 17 ♕e5 ♖g6 18 ♕xh5 ♖xd4 ∓ Zhuravlev-Gutman, Riga 1971) 15...♗e7 16 ♗e3 h4 17 ♖ac1 h3 18 gxh3 ♖xh3 19 ♕g4 ♕f3 20 ♕xf3 ♖xf3 = Sveshnikov-Kovalev, Budapest 1989.

b) 12....♗e7 13 ♕g4 0-0 (riskier is 13...♗f6 14 ♖d1 a6 15 ♗xc6 ♕xc6 16 d5 ♘xd5 17 ♘xd5 exd5 18 ♕b4 a5 19 ♖e1+ ♔d8 20 ♕a3 Godena-Marinelli, Verona 1995 or 14...h5 15 ♕e2 ♘d5 16 ♘xd5 ♕xd5 17 ♗e3 h4 18 h3 0-0 19 ♗c4 ♕e4 20 d5 Kosilov-Zaid, Ukrainian Ch 1978) 14 ♗xc6 bxc6 (14...♕xc6 15 ♗h6 ♗f6 16 ♖ad1 ♕d7 17 ♘e4 ♕e7 18 ♖d3 ♔h8 19 ♗f4 gave White more attacking chances in Godena-Bacrot, Cannes 1995) 15 ♗h6 ♗f6 16 ♖fd1 ♔h8 (16...♖fd8 17 ♘e4 ♕e7 18 ♖ac1 ♔h8 19 ♗e3 ♖ac8 = Monclus-Tal, Barcelona 1988) 17 ♘e4 ♕e7 18 ♗g5 ♗xg5 19 ♕xg5 ♕xg5 20 ♘xg5 ♔g8 21 ♖ac1 ♖ac8 22 ♘f3 f6 = Godena-Pigusov, Vienna 1991.

10...♗xc6 11 ♘xc6 bxc6 12 0-0
(D)

12 ♘c3 e6 would transpose to a position that could also be reached via the 10 ♘c3 lines of Game 44, that move indeed cancelling out any lines for Black with ...g6. However (although often mis-assessed as ±, or ±) these positions with a black pawn on c6 versus a white pawn on d4 are satisfactory for Black, as the prospective knight on d5 is stronger than its less centralised white counterpart on c5. Therefore White must proceed dynamically, e.g. 13 ♕g4 h5 (13...♘d5!? 14 0-0 h5 15 ♕f3 ♕f6 = Lerner-Gutman, USSR 1979) 14 ♕f3 (14 ♕e4 ♘d5 15 0-0 ♗e7 16 ♗f4 ♘xf4!? 17 ♕xf4 0-0 = Chandler-Gruchacz, USA 1979) 14...♖c8 15 0-0 ♕xd4 16 ♗f4 ♗e7 17 ♖fe1 ♘d5 (better is 17...♕f6 18 ♖e5 ∞ Sveshnikov) 18 ♗e5 ♕g4 19 ♕xg4 hxg4 20 ♗xg7 ± Sveshnikov-Browne, Novi Sad 1979.

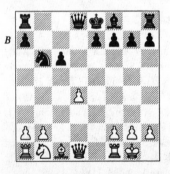

12...g6
Also possible is 12...e6 13 ♕g4 (13 ♘c3 ♗e7 14 ♕g4 0-0 =) 13...h5 (13...♕f6 looks fishy) 14 ♕e4 (14 ♕f3 ♘d5 15 ♕d3 c5 16 ♘c3 ♕xd4

17 ♕f3 ♕d7 18 ♗g5 f6 19 ♖ad1
♕c8 20 ♗c1 ♗e7 21 ♖fe1 h4 ∞ Høi-
Gutman, Reykjavik 1984) 14...♕d5
(14...♖c8 15 ♘c3 ♘d5 16 ♖d1 ♗e7
17 ♕f3 ♘xc3 18 ♕xc3 0-0 = Thi-
bault-Zaltsman, Lone Pine 1979) 15
♕c2 ♗e7 16 ♗e3 h4 17 ♘c3 ♕h5
18 h3 0-0 = Maciejewski-Yakovich,
Belgrade 1991. Despite the weakness generated by 13...h5, Black's
strong-point on d5 is sufficient for
equality.

13 ♖e1

13 ♗g5 ♗g7 14 ♖e1 transposes to
the main game. Alternatively:

a) 13 ♘c3 ♗g7 14 ♗e3 (14 ♕f3
♖c8 15 ♖d1 0-0 16 ♗g5 ♖e8 is equal
Oblamsky-Kapengut, Minsk 1978)
14...0-0 15 ♕e2 ♘d5 is an equal position that has occurred in several
games with Maciejewski playing
White.

b) 13 ♕c2 ♖c8 14 ♖d1 ♗g7 15
♗f4 (15 ♘c3 0-0 16 ♗g5 ♕d7 17
♖ac1 ♖fe8 18 ♕e4 ♕f5 with equality Westerinen-Rantanen, Helsinki
1979) 15...0-0 16 ♗e5 ♕d7 (16...c5
17 ♘c3 c4 18 ♗xg7 ♔xg7 19 d5
♖c5 ∞ Machulsky-Podgaets, USSR
1976) 17 ♘c3 ♖fd8 18 ♖ac1 ∞ Pla-
tonov-Ftačnik, Kiev 1978.

13...♗g7 14 ♗g5 0-0!?

Castling exploits a clever tactical
possibility – Black will not lose the
exchange on account of a counter-at-
tack against b2. Inferior is 14...♕xd4?!
15 ♖xe7+ ♔f8 16 ♕xd4 ♗xd4 17
♖e2 ♔g7 18 ♘c3 with a favourable
endgame for White (the weak pawn
on d4 is gone) in Izvozchikov-Kir-
pichnikov, USSR 1975. However
14...♘d5!? is possible: 15 ♘c3 0-0

16 ♕a4 (16 ♘xd5 ♕xd5 17 ♗xe7
and then 17...♖fe8 18 ♗c5 ♖xe1+ 19
♕xe1 ♗xd4 20 ♗xd4 ♕xd4 21 b3
♖d8 is equal, while 17...♕fb8!?
needs tests) 16...♕b6 17 ♘xd5 cxd5
18 ♗xe7 ♗xd4! = 19 ♖e2 ♖fe8 20
♕d7! ♗f6 21 ♗c5 ♕d8 22 ♖xe8+
♕xe8 23 ♕xd5 ♗xb2 24 ♖b1 ♖d8
25 ♕b7 ♕a4! 26 g3 ♕c2! 27 ♕xb2
♖d1+ 28 ♖xd1 ♕xd1+ (of course
not 28...♕xb2??, which loses to 29
♖d8+ ♔g7 30 ♗d4+) 29 ♔g2 ½-½
Daniliuk-Shaposhnikov, Balakovo
1995, since 29...♕d5+ regains the
bishop.

The retreat 14...♘c8 keeps more
play in the position:

a) 15 ♕f3 0-0 (15...♕d5?! 16
♕xd5 cxd5 17 ♘c3 h6 18 ♗f4 ♘b6
19 a4! ±) 16 ♘c3 ♖b8! (16...♕xd4 17
♕xc6 ♖b8 18 ♖ad1 ♕b6 19 ♕xb6
♖xb6 20 ♘a4 ♖b7 21 b3 with an
edge for White in the endgame,
Smagin-Tischbierek, Germany 1993)
17 ♖ad1 ♖xb2 18 ♕xc6 ♗xd4 and
the complications favoured Black in
Talavera-Georgadze, Malaga 1987.

b) 15 ♕a4 0-0! 16 ♕xc6 ♖b8 17
♘c3 ♖b6! 18 ♕f3 ♖xb2 ∞ Khol-
mov-Mnatsakanian, USSR 1977.

c) 15 ♘c3 0-0 (15...♕xd4 16 ♕f3
0-0 is the Smagin game from 15 ♕f3
above) 16 ♗e3 ♘b6 = S.Lalić-Sher,
Hastings 1994.

d) 15 ♕e2 h6 16 ♗e3 0-0 17 ♘c3
♘d6 18 d5 cxd5 19 ♘xd5 e6 ∓ Sza-
bolcsi-Sax, Hungary 1980.

15 ♗xe7 ♕xd4 (D)

16 ♕xd4

Obviously 16 ♗xf8 ♕xd1 17 ♖xd1
♗xb2 recovers the material with interest for Black. Instead 16 ♘c3

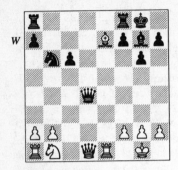

♕xd1 (16...♖fe8 17 ♕f3 is unclear) 17 ♖axd1 ♖fe8 is becoming very equal. For example 18 ♗c5 ♘c4 19 ♖xe8+ ♖xe8 20 ♘a4 ♘xb2 21 ♘xb2 ♗xb2 22 ♗xa7 ♖a8 ½-½ Crouch-Plaskett, London 1980 or 18 ♔f1 ♗xc3 19 bxc3 ♘d5 20 ♗c5 ♖xe1+ 21 ♖xe1 ♘xc3 22 ♖c1 ♘d5 23 ♗d4 ½-½ Gogichayshvili-Ernst, Gausdal 1992.

16...♗xd4 17 ♘d2 ♖fe8

17...♖fb8!? and now:

a) 18 ♖ac1 ♘d5 19 ♘f3 ♗xb2 ½-½ Typek-Skalik, Poland 1994.

b) 18 ♖ab1 ♘d5 (Alterman recommends the alternative 18...♘a4, but White has 19 ♖e4 c5 20 ♗xc5! winning a pawn) 19 ♘f3 ♗g7 20 ♗d6 ♖b5 21 ♖ec1 ♖e8 22 ♔f1 ♖c8 23 ♖c4 a5 24 ♖bc1 ♗xb2 25 ♖xc6 ♖xc6 ½-½ Sammalvuo-Krakops, Halle 1995.

18 ♗a3 c5

Dubious according to Alterman, who gives 18...♗g7! 19 ♖ac1 ♖xe1+ 20 ♖xe1 ♖d8 21 ♔f1 h5 22 ♔e2 ♗h6 =.

19 ♔f1 ± c4 20 ♖xe8+ ♖xe8 21 ♖c1 ♖c8 22 ♘e4! a6 23 ♖d1 ♗e5 24 g3 h5 25 f4 ♗g7 26 ♘c3 ♗xc3 27 bxc3 ♘a4 28 ♗b4 ♘b2 29 ♖d7?! (29 ♖d6 ♘d3 30 a3!?) **29...♘d3 30 ♗d6 ♔g7 31 ♗e5+ ½-½**

17 4 d4 cxd4 5 ♘f3

1	e4	c5
2	c3	♘f6
3	e5	♘d5
4	d4	cxd4
5	♘f3 (D)	

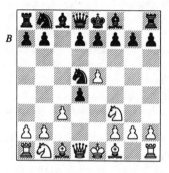

With 5 ♘f3 (instead of the 5 cxd4 of Chapters 13-16) White intends to meet 5...♘c6 with the aggressive 6 ♗c4 ♘b6 7 ♗b3, which can occasionally involve a pawn sacrifice. It is possible for Black to remain in solid lines similar to the earlier chapters with the reply 5...e6, and indeed transpositions back to those chapters are common. However White's key point is that, via the present move-order, Black cannot reach the clear equalising plan he had in Chapter 16. In Game 47 we deal with these odds and ends, with the general conclusion being that after White should probably play an early a3 and head for Chapter 13. Otherwise White risks allowing a particularly comfortable

(and little-known) defence for Black in the sneaky move 8...♕c7! (see the note to Black's eighth move). But in turn if Black plays routinely, as in the illustrative game, White gains a pleasant initiative.

The remaining two illustrative games include coverage of lines (after 5...♘c6 6 ♗c4 ♘b6 7 ♗b3 d5 8 exd6) where Black does not continue with the standard recapture 8...♕xd6. The pawn-grab 8...dxc3 (Game 48) is obviously risky, but perhaps not completely clear. Bologan's 1995 discovery, the fianchetto with 7...g6!? (Game 49), was adopted enthusiastically for a time, but White seems to have at least one safe route to a small edge with the continuation 8 cxd4 ♗g7 9 ♗f4.

Game 47
Minev – Korchnoi
Oslo tt 1954

1 e4 c5 2 c3 ♘f6 3 e5 ♘d5 4 d4 cxd4 5 ♘f3

The move-order of the actual game, 5 cxd4 ♘c6 6 ♘f3 e6 7 ♘c3 ♘xc3 8 bxc3 d6, has been altered slightly for administrative convenience. In fact there are numerous transposition possibilities to other chapters around this point, and in some ways this game merely ties up some loose ends – both Black and

White have promising possibilities to vary early.

5...e6

5...♘c6, heading for the main line, is analysed in the following game.

6 cxd4 d6 *(D)*

Here 6...b6!? is a transposition to Chapter 14. On 6...♘c6 White may choose from several options. After 7 a3! (intending ♗d3), for example, Black has nothing better than 7...d6 with a transposition to Chapter 13 – a move-order commonly utilised to reach that chapter. Also possible is 7 ♘c3 ♘xc3 8 bxc3 d5 (8...d6 is the main game) and here 9 exd6 is possible, while 9 ♗d3 is equally pleasant for White.

After 6...♘c6 White can also go for systems with his bishop on c4: 7 ♗c4 ♘b6 (7...d6 is a transposition to Chapter 15 while 7...♗b4+ 8 ♗d2 ♗xd2+ 9 ♘bxd2 ♘de7 10 ♘e4 ± was Sveshnikov-Mrdjen, Pula 1990) 8 ♗b3 (8 ♗d3!? would transpose to Preissmann-Gallagher, Swiss Cht 1995, which continued 8...d5 9 ♗g5 ♗e7 10 ♗xe7 ♕xe7 11 0-0 ♗d7 12 a3 0-0 13 ♘c3 ♖ac8 14 ♕d2 f5 15 exf6 ♖xf6 16 ♕e3 ♖cf8 17 ♘g5 g6 ∞) 8...d6 (8...d5 is also played) and now 9 ♕e2 is examined in Chapter 16, Game 44, note after Black's eighth move, while 9 exd6 is covered (by transposition) in the course of Game 48 coming up.

7 ♘c3

Again 7 a3!? is Chapter 13. If 7 ♗d3 immediately then 7...♘b4 is irritating, e.g. 8 ♗e2 (8 ♗b5+ ♗d7 9 ♗e2 ♗c6 10 0-0 ♘d7 11 ♘c3 dxe5

12 dxe5 ♗e7 13 ♗f4 ♘d5 = Baev-Kalegin, Moscow 1995) 8...dxe5 9 a3 e4! 10 ♘g5 ♘4c6 11 ♗e3 g6 12 ♘c3 ♗g7 13 d5 ♗xc3+ 14 bxc3 exd5 ∓ Rauze-Lerner, Nîmes 1991.

The third possibility is 7 ♗c4, when Black can continue:

a) 7...♘c6 transposes to Chapter 15.

b) 7...dxe5 8 dxe5 ♗b4+ (8...♘c6 is Chapter 15) 9 ♗d2 (9 ♘bd2 ♘b6 10 0-0 ♘xc4 11 ♕a4+ ♘c6 12 ♘xc4 and then 12...♕d3 13 ♘d6+ ♗xd6 14 ♖d1 ♕a6 15 ♕xa6 bxa6 16 exd6 ± was Svidler-Taimanov, Russia 1995 but safer was 12...0-0 13 ♗f4 ♕c7 14 ♖fd1 ♗d7 15 ♖ac1 ♖fd8 16 ♗g5 ♗e7 ∞ Alexander-Golombek, Hastings 1935!) 9...♗e7 (9...♘c6 10 0-0 ♗e7 11 ♕e2 0-0 12 ♘c3 ♘xc3 13 ♗xc3 ± Wolff-Rotshtein, Wijk aan Zee 1993) 10 0-0 ♘c6 11 ♕e2 ♕b6 12 ♘c3 ♘xc3 13 bxc3 ♗d7 14 ♗d3 ♖d8 15 ♖ab1 ± Yanovsky-Krasenkov, Voskresensk 1992.

c) 7...♗e7 8 0-0 0-0 9 ♕e2 ♗d7 (9...♘c6 is Chapter 15) 10 ♘c3 ♘xc3 11 bxc3 ♗c6 12 ♗f4 (12 exd6 ♗xd6 13 ♘e5 ♗xe5 14 ♕xe5 ♘d7 15 ♕g3 ♗e4 16 ♗b3 ± Sveshnikov-Vera, Sochi 1985) 12...dxe5 13 ♘xe5

♗d5 14 ♗d3 ♘d7 15 c4 ± Dolma-
tov-Zapata, Tilburg 1993.

d) 7...♘b6!? 8 ♗d3 (for 8 ♗b3
see Game 47, note to Black's fifth)
8...♘c6 9 a3 dxe5 10 dxe5 ♘d7!?
(10...♕c7 11 ♗f4 ♘d5 12 ♗g3 ♗d7
13 ♘bd2 ♗e7 14 0-0 0-0 15 ♕b1 h6
16 ♕e1 ♕d8 17 ♕e4 f5 18 exf6
♘xf6 19 ♕e2 ± Kharlov-Marić, Biel
1992) 11 ♗f4 ♘c5 12 ♗c2 ♕xd1+
13 ♔xd1 ♗e7 14 ♘bd2 0-0 15 b4
♘d7 16 ♘e4 ♖d8 17 ♔e2 ♘b6 =
Sermek-Banas, Luxembourg 1993.

7...♘xc3

If 7...dxe5, 8 ♘xe5 ±, for example
8...♗b4 9 ♗d2 0-0 10 ♗e2 (10 ♗d3
♘d7 11 ♕e2 ♘xe5 12 dxe5 ♕a5 13
0-0 ♘xc3 14 bxc3 ♗e7 15 ♕e4 g6
16 ♖fd1 ♕d5 17 c4 ♕xe4 18 ♗xe4
½-½ Sveshnikov-Polugaevsky, but
White looks better in the final position) 10...♗xc3 11 bxc3 ♘d7 12 0-0
♘xe5 13 dxe5 ♗d7 14 c4 ♘b6 15
♗b4 ♖e8 16 ♕b3 ♗c6 17 ♕e3 ♘d7
18 ♗d6 ± Kholmov-Malich, Halle
1978.

Instead 7...♘c6!? gives a fairly
standard position, when White has a
choice:

a) 8 ♗d3 dxe5 9 dxe5 ♘db4!?
(9...♗b4 10 ♕c2 ♗e7 11 ♗e4 ♘xc3
12 bxc3 ♕c7 13 ♗f4 ± Timman-
E.Meyer, New York 1974) 10 ♗e4
♕xd1+ 11 ♔xd1 ♗c5 12 a3 ♘d5! 13
♘xd5 exd5 14 ♗xd5 0-0 15 ♔e2
♖d8 16 ♗e4 (16 ♖d1 ♘d4+!)
16...♖e8! 17 ♗xc6 bxc6 18 ♗e3
♗a6+ 19 ♔d2 ♖ad8+ 20 ♔c2 ♗d3+
21 ♔c3 ♗xe3 22 fxe3 ♗e2! 23 b4
♖d3+ 24 ♔c2 ♖xe3 25 ♖he1 ♖e4!
26 ♘d4! ♖4xe5 ∓ Blatny-Lechtyn-
sky, Czechoslovak Ch 1986.

b) 8 ♗b5 ♕a5!? (8...♘xc3 9
bxc3 ♗d7 10 0-0 ♘xe5 11 ♘xe5
dxe5 12 ♖b1 ♗xb5 13 ♖xb5 ♕d7 14
♕b3 b6 15 ♖xe5 ♗d6 = Stanciu-
Ghinda, Skopje OL 1972) 9 ♕b3 ♗d7
10 ♗d2 ♘xc3 11 ♗xc3 ♕b6 12 ♗a4
d5 13 0-0 ♗e7 14 ♕d1 0-0 15 a3
♖ac8 ∞ Kholmov-Saltaev, Volgo-
grad 1994.

c) 8 exd6 ♗xd6 9 ♗d3 (9 ♗c4
♘xc3 10 bxc3 0-0 11 0-0 transposes
to the note after White's eighth move
in Game 42, a satisfactory IQP position for Black) 9...♘f4! 10 ♗xf4
♗xf4 11 0-0 0-0 12 ♕e2 ♗h6 (or
12...♘xd4 13 ♗xh7+ ♔xh7 14 ♕e4+
♔g8 15 ♕xf4 ♘xf3+ 16 ♕xf3 ♕b6
17 ♖fd1 ½-½ Bisguier-Panno, Lone
Pine 1976 while 12...g6 13 ♖ad1
♗h6 transposes to the 12...♗h6 line)
13 ♖ad1 g6 14 ♗e4 ♗g7 15 ♗xc6
(15 d5 exd5 16 ♗xd5 ♕f6 17 ♘e4
♕e7 18 ♖fe1 ♗g4 = 19 h3? ♘d4! 20
♖xd4 ♗xf3 21 ♕xf3 ♖xd4 ∓ Hecht-
Malich, Amsterdam 1971) 15...bxc6
16 ♘e5 c5 17 d5 ♕d6 18 ♘c4 ♕a6
19 d6 ♗b7 20 ♘e4 ♗d5 21 b3 ♖ad8
∞ Romanovich-Zitin, Russia 1995.

d) 8 ♘xd5 exd5:

d1) 9 ♗e2:

d11) 9...dxe5 10 ♘xe5 ♗d6 11
♕a4?! Pazos-Anand, Dubai OL 1986,
and now Anand gives 11...♗xe5! 12
dxe5 0-0 13 f4 ♕h4+ ∓.

d12) 9...♗e7 10 0-0 0-0 11 ♗f4
♗g4 12 ♖e1 ♖e8 13 h3 ♗h5 14 ♖c1
♖c8 with little for White in Pomar-
Andersson, Las Palmas 1974.

d2) 9 ♗d3:

d21) 9...♗e7 10 0-0 0-0 11 h3
♗e6 12 ♗f4 ♖e8 13 ♖c1 ♕d7 14 ♗b5
f6 15 ♕a4 ± Markland-Ermenkov,

Polanica Zdroj 1973 or 10 h3 dxe5 11 dxe5 0-0 12 0-0 ♗e6 13 ♗f4 ♖c8 14 ♖c1 ♕d7 15 a3 ♘a5 16 ♕e2 a6 17 ♘d4 ± Boeven-Gudat, corr. 1970. The bishop is well posted on d3 if Black does not interrupt White's smooth development.

d22) 9...dxe5! 10 dxe5 ♗b4+ 11 ♗d2. This position looks satisfactory for Black, for example 11...♕e7 12 0-0 ♗g4 = Müller-Heuser, Germany 1988 or 11...0-0 12 0-0 ♗xd2 13 ♕xd2 ♗g4 14 ♕f4 ♗xf3 15 ♕xf3 ♘xe5 16 ♗xh7+ ♔xh7 17 ♕h5+ ♔g8 18 ♕xe5 ♖e8 19 ♕d4 ♖e4 20 ♕d2 ♕d6 21 ♖ad1 ♖d8 = Nicolini-Hudecek, Slovakian Cht 1995.

8 bxc3 *(D)*

8...♘c6?!

There are several move-orders to reach this standard position. Quite often Black has played ...♘c6 earlier, but if not, Black has an excellent opportunity to continue 8...♕c7! instead. The queen is developed with game of time on account of the attack on the c3-pawn, and it becomes apparent that Black's queen's knight can be more effectively posted on

d7. Comparing analogous ...b6 lines (Chapter 14) where Black plays the same manoeuvre; the present version is very comfortable for Black: the earlier pressure on e5 will probably force White to exchange pawns on d6. First, of course, the c-pawn must be looked after:

a) 9 ♕b3 ♘d7 (9...♗d7!? 10 ♗a3 ♗c6 11 ♗b5 dxe5 12 ♗xf8 ♔xf8 13 ♗xc6 ♘xc6 14 0-0 g6 15 ♘xe5 ♘xe5 16 dxe5 ♗g7 ∓ Karaklajić-Barlov, Pula 1990) 10 ♗f4 dxe5 11 ♗xe5 ♘xe5 12 ♘xe5 ♗d6 13 ♗b5+ ♔f8 14 f4 g6 15 0-0 ♔g7 16 c4 b6 ∓ Barić-Mencinger, Bled 1992.

b) 9 ♕c2 ♘d7 10 ♗f4 dxe5 11 ♗xe5 ♘xe5 12 ♘xe5 ♗d6 13 ♗b5+ ♔f8 14 f4 b6 15 0-0 g6 = Lehmann-Kraut, Bundesliga 1990.

c) 9 exd6 ♗xd6 10 ♗b2 ♘d7 11 ♗d3 and now instead of 11...b6 12 0-0 ♗b7 13 ♖e1 0-0 14 c4 when the white bishops point ominously at the black kingside, Campora-P.Cramling, Argentina 1994, the neat tactic 11...♗a3! swaps bishops as in the following note.

d) 9 ♗b2 ♘d7 10 exd6 ♗xd6 11 ♗d3 ♗a3! (a useful liquidation: obviously 12 ♗xa3? ♕xc3+ and 13...♕xa3 would regain the bishop) 12 ♕b3 ♗xb2 13 ♕xb2 = Ramirez-Llanes, Spain 1995.

e) 9 ♗d2 (the main move) 9...♘d7 (9...♘c6 10 exd6 ♗xd6 11 ♗d3 e5 Nunez-Ochoa, Cuba 1992 leaves the black kingside a little exposed, while the plan 9...♗d7 10 ♗d3 ♗c6 was unclear in Glavina-Komljenović, Ceuta 1995) 10 exd6 ♗xd6 11 ♗d3 b6 12 0-0 ♗b7 with a comfortable position for Black. In fact this position is examined in Chapter 14, Game 38, note to White's 10th move.

9 exd6

Interesting is 9 ♗d3!? dxe5 10 dxe5 ♗e7 (10...♕a5 11 0-0 ⑤xe5 12 ⑤xe5 ♕xe5 13 ♖e1 is dangerous, for example 13...♕d6 14 ♖e4 ♗e7 15 ♗f4 ♕d5 16 ♖d4 ♕a5 17 ♖b1 0-0 18 ♖b5 ♕xc3 19 ♖c4 ♕f6 20 ♗e5 ♕h6 21 ♗xg7 ♕xg7 22 ♖g4 Kosikov-Khodos, USSR 1978) 11 ♕e2 as in King-Friedgood, London 1980. You can understand Black's reluctance to now castle kingside, but in the game the queenside did not prove safer: 11...♕c7 12 0-0 ♗d7 13 ♖e1 0-0-0 14 ♖b1 ♔b8 15 ♗e4 ♗c8 16 ♗e3 ♔a8 17 ♖b5 f5 18 exf6 gxf6 19 ♖eb1 e5 20 ♕c2 ♗d6 21 ♕a4 ♖hg8 22 ♗xc6 bxc6 23 ♖b7 1-0.

Another idea is 9 ♗f4, for example 9...♗e7 10 ♗d3 dxe5 11 ⑤xe5 ⑤xe5 12 ♗xe5 0-0 (12...♗f6 Levi-Canfell, Melbourne 1991 and now 13 ♗xf6 ± because on 13...♕xf6, there follows 14 ♗b5+) 13 ♕h5 g6 14 ♕h6 ♗f6 15 f4 ♗xe5 16 fxe5 ±, as in Zimmermann-Kotter, Germany 1994.

9...♗xd6

After 9...♕xd6 10 ♗d3 ♗e7 11 0-0 0-0 12 ♖e1 b6 13 ⑤e5 (13 ⑤g5! ± g6? 14 ⑤xh7! ♔xh7 15 ♕h5+ ♔g8 16 ♗xg6 fxg6 17 ♕xg6+ ♔h8 18 ♖e3 ♗h4 19 ♖h3 ♕e7 20 ♗g5 ♕g7 21 ♖xh4+ ♔g8 22 ♕xg7+ ♔xg7 23 ♗h6+ 1-0 was a lovely successful attack in Häusler-Schlemermeyer, Bundesliga 1981) 13...⑤xe5 14 ♗f4 ♗b7 15 ♗xe5 was played in two games. White looks slightly better,

but in both cases was fortuitous to win with bishop sacrifices:

a) 15...♕d8 16 ♗xh7+? ♔xh7 17 ♕h5+ ♔g8 18 ♖e3 f6 19 ♖h3 ♗d6 ∓ 20 ♖xd6 ♕xd6 21 ♖e1 ♗d5?! 22 ♕g6 ♖ac8? 23 ♖h7 ♕c7 24 ♕h5 1-0 Tsharotshkin-Hanko, Dortmund 1992.

b) 15...♕c6 16 ♗e4 ♕d7 17 ♗xh7+ ♔xh7 18 ♕h5+ ♔g8 19 ♗xg7 ♔xg7 20 ♖e3 ♕d5? (20...♖h8 21 ♖g3+ ♗g5! 22 ♕xg5+ ♔f8) 21 ♖g3+ ♔f6 22 ♕h4+ ♔f5 23 ♕g4+ 1-0 Palkovi-Pigott, Budapest 1993.

10 ♗d3 ♗e7

Black takes precautions against the Greek gift sacrifice on h7, which is in the air either immediately or later if he castles.

a) In the game Mestel-Kirov, Moscow 1977, Black successfully bolstered his kingside with 10...⑤e7!? 11 0-0 ⑤g6 12 ♖e1 0-0 13 c4 b6 14 ♗e4 ♖b8 15 ♗b2 ♕c7 16 ♖c1 ♗f4 ∞.

b) Black can also postpone castling with 10...♕a5 when 11 ♗d2 is probably ±, while 11 ♕c2 b6 12 0-0 ♗a6 13 ♗e4 ♖c8 14 ♖e1 ⑤e7 15 ♗d2 ♗c4 16 ♗b7 ♖c7 17 ⑤e5 ♖xb7 18 ⑤xc4 ♕d5 19 ♕a4+ b5 20 ⑤xd6+ ♕xd6 21 ♕b3 0-0 = was Alekhine-Foltys, Prague 1942! However White can also offer a pawn with 11 0-0!?, when 11...♕xc3 12 ♖b1 0-0 13 ♖b3 ♕a5 14 ♗xh7+! ♔xh7 15 ⑤g5+ ♔g6 16 ♖h3 ♗d7 17 ⑤e4 1-0 Markland-Klundt, Madrid 1971 is an example of the dangers awaiting Black's acceptance.

c) 10...♕c7 11 0-0 ♗d7 12 ♖e1 0-0-0 is a method of side-stepping White's potential kingside threats.

In Benderac-Marković, Yugoslavia 1993 Black gained a good game after 13 a4 ⧖a5 14 ♗a3?! ♗xa3 15 ♖xa3 ♔b8 16 ⧖e5 ♗c8 17 ♕e2 f6 =, but White had more testing methods of trying to exploit Black's king position on the queenside. The overall impression of these alternatives is that they are certainly playable for Black, although White usually has a bit more space.

11 0-0 0-0 12 ♕e2 ♗f6 13 ♖e1 ♕d5 14 ♗f4 ♖d8 15 ♖ad1 ♗d7 16 ⧖e5 ±

White has an initiative, more space and chances of an attack.

16...♗e8 17 ♕h5!? g6 (D)

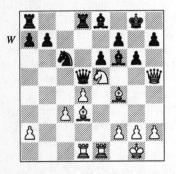

Now Minev finds a marvellous continuation.

18 ⧖g4!! ♗e7 (18...♗g7 19 ♕h4! and 20 ⧖f6+ is coming) **19 ♕h6 ♕h5** (leaving the black pawns crippled, but 19...♕xa2 was too dangerous a pawn snatch even for Korchnoi: 20 ♗g5! and Black's dark squares are critically weak) **20 ♕xh5 gxh5 21 ⧖e5 ♖ac8 22 ⧖xc6 ♗xc6 23 ♖e5 ♗a4 24 ♖c1 ♗a3 25 ♖b1 ♖xc3 26 ♖e3 ♖dc8 27 ♖g3+ ♔f8 28 ♖xb7 ♖c1+ 29 ♗f1 1-0**

The threat is 30 ♗h6+ followed by ♖g8.

Game 48
Biro – Gueldner
Budapest 1990

1 e4 c5 2 c3

The game moves were 2 ⧖f3 ⧖c6 3 c3 ⧖f6 4 e5 ⧖d5 5 d4 cxd4; I have substituted the usual order in order to fit in the note at move five.

2...⧖f6 3 e5 ⧖d5 4 d4 cxd4 5 ⧖f3 ⧖c6

After 5...d6 White can continue 6 ♗c4 (6 cxd4 was covered in earlier chapters) and now:

a) 6...dxe5 7 ⧖xe5 is promising for White: 7...e6 8 0-0 (8 ♕xd4!? ⧖c6 9 ⧖xc6 bxc6 10 0-0 ♗b7 11 ♗b3 ♕b6 12 ♕g4 0-0-0 13 ♗g5 ⧖f6 14 ♕h4 c5 15 ⧖a3 h6 16 ♗xf6 gxf6 17 ⧖c4 ♕c6 18 f3 ♗e7 19 ⧖a5 ± Makarychev-Vasiukov, Moscow 1986) and then:

a1) 8...dxc3? is too risky: 9 ⧖xc3 ⧖c6 10 ⧖xf7! ⧖xc3 (10...♔xf7 loses to 11 ⧖xd5 exd5 12 ♗xd5+ ♗e6 13 ♗xe6+ ♔xe6 14 ♖e1+ ♔f7 15 ♕b3+, etc.) 11 ♕h5 ♕a5 12 ⧖d6+ ♔e7 13 ♕f7+ ♔xd6 14 bxc3 ⧖e5 15 ♗f4 ♔c6 16 ♕e8+ ♗d7 17 ♕xa8 ⧖xc4 18 ♖ab1 ♕a6 19 ♖fd1 e5 20 ♖xd7 ♔xd7 21 ♖xb7+ 1-0 Espinoza-Jasnikowski, Cuba 1988.

a2) 8...♗e7 9 cxd4 (9 ♕h5 0-0 10 ♖d1 ⧖d7 11 cxd4 ⧖7f6 12 ♕h3 ♗d7 13 ⧖c3 ♗c6 = Espinoza-Xu, Moscow OL 1994) 9...0-0 10 ⧖c3 ⧖f6 11 ♗e3 ⧖c6 12 ⧖xc6 bxc6 13 ♖c1 ♕c7 14 ♗d3 ♖d8 15 ♕e2 ♗d7 16 ♖fd1 ± Pribik-Hromada, Corr. 1984.

b) However instead Black has 6...♘b6 7 ♗b3 and now:

b1) 7...♘c6 transposes to earlier chapters.

b2) 7...d5 8 ♘xd4!? (for 8 cxd4 see Game 44, 8...d5 note to Black's eighth move) 8...♘c6 9 ♕e2 ♘xd4 10 cxd4 ♗f5 11 ♗d2 e6 12 ♗a5!? ♗e7 13 ♗a4+ ♔f8 14 0-0 ± Hresc-Gutman, Kirchheim rpd 1990.

b3) For 7...dxe5 8 ♘xe5 e6 see the next note.

b4) 7...e6!? 8 cxd4 dxe5 (8...♗d7 9 0-0 ♗c6 10 ♘c3 ♘8d7 11 ♕e2 ♗e7 12 ♖d1 0-0 13 ♗f4 dxe5 14 dxe5 ♖c8 15 ♘d4 ♘d5 Godena-Borgo, Italy 1994, and here simply 15 ♘xd5 ±) 9 ♘xe5 (9 dxe5 ♕xd1+ 10 ♗xd1 is certainly playable for White) 9...♘c6 (9...♘8d7 10 0-0 ♘xe5 11 dxe5 ♕xd1 12 ♖xd1 ♗d7 13 ♘c3 ♗c6 14 ♗e3 ♗e7 15 a4 0-0 16 ♘b5 ♗xb5 17 axb5 ± in Maliutin-Golod, Minsk 1993) 10 ♘xc6 bxc6 11 0-0 ♗e7 12 ♘c3 0-0 with quite an important position to evaluate, even though reached relatively few times:

b41) 13 ♗e3 a5 14 ♖c1 ♗a6 15 ♖e1 ♘d5 16 ♕f3 ♗b4 17 ♖ed1 ♕f6 18 ♕g3 ♕g6 19 ♕h3 h6 20 ♗c2 f5 21 ♘xd5 cxd5 22 ♕f3 ½-½ was Lane-Kuczynski, Gent 1988.

b42) 13 ♘e4 a5 14 ♗c2 ♖e8 15 ♖e1 ♘d5 16 a3 ♕b6 17 h4 ♗d7 18 ♕d3 f5 19 ♘g5 ♗f6 20 ♘f3 c5 21 dxc5 ♕xc5 22 ♖b1 ♗b5 ∓ was the game Sariego-Kuczynski, Polanica Zdroj 1989.

b43) 13 ♗f4 ♗a6 (13...♘d5 14 ♗e5 gave White a slight pull in Winants-Klarenbeek, Netherlands 1995, which increased after 14...♘xc3?!

15 bxc3 ♗d6 16 ♖e1) 14 ♖e1 c5 15 dxc5 ♕xd1 = Kharlov-Yudasin, Kemerovo 1995. On the evidence of these game references this variation could be a valid alternative to the much sharper main lines where Black has to know a lot of theory.

6 ♗c4 ♘b6

6...e6 7 cxd4 transposes to earlier chapters, (but of course to lines where Black is denied the straightforward equalising path found in Chapter 16).

7 ♗b3 d5

7...d6 gives White the choice of 8 exd6 (transposing into the main game) and 8 cxd4 as per Chapter 16. Or 7...dxc3?! 8 ♘xc3 gives White a serious advantage in development for the pawn, when the follow-up 8...d6 9 exd6 would transpose to the illustrative game. Finally the move 7...g6 is examined in Game 49.

8 exd6 *(D)*

8 cxd4 ♗g4 is very comfortable for Black.

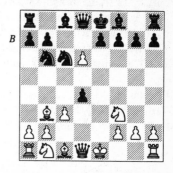

8...dxc3

The normal move, 8...♕xd6, forms the subject of the next few chapters. 8...e6, a pet line of Lanka, gives

Black a rather passive anti-IQP position provided White captures with the pawn on d4:

a) On 9 ᐁxd4?! Black can consider both 9...♗xd6 10 ᐁb5 ♗b8 11 ♕xd8+ ᐁxd8 12 ♗e3 ᐁd7 13 0-0 a6 14 ᐁd4 ᐁe5 with equality, Dubois-Lanka, Cappelle la Grande 1994 and 9...♕xd6 10 ᐁb5 ♕b8 11 ♗e3 ♗e7 12 ♕f3 0-0 13 ♕g3 e5 14 ᐁd2 ♗f5 = Kranzl-Lanka, Budapest 1991.

b) 9 cxd4 ♗xd6 10 0-0 (or first 10 ᐁc3) 10...0-0 (10...ᐁd5 11 ᐁc3 ᐁxc3 12 bxc3 0-0 13 ♕d3 e5 14 ᐁg5 g6 15 ♕f3 ♗e7 16 ♖e1 ♔g7 17 ᐁe4 ♗c7 18 ᐁf6! ♗d8 19 ♗g5 ± Kotliar-Shirazi, Saint Martin 1991) 11 ᐁc3 ♗e7 12 ♗f4 (12 a3 ♗f6 13 ♗e3 ᐁa5 14 ♗a2 ᐁac4 15 ♕e2 ᐁd6 16 ♖fd1 ♖e8 17 ♗f4 ± Strikovic-Lanka, Val Maubuee 1990, and 12 ♖e1 would transpose to Am.Rodriguez-Talavera, Malaga 1987, which continued 12...ᐁb4 13 a3 ᐁ4d5 14 ♕d3 ♗d7 15 ♗c2 g6 16 ♗h6 ♖e8 17 ᐁe5 ♗f8 18 ♕h3 ±) 12...ᐁa5 13 ♗c2 ᐁd5 14 ᐁxd5 ♕xd5 15 ♖e1 ᐁc6 16 ♕d3 g6 17 ♗b3 ♕d8 18 ♗h6 ♖e8 19 ♖ad1 ♗f6 20 ♕e4 ♗d7 21 ᐁe5 ♕e7 22 ♕f4 ±, as in Schandorff-T.Thorhallsson, Copenhagen 1994.

9 ᐁxc3

9 0-0 exd6 10 ᐁg5? is too ambitious: 10...cxb2! 11 ♕h5 g6 12 ♕e2+ ♗e7 13 ♗xb2 0-0 ∓ Acs-Chachere, Budapest 1993.

9...exd6 10 ᐁg5! d5

10...ᐁe5?! 11 f4 h6 12 fxe5 hxg5 13 0-0 d5 14 ᐁe4 ♗e7 15 ♗xg5 ♗xg5 16 ᐁd6+ ♔f8 17 ♖xf7 ± was a promising piece-for-two-pawns

sacrifice in Kantsler-N.Popov, USSR 1980.

11 0-0

White can regain his pawn immediately with 11 ᐁxd5 ᐁxd5 12 ♗xd5 (12 ♕xd5 ♗b4+ 13 ♗d2 is roughly equal) 12...♗b4+ 13 ♔f1 0-0 but now White should play 14 ♕f3 ♕e7 15 ♗e3 because 14 ♕h5?! is dubious: 14...♗f5 15 ♗xf7+ ♔h8 16 ♗e3 (16 ♗f4 ♕d3+ 17 ♔g1 ᐁd4 18 g3 ♗e4! 19 ᐁxe4 ♖xf7! 20 ♕xf7 ♕xe4 −+ Miniböck-Lanka, Trnava 1986) 16...♕d3+ 17 ♔g1 ᐁd4 18 ♗xd4 ♕xd4 and now 19 h4 ♗g6? led to a stunning finish in the game Šibarević-M.Pavlov, Pernik 1988: 20 ♕xg6!! hxg6 21 h5!! ♖xf7 22 hxg6+ ♔g8 23 gxf7+ ♔f8 24 ᐁe6+ 1-0. However 19th move alternatives such as 19...♗c5 and 19...♕xb2 look promising for Black.

11...♗e7

11...f6? 12 ᐁxd5 ᐁxd5 13 ♗xd5 fxg5 14 ♖e1+ ♗e7 15 ♗xg5 ♔f8 16 ♗xc6 ♗xg5 17 ♕xd8+ ♗xd8 18 ♖e8+ ♔f7 19 ♖xh8 ♗e7 20 ♗d5+ ♔f6 21 ♖c1 1-0 is quoted as a game I.Horvath-Larsen, Budapest 1989 – not, of course, *the* Larsen!

12 ♕h5

12 ᐁxd5 ᐁxd5 13 ᐁxf7 looks an over ambitious sacrifice: 13...♔xf7 14 ♗xd5+ ♔f8 15 ♕h5 ♕e8 16 ♕f3+ ♗f6 17 ♗f4 and now instead of 17...♗e6? 18 ♗d6+ ♔f7 19 ♖ae1 ± ᐁd8 20 ♗xe6+ ᐁxe6 21 ♕xb7+ ♗e7 22 ♖xe6 ♔xe6 23 ♗xe7 ♔f7 24 ♖e1 1-0 Motwani-Coleman, Hastings 1991, 17...ᐁe5! defends.

12...g6 13 ♕h6 ♗e6 14 ♖e1 ♕d7 15 ♗f4 (D)

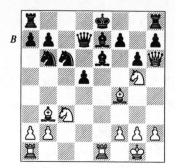

**1 e4 c5 2 c3 ₤f6 3 e5 ₤d5 4 d4 cxd4
5 ₤f3 ₤c6 6 ₤c4 ₤b6 7 ₤b3 g6!?**
(D)

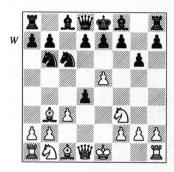

White has dangerous compensation for the sacrificed pawn, but the situation is by no means completely clear.

15...a6

15...₤d6 16 ₤xd6 ₩xd6 17 ₤b5 ₩f8 18 ₩h3 0-0-0 19 ₤xe6 fxe6 20 ₤xe6 ₤d7 21 ₤ae1 ± Van Mil-Quist, Dieren 1990, while the continuation 15...0-0-0 16 ₤ac1 sets up the threat of ₤b5.

16 ₤ac1

The immediate 16 a4!? has also been seen.

16...0-0-0 17 a4 (or 17 ₤a4!?) **17...₤d6 18 ₤xe6 fxe6 19 ₤xd6 ₩xd6 20 ₤b5!? axb5 21 axb5 ₢b8 22 bxc6 bxc6 23 ₩e3 ₢b7 24 ₩d4 ₤hf8 25 g3** (perhaps White could have exploited his queenside pressure better; Black's king position is still shaky, but White has to remember he is still a pawn down) **25...₤f5 26 f4 g5 27 ₤c2 c5 28 ₩g7+ ₤d7 29 ₩h6 ₩f8 30 ₤xe6 ₩xh6 31 ₤xh6 ₤ff7 32 fxg5 c4 33 b3 c3 34 ₤e1 d4 35 ₤e4+ ₤d5 36 ₤d1 ₢c8 37 ₤c6+ ₢b8 38 ₤xd4 ₤e3 39 ₤b4+ ₢a7 40 ₤a4+ ₢b8 41 ₤b6+ ₢c8 42 ₤a8+ ₢c7 43 ₤c6+ ₢b7 44 ₤xc3+ ₤d5 45 ₤a5 1-0**

This novelty was first played by Bologan against Rozentalis.

8 cxd4

a) **8 a4?!** d5 9 exd6 ₩xd6 10 ₤a3 (10 0-0 ₤g7 11 a5 ₤d7 12 cxd4 ₤xd4 13 ₤xd4 ₩xd4 14 ₩f3 ₤e5 15 ₩g3 0-0 16 ₤c3 ₩g4 ∓ Handoko-Hsu, Malaysia 1995) 10...a6 11 0-0 ₤g7 12 ₤xd4 ₤xd4 13 cxd4 0-0 14 a5 ₤d5 15 ₤c4 ₩d8 16 ₤g5 ₤e6 17 ₩d2 ₤c8 18 ₤ac1 ₤f6 ∓ Meštrović-Tukmakov, Bled 1996.

b) **8 ₤g5!?** with the following possibilities:

b1) **8...e6** creates an ugly impression: 9 ₤e4 ₤xe5 10 ₤g5 ₤e7 and now instead of 11 ₤d6+ ₢f8 12 ₤h6+ ₢g8 13 ₩xd4 f6 14 ₤e3 ₩c7 15 ₤b5 ₤c6 16 ₤1a3 ₤c5! 17 ₩d2 ₤xe3 18 fxe3 d5 Shilin-R.Kozel, Yalta 1995, White could exchange the defender of the dark squares with 11 ₤xe7 ₩xe7 12 ₩xd4 ±.

b2) Even worse is 8...♘xe5? when 9 ♕xd4 f6 10 ♕xe5! d5 11 ♕e2 fxg5 12 ♗xg5 is strong, as is 9 ♗f4 ♗g7 10 ♗xe5 ♗xe5 11 ♘xf7 dxc3 12 ♘xe5! cxb2, Acs-Nikolaidis, Budapest 1995, when 13 ♗f7+ ♔f8 14 ♕d2! threatening the pawn on b2 and mate on h6 was the simplest win.

b3) 8...d5 9 exd6 e6:

b31) 10 cxd4 and then after 10...♗g7, 11 ♘e4!? is interesting, e.g. 11...0-0 12 ♘bc3 f5 13 ♗g5 ♕e8 14 ♘d2 h6 15 ♗e7 ♘xe7 16 dxe7 ♕xe7 17 ♘f3 ♘d5 18 0-0 ± Handoko-Dao, Asian Cht 1995 (round three). However as Handoko varied with 10 ♕f3 later in the same event, it is fair to assume he believes Black can improve at some point, and indeed the simple 10...♕xd6 is at least equal.

b32) 10 ♕f3 f5 (10...f6 11 ♘xe6 ♗xe6 12 ♗xe6 ♗xd6 13 ♕h3 f5 14 0-0 ± Filipović-Čabrilo, Yugoslavia 1995; 10...♘e5!? is double-edged: 11 ♕g3 ♗g7 12 0-0 0-0 13 ♕h3 h5 14 ♘e4 ♘ec4 15 cxd4 ♘xd6 16 ♗g5 f6 17 ♗xe6+ ♔h7 18 ♘xd6 ♕xd6 19 ♗xc8 ♖axc8 20 ♗e3 ♖c2 = Acs-Dao, Budapest 1995, but many deviations are possible) 11 ♗xe6 (11 ♘xe6 ♗xe6 12 ♗xe6 ♗xd6 13 0-0 allows 13...♗xh2+ 14 ♔xh2 ♕d6+ 15 ♗f4 ♕xe6 ∓) 11...♗xe6 12 ♘xe6 ♕xd6 13 ♘xd4 ♘xd4 14 cxd4 ♕d5!? and it is a question of whether Black's light-squared control is sufficient for him to eventually regain his pawn. Handoko-Xu, Asian Cht 1995 (round nine) went 15 ♕xd5 ♘xd5 16 0-0 ♖c8 17 ♘d2 ♗g7 18 ♖e1+ ♔d7 19 ♘f3 ♖he8 20 ♘e5+?!

♗xe5 21 dxe5 ♖c2 22 b3 f4! with excellent compensation, and Black even went on to win.

8 cxd4 ♗g7 *(D)*

If 8...d6 White has 9 ♘g5 e6 10 ♕f3 with an initiative.

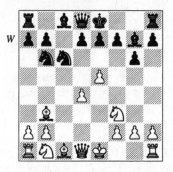

9 ♗f4!?

White reasons that Black will inevitably employ the freeing break ...d6, and this early bishop development will now stop him recapturing with his queen. In addition White threatens the advance 10 d5.

a) 9 0-0 d6!? (9...0-0 10 h3 d6 11 ♕e2 dxe5 12 dxe5 ♗e6! 13 ♖d1?! ♕c8 14 ♗f4 ♗xb3 15 axb3 ♕e6 ∓ was Zakharov-Vaulin, Moscow 1995) 10 exd6 ♕xd6 11 d5 ♘a5 12 ♗a4+ ♗d7 13 ♗xd7+ ♕xd7 14 ♘c3 ♘ac4 and Black has good play.

b) 9 ♘c3 0-0 10 h4?! (the caveman approach; White intends to continue 10...d6 11 e6! fxe6 12 h5 with an attack according to Bologan) 10...d5! 11 h5 ♗g4 and now 12 hxg6 fxg6 13 ♗e3 a5! was ∓ in Rozentalis-Bologan, Belfort 1995 or 12 ♖h4!? gxh5! 13 ♗c2 f5! 14 a3 e6 15 ♖h1 ♖c8 ∓ Marković-Matulović, Yugoslavia 1995.

9...d6 10 exd6 0-0 11 h3 (if 11 dxe7?! ♕xe7+ 12 ♗e3 ♗g4 13 0-0 ♗xf3 14 ♕xf3 ♘xd4 =) **11...exd6 12 0-0** (± Dolmatov) **12...♘a5** (to be considered was 12...♗f5 13 ♘c3 d5!?, de las Paz-Benzanilla, Cuba 1995) **13 ♘c3 ♘xb3 14 ♕xb3 ♗f5 15 ♖fe1** (15 a4!? ± Dolmatov) **15...♕d7 16 a4 ♖ac8 17 ♘b5?!** (17 a5 ♘c4 18 ♕b4 still seems more pleasant for White) **17...♗e6 18 ♕d1 ♘c4 19 ♗c1?** (19 b3 a6! 20 bxc4 axb5 21 cxb5 ♖c4 22 ♗e3 ♗d5 ∞) **19...a6 20 ♘c3 ♕c7 21 ♖e2 ♕a5 ∓ 22 ♕e1 h6 23 ♖b1? ♗f5 24 b4 ♕d8 25 ♖b3 ♗d3 26 ♖a2 ♘b6 27 ♖aa3 ♗f5 28 a5 ♘c4 29 ♖a2 ♗e6 30 d5?! ♗f5 31 ♗f4 g5 32 ♗g3 ♖e8 33 ♘e2 ♕f6 34 ♕d1 ♕g6 −+ 35 ♘ed4 ♗e4 36 ♖e2 ♗xd5 37 ♖c3 f5 38 ♖xe8+ ♖xe8 39 ♘b5 ♗xf3 40 ♖xf3 axb5 41 ♕d5+ ♕e6 42 ♖xf5 ♕xd5 43 ♖xd5 ♗e5 44 ♖xb5 ♗xg3 45 fxg3 ♖e7 46 h4 g4 47 ♖d5 ♖d7 48 ♔f2 ♔f7 49 ♖h5 ♔g6 50 ♖d5 ♔f6 51 ♔e2 ♘e5 52 ♔e3 ♔e6 53 ♖b5 ♖c7 54 ♔e4 ♘d7 55 ♔d4 ♘f6 56 ♔d3 ♘d7 57 ♔d4 ♘e5 58 ♔e4 ♖c4+ 59 ♔e3 ♘c6 60 ♖xb7 ♘xb4 61 a6 ♘xa6 62 ♖h7 ♔e5 63 ♖xh6 ♖c3+ 64 ♔f2 ♘c5 65 ♔g1 ♘e4 66 ♔h2 ♖c1 67 ♖h5+ ♔d4 0-1**

18 7...d5 8 exd6 ♕xd6

1	e4	c5
2	c3	♘f6
3	e5	♘d5
4	d4	cxd4
5	♘f3	♘c6
6	♗c4	♘b6
7	♗b3	d5
8	exd6	♕xd6 (D)

In Game 50 the move 9 ♘a3!? (with ideas of ♘b5) is a significant alternative for White to the main lines (with 9 0-0 ♗e6) of the following two chapters. It is presently unclear if Black can try to transpose to those chapters with 9...♗e6, but he does have a forthright attempt at refutation in the pawn grabbing 9...dxc3. Perhaps Black should brave these (most likely favourable) complications, because the cautious but very common alternative 9...a6 has scored quite well for White. A subsequent capture on d4 by White creates an unusual type of IQP position where it transpires that White's pieces are deceptively active.

A similar theme arises in Game 51, where we investigate the line 9 0-0 ♗f5. The key point to note here is that capturing on d4 with the knight (10 ♘xd4!) frees the f3-square for White's queen. White's development is fluid and fast, and the triumphant advance of the isolated d-pawn from d4 to d5 can scarcely be prevented. However an interesting sideline (also Game 51) is 9...g6!? which deserves more tests.

Game 50
Blatny – Stocek
Czechoslovakia 1996

1 e4 c5 2 c3 ♘f6 3 e5 ♘d5 4 d4 cxd4 5 ♘f3 ♘c6 6 ♗c4 ♘b6 7 ♗b3 d5 8 exd6 ♕xd6 9 ♘a3!?

By playing this before castling, White wants to give Black no time for the 9 0-0 ♗e6 defence of Chapters 19 and 20.

9...a6

To stop ♘b5, but time-consuming. On 9...e5 simply 10 0-0 with threats of ♘b5 and ♘g5 looks dangerous, while if 9...♗f5 Black will lose time with the bishop after 10 ♘b5 ♕d7 11 ♘fxd4 or 11 ♘bxd4. It may be possible to get away with 9...♗e6 in spite of Blatny's clever 10 ♘b5 ♕d7 11 ♗xe6 ♕xe6+ 12 ♗e3!

±. After 12...♕d7 (12...0-0-0?! 13
♘fxd4 ♕d5 14 ♕b3 ± Sermek-Sosa
Macho, Paranana 1993 or 12...♖c8?!
13 ♘fxd4 ♘xd4 14 ♕xd4 a6 15 ♘a7
1-0 Strikovic-Drei, Forli 1988) 13
♘bxd4 e6 14 0-0 ♘c4!? (14...♗e7
15 ♘xc6 ♕xc6 16 ♘e5 ♕b5 17
♗xb6 axb6 18 ♖e1 0-0 19 ♕d7 ±
Blatny-Raičević, Trnava 1987) 15
♕e2 ♘xe3 16 fxe3 ♗e7 17 ♖ad1
♕c7 18 ♕c4 0-0 19 ♘xc6 bxc6 20
♖f2 ♖ad8 was unclear in Shaked-de
Firmian, Las Vegas 1994.

It is also an open question (and an
important one) as to what happens
after 9...dxc3! 10 ♕e2 *(D)*:

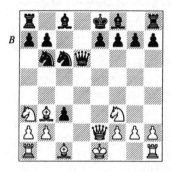

a) 10...cxb2 (Black grabs a second pawn, but White's bishops are
becoming very active) 11 ♗xb2
♕b4+ 12 ♔f1 ♗f5 (12...♗g4 and
now 13 ♖d1 ♖d8 14 ♖xd8+ ♘xd8
15 ♘c2 ♕c5 16 ♗d4 ♕c7 17 h3
♗e6 ∓ Mortazavi-Aseev, London
1994 but more dangerous for Black
was 13 ♘b5 ♗xf3 14 gxf3 ♕f4 15
♗c1!? ♕b8 16 ♕e4 g6 17 ♗b2 e5
18 ♖c1 f5 19 ♕e3 as in de la Paz-
Cabrera, Matanzas 1995) 13 ♖d1 (13
♖c1 ♖d8 14 ♘c2 ♕xb3! 15 axb3
♗d3 and Black reached an endgame

two pawns up in Meštrović-Grosar,
Nova Gorica 1996, but just look how
Black's lagging development then
plagued him nevertheless: 16 ♘cd4
♗xe2+ 17 ♔xe2 ♘xd4+ 18 ♘xd4
a6 19 ♖c7 ♖d7 20 ♖xd7 ♔xd7 21
♖d1 e6 22 ♘f3+ ♔e8 23 ♖c1 f6 24
♖c7 ♘d5 25 ♖xb7 ♗e7 26 ♘d4 ♔f7
27 ♘c6 e5 28 ♗a3 ♖e8 29 ♖a7 h5 30
♔d3 a5 31 ♔c4 ♗e6 32 ♘xe7 ♘xe7
33 ♖xa5 and White even went on to
win; you feel Black must have been
much better at some point, but this
example shows how complex these
lines are to play and assess) 13...♖d8
(13...e6 14 ♘b5 ♖c8 15 ♘fd4! ± Van
Mil-Yakovich, Leeuwarden 1992)
14 ♖xd8+ ♘xd8 15 ♘d4 ♗d7 16
♘ab5 ♗xb5 17 ♘xb5 a6 18 ♘d4 e6
19 g3 ♗e7 20 ♘c2 ♕b5 21 ♕xb5+
axb5 22 ♗xg7 ♖g8 23 ♗d4 ♘c4 ∓
Sermek-Sher, Ljubljana 1994. All
very unclear, but I suspect this line is
Black's best option against 9 ♘a3!?.

b) 10...♗f5!? (the latest try) 11
♘b5 ♕d7 12 ♘e5 ♘xe5 13 ♕xe5 f6
14 ♘c7+ (14 ♘d6+ ♕xd6 15 ♕xf5
g6 16 ♕e4 ♕c6 17 ♕xc6+ bxc6 18
bxc3 e5 19 f4 ♗d6 20 0-0 0-0-0 ∓
Van Mil-Nijboer, Wijk aan Zee
1995) 14...♔d8 15 ♘e6+ ♗xe6 16
♕xe6 ♕xe6+ (16...♖c8?! 17 ♕e2!
e5 18 0-0 ♔c7 19 a4! with a strong
initiative to compensate for the pawns,
de la Paz-Blanco Fernandez, Villa
Clara 1995) 17 ♗xe6 ♘a4! (Guido-
Berthelot, Cannes 1995) and now
Nogueiras analyses 18 ♗e3! cxb2 19
♖d1+ ♔c7 20 0-0 ♘c3 21 ♖d7+!
♔c6 22 ♖d3 b1♘! (22...b1♕ 23
♖xc3+) 23 ♖c1! with a totally unclear position.

10 0-0

10 cxd4 e6 11 0-0 will transpose to the main line.

10...e6 *(D)*

Black's defensive set-up (with 9...a6 and 10...e6) is viable as White has committed his knight to a3 early. 10...g6 is possible here (see the next game, note at Black's move nine) but alternatives are inferior:

a) 10...dxc3? 11 ♘g5 ♘d8 12 ♕e2 e6 13 ♖d1 ♕c7 14 g3 ♗e7 15 ♗f4 ♕c6 16 ♖ac1 ± T.Christensen-Formanek, Gausdal 1991.

b) 10...♗f5?! 11 ♘xd4 (11 ♘g5 e6 12 ♕f3 ♗g6 13 ♗f4 ♕d7 14 ♖fe1 ♗xa3!? 15 ♘xe6!? Dovzhik-Volodin, Budapest 1991, when Dovzhik analyses 15...♗e7! 16 ♘xg7+ ♔d8 as unclear) 11...♘xd4 12 cxd4 e6 13 ♕f3 ♕c6 (13...♕d7 14 d5! ♘xd5 15 ♖d1 ♗xa3 16 bxa3 0-0 17 h4! ± Okhotnik-A.Shnaider, USSR 1987) 14 d5 ♘xd5 15 ♖d1 ♘b6 16 ♕g3 ♘d5 17 ♘c4 ♖d8 18 ♗e3! ♗g6 19 ♘xd5 exd5 20 ♗g5 ± f6 21 ♖ac1 ♕e6 22 ♖e1 ♗e4 23 f3 ♕f5 24 ♗f4 1-0 Sermek-Kiselev, Ljubljana Iskra 1992.

c) 10...♗e6 11 ♗xe6 (11 ♘g5 has also been played) 11...♕xe6 12 ♘xd4 ♘xd4 13 ♕xd4 ♖d8 14 ♕h4 ± has been seen several times, but is simply a bad version of Chapter 19 for Black, as White's knight is already developed on a3, e.g. 14...♕c6 15 ♗g5 f6 16 ♗e3 ♘d5 17 ♘c2 e5 18 ♖ad1 ♗e7 19 c4 ♘f4 20 ♖xd8+ ♗xd8 21 ♗xf4 ♕xc4 22 ♕h5+ g6 23 ♕f3 ♕xc2 24 ♕xb7 ♕c7 25 ♕e4 ± Sariego-Martin del Campo, Bayamo 1990.

11 cxd4

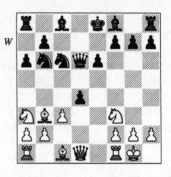

A significant alternative is 11 ♘xd4!?, played repeatedly and with success by Sermek. The f3-square is freed for White's queen: 11...♘xd4 12 cxd4 ♗e7 13 ♕f3 0-0 14 ♖d1 (14 ♗f4 ♕xd4 ∞ Striković-Matulović, Yugoslav Ch 1988; instead 14 ♘c2!? a5 15 a3 ♕c6 16 ♕e2 ♗f6 17 ♖d1 ♗d7 18 a4 ♘d5 19 ♘e3 ♘f4 20 ♕f1 ♕b6 looked OK for Black in Sermek-Orel, Ljubljana 1993, but even here consider how Black had to subsequently retreat: 21 ♗c4 ♖fd8 22 ♘g4 ♘d5 23 ♕d3 ♗e8 24 ♘xf6+ ♘xf6 25 ♗g5 ±) 14...♕d8 (14...♕b8 15 ♘c2 ♗d6 16 ♕h5 ♗f4 17 ♘e3 ♗d7 18 ♘g4 ♖c8 19 ♘e5 ♗xe5 20 dxe5 ± Sermek-Zadrima, Moscow OL 1994 or 14...♕c6 15 ♕g3 ♗d7 16 ♗h6 ♗f6 17 ♖e1!? ± Sermek-Kiselev, Ljubljana 1992) 15 ♘b1!? (a creative idea, re-routing the knight to c3; the natural 15 ♘c2 also turned out promisingly in Sermek-Dvoirys, Groningen 1993: 15...a5 16 a4 ♗d7 17 ♘e3 ♗c6 18 d5 exd5 19 ♘xd5 ♘xd5 20 ♗xd5 ♕b6 21 ♗e3 ♕xb2 22 ♗xc6 bxc6 23 ♗d4 ♕b7 24 ♖ab1 ♗b4 25 ♗xg7! ♔xg7 26 ♕g4+ ♔h8 27 ♖d7 ♕b6 28 ♕f5 c5 29 ♕e5+ ♔g8 30 ♖d6 ♕xd6 31 ♕xd6 and

Black is worse but may hold the draw) 15...♘d5 16 ♘c3 ♘xc3 17 bxc3 ♗d6 18 c4 ♖b8 19 c5 ± ♗c7 20 ♗b2 ♛h4 21 g3 ♛h3 22 ♖e1 ♗d7 23 d5 exd5 24 ♗xd5 ± Shaked-Krakops, Halle 1995.

Less convincing is 11 ♛e2 and now:

a) 11...dxc3 12 ♖d1 ♛c7!? (or 12...♛b4 13 ♘e5 ♗e7 14 bxc3 ♛a5 15 ♘ac4 ♘xc4 16 ♘xc4 ♛c7 17 ♛e4 0-0 18 ♗f4 e5 19 ♘xe5 ± Dovzhik-Bagaturov, Bratislava 1990) 13 bxc3 ♗e7 14 c4 0-0 15 ♗b2 ♘d7 16 ♖ac1 ♘c5 17 ♗c2 b6 18 ♗b1 ♗b7 19 ♘e5 ♘xe5 20 ♗xe5 ♛c6 21 ♛g4 f6 22 ♗a1 ♖ad8 23 ♛h3 ♘e4 ∓ Dovzhik-A.Schneider, Hungarian Cht 1992.

b) 11...♗e7 12 ♖d1 ♗f6 13 ♗e3 ♘d5 14 ♘xd4 ♘xe3 15 ♘db5 ♛c5 16 ♘d6+ ♚e7 17 fxe3 ♘e5 (17...♘d4 18 ♖xd4! ♗xd4 19 ♘e4 ♗xe3+ 20 ♚h1 ♛a7 21 ♘c4 ♗f4 22 ♖d1 with an attack, Dovzhik-Vancszak, Eger 1990) 18 ♘e4 ♛c6 19 ♖d4! b5 20 ♖f1 ♗b7 21 ♗c2 ♖ad8 22 ♘b1 a5 23 ♘bd2 ± Dovzhik-Moiseev, Budapest 1990.

11...♗e7 12 ♗e3!?

With an aggressive idea in mind. Others:

a) 12 ♖e1 0-0 13 ♖e4 ♘d5 (also 13...♘b4 14 ♘e5 ♘4d5 15 ♖g4 f5 ∞ Marković-Michelakis, Buenos Aires 1993) 14 ♘c4 ♘d8 15 ♘ce5 ♗d7 16 ♗d2 ♖c8 17 ♛e1 ♘xe5 18 dxe5 ♗b5 19 ♖d1 b6 20 h4 ♗d3 ½-½ Smagin-Popović, Yugoslav Cht 1992.

b) 12 ♛d3 0-0 13 ♖d1 ♗d7 14 ♘g5 ♗xg5 15 ♗xg5 ♘b4 16 ♛e3 ♘6d5 17 ♛e5 ♛xe5 18 dxe5 ♖fc8

with equality, Smagin-Vyzhmanavin, USSR 1988.

c) 12 ♛e2!? ♘xd4 (White gains an strong initiative for this pawn; safer is 12...0-0, but after 13 ♖d1 or 13 ♛e4 White again has active play around the IQP) 13 ♘xd4 ♛xd4 14 ♖d1 ♛f6 15 ♗e3 ♘d7 16 ♖ac1 ♛e5 17 ♛d2 ♛b8 18 ♗f4 e5 19 ♗g3 ♗f6 20 ♛d5 0-0 21 ♖xc8 ♛xc8 22 ♛xd7 ± Benderac-Dujković, Yugoslav Cht 1989.

12...0-0

Perhaps Black should consider an immediate 12...♘d5 (to stop White's next) although this does allow 12 ♘c4.

13 ♘e5! ± *(D)*

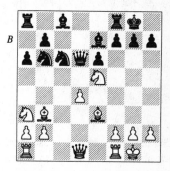

13...♗f6

Since 13...♘xe5 14 dxe5 ♛xd1 (14...♛xe5? 15 ♗xb6) 15 ♖fxd1 is favourable for White. Alternatively 13...♗d8 14 ♘ac4 ♘xc4 15 ♘xc4 ♛d7 16 ♘e5 ♘xe5 17 dxe5 ♛b5 18 ♛d6 ♗d7 19 ♗c2 g6 20 ♗e4 ± Darnstädt-Aseev, Berlin 1993 or 13...♘b4 14 ♘ac4 ♘xc4 15 ♘xc4 ♛d8 16 ♛f3 ♘d5 17 ♘e5 ♛d6 18 ♖ac1 ♗d7 19 ♗xd5 exd5 20 ♗f4 ± Bruchfeld-Van der Wees, Corr. 1989.

14 ♖c1 ♗d7 15 ♘ac4 ♘xc4 16
♘xc4 ♕c7 17 d5 exd5 18 ♘b6
♗xb2 19 ♖c2 ♗e5 20 f4 ♗f5 21
♘xa8 ♗xc2 22 ♕xc2 ♖xa8 23 fxe5
♕xe5 24 ♕f2 ♕e6 25 ♖d1 ♖d8 26
♗b6 ♖e8 27 ♗xd5 ♕d7 28 ♗b3 1-0

Game 51
Lautier – J.Polgar
Hilversum 1993

1 e4 c5 2 c3 ♘f6 3 e5 ♘d5 4 d4 cxd4
5 ♘f3 ♘c6 6 ♗c4 ♘b6 7 ♗b3 d6 8
exd6 ♕xd6 9 0-0 *(D)*

9...♗f5?!

The normal lines with 9...♗e6 are
the subject of the next two chapters.
Others:

a) 9...♘a5 (inferior) 10 ♘xd4
♘xb3 11 axb3 a6 12 ♖e1 g6 13 ♗g5
f6 14 ♗h4 ♗g7 15 ♘d2 0-0 16 ♘e4
♕c7 17 b4 e5 18 ♕b3+ ± Kantsler-
Vitolinš, USSR 1980.

b) 9...d3 (also inferior) 10 ♘a3
♗f5 11 ♘b5 ♕d7 12 ♗f4 ♖c8 13
♘xa7! ♘xa7 14 ♘e5 ♕b5 15 ♘xf7 ±
Schmittdiel-Gutman, Lugano 1987.

c) However there has been revived interest with 9...g6!?. For example:

c1) 10 ♘g5 e6 (10...♘d8!?, e.g.
11 ♕f3 ♕f6 12 ♕xf6 exf6 ∞ Perissi-
notto-Mariotti, Ticino 1994 and
Brauer-Woller, Corr. 1987) 11 ♕f3
(11 ♘e4 ♕e5 12 ♖e1 ♗e7 13 cxd4
and then 13...♘xd4 14 ♗d2 ♘xb3
15 axb3 ♘d5 16 ♘bc3 0-0 17 ♖a5
♕d4 ∞ Acs-Leroy, Budapest 1994 or
13...♕d8 12 cxd4 ♗g7 13 ♗g5
♕xd4! 14 ♘d6+ ♔f8 15 ♘c3 ♕xd1
16 ♖axd1 h6 17 ♗e3 ♗e5 18 ♘db5
♔g7 ∓ Grushevsky-Blokh, Moscow
1986) 11...♕e7 12 ♘e4 f5 13 ♘g5
♗g7 (13...dxc3? 14 bxc3! ♗g7 15
♖e1 ♘e5 16 ♕g3 ♘bc4 17 ♘d2 ±
Vajda-Chernov, Romania 1995) 14
♖e1 e5 15 ♘f7 (15 ♕g3 ♗f6 16 ♘f3
♗e6 17 ♘xd4 ♘xd4 18 cxd4 e4 ∓
was Demarre-Ward, Paris-London
1994) 15...♖f8 16 ♗g5 ♕c5 17
♘xe5!? ♘xe5 18 cxd4 ♕xd4 19
♘c3 ♗e6 20 ♕f4! ♕xf4 21 ♗xf4
½-½ Välkesalmi-Yrjölä, Helsinki
1986.

c2) It may be sensible for White
first to gain time developing: 10
♘a3!? a6 (10...♗g7 11 ♘b5 ♕d8 12
♘bxd4 ♘xd4 13 ♘xd4 0-0 14 ♗g5
♘d7 15 ♖e1 ± Lane-Ward, London
Lloyds Bank 1994) 11 ♘g5 (11
♘xd4 ♘xd4 12 cxd4 ♗g7 13 ♗e3
♗e6! = Asaturian-Blokh, Corr. 1991)
11...e6 12 ♕f3 (12 ♘e4!? ♕e5 13
♖e1) 12...♕e7 13 ♗f4 ♗h6 14 ♘e4 ±
although Olesen-C.Ward, Gausdal
1995 was agreed drawn at this point.

d) 9...e6 10 cxd4 ♗e7 11 ♘c3
0-0 gives Black a rather passive anti-
IQP position:

d1) 12 ♗e3 ♘d5 13 ♕e2 b6 14
♖ac1 ♗b7 15 ♘e4 ♕d8 16 ♖fd1
♖c8 17 a3 ♘a5 18 ♗a2 ♘xe3 19

♕xe3 b5 = Van Dongen-Tiviakov, Paris 1989.

d2) 12 a3 ♘d5 13 ♘e4 ♕d8 14 ♕d3 b6 15 ♗c2 g6 16 ♗h6 ♖e8 17 ♖ac1 ± Pedersen-Mednis, Copenhagen 1989.

d3) 12 ♘b5 ♕d8 13 ♗f4 ♘d5 14 ♗g3 a6 15 ♘c3 (here 15 ♗xd5!? would transpose into Lautier-J.Polgar from Chapter 6!) 15...♘xc3 16 bxc3 ± Blatny-Ki.Georgiev, Stara Zagora Z 1990.

10 ♘xd4!

After 10 ♘a3 dxc3 White will have to exchange queens, as on 11 ♕e2?, Black plays 11...♗d3. Playable is 10 cxd4 e6 (or 10...♗xb1 11 ♖xb1 e6 with near equality, As.Arnason-Tisdall, Vestmann Isles 1985 and Hickl-Bastian, Bundesliga 1990) 11 ♘c3 ♗e7 (11...♖d8 12 ♘b5 ♕d7 13 ♗f4 ± Antonov-Spassov, Pernik 1981) 12 ♗e3 (12 ♕e2 0-0 13 ♖d1 ♘a5 14 ♗c2 ♗xc2 15 ♕xc2 ♖ac8 with a slight plus for Black, O.Castro-Matulović, Dortmund 1977 or 12 d5 exd5 13 ♘xd5 ♘xd5 14 ♕xd5 ♕xd5 15 ♗xd5 = Yukhtman-Polugaevsky, USSR Ch 1959) 12...0-0 13 a3 ♖fd8 14 ♕e2 a6 15 ♖fd1 ♘d5 = Matulović-Udovčić, Sombor 1957.

10...♘xd4 11 cxd4 e6

If 11...♗xb1 12 ♖xb1 e6 13 ♕f3 ♕d7 14 ♗f4 ♗d6 15 ♗xd6 ♕xd6 16 ♕xb7 0-0 17 ♖fd1 ± Veličković-Matulović, Vršac 1981. Overambitious is 11...g6 12 ♖e1 (12 ♕f3!? ♗g7 13 ♘c3 0-0 14 ♕xb7 ♖fb8 15 ♕f3 ♕xd4 16 ♗e3 ± Nun-Rantanen, Eksjö 1981) 12...♗g7 13 ♗g5 e6 14 ♘c3 h6 15 ♗e3 g5 (White threatened g4) 16 d5 e5 17 ♘b5 ♕d8 18

♗c5 and White is clearly better, David-Farago, Ostrava 1987.

12 ♘c3 ♗e7 13 ♕f3! ± (D)

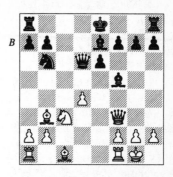

This is the reason White often takes with the knight on d4: the queen finds a useful outpost on f3.

13...♕xd4?!

After this Polgar's king ends up in the centre, but otherwise Black has trouble dealing with White's powerful pawn thrust d5. On 13...♕d7, for example, comes 14 d5! e5 (14...0-0 see 13...0-0, covered next) 15 a4 a5 16 ♕e3 ♖a6 17 ♕xe5 ± Palkovi-Sapi, Budapest 1994. After 13...0-0 again comes the advance: 14 d5! (14 ♖d1!? ♕d7 15 ♗e3 ♖fd8 16 d5! e5 17 d6! ♗f8 18 ♗xb6 axb6 19 ♘d5 e4 20 ♕e3 ± Chandler-Seppeur, Bundesliga 1986 is similar; less good is 14 ♕xb7 ♖fb8 15 ♕f3 ♕xd4 16 ♗f4 ♖d8 with an unclear position in the games Blatny-Ksieski, Naleczow 1985 and Tzermiadianos-Anastasian, Komotini 1992) and now:

a) 14...♗f6 15 ♖d1 ♕b4 16 h3 ♖ad8 17 ♗d2 ♖fe8 18 dxe6 ♗xe6 19 ♘e4 is good for White, Torre-Mok, Asian Cht 1993.

b) 14...♕b4 15 dxe6 fxe6 16 ♕xb7 ♗d6 17 ♗e3 ♖f7 18 ♕a6 ± Mihaljčišin-Ftačnik, Prague 1979.

c) 14...♕d7 15 dxe6 (15 ♖d1!) 15...♗xe6 16 ♖d1 ♕c8 17 ♗xe6 fxe6 18 ♕e4 ± Mi.Tseitlin-Velikov, Pernik 1981 or 18 ♕e2 Van Mil-Rio, Lugano 1989.

14 ♕xb7 ± ♗d6 (15...♕d7 fails to 16 ♗a4!) **15 ♕c6+ ♔e7 16 ♘b5 ♕e5 17 ♕b7+ ♔f6** (17...♘d7 18 ♘xd6 ♕xd6 19 ♖d1 ♖hb8 20 ♕f3 ♘e5 21 ♕g3 ♘d3 22 ♕xg7 ± Lautier) **18 ♘xd6 ♕xd6 19 ♗e3** (19 g4!! intending 19...♗xg4 20 ♕g2

Lautier) **19...♘d5 20 ♗xa7 ♖hc8 21 ♖fd1 ♔g6 22 ♗xd5 exd5 23 ♖xd5 ♕e6 24 ♖dd1 ♗e4 25 ♕d7 ♕xd7 26 ♖xd7 ♖c2 27 b4 ♗f5 28 ♖e7 ♔f6 29 ♖b7 ♗c8 30 ♗d4+ ♔g6 31 ♖a7 ♖xa7 32 ♗xa7 ♗d7 33 h3 ♗a4 34 a3 ♖c3 35 ♗c5 h5 36 ♔f1 f6 37 ♔e2 ♔f5 38 ♔d2 ♖b3 39 ♖e1! ♖xa3 40 ♖e7 g5 41 ♖a7 ♔e4 42 f3+ ♔d5 43 ♗e7 ♖a2+ 44 ♔c3 ♖c2+ 45 ♔d3 ♖a2 46 ♔c3 ♖c2+ 47 ♔d3 ♖a2 48 ♖a5+ ♔e6 49 ♗d8 ♖b3 50 ♖xa2 ♗xa2 51 ♔d4 ♔f5 52 b5 ♗e6 53 ♔c5 ♗c8 54 ♔c6 h4 55 ♔c7 ♗e6 56 b6 1-0**

1	e4	c5
2	c3	♘f6
3	e5	♘d5
4	d4	cxd4
5	♘f3	♘c6
6	♗c4	♘b6
7	♗b3	d5
8	exd6	♕xd6
9	0-0	♗e6
10	♗xe6	♕xe6 *(D)*

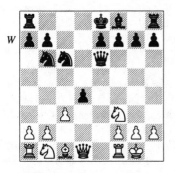

Black has some reasonable-looking possible deviations *en route*, but nevertheless the vast majority of games in this key line continue 11 ♘xd4 ♘xd4 12 ♕xd4 ♖d8 13 ♕h4 ♕e2 reaching a quite sharp position. Black's kingside is undeveloped, but White will must now take a committal decision on how to activate his queenside pieces. 14 ♘d2 (Game 52) is the first of the three big alternatives examined for White, leading to very unclear play. 14 ♗d2 (Game 53) looks equal. The real fun comes

if White chooses the dramatic sacrificial path of 14 ♗e3!? (Game 54) when very tactical play results after 14...♕xb2 15 ♘d2 ♖xd2. Black ends up with two pieces (and even a pawn or two) versus a rook, but White has a dangerous initiative. At present Black's resources appear promising – see the game M.Marić-Cherniaev (note to White's 16th move in Game 54) for a wonderful example of defensive technique. Nevertheless, in practice White has not scored at all badly.

Game 52
Acs – A.Schneider
Budapest 1995

1 e4 c5 2 c3 ♘f6 3 e5 ♘d5 4 d4 cxd4 5 ♘f3 ♘c6 6 ♗c4 ♘b6 7 ♗b3 d6 8 exd6 ♕xd6 9 0-0 ♗e6 10 ♗xe6 ♕xe6 11 ♘xd4

Inferior is 11 cxd4 ♕d7 12 ♘c3 e6 with an easy game for Black.

11...♘xd4

11...♕d5 12 ♕e2 ♘xd4 13 cxd4 e6 14 ♘c3 ♕d7 15 d5! ♘xd5 16 ♘xd5 ♕xd5 17 ♖d1 gives White an initiative for the pawn, Sveshnikov-Rashkovsky, USSR 1984.

Instead 11...♕d7!? is an underrated move:

a) 12 ♕e2 ♘xd4 13 cxd4 e6 14 ♘c3 ♗e7 15 d5 exd5 16 ♗g5 f6 17 ♗e3 0-0 18 ♗xb6 axb6 19 ♖ad1 ♖a5

∞ was Antonio-Liang, Shenzhen 1992.

b) 12 ♘b5 a6 13 ♕xd7+ ♔xd7 14 ♖d1+ ♔c8 15 ♘5a3 e6 16 ♗f4 ♗e7 17 ♘c2 ♖d8 just gives an equal endgame, Marković-Liang, Novi Sad OL 1990.

c) 12 ♘xc6 ♕xc6 leaves White ahead in development, but to date he has not been able to exploit this, e.g. 13 ♕e2 e6 14 ♘d2 ♗e7 15 ♘f3 0-0 16 ♗f4 ♖fd8 17 ♖fd1 ♖xd1+ 18 ♖xd1 ♕a4 19 ♗g5 ♗xg5 20 ♘xg5 ½-½ Lendwai-Tischbierek, Vienna 1991.

d) Perhaps Sveshnikov found the best plan for White in an old game: 12 ♗e3!? ♘d5 13 ♘d2 ♘xe3 14 fxe3 e5 (14...e6 15 ♕g4!?) 15 ♘xc6 ♕xc6 16 ♕g4 g6 17 ♕c4 f5 18 ♕xc6+ bxc6 19 ♘c4 0-0-0 20 ♘xe5 ± Sveshnikov-Rashkovsky, Kuibyshev 1986.

12 ♕xd4

12 cxd4 and Black must proceed accurately in spite of weak white IQP:

a) 12...g6 13 ♖e1 (or 13 ♘c3) 13...♕f6 14 ♘c3 ♗g7 15 ♘e4 ♕c6 16 ♗g5 ± Dončević-Illescas, JW GC IV 1989.

b) 12...♕d7 13 ♘c3 ♖d8 (if 13...e6 14 ♕g4 f5 15 ♕e2 ♗e7 16 ♖e1 ♔f7 17 ♗f4 ♖hc8 18 ♖ad1 ±) 14 ♖e1 (14 ♕f3!? ♘d5 15 ♗g5) 14...e6 15 ♗e3 ♗e7 16 ♕g4 0-0 17 ♖ad1 ♘d5 18 ♗h6 ♗f6 19 ♘e4 ♕e7 20 h4 ♖d7 21 ♖d3 ♔h8 ∞ Handoko-Martin del Campo, Manila OL 1992.

c) 12...♖d8 13 ♘c3 g6 14 d5!? (14 ♖e1 ♖xd4! 15 ♖xe6 ♖xd1+ 16 ♘xd1 fxe6 ∓ Sveshnikov-Dvoirys,

Moscow 1990, or 14 ♕f3 ♕c6 = as in Bergström-Yakovich, Gausdal 1991) 14...♘xd5 15 ♕d4 ♕f6 16 ♕xa7 ♘xc3 17 bxc3 ♗g7 18 ♕xb7 0-0 19 ♗a3 ♖b8 20 ♕xe7 ♕xc3 21 ♕e3 ♕xe3 22 fxe3 ♖fe8 23 ♖ab1 ♗h6 = Dončević-Komljenović, Bad Wörishofen 1985.

12...♖d8 *(D)*

Almost invariably played, even though Black can try to exchange queens. 12...♕d5 13 ♕g4 e6 14 ♖d1 h5 15 ♕e2 ♕c4 16 ♕c2 ♗e7 17 b3 ♕c6 18 c4 ♗f6 19 ♘c3 ± was Westerinen-Shamkovich, Brighton 1982, or 12...♕d7 13 ♗e3!? (13 ♕xd7+ ♘xd7 14 ♗e3 e6 15 ♖d1 allowed 15...♗c5! = in Blatny-Kovalev, Germany 1995, as on 16 ♖xd7? ♗xe3 17 ♖xb7?? 0-0-0 Black wins; Black also equalised after 13 ♕e5 e6 14 ♘d2 ♕d5 15 ♕e2 ♗e7 16 c4 ♕f5 17 b3 0-0 18 ♕e4 ♕xe4 19 ♘xe4 ♖fd8 20 ♗e3 f5! in Vorotnikov-Georgadze, USSR 1985) 13...♕xd4 14 ♗xd4 ♘d7 15 ♘d2 (15 ♖e1 ± is superior) 15...e5 16 ♖fe1 f6 17 ♖ad1 ♗e7 18 ♗e3 0-0-0 = Nouro-A.Shneider, Jyväskylä 1994.

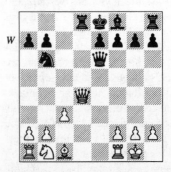

13 ♕h4

Or:

a) 13 ♕b4 ♕c6 14 a4 (14 ♘d2 e6 and now 15 ♕e4 ♕d5 16 a4 ♗e7 17 a5 ♕xe4 18 ♘xe4 ♘d5 = Vorotnikov-Salov, Leningrad 1984 or 15 ♕g4 h5 16 ♕g3 h4 17 ♕f3?! ♕xf3 18 ♘xf3 h3 ∓ Hresc-Vaisser, Cappelle la Grande 1987) 14...a6 15 ♕b3 (15 ♗e3 ♘d5 16 ♕c5 ♕d7 17 ♕d4 ♘xe3 18 fxe3 ♕c7 19 ♕g4 e6 20 ♘a3 f5 21 ♕c4 ♕xc4 22 ♘xc4 ♖c8 ½-½ Sveshnikov-Pigusov, Podolsk 1990) 15...e6 16 ♘d2 ♗e7 17 ♘f3 0-0 18 ♖e1 ♘c4 19 ♕c2 h6 20 b3 ♘a5 21 ♗e3 ♗f6 22 ♖ac1 ♕c7 = Blatny-Stohl, Pardubice 1993.

b) 13 ♕e3 ♕xe3 (in Sariego-Dvoirys, Polanica Zdroj 1989, Black rejected the drawish exchange of queens and duly gained a good game after 14...♕c6 14 ♘d2 e6 15 ♕g3 f6 16 ♘f3 ♔f7 17 ♖e1 ♗c5 18 ♗e3 ♖he8 19 ♕h3 ♗xe3 20 ♖xe3 ♘d5 21 ♘d4 ♕d7 22 ♖ee1 e5 ∓) 14 ♗xe3 ♘c4 (14...e6 15 ♗xb6 axb6 16 a4 ♔d7 17 ♖d1+ ♗d6 18 ♘a3 ♔c6 19 ♘b5 ♗e5 20 ♔f1 ♗f6 21 ♔e2 h5 22 b4 ½-½ Lane-Ernst, London 1988) 15 ♗xa7 ♘xb2 16 ♘a3 e6 17 ♘c2 ♖d2 18 ♘d4 ♗a3 19 ♖fb1 ♘a4 20 ♖xb7 0-0 21 ♘f3 ♖c2 22 ♘d4 ♖d2 ½-½ Mikhalchishin-Ki.Georgiev, Sarajevo 1985.

c) 13 ♕f4:

c1) 13...♕c6 is logical, when after 14 ♘d2 Black has played several moves: 14...e6 15 ♘f3 ♘d5 16 ♕g3 g6 17 ♗g5 ± was Vorotnikov-Gorelov, USSR 1985, but equal were 14...g6 15 ♕e5 f6 16 ♕e2 ♗g7 17 ♘b3 ♕c4 18 ♕xc4 ½-½ Luther-Lysenko, Sverdlovsk 1989 and 14...f6

15 ♕e4 e5 16 ♕xc6+ bxc6 17 ♖e1 ♔f7 18 ♔f1 ♗e7 19 ♘b3 ♖d5 = Blatny-Aseev, Kecskemet 1992.

c2) 13...g6 *(D)* with three possibilities:

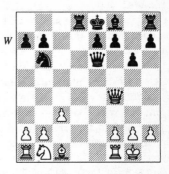

c21) 14 ♘a3?! (once popular, but now discredited) 14...♗g7 15 ♘b5 (15 ♕c7 ♕d5!? 16 ♗e3 ♗e5 17 ♕c5 ♕xc5 18 ♗xc5 ♘a4 19 ♗xa7 ♘xb2 ∓ O'Donnell-Tukmakov, Canada 1989) 15...0-0! (previously 15...♘d5 16 ♘c7+ ♘xc7 17 ♕xc7 ♕d7 was played, but castling will be very effective if White cannot safely snatch the a-pawn) 16 ♘xa7? (16 ♘d4 ♗xd4 17 cxd4 ♘d5 ∓) 16...♕e2! (threatening ...♖d1, and 17 ♕e3? is met by 17...♕a6) 17 ♗e3 ♘d5 18 ♕f3 ♕xb2 19 ♖ab1 ♕xa2 20 ♖xb7 ♕a6 21 ♖bb1 ♘xc3 ∓ Yanovsky-Kiselev, USSR 1988.

c22) 14 ♗e3 ♗g7 and now 15 ♗xb6 ♕xb6 16 ♕a4+ ♔f8 17 ♘a3 ♗f6 18 ♘c4 ♕c5 19 ♕b3 ♔g7 with equality, Sveshnikov-Vyzhmanavin, Moscow 1987 or 15 ♕c7 ♘d5 16 ♕xb7 0-0 17 ♗d4 ♗xd4 18 cxd4 ♖b8 19 ♕xa7 ♖a8 20 ♕c5 ♖fc8 21 ♕b5 ♖ab8 22 ♕a5 ♖xb2 ∞ Jackson-S.Arkell, London 1991.

c23) White could also reach a reasonable ending with 14 ♕c7 ♕d7 15 ♕xd7+ ♖xd7 16 a4 a6 17 a5 ♘c4 18 ♖a4 ♘e5 19 ♗e3 = Bashkov-Bagaturov, Mlada Boleslav 1993.

13...♕e2! *(D)*

Considering Black's lack of kingside development this queen move gives a cheeky impression, but in fact it is now not so easy for White to get his own remaining pieces out. The dangerous ...♖d1 is always in the air, and White's b-pawn will be *en prise* should the c1 bishop develop to the natural e3-square. Alternatives:

a) 13...♕f5 14 ♗e3 e5 15 ♗xb6 axb6 16 ♘a3 ♗xa3 17 ♕a4+ ♕d7 18 ♕xa3 ± Striković-Cigan, Cetinje 1990.

b) 13...♕g6 14 ♗e3 e5 15 ♗xb6 ♕xb6 16 ♘a3 ♗e7 (16...♕xb2 17 ♕a4+) 17 ♕a4+ ♕c6 18 ♕xc6+ bxc6 19 ♘c4 ± Acs-Cao, Budapest 1995.

c) 13...g6!? 14 ♗e3 (14 ♗h6 ♕e2!) 14...♗g7 15 ♘d2 0-0 16 ♘f3 ± Kopp-Klingelhöfer, Hessen 1989.

d) 13...♕c6 14 ♖e1! (14 ♘d2 e6 15 ♘f3 ♗e7 16 ♗g5 f6 17 ♗e3 0-0 18 ♖fe1 ♘c8 19 ♘d4 ♕d5 20 b3 ♖fe8 21 c4 ♕d7 ∞ Kostenko-Stripunsky, Moscow 1994) 14...e6 15 ♗g5 ♖d5 16 ♘d2 h6 17 ♗e3 ♗c5 18 ♘e4 ♗xe3 19 ♖xe3 0-0 20 ♖g3 ± Sveshnikov-Szekely, Leningrad 1984.

e) 13...h5!? (with the idea of 14...♕g4! ∞) 14 h3 ♕c4 (14...g6 15 ♘a3 ♖d7 16 ♗g5 f6 17 ♗e3 ♔f7 18 ♖fe1 ± Acs-Enders, Budapest 1996; instead 14...♕e2 15 ♗e3!? ♕xb2 16 ♘d2 ♖xd2 17 ♗xd2 ♕xd2 18 ♖fd1 ♕h6 gives White a version of Game

54 where the interpolation of ...h5 and h3 is favourable for him, e.g. 19 ♖ab1 ♕c6 20 ♕f4 ♘c8 21 ♖xb7! f6 22 ♕b8 ♔f7 23 ♖c7 ♕a4 24 ♖d4 ♕xa2 25 ♖xc8 g5 26 ♖dd8 1-0 Angelov-Prahov, Primorsko 1985) 15 ♕g3 (15 ♕xc4 ♘xc4 16 b3 ♘d6 17 ♗e3 a6 18 ♘a3 ♖c8 19 c4 ♘f5 20 ♗b6 g5 with equality, Podobnik-Sveshnikov, Pula 1990) 15...♕d3 16 ♗e3 ♘c4 17 ♘a3 ♘xe3 (17...♘xa3) 18 fxe3 ± Sveshnikov-Ubilava, Sochi 1984. Bearing in mind Sveshnikov is now also playing the line with Black, this plan could become a safe alternative to the sharp 13...♕e2 lines.

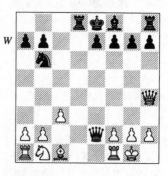

14 ♘d2

For 14 ♗d2 see Game 53, and for 14 ♗e3 Game 54. Instead 14 ♕g3 e6 15 ♘d2 transposes to the note after Black's next move while 14 b3?! g6 15 ♗g5 ♖d1 16 ♘d2 ♖xa1 17 ♖xa1 ♗g7 18 ♘e4 0-0! ∓ 19 ♗xe7 ♖e8 20 ♖f1 g5! won material for Black in Morvay-Vegh, Hungary 1982. 14 ♕g5?! is likewise ineffectual: 14...e5 15 ♕e3 ♕xe3 16 ♗xe3 ♘c4 17 ♗c1 ♗c5 18 b3 ♘d6 = Panchenko-Ionov, USSR 1983.

14...h5

The start of a double-edged advance of the kingside pawns. Alternatives:

a) Immediately grabbing the two pieces for a rook leaves Black with a vastly inferior version of Game 54: 14...♖xd2? 15 ♗xd2 ♕xd2 16 ♖fd1 ♕h6 17 ♕g3 ♕c6 18 ♖d3 ♘c8 19 ♖ad1 f6 20 ♕b8 ♔f7 21 ♖d7 ± Barle-Wittman, Ljubljana 1981.

b) 14...g6 needs more tests, e.g. 15 a4 ♗g7 16 a5 ♘c8 17 ♕a4+ ♖d7 18 ♘f3 b5 19 ♕b3 0-0 20 ♖e1 ♕d3 21 a6 ♖fd8 ∞ Nun-Stohl, Prague 1986.

c) 14...e6 15 ♕g3 *(D)* is quite common:

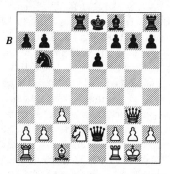

c1) 15...♗d6 (White's last move was supposed to prevent this bishop developing) 16 ♕xg7 ♗e5 17 ♕g5 ♖d3 18 ♘f3 (18 ♘b3 h6! 19 ♕h4 ♖d1 20 ♘d2 ♖xd2 21 ♗xd2 ♕xd2 22 ♖ad1 ♕g5 23 ♕e4 ♕f4 ∓ Afek-Ikonnikov, Paris 1995) 18...♖d1 19 ♘d2 ♘c4 20 ♖xd1 ♕xd1+ 21 ♘f1 h6 22 ♕h4 ♘d2 (forcing White into a promising exchange sacrifice) 23 ♗xd2 ♕xa1 24 ♕h5 ♗f6 25 ♕f3 ♗g7 26 ♕g3 ♗f6 Acs-Volzhin, Budapest 1996, and now 27 ♕b8+ ♗d8

28 ♕e5! ± in view of 28...♖g8 29 ♕b5+.

c2) 15...h5!? 16 ♘f3 h4 17 ♕c7 (17 ♘xh4? ♖xh4! 18 ♕xh4 ♖d1 −+) 17...♕a6! 18 ♗g5 f6 19 ♗xh4 ♘d5 20 ♕g3 g5 21 ♗xg5 fxg5 22 ♕xg5 ♗e7 23 ♕g6+ ♔d7 24 ♖fd1 ♔c8 25 ♘d4 ♘c7 ∓ Morvay-Hardicsay, Hungary 1982, but no one has tried the line again for Black.

15 h3

To prevent ...♕g4 by Black, as 15 ♘f3 is met by 15...♖d1 16 ♘d2 ♖h6 17 ♕f4 ♖d6 18 ♖xd1 ♕xd1+ 19 ♘f1 g6 ∓ Khlusevich-Dvoirys, USSR 1982. However the useful move 15 a4!? is worth consideration, when after 15...♕g4 16 ♕xg4 hxg4 17 a5 ♘d5 18 ♖a4 f5 19 ♖e1 g6 20 ♘b3 White had a better endgame in the game Vancini-Hugony, San Benedetto del Tronto 1987.

15...g5!? 16 ♕g3

Not 16 ♕xg5? ♗h6.

16...g4 17 h4

17 ♘b3?! ♗g7 (also 17...gxh3 18 ♘d4 ♕g4 Acs-Votava, Budapest 1995) 18 ♗f4 ♘d5 19 ♖fe1 ♕xb2 20 c4 ♘xf4 21 ♕xf4 gxh3 22 ♕g5 ♕f6 ∓ Acs-Szuk, Budapest 1995.

17...♗g7 18 ♘b3 0-0

18...♘d5 19 ♘d4 ♕e5 20 ♕d3 ♖d7 21 ♗g5 ♘f4 ∞ Acs-Varga, Budapest 1996.

19 ♘d4 ♗xd4 20 cxd4 ♕e4

If 20...♖xd4 21 ♗h6 ♖e8 22 ♖ae1 Black's kingside is looking exposed, and Schneider gives the continuation 22...♕b5 23 ♖e5 ♕d3 24 ♖g5+ ♔h7 25 ♖xh5 ♕g6 26 ♕e5! f6 27 ♗f4+ ♔g7 28 ♖g5! ♕xg5 29 hxg5 fxe5 30 ♗xe5+ ♔g6 31 ♗xd4 ♔xg5 32

♗e3+ ♔f5 33 ♖d1 ±. However even in the game Black's king has little shelter, and we should take note that Acs is still playing this line for White.

21 ♗d2 ♘d5 22 ♖ae1 ♕g6 23 f3!? ♕d3! 24 ♗h6 ♕xd4+ 25 ♔h2 ♖fe8 26 ♖e5 ♔h7 27 ♗d2 (27 ♖xh5? ♘f6) **27...♘f6 28 ♗c3 ♕d6 29 ♖fe1?** (29 fxg4! hxg4 30 ♖e3 was still fine for White; not 29...♘xg4+? 30 ♔h1 ♘xe5 in this line, when 31 ♖xf7+! forces mate next move) **29...gxf3! 30 gxf3 ♖g8 31 ♕f4 ♖g6 32 ♕b4? ♕xb4 33 ♗xb4 ♖d4 0-1**

Game 53
Sveshnikov – Salov
Leningrad 1984

1 e4 c5 2 c3 ♘f6 3 e5 ♘d5 4 d4 cxd4 5 ♘f3 ♘c6 6 ♗c4 ♘b6 7 ♗b3 d5 8 exd6 ♕xd6 9 0-0 ♗e6 10 ♗xe6 ♕xe6 11 ♘xd4 ♘xd4 12 ♕xd4 ♖d8 13 ♕h4 ♕e2 14 ♗d2 *(D)*

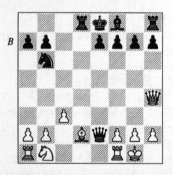

The idea of 14 ♗d2 is to develop (White intends ♖e1) without sacrificing the b-pawn by 14 ♗e3!?, the subject of the following illustrative game). As commented on in the 14

♘d2 lines (Game 52), after 14 ♗d2 it is too dangerous for Black to grab the two pieces for a rook with the immediate 14...♖xd2.

14...h5
With the idea of 15 ♖e1 ♕g4 swapping queens. Others:

a) 14...♕c4 15 ♕g3 ♕d3 and Panchenko has had a couple of grandmaster draws repeating moves with 16 ♕h4 ♕c4 17 ♕g3 and 16 ♕f4 ♕c4 17 ♕g3.

b) 14...e6 15 ♖e1 ♕d3 (another idea for Black is 15...♕c4!?) 16 ♗g5 ♖d5 17 ♘d2 ♕g6 18 ♘e4 h6 19 ♗f6! ♘d7! ∞ Sveshnikov-Ionov, Volgodonsk 1983.

c) 14...f6 15 ♖e1 ♖xd2 16 ♘xd2 ♕xd2 17 ♕h5+ (or 17 a4!? ♕d5 18 a5 ♘c8 19 ♕g4 ♕d7 20 ♖e6 g6 21 ♖d1 ♕c7 22 a6 with pressure for White, Cabrera-Remon, Cuba 1984) 17...g6 18 ♕a5 ♕d7 19 ♕xa7 ♘c8 20 ♕a5 (Sveshnikov assesses this position as better for White; Kuzmin thinks it favours Black, but in the game he seriously erred) 20...e6 21 c4! ♕c6? (21...b6) 22 ♖xe6+! ♕xe6 23 ♖e1 ♕xe1+ 24 ♕xe1+ ♔d7 25 ♕d2+ ♔c7 26 ♕f4+ ♗d6 27 ♕xf6 ± because White had too many pawns in Sveshnikov-Kuzmin, Tashkent 1984.

15 h3
15 ♕g5?! h4! 16 ♖e1 ♕h5 17 ♘a3 ♕xg5 18 ♗xg5 ♖h5 19 ♗e3 e6 20 ♗xb6 axb6 21 ♘c4 b5 22 ♘e3 h3 23 gxh3 ♖xh3 24 a4 b4 ∓ Sveshnikov-Tukmakov, USSR 1984 or 15 ♖e1 ♕g4 16 ♕xg4 hxg4 17 ♗e3 e6 18 ♘d2 ♗d6 19 g3 ♗b8 = Sariego-Pigusov, Bayamo 1985.

15...♘c4

15...♕c4 16 ♕g3 ♕d3 17 ♕h4 ♕c4 18 ♕g3 ♕d3 ½-½ was Panchenko-Sherbakov, Sochi 1989, the same draw as at move 14 with the moves 14...h5 15 h3 thrown on. Panchenko obviously has a sense of humour more highly developed than his fighting spirit.

16 ♖e1 ♕d3 17 ♗c1 a6 18 b3 ♘d6 19 ♕a4+ ♕b5 20 ♕xb5+ (20 ♕f4!?) 20...♘xb5 21 a4 ♘c7! 22 ♖a2 e6 23 ♗e3 ♗e7 24 ♗d4 ♗f6 25 ♗b6 ♔d7 26 b4 ♔c6! = 27 a5 ♖d7 28 c4 ♗d4 29 ♘a3 ♗xb6 30 axb6 ♔xb6 31 c5+ ½-½

Just when the position was getting interesting: 31...♔a7 32 b5 ∞.

Game 54
Woodland – Neil
Corr. 1989

1 e4 c5 2 c3 ♘f6 3 e5 ♘d5 4 d4 cxd4 5 ♘f3 ♘c6 6 ♗c4 ♘b6 7 ♗b3 d5 8 exd6 ♕xd6 9 0-0 ♗e6 10 ♗xe6 ♕xe6 11 ♘xd4 ♘xd4 12 ♕xd4 ♖d8 13 ♕h4 ♕e2 14 ♗e3!? (D)

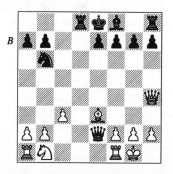

The critical and most dangerous move. White offers a double-edged

pawn sacrifice on b2, soon followed by two pieces for a rook. Usually Black grabs the material and then, in good modern style, offers some back to get his kingside pieces developed. In practical play White has not done badly, as Black's king is exposed and accurate defence is essential, but objectively I suspect that Black can successfully regroup with precise play.

14...♕xb2

14...♘c4 15 ♘a3 (15 ♗xa7? ♖d1 ∓) 15...♘xe3 16 ♕a4+ ♖d7 17 fxe3 ♕a6 18 ♕xa6 bxa6 19 ♘c4 ± Morvay-Monda, Hungarian Cht 1995.

A more serious line is 14...e6:

a) 15 ♘d2 ♗e7 16 ♕g3 0-0 17 ♗h6 (17 ♖fe1 ♕d3 18 ♗xb6 ♕xg3 19 hxg3 ♖xd2 20 ♗xa7 = Haba-Stohl, Czechoslovakia 1987) 17...♗f6 18 ♖fe1 ♕h5 19 ♗e3 ♖d3 20 ♕f3 ♕xf3 21 ♘xf3 ½-½ Sveshnikov-Kiselev, Moscow Ch 1987.

b) 15 ♗xb6 axb6 16 ♘a3 b5 (16...♖d7 17 ♖fe1 ♕xb2 18 ♘c4 ♕xc3 19 ♘e5 ♖d4 20 ♕h5 g6 21 ♘xg6 ♖g8 22 ♘xf8 ♔xf8 23 ♖ac1 ± Van Mil-Eiemersma, Netherlands 1992) 17 ♕g5 ♗xa3 18 ♕xg7 ♗xb2 (really? 18...♖f8 19 bxa3 ± Hmadi-Mascariñas, Novi Sad OL 1990) 19 ♖ae1 ♕h5 20 ♕xh8+ ♔e7 21 ♕e5 ♕xe5 22 ♖xe5 b4 23 ♖b5 bxc3 24 ♖xb7+ ♖d7 25 ♖b8 ♖d8 26 ♖b7+ ♖d7 27 ♖b8 ♖d8 ½-½ Lindgren-Kotronias, Gausdal 1990, but White might expect to improve somewhere.

15 ♘d2 ♖xd2 (D)

If 15...♕b5?!, 16 ♖ab1 ♕c6 17 ♗xb6 ♖xd2 18 ♕f4! ♖d6 19 ♗xa7 ± Lagunov-Poliakevich, USSR 1986, but 15...e6!? is less clear, e.g. 16 ♖ab1 (perhaps 16 ♘c4 ♕xc3 17 ♘xb6 axb6 18 ♗xb6 ♖c8 ∞) 16...♕xa2 17 ♖a1 ♕d5 18 ♖xa7 ♘c8 19 ♖a4 ♘d6 Hünerkopf-De Boer, Germany 1990.

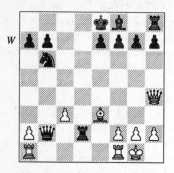

16 ♖ab1!?

This *zwischenzug* offers a further pawn or two to activate the rook with tempo. The alternative is 16 ♗xd2 ♕xd2 17 ♖fd1 (17 a4 leads to similar play: 17...♕h6 18 ♕g3 ♕c6 19 ♖fd1 g6 20 ♖ab1 ♘d7 21 ♖d3 f6 22 ♖bd1 ♘e5 23 ♖d8+ ♔f7 ∓ Van der Werf – Har-Zvi, Wijk aan Zee 1993; White's problem in this whole line is that he is so seriously behind in material Black will usually become better if he successful develops his kingside) 17...♕h6 18 ♕g3 ♕c6 and now:

a) 19 ♕b8+ ♘c8 and Black is threatening to develop with 20...e6 and 21...♗e7 (as White's queen no longer exerts pressure on g7), e.g. 20 ♖ab1 b6 21 a4 e6 22 a5 ♗c5 ∓.

b) 19 ♖ab1 ♕c8!? (19...♘c8!?), when 20 ♕e5 e6 21 ♕b5+ ♕c6 22 ♕xc6+ bxc6 23 a4 ♗c5 24 a5 ♘c8 25 ♖b8 ♔e7 26 ♖b7+ ♔f6 27 ♖b8 ♔e7 28 ♖b7+ ♔f6 29 ♖b8 ♖e8 30

♖d7 ♖e7 31 ♖bb7 ♖xd7 32 ♖xd7 ♘e7 and White was left trying to defend (unsuccessfully) with rook v the two minor pieces in Kotliar-Brook, Israeli Ch 1986.

c) 19 ♖d4!? (this centralising rook move is a good attempt, but as we shall see Black has some remarkable defensive resources which give him a large advantage) 19...f6 20 ♕b8+ ♘c8 21 ♖ad1 ♔f7 22 ♖d7 (after 22 ♖d8? ♘d6 the knight takes up a protected central post; after the text move 22...♘d6?? is a blunder due to 23 ♖xd6 or 23 ♕xd6; however Cherniaev understands that ♖c7 is only a pseudo-threat, and plays an excellent move) 22...g5! 23 ♖c7 (23 ♖xb7 ♗g7 24 ♖c7 ♕b6! 25 ♖b7 ♕e6 ∓; probably the best chances are offered by 23 ♕xb7 ♕xb7 24 ♖xb7 ♗g7 25 c4 f5 26 c5 when Black's knight is without moves, but after 26...♗e5 White's c-pawn is no real danger and Black can gradually unravel his position) 23...♕a4! 24 ♖d8 ♕a3! ∓ (brilliant defence: of course 24...♘d6? would have lost to 25 ♖xd6, but now, using the threat ...♕c1, Black gains time to overprotect d6 with his queen, e.g. 25 g3 ♘d6 26 c4 ♕b4! ∓ is analysed by Shirov and Cherniaev in *Informator 53*) 25 h3?! ♘d6 26 g3 h5! 27 c4 h4 28 c5 ♘f5 29 ♖cc8 (White will win back vast quantities of material, but her king is actually in deep trouble) 29...hxg3! 30 ♖xf8+ ♔e6! 31 ♖xh8 gxf2+ 32 ♔xf2 ♕xa2+ 33 ♔f3 ♕b3+ 34 ♔f2 (34 ♔g4 ♕d1#) 34...♕c2+ 35 ♔e1 ♘d4 36 ♖c6+ (there is no other way for White to stave off

mate) 36...bxc6 37 ♕c8+ ♔e5 38
♕c7+ ♔e6 39 ♕c8+ ♔d5 40 ♕d7+
♔c4 41 ♕xe7 ♕g2! −+ 42 ♖d8
♕g1+ 43 ♔d2 ♕f2+ 44 ♔d1 ♕f1+
45 ♕e1 (45 ♔d2 ♘b3+) 45...♕f3+
46 ♔c1 ♕a3+ 0-1 M.Marić-Cher-
niaev, Hastings 1991.

16...♕c2?!

Although 16...♕xc3 looks risky,
Black wriggled out after 17 ♗xd2
♕xd2 18 ♕e4 ♕xa2 19 ♕xb7 f6 20
♖a1 ♕e6 21 ♕xa7 ♘c8 22 ♕c7 (22
♕c5!? ♔f7 23 ♖fe1 ♕d7 24 ♖a8
♘d6 25 ♖a7 is by no means clear)
22...♕d7 23 ♕c4 ♘b6 24 ♕b3 ♘d5
25 ♖a8+ ♔f7 26 ♕a2 ♔g6!? ∓ in
Hmadi-De Firmian, Manila IZ 1990.

However why not take the a-
pawn? After 16...♕xa2!, if there is
nothing better than the capture on d2
in reply, the fact that White has no a-
pawn will be important in the long
term. 17 ♖a1 tries to exploit Black's
pawn grab (intending 17...♕c2 18
♗xd2 ♕xd2 19 ♖xa7 when Black's
lack of development is worrying) but
after 17...♕c4!? 18 ♕xc4 ♘xc4 19
♗xd2 ♘xd2 20 ♖fd1 ♘e4 21 ♖xa7
♘d6 22 c4 b6 Black is certainly not
worse, and may be much better.
Whilst White spends time trying to
round up to b-pawn Black will develop with ...g6 and ...♗g7. Therefore White continues 17 ♗xd2 ♕xd2
18 ♖fd1 *(D)* and now:

a) 18...♕xc3? 19 ♖xb6 axb6 20
♕a4+ ♕c6 21 ♕a8+ wins for White.

b) 18...♕a2 transposes to the
main game (the reference Morvay-
Halasz used this move-order).

c) 18...♕h6! 19 ♕g3 f5 (and not
19...♕c6? 20 ♖xb6! with 21 ♕b8+

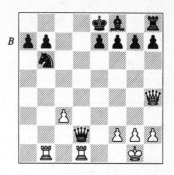

coming) 20 ♕b8+ ♔f7 21 ♕xa7
♘c8 22 ♕xb7 ♘d6 Hellström-Kre-
imer, Corr. 1992. Black's knight has
reached a solid outpost, and he has
two pieces for a rook. White is still
ahead in development, and could
create problems for Black if he could
advance his c-pawn. The game continued 23 ♕a7 (this plan looks dubious) 23...♕e6 24 ♖b8 g6 25 ♕a8
♕e5 26 g3 ♗g7 27 ♖xh8 ♗xh8 28
c4 ♘xc4 29 ♕d8 ♘d6 30 ♖b1 g5 31
♖b8 ♕e1+? 32 ♔g2 ♕e4+ 33 ♔g1
♕e1+? (33...♗g7 ∓) ½-½. I suspect
Black is better at move 22, but we
await more practical tests.

17 ♗xd2 ♕xd2 18 ♖fd1 ♕xa2

Now if 18...♕h6 White is either a
pawn or a tempo up on lines examined earlier: 19 ♕g3 f5 20 ♕b8+
♔f7 21 ♕xa7 ♘c8 22 ♕xb7 ± Di-
mov-Halkias, Varna 1994, because
White's passed a-pawn is a danger.

19 ♕e4

Whilst the position remains very
unclear, the activity of the white major pieces can make life very unpleasant for Black, in spite of his
considerable material advantage. For
example, Black ended up returning
material for a worse ending after

both the alternatives 19 ♕h5 ♕e6 20
c4 g6 21 ♕b5+ ♕c6 22 c5 ♕xb5 23
♖xb5 ♗g7 24 cxb6 axb6 25 ♖xb6
0-0 26 ♖xb7 ♗f6 Van de Oudewee-
tering-Boersma, Netherlands 1993
and 19 ♕g3 f6 20 ♕b8+ ♔f7 21
♕xb7 ♕a5 22 ♕c7 ♕e5 23 ♕xa7
♘c8 24 ♕b7 ♘d6 25 ♕c7 h5 26 c4
♘e4 27 ♕xe5 fxe5 28 ♖b8 ♖h6 29
♖dd8 ♖h8 30 f3 ♘c5 31 ♖dc8 ♘e6
32 c5 ♘d4 33 c6 ♘xc6 34 ♖xc6
Vella-Ribeiro, Gausdal 1986.

19...f6

19...g5 20 c4 (20 ♕xb7 ±) 20...♗g7
21 c5 ♘a4?? (21...♘c8 22 ♖xb7 0-0)
22 ♕c6+! 1-0 was Morvay-Halasz,
Hungary 1994.

**20 ♕xb7 ♔f7 21 ♖a1 ♕c2 22
♕xa7 ♘c4 23 ♕d4 ♘e5?!** (Black
should have tried 23...♘d6) **24 f4
♘g4 25 h3 ♘h6 26 ♕c4+ e6 27
♖d7+ ♔g6 28 g4 ♗a3 29 ♕xe6
♗c5+ 30 ♔h1 ♖b8 31 ♖ad1 ♗f8 32
♖g1 1-0**

20 9 0-0 ♗e6 10 ♘a3

1	e4	c5
2	c3	♘f6
3	e5	♘d5
4	d4	cxd4
5	♘f3	♘c6
6	♗c4	♘b6
7	♗b3	d5
8	exd6	♕xd6
9	0-0	♗e6
10	♘a3 *(D)*	

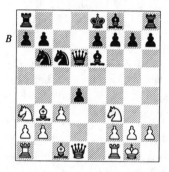

This is the absolute main line of the 2...♘f6 variation, where Black must make a decision whether to turn his temporary pawn advantage into a permanent one with 10...dxc3. In Games 55 and 56 we examine the unambitious variations where he chooses not to. After 10...♗xb3 11 ♕xb3 e6 (Game 55) it transpires that the sharpest line, 12 ♖d1!?, gives promising play. Instead 11...♕d5!? (Game 56) aims to exchange queens, but matters are not so straightforward, since if Black swaps on b3 the

semi-open a-file can be a penetration point for White's queen's rook. In all of these lines White quickly re-establishes material equality, and can exploit his lead in development with no risk of becoming worse. The conclusion is that if Black declines the pawn he is struggling for equality.

Therefore we turn to 10...dxc3. In Game 57 White pursues a slightly illogical course with 11 ♘b5?!, as after the queen exchange Black's king is safe in the centre. The critical test is 11 ♕e2!? (Game 58), where White seeks long-term compensation for his sacrificed pawn. After 11...♗xb3 12 ♘b5 Black's queen drops back to b8 to stop a later ♗f4 or attack by White's rook on the d-file. Black's defensive resources appear satisfactory at present, but White certainly has active play in many lines, and could experiment with Andrew Harley's interesting new suggestions.

Game 55
Schmittdiel – Kotronias
Gausdal 1994

1 e4 c5 2 c3 ♘f6 3 e5 ♘d5 4 d4 cxd4 5 ♘f3 ♘c6 6 ♗c4 ♘b6 7 ♗b3 d5 8 exd6 ♕xd6 9 0-0 ♗e6 10 ♘a3 ♗xb3

10...dxc3 is examined in games 57 and 58, while 10...a6 transposes to a line examined in Chapter 18.

11 ♕xb3

11 axb3?! a6 (11...dxc3 12 ♕e2 see Game 56) 12 cxd4 (12 ♘xd4 ♘xd4 13 ♝e3 ♘f5 14 ♕xd6 ♘xd6 15 ♝xb6 = Motwani -Yrjölä, Manila OL 1992 and Pedersen-De Firmian, Farum 1993) leaves the white pawn structure very poor. Although he remains well ahead in development this has so far been insufficient to compensate: 12...♖d8 (12...♕d5!? 13 ♕d3 e6 14 ♘c4 ♕b5 15 ♝f4 ♖c8 16 ♘fd2 ♘d5 17 ♝d6 ♘f6 18 ♝xf8 ♚xf8 19 ♘f3 ♖d8 20 ♖fd1 ♚e7 21 ♕e3 ♖d5 22 ♘ce5 ♖hd8 ∓ Rohde-Granda, USA 1992) 13 ♘c4 ♘xc4 14 bxc4 ♘xd4! (14...e6 15 ♕b3 ♖d7 16 ♖d1 ± Smagin-Abramović, Čačak 1991) 15 ♘xd4 ♕xd4 16 ♕f3 ♖d7 17 ♝f4 ♕d3 18 ♝e3 g6 19 ♖ad1 ♕f5 20 ♖xd7 ♕xf3 21 ♖xe7+ ♝xe7 22 gxf3 ♚d7 23 ♖d1+ ♚c6 ∓ Rohde-Wolff, USA Ch 1991.

11...e6?! *(D)*

Whilst Black retains chances of equality, this quiet move encourages White to gain further time by exploiting the queen's position on d6. 11...♕d5!? is examined in the following game. 11...♖c8 12 ♖d1!? ♕d5 13 ♘xd4 ♕xb3 14 axb3 e6 15 ♘xc6 ♖xc6 16 b4 ♝e7 17 ♝e3 ♘c8 18 b5 ♖c7 19 ♝xa7! ± was the game Hoffman-P.Cramling, Buenos Aires 1994, whilst another inferior prophylactic move is 11...♕d7?, e.g. 12 ♖d1! e6 13 ♘xd4 ♘xd4 (13...♘a5 14 ♕b5! ♝xa3 15 ♕xa5 ± Blatny-Aseev, Bad Wörishofen 1992) 14 ♖xd4 ♕c6 15 ♘c4 ♝c5 16 ♘e5 ♕c8 17 ♕b5+ ± Marković-Ilinčić, Kladovo 1993.

12 ♘b5

12 ♖d1!? is sharper and may keep an edge:

a) 12...d3 13 ♘b5 ♕d7 14 c4 ♖d8 15 ♘xa7 ♘xc4 16 ♕xc4 ♘xa7 17 ♝e3 ♘c6 18 ♝b6 ♕d5 19 ♕a4 ♖d7 20 ♘e1 ♝d6 21 ♖xd3 ♕h5 22 g3 ♝b8 23 ♖xd7 ♚xd7 24 ♖d1+ ± Schmittdiel-Enders, Germany 1990.

b) 12...♕d5 13 ♘b5 0-0-0:

b1) 14 ♘bxd4? is a mistake: 14...♕xb3 15 axb3 e5 16 ♝g5 exd4 17 ♝xd8 ♘xd8 ∓ Schmittdiel-Kotronias, Gausdal 1992.

b2) 14 ♝f4 ♕xb3 15 axb3 ♘d5 16 ♘xa7+ ♘xa7 17 ♖xa7 ♘xf4 18 ♖a8+ ♚c7 19 ♖xd8 ♚xd8 20 ♖xd4+ ♘d5 21 c4 ♝c5 22 ♖d2 ♝b4! 23 ♖d4 ♝c5 24 ♖d2 ½-½ Panchenko-Baikov, Yaroslavl 1986 as 24 ♖d1 allows 24...♚e7 25 cxd5 ♖d8 and Black regains the pawn with advantage.

b3) 14 ♘xa7+ ♘xa7 15 ♕xb6 ♝c5 16 ♕a5 ♘c6 17 ♕a8+! (17 ♕a4 d3 ∞ Rozentalis – Sideif-Zade, USSR 1985) 17...♚c7 18 ♕a4 d3?! (after 18...e5 Blatny suggests 19 b4!? or 19 cxd4 ♘xd4 20 ♘xd4 ♝xd4 21 ♝e3 ±) 19 ♘e1! g5 20 ♖xd3 ♕f5 21 ♖f3 ♕g6 22 ♝e3 ± Blatny-Kotronias, Debrecen Echt 1992.

c) 12...♗e7 13 ♘b5 (13 ♗e3 ♕d5 14 ♘xd4 ♗xa3 15 bxa3 0-0 16 ♘f3 ♘a5 17 ♕b4 ♘c6 18 ♕b3 ♘a5 19 ♕b1 ♘c6 20 ♘g5 f5 21 ♖e1 ∞ Smagin-Beshukov, St Petersburg 1993) 13...♕b8 14 ♘bxd4 0-0 15 ♘xc6 bxc6 16 c4 ♕c7 17 ♕c2 e5 18 b3 f6 19 ♘h4!? ♗c5 20 ♘f5 ♖fd8 21 ♗e3 ♗xe3 22 ♘xe3 ± Novik-Pigusov, Berlin 1994.

12...♕d7

12...♕d8?! allows 13 ♖d1! ♗e7 (or 13...d3 14 c4 ♗c5 15 ♖xd3 ♕e7 16 ♗f4 ± Kveinys-Levchenkov, Katowice 1993) 14 ♘fxd4 ♕b8 15 ♘xc6 bxc6 16 ♘d4 ± Dolmatov-Grünfeld, Haifa 1995. 12...♕b8 is possible, when White could play simply with 13 ♘bxd4 ♗e7 14 ♘xc6 bxc6 15 c4 0-0 16 ♕c2 ±.

13 ♘bxd4

A useful feature of 12...♕d7 is that now 13 ♖d1? would be a blunder due to 13...♘a5! –+ winning the knight on b5! White must watch out for this surprise ...♘a5 move in several variations; 13 ♗f4 ♘a5 is a possible alternative to 13...♘d5, whilst 13 ♘fxd4?! ♘a5! 14 ♕d1 a6! ∓ 15 ♘xe6?! (15 ♘a3) 15...fxe6 16 ♕h5+ g6 17 ♕e5 axb5 18 ♕xh8 ♕g7 19 ♕xg7 ♗xg7 also favoured Black in the game Smagin-Rõtsagov, Copenhagen 1993. Hence White's decision in the illustrative game to capture on d4 with the b5-knight.

13...♗c5

This is the only route to equality. 13...♘xd4 14 ♘xd4 and now:

a) 14...♗e7 15 ♖d1 0-0 16 ♘f5 (16 ♗e3 ♕c8 17 ♘b5 ♗c5 18 ♗d4 ♕c6 19 a4 Vasiukov-Tseitlin, Tiraspol

1994) 16...♕c7 17 ♘xe7+ ♕xe7 18 ♗e3 ♘d5 19 ♗d4 b6 20 c4 ± Halasz-Tischbierek, Balatonbereny 1984.

b) 14...♗c5 15 ♗e3 ♖c8 (Black must spend a tempo, as 15...0-0? 16 ♘xe6! fxe6 17 ♗xc5 +– Harley-Parmentier, Hastings 1988) 16 ♖fd1 ♕a4 and now instead of 17 ♕b5+ ♕xb5 18 ♘xb5 ♘c4! ½-½ Rabiega-Mainka, German Ch 1995 simply 17 ♘b5 ±.

14 ♗e3

Kotronias gives 14 ♖d1 ♘xd4 15 ♘xd4 0-0 16 ♗e3 ♕e7 as leading to equality.

14...♘xd4! 15 ♖fd1 0-0 16 ♗xd4 ♘xd4 17 ♖xd4 ♕c7 = 18 ♕c2 h6 19 ♖ad1 ♖ad8 20 ♕d3 ♖d5 21 ♖xd5 ♘xd5 22 g3 ½-½

Game 56
Benjamin – P.Wolff
New York 1996

1 e4 c5 2 c3 ♘f6 3 e5 ♘d5 4 d4 cxd4 5 ♘f3 ♘c6 6 ♗c4 ♘b6 7 ♗b3 d6 8 exd6 ♕xd6 9 0-0 ♗e6 10 ♘a3 ♗xb3 11 ♕xb3 ♕d5!? (D)

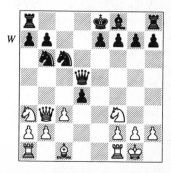

A logical response, anticipating White's ♘b5. However, White's lead

in development tends to persist even
after a queen exchange.

12 ♘b5 ♖c8

12...♕xb3 13 axb3 ♖c8 is tactically possible (14 ♘xa7? ♖a8) but
after 14 ♘bxd4 ♘xd4 15 ♘xd4 a6
16 b4 White is ready to prise open
the a-file as per the game Rashkov-
sky-Georgadze in the note at move
15.

13 ♘fxd4

13 ♘bxd4 ♘xd4 14 ♘xd4 transposes to the game, whilst another
idea is 13 ♖d1!? e6 (Vera analyses
13...♕xb3 14 axb3 dxc3 15 ♘xa7 ±
as on 15...♖a8 White has 16 ♘xc6!
bxc6 17 ♖xa8+ ♘xa8 18 bxc3) 14
♘bxd4 ♘xd4 15 ♖xd4!? ♕xb3 16
axb3 ♖a8?! (16...a6 17 b4 ±) 17 ♖d1
♗e7?! 18 ♗e3 ± Vera-Otero, Cuban
Ch 1985.

13...♘xd4 14 ♘xd4 e6

For 14...♕xb3 15 axb3 a6 16 b4
see the note at Black's 15th move.

15 ♖d1

15 ♗e3 ♘c4 (or 15...♗c5: 16
♖fd1 0-0 17 ♘b5 ♕xb3 18 axb3
♗xe3 19 fxe3 a6 20 ♘d6 = Sermek-
Orlov, Pula 1991 while 16 ♕b5+
♕d7 17 ♖ad1 ♘d5 18 ♕xd7+ ♔xd7
19 ♘f5 g6 20 ♗xc5 ♖xc5 is nothing much for White, Petronijević-
Kunovac, Yugoslav Cht 1994) 16 ♗f4
(16 ♕a4+ ♕d7 17 ♕xd7+ ♔xd7 18
♖ad1 ♘xe3 19 fxe3 ♔e8 = Petroni-
jević-Zafirovski, Nis 1994 and Rõt-
sagov-Van der Wiel, Amsterdam
1995) 16...♗e7 17 ♖ad1 0-0 18 ♖fe1
♘b6 19 ♘b5 ♕xb3 20 axb3 a6 21
♘d6 ♗xd6 22 ♗xd6 ♖fd8 23 ♗g3
♘d5 24 ♔f1 ♔f8 25 c4 ♘e7 26 ♗c7
♖xd1 27 ♖xd1 ♔e8 with equality,

Yudasin-Ki.Georgiev, Manila IZ
1990.

15...♗c5

If 15...♗e7 16 ♗e3 ± Dončević-
Juhnke, Germany 1985 as White
threatens 17 ♘b5. Instead 15...♕xb3
allows White play on the a-file: 16
axb3 a6 17 b4 ♗e7 18 b5 axb5 19
♖a7! (19 ♘xb5 0-0 20 ♗f4 ♘d5 21
♗d6 ♖xd6 22 ♘xd6 ♖c6 23 ♘b5
♖c5 24 ♘d6 ♖c6 ½-½ Renet-
Smirin, Moscow OL 1994) 19...b4
20 ♖xb7 ♘d5 21 ♘f5 ♗f8 22 ♘e3!
± (22 c4 ♖xc4 23 ♘e3 ♘xe3 24
♖b8+ ♔e7 25 ♗xe3 f5 26 b3 ♖c7 27
♖xb4 ± Zarnicki-Van Wely, Buenos
Aires 1995) 22...♘xe3 23 ♗xe3
bxc3 24 bxc3 ♗e7 (24...♖xc3 25
♖b8+ ♔e7 26 ♗b6 e5 27 ♖a5 ♖c4
28 ♗b4+) 25 c4 ♖d8 26 ♖xd8+
♗xd8 27 c5 0-0 28 c6 ♗f6 29 c7
♗e5 30 ♗d4 1-0 Rashkovsky-Geor-
gadze, Aktiubinsk 1985, as 30...♗d6
31 ♗c5! ♗xc5 32 ♖b8.

16 ♕b5+ *(D)*

16 ♘b5?! ♕xb3 17 axb3 a6 18
♘d6+? (18 b4 axb5 19 bxc5 ♘a4 20
♗e3 ♔e7 21 ♗d4 f6 22 b3 ♘xc5 23
♖a7 e5 = Sariego-Browne, Linares
1992) 18...♗xd6 19 ♖xd6 ♘d5 (now
White's rook on d6 is in danger) 20
♗g5 h6 21 ♗h4 g5 22 ♗g3 ♔e7 ∓
23 c4 ♘f4 24 ♗xf4 gxf4 25 ♖ad1?!
(25 ♖d4 ♖hd8 26 ♖xf4 ♖d2)
25...♖hd8 26 ♖xd8 ♖xd8 27 ♖xd8
♔xd8 reaching a pawn ending in the
game Kamsky-Tukmakov, Reykjavik 1990. According to later analysis
by Tukmakov, Black is winning
(though in the game he actually
lost!).

16...♔e7?

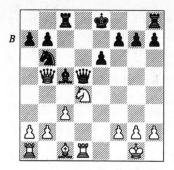

16...♕d7 17 ♕e2 ♕e7 18 ♘b3 (18 ♘b5 a6 19 b4 axb5 20 ♕xb5+ ♖c6 21 bxc5 ♘d5 22 ♖b1 0-0 23 ♕xb7 ♕xb7 24 ♖xb7 ♘xc3 25 ♖d2 h6 26 ♖c2 ♖d8 27 g3 ♖xc5 28 ♗e3 ♖cc8 29 ♗b6 ♘a4! with an equal position in the game Sveshnikov-Rashkovsky, USSR 1985) 18...0-0 19 ♘xc5 ♕xc5 20 ♗e3 ♕c6 21 ♗d4 f6 22 ♗xb6 ♕xb6 23 ♖d7 ♖cd8 24 ♖ad1 ♖xd7 25 ♖xd7 ♖f7 26 ♖d2 ± Blatny-Arlandi, Groningen 1985.

17 ♕e2 ± ♖hd8 18 ♗e3

18 ♕g4 ♗xd4? 19 ♖xd4 ♕e5 20 ♗g5+ f6 21 ♗f4 ♕f5 22 ♕xg7+ ♔e8 23 ♗d6 1-0 Tzermiadianos-Kalesis, Khania 1993.

18...♕e5 19 ♕g4 ♔f8 20 ♗f4 h5? (20...♕d5) **21 ♕h4 ± ♕d5 22 ♘xe6+ fxe6 23 ♖xd5 ♖xd5 24 ♗e3 ♘d7 25 ♗xc5+ ♘xc5 26 c4 ♖f5 27 ♖d1 1-0**

Game 57
Bräuning – Yarkovich
Munich 1991

1 e4 c5 2 c3 ♘f6 3 e5 ♘d5 4 d4 cxd4 5 ♘f3 ♘c6 6 ♗c4 ♘b6 7 ♗b3 d5 8 exd6 ♕xd6 9 0-0 ♗e6 10 ♘a3 dxc3 11 ♘b5?!

This looks rather illogical; first White sacrifices a pawn to exploit Black's king in the centre, and then he offers to exchange queens, relieving the pressure. Of course there is an idea behind the manoeuvre; White gets to cripple the black pawn structure in compensation.

For 11 ♕e2!? see the following game, while 11 ♗xe6?! ♕xd1 12 ♖xd1 fxe6 is an inaccurate move-order as, for example, 13 ♘b5 can now be met by 13...c2!.

11...♕xd1 12 ♖xd1 ♖c8 13 ♗xe6 fxe6 14 bxc3 (D)

Recapturing with 14 ♘xc3 leaves White is struggling for equality even if Black returns his extra doubled pawn on e6:

a) 14...g6 15 ♘g5 (15 ♖e1 ♗g7 16 ♖xe6 0-0 also allows Black a comfortable game, Nadyrkhanov-Kruppa, Sochi 1994 and Van Beers-Nijboer, Cappelle la Grande 1996) 15...♘d8 (15...e5 16 ♘e6 ♘d4 17 ♘xd4 exd4 18 ♖xd4 ♗g7 = Basirov-Rashkovsky, Kstovo 1994) 16 ♖e1 ♗g7 17 ♘xe6 ♘xe6 18 ♖xe6 ♔f7 19 ♖e3 ♖hf8 20 ♘e4 ♖c2 ∓ Mikac-Timoshenko, Pula 1994.

b) 14...h6!? 15 ♘e4 g5 16 ♘c5 (but perhaps 16 h4!? g4 17 ♘h2 ♖g8 18 b3 as Smagin used to beat Salov in a quickplay game in Moscow in 1992) 16...♘d8 17 ♗e3 (17 b4 ♗g7 18 ♖b1 ♘c4 19 ♖e1 ♔f7 is clearly better for Black, Bronstein-Tischbierek, Gausdal 1990) 17...♗g7 18 ♖ab1 ♘c4 19 b4 b6 20 ♘e4 ♘f7 21 ♗d4 e5 22 ♗e3 ♘fd6 ∓ Handoko-Liang, Asian Cht 1993.

14...♘c4

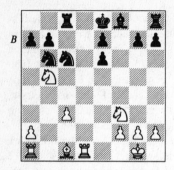

There are other respectable tries:

a) 14...h6 15 ♗e3 ♘d5 16 ♘xa7 ♘xe3 17 ♘xc8 ♘xd1 18 ♖xd1 g5 19 ♘b6 ♗g7 20 ♖d7 ♗xc3 (20...♘a5 21 ♘d4 ± Vorotnikov-Polovodin, USSR 1985) 21 ♖xb7 0-0 22 ♖c7 ♘d4! 23 ♘c8!? ♘xf3+ 24 gxf3 (Stoica-Georgescu, Romania 1986) and now Stoica claims Black can hold with 24...♖xf3 25 ♔g2 ♖d3 26 ♘xe7+ ♔f8 27 a4 ♗f6! 28 ♘c6 ♖a3 29 a5 ♗c3 30 ♖a7 ♖a2.

b) 14...♘a4!? (successful in its only outing) 15 ♗f4 h6 16 h4 g6 17 ♖e1 ♗g7 18 ♖xe6 ♔f7 19 ♖e3 a6 20 ♘bd4 ♘xc3! 21 ♘xc6 ♖xc6 22 ♗e5 ♗f6! 23 ♖d3 ♖hc8 ∓ Lautier-Wahls, Hamburg 1986.

c) 14...g6 15 ♘g5 (15 ♖b1!?, for example 15...♘a4 16 ♖e1 a6 17 ♘bd4 ♘d8 18 ♗a3 ♘xc3 19 ♖bc1 ♖c7 20 ♗b2 ♘d5 21 ♖xc7 ♘xc7 22 ♘xe6 ♘cxe6 23 ♗xh8 ± Eruslanova-Semina, Moscow 1986) 15...a6 (15...e5!? 16 ♘e4 ♘c4 17 ♖b1 b6 with an at least equal position for Black, Ochoa-Bellon, Spanish Cht 1995) 16 ♘d4 ♘xd4 (16...♘d5 17 ♘dxe6 ± Panchenko-Gorelov, Minsk 1985, as on 17...♘xc3? comes 18 ♗b2) 17 cxd4 ♖c6 18 ♖e1 ♗g7 19

♘xe6 ♗f6 20 ♖b1 and White is just a touch better, Degraeve-Jirovsky, Mamaia 1991.

15 ♘g5 e5 16 ♘e6

16 ♖b1 h6 17 ♘e6 ♔f7 18 ♘bc7 b6 19 ♖b5 (for 19 f4 see the following note) 19...g6 20 ♖d7 ♗g7 21 ♘xg7? ♘b8!! 0-1 Martin del Campo-Browne, Mexico 1994 was an evil trap – 22 ♖d1 ♖xc7 and the knight on g7 has no escape.

16...♔f7 17 ♘bc7?!

After 17 ♘g5+ ♔e8 18 ♘e6 Black's safest is 18...♔f7 ½-½, as in Smagin-Gavrikov, USSR Ch 1986, although Black can avoid the repetition with 18...h6 19 ♘bc7+ ♔f7 as in Blauert-Ernst, Lugano 1989. After the continuation 20 ♖b1 b6 21 f4 (for 21 ♖b5 see Martin del Campo-Browne in the previous note) 21...exf4 22 ♗xf4 g5 23 ♗g3 ♗g7 24 ♘xg7 ♔xg7 25 ♖d7 ♔g6 26 ♖e1 ♖hf8 27 ♖e4 ♘a5 28 ♘d5 ♔f5 29 ♖e1 ♖f7 30 ♗d6 ♘c4 31 ♘xe7+ ♖xe7 32 ♖exe7 ♖xe7 33 ♗xe7 the game was equal, but certainly the position after 18...h6 has plenty of play.

17...g6 18 f4 ♗g7 19 fxe5 ♘4xe5 20 ♖f1+ ♗f6 21 ♗h6 g5! 22 ♗xg5 ♘d8!

After Black's surprising 21st, the white minor pieces are in a bit of a tangle. On 23 ♗xf6 exf6 24 ♘g5+ ♔g6 25 ♘ge6 ♘xe6 26 ♘xe6 comes 26...♖xc3 with a good extra pawn for Black.

23 ♘xd8+ ♖hxd8 24 ♖ae1 ♖xc7 25 ♖xe5 ♖d3! ∓ 26 ♗xf6 exf6 27 ♖h5 (27 ♖ef5 ♖c6 28 ♖1f3 ♖d1+ ∓) 27...♔g6 28 ♖h4 ♖dxc3 29 ♖g4+ ♔f7 30 ♖h4 ♔g8! (with a winning rook ending; if 31 ♖g4+ then 31...♖g7) **31 ♖xf6 ♖c1+ 32 ♔f2 ♖1c2+ 33 ♔g3 ♖xa2 34 ♖g4+ ♖g7 35 ♖xg7+ ♔xg7 36 ♖d6 ♖b2 37 ♔f4 a5 38 g4 a4 39 h4 a3 40 ♖d3 ♖b4+ 41 ♔e5 ♖a4 42 ♖d1 ♖xg4 43 ♖d7+ ♔h6 44 ♖xb7 ♖a4 45 ♖b1 a2 46 ♖a1 ♔h5 0-1**

Game 58
Smagin – Dvoirys
Novgorod 1995

1 e4 c5 2 c3 ♘f6 3 e5 ♘d5 4 d4 cxd4 5 ♘f3 ♘c6 6 ♗c4 ♘b6 7 ♗b3 d5 8 exd6 ♕xd6 9 0-0 ♗e6 10 ♘a3 dxc3 11 ♕e2!? ♗xb3 12 ♘b5

The most accurate. 12 axb3 can transpose after 12...e5 13 ♘b5 ♕b8. An attempt to exploit the move-order with 12...♖d8 in Winants-Nijboer, Wijk aan Zee 1995, failed to 13 ♘b5 ♕b8 14 bxc3 a6 15 ♘bd4 ♘xd4 16 ♘xd4 ♕c7 17 ♗b2 e6 18 c4 ♗e7 19 ♕g4 ♗f6 20 ♘xe6! fxe6 21 ♗xf6 gxf6 22 ♕xe6+ ♕e7 23 ♕xb6 ±. The witty 12...c2!? 13 ♘b5 ♕b8 was played in Bianco-Tukmakov, Zurich 1994, but such a time-consuming plan should be too risky for Black. Interesting, however, is 12...0-0-0!? 13 bxc3 ♕d3 14 ♕b2 e5 ∓ M.Anderton-Marley, British League (4NCL Ware) 1996.

12...♕b8 13 axb3 e5 *(D)*

After 13...e6?! 14 g3! (threatening ♗f4) 14...♘d5 15 bxc3 ♕c8 16 c4 ♘c7 17 ♗b2 a6 18 ♗xg7 ♖g8 19 ♗xf8 ♔xf8 20 ♘d6 and White is obviously much better although he eventually lost in Blauert-Kveinys, Groningen 1991.

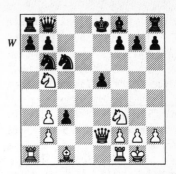

14 bxc3

Limiting the sacrifice to that of one pawn, but there are serious alternatives:

a) 14 ♘bd4 ♗d6 (for 14...♘xd4 15 ♘xd4 see the 14 ♘fd4 lines below) 15 ♘f5 (15 bxc3!?) 15...g6 16 ♘xd6+ ♕xd6 17 bxc3 ♖d8!? (intending ...♕d3; 17...f6 18 ♗a3 ♕e6 ∞ Soloviov-Ionov, USSR 1986) 18 b4?! (18 ♗h6!?) 18...♘d5 19 b5 ♘xc3 20 ♕c4 ♘d4! ∓ Harley-Boyce, Corr 1989.

b) 14 ♗f4 ♗d6 (14...f6) 15 ♖ad1 0-0! 16 ♘xd6 exf4 17 bxc3 ♘c8 18 ♘xf7 ♖xf7 19 ♘g5 ♘b6 20 ♘xf7 ♔xf7 21 ♖fe1 ♔g8 ∓ Motwani-Ernst, Gausdal 1992.

c) 14 ♗e3 cxb2 (also 14...♘c8!? Vorobiov-Mitenkov, Moscow 1994) 15 ♕xb2 ♘d7 (15...♘d5? 16 ♘xa7! ♘xa7 17 ♗xa7 ♖xa7 18 ♖xa7 ♕xa7 19 ♕xe5+ ♘e7 20 ♖a1 gave White a winning attack in Spangenberg-Quinteros, San Martin 1995) 16 ♖fd1 ♗e7 17 ♕c2 a6 18 ♘c3 ♘f6 19 ♘g5 ♘b4 20 ♕f5 g6 21 ♕f3 0-0 ∓ Smagin-Mukhutdinov, St Petersburg 1993.

d) 14 ♖e1 ♘d7 (14...cxb2 and 14...♗e7 are also candidate moves;

14...f6!? 15 ♘fd4 ♘xd4 16 ♘xd4 ♔f7 17 bxc3 and then 17...♕c8!? 18 ♘f3 ♗d6 19 ♗e3 ∞ was Vajda-Grabics, Nadele Z 1995, but 17...exd4 18 ♕e6+ ♔g6 19 ♖e4 h6 20 ♖g4+ ♔h7 21 ♕f5+ gives a draw by repetition) 15 ♗f4! ♗e7 16 ♖ad1! (16 ♘xe5 ♘dxe5 17 ♗xe5 ♘xe5 18 ♕xe5 ♕xe5 19 ♖xe5 cxb2 20 ♖ae1 ♔f8) 16...exf4 17 ♘d6+ ♔f8 18 ♘xf7! ♘b6! (18...♔xf7 19 ♖xd7 with an attack) 19 ♘xh8 ♗g8 20 ♘d4 ♗f6 21 ♘xc6 bxc6 22 ♘g6 hxg6 23 ♕e6+ ♔f8 24 bxc3 = Torre-Illescas, Moscow OL 1994.

e) 14 ♘fd4!?:

e1) 14...g6 15 ♘xc6 bxc6 16 ♘xa7! ♕c7 17 ♗e3 ♗d6 18 ♘b5! cxb5 19 ♗xb6 ♕c6 20 ♖xa8+ ♕xa8 21 ♕xb5+ ± Yanovsky-Timoshchenko, Voskresensk 1992.

e2) After 14...♗c5 15 ♘f5!? g6 16 ♗e3 ♗xe3 17 ♘fd6+ ♔e7 18 ♕xe3 cxb2 19 ♖ad1 ♖d8 20 ♕c5 ♔f6 21 f4 White had a dangerous attack for his three sacrificed pawns in Swinkels-Hofland, corr. 1994.

e3) 14...♗e7 15 ♘f5 0-0 as in Ferguson-Sutovsky, Guarapuava 1995 is a risky-looking defence, when instead of 16 ♘xc3?! g6 ∓ White must try the violent 16 bxc3 a6 17 ♗h6! axb5 (17...gxh6 18 ♕g4+ ♗g5 19 ♘xh6+ ♔h8 20 ♕xg5 f6 21 ♕e3 hits b6) 18 ♖xa8 ♘xa8 19 ♗xg7 with a dangerous attack for the piece; if White wishes to avoid any of these lines he could consider the move-order 14 ♘bd4 ♘xd4 15 ♘xd4, as above, and it should be noted that the Lautier-Gelfand reference coming up came via this route.

e4) 14...♘xd4 15 ♘xd4 f6 16 bxc3 ♔f7 (16...♗d6 17 ♘f5 with a strong attack) 17 ♘b5 a6 18 ♗e3 axb5 19 ♗xb6 ♖xa1 20 ♖xa1 ♕e8 21 ♖a5 b4 22 c4 (22 cxb4 ♕e6 23 ♕c4 ♕xc4 24 bxc4 ♗xb4 25 ♖a7 ♖c8 26 ♖xb7+ ♔e6 27 ♖xg7 ♗f8! 28 ♖c7 ♖b8! 29 ♖c6+ ♔d7 30 ♖c7+ ♔e6 31 ♖c6+ ♔d7 ½-½ Luther-Sadler, Gausdal 1994 – a nice use of bank-rank mate threats by Black, e.g. 28 ♖xh7? ♖b8! 29 c5 ♗xc5) 22 c4 ♕c6 23 ♖b5 ♗e7 24 ♗a5 ♖a8 25 h3 ♔g8 (25...♗c5 26 ♕d2 ♗d4 27 ♕xb4 b6 28 ♗xb6 ♖a1+ 29 ♔h2 ♕e4 30 ♗xd4 ♕f4+ 31 g3 ♕f3 32 ♖b7+ ♔g6 33 ♖xg7+ ♔xg7 34 ♕e7+ ♔g6 35 ♕e8+ ½-½ Soloviov-Vaulin, USSR 1988) 26 ♕e1 ♗c5 27 ♗xb4 ♗d4 28 ♗c3 = Lautier-Gelfand, Linares 1994.

14...♗e7 15 ♗g5! *(D)*

Stronger than 15 ♖e1 ♘d7 16 ♘g5 ♗xg5 17 ♗xg5 0-0 18 ♖ad1 ♘c5 19 ♕g4 ♕c8 20 ♕h4 ♕f5 and Black escaped with his extra pawn in Hoffman-Gavrikov, Biel 1994. The immediate 15 ♗e3 ♘c8!? 16 c4 0-0 17 c5 b6 18 ♖fc1 bxc5 19 ♗xc5 a6 20 ♘a3 ♕xb3 21 ♕e4 was Sveshnikov-Yudasin, USSR 1986 when 21...♗xc5 looks good for Black.

15...f6

On 15...a6!? 16 ♗xe7 ♘xe7 17 ♘xe5! 0-0 (17...f6 ∞) 18 ♘d4 White is slightly more comfortable, but Black defended the position after 18...♘g6 19 ♘xg6 hxg6 20 ♖fe1 ♖e8 21 ♕f3 ♕c7 22 c4 ♘d7 23 ♖e3 (23 ♘c2!? intending ♘e3-d5 Onishchuk) 23...♖xe3 24 ♕xe3 ♕e5 in Onishchuk-Nijboer, Wijk aan Zee

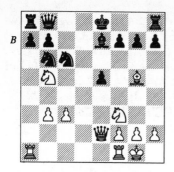

1996. Instead 15...⩔xg5?! 16 ⩔xg5 h6 (16...a6 ∞) 17 ⩔e4 0-0 18 ⩦fd1! ⩦d8 19 ⩔bd6 ⩔c7 20 ⩔h5 ⩔e7 21 ⩦d3! gave White dangerous pressure in Smagin-Baikov, Moscow 1995.

16 ⩔e3 0-0?

Returning the pawn without a fight, when White is clearly better. There are two critical alternatives:

a) 16...⩔d5 17 ⩔xa7!? (an idea of Andrew Harley's; White's compensation looked insufficient after both 17 ⩔d2 0-0 18 c4 ⩔c7 19 ⩔e3 ⩦d8 20 ⩦fd1 a6 21 ⩔c3 ⩦xd1+ 22 ⩦xd1 ⩔e8 23 ⩔b6 ⩔e6 Turov-Nevostruev, St Petersburg 1994, and 17 ⩔h4!? a6 18 ⩔h5+ ⩔f8 19 ⩔a3 ⩔e8 20 ⩔f3 ⩔xe3 21 ⩔xe3 g6 22 ⩔h6+ ⩔f7 23 ⩔c4 ⩔f8 24 ⩔e3 ⩔g7 25 ⩔b6 ⩔c8 26 ⩦fd1 ⩦d8 27 g3 ⩦b8 28 ⩔g2 ⩔e6 29 ⩔ge3 f5 Smagin-Ionov, Russia 1995) 17...⩔xe3 (17...⩔xa7 18 ⩔xa7 ⩦xa7 19 ⩦xa7 ⩔xa7 20 ⩔b5+ and 20 ⩔xd5 is the idea) 18 ⩔xc6 ⩦xa1 19 ⩦xa1 bxc6 20 ⩔xe3 with an unclear position.

b) 16...⩔c8!? 17 ⩔h4 (17 c4!? 0-0 18 c5! ⩔h8 19 ⩔c4 ∞ – Harley) 17...g6 (17...0-0!? 18 ⩔f5 a6 when instead of 19 ⩔a2?!, Tzermiadianos-Ilinčić, Čačak 1995, the variation 19

⩔g4 g6 20 ⩔xe7+ ⩔6xe7! 21 ⩔c4+ ⩦f7 22 ⩔c7 ⩔d6 23 ⩔c5 ⩔e4 24 ⩔c4 ⩔d6 with a draw by repetition is proposed by Tzermiadianos in *Informator 65*) 18 f4 0-0 (Chekhov suggests 18...a6!? with the point 19 fxe5?! ⩔xe5 20 ⩔d4 ⩔xd4 21 cxd4 ⩔e6 ∓; instead 19 ⩔a3 yields unclear compensation for the pawn) 19 ⩔xg6! (19 ⩔g4 f5! 20 ⩔g3 ⩔xh4 21 ⩔xh4 a6 22 ⩔a3 b5 ∞) 19...hxg6 20 ⩔g4 (according to Chekhov, the white attack is winning) 20...⩦f7 21 ⩔xg6+ ⩔f8 22 ⩦ad1 ⩦g7 23 ⩔h5 a6 24 ⩔h8+ ⩔f7 25 ⩔h5+ ⩔f8 26 ⩔h8+ ⩔f7 27 fxe5! ⩔xe5 28 ⩔h6 ⩦xg2+ 29 ⩔xg2 ⩔e4+ 30 ⩦f3 axb5 31 ⩔g7+ ⩔e6 32 ⩔g8+ ⩔e5 33 ⩔f4+ 1-0 Degraeve-Aseev, St Petersburg v Paris 1996.

17 ⩔xa7 ⩦xa7 18 ⩔xb6 ⩦xa1 19 ⩦xa1 ± *(D)*

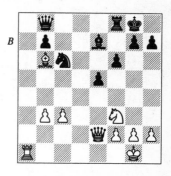

White is better. Now if 19...⩔d6, then Smagin gives 20 ⩔c4+ ⩔h8 21 b4.

19...f5 20 b4 e4 21 b5 exf3 22 ⩔e6+ ⩦f7 23 bxc6 bxc6 24 ⩔xc6 ⩔f8 25 ⩔e6 (better is 25 ⩦a8! with excellent winning chances) **25...⩔d6 26 ⩔xd6 ⩔xd6 27 c4 ⩦b7 28 c5**

♗c7 29 ♖a6 (29 gxf3 ♗xb6! 30 ♖b1 ♗xc5 31 ♖xb7 g6 32 ♔f1 ♗d4 33 ♔e2 h5 = Smagin) 29...fxg2 30 ♔xg2 ♔f7 = 31 h3 ♔e7 32 ♔f3 ♗xb6 33 cxb6 ♔e6 34 ♔f4 h6 35 h4 g6 36 ♔e3 g5 37 hxg5 hxg5 38 ♔d4 ♔d6 39 ♔c4 ♔c6 40 ♖a5 ♖xb6 41 ♖xf5 ♖b2 42 ♔d4 ♔d6 43 ♔e3 ♖b3+ 44 ♔e4 ♖b4+ 45 ♔f3 ♔e6 46 ♖xg5 ♔f6 47 ♖d5 ♖a4 48 ♔g3 ♖a1 49 ♖d8 ♖a4 50 ♖f8+ ♔g6 51 ♖f4 ♖a5 52 ♖b4 ♔f5 53 ♖h4 ♖a3+ 54 f3 ♖b3 55 ♖h5+ ♔g6 56 ♖e5 ♔f6 57 ♖d5 ♖b4 58 ♖h5 ♖a4 ½-½

21 2...e6

1	e4	c5
2	c3	e6
3	d4	d5
4	exd5	exd5 *(D)*

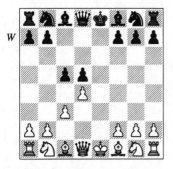

Of course White could also have chosen 4 e5, transposing into an Advance French – this possibility alone can put Sicilian players off 2...e6. In Game 59 (following 5 ♘f3 ♘c6 6 ♗b5) we see a direct transposition to the French Defence, Tarrasch Variation, *ECO* code C09, after either 10...♗b6 or 10...♗d6. The normal French Tarrasch move-order would run 1 e4 e6 2 d4 d5 3 ♘d2 c5 4 exd5 exd5 5 ♘gf3 ♘c6 6 ♗b5 ♗d6 7 dxc5 ♗xc5 8 0-0 ♘e7 9 ♘b3 ♗b6 (or 9...♗d6) and now the transposition would arise if play continued 10 c3 0-0. The fact that White is restricted to French Tarrasch lines with c3 is a point to be noted, as, given the choice, White might have preferred to delay or omit the move c3. Whilst

c3 at some stage in these French Tarrasch lines is a quite standard, it does not always represent optimum play for White. Therefore Black has reasonable chances of equalising, but recently there has been a flurry of activity in the white plan of retreating the bishop with ♗d3 and ♗c2, followed by ♕d3 softening up the black kingside.

The next three games show that there can, however, be advantages for White in utilising the c3 Sicilian move-order. In Game 60 (with 6 ♗e2) similar positions to the previous game arise where the bishop is not badly posted on the modest e2-square. In Game 61 (with 6 ♗e3) White forces a clarification of the central pawn structure, but the most exciting and creative plan against Black's 2...e6 defence is to be found in Game 62, where the move 5 ♗e3!? gives an untypical and very dynamic structure. White does not place his king's knight on f3. Instead the square is reserved for his queen, and this unusual plan has posed Black some fresh problems.

Game 59
Dolmatov – Lobron
Dortmund 1993

1 e4 c5 2 ♘f3 e6 3 c3 d5 4 exd5 exd5 5 d4 ♘c6

5...♗d6 just transposes: 6 dxc5 (6 ♗e2 is Game 60) 6...♗xc5 7 ♗b5+ ♘c6 is the present game while 6 ♗e3 c4 7 b3 axb3 8 axb3 will transpose to lines covered in Game 61 if Black shortly plays ...♘c6.

Instead 5...a6 6 ♗e2!? (6 ♗e3 c4 7 b3 b5!? 8 ♘e5 ♘e7 9 bxc4 bxc4 10 ♘d2 f6 11 ♘exc4!? dxc4 12 ♗xc4 was an unclear piece for two pawns sacrifice in Topakian-Jokšić, Biel 1994; of course Black can continue 7...cxb3 8 axb3 when 8...♘c6 is Game 61, and 8...♘f6 9 ♗e2 ♗d6 10 0-0 0-0 11 c4?! ♘e4! = was Dvoretsky-Smejkal, Wijk aan Zee 1976, but better was 11 ♗g5 ± Smejkal) 6...c4 7 ♗f4 (7 b3) 7...♗d6 8 ♗xd6 ♕xd6 9 b3 cxb3 (9...b5?! 10 a4 ♗b7 11 0-0 ± with ♘a3 to follow) 10 axb3 ♘e7 11 0-0 0-0 12 c4 (12 ♘a3!?, intending ♘c2-e3, is slightly better for White according to Timoshchenko) 12...♘bc6 13 c5 ♕f6 14 ♘c3 ♗f5 (14...♗g4 15 ♖a4 ±) 15 ♕d2 ♗e4 16 ♖fd1 ♘f5?! (16...♖ad8) 17 ♖a4 ♖ad8 18 ♘e1! ± Timoshchenko-Kasparov, USSR Ch 1978.

On 5...♘f6 *(D)* White has several ways to handle the position:

a) 6 ♗e2 ♗e7 7 dxc5 ♗xc5 will be examined in the course of Game 60.

b) 6 ♗d3!? ♘bd7!? 7 0-0 ♗e7 8 ♖e1 0-0 9 ♗g5?! (Short suggests 9 ♘bd2 intending ♘f1-g3) 9...♖e8 10 ♘bd2 a6 11 ♘f1 cxd4 12 cxd4 ♘f8 13 ♘e5 ♘6d7!? 14 ♗xe7 ♖xe7 15 ♘f3 ♖xe1 16 ♕xe1 ♕b6! = Short-Tregubov, Wijk aan Zee 1995.

c) 6 ♗b5+ ♗d7 (on 6...♘c6 7 0-0 ♗e7 8 dxc5 ♗xc5 good are both 9 ♗g5 ♗e6 10 ♘d4 Smagin-Rom.Hernandez, Palma de Mallorca 1989 and 9 ♘d4 ♗xd4 10 ♕xd4 0-0 11 ♕h4 ♖e8 12 ♗g5 ♖e4 13 ♗xf6 gxf6 14 ♕h6 ± Handoko-Hurelbator, Manila OL 1992) 7 ♗xd7+ (7 ♕e2+) 7...♘bxd7 (7...♕xd7 8 0-0 ♗e7 9 ♘e5 ♕c8 10 ♕a4+ ♘c6 11 ♖e1 ± Kholmov-Korsunsky, USSR 1978) 8 0-0 ♗e7 9 dxc5 ♘xc5 10 ♘d4 0-0 (10...♕d7 11 ♕f3 0-0 12 ♘f5 ♖fe8 13 ♗e3 ♘ce4 14 ♘d2 ± Chandler-Szabo, Hastings 1981) 11 ♘f5 ♖e8 12 ♘xe7+ ♕xe7 13 ♗e3 ♖ac8 14 ♘d2 a6 15 ♘f3 ± Smagin-Velimirović, Yugoslavia 1995.

d) 6 ♗g5!? c4 (if 6...♘c6 White continues 7 ♗b5; alternatively Black can play 6...cxd4 7 ♗b5+ ♗d7 8 ♕e2+ ♕e7 9 ♗xf6 ♕xe2+ 10 ♗xe2 gxf6 11 ♘xd4 ± Makarychev-Balashov, Tallinn 1983, or 6...♗e7 7 ♗b5+ ♗d7 8 ♗xd7+ ♘bxd7 9 dxc5 ♘xc5 10 0-0 0-0 11 ♘bd2 ♘ce4 12 ♘xe4 dxe4 13 ♘d2 ♘d5 14 ♗xe7 ♕xe7 15 ♖e1 ♘f6 16 ♕a4 ± Shirazi-Benjamin, USA Ch 1986) 7 ♘bd2 ♗e7 8 g3!? ♕b6 9 b3 ± cxb3 10 axb3 ♗f5 11 ♗g2 ♕e6+ 12 ♘e5 ♘fd7 13 ♗xe7 ♘xe5 14 0-0! ♔xe7 15 ♖e1

♘bc6 16 b4! Anand-Malishauskas, Lyon 1994.

6 ♗b5 ♗d6

Inferior is 6...c4?! 7 ♘e5! ♕b6 8 ♗xc6+ bxc6 9 0-0 ♗d6 10 b3! ± Karpov-J.Polgar, Linares 1994.

7 dxc5 ♗xc5 8 0-0 ♘ge7 9 ♘bd2 0-0 10 ♘b3 *(D)*

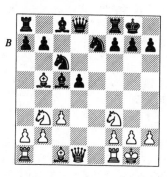

10...♗b6!?

Via the French Tarrasch move-order Black commonly retreats with ...♗d6. The reason is that after 1 e4 e6 2 d4 d5 3 ♘d2 c5 4 exd5 exd5 5 ♘gf3 ♘c6 6 ♗b5 ♗d6 7 dxc5 ♗xc5 8 0-0 ♘e7 9 ♘b3 ♗b6 White has the excellent plan 10 ♖e1 0-0 11 ♗e3! challenging the bishop. In the present illustrative game, as we shall see, the tempo White has spent on c3 means Black has time to discourage this manoeuvre with ...♘f5. Therefore, although strictly speaking we are now in a French, we cover the ...♗b6 retreat variation in full, as French Defence books understandably view it as a side-line.

Of course in the illustrative game Black could also have continued 10...♗d6 giving a French Tarrasch position where Black has reasonable prospects for equality, but there is plenty of play. These typical Tarrasch positions are covered in books such as *The Complete French* by Psakhis; however I will give a brief round-up of White's most popular options at this point:

a) 11 ♗g5 ♗g4 (or 11...♕c7) and White can try 12 ♗h4, 12 ♖e1 or 12 ♗e2.

b) 11 ♘bd4 ♗g4 12 ♕a4 ♗h5! (Korchnoi demonstrated that this manoeuvre gives equality in his 1974 Candidates match in Moscow with Karpov) 13 ♗d3 (13 ♗e3 ♕c7 14 h3 ♘a5 15 ♗d3 ♘c4 16 ♘b5 ♕d7 17 ♗xc4 dxc4 18 ♖fd1 ♘f5! = Karpov-Korchnoi, Moscow Ct (12) 1974 or 13 ♖e1 ♕c7 14 ♗f1!? a6! 15 g3 ♘a5 16 ♘h4 ♘c4 = A.Sokolov-Vaganian, Montpellier Ct 1985) 13...♗c5 14 ♖e1 h6 15 ♗e3 ♗b6 16 h3 ♕d6 17 ♗e2 ♖fe8 18 ♖ad1 ♕f6 = Karpov-Korchnoi, Moscow Ct (14) 1974.

c) 11 ♗d3!? (stops 11...♗g4 owing to 12 ♗xh7+ ♔xh7 13 ♘g5+) 11...h6 (11...♘g6?! 12 ♗g5 ♘ce7 13 h3 h6 14 ♗e3 ♘f4 15 ♗xf4 ♗xf4 16 ♘bd4 ± Dolmatov-Skomorokhin, Novgorod 1995 or 11...♕c7 12 h3 ♖d8 13 ♕c2 ♘g6 14 ♘bd4 a6 15 ♗e3 ♗d7 16 ♖ad1 ♘a5 17 ♘f5 ♗f8 18 ♗d4 ± Tiviakov-Rozentalis, Groningen 1993) 12 h3 ♘f5 (12...♕c7!? 13 ♖e1 ♖e8 14 ♗c2 ♗f5 15 ♗e3 ♕d6 16 ♘bd4 ♘xd4 17 ♗xd4 ♗xc2 18 ♕xc2 ♘c6 and Black is close to equality, Manca-Portisch, Reggio Emilia 1993) 13 ♖e1 (13 ♗c2!? ♗e6 14 ♕d3 g6 15 ♖e1 {15 g4!?} 15...♖e8 16 ♘bd4? ♘fxd4 17 cxd4 ♗f5 18

♕d1 ♗xc2 19 ♕xc2 ♘xd4! 20 ♖xe8+
♕xe8 21 ♕d1 ♘xf3+ 22 gxf3 –+ as
in Šibarević-Ivanović, Yugoslav Ch
1992) 13...♕f6 with a transposition
into the variation below starting 11
♖e1.

d) 11 ♖e1!? h6 (11...♗g4!? 12
♗e2 ♖e8 is Black's safest try for
equality, e.g. 13 ♘fd4 ♗xe2 14 ♖xe2
♕d7 15 ♘b5 ♗e5 16 ♘c5 ♕f5 =
Ljubojević-Short, Linares 1990) 12
h3 ♘f5 13 ♗d3 ♕f6 (13...♗c7!? 14
♗c2 ♕d6 15 ♕d3 g6 16 ♕d2!? ±
Smagin-Lalić, Sochi 1987) 14 ♗c2!
♖d8 (14...♗e6 15 ♕d3 ♖fe8 16 ♗d2
g6 and now White should play 17
♖e2!? ♗f8 18 ♖ae1 ± Wolff-Ben-
jamin, San Francisco 1991; riskier is
17 ♕b5?! ♘h4! as in Ernst-Vagan-
ian, Copenhagen 1988 and Renet-
Uhlmann, Novi Sad OL 1990) 15
♕d3 g6 *(D)* and now:

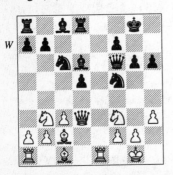

d1) 16 ♗d2 a5 17 a4 b6 18 ♕e2
♗a6 19 ♗d3 ♗xd3 20 ♕xd3 ♘e5 21
♘xe5 ♗xe5 = as White could not
prevent the advance ...d4 in Psakhis-
Lputian, Rostov 1993 and I.Gure-
vich-Lputian, Philadelphia 1994.

d2) Possible is the modest 16
♕d1!? ♗f8 17 ♗xf5 ♗xf5 18 ♘bd4

♗e4 19 ♗e3, Tolnai-Uhlmann, Debrecen 1988, when Psakhis believes
Black has not equalised.

d3) 16 ♕d2!? ♗f8:
d31) After 17 ♘h2, 17...♘h4 18
♕e2 ♗f5 19 ♘g4 ♗xg4 20 ♕xg4 d4
21 cxd4 ♘xd4 22 ♗e4! was still
slightly better for White in the game
Smagin-Uhlmann, Berlin 1988 but
17...♕g7!? 18 ♘g4 h5 = improved in
V.L.Ivanov-Lastin, Russia 1994.

d32) 17 ♕f4 ♗g7 18 ♕c7? is
bad: 18...♘d6! 19 ♘c5 ♗xh3! 20
gxh3 ♕xf3 –+ Asrian-Lputian, Ar-
menian Ch 1995.

d33) 17 ♕e2!? ♗d7 (17...a6!? 18
♗e3 ♘xe3 19 ♕xe3 ♔g7 Matulo-
vić-Peng, Pozarevac 1995) 18 ♗xf5
♗xf5 19 ♗e3 ♖e8 20 ♕d2 ♗xh3 21
♗xh6 ♗xh6 22 ♕xh6 ± ♗g4 23
♘g5 ♖ad8?? 24 ♕h7+ ♔f8 25 ♕h4!
1-0 Smagin-Blauert, Vienna 1991.

11 ♖e1

11 ♘fd4 and 11 ♗g5 are nothing
special, but there are two serious options:

a) 11 ♗d3!? h6 (11...♘f5 12
♗g5 ♕d6 13 ♕c2 g6 14 ♕d2 ♖e8 15
♖ad1 a5 16 a4 ♗e6 17 ♗f4 ♕f8 18
♗xf5! ♗xf5 19 ♕xd5 ± Smagin-
Cvitan, Zenica 1989; 11...♗f5 12 ♖e1
♕d7 13 ♗e3 ♗c7 14 ♕c2 ♗xd3 15
♕xd3 ± Sermek-Sinowjew, Vienna
1991; 11...♘g6!? 12 ♖e1 ♗g4 13
♗e3 ♗xe3 14 ♖xe3 ♘ge5 15 ♗e2
♘c4 16 ♗xc4 dxc4 is equal, Tivi-
akov-Iskusnykh, Russian Ch 1995)
12 ♖e1 (12 h3!? ♕d6 13 a4!? a5 14
♗c2 ♖e8 15 ♘bd4 ♘xd4 16 ♘xd4
♗c7 17 ♘f3 ♗f5 18 ♖e1 ♗xc2 19
♕xc2 ♘c6 20 ♗e3 ± Sermek-Jelen,
Ljubljana Iskra 1992) 12...♗g4 13

♗e3 ♜e8 (13...♗c7 14 ♗e2 ♘f5 15 ♗c5 ♜e8 16 h3 ♗xf3 17 ♗xf3 ♜xe1+ 18 ♕xe1 ♘h4 19 ♕d1 ♘xf3+ 20 ♕xf3 ♕g5 21 ♜e1 ± Godena-Portisch, Reggio Emilia 1992) 14 ♗xb6 ♕xb6 15 ♜e3 ♘f5 16 ♜xe8+ ♜xe8 17 ♗xf5 ♗xf5 18 ♕d2 a5 ∞ Blauert-Balashov, Dortmund 1992.

b) 11 ♘bd2 ♗g4 12 ♕a4!? (12 ♗e2 is solid, or 12 ♕d3 ♕d6 13 ♗a4 ♘g6 14 ♗c2 ♘xd4 15 ♘xd4 ♗c7 16 g3 ♕f6 17 ♗e3 ♗h3 18 ♜fe1 ♜fe8 19 f4 ♘f8 = Bondarevsky-Boleslavsky, USSR Ch 1940) 12...♗d7 13 ♗e3 a6 (13...♜c8 14 ♜fe1 ♘g6 15 ♘b3 ♜e8 16 ♗xb6 ♕xb6 17 ♜ad1 ♜xe1+ 18 ♜xe1 h6 19 ♜d1 ♗e6 20 ♗d3 ± Wahls-Christiansen, Bundesliga 1992) 14 ♘xc6 (14 ♗xc6 bxc6 15 ♘e5 = Rause-Winge, Corr 1993) 14...bxc6 15 ♗xb6 ♕xb6 16 ♗d3 ♗f5 = Nadyrkhanov-Fominykh, Alushta 1994.

11...♘f5!?

Aimed at discouraging White's ♗e3 plan. 11...♗g4 allows White to achieve his objective: 12 ♗e3 (12 ♗d3 h6 13 ♗e3 was actually the move-order of the game Godena-Portisch, quoted in the note to White's previous move) 12...♜e8 (12...♕d6 13 ♗xb6 axb6 14 ♗e2 ± or 12...♗xe3 13 ♜xe3 ♘f5 14 ♜e1 ♘h4 15 ♗e2 ♜e8! 16 ♘xh4 ♕xh4 17 f3! ♗e6 18 ♗b5 ± Smagin-Ortega, Amantea 1994) 13 h3 ♗h5 14 a4!? (14 ♗xb6 ♕xb6 15 ♗e2) 14...♗c7 15 ♗c5 a6 16 ♗xc6! ♘xc6 (16...bxc6 17 ♘b↯ ♗d6 18 ♘xc6! ♘xc6 19 ♜xe8+ ♕xe8 20 ♗xd6 ± Smagin) 17 ♜xe8+ ♕xe8 18 ♕xd5 ± Smagin-Cvitan, Biel 1995.

12 ♗d3!? *(D)*

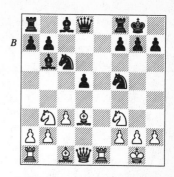

This key position can also arise from the 6 ♗e2 lines of Game 60. Note that 12 ♗g5? is a blunder due to 12...♗xf2+ 13 ♚xf2 ♕b6+ and Black wins a pawn, Striković-Popović, Yugoslav Ch 1989.

12...h6

12...♗c7!? and now:

a) 13 ♕c2 ♘h4 14 ♘bd4 ♗g4 (14...♘xd4 15 ♘xd4 ♘xg2!? 16 ♚xg2 ♕h4 17 ♗xh7+ ♕xh7 18 ♕xh7+ ♚xh7 and Black should be OK in the endgame, Smagin-Velimirović, Yugoslavia 1992) 15 ♘xh4 ♕xh4 16 g3 ♕h5 with an attack, Yandemirov-Kovalev, Minsk 1995.

b) 13 g3!? h6 14 ♗c2 Emms-Mortensen, Hastings 1995.

c) 13 ♗c2 g6 14 ♗xf5 ♗xf5 15 ♗h6 ♜e8 16 ♜xe8+ ♕xe8 17 ♘fd4?! (17 ♕xd5!? ♗e4 18 ♕d1) 17...♕e5 = Kharlov-Rublevsky, Novosibirsk 1995.

d) 13 ♗xf5 ♗xf5 14 ♗g5 f6 15 ♗h4 ♗g4 16 ♕d3 ♗xf3 (16...a5!? Chekhov) 17 ♕xf3 ♘e5 18 ♕f5 ♜e8 19 ♜ad1 ♕d6 20 ♗g3 ± David-Barbero, Lazne Bohdanec 1995.

13 ♗c2!? a5?!

White's plan is ♕d3 with the threat of g4, but Black's best defence, variation 'd', currently seems adequate:

a) 13...♕f6 14 ♕d3 g6 15 ♕xd5 ♖d8 16 ♕b5 ♘h4 17 ♘bd4 ± Manca-Van der Wiel, Lugano 1989.

b) 13...♗e6?! 14 ♕d3 g6? (Black should prefer 14...♖e8 15 ♗f4 ♕f6 16 g4 ♕g6 17 h3 ♘fe7 18 ♕xg6 ♘xg6 19 ♗g3 ± Smagin-Striković, Čačak 1991) 15 ♗xh6! ± Nogueiras-Vogt, Kecskemet 1979 because if 15...♘xh6, 16 ♖xe6!.

c) 13...♗c7 14 ♕d3 g6 15 ♘bd4 ♘fxd4 16 ♘xd4 ♕h4 17 ♘f3 ♕h5 18 ♗d1 ± Ki.Georgiev-I.Gurevich, New York rpd 1994.

d) 13...♕d6!? 14 ♕d3 (14 ♗xf5 ♗xf5 15 ♗e3 ♗g4 16 ♗xb6 axb6 17 h3 ♗h5 18 ♕d3 ♗xf3 19 ♕xf3 ♖fd8 20 ♕e3 d4 21 cxd4 ♘b4 22 ♕e4 ♕d5 23 ♕xd5 ♖xd5 24 ♖e7 ♖xa2 25 ♖xa2 ♘xa2 26 ♖xb7 ♖b5 27 ♘c5 ♖xb2 28 ♘d7 ♘c3 29 ♖b8+ ½-½ Tiviakov-Lautier, Groningen 1995) 14...♖d8! 15 ♘bd4 (15 g4 ♕g6 16 h3 is unclear; 15 ♗e3 ♗xe3 16 fxe3 g6 17 e4 ½-½ Ivanchuk-Lobron, Dortmund 1995) 15...♘cxd4 16 ♘xd4 g6 17 ♗e3 ♕f6 18 ♖ad1 ♔g7 19 ♗f4 ♔h7 20 ♕d2 ♘xd4 21 cxd4 ♗g4 22 f3 ♗f5 23 ♗e5 ♕g5 24 ♗f4 ♕f6 25 ♗e5 ♕g5 26 ♗f4 ♕f6 ½-½ Filipović-Cvitan, Biel 1989.

14 ♕d3 a4 15 ♘bd4 g6 (after this move White is able to force a favourable exchange of minor pieces, but 15...♘cxd4 16 ♘xd4 ♗xd4 17 cxd4 ♕h4 18 ♖e5 ± Dolmatov) **16 ♘xf5 ♗xf5 17 ♕d1 ♗xc2 18 ♕xc2 ± ♔g7 19 ♗f4 ♕f6 20 ♕d2 g5 21 ♗e3 d4**

22 ♗xd4 ♘xd4 23 ♘xd4 ♖fd8 24 ♖ad1 ♖a5 25 ♖e3 ♖ad5?! (Black has better defensive chances after 25...♗xd4!? 26 cxd4 ♖ad5 27 ♖d3 ±) **26 ♖d3 ♗xd4 27 ♖xd4! ♖xd4 28 cxd4 ♖d5 29 h3 b5 30 b3 axb3 31 axb3 h5 32 ♕d3 h4 33 ♕e4 ♕d6 34 ♖d3 b4 35 g3! hxg3 36 ♖xg3 ± ♔f8 37 ♖d3?** (37 h4!) **37...♕d8 38 ♔g2 ♔g7 39 ♕g4 ♔f8 40 ♖g3 ♕f6 41 h4 ♖f5 42 ♔h3 ♕e6?** (42...gxh4! 43 ♕g8+ ♔e7 44 ♖e3+ ♔d6 =) **43 hxg5 ♖xf2 44 ♕xe6 fxe6 45 ♔g4 ♖d2?! 46 ♔f4 ♖xd4+ 47 ♔e5 ♖h4 48 ♔xe6 ♔g7 49 ♔f5 ♖h8 50 ♖g4 ♖b8 51 g6 ♖f8+ 52 ♔e6 ♖f3 53 ♖xb4 ♔xg6 54 ♖b8 ♖e3+ 55 ♔d6 ♔f7 56 b4 ♖d3+ 57 ♔c6 ♔e7 58 b5 ♖d6+ 59 ♔b7 ♖d7+ 60 ♔a6 ♖d6+ 61 b6 ♔d7 62 ♔b7 ♖h6 63 ♖a8 ♖h7 64 ♖c8 1-0**

Game 60
Salov – Kasparov
Linares 1993

1 e4 c5 2 c3 e6 3 d4 d5 4 exd5 exd5 5 ♘f3 ♘c6 6 ♗e2 ♗d6

For 6...♘f6!? 7 0-0 ♗d6 8 dxc5 ♗xc5 see the note to Black's eighth move in the main game. Alternatively:

a) 6...c4 7 b3 cxb3 8 axb3 ♗d6 is playable, but compared to related lines examined in Game 61 White should benefit from not having already committed his bishop to e3, e.g. 9 0-0 ♘ge7 10 c4 0-0 11 ♘c3 ♗g4 12 cxd5 ♘b4 13 h3 ♗f5 14 ♗g5 f6 15 ♗e3 ♘exd5 16 ♗c4 ♗e6 17 ♗d2 ♗f7 18 ♘h4 ± Men-Dzindzichashvili, USA Ch 1992.

b) 6...cxd4 7 ♘xd4 (7 cxd4 re-establishing symmetry isn't much for White, because after 7...♘f6 8 0-0 ♗e7 9 ♘c3 we have a transposition to a level Queen's Gambit Tarrasch defence, *ECO* code D32. Instead 7...♗d6 8 ♘c3 ♘ge7 9 ♗g5 f6 10 ♗h4 0-0 11 ♗g3 ♗b4 12 0-0 ♗xc3 13 bxc3 ± was Sveshnikov-Dorfman, USSR Ch 1976) 7...♗d6 8 ♕a4!? (an early excursion; if 8 0-0 then after 8...♘ge7, 9 ♗g5 and 9 ♗e3 are natural; 8...♘f6 should probably be answered by 9 ♗e3 rather than 9 ♗g5 0-0 10 ♗h4 ♖e8 11 ♘d2 ♘xd4 12 cxd4 ♗f4 = O'Donnell-Wolff, Saint John 1988) 8...♘ge7 9 ♘b5 ♗e5 10 ♘d2 0-0 11 ♘f3 f6 12 ♘bd4 ♗d7 13 ♕b3 ♘xd4 14 ♘xd4 ♕c7 15 h3 ♔h8 16 0-0 ♕c8 17 ♘f3 ± Smagin-Gurgenidze, USSR Ch 1985.

7 dxc5

7 0-0 ♘ge7 and now Black equalises easily after 8 ♘bd2 cxd4 9 ♘xd4 ♘xd4 10 cxd4 0-0 11 ♘f3 ♕b6 Tamm-Kramnik, Dortmund 1992 or 8 ♗e3 ♘f5! Zurla-Kupreichik, Cattolica 1993.

7...♗xc5 8 0-0 *(D)*

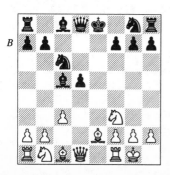

8...♘ge7

Interesting is 8...♘f6!? and now:

a) 9 ♘bd2 0-0 10 ♘b3 ♗b6 11 ♗g5 ♖e8 12 h3 (12 ♕d3 h6 13 ♗xf6 ♕xf6 14 ♖ae1 ♗f5 15 ♕d2 ♗e4 16 ♘bd4 ♖e7 17 ♗d1 ♖ae8 ∓ Csom-Spassky, Amsterdam 1970) 12...♕d6 13 c4 ♘e4 14 ♗h4 dxc4 15 ♗xc4 ♕g6 16 ♔h1 ♘d6 17 ♘bd2 ♘xc4 18 ♘xc4 ♗c7 19 ♘e3 ♗d8 20 ♗xd8 ♖xd8 21 ♕a4 ♕h5 = Men-Gulko, USA Ch 1992.

b) 9 ♗g5!? ♗e6 (9...♗e7 10 ♘bd2 h6 11 ♗h4 0-0 12 ♘b3 g5 13 ♗g3 ♘e4 14 ♘fd4 ♗f6 15 ♗d3 ♗g7 16 ♕c2 f5 ∞ Panchenko-Renet, Palma de Mallorca 1989) 10 ♘bd2 0-0 (10...h6!? 11 ♗h4 ♗b6 12 ♘b3 g5!? 13 ♗g3 ♘e4 ∞ Okhotnik-Velimirović, Belgrade 1988) 11 ♘b3 ♗b6 12 ♘bd4 ♗g4 13 h3 (13 ♖e1!?) 13...♘xd4 14 ♘xd4 ♗xe2 15 ♘xe2 h6 16 ♗h4 ♖e8 17 ♕d3 ♕e7 18 ♘d4 ♕e4 = Kengis-Miezis, Riga Z 1995.

9 ♘bd2

After 9 ♗g5 0-0 10 ♘bd2 there have been three games where Black responded with the bold plan of expanding with 10...h6! 11 ♗h4 g5 12 ♘b3 ♗b6 13 ♗g3 f5 14 h3 f4 15 ♗h2 ♘f5 ∞ (Vujičić-Striković, Belgrade 1989, Schoffstoll-Gulko, Los Angeles 1991, and Turov-Yuneev, St Petersburg 1994). Black's airy kingside is compensated for by very active pieces.

9...0-0 10 ♘b3 ♗b6 *(D)*

Of course 10...♗d6 is the other option, when an identical position to Game 59 is reached, but with White's light-squared bishop possibly better-posted on e2 instead of the b5-square. 11 ♗g5 (11 ♘bd4!? a6 gives a fairly standard type of Tarrasch IQP position, while 11 ♗d3 is a transposition to Game 59, note to Black's 11th) 11...♕c7 (if 11...♗g4?! Black would be a tempo down on lines from Game 59 where White has just retreated his bishop from b5 to e2 in this position) 12 ♘bd4 a6 (12...♘xd4!? 13 ♕xd4 ♗e6 ± Harley-McDonald, British Ch 1993) 13 h3 ♘g6 14 ♗d3 ♘xd4 15 ♘xd4 ♗d7 16 ♕c2 ♗c5 17 ♗f5 ♗a7 18 ♗xd7 ♕xd7 19 ♖ad1 ± S.Arkell-Zsu.Polgar, Novi Sad OL 1990.

11 ♗g5?!

Probably not best if White really has to exchange on e7 as in the game continuation. 11 ♗d3!? again transposes to Game 59 (where the bishop has just retreated from b5 instead of advancing from e2). Sample alternatives:

a) 11 ♘fd4 ♘g6 12 ♗e3 ♖e8 13 ♕c2 ♘ce5 14 ♖ad1 ♗d7 15 ♘d2 ♘g4 16 ♗xg4 ♗xg4 17 ♖de1 ♖c8 ∞ Padevsky-Karpov, Skopje 1972.

b) 11 ♖e1 ♕d6!? (11...♗g4 12 ♘fd4 ♗xe2 13 ♖xe2 ♕d7 14 ♗e3 ♘e5 15 ♘c2 ♗c7 16 ♗c5 ± Braga-Kuijf, Bad Wörishofen 1993 or

11...♘f5 12 ♗d3!? as in Game 59) 12 ♘fd4 (12 ♘bd4) 12...♘f5 13 ♘b5 ♕f6 (a sharp sacrifice) 14 ♕xd5 a6 15 ♘a3 ♘h4 16 ♘c5 ♗f5 17 ♗e3 ♖fd8 18 ♕c4 ♗xc5 19 ♕xc5 ♗e4 20 ♗g5 ♘g6 21 ♗h5 ♕xh5 22 ♖xe4 h6! 23 ♗e7 ♖d1+ 24 ♖e1 ♖xa1 25 ♖xa1 ♘f5 26 ♗d6 ♖d8 27 ♘c4 g6 with compensation for the pawn, Pospišil-Beroun, Corr. 1991.

c) 11 ♘bd4 ♘f5!, e.g. 12 ♘xc6 bxc6 13 ♗d3 h6 = Dückstein-Klinger, Austrian Ch 1989 or 12 ♘xf5 ♗xf5 13 ♗g5 ♕d7 (13...f6 14 ♗f4 ♔h8 15 ♕d2 ♖e8 16 ♖ad1 ♗e4 leads to equality, Petronijević-Scherbakov, Cheliabinsk 1990) 14 ♕d2 ♖fe8 15 ♗b5 ♗e4 = Röder-Schmittdiel, Augsburg 1989.

11...h6! =

Not 11...f6 12 ♗f4 ♘g6 13 ♕d2 ♘xf4 14 ♕xf4 ♖e8 15 ♖fe1 ♖e4 16 ♕d2 ♗g4 17 ♖ad1 ± Timoshchenko-Gufeld, USSR 1978 but possible is 11...♕d6 12 ♕d2 ♗c7 13 ♖ad1 ♖e8 14 ♖fe1 ♗g4 15 g3 ♗b6 = Timoshchenko-Kochiev, USSR Ch 1978.

12 ♗xe7

12 ♗h4 g5 13 ♗g3 f5 (∓ Kasparov) transposes into the note at White's move nine.

12...♕xe7 13 ♖e1 ♗e6 14 a4 a5 15 ♕d3 ♖ad8 16 ♕b5?! (16 ♗d1!? ♕c7 17 ♗c2 g6 is given as unclear by Kasparov) **16...♕c7 ∓ 17 ♘bd4?! ♗g4 18 ♗f1 g6 19 g3 h5 20 ♕d3 ♖fe8 21 ♗g2 ♔g7 22 ♔f1 ♕d6 23 ♕b5 ♘xd4 24 ♘xd4 ♖xe1+ 25 ♖xe1 h4 26 ♕d3 ♕f6 27 ♔g1 h3! ∓ 28 ♗f1 ♖c8 29 ♕d2 ♗d7 30 ♘b5 ♖d8 31 ♘d4 ♖c8 32 ♘b5 ♖h8 33**

Re2 Bg4 34 Re1 Bd7 35 Re2 d4? (35...Bc6, 35...Rh5 and 35...g5!? are all much better for Black) 36 Nxd4 Bxa4 37 Re4 Bd7 38 Qe3 Bc6 39 Rf4 Bxd4 40 Qxd4 Qxd4 41 Rxd4 Re8 42 f4 a4 43 Rd2 Re1 44 Kf2 Rc1 45 Bxh3 a3 46 bxa3 Rxc3 47 Bg2 Rxa3 ½-½

Game 61
Mann – Christiansen
Bundesliga 1995

1 e4 c5 2 c3 e6 3 d4 d5 4 exd5 exd5 5 Nf3 Nc6 6 Be3 c4

A defence that the talented American grandmaster Larry Christiansen has patronised. Instead the rare 6...Qb6 needs some high-level tests, but 6...cxd4 is quite common, when White must decide whether to recapture with the knight or bishop:

a) 7 Nxd4 Bd6 (7...Nf6 8 Be2 Bd6 will transpose) 8 Be2 (8 g3 Nf6 9 Bg2 0-0 10 0-0 Ng4 11 Nc2 Bf5 12 Nd2 Qd7! 13 Bd4 Bd3 14 Re1 Qf5 15 Bh3 Bxc2 16 Qxg4 Qxg4 17 Bxg4 Nxd4 18 cxd4 f5 19 Bh3 Bb4 20 Rec1 Rac8 21 Nf1 g6 = Beliavsky-Tseshkovsky, Yugoslavia 1994) 8...Nf6 9 0-0 (9 Nd2) 9...0-0 10 Nd2 Re8 11 Re1. Black has a good game, e.g. 11...a6 12 Nxc6 bxc6 13 b4 a5 14 a3 Qc7 15 Nf1 Bd7 16 Bd4 Re6 17 Bf3 Ne4 18 c4 Ng5 19 Rxe6 Nxe6 = Minev-Tal, Sarajevo 1966 or 11...h6 12 h3 a6 13 Qc2 Bc7 14 Rad1 Qd6 15 Nf1 Ne4 with the initiative, Yagupov-Chekhov, Moscow Tal mem 1992.

b) 7 Bxd4!? Nxd4 (7...a6 8 Qe2+!? Be6 9 g3 Nge7 10 Nbd2 Nf5 11 Nb3 Bd6 12 Bg2 0-0 13 0-0 Re8 14 Rfe1 Nfxd4 15 Nfxd4 Qf6 16 Nxe6 fxe6 17 c4 ± Plaskett-Mestel, British Ch 1989) 8 Nxd4 (8 Qxd4 Nf6 9 Bb5+ Bd7 10 Bxd7+ Qxd7 11 0-0 Be7 12 Nbd2 0-0 13 Rfe1 Bd8 14 Ne5 Qd6 15 Ng4 Nxg4 16 Qxg4 Bb6 = Sveshnikov-Tal, Moscow 1976) 8...a6 (to prevent the check on b5, as in 8...Bd6 9 Bb5+ Kf8 10 0-0 ± Regan-Kuzmin, Budapest 1978; Black is marginally worse after 8...Nf6 9 Bb5+ Bd7 10 Qe2+ Qe7 Ochoa-Ferreira, Thessaloniki OL 1988) 9 Be2 Nf6 10 0-0 Bc5 11 Nd2 0-0 12 N2b3 Bb6 13 Qd3 Qd6 14 Rad1 Re8 15 Rfe1 Bc7 16 g3 g6 = Sermek-Raičević, Bled 1989.

7 b3

White should always challenge Black's pawn structure immediately in these ...c4 lines. If Black gets time to develop he may later be tempted to respond to b3 with ...b5.

7...cxb3 8 axb3 Bd6

On 8...Bf5 9 Bd3 Bxd3 10 Qxd3 gives White the freer game, but 8...Nf6 is worth a thought, e.g. 9 Be2 (9 Bd3) 9...Bd6 10 Bg5 (10 0-0 0-0 11 c4 ± Vera-Vilela, Havana 1984) 10...h6 11 Bh4 0-0 12 0-0 Re8 13 Ra2 Bg4 14 Ne1 Bxe2 15 Rxe2 Rxe2 16 Qxe2 Qe8 17 Qd3 Nh5 ½-½ Makarychev-Gulko, Frunze 1985.

9 Bd3

Or 9 Be2 Nge7 10 0-0 0-0 11 c4 Bg4 12 Nc3 a6 13 h3 (13 Ne1 Bxe2 14 Nxe2 Re8 = Ochoa-Gufeld, Cienfuegos 1984) 13...Nh5 14 Qd2 Rc8?! (14...Bb8!? intending ...Qc7 Vera)

15 c5 ♗b8 16 ♗f4 ♖e8 17 ♗xb8 ♖xb8 18 ♖fe1 ± Vera-Zapata, Cienfuegos 1984.

9...♘ge7 (D)

Or 9...h6!? 10 0-0 ♘f6 11 h3 (in the game Makarychev-Christiansen, Saint John 1988 a more vigorous response brought only equality: 11 ♘e5!? ♘xe5 12 dxe5 ♗xe5 13 ♗b5+ ♗d7 14 ♗xd7+ ♕xd7 15 ♗d4 ♗xd4 16 ♖e1+ ♔f8! 17 ♕xd4 ♖e8 18 ♘d2 ♖xe1+ 19 ♖xe1 a6) 11...0-0 12 ♘bd2 ♗e6 13 b4 ♖c8 14 ♕a4 ♗b8 15 ♘b3 ♘e4 16 ♘c5 ♗f5 17 ♘xb7 ♕c7 18 ♗a6 ♖ce8 19 ♖fc1 ♘g5 20 ♗xg5 hxg5 21 ♘a5 and Black's compensation looked insufficient in Tomczak-Christiansen, German Cup 1992, although Black later succeeded in smashing through the white kingside.

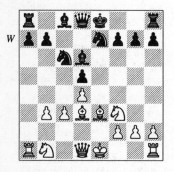

10 0-0

Or:

a) 10 ♘bd2?! allows 10...♗f5! 11 ♕b1 ♕d7 12 0-0 0-0 13 ♖e1 a5!? 14 ♘f1 b5! 15 ♘g3 ♗xd3 16 ♕xd3 a4! ∓ Bukacek-Psakhis, Lenk 1991.

b) White can try for an edge with 10 ♘h4!? 0-0 (10...♘g6 11 ♘f5 ♗xf5 12 ♗xf5 0-0 13 0-0 ♕c7 14 ♕h5 ♘ce7 15 ♗d3 a6 16 c4 f5 ∞ De Kleuver-Gausel, Reykjavik 1996 and 10...♗e6!? 11 0-0 ♕d7 12 f4?! ♘f5 13 ♘xf5 ♗xf5 14 ♕c2 ♘e7 ∓ N.Pedersen-Psakhis, Gausdal 1994; however, note White could avoid this latter line with the move-order 10 0-0 0-0 11 ♘h4) 11...♘g6 12 ♘f5 and here:

b1) 12...♗c7 13 ♕h5 ± ♘ce7?! 14 ♘xe7+ ♕xe7 15 ♕xd5 ♗e6 16 ♕h5 ♗xb3 17 c4! a5 18 ♘d2 a4 19 ♘xb3 axb3 20 ♕b5 ♗f4 21 ♖ae1 ♗xe3 22 ♖xe3 ♕f6 23 ♕xb3 ♕xd4 24 ♕xb7 ♖a3? 25 ♗xg6! 1-0 Yanovsky-Mestel, Hastings 1990, as on 25...♖xe3 comes 26 ♗xf7+ ♖xf7 27 ♕xf7+! ♔xf7 28 fxe3+ finishing off.

b2) 12...♗xf5 13 ♗xf5 ♕f6 (alternatively, 13...♕c7!? is De Kleuver-Gausel above) 14 ♕h5 ♘ce7 15 ♗d3 h6?! (15...♗f4 16 ♘d2 ± is better) 16 g3! ± Finkel-Kogan, Israel 1993.

10...0-0

After 10...♗f5 White can either continue as in the main game with 11 ♖e1, or try 11 c4!?, e.g. 11...♗b4 12 ♘a3 ♗xd3 13 ♕xd3 ♗xa3 14 ♖xa3 0-0 15 ♘g5 ♘g6 16 h4!? ♕e7 17 ♖aa1 ♖fd8 18 h5 ♘f8 19 h6 g6 20 ♖fe1 ± Rozentalis-Neverov, Uzhgorod 1987.

11 ♖e1

For the interesting 11 ♘h4!? see the analysis given in the note to White's 10th move. Other ways to play are 11 ♘a3 a6 12 ♘b5 ♗b8 13 ♕c2 h6 14 h3 ♗e6 15 ♘h4 ♖e8 16 ♖fe1 ♘c8 17 ♘f5 ♘b6 18 ♘a3 ♕f6 19 ♗d2 ♗c7 ∞ Maliutin-Lastin, Moscow 1995 and 11 ♕c2 g6 12

♗h6 ♖e8 13 ♗g5 ♗g4 14 ♘h4 ♕d7 15 ♘a3 ♖ac8 16 ♕d2 ♗b8 17 ♘c2 ♗f5 18 ♘xf5 ♘xf5 19 ♘e3 ♘fe7 20 f4 with an attack for White, Rozentalis-Kochiev, Voronezh 1987, but of course Black has potential improvements in this line, starting with 11...h6!?.

11...♗f5 = 12 ♗xf5?!

The position is roughly level after 12 ♗g5 f6 (12...♗xd3 13 ♕xd3 ♕d7 14 ♘bd2 f6 15 ♗h4 ♘g6 16 ♗g3 ♘f4 17 ♗xf4 ♗xf4 18 ♖e2 ♖ae8 = Brynell-Schmittdiel, Aabybro Nordic Cht 1989) 13 ♗h4 ♕d7 14 ♗g3 ♗xg3 15 hxg3 a6 = Kulish-Zsu.Polgar, Moscow OL 1994 and = Brynell-Larsen, Næstved 1988.

12...♘xf5 13 ♕d3 ♕d7 14 ♘bd2 ♖fe8 15 ♗g5 f6 16 ♗h4 a6 17 ♘f1 ♗f8 18 ♗g3 ♖ac8 19 ♘e3 ♘xe3 20 ♖xe3 ♖xe3 21 ♕xe3 ♘e7 22 ♕d3 ♕c6 23 ♖c1 (White is now passive, and Black manoeuvres to exploit his potential outside passed pawn on the queenside) **23...b5 24 ♘d2 a5 25 ♘b1 a4 26 b4 g6 27 ♘a3 ♘f5!? 28 ♘xb5 ♘xg3 29 hxg3 ♖b8 30 ♘a3 ♖xb4 31 ♘c2 ♖b3 32 ♘e3 a3 33 ♔h2 f5?!** (this looks wrong; 33...♗h6!? and White has problems) **34 ♖c2 ♗d6 35 ♕e2 ♕b7 36 ♘d1** (threatening 36 ♕e6+ and gaining vital counterplay against the black king) **37...♔f7 37 c4 dxc4 38 ♕xc4+ ♔g7 39 d5 ♖b4 40 ♕c3+ ♔h6 41 ♘e3 ♕e7 42 ♘c4 ♕h4+ 43 ♔g1 ♕g5 44 ♘xa3 ♖b8 45 ♖b2 ♖a8 46 ♖b3 ♕g4 47 ♕c1+ ♕g5 48 ♕xg5+ ♔xg5 49 ♘c4 ♖a1+ 50 ♔h2 ♗c5 51 f4+ ♔f6 52 ♘e5 ♗g1+ 53 ♔h3 ♗f2 54 ♔h2 ♗g1+ 55 ♔h3** ½-½

Game 62
Kramnik – Gelfand
Sanghi Nagar Ct (5) 1994

1 e4 c5 2 c3 e6 3 d4 d5 4 exd5 exd5 5 ♗e3!? *(D)*

This unique approach has been scoring well, even against very strong opposition, and represents a serious challenge to Black's hopes of transposing into a French Defence. White avoids the routine development of his knight to the f3-square, in favour of an unusual formation whereby the f3-square will instead provide an aggressive outpost for the queen.

5...c4

Possible is 5...cxd4 6 ♗xd4 ♘c6 (6...♘h6 7 ♘f3 ♘f5 8 ♗d3 ♘c6 9 ♗xf5 ♗xf5 10 0-0 ♗e7 11 ♗xg7 ♖g8 12 ♗d4 ± Stripunsky-Berg Hansen, Denmark 1994) 7 ♗b5 (7 ♘f3!? transposes to Game 61, note to Black's sixth) 7...a6 8 ♗a4 b5 (8...♕g5 9 ♘f3 ♕xg2 10 ♕e2+ ♘ge7 11 ♖g1 ♕h3 12 ♗xg7 ♖g8 13 ♗xc6+ bxc6 14 ♗xf8 ♔xf8 15 ♖xg8+ ♔xg8 16 ♘bd2 ♗g4 ∞ Rabiega-Afek, Budapest 1993) 9 ♗b3

♘xd4 10 ♕xd4 ♘f6 11 ♘e2 ♗b7 12 0-0 ♗d6 13 ♘g3 0-0 14 ♘f5 ♗c7 = Lima-Mecking, Brazil 1995.

A sharper try is 5...♕b6!? when White's best reply is not yet established:

a) 6 ♕b3 ♘c6 7 ♘f3 c4 8 ♕xb6 axb6 9 ♗e2 ♗d6 10 0-0 b5 11 ♖d1 ♘ge7 12 a3 ♘f5 13 ♗d2 0-0 ∓ Van Hul-Korchnoi, Antwerp 1995.

b) 6 dxc5 ♕xb2 7 ♕b3 ♕xa1 (7...♕xb3 8 axb3 ♘e7 9 ♘a3 ♗d7 10 ♘b5 ♗xb5 11 ♗xb5+ ♘bc6 12 ♘f3 a6 13 0-0 ± Van Mil-Cifuentes, Dieren 1989) 8 ♘f3 ♘d7 9 ♗b5 ♘gf6 10 0-0 ♗e7 11 ♘e1 0-0 12 ♘c2 ♘xc5 13 ♗xc5 ♕xb1 14 ♖xb1 ♗xc5 and Black has close to enough compensation for his queen, Palkovi-Backwinkel, Bundesliga 1995.

c) 6 ♕e2 c4 7 b3 axb3 8 ♕b5+ ♗d7 (8...♕xb5 9 ♗xb5+ ♗d7 10 ♗xd7+ ♘xd7 11 axb3 a6 12 ♘f3 ♗d6 13 c4 ♘e7 14 c5 ♗c7 15 ♘c3 h6 16 0-0 0-0 17 b4 ♘f6 18 b5 ± Striković-Gausel, Novi Sad OL 1990) 9 ♕xb3 ♘f6 10 ♘f3 ♗d6 11 ♕xb6 axb6 12 ♘e5 ♘c6 13 ♘xd7 ♔xd7 14 ♗d3 ♖a5 15 ♗c2 ♖ha8 16 ♗b3 ♖5a7 17 ♘d2 ½-½ Dzindzichashvili-Benjamin, Philadelphia 1993.

d) 6 ♕c2!? ♘c6 7 ♘f3 ♘f6 8 ♘bd2 (8 dxc5 ♗xc5 9 ♗xc5 ♕xc5 10 ♗d3 ♗g4 11 ♕e2+ ♔f8 12 0-0 ♖e8 13 ♕d1 ♕b6 14 b3 ♗xf3 15 ♕xf3 ♘e5 16 ♕d1 d4 ∞ Blatny-Benjamin, Philadelphia 1995) 8...♘g4 9 ♗d3 cxd4 10 ♗xd4 ♘xd4 11 ♘xd4 ♗c5 12 0-0 ± Benderac-Stanimirović, Yugoslav Cht 1992.

6 b3 cxb3 7 axb3 ♗d6

Usually 7...♘c6 leads to a transposition. White can also consider the plan 8 g3!? followed by ♘ge2 and 0-0.

8 ♗d3 ♘c6

After 8...♘f6 the course of the game Motwani-Korchnoi, Manila OL 1992 was very interesting: 9 ♘d2 0-0 10 h3! ♖e8 11 ♕f3 ♕e7 (an unusual manoeuvre was 11...♗d7!? 12 ♘e2 ♗c6 as in Motwani-Bellin, Gausdal 1992, when a draw was agreed after 13 ♗f4 ♗xf4 14 ♕xf4 ♘bd7 15 0-0 ♘f8 16 ♘f3 ♘g6 17 ♗xg6 hxg6 ½-½; however 13 ♘g3 seems more logical, covering e4 and with ideas of ♘f5) 12 ♘e2 ♘e4 13 0-0 ♘d7 14 ♘f4!? ♗xf4 15 ♕xf4 ♘xc3 16 ♖fc1 ♘e4 17 ♗xe4! dxe4 18 ♘c4. Here the players agreed a draw, but in spite of the extra pawn it is not apparent how even Viktor the Terrible would have dealt with White's unpleasant threat of ♘d6 followed by ♖c7.

Black can also continue 8...♘e7 9 ♕f3 (other squares are less testing: 9 ♕h5 ♘d7 10 ♗g5 ♘f8! = Cherniaev-Oll, Antwerp 1994 or 9 ♕c2 h6 10 ♘e2 0-0 11 0-0 ♘bc6 12 ♘g3 ♗e6 13 ♘d2 ♖c8 14 ♕b1 a5 15 ♘f3 f5 ∞ Kotliar-Kaidanov, New York 1993) and now:

a) 9...♗e6 10 ♗f4 0-0 11 ♘e2 ♗xf4 12 ♘xf4 ♕d7 13 0-0 ♗g4 14 ♕g3 ♗f5 15 ♘d2 ♘bc6 16 b4 (it is not clear that this is the best plan) 16...a5 17 b5 ♘d8 18 b6 ♘e6 19 ♘xe6 fxe6 20 ♘b3 ♗xd3 21 ♕xd3 ♘c8 22 ♘c5 ♕c6 23 ♖fe1 ♖f6 24 ♕h3 ½-½ Motwani-Jelen, Sas van Gent 1992.

b) 9...♘d7 10 ♘e2 0-0 11 ♘d2 ♖e8 12 0-0 ♘g6 13 ♘g3! ± (13 ♕xd5?! ♘f6 gives Black counterplay) 13...♕c7?! (13...♘b6) 14 ♕xd5 ♘f6 15 ♕c4 and Black did not have enough compensation for his pawn in Motwani-Conquest, Hafnarfirdi 1992.

9 ♕f3! *(D)*

Instead 9 ♘d2!? waits to see whether the black king's knight goes to f6 or e7. However there doesn't seem much point to this flexible approach, as White usually develops the queen to f3 in any case: 9...♗e6 (Sermek-Popović, Velden 1993 took a different course: 9...♕f6 10 ♕h5 ♘ge7 11 ♗g5 ♕e6+ 12 ♘e2 ♕g4 13 ♕xg4 ♗xg4 14 ♘f1 f6 15 ♗h4 ♘f5 16 ♗g3 ♘xg3 17 hxg3 ♘e7 18 ♘f4 ♗xf4 19 gxf4 and White was marginally better in the endgame) 10 ♕f3!? ♘ge7 11 ♗f4 (11 ♘e2 ♘g6 threatens ...♘h4) 11...♗xf4 12 ♕xf4 ♘g6 13 ♕g3 0-0 14 h4! ♕f6 (not 14...♘ce7? 15 h5 ♘h8 16 h6! and if 16...g6??, 17 ♕e5 +–) 15 ♘e2 ♗f5 16 ♗xf5 ♕xf5 17 h5 (17 ♕f3) 17...♘ge7 18 ♕f3 with a small plus for White (who later won) in Blatny-Korchnoi, Brno 1992.

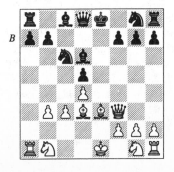

9...♘f6

A major diversion. 9...♘ge7 10 ♘d2 (after 10 ♘e2 0-0, 11 ♘d2 ♘g6?! 12 h4! is Kramnik's suggestion, but less accurate is 11 0-0?! ♘g6! when White cannot capture on d5; however White can deal with the ...♘g6 plan in another way too: 11 h3 would transpose to Marković-Todorović, Cetinje 1990, which continued 11...♗e6 12 0-0 ♕d7 13 ♘g3 ♘g6 14 ♕h5 ♖fe8 15 ♘f5 ♘ce7 16 ♘xe7+ ♖xe7 17 ♘d2 ♘f8 18 c4 a6 19 c5 ♗c7 20 b4 ♖c8 21 ♖fb1 ±) 10...♗e6 11 ♗f4!? (a typical theme when Black is preparing to play ...♘g6, after having protected the d-pawn with his bishop) 11...♘g6 12 ♗xd6 ♕xd6 13 ♘e2 (a nice finesse; 13...♘h4 can be met by 14 ♕g3) 13...0-0 14 h4 (14 ♕g3 ♕d7 15 ♘f4 ♗f5 wasn't anything for White in Hauchard-Renet, Clichy 1993) 14...h6 15 h5 ♘ge7 16 ♕f4 ♖ad8 17 0-0 ♖fe8 18 ♖fe1 ♔f8 19 ♘f3 ♗f5? (19...♕xf4 20 ♘xf4 ±, but Black has a hallucination planned) 20 ♘e5 ♗xd3?? 21 ♕xf7# (1-0) Motwani-Schmittdiel, Gausdal 1992.

10 h3 h6

10...0-0 11 ♘e2 and now:

a) 11...♖e8 12 ♘d2 ♗e6 (or 12...♕e7 13 ♗g5 ± Kramnik) 13 0-0 ♕d7 14 ♘g3 ♗c7 15 ♗g5 ♗d8 16 ♖fe1 h6 17 ♗f4 ± Van Mil-Kosten, Budapest 1989. The continuation of the game was an excellent illustration of White's kingside attacking chances in this line: 17...♖c8 18 ♖ac1 ♗e7 19 ♗b1 ♗a3 20 ♖cd1 ♗e7 21 ♕d3 ♔f8 22 ♘f3 ♘g8 23 ♕h7 ♗f6 24 ♘h5 ♕d8 25 ♗e5

♗xe5 26 dxe5 ♔e7 27 ♘xg7 and White wins.

b) 11...♗e6 12 ♘d2 ♕d7 was Striković-Gallagher, Geneva 1991, when White suffered for a dubious mixture of plans: 13 g4?! (13 ♗f4 ±) 13...♘e7 14 ♘f4 ♘g6 15 0-0 ♘h4 16 ♕d1 ♘xg4 17 hxg4 ♘xg4 18 ♗e2 ♘xe3 19 fxe3 ♕e7 20 ♔f2 ♘f5 21 ♘g2 ♘xe3 22 ♕e1 ♘xg2 23 ♔xg2 ♕g5+ 24 ♔h3 ♕h6+ 0-1.

11 ♘e2 ♘e7

On 11...0-0 12 ♘d2 ♖e8 Kramnik gives 13 g4! ±; the white attack is looming, as 13...♘h7 drops material to 14 ♗xh7+ ♔xh7 15 ♕xf7. Instead 13 0-0 ♘h7!? 14 ♗f4 (not now 14 ♗xh7+ ♔xh7 15 ♕xf7 ♖f8 16 ♕h5 ♖f5) 14...♘g5 15 ♕g3 ♗e7 16 ♘f3 ♗f6 17 ♘xg5 ♗xg5 18 ♗xg5 and a draw was agreed in I.Marković-Topalov, Kavala Balkaniad 1990, though even here White can play after 18...♕xg5 19 ♖fe1.

12 ♘g3

In his notes in *Informator 61*, Kramnik mentions only 12 ♘d2 ♘g6 13 g3 0-0 14 ♔f1 ∞. Worth consideration, however, is the logical 12 ♗f4!? and I see no reason why White should not be slightly better.

12...♗e6

On 12...♘g6 Kramnik gives the following variations:

a) 13 ♗b5+ ♔f8! (13...♗d7?! 14 ♗xd7+ ♕xd7 15 ♘f5 ±) 14 0-0 ♘h4 15 ♕d1 g5!? with counterplay, or 15...♗e6 intending ...♕c8.

b) 13 ♘h5!? ♘xh5 (13...♘h4?

14 ♘xf6+ ♕xf6 15 ♕xd5 ± or 13...♗e6 14 ♘xf6+ gxf6 15 g3 ±) 14 ♕xh5 ♘f4 15 ♗b5+ (15 ♗xf4 ♗xf4 16 ♗b5+ ♔f8 17 0-0 ♗e6 is level) 15...♗d7 (as on 16 ♗xf4 ♗xb5) 16 ♗xd7+ ♕xd7 17 ♗xf4 ♗xf4 =.

13 0-0 ♘g6 14 ♘f5 (14 ♗b5+ ♔f8!?) **14...♗xf5 15 ♕xf5 ♘h4?!** (better is 15...0-0 16 g3 ♖e8 17 ♕f3 ♘e4 ∞ 18 c4 ♕e7!? Kramnik) **16 ♗b5+ ♔f8 17 ♕c2 g6** (17...g5!? 18 ♘d2 g4?! can be met with 19 g3) **18 ♗d3 ♕d7 19 c4 a6?!** (19...♘f3+ would rebound on Black after 20 ♔h1 ♘g5 21 c5 ♗b8 22 f4 ± and if 22...♘xh3, then 23 ♖f3; 19...♔g7 was best, though White is now better) **20 c5 ♗c7 21 c6?** (hoping for 21...bxc6 22 ♖c1, but allowing Black a defensive trick; 21 ♘d2 ♖e8 22 ♖fe1 ♔g7 23 b4 ±) **21...♕d6!** (with the irritating point that 22 g3 bxc6 23 ♗f4 can be countered by the perpetual 23...♘f3+ 24 ♔g2 ♘h4+! 25 ♔h2 (25 ♔h1 ♕e6) 25...♘f3+, etc.; White has to go into an ending, where, after one further inaccuracy, he loses his advantage entirely) **22 ♕c5 ♕xc5 23 dxc5 bxc6 24 ♖xa6 ♖xa6 25 ♗xa6 ♔g7 26 ♗b7 ♖b8 27 ♗xc6 ♖xb3 28 ♘d2?!** (28 ♗d4! ±) **28...♖b4 29 ♖b1 ♖xb1+ 30 ♘xb1 ♘f5 31 ♗d2 ♘d4 32 ♗a4 ♘e4 33 ♗b4 ♘e6 34 c6 ♗b6! 35 ♘c3 ♗xf2+ 36 ♔f1 ♗c5! 37 ♗a5 ♘xc3 38 ♗xc3+ ♔f8 = 39 ♗b3 ♘c7 40 ♗e5 ♗b6 41 ♗d6+ ♔g7 42 g4 ♔f6 43 h4 ♔e6 44 ♗f8 h5 45 gxh5 gxh5 46 ♗d1 ♘b5 47 ♗xh5 ½-½**

22 2...d6

| 1 | e4 | c5 |
| 2 | c3 | d6 (D) |

There has been a great deal of activity in the ...d6 systems, and several variations have similarities or transpositions to branches of the Pirc/Modern or Sämisch King's Indian defences. After 3 d4 ♘f6 White must decide how to deal with the threat to his e-pawn. In Game 63 we examine the least-played of the three major options, 4 f3. In fact White's intentions are deceptively aggressive (after ♘c3, ♗e3 and ♕d2 he will castle queenside and seek a kingside attack); however Black has a fair choice of defensive set-ups to choose from, and even in the illustrative game could probably obtain reasonable counterplay.

4 dxc5 (Game 64) allows Black to show his clever idea of 4...♘c6! 5 f3 d5!?. The critical assessment comes after 9...♗e7, where Black

has sacrificed a pawn for long-term compensation.

In the next two games we examine the main line, 4 ♗d3. White is better after the pseudo queen offer 4...♘c6 5 ♘f3 ♗g4 6 d5 ♘e5 7 ♘xe5! (Game 65), so Black often fianchettoes with 4...cxd4 5 cxd4 g6 6 ♘c3 ♗g7 (Game 66). It seems that White can keep an edge, but both sides have a wide variety of plans in this somewhat amorphous system, and the complex positions that result may suit a strong player trying to win with Black.

Game 63
Rausis – A.Sokolov
Moscow 1992

1 e4 c5 2 c3 d6

For historical record the actual move-order of this illustrative game was the less common 2...g6 3 d4 cxd4 4 cxd4 ♗g7 5 ♘c3 d6 6 ♗e3 ♘f6 7 f3.

3 d4 ♘f6

Attacking the e-pawn immediately is an important part of Black's strategy if he is not to be left with a passive game.

a) The premature exchange of pawns with 3...cxd4?! 4 cxd4 frees the c3-square for White's knight a move too early (as now if 4...♘f6 White can respond 5 ♘c3). Even so this is not an uncommon exchange amongst lower-ranked players, although White gains easy development and a pleasant choice of lines, e.g.:

a1) 4...♘f6 5 ♘c3 g6 and now 6 ♗d3 transposes to Game 66, and so can 6 ♘f3 if White choose to place his bishop on d3 later. 6 ♗b5+!? is an option, though after 6...♗d7 7 ♕e2 ♘c6 8 ♘f3 a6 9 ♗xc6 ♗xc6 10 0-0 ♗g7 11 d5 ♗d7 12 h3 0-0 13 a4 Black equalised with 13...b5! 14 axb5 axb5 15 ♖xa8 ♕xa8 16 ♕d3 b4 17 ♘e2 ♗c8 ½-½ in Raičević-Klarić, Geneva 1989.

a2) 4...g6 5 ♘c3 ♗g7 6 ♘f3 (6 ♗e3 a6 7 ♖c1 ♘f6 8 h3 0-0 9 ♘f3 b5 10 ♗d3 ♗b7 ∞ Godena-Guevara, Moscow OL 1994) 6...♘f6 7 ♗b5+!? (7 ♗d3!? would give Game 66; 7 ♗e2 0-0 8 0-0 ♗g4 9 ♗e3 a6 10 h3 ♗xf3 11 ♗xf3 ♘c6 12 ♖c1 ± Handoko-Angles d'Auriac, Lucerne OL 1982) 7...♘fd7?! 8 ♗g5 0-0 9 0-0 a6 10 ♗e2 h6 11 ♗e3 b5 12 a4 ± Sveshnikov-Akopian, USSR 1969.

b) 3...♘c6 (gratuitously provocative) gives White the choice of transposing into later games with 4 dxc5 ♘f6 (Game 64) or 4 ♘f3 ♘f6 5 ♗d3 (Game 66), or gaining time with the advance 4 d5.

c) 3...♘d7 4 ♘f3 (4 f4 cxd4 5 cxd4 e5 6 ♘f3 ♘gf6 7 ♘c3 exd4 8 ♕xd4 ♕b6 9 ♕xb6 ♘xb6 10 ♗e3 ± Sermek-Kempinski, Groningen 1995) 4...e6 (after 4...g6, White may play 5 ♗d3 ♗g7 6 0-0 ♕c7 7 ♖e1 a6 8 a4 e6 9 ♗f4 e5 10 dxe5 dxe5 11 ♗e3 ♘gf6 12 ♘a3 0-0 13 ♘c4 ± Frois-Damljanović, La Coruña 1995,

while 5 ♗c4 ♕c7 6 ♕b3 e6 7 0-0 as in Pilgaard-H.Stefansson, Copenhagen 1990 could also be considered) 5 ♗d3 ♘e7 (5...♘f6 is small reference given in Game 65, note to White's fourth) 6 ♘a3!? (6 0-0) 6...a6 7 ♘c4 ♘g6 8 h4 b5 9 h5!? bxc4 10 hxg6 cxd3 11 ♖xh7! ♖g8 12 gxf7+ ♔xf7 13 ♘g5+ ♔e7 14 ♘xe6! ± Kr.Georgiev-Kofidis, Athens 1992.

4 f3 *(D)*

For 4 dxc5 ♘c6!? see Game 64, and for 4 ♗d3 see Games 65 and 66.

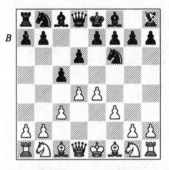

4...cxd4

4...♕c7 is plausible, e.g. 5 ♗e3 g6 6 ♗d3 ♗g7 7 ♘e2 0-0 8 ♘d2 b6 9 b4 a5 10 b5 ♗b7 11 0-0 ♘bd7 12 ♔h1 e5 13 d5 h5 14 ♘c4 ♘h7 15 ♕d2 ♖ae8 16 ♗c2 f5 17 exf5 gxf5 18 f4 e4 ∞ Am.Rodriguez-Pfleger, Cienfuegos 1983.

Black can also try to exploit White's early f3 by breaking with an early d5, e.g. 4...♘c6!? (4...d5 5 e5 ♘fd7 6 f4 cxd4 7 cxd4 ♘b6 8 ♘c3 ♘c6 9 b3 ♗f5 10 ♗a3 ♘d7!? 11 ♕d2 ♕a5 ∞ Rogers-Sadler, London 1992 whilst 9 ♗e3 is a transposition) 5 ♗e3 (5 dxc5 see Game 64) 5...d5

(5...g6 6 &d3 &g7 7 ♘e2 0-0 8 0-0 b6 9 ♕d2 &b7 10 b4 ♘d7 11 ♘a3 e6 12 ♖ab1 ♕e7 13 &g5 f6 14 &e3 ± Yanovsky-Dautov, Sverdlovsk 1989) 6 e5 ♘d7 (6...♘g8 7 ♘e2 ♘h6 8 g4 e6 9 ♘g3 ♕b6 10 ♕d2 &d7 11 &e2 0-0-0 ∞ Atlas-Oratovsky, Cappelle la Grande 1996) 7 f4 (7 e6 fxe6 8 dxc5 ♘f6 9 &d3 g6 10 ♘e2 &g7 11 ♘d2 0-0 12 ♕a4 e5 13 0-0-0 &f5 ∓ Välkesalmi-Dorfman, Helsinki 1986) 7...cxd4 8 cxd4 ♘b6 9 ♘c3 &f5 10 &d3 (the move-order 10 ♘f3 e6 11 &d3 would encourage Smagin's suggestion of 11...♘c4! 12 &xc4 {12 &c1 &g4!} 12...dxc4 13 a3 ∞) 10...&xd3 11 ♕xd3 e6 12 ♘f3 ♘c4 13 &c1 ♖c8 (13...&b4 14 0-0 0-0 15 ♘g5 g6 16 ♘e2 ± B.Filipović-Kosanović, Yugoslavia 1993) 14 0-0 ♕d7 15 b3 and here 15...♘b6 16 &d2 &e7 17 ♖ae1 ± was Smagin-Arnason, Sochi 1988, but 15...♘a3!? would transpose to Novoselsky-Arnason, Iraklio 1993, which appears unclear after 16 &d2 ♘b4 17 ♕e2 &e7 18 ♖ac1 0-0 19 ♘e1 ♖c7 20 ♖f3 f5.

Another idea is 4...♘bd7 (a position also reachable via the Pirc: 1 e4 d6 2 d4 ♘f6 3 f3 c5 4 c3 ♘bd7, etc.) and here 5 &e3:

a) 5...e6 6 &d3 &e7 7 ♘e2 0-0 8 0-0 b6 9 ♘d2 &b7 10 ♘g3 ♘e8?! 11 f4 cxd4 12 cxd4 g6 13 ♕e2 e5 14 ♖ad1 exf4 15 &xf4 ± Spassky-Jansson, Gothenburg 1972.

b) 5...e5 6 dxc5 dxc5 7 a4 &e7 8 ♘a3 0-0 9 ♕c2 (Sveshnikov claims ±) 9...♘b8 10 &c4 ♘c6 11 ♘e2 ♘a5 12 &a2 ♕c7 13 ♘c4 &e6 14 ♘xa5 &xa2 15 b3 ♕xa5 16 ♖xa2 c4 leads

to an unclear position, Sveshnikov-Gufeld, USSR 1983.

c) 5...♕c7 6 a4 (6 &d3 g6 7 ♘e2 &g7 8 0-0 0-0 9 ♘d2 a6 10 a3 b5 11 b4 c4 12 &c2 e5 13 a4 &b7 14 g4 d5 15 g5 ♘h5 16 exd5 ♘b6 ∞ Striković-Cebalo, Mendrisio 1987) 6...g6 7 ♘a3 a6 8 ♘e2 &g7 9 g4 b6 10 ♘g3 h5 11 g5 ♘h7 12 h4 &b7 13 f4 with a slight advantage for White, Marjanović-Cebalo, Yugoslavia 1985.

d) 5...g6!? 6 dxc5 (6 ♘d2 &g7 7 &d3 0-0 8 ♘e2 cxd4 9 cxd4 e5 10 d5 ♘c5 11 &c2 ♘h5 12 b4 ♘a6 13 ♖b1 f5 = Semkov-Gavrikov, Nimes 1991; also 6 ♘h3 &g7 7 &e2 0-0 8 0-0 e5 9 dxc5 ♘xc5 10 ♘f2 ♘e6 11 c4 b5 12 ♘c3 bxc4 13 &xc4 ♖b8 14 ♕d2 ♘d4 ∞ Lautier-D.Garcia, Pamplona 1992; 6 &d3!? &g7 7 ♘e2 0-0 8 0-0 is the natural and perhaps best way to develop) 6...dxc5 7 a4 (7 ♘a3 a6 8 ♘c4 b5 9 e5 ♘h5 10 e6 fxe6 11 ♘d2 &g7 12 ♘e4 ♕c7 13 ♘h3 0-0 14 a4 ♘df6 ∓ Vorotnikov-Yermolinsky, Leningrad 1985) 7...&g7 8 ♘a3 0-0 9 ♘h3 ♕c7 10 &e2 ♘e5 11 ♘f2 &e6 12 0-0 ♖fd8 13 ♕c2 b6 with unclear play, Bergström-Shabalov, Gausdal 1991.

5 cxd4 g6

Or 5...e5 6 dxe5 (6 ♘c3 exd4 7 ♕xd4 ♘c6 8 &b5 a6 9 &xc6+ bxc6 10 &e3 &e7 11 ♘ge2 0-0 12 0-0 &e6 13 ♖fd1 ♕b8 = Demkov-Pushkin, Corr 1993) 6...dxe5 7 ♕xd8+ ♔xd8 8 ♘c3 &b4 9 ♘ge2 ♘c6 10 &e3 &e6 11 0-0-0+ ♘d7 12 ♘d5 &xd5 13 ♖xd5 ♔e7 14 ♘c3 ♖hc8 15 &b5 a6 16 ♖hd1 ♖c7 17 &xc6 bxc6 18 ♖5d2 &xc3 19 bxc3 with a small but lingering endgame edge for White, Vorotnikov-Yermolinsky, Leningrad 1984.

6 ♘c3 (D)

To be seriously considered was 6 ♗e3 ♗g7 7 ♗d3 0-0 8 ♘e2. Now 8...♘c6 9 ♘c3 e5 10 d5 ♘d4 fails to 11 ♘xd4 exd4 12 ♗xd4 ♘h5 13 ♗xg7 ♕h4+ 14 g3 ♘xg3 15 ♗f6! Praznik-Jeras, Bled 1992, and after 8...e5 9 d5 a Sämisch King's Indian type position would arise, for example 9...♘h5 (9...♘bd7 10 ♘c3 is a direct Sämisch transposition – see Game 66, note to White's sixth move for more coverage) 10 ♘bc3 f5 11 exf5 ♗xf5 12 0-0 ♗xd3 13 ♕xd3 ♘f4 14 ♕d2 ♘xe2+ 15 ♕xe2 ♘d7 16 ♕b5 b6 17 ♘e4 ♘f6 18 ♗g5 and White is clearly better, Semkov-Negulescu, Erevan 1988.

6...♗g7 7 ♗e3 0-0

7...♘c6 8 ♘ge2 a6 9 ♕d2 h5 10 ♘c1 0-0 11 h3 e5 12 d5 ♘d4 13 ♘1e2 ♘xe2 14 ♗xe2 ♘h7 15 g4 ♗f6 16 0-0-0 h4 17 ♔b1 ♗g5 ∞ was Khmelnitsky-Goldin, Philadelphia 1992, but more direct is 8 ♕d2 ♗d7 9 0-0-0 ♖c8 10 ♔b1 0-0 11 h4 Lane-Ulrichsen, Oslo 1987.

8 ♕d2 ♘c6

8...a6 9 ♘ge2 e5 10 0-0-0 ♘c6 11 g4!? ♘a5 (11...b5 12 d5 ♘a5 13 ♘g3 b4 ∞ Sveshnikov) 12 ♘g3 exd4 13 ♗xd4 ♘c6 14 ♗e3 ♗e6 15 ♔b1 ♖e8 and now the sacrifice 16 ♘f5! gxf5 17 gxf5 ♗d7 18 ♖g1 gave White huge attack in Sveshnikov-W.Watson, Hastings 1984.

However the immediate 8...e5! appears to be a promising alternative: 9 0-0-0 (9 ♘ge2!? exd4 10 ♗xd4 ♘c6 11 ♗e3 d5 12 exd5 ♘b4 13 ♗c5 ♘bxd5 14 ♗xf8 ♗xf8 15 ♖d1 ♗e6 was a bold if unclear exchange sacrifice in Sariego-Canda, Bayamo 1989) 9...exd4 (9...♘c6 10 d5 ♘d4 11 ♘ge2 ♘xe2+ 12 ♘xe2 h5 13 ♘c3 ♗d7 14 ♔b1 a6 15 ♖c1 ± Sveshnikov-Kremenietsky, Moscow 1983) 10 ♕xd4 ♘g4! (10...♘c6 11 ♕xd6 ♕a5 was Bjelajac-Cebalo, Yugoslavia 1984, and here Sariego gives 12 ♕c5! ±) 11 ♕d2 ♘xe3 12 ♕xe3 ♗e6 13 ♘ge2 ♕a5! 14 ♔b1 ♖c8 and Black's raking bishops mean danger for White, Sariego-Andres, Sagua la Grande 1987.

9 0-0-0 ♗d7 (D)

A sharp but well-known type of position has arisen: White and Black have castled on opposite wings, and both will attempt to attack the other's king. Possible here was 9...a6, intending 10...b5. As well as caveman assaults it is also important to restrain the opponent's counterplay, e.g. 9...♕a5 10 ♔b1 e5 11 d5 ♘d4 12 ♘ge2 ♘xe2 13 ♗xe2 a6 14 g4 b5 15 ♖c1 ♗d7 16 a3 ♕d8 17 h4 ♕b8 18 ♘a2 a5 19 h5 ♕b7. Here the positional continuation 20 ♗d3!? ♖fb8 21 b3 b4 22 a4 ♖c8 23 ♕e2

🗷xc1+ 24 ♘xc1 left Black's queen-side counterplay stymied in Strik-ović-Ristić, Cetinje 1991.

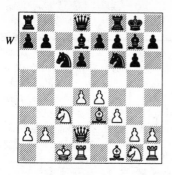

10 ♔b1

After 10 ♗h6 ♗xh6 11 ♕xh6 ♕a5 12 ♔b1 🗷fc8 13 ♕d2 b5 14 ♘ce2 b4 15 ♘c1 🗷c7 16 ♘ge2 🗷ac8 17 d5 ♘e5 18 ♘d4 ♗a4 Black had clearly seized the initiative in B.Kutuzović-F.Arnold, Budapest 1995.

10...♕a5

Once again 10...a6 or 10...♘a5 followed by ...🗷b8 and ...b5 were options.

11 ♘ge2 b5 12 ♘c1! b4 13 ♘3e2 🗷fc8 14 g4 ♕d8 15 g5 ♘e8 (not 15...♘h5?, which would be strongly met by 16 ♘g3) **16 h4 d5?!** (with the laudable intention of 17 exd5? ♗f5+ 18 ♔a1 ♕xd5, but White is not going to capture; 16...♘a5!? creating threats on the queenside was still unclear) **17 h5 e5 18 hxg6 hxg6 19 ♘b3** (19 dxe5? ♘xe5) **19...dxe4 20 fxe4 exd4 21 ♘exd4 ♕e7 22 🗷h4! ±** (with the menacing threat of trebling on h-file) **22...♘e5 23 ♗a6 🗷d8** (23...♘c4!? 24 ♗xc4 🗷xc4 25 🗷dh1 🗷ac8 intending 26 ♕h2 ♕e5) **24 ♕g2! ♘c7 25 ♗e2 ♘e6 26 🗷dh1 f6**

(27 ♕h2 was the threat but now a beautiful knight offer forces the exchange of a key black defender) **27 ♘f5! ± ♕f8** (if 27...gxf5 comes 28 🗷h8+! ♗xh8 29 gxf6+, winning) **28 ♘xg7 ♕xg7 29 ♘d4 ♘f7 30 ♗c4 fxg5 31 🗷h7 ♕e5 32 ♗d5 🗷f8 33 ♕h3 🗷ae8 34 ♘f3 g4 35 ♕xg4 ♕f6 36 ♕h3 ♗c8 37 ♗d4 ♘fg5 38 ♗xf6 ♘xh3 39 🗷g7+ 1-0**

Game 64
Thorhallsson – Fedorowicz
London 1987

1 e4 c5 2 c3 d6 3 d4 ♘f6 4 dxc5 ♘c6! *(D)*

The key move in Black's strategy – now the white pawn on e4 is ready to be captured. The blunder 4...♘xe4? loses a piece to 5 ♕a4+ (three games on my database) and 4...dxc5 5 ♕xd8+ is considered to be an inferior endgame for Black.

5 f3!?

There are numerous other ways for White to respond:

a) 5 ♗d3 d5! (a typical theme in this line, and better than 5...dxc5 6 ♕e2, for example 6...♘e5 7 ♗c2 c4

8 ♘f3 ♘d3+ 9 ♗xd3 ♕xd3 10 ♘bd2
♕xe2+ 11 ♔xe2 ♗g4 12 e5 ♘d7 13
♘xc4 ♖c8 14 b3 b5 15 ♘a3 ♖c5 16
e6! fxe6 17 ♗e3 ± Van Wijgerden-
Van der Wiel, Dutch Ch 1983) 6 ♘d2
e5 7 ♘gf3 (after 7 b4!?, 7...d4 8 ♕c2
dxc3 9 ♕xc3 ♘xb4 10 ♗b5+ ♘c6
11 ♘gf3 ♘d7 12 0-0 was good for
White in Hermann-Podzielny, Bundesliga 1985 so Black should prefer
7...a5 8 b5 ♘b8 9 ♘gf3 ♗xc5 10
♕e2 ♘bd7 = Schandorff-De Jong,
Corr 1990) 7...♗xc5 8 0-0 0-0 9 ♕e2
♗e6 = Van Wijgerden-Van Mil, Amsterdam 1983.

b) Another sideline is 5 ♘d2 dxc5
(now 5...d5 is less effective) 6 ♘gf3
g6!? (6...e6 7 ♕c2 ♕c7 8 g3 ♗e7 9
♘c4 e5 10 ♗g5 ♘g4 11 h3 ♗xg5 12
hxg4 ♕e7 13 ♘xg5 ♕xg5 14 ♗e2 0-
0 15 ♖h5 ♕e7 16 0-0-0 ± Werner-
Fedorowicz, Cannes 1988) 7 g3 ♗g7
8 ♗g2 ♕d3 = Sveshnikov-Dorfman,
USSR 1981.

c) After 5 cxd6 ♘xe4 the critical
line runs 6 dxe7? (on 6 ♗d3, 6 ♘f3
or 6 ♘d2 comes 6...♘xd6 with a
good game for Black) 6...♕xd1+ 7
♔xd1 ♘xf2+! (7...♗xe7 8 ♗e3 ∞ as
in several games, but these lines are
redundant as the text is strong) 8
♔e1 ♘xh1 9 exf8♕+ ♔xf8! 10 g3
♗f5 (10...h5? 11 ♗g2 h4, Anton-
Kengis, Riga 1981, fails to 12 gxh4!
♖xh4 13 ♘f3) 11 ♗g2 ♖e8+ (with
this Black saves his knight, or, as in
the game, wins White's in return)
12 ♘e2 ♗g4 −+ Sindermann-Sick,
Baden-Baden 1987.

d) 5 ♕c2!? is complex:

d1) The positions after 5...dxc5
are not unfavourable for White, e.g.

6 ♘f3 (or 6 ♗f4, when both 6...g6 7
♘a3 ♗g7 8 ♖d1 ♘d7 9 ♘b5 ♘ce5
10 ♘f3 ♕b6 11 ♘xe5 ♘xe5 12 ♖d5
a6 13 ♘a3 ♘d7 14 ♘c4 ♕a7 15 a4
b6 Kharlov-Van der Mortel, Leeuwarden 1994 and 6...e5 7 ♗g5 h6 8
♗h4 ♗e7 9 ♘d2 ♘h5 10 ♗xe7
♕xe7 ∞ Cherniaev-Tregubov, Sochi 1993 are roughly equal) 6...g6
(6...♗g4 7 ♘bd2 ♕c7 8 ♗e2 e6 9
♘c4 ♗e7 10 g3 e5 11 ♘e3 ♗e6 12
0-0 h6 13 ♘h4 g6 14 ♖d1 ♖d8 15
♗f3 ♖xd1+ 16 ♕xd1 ♕d7 17 ♘d5
g5 18 ♘f5 ♗xd5 19 exd5 ♘xd5 20
♗xd5 ♕xf5 21 ♕b3 ± Mir.Mark-
ović-A.Kovačević, Cetinje 1993) 7
♗e3 b6 8 ♗b5 ♗d7 9 e5 ♘d5 10
♕e4 a6 11 ♗a4 e6 12 ♗g5 ♗e7 13
♗xe7 ♘dxe7 14 0-0 b5 15 ♗c2 ±
Rausis-Fedorowicz, Saint Martin
1991.

d2) Therefore, recently Black has
tried 5...d5: 6 ♘d2 e6!? (6...e5 7
exd5 ♕xd5 8 ♘b3 a5 9 ♗g5 ♕e4+
10 ♕xe4 ♘xe4 11 ♗e3 a4 12 ♘d2
♘xd2 13 ♔xd2 ♖a5 = M.Marković-
A.Kovačević, Nis 1993 but 7 b4!? a5
8 ♗b5 axb4 9 cxb4 ♗d7 10 ♗xc6
♗xc6 11 ♘gf3 dxe4 12 ♘xe5 ap-
peared favourable for White in the
game Cherniaev-Mortensen, Hastings 1995) 7 b4 a5 8 b5 ♘b8 9 ♘gf3
♗xc5 10 ♗d3 ♘bd7 11 exd5 exd5
12 0-0 0-0 13 c4 h6 14 ♘b3 ♗e7 was
unclear in Yagupov-Tregubov, Moscow 1994.

e) 5 ♗c4, and the subsequent temporary sacrifice on f7, looks more
fearsome than it is: 5...♘xe4 (or
5...dxc5 6 ♕xd8+ ♘xd8 7 e5 ±, but
5...e6 is plausible: 6 ♗g5 dxc5 7
♕xd8+ ♔xd8 8 ♘d2 h6 9 ♗h4 g5 10

♗g3 ♘h5 = as in Novak-Plachetka, Strbske Pleso 1978) 6 ♗xf7+ (on 6 ♕d5 Black has either 6...e6 7 ♕xe4 d5 or 6...♗e6 7 ♕xe4 d5) 6...♔xf7 *(D)* and now:

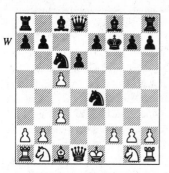

a) 7 ♕d5+ e6 8 ♕xe4 d5 9 ♕f3+ ♕f6 (9...♔g8 10 ♗e3 b6 11 cxb6 axb6 12 ♕d1 ♗c5 and now 13 ♘e2?! ♗xe3 14 fxe3 ♕h4+ 15 ♘g3 ♗a6 ∓ was Sveshnikov-Tseshkovsky, USSR Ch 1981, but an improvement is 13 ♗xc5 bxc5 14 ♘e2 ♖b8 15 b3 ♕f6 ∞ Tseshkovsky) 10 ♗e3 b6!? (after 10...♗e7 11 ♕g3 e5 12 ♘f3 h6 13 0-0 g5, 14 ♘xe5+!? ♕xe5 15 f4 ♕g7 16 fxg5+ ♔g8 17 g6 was a dangerous-looking sacrifice in Angelov-Babula, Marianske Lazne 1989; however 10...♘e5 is possible, when the endgame 11 ♕e2 ♕f5 12 ♘f3 ♘xf3+ 13 ♕xf3 ♕xf3 14 gxf3 has been reached a few times, and Black seems to be OK after 14...e5) 11 cxb6 axb6 12 ♗d4 ♘xd4 13 cxd4 ♖a4 14 ♕xf6+ gxf6 15 ♘e2 ♗b4+ 16 ♘bc3 ♗xc3+ 17 bxc3 ♗a6 18 ♔d2 ♗xe2 19 ♔xe2 ♖ha8 = Azmaiparashvili-Topalov, Elenite 1995.

b) 7 ♕h5+ and now:

b1) 7...g6 8 ♕d5+ was met by 8...e6 9 ♕xe4 d5 10 ♕e2 e5 11 ♘f3 e4 12 ♘d4 ♗xc5 13 ♗e3 ♘e5 14 0-0 ♗g4 15 ♕b5 ♕b6 16 ♕xb6 ♗xb6 ∞ in Nun-Kengis, Timisoara 1987, but 8...♔g7 9 ♕xe4 is more common, for example 9...e5!? 10 cxd6 ♕xd6 11 ♘f3 ♗f5 12 ♕e3 ♗d3 ∞ Stripunsky-Mironenko, USSR 1988 or 9...♗f5!? 10 ♕h4?! (10 ♕e3 is better) 10...♘e5! 11 ♕d4 ♔f7 12 ♕d5+ e6 13 ♕xb7+ ♔g8 ∓ Minerva-Fomin, Corr 1987.

b2) 7...♔g8 8 ♕d5+ e6 9 ♕xe4 d5 10 ♕e3 (defending the c5-pawn) 10...b6 (after 10...d4 11 ♕e4, the continuation 11...♗xc5 12 ♘f3 ♕d5 13 ♕xd5 exd5 14 b4! ♗b6 15 b5 ♘e7 16 cxd4 ± was Sveshnikov-Ermenkov, Varna 1987; instead 11...♕d5!? was met by 12 ♘d2 dxc3 13 bxc3 ♘e5 14 ♗a3 ♘d3+ 15 ♔e2 ♘xc5 16 ♕xd5 exd5 17 ♘b3 ♘e4 = in Blauert-Smirin, Groningen 1990, but White can consider 12 ♕xd5 exd5 13 ♘f3 dxc3 14 ♘xc3 d4 15 ♘e4 ♗g4?! {15...♗f5!? ∞ Daniliuk} 16 0-0 ♖e8 17 ♖e1! ± Daniliuk-Karasev, Russia 1992) 11 cxb6 axb6 12 ♘f3 (12 ♘e2 ♗c5 13 ♕g5 ♕f6! 14 0-0 ♗a6 15 ♕xf6 gxf6 16 ♖e1 ♔f7 ∞ Khmelnitsky-Goldin, Philadelphia 1992) 12...♗c5 13 ♕g5 ♕xg5 14 ♗xg5 ♗a6 Daniliuk-Tregubov, St Petersburg 1993, which has been assessed as ± but Black looks to have sufficient compensation to me.

5...d5!?

Black challenges the white centre, hoping later to recapture on c5 with a piece (though sometimes the pawn sacrifice turns out to be permanent).

Instead 5...dxc5 6 ♕xd8+ ♘xd8 and now:

a) 7 ♗e3 e6 8 ♘a3 ♗e7 9 ♗b5+ (9 ♘b5 0-0 10 ♘c7 ♖b8 11 ♗f4 ♘c6 Ftačnik) 9...♗d7 10 0-0-0 ♗xb5 11 ♘xb5 0-0 12 g4?! (12 ♘e2) 12...♘c6 13 g5 ♘h5 14 ♖d7 a6! 15 ♘a3 b5 16 ♘e2 f6! 17 h4 ♖ad8 18 ♖c7 ♖c8 19 ♖xc8 ♖xc8 20 f4 ♘d4! with advantage to Black, A.Fernandes-Illescas, Lisbon Z 1993.

b) 7 ♘a3!? a6 (now 7...e6 8 ♘b5) 8 ♘c4 ♘d7 9 a4 ♘c6 10 a5 e6 11 f4 ♘f6 12 ♗d3 ♗d7 13 ♘b6 ♖d8 14 ♘f3 ♗e7 15 ♔e2 ♘a7 16 ♘xd7 ♘xd7 17 ♖d1 0-0 18 e5 ± Handoko-Sitanggang, Djakarta 1994.

6 exd5 *(D)*

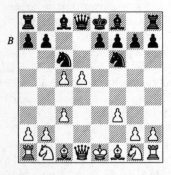

6...♘xd5

6...♕xd5!? 7 ♕xd5 (7 ♗e3 ♕xd1+ 8 ♔xd1 ♗f5 9 ♘d2 0-0-0 10 ♘e2 ♘d5 11 ♗f2 g6 ∓ Gorelov-Ubilava, USSR 1981) 7...♘xd5 8 ♗c4 e6 9 ♗xd5 exd5 10 ♗e3 ♘e5 (10...♗f5 11 ♘e2 ♘e5 12 ♘d4 ♘d3+ 13 ♔e2 ♗g6 14 b4 a5 15 ♘b5 ♔d7 16 ♖d1 ♘b2 17 ♖xd5+ ♔c6 18 ♖d2 ♘c4 19 ♘d4+ ♔d7 20 ♖d1 ♖e8 21 ♘c2+ ♔c8 22 ♖d4! ± Shrentzel-Ma.Tseitlin, Tel Aviv 1990) and here:

a) 11 ♘d2 ♘d3+ 12 ♔f1 ♘xb2 = Seyb-Leko, Nuremberg 1989.

b) 11 b4 a5! 12 ♗d4 ♘d3+!? 13 ♔d2 (13 ♔e2 ♗f5 14 g4 ♗g6 15 ♘h3 axb4 16 cxb4 ♗xb4 17 ♘c3 ♘c2 ∓ S.Arkell-Sadler, Capelle la Grande 1991) 13...♗f5 14 g4 (14 a3 h5! 15 ♘e2 ♖h6! 16 ♗e3 ♖ha6 17 ♘f4 d4!! 18 cxd4 ♘xf4 19 ♗xf4 axb4 ∓ Klinger-Cebalo, Biel 1986) 14...♗g6 15 a3 h5 16 g5 f6 17 gxf6 gxf6 18 ♘e2 ♔f7 19 ♖f1 ♗h6+ 20 f4 ♖he8 21 ♖f3 ♘b2 22 ♖a2 ♘c4+ 23 ♔c1 ♖e7 0-1 Kuntz-Cebalo, Cannes 1995.

c) 11 b3!? ♘d3+ 12 ♔d2 ♘xc5 (this has occurred in a number of games; Black still has an isolated queen's pawn, and although the bishop pair compensates to a degree White holds a light edge) 13 ♘a3 (13 ♘e2 ♘e6 14 a4 ♗e7 15 ♘a3 0-0 16 ♘b5 a6 17 ♘bd4 ♘xd4 18 ♘xd4 ♗d7 19 ♖he1 ♖fe8 20 ♗f4 ♗h4 21 g3 ♗f6 22 ♖xe8+ ♖xe8 23 ♖e1 ♖xe1 24 ♔xe1 h5 25 ♗d6 ½-½ Thorhallsson-Ivanchuk, Groningen 1986) 13...♗d7 (13...a6 14 ♘e2 ♗f5 15 ♘c2 ♗d6 16 ♗f4 ♖d8 17 ♘e3 ± Bojković-Tazheva, Moscow OL 1994) 14 ♘e2 0-0-0 (or 14...♗d6 15 ♘c2 ♘e6 16 ♘cd4 g6 Manca-Gelfand, Arnhem 1988) 15 ♘c2 b6 16 ♘f4 ♗e7 17 ♘d4 ♗e8 18 ♖he1 ± Blauert-Oratovsky, Bundesliga 1995.

7 ♗c4

7 c4 ♕a5+ 8 ♗d2 ♘db4 9 a3 ♗f5! is good for Black, e.g. 10 ♗c3 ♕a6 11 ♘d2 ♘c2+ as in Viksnin-Goldin, Leningrad Cht 1989 and Kharlov-Smirin, Oviedo rpd 1993.

7...e6 8 ♗xd5 exd5

For 8...♕xd5 9 ♕xd5 see the note at Black's sixth move.

9 ♗e3 ♗e7! *(D)*

9...♕h4+ favours White: 10 g3 (or even 10 ♗f2 ♕g5 11 ♔f1 ♗e7 12 ♘e2 0-0 13 ♕d2 ♕f5 14 ♘d4 ♕g6 15 ♘a3 ♗xc5 16 ♘xc6 ♗xa3 17 ♘xa7 ± Zhuravliov-Goldin, Leningrad Cht 1989) 10...♕h5 11 ♘d2 (11 ♔f2 ♘e5 12 ♗d4 ♗e7 13 ♗xe5 ♕xe5 14 ♕d4 ♕e6 ∞ Makropoulos-Ivanović, Budva 1981, but possible is 11 ♘a3 ♗e7 12 ♔f2 0-0 13 ♘e2 ± Sikora-Cvetković, Stary Smokovec 1977 and An.Fernandez-Damaso, Portugal 1992) 11...♗e7 12 ♘e2 0-0 13 ♘f4 ♕e5 and now instead of 14 ♕e2 b6! with counterplay, Razuvaev gives 14 ♔f2 ±.

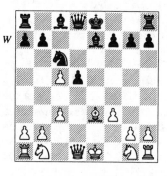

10 ♘e2 0-0 11 0-0 ♖e8 12 ♕d2?!

After 12 ♗f2!? the position is unclear. Black has little prospect of regaining the c5-pawn, but the two bishops and White's slightly awkwardly placed minor pieces offer compensation. The two known examples both saw Black rewarded for bold play:

a) 12...♗g5 13 ♘d4 ♘e5 14 ♘a3 b6 15 cxb6 ♕xb6 16 ♕b3 ♕g6 17 ♕xd5 ♗a6 18 ♖fe1 ♘d3 19 ♖xe8+ ♖xe8 20 ♗g3 h5 21 ♕f5 ♕xf5 22 ♘xf5 ♖e2 23 b3 ♖d2 24 ♘c4 ♗xc4 25 bxc4 g6 26 ♘d4 h4 27 ♗e1 ♖b2 28 g3 ♗e3+ 29 ♔h1 h3 30 ♖d1 ♖g2 0-1 Russek-Ermenkov, Saint John 1988.

b) 12...♘e5 13 ♘f4 ♗f5 14 ♖e1 ♗g5 15 ♘xd5 ♘d3 16 ♖xe8+ ♕xe8 17 f4 ♖d8 18 fxg5 ♖xd5 19 ♘a3 ♘f4 20 ♕f3 ♘e2+ 21 ♔h1 ♗e4 22 ♕g4 ♗f5 23 ♗e3 ♗d3 24 ♗d2 ♕e6 25 h3 f6 26 gxf6 ♕xf6 27 ♗e3 h5 28 ♕a4 ♕e5 0-1 (time) Röder-Kunze, Germany 1990.

12...♘e5 13 ♘a3 (13 b3 ♗f5 with ideas of ...♗d3 or ...♘d3) **13...b6!?** (another thematic idea in this line; if White exchanges on b6 Black's rook will exert pressure down the a-file) **14 ♘f4 ♗b7 15 ♖ad1 ♗f8 16 ♕f2** (16 ♘xd5 ♗a6!?) **16...♕b8 17 ♖fe1 bxc5 18 ♘xd5** (18 ♗xc5 ♘xf3+! 19 gxf3 ♕xf4 ∓) **18...c4 19 ♕g3 ♗xd5 20 ♖xd5 ♘d3 ∓ 21 ♖xd3** (21 ♖e2 ♗xa3 –+) **21...cxd3 22 ♘c4 ♕xg3 23 hxg3 ♖ac8 24 b3 0-1**

Game 65
Smagin – Kofidis
Iraklion 1993

1 e4 c5 2 c3 d6 3 d4 ♘f6 4 ♗d3 *(D)* **4...♘c6**

For 4...cxd4 and 4...g6 see Game 66. Others:

a) 4...e6 (passive but playable) 5 ♘f3 ♗e7 6 0-0 ♘bd7 7 ♕e2 a6 8 a4 0-0 9 ♖d1 ♕c7 10 ♗g5 ± David-Meduna, Czech Ch 1994.

b) 4...♘bd7 (again passive) 5 ♘f3 cxd4 (5...e6 6 0-0 ♗e7 7 e5 ♘d5 8

♗e4 cxd4 9 exd6 ♗xd6 10 ♗xd5
exd5 11 ♖e1+ ± Godena-Mrva, Mitropa Cup 1995 while 5...e5 has also
been seen) 6 cxd4 e5 7 0-0 ♗e7 8
♘c3 0-0 9 h3 (9 ♖e1!? a6 10 a4 b6
11 ♗f1 ♗b7 12 d5 ♖c8 13 ♘d2 ♘e8
14 ♘c4 ± Smagin-Ubilava, Oviedo
rpd 1993) 9...a6 10 ♗e3 b5 and now
11 b4 ♗b7 12 d5 ♖c8 13 ♕b3 ♘b6
14 ♖fe1 ♘h5 15 a4 ♘f4 16 ♗f1 f5
17 axb5 fxe4 led to great complications in Finkel-Golubev, Groningen
1993.

c) After 4...e5!? White has tried
a variety of moves, such as 5 d5 and
5 ♘e2, while 5 dxe5 dxe5 is also
possible, e.g. 6 ♘f3 ♕c7 7 0-0 ♗e7
8 ♘a3 ♘c6 9 ♘c4 0-0 10 a4 ♖d8 11
♕c2 h6 12 ♘e3 ♘a5 13 ♘d2 b6 ∞
Okhotnik-Karpman, USSR 1988.
However the most common continuation is 5 ♘f3 ♘c6 6 dxc5 (6 0-0!?
g6?! 7 dxc5 dxc5 8 ♘a3 ♗g7 9 ♘c4
♕e7 10 ♗e3 b6 11 b4 cxb4 12 cxb4
0-0 13 ♖c1 ♗g4 14 b5 ♘d4 15 ♗xd4
exd4 16 h3 ♘f6 17 ♘ce5 ♕d6 18
♘c6 ± Rõtsagov-Czebe, Cappelle la
Grande 1994) 6...dxc5. Here some
examples show that so far Black
has not fared so badly in the manoeuvring type of game that results:

7 ♕e2 ♗e7 8 0-0 0-0 9 ♘bd2 h6 10
♖e1 ♗e6 11 ♘f1 ♖e8 12 ♘g3 ♗f8
13 h3 a6 14 ♘h2 g6 15 ♗c2 c4 16
♕f3 ♗g7 17 ♗e3 ♕e7 18 h4 ♖ad8
½-½ Godena-Kunze, Lugano 1989
or 7 0-0 h6 8 ♘a3 ♗e7 9 ♘c4 ♕c7
10 ♘e3 0-0 11 ♖e1?! ♗e6 12 ♗c4
♖fd8 13 ♕e2 ♗xc4 14 ♕xc4 ♘a5
15 ♕e2 c4 ∓ Westerinen-Ermenkov,
Dieren 1988. There is a dearth of
high-level examples in these 4...e5
lines, so we can assume that these
structures with pawns on e5 and c5
are disliked by grandmasters playing
Black. However White's exact route
to advantage has yet to be demonstrated.

d) 4...♕c7, by contrast, has been
utilised by several famous names. 5
♘f3 (5 ♘e2 g6 6 0-0 ♗g7 7 f3 0-0 8
♗e3 b6 9 ♘d2 ♗b7 10 ♕e1 ♘c6 11
♕h4 cxd4 12 cxd4 ♘b4 13 ♖fc1
♕d7 14 ♘c4 d5 15 a3 ♘a6 ∞ Garma-
Ki.Georgiev, Calcutta 1992) 5...g6
(the position after 5...♗g4 6 0-0 e6 7
♘bd2 ♗e7 8 e5 ♘fd7 9 exd6 ♗xd6
10 h3 ♗h5 11 ♘e4, as in Nun-Renet,
Dortmund 1989, is assessed as ± by
Karpov) 6 0-0 ♗g7 and now:

d1) 7 h3 0-0 8 ♖e1 e5 (8...♘bd7
9 e5 ♘d5 10 exd6 exd6 11 dxc5
♘xc5 12 ♗xg6 fxg6 13 ♕xd5+ ±
Berndt-Christiansen, Wiesbaden 1994
or 8...♖d8 9 ♗g5 e5 10 dxe5 dxe5 11
♕e2 h6 12 ♗xf6 ♗xf6 13 ♘bd2
♘d7 14 ♗c4 ♘b6 15 ♗b3 ♗d7 16
a4 a5 17 ♘c4 ± Torre-Anand, Manila
1992; 8...♘fd7!? 9 ♗g5 ♘c6 is interesting; the idea is that 10 d5 ♘ce5
11 ♗xe7 ♘xf3+ forces 12 gxf3 ∞,
while 10 e5?! cxd4 11 cxd4 dxe5 12
d5 ♘c5! 13 dxc6 ♖d8! 14 cxb7

♗xb7 15 ♕c2 ♖xd3 ∓ was Schmitt-diel-Ki.Georgiev, Dortmund 1991) 9 dxe5 dxe5 10 ♘bd2 ♖d8 11 ♕c2 ♘bd7 12 a4 b6 13 ♗c4 ♘f8 14 ♘g5 ♖d7 15 a5 ♖b8 16 axb6 axb6 17 ♗b5 ♖d8 18 ♘c4 ± Kamsky-J.Pol-gar, Madrid 1994.

d2) 7 ♗f4!? 0-0 8 ♘bd2 (8 ♖e1!? ♗g4 9 ♘bd2 cxd4 10 cxd4 ♘c6 11 h3 ♗xf3 12 ♘xf3 e5 13 ♗e3 d5!? 14 ♘xe5 dxe4 15 ♘xc6 ♕xc6 16 ♖c1 ♕b6 17 ♗c4 ♕xb2 18 ♖b1 ♕c3 19 ♕a4! ♘d7! 20 ♖ec1 ♘b6 21 ♗xf7+! ♖xf7 22 ♖xb6 ♕d3 23 ♖e6 with a slight plus, Tzermiadianos-Tregu-bov,Iraklion 1995) 8...♘bd7 9 ♖e1 e5 10 dxe5 dxe5 11 ♗g3 ♘h5 12 a4 b6 13 a5! bxa5 14 ♕a4 ♘b6 15 ♕xa5 ♗g4 (15...♘xg3 16 hxg3 f5 17 ♗a6! ± Karpov) 16 ♗e2! ♖fd8 17 ♘c4 ♘f4 18 ♗xf4 exf4 19 e5! ± Karpov-Polgar, Dos Hermanas 1994.

5 ♘f3

5 dxc5 transposes to analysis in Game 64.

5 ♘e2 g6 is unclear, e.g. 6 0-0 ♗g7 7 h3 0-0 8 ♗e3 (8 d5 ♘e5 9 ♗c2 b5 with counterplay, S.Arkell-Wilder, London 1989) 8...cxd4 9 cxd4 ♘b4 10 ♘bc3 ♘xd3 11 ♕xd3 ♗d7 12 ♖ac1 ♕a5 13 a3 ♖fc8 14 d5 ♗e8 = Kamsky-Dzindzichashvili, Exhibition game, New York 1989.

Instead 5 d5 ♘e5 6 ♗c2 g6 7 f4 ♘ed7 8 ♘f3 ♘b6 9 0-0 ♗g7 10 ♕e1 0-0 11 ♕h4 e6 12 dxe6 ♗xe6 13 ♘bd2 ♘g4 14 ♕e1 ♘c4 15 ♘b3 ♖e8 16 h3 ♘f6 17 ♕h4 ♘h5 18 ♕f2 ½-½ was Motwani-Xu, Manila OL 1992.

5...♗g4

5...g6 and now:

a) 6 h3 ♗g7 (6...♘d7 7 ♗c2 ♗g7 8 d5 ♘a5 9 0-0 b5 10 a3 0-0 11 ♖e1 ♕c7 12 ♗g5 ♖e8 13 ♘bd2 ♖b8 14 ♖c1 ♘c4 15 ♘xc4 bxc4 16 ♖b1 e6 = Godena-Arnason, Novi Sad OL 1990) 7 0-0 0-0 8 ♖e1 ♘d7 9 dxc5 ♘xc5 10 ♗c2 b5 11 ♗e3 ♖b8 12 a3 a5 = Kotliar-Fedorowicz, New York 1992.

b) 6 0-0 ♗g7 7 d5 ♘a5 (another idea is 7...♘b8!?) 8 ♘bd2 b6 9 ♖b1 0-0 10 b4 ♘b7 11 a3 ♕c7 12 ♗b2 e5 13 dxe6 fxe6 14 e5! dxe5 15 c4 ♘d7 16 ♘g5 ♕d6 17 ♘de4 ♕e7 18 ♕g4 ♖f5 19 h4 and White's posi-tional pawn sacrifice has given him an excellent game, Kaufman-Ehl-vest, Philadelphia 1995.

6 d5

Almost invariably played, even though 6 ♗e3 e6 7 0-0 ♗e7 8 ♘bd2 cxd4 9 cxd4 d5 10 e5 ♘d7 11 ♖c1 ♖c8 12 h3 ♗h5 13 g4 ♗g6 14 ♘e1 ♘b4 was unclear in Fong-Benjamin, USA 1987.

6...♗xf3

As 6...♘e5 can be met by 7 ♘xe5! dxe5 (7...♗xd1? 8 ♗b5+ wins) 8 f3 ± Godena-Cesareo, Geneva 1993, or even better 8 ♕xg4! ♘xg4 9 ♗b5+. Instead White has a space advantage after 6...♘b8, e.g. 7 ♘bd2 (7 h3 ♗xf3 8 ♕xf3 g6 9 0-0 ♗g7 10 ♕e2 0-0 11 c4 e6 12 ♘c3 exd5 13 cxd5 ♘bd7 14 ♗f4 ± Shaked-Fedoro-wicz, Philadelphia 1994) 7...g6 8 h3 ♗c8 9 ♘c4 ♗g7 10 a4 0-0 11 ♗f4 ♘a6 12 0-0 ♘c7 13 ♖e1 Sveshni-kov-Loncar, Bled 1994.

7 ♕xf3

The natural recapture, especially because White can retain the two bishops. 7 gxf3 ♘e5 8 ♗e2 (8 ♗c2 g6 9 f4 ♘ed7 10 ♗e3 ♗h6 11 ♘d2 ♘h5 ∓ L.Hansen-Mortensen, Denmark 1994) 8...♘ed7 9 c4 g6 10 ♘c3 ♗g7 11 ♗e3 0-0 12 ♕d2 ♖e8 13 f4 a6 14 0-0 ♕a5 15 a4, Bacrot-Aronian, Szeged 1994, is assessed as ± in *Informator*, but it looks odd for White to gratuitously accept doubled pawns.

7...♘e5 8 ♗b5+ ♘fd7 (D)

Or 8...♘ed7 9 a4 (9 0-0 a6 10 ♗a4 g6 11 ♗c2 ♗g7 12 a4 0-0 13 ♕e2 ♖e8 14 ♗g5 h6 15 ♗h4 b5!? was Sermek-Cebalo, Pula 1994, as 16 axb5 axb5 17 ♖xa8 ♕xa8 18 ♕xb5 can by 18...♖b8) 9...g6 10 a5 a6 11 ♗a4 ♗g7 12 ♘d2 0-0 13 ♘c4 ± Nun-Khalifman, Sochi 1989 and Schandorff-E.Mortensen, Aalborg 1994.

9 ♕e2 ± a6 10 ♗a4 b5

10...c4 11 0-0 b5 (11...♘d3 12 ♗e3 b5 13 ♗d1! ± Smagin) 12 ♗c2 ♘c5 13 b4! ♘cd3 14 ♗e3 (now the threat is f4, so Black must offer a pawn sacrifice) 14...g5 15 ♗xg5 ♖g8 16 ♗e3 ♕d7 and instead of 17 f4 ♗h6 with complications, Rausis-Barczay, Paris 1994, Rausis suggests 17 ♘d2 ♕h3 18 f3 ♗h6 19 ♔h1 ±.

11 ♗c2 ♘b6 12 0-0 ♕d7 13 h3!? g6!? 14 a4 (14 f4 is also slightly better for White) **14...bxa4 15 ♘d2! ♕b5 16 c4! ♕b4** (16...♘exc4? 17 ♗d3) **17 f4 ♘exc4 18 ♘xc4 ♕xc4 19 ♗xa4+ ♔d8 20 ♕e1! ± ♗g7 21 ♗c6 ♗d4+ 22 ♔h1 ♖c8! 23 ♗d2** (better is 23 ♗e3!) **23...♖xc6! 24 dxc6 ♔c7 25 ♖b1 ♕c2! 26 ♗c3 ♗xc3 27 bxc3 ♔xc6 28 ♖f2 ♕d3 29 ♖d2 ♕c4 30 ♖db2 ♖b8 31 e5!? a5 32 ♕h4 dxe5?!** (32...♕e6 ∞ Smagin) **33 ♕xe7 ♘d5 34 ♕xf7 ♖xb2 35 ♕e8+ ♔d6?** (35...♔c7 36 ♕xe5+ ♔c6 37 ♖xb2 ♕f1+ 38 ♔h2 ♕xf4+ 39 ♕xf4 ♘xf4 40 c4! ± Smagin) **36 fxe5+ ♔c7 37 ♕f7+ 1-0**

Game 66
Adams – Gelfand
Wijk aan Zee Ct (5) 1994

1 e4 c5 2 c3 d6 3 d4 ♘f6 4 ♗d3 cxd4

Black does not have to swap pawns before fianchettoing. However, if he doesn't, White can try to exploit the omission (by capturing on c5 for example), or continue normally (with 5 ♘f3, 6 h3 and 7 0-0) when sooner or later Black will probably play ...♕c7, transposing to lines examined in the course of the previous game. After 4...g6 play can continue:

a) 5 ♘e2 ♗g7 6 0-0 0-0 7 f3 (7 h3 ♘c6 8 d5 ♘e5 9 ♗c2 b5 10 f4 ♘c4 11 a4 bxa4 12 ♖xa4 ♘b6 ∞ Handoko-Juswanto, Djakarta Z 1993) 7...♘bd7 8 ♗e3 a6 9 a4 cxd4 10 cxd4 e5 11 ♘bc3 (11 d5 ♘h5 12 ♘bc3 f5 gives a Sämisch King's Indian type position, Striković-Franco, Palma de Mallorca 1995) 11...exd4 12 ♗xd4 ♘e5 13 ♘f4! ± Sveshnikov-Rustemov, Russian Ch 1995.

b) 5 dxc5!? dxc5 6 e5 with four lines:

b1) 6...♘g4 7 ♗b5+ gives White an edge, since 7...♗d7?? 8 e6! wins, Ankerst-Heinatz, Bundesliga 1992.

b2) Instead 6...♘fd7 7 e6 fxe6 is a cheap investment to wreck the black pawn structure.

b3) 6...c4!? is a spirited try, e.g. 7 ♕a4+ ♗d7 8 ♕xc4 ♘g4 9 ♘f3 ♗g7 10 h3 ♘xe5 11 ♘xe5 ♗xe5 12 ♗h6 ± Kuijf-Van de Mortel, Wijk aan Zee 1996.

b4) 6...♘d5 7 ♗e4:

b41) 7...e6 8 ♘f3 ♘c6 9 c4 ♘de7 10 ♕xd8+ ♔xd8 11 ♘c3 ± Sermek-Mali, Bled 1994.

b42) 7...♘c7 8 ♕xd8+ ± Van der Werf-Mascini, Dutch Ch 1992 and Sermek-Cebalo, Maribor 1994.

b43) 7...♘b6 8 ♕xd8+ ♔xd8 9 ♘a3 ♘c6 10 ♘f3 ♗f5 and then 11 ♗xf5?! gxf5 12 e6 fxe6 13 ♗e3 ♖g8 14 ♘g5 ♖g6 15 h4 h5 16 0-0-0+ ♔e8 17 ♗xc5 e5 was unclear in Lautier-Polgar, Dos Hermanas 1994, but Lautier later gave the improvement 11 ♗xc6 bxc6 12 ♗e3 ♖b8 13 0-0-0+ ±.

c) 5 h3 ♗g7 6 ♘f3 transposes to the following line with 5 ♘f3.

d) 5 ♘f3 ♗g7 6 h3 (6 0-0 0-0 7 h3 is the same) 6...0-0 7 0-0:

d1) 7...♕c7!? transposes to the 4...♕c7 lines of Game 65, and is a very common way to reach that variation, while 7...♘fd7 and 7...a6 have been seen a number of times.

d2) The developing 7...♘bd7 is more logical: 8 ♖e1 cxd4 9 cxd4 e5 10 ♗e3 exd4 11 ♗xd4! ♘c5 12 ♘c3 b6 13 ♗c4 ♗b7 14 ♗d5 ± Rausis-Bernard, Paris 1994.

d3) 7...♘c6 8 d5! (8 ♖e1 ♘d7 9 d5 ♘ce5 10 ♘xe5 dxe5 11 ♗f1 f5 12 exf5 gxf5 13 f4 e4 14 ♗e3 ♘b6! 15 ♕b3 ♕xd5 16 ♗xc5 ♗e6 17 ♕xd5 ♘xd5 ∓ Men-Ftačnik, Philadelphia 1991 shows how Black can also have chances in this variation) 8...♘a5 (8...♘b8 but White has an edge, as in Torre-Sitanggang, Beijing 1992 and Schmittdiel-Arnason, St Martin 1993) 9 c4! ("in such King's Indian structures the knight is almost always misplaced on a5" – Nunn; 9 ♘a3 b6 10 ♗d2 e6 11 c4 ♖e8?! 12 ♖e1 ♘d7?! 13 ♖b1 ♘e5 14 ♘xe5 ♗xe5 15 f4 ± Yusupov-Speelman, Munich 1992) 9...a6 10 ♘c3 ♖b8 11 a4 ♗d7 12 ♕c2 b5 13 cxb5 c4 14 ♗e2 axb5 15 axb5 ♗xb5 16 ♘xb5 ♖xb5 17 ♘d4 ± Sveshnikov-Tregubov, Ljubljana 1994.

5 cxd4 g6 *(D)*

5...♘c6 6 ♘f3 (or 6 ♘e2 with King's Indian transpositional possibilities – see later) 6...♗g4 (after 6...♕b6!?, 7 d5 ♘b4 8 0-0 ♘xd3 9 ♕xd3 g6 10 ♗e3 ♕d8 was not so clear in Sermek-Vescovi, Groningen 1993; 7 ♘c3 ♗g4 8 d5 is one possible improvement) 7 d5 ♗xf3 (7...♘e5 8 ♘xe5! dxe5 9 ♕b3 ± Schmittdiel-Yrjölä, Gausdal 1987) 8 ♕xf3 ♘e5 9 ♗b5+ with an edge – this has happened in several games.

Again 5...e5!? is possible:

a) 6 ♘e2 ♗e7 7 0-0 0-0 8 ♘bc3 ♘bd7 9 ♗c4 ♕c7 10 ♗b3 b6 11 ♖e1

♗b7 12 ♘g3 g6 13 ♗h6 ♖fe8 14 h3 a6 15 ♕d2 ♗f8 16 ♗xf8 ♖xf8 17 ♖ad1 ± Kengis-Kotliar, Philadelphia 1989.

b) 6 ♘f3 exd4 (6...♗g4!? 7 ♕a4+ ♘fd7 8 ♘bd2 ♘c6 9 d5 ♘c5 10 ♕a3 ♘xd3+ 11 ♕xd3 ♘b8 12 h3 ♗d7 ∞ Schmittdiel-Minasian, Groningen 1990) 7 ♘xd4 ♘c6 (7...♗e7 8 ♘c3 0-0 9 0-0 ♘c6 10 ♘xc6 bxc6 11 ♗f4?! ♘d7 12 ♕c2 ♘e5 13 ♗xe5 dxe5 14 ♘a4 ♕d6 15 ♖fd1 ♕g6 16 ♗e2 ♖b8 ∞ S.Arkell-Sadler, Cappelle la Grande 1993) 8 ♘xc6 bxc6 9 0-0 ♗e7 10 ♕c2 ♗b7 11 ♘c3 (also 11 b3 0-0 12 ♗b2 ± Van Mil-Bosboom, Dutch Ch 1991) 11...0-0 12 ♖d1 ♕a5 13 ♗f4 ♖ad8 14 b4 ♕h5 15 ♘e2 g6 16 h3 ♘d7 17 ♘d4 c5 18 ♘f3 g5 19 ♗g3 ± Godena-Cebalo, Geneva 1996.

c) 6 d5!? ♗e7 7 ♘e2 0-0 8 ♘g3?! (8 f3 ♘e8 9 ♗e3 ♗g5 10 ♗f2 Yermolinsky) 8...♘bd7 9 0-0 ♘e8 10 ♘c3 g6?! (10...♗g5 11 ♗xg5 ♕xg5 12 ♕c1!?; 10...♘c5 11 ♗c2 a5) 11 ♗h6 ♘g7 12 ♕d2 ♘f6 13 f3 ± Shaked-Yermolinsky, San Francisco 1995.

6 ♘c3

White can also play 6 h3 or 6 ♘f3 first. Surprisingly 6 ♘e2!? can eventually transpose into a King's Indian Defence: 6...♗g7 7 0-0 0-0 8 ♘bc3 ♘c6 (8...e5 9 d5 ♘bd7 10 f3 ♘c5 11 ♗c2 a5 12 ♗e3, Rozentalis-Yrjölä, Voronezh 1987, is a position normally reached via a Sämisch, e.g. 1 d4 ♘f6 2 c4 g6 3 ♘c3 ♗g7 4 e4 d6 5 f3 0-0 6 ♗e3 c6 7 ♗d3 e5 8 d5 ♘bd7 9 ♘ge2 ♘c5 10 ♗c2 cxd5 11 cxd5 a5 12 0-0 as in Petrosian-Gligorić, USSR v Yugoslavia 1973, and several other games) 9 f3 (9 a3 e5 10 d5 ♘d4 ∞ Rozentalis-Gelfand, Uzhgorod 1987) 9...e5 10 d5 ♘e7 11 ♗e3 ♘e8 (this less common King's Indian position can be reached via 1 d4 ♘f6 2 c4 g6 3 ♘c3 ♗g7 4 e4 d6 5 ♗d3 ♘c6 6 ♘ge2 e5 7 d5 ♘e7 8 f3 c6 9 ♗e3 cxd5 10 cxd5 0-0 11 0-0 ♘e8 as in the game Hort-Kljako, Lugano 1984) 12 ♕b3 Rozentalis-Smirin, Vilnius 1988. These transpositions are quite promising for White, and the reader is referred to any of the many books on the King's Indian for further study.

6...♗g7 7 h3

Anticipating any thoughts Black may have had of pinning with 7 ♘f3 0-0 8 0-0 ♗g4 or 7 ♘f3 ♗g4, although 8 ♕a4+!? worked out well for White after 8...♘fd7 9 ♘g5 ♘c6 10 h3 ♗e6 11 ♘xe6 in Manca-Cebalo, Reggio Emilia 1991.

7 e5 dxe5 8 dxe5 ♘fd7 9 f4 ♘c6 (or 9...♘c5 10 ♗b5+ ♗d7 11 ♗e3 ♗xb5 12 ♕xd8+ ♔xd8 13 ♘xb5 ♘d3+ 14 ♔e2 ♘xb2 15 ♘f3 ♘c6 16 ♘g5 with excellent play for the pawn, Motwani-Chiong, Bern 1992)

10 ♗e3 ♘b6 11 ♘f3 0-0 12 0-0 ♗e6 13 b3 ♘b4 14 ♗e4 ♘6d5 15 ♘xd5 ♗xd5 16 ♕d4 ♗xe4 17 ♕xe4 ♘d5 18 ♗d4 e6 ∞ Motwani-Thorhallsson, Iceland 1992.

For 7 ♘ge2!? see the 6 ♘e2 note at White's move six.

7...0-0

Playing 7...e5!? immediately gives White the option of 8 dxe5 dxe5 9 ♗b5+!? (9 ♘f3) 9...♗d7 10 ♕d6, though 10...♕e7 11 ♗xd7+ ♘bxd7 12 ♕xe7+ ♔xe7 13 ♗e3 ♖hc8 14 f3 ♔e6 15 ♘ge2 ♗f8 did not seem much for White in Smagin-Smirin, Minsk 1986.

8 ♘f3 e5 (D)

8...a6?! is now Torre-Barcenilla, Bacolod 1991: 9 0-0 b5 10 e5 ♘e8 11 ♗e4 ♖a7 12 ♗e3 ±.

Instead 8...♘c6 9 0-0 e5 10 d5!? (10 dxe5 dxe5 would be the main game) 11...♘d4 11 ♘xd4 exd4 12 ♘e2 ♖e8 13 ♘g3 ♘d7 14 b3 ♕h4 (Black should probably try 14...h5!? 15 ♗b2 h4 16 ♘e2 ♘c5 ∞) 15 ♗b2 ♘e5 16 ♗xd4 f5 17 ♗xe5! ♗xe5 18 exf5! ♗xa1 19 ♕xa1 ± Emms-Mestel, British Ch 1992.

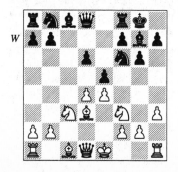

9 dxe5

After 9 0-0 Black might very well try 9...exd4 10 ♘xd4 ♘c6 transposing to Haba-Gelfand, Halle 1987: 11 ♘xc6 bxc6 12 ♗f4 ♗e6 13 ♕d2 d5 14 ♖fd1 ♖e8 15 exd5 ♘xd5 16 ♘xd5 ♕xd5 =. Alternatively 9...♘c6 10 ♗e3 (10 d5 or 10 dxe5) and Black equalises by means of 10...exd4 11 ♘xd4 d5!, as in Hresc-Cebalo, Vrbas 1982.

9...dxe5 10 0-0 ♘c6 11 ♗e3

After 11 ♗c4 ♕xd1 12 ♖xd1 ♘a5 13 ♗d5 ♘xd5 14 ♘xd5 b6 15 b3 ♗e6 16 ♗a3 ♖fd8 17 ♘c7 White was better in Khuzman-Minasian, Belgrade 1989, so Black could consider either 11...♕e7, or offering a slightly suspicious looking pawn sacrifice with 11...♘a5, for example 12 ♕xd8 (12 ♗e2 ♗e6 13 ♗e3 ♘c4 14 ♗c5 ♕xd1 15 ♖fxd1 ♘xb2 16 ♗xf8 ♘xd1 17 ♗xg7 ♘xc3 18 ♗xf6 ♘xe2+ 19 ♔h2 ♘c3 20 ♘g5 ♖e8 21 ♖c1 h6 22 ♖xc3 hxg5 23 a3 ♖c8 ½-½ B.Andersson-Engqvist, Stockholm 1987) 12...♖xd8 13 ♘xe5 ♘xc4 14 ♘xc4 b5 15 ♘xb5 ♘xe4 Jahn-Choluskina, Debrecen wom Echt 1992.

11...♗e6

a) 11...♖e8 12 ♗c4 ♗e6 13 ♗xe6 fxe6 (13...♖xe6 14 ♗g5 ♖d6 15 ♘d5 ±) 14 ♕b3 ± Luther-Gauglitz, E.German Ch 1989.

b) 11...♘h5 12 ♘d5 (also 12 ♗c4 ♘d4 13 ♘d5 ♘e6 14 ♕b3 ± Nun-Trapl, Namestovo 1987) 12...♘f4 13 ♘xf4 exf4 14 ♗xf4 ♗xb2 15 ♖b1 ♗g7 16 ♗c4 h6 17 ♕c1 ♔h7 18 ♖d1 ♕f6 19 e5 ♕e7 20 e6! ♗xe6 21 ♗d6 +− Hort-Hodgson, San Bernardino 1992.

c) 11...♕e7 12 ♖c1 (12 ♘d5
♘xd5 13 exd5 ♘b4 14 ♗c4 ♗f5 15
♖c1 ♖ac8 16 ♕d2 ♘c2! ∓ Rabiega-
Milov, Budapest 1993; 12 ♗g5 ♗e6
13 ♘d5 ♗xd5 14 exd5 ♘d4 15
♘xd4 exd4 16 ♖e1 ♕c5 = Sermek-
Veličković, Portorož 1994; 12 ♗c4
♗e6 13 ♗xe6 ♕xe6 14 ♕e2 ♖fd8 15
♖fd1 h6 16 ♕b5 b6 17 ♘d5 ♖ac8 18
♘xf6+ ♕xf6 19 ♕a4 ± Rosandić-
Grgurić, Pula 1994) 12...♖d8 13 ♕e2
♗e6 14 ♗g5 ♘h5 15 ♘xe6 fxe6 16
g3 ♕f6 17 ♗c4 ♘f4 18 gxf4 exf4 19
♕g4 fxe3 20 fxe3 ♕e5 21 ♕xe6+ ±
Lobron-Davies, Bundesliga 1986.

12 ♗b5! ♘a5
Otherwise Black may be saddled
with a weak pawn on c6: 12...♕b8
13 ♗xc6 bxc6 14 ♕c2 ♘h5 15 ♘a4
h6 16 ♘c5 ♕e8 17 ♖ad1 ♕e7 18
♘xe6 ♕xe6 19 b3 ♘f4 20 ♖d2 ± Lo-
bron-Christiansen, Germany 1994,
or 12...♘h5 13 ♗xc6 bxc6 14 ♕xd8
♖fxd8 15 ♖fd1 ♖db8 (½-½ Her-
mann-Chandler, Bundesliga 1985)
when 16 b3 gives White a clearly
better endgame.

13 ♕e2 ± (D)
White has a pleasant game, and
will gain time bringing a rook to the
open d-file; if 13 ♗c5 Adams gives
13...♕xd1 14 ♖fxd1 ♖fc8 15 ♗d6
♘c4 16 ♗xc4 ♖xc4 17 ♘xe5 ♖xc3
18 bxc3 ♘xe4 ∞.

13...a6 14 ♗d3 ♘c6?! (14...♘h5!?
Adams) **15 ♖fd1 ♕c8?!** (15...♕a5)

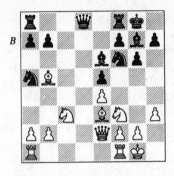

16 ♖ac1 ♖d8 17 ♘a4 ♘d7 18 ♗c4
♗xc4 19 ♕xc4 ♘d4 (Black is passive after 19...♕c7, but Gelfand will
get little for his pawn sacrifice) 20
♕xc8 ♖axc8 21 ♖xc8 ♖xc8 22 ♘xd4
exd4 23 ♗xd4 ♗xd4 24 ♖xd4 ♖c1+
25 ♔h2 ♘e5 26 ♖d5 ♘c6 27 ♖d2 g5
28 ♔g3 ♔g7 29 h4 gxh4+ 30 ♔xh4
♘e5 31 b3 ♖h1+ 32 ♔g3 h5 33 ♘c5
h4+ 34 ♔f4 ♘g6+ 35 ♔e3 ♖e1+ 36
♖e2 ♖c1 37 ♘xb7 ♖c3+ 38 ♔d4
♖c1 39 ♔e3 ♖c3+ 40 ♔d2 ♖c7 41
♘d6 ♖d7 42 e5 ♘xe5 43 ♖xe5
♖xd6+ 44 ♔e3 ♔g6 45 ♖e4 ♔g5 46
♔e2 f5 47 ♖a4 ♖e6+ 48 ♔f1 ♖d6 49
♔g1 ♖d1+ 50 ♔h2 ♖d6 51 ♖a5
♔g4 52 ♖a4+ ♔g5 53 g3 hxg3+ 54
♔xg3 ♖d3+ 55 f3 ♖d6 56 ♖a5 ♖c6
57 b4 ♖b6 58 a3 ♖d6 59 ♖c5 ♖d3
60 ♖a5 ♖b3 61 ♖xa6 f4+ 62 ♔g2
♔h5 63 ♖a7 ♔g5 64 ♖a8 ♔f5 65
♖a5+ ♔f6 66 a4 ♖xb4 67 ♔h3 ♔e6
68 ♔g4 ♖c4 69 ♖a8 ♖b4 70 ♔g5
♖c4 71 a5 ♖a4 72 ♖a6+ ♔f7 73
♔f5 ♔e7 74 ♖a8 ♔f7 75 ♖a7+ 1-0

23 Other 2nd Moves for Black

All four of these second move alternatives (2...♕a5, 2...g6, 2...b6 and 2...e5) are better than their reputations, although objectively none clearly achieves full equality. 2...b6 (as utilised by the fighting GM Tony Miles) is a good choice against a weaker player. Natural (but nevertheless inaccurate) moves by White can result in Black successfully exchanging his knight for bishop with the manoeuvre ♘c6-b4xd3.

2...e5!? has become a tenacious defence: after 3 ♘f3 ♘c6 4 ♗c4 the clever 4...♕c7!? means that White's ♘g5 attacks can be answered by ...♘d8. White can choose between quiet Lopez-like manoeuvres (d3, a4, ♘bd2-f1-e3) or choosing the moment to blast the game open with ♘g5 and f4 in some position. Further tests are needed.

Game 67
Sveshnikov – Kupreichik
USSR 1984

1 e4 c5 2 c3 ♕a5 *(D)*

Black gambles that, in order to hold up White's d4, it is worth breaking the rule about not developing your queen early. There is certainly no outright refutation, and White must be content with a potential gain of time exploiting the misplaced queen at a later date.

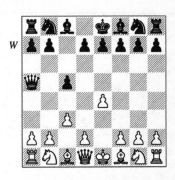

3 ♘f3

3 ♘a3 and 3 ♗c4 are sidelines.

3...♘c6

The Hungarian grandmaster Istvan Csom has had a few games with 3...d6!? (planning ...♘f6), though not against fellow GMs, who might have given him a tougher time:

a) 4 ♗c4 ♘c6 5 0-0 ♘f6 6 ♖e1 ♗g4 7 ♘a3 e6 8 h3 ♗xf3 9 ♕xf3 ♗e7 10 ♗b3 0-0 11 d3 ♘d4!? 12 ♕d1 ♘xb3 13 ♕xb3 ♕a6 = Werner-Csom, Lenk 1994.

b) 4 ♗e2 ♘f6 (4...♘c6 5 0-0 ♘f6 6 d3 ♗g4 7 ♘bd2 e6 8 h3 ♗h5 9 ♘h2 ♗xe2 10 ♕xe2 ♗e7 11 ♘c4 ♕a6 12 ♗g5 ♖d8 13 ♗xf6 ♗xf6 14 ♘g4 ♗e7 ∞ Eynard-Csom, Mendrisio 1989) 5 d3 (5 ♕c2) 5...c4!? 6 h3 cxd3 7 ♗xd3 ♘bd7 8 0-0 g6 9 ♘bd2 ♕c7 = Šibarević-Csom, Mendrisio 1989.

c) Perhaps White should play to harass the queen straight away with 4 ♘a3 ♘f6 5 e5 dxe5 6 ♘c4, e.g.

6...♕c7 7 ♘cxe5 e6 8 d4 cxd4 9 ♕xd4 ♗c5 10 ♕h4 ♘bd7 11 ♗f4 ♕b6 12 ♘c4 ♕c6 13 ♗d3 ♗e7 14 ♗g5 ♘c5 15 ♗c2 ♕a6 16 0-0 ♘ce4 17 ♘ce5 ♘d6 18 ♗a4+ b5 19 ♗c2 ± V.Ivanov-Odeev, Moscow 1991.

4 a3!?

Not strongest, but still dangerous for Black. 4 ♗d3 has been seen a few times, as has 4 ♗c4, e.g. 4...d6 5 0-0 ♘f6 6 ♖e1 ± b5!? (6...e5!? 7 ♘g5 ♘d8 8 ♕b3 ♕c7) 7 ♗d5 ♗d7 8 b4 cxb4 9 cxb4 ♕b6 10 a4 (10 ♘c3) 10...♘xd5 11 exd5 ♘xb4 12 ♘c3 g6 13 a5 ♕d8 ∞ Keitlinghaus-Movsesian, Czechoslovakia 1996. After 4 ♘a3!? Black should prefer 4...e6 5 ♘c4 ♕c7 6 d4 cxd4 7 ♘xd4 a6 8 ♗d3 b5 9 ♘e3 ♘f6 10 0-0 ♗b7 11 ♘f3?! ♗d6 12 ♖e1 ♘e5 ∓ Alapin-Tarrasch, Vienna 1898 (!) to 4...d6 5 ♘c4 ♕d8 6 d4 ♘f6 7 d5 ♘b8 8 ♗d3 g6 9 ♗g5 ♗g7 10 0-0 0-0 11 a4 h6 12 ♗h4 ♘a6 13 ♘fd2 ♘c7 14 f4 ± Afek-Djurić, Rishon le Zion 1992.

4 d4! is best: 4...cxd4 5 b4 ♕c7 6 b5 ♘e5 7 ♘xe5 ♕xe5 8 ♕xd4 ± ♕c7 (8...♕xd4 9 cxd4 d6 10 ♗e3 ♘f6 11 f3 d5 12 ♘d2 e6 13 ♗d3 ♗b4 14 ♔e2 0-0 15 e5 ♘d7 16 ♖hc1 ± Hauchard-San Marco, French Cht 1989) and here, instead of 9 a4?! e5 10 ♕c4 ♕xc4 11 ♗xc4 ♘f6 12 f3 d6 13 ♗e3 ♗e6 14 ♘d2 d5 = Makropoulos-Ljubojević, Athens 1981, White has other tries to exploit his lead in development, e.g. 9 ♗c4 e6 10 0-0 b6 11 ♖d1 ♗b7 12 ♗f4! d6 13 ♗xd6 ♗xd6 14 ♕xd6 ♕xd6 15 ♖xd6 ♗xe4 16 ♗xe6 ♗xb1 17 ♗d5 ♔e7 18 ♗xa8 ♔xd6 19 ♖xb1 ♘f6 20 ♗c6 ± Blauert-Tataev, Cuxhaven

1993 or even 9 e5!? Kopp-Gerber, Germany 1993.

4...e6

On 4...d6 Sveshnikov gives 5 b4! cxb4 6 cxb4 ♘xb4 7 axb4 ♕xa1 8 ♘c3 as unclear.

5 d4 ♘xd4! 6 ♘xd4 cxd4 7 b4 ♕c7

7...♕e5 8 cxd4!? (8 ♕xd4 ♕xd4 9 cxd4 d5 =) 8...♕xe4+ 9 ♗e3 ♕c6! 10 d5!, again unclear, is more Sveshnikov analysis.

8 cxd4 ♘f6 9 ♗d3 d5 10 e5 ♘d7 11 ♖a2 ± ♘b6 12 ♖c2 ♕d8 13 ♕g4 g6 14 ♗g5 ♗e7 15 ♗h6 ♗d7 16 0-0 ♗a4? (16...a6 17 ♘d2 ♗b5) 17 ♖c3 a6 18 ♖fc1 ♖c8 19 ♖xc8 ♘xc8 20 ♘d2 ♘a7 21 ♘f3 ♗f8 22 ♕f4 ♘c6 23 ♗xf8 ♔xf8 24 ♕h6+ ♔g8 25 h4 ± ♕f8 26 ♕f4 h6 27 h5 g5 28 ♕f6 ♕g7 29 g4! ♕xf6 30 exf6 ♔f8 31 ♘e5 ♔e8 32 ♗xa6 ♘xe5 33 dxe5 ♔d7 34 ♗xb7 ♖b8 35 ♗a6 ♗b3 36 ♗d3 ♖a8 37 b5 ♖a4 38 b6 ♖xg4+ 39 ♔h2 ♗c4 40 ♗g6! ♗e2 41 f4 ♗c4 42 ♗xf7 ♖xf4 43 ♖b1 ♔c8 44 ♗xe6+ ♔b8 45 ♖b4 ♔b7 46 f7 1-0

Game 68
Adams – Dzindzichashvili
New York PCA rpd 1994

1 e4 c5 2 c3 g6

A related system, 2...d5 3 exd5 ♕xd5 4 d4 g6!?, has been developed over the past few years. Although Black has committed his queen to the d5-square, this system does cut out White's irritating option of transposing to a Caro-Kann as in the main line. Play usually continues 5 ♘f3 (5 ♘a3 and 5 ♗e3 are reasonable; after

5 dxc5!? ♕xc5 6 ♗e3 ♕c7 either no-one has spotted or dares to play the startling 7 ♗xa7!?!? suggested by Fritz – after 7...♖xa7, 8 ♕d4 forks both black rooks!) 5...♗g7 and now:

a) 6 dxc5 ♕xc5 7 ♗e3 ♕c7 8 h3 ♘c6 9 ♘a3 ♘f6 10 ♘b5 ♕b8 11 g3 0-0 12 ♗g2 ♗f5 13 0-0 ♖d8 14 ♕b3 ♗e6 ½-½ Rozentalis-Hulak, Debrecen Echt 1992.

b) 6 ♗e2 cxd4 7 cxd4 ♘h6!? (7...♘f6 8 ♘c3 ♕d8 9 0-0 0-0 is unclear, e.g. 10 ♗g5 ♗e6 11 ♕d2 ♘c6 12 ♖fd1 ♘d5 13 ♗h6 ♕a5 14 ♗xg7 ♔xg7 15 a3 ♖ad8 Neyer-Wojtkiewicz, Bern 1996) 8 ♘c3 ♕a5 9 0-0 0-0 10 ♕b3 ♘f5 11 d5 ♘a6 12 ♗g5 ♖e8 13 ♗b5 ♘c5 14 ♕c4 ♘d7 15 ♕e2 a6 16 ♗d3 ♘f6 17 ♗c4 ♘d6 18 ♗b3 ♗f5 19 ♖ac1 ♘d7 20 ♗d2 ♕b4!? with a good game for Black, Gufeld-Bronstein, USSR Ch 1960.

c) 6 ♗e3 cxd4 7 cxd4 ♘f6 (not 7...♘h6?? 8 ♕c1 +– attacking c8 and h6, as in T.Reich-Ma.Pavlović, Munich 1992) 8 ♘c3 ♕a5 9 ♗c4 0-0 10 h3 (10 0-0 ♘bd7 11 a3 ♘b6 12 ♗a2 ♘bd5 13 ♖c1?! ♗e6 14 ♕d2 ♘xe3 15 fxe3 ♗xa2 16 ♘xa2 ♕xd2 17 ♘xd2 ♘d5 ∓ G.Mohr-Hulak, Portorož 1993) 10...♘bd7 11 0-0 ♘b6 12 ♗b3 ♘bd5 13 ♗d2 ♕d8 14 ♖e1 b6 15 ♗g5 ♗b7 16 ♘e5 ♘xc3 17 bxc3 ♖c8 18 c4 ♘e4 19 ♗f4 e6 20 ♕d3 ± Fedorowicz-Larsen, Buenos Aires 1991.

d) 6 ♘a3 cxd4 7 ♗c4!? (also 7 ♘b5 ♘a6 8 ♗e3!? ♗g4 9 ♕a4 ♔f8 10 ♘fxd4 ♘f6 11 h3 e5 12 hxg4 exd4 13 ♕xd4! ♖e8 14 ♗e2 ♕xg2 15 0-0-0 ± Rausis-Permjakov, Latvian Ch 1994) 7...♕d8 (7...♕e4+ 8 ♗e3! as on 8...dxe3, 9 ♗xf7+!) 8 ♕b3 e6 9 ♘xd4 ♘e7 10 ♗g5 h6 11 ♗e3 ♘d5 12 ♗xd5 exd5 13 0-0 ± Sveshnikov-Cvitan, Tilburg 1993.

3 d4

3 ♘f3!? is an interesting alternate move-order which can stop Black getting either of the Caro-Kanns coming up. After 3...♗g7 4 d4 cxd4 5 cxd4 d5 6 exd5 ♘f6 the transposition is actually to B27 (the Sicilian starting 1 e4 c5 2 ♘f3 g6), and after 7 ♗b5+ *ECO* considers White has a slight edge.

3...cxd4 4 cxd4 d5 *(D)*

Otherwise ♘c3 will prevent this break. For example, 4...♗g7 5 ♘c3 d6 6 ♗e3 ♘f6 as in Rausis-Sokolov, Moscow 1992, is one transposition to the 2...d6 systems examined last chapter.

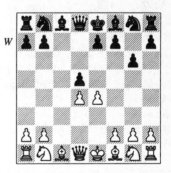

5 e5

Here 5 exd5!? ♘f6 will transpose to the Caro Kann (either the Panov-Botvinnik attack variation, *ECO* code B14, with 1 e4 c6 2 d4 d5 3 exd5 cxd5 4 c4 ♘f6 5 ♘c3 g6 6 cxd5, etc., or *ECO* code B10 starting 1 e4 c6 2 c4 d5 3 exd5 cxd5 4 cxd5 ♘f6, etc.). This is a major branch of the Caro, and so regretfully must fall outside the scope of this book. However it should be noted that White's move-order via the c3 Sicilian does rules out one of his most testing lines, 1 e4 c6 2 d4 d5 3 exd5 cxd5 4 c4 ♘f6 5 ♘c3 g6 6 ♕b3 ♗g7 7 cxd5.

5...♘c6 6 ♘c3 ♗g7 7 h3

7 ♘f3 ♗g4 is equal. After 7 ♗e2!? ♘h6 8 h3, 8...f6 9 exf6 exf6 10 ♗f3! ♗e6 11 ♘ge2 0-0 12 ♘f4 ♗f7 13 ♗xd5 favoured White in Groszpeter-Regan, Budapest 1978, but Black should delay ...f6, e.g. 8...0-0 9 ♘f3 (9 ♗f3 ♘f5 10 ♘ge2 e6) 9...f6. However 7 ♗b5!? ♘h6 8 ♘ge2 is reasonable, e.g. 8...0-0 9 0-0 ♔h8 10 ♗f4 f6 11 ♗xc6 bxc6 12 exf6 exf6 13 ♘c1 ♖e8 14 ♘b3 ♘f5 15 ♖e1 ♗f8 16 ♕d2 g5 17 ♗g3 ♘d6 18 h4 ♘c4 19 ♕c2 ± Jonkman-Van Mil, Dutch Ch 1994.

7...f6 8 exf6

8 f4?! ♘h6 9 ♗e3 fxe5 10 fxe5 0-0 11 ♘f3 ♘f5 12 ♗f2 ♗h6 13 ♕e2 ♗f4 ∓ Yanovsky-Hoffmann, Biel 1991.

8...exf6

8...♘xf6 9 ♘f3 0-0 10 ♗d3 ♘h5 ∞ Palkovi-Certek, Hungary 1995.

9 ♘f3 ♘ge7 10 ♗e2 0-0 11 0-0 g5!? 12 ♖e1 ♗f5 13 ♗e3 ♗g6 14 ♖c1 ♕d7 15 h4 h6 16 hxg5 fxg5

The position is unclear. As the rest of the game was a quickplay there is little point in annotating it, but certainly Black looked a little unlucky to emerge into a worse endgame.

17 ♘h2 ♔h8 18 ♗f3 ♖ad8 19 ♘f1 ♘f5 20 ♗g4 ♕f7 21 ♗xf5 ♗xf5 22 ♘g3 ♗g6 23 ♕d2 ♕f6 24

♘ce2 ♖d7 25 f4 g4 26 ♖f1 ♗f5 27 ♘xf5 ♕xf5 28 ♘g3 ♕e6 29 ♖ce1 ♕d6 30 ♕d1 ♖e7 31 ♔h1 h5 32 ♗g1 ♖xe1 33 ♕xe1 ♘xd4 34 ♗xd4 ♗xd4 35 ♘xh5 ♕h6 36 ♕h4 ♖g8 37 ♖d1 ♗f2 38 ♕xf2 ♕xh5+ 39 ♔g1 g3 40 ♕d4+ ♔h7 41 ♕xd5 ♕xd5 42 ♖xd5 ♖c8 43 ♖h5+ ♔g6 44 ♖g5+ ♔f6 45 ♖xg3 ♔f5 46 ♖g7 b6 47 ♖xa7 ♔xf4 48 ♖a4+ ♔g3 49 ♖a3+ **1-0**

Game 69
Feller – Stean
Amsterdam 1978

1 e4 c5 2 c3 b6!?

The ...b6 lines reached via 2...♘f6 have already been covered in Chapter 14. Played on move two, the defence is also quite interesting. Black has the persistent theme of exchanging pawns on d4, followed, if allowed, by the manoeuvre ...♘c6-b4.

3 d4 ♗b7 4 ♗d3 (D)

Otherwise:

a) 4 f3 is playable:

a1) 4...g6 5 ♗e3 d6 6 ♗d3 ♗g7 7 ♘e2 ♘f6 8 0-0 0-0 9 ♘d2 ± Striković-Cebalo, Yugoslav Ch 1989.

a2) 4...d5 5 e5 ♘c6 6 ♗e3 e6 7 f4 ♘h6 8 ♘f3 ♘f5 9 ♗f2 h5 10 ♗d3 ♗e7 11 0-0 g6 12 g3 ♔f8 13 h3 a5 14 ♔g2 c4 15 ♗c2 b5 16 g4 hxg4 17 hxg4 ♘h6 18 ♖h1 ♔g7 19 ♔g3 ♗c8 20 ♗e3 b4 21 ♘bd2 ♗d7 22 ♖h3 a4 23 ♕h1 a3 24 f5 ♘xg4 25 fxg6 fxg6 26 ♔xg4 axb2 27 ♗h6+ ♔g8 28 ♖g1 bxc3 29 ♗xg6 cxd2 30 ♗g5 ♔g7 31 ♖h7+ **1-0** Striković-Paunović, La Coruña 1995 – an amazing game!

a3) 4...e6 5 ♗e3 ♘c6 (5...♘f6 6 ♗d3 ♗e7 7 ♘e2 0-0 8 0-0 d6 9 ♘d2 ♘bd7 10 g4 e5 11 d5 ♘e8 12 a4 a6 13 b4 ♗g5 14 ♗f2 cxb4 15 cxb4 a5 16 bxa5 bxa5 17 ♖b1 ♗a6 18 ♗xa6 ♖xa6 19 ♘c4 ± Striković-Aleksić, Yugoslavia 1990) 6 a3 ♘h6 (6...d5!? 7 e5 f6 8 f4 ♘h6 with counterplay – Cherniaev) 7 ♗d3 f5 8 ♘h3! ± fxe4 9 fxe4 ♕h4+ 10 ♘f2 ♗d6 11 g3 ♕e7 12 ♘d2 ± Cherniaev-Arkhipov, Sochi 1993.

b) Instead unclear play results from 4 d5 ♘f6 5 f3 (5 ♗d3 is answered by 5...c4! with counterplay, but not 5...e6 6 c4 b5 7 ♘c3 exd5 8 exd5 b4 9 ♘b1 ♗e7 10 ♘f3 0-0 11 0-0 ♖e8 12 b3 d6 13 a4 g6 14 ♖a2! ± and the rook swings over to e2, Benjamin-Fedorowicz, New York 1977) and then 5...e6 6 c4 d6 7 ♘c3 exd5 8 cxd5 g6 9 ♗c4 ♗g7 10 ♘ge2 0-0 11 0-0 ♗a6 12 ♕d3 ♗xc4 13 ♕xc4 a6 14 ♗e3 b5 Hresc-Johansen, Arnhem/Amsterdam 1983 or 5...g6 6 c4 d6 7 ♘c3 ♗g7 8 ♗g5 ♗a6 9 ♕d2 h6 10 ♗e3 ♘c7 11 ♘ge2 a6 12 ♘g3 h5 13 ♗d3 e6 14 0-0 h4 Yilmaz-Cebalo, Kavala 1985.

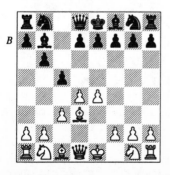

4...♘f6!?

P.Littlewood-Speelman, London 1978 went 4...cxd4 5 cxd4 ♘c6 6 ♘f3 ♘b4 7 ♗c4 (7 ♘c3) 7...♖c8 8 ♘e5 e6 9 ♘c3 f6 (9...♗d6!? 10 ♘b5 ♗b8) 10 ♕h5+ g6 11 ♘xg6 hxg6 12 ♕xh8 ±.

Instead 4...e6 (now an Owen's Defence, *ECO* code B00) and now White has tried several moves:

a) 5 ♘e2!? ♘f6 6 ♘d2 leading to a position examined in the note at White's fifth move.

b) 5 f4 ♘f6 6 ♕e2 cxd4 7 cxd4 ♘c6 8 ♘f3 ♘b4 9 ♘c3 ♘xd3+ 10 ♕xd3 ♗b4 ∓ Barnes-Owen, London 1862.

c) 5 ♘d2?! (now Black's knight speeds to b4) 5...cxd4 6 cxd4 ♘c6 7 ♘gf3 ♘b4 8 ♗b1 (8 ♗e2 ♖c8 9 0-0 ♘f6 10 e5 ♘fd5 11 a3? ♘c2 12 ♖a2 ♘f4 13 b3 ♘e3!! 14 fxe3 ♖xc1 won White's queen in Van der Sterren-Šahović, Lone Pine 1979) 8...d5 9 e5 ♗a6 10 ♘f1 ♕d7 11 a3 ♘c6 12 ♘e3 ♘ge7 13 ♗d3 ♗xd3 14 ♕xd3 ♘g6 15 g3 and now not 15...♗e7? 16 h4! Lasker-S.Bernstein, New York 1977, but 15...f6 16 exf6 gxf6 and Black gets a good game by advancing in the centre.

d) 5 ♘h3 cxd4 (5...♘f6 6 f3 ♘c6 7 ♗e3 ♗e7 8 0-0 0-0 9 a3 ♖c8 10 ♘d2 cxd4 11 cxd4 d6 12 f4 ♖e8 13 g4?! g6 14 g5?! ♘h5 ∓ Suradiradja-Chandler, Wellington 1978) 6 0-0 dxc3 (after 6...♘f6!? 7 e5 ♘d5 8 cxd4 ♘c6 9 ♗e4 ♘ce7 Sax-Basman, London 1975 continued 10 ♕f3 ♗c6 11 ♘g5 f5 12 exf6 ♘xf6 13 ♗xc6 ♘xc6 14 ♘xe6! winning) 7 ♘xc3 ♘c6 8 f4 ♗c5+ 9 ♔h1 ♕e7 10 a3 0-0-0 11 b4 ♗d4 12 ♗d2 ♘f6 13

♕a4 e5 14 ♕b3 ♔b8 ½-½ Sax-Ša-hović, Vrbas 1977.

e) 5 ♘f3 ♘f6 6 ♕e2 (here this queen move is good, as Black cannot force his knight to b4; 6 ♗g5!? h6 – 6...♗e7 – 7 ♗xf6 ♕xf6 8 0-0 cxd4 9 cxd4 ♘c6 10 ♗b5 ± Blackburne-Owen, London 1862) 6...♗e7 (6...d5 7 e5 ♘fd7 8 ♗g5 ♕c7 9 0-0 ♘c6 10 ♘bd2 h6 11 ♗e3 0-0-0 12 b4 c4 13 ♗c2 probably favours White, although after 13...g5 14 b5 ♘a5 15 h3 ♗a3 White discovered his queenside blocked in Konstantinopolsky-Munchik, Moscow 1966, and was duly slaughtered on the other wing; instead after 6...cxd4 7 cxd4, 7...♘c6 meets 8 a3!, while 7...♗b4+ 8 ♘bd2 d5 9 e5 ♘fd7 10 0-0 a5 11 ♖d1 ♗a6 12 ♘f1 ♗xd3 13 ♖xd3 ♘c6 14 ♘g5 ± was played in Hübner-Larsen, Bugojno 1978) 7 0-0 (7 e5 ♘d5 8 dxc5 ♗xc5 9 ♘g5 ♘c6 10 f4 ♗e7 11 ♘e4 ♖c8 12 0-0 0-0 13 ♘bd2 b5!? 14 ♘f3 a6 ∞ Van Mil-Rogers, Tilburg 1993) 7...♘c6 8 dxc5 bxc5 9 e5 ♘d5 10 c4 ♘db4 11 ♗e4 ♖b8 12 a3 ♘a6 13 ♘c3 ± Florian-I.Polgar, Hungary 1974.

Returning to the position after 4...♘f6 (D).

5 ♕e2

This queen move would be a strong plan if it did not allow Black a tactical finesse to get his knight to b4 and exchange White's d3 bishop. Therefore a critical continuation is 5 ♘d2!?:

a) 5...e6 6 ♘gf3 ♘c6 is slow: after 7 a3, 7...d6 8 0-0 ♗e7 9 ♕e2 ♕c7 10 ♖e1 h6 11 b4 g5 12 bxc5 dxc5 13 ♘b3 0-0-0 14 dxc5 bxc5 15 ♗a6 ± was Vaganian-Regan, Mexico 1977. Sometimes Black plays these positions like a French Defence, e.g. 7...d5 8 e5 c4 9 ♗c2 ♘d7 10 ♘f1 h6 11 ♘g3 b5 12 0-0 ♘b6 13 ♘h5 ± Borge-Conquest, Politiken Cup 1992. 7 0-0!? ♗e7 8 ♖e1 ♕c7 9 a3 d5 10 e5 ♘d7 11 b4 c4 12 ♗c2 0-0-0 13 ♘f1 ♖dg8? 14 ♘g5! ♗xg5 15 ♗xg5 ♘f8 16 f4 ± was Torre-Larsen, Geneva 1977.

b) 5...cxd4 6 cxd4 ♘c6 (D) and here:

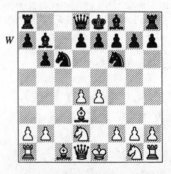

b1) 7 ♘gf3 ♘b4! 8 ♗c4!? (8 ♗b1 ♗a6! is clearly fine for Black, e.g. 9 ♘e5 e6 10 a3 ♘c6 11 ♘df3 ♕c7 12 ♗d3 ♗xd3 13 ♕xd3 d6 14 ♘xc6 ♕xc6 15 ♘d2 ♗e7 ∓ Coupet-Minasian, Cannes 1992) 8...b5! (in

order to decoy the bishop; 8...♘xe4?!
9 ♘xe4 ♗xe4 10 ♗xf7+ ♔xf7 11
♘g5+ and 12 ♘xe4) 9 ♗xb5 ♕a5
(9...♘xe4 looks riskier, though after
10 0-0 ♘f6 11 ♕a4 e6 12 ♘e5 a6 13
♗e2 ♗e7 14 ♘df3 0-0 15 ♗d2 a5
Black had a fine game in Mulder-
Grooten, Leeuwarden 1995) 10 ♗c4
♘xe4 11 0-0 ♘d6 12 a3 ♘xc4 13
♘xc4 ♕a6 = Handoko-Miles, Sydney 1991 and Sevillano-Wang Zili,
Penang 1991.

b2) 7 ♘e2!? (from here the knight
can always leap to c3, cutting down
Black's play on the c-file) and then:

b21) 7...e6 transposes to Ermen-
kov-Šahović, Jurmala 1978: 8 a3
♗e7 9 0-0-0 0-0 10 b4 d6 11 ♗b2 ♖c8
12 ♘g3 ♘d7 13 f4 with a looming
kingside attack.

b22) Instead 7...g6 8 0-0 ♗g7 9
a3 0-0 10 ♖e1 d6 11 ♖b1 e6 12 ♘f3
e5 13 d5 ♘e7 14 ♘g3 ± was Sma-
gin-Miles, Århus 1993.

b23) 7...♘b4 8 ♗b1 ♗a6 deserves more attention, although 9
♘f3 ♕c7 10 ♘c3 e6 11 a3 ♘c6 12
♗g5 ♘h5 13 d5 ♘a5 14 e5 was
clearly good for White in Schmitt-
diel-Grooten, Wijk aan Zee 1993.

b24) 7...e5 8 d5 ♘b4 9 ♗b1 ♗c5
10 0-0 (10 ♘c3!? 0-0 11 a3 ♘a6 12
0-0 ♘c7 13 ♗d3 ♘fe8?! 14 ♘f3
♕e7 15 b4 ♗d6 16 ♗g5 f6 17 ♗e3
g6 18 ♖e1! with advantage, Smagin-
Milov, Iraklion 1993; Smagin gives
10...a5 11 ♘b3 ♘a6 12 0-0 intending ♘xc5 and f4 ±) 10...a5 11 ♘f3
(11 a3 ♘a6 12 ♘g3 h5!? 13 ♘c4
♘g4 14 ♘f5 ♕f6 15 h3 g6 led to
great complications in Kharlov-Mi-
nasian, USSR 1991) 11...♕e7 12 a3

♘a6 13 ♘g3 g6 14 ♗d3 ♗d6 15 b3
♘g8 16 ♖e1 h5 17 h3 ± Rausis-
Wang Zili, Copenhagen 1995.

5...cxd4 6 cxd4 ♘c6 (D)

7 ♘f3

Very complex is 7 d5!? ♘b4
(7...♘e5!? 8 ♗b5 a6 9 ♗a4 e6 10 f4
♕c7 11 ♘c3 ♘c4 12 ♘f3 ♗b4 13
0-0-0 0-0 14 dxe6 ♗xc3 15 bxc3 ♘xe4
16 ♗c2 f5 ∓ Castellano-Kurajica,
Las Palmas 1994 but White can improve) and here:

a) 8 ♘c3?! ♘xd3+ (8...e6 9 ♘f3
exd5 10 e5 ♘e4 11 ♘xd5 ∞ Sowray-
Rogers, London 1988) 9 ♕xd3 e6 10
d6 ♖c8 11 ♘ge2 b5 12 0-0 b4 13
♘b5 ♗xe4 ∞ David-Murey, France
1993.

b) 8 ♗b5!? a6 9 ♗a4 a5 10 ♘c3
e5 (10...♗a6 11 ♗b5 ♗xb5 12
♘xb5 ♕c8 13 ♘c3 e6 14 ♗g5 ♗e7
15 ♖c1 ♕b7 16 ♘f3 0-0 17 d6 ♗d8
18 0-0 ± Novoselsky-Veličković, Yugoslav Ch 1992 or 10...e6 11 ♘b5!?
♘a6 12 ♗g5 ♗b4+ 13 ♔f1 e5 14
♘f3 0-0 15 ♘xe5 ♖e8 16 ♘g4
♗xd5 17 ♗xf6 Van Mil-Käser, Bundesliga 1993) 11 ♘f3 ♕b8 12 0-0
♘a6 13 ♗g5 ♗e7 14 ♘d2 ♘c5 15
♗b5 0-0 16 ♘c4 ♘xd5 17 exd5

♗xg5 18 ♕xe5 ± Van Mil-Johansen, Wijk aan Zee 1993. Food for thought.

7...♘b4! 8 ♘c3 ♘xd3+ 9 ♕xd3 e6 10 ♗g5 *(D)*

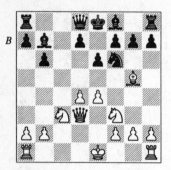

The position is roughly equal. An alternative was 10 0-0!? ♗b4 11 ♖e1 (11 e5 ♘d5 12 ♗g5 ♗e7 13 ♗xe7 ♕xe7 14 ♘d2 0-0 15 f4 f6 16 ♘ce4 fxe5 17 fxe5 ♖f4 18 ♘d6 ♗c6 = Chandler-Speelman, British Ch 1976) 11...h6 (11...♖c8 12 ♗d2 ♗xc3 13 ♗xc3 0-0 14 ♗b4 d6 15 ♘d2 with a slight advantage for White, Van Wijgerden-B.Ivanović, Plovdiv 1983) 12 a3?! (12 ♗d2!?) 12...♗xc3 13 bxc3 ♕c7 14 e5 ♘d5 15 c4 ♘e7 16 ♗d2?! ♖c8 17 ♖ac1 ♗a6 and due to White's faulty play his c-pawn is falling, Hmadi-Romero, Novi Sad OL 1990.

10...h6

10...♗e7!? 11 0-0 0-0 12 ♖ac1 d6 13 ♖fe1 a6 14 a4 h6 15 ♗d2? (15 ♗h4) 15...d5 16 e5 ♘e4 17 ♗f4 ♖c8 18 ♘d2 ♘xc3 19 ♖xc3 ♕d7 ∓ L.Fernandez-Rubinetti, Buenos Aires 1993.

11 ♗h4

11 ♗xf6?! ♕xf6 12 0-0 ♗b4 13 ♘d2 0-0 14 a3 ♗xc3 15 ♕xc3 ♖fc8

16 ♕d3 ♖c7 17 ♖ac1 ♖ac8 ∓ Trabert-Miles, Iraklio 1993.

11...g5?

Once again the situation after 11...♗e7!? is not so clear. 12 0-0 0-0 13 ♖ac1 d5 14 e5 ♘e4 15 ♗xe7 ♕xe7 16 ♘d2 ♘xc3 17 ♖xc3 ♖fc8 was marginally more comfortable for White in Engelbert-Schläger, Germany 1989, due to Black's bishop being restricted by his own pawns. However, after 18 ♖fc1 ♕b4! (gaining counterplay against the b-pawn) 19 ♖xc8+ (19 b3!?) 19...♖xc8 20 ♖xc8+ ♗xc8 21 ♕c3 ♕xc3 22 bxc3 Black should not have lost the ensuing endgame.

12 ♗g3 ♗b4 13 ♘d2 ♘h5 14 ♗e5? (14 a3 ♗f8 15 d5 followed by 0-0-0 ± Stean) **14...♖g8** (preferable is 14...f6! 15 ♕f3 fxe5 16 ♕xh5+ ♔e7 17 dxe5 ♕c7 18 0-0 ♕xe5 ∓ Hünerkopf-Schlemermeyer, Bundesliga 1983) **15 0-0 ♘f4 16 ♕b5? a5 ∓ 17 ♕a4 ♗a6 18 ♖fe1 ♘d3 19 ♖e3 ♘xe5 20 dxe5 ♕c7 21 a3 ♗c5 22 ♖h3 g4! 23 ♖h5 ♗xf2+! 24 ♔h1** (24 ♔xf2 ♕c5+) **24...♖g5 25 ♖xh6 ♕xe5 26 g3 ♖c8 27 ♖d1 ♖c7 28 ♔g2 ♗d4 29 ♘db1 ♖c4 30 ♕c2 ♗b7 31 ♘d2 ♗xc3! 32 ♘xc4 ♗xe4+ 0-1**

Game 70
Stripunsky – Maksimenko
Kherson 1990

1 e4 c5 2 c3 e5!?

A number of Russian players have experimented with this line. 2...e5 is not as anti-positional as it first appears, as positions often resemble those of a Lopez or Two Knight's

Defence, in which the move ...c5 is often played at some stage.

3 ♘f3 ♘c6 *(D)*

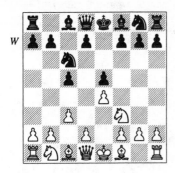

4 ♗c4

Most natural, since 4 ♗b5 gives a Ruy Lopez type of position where Black's pawn is not badly placed on c5 very early: 4...♘f6 5 0-0 ♘xe4 6 ♖e1 ♘d6 7 ♗xc6?! dxc6 8 ♖xe5+?! ♗e7 9 ♖xc5 f6! 10 ♖h5 ♗g4 11 ♖h4 h5 12 h3 g5 13 hxg4 gxh4 14 ♘xh4 hxg4 15 ♕xg4 ♕d7 ∓ Vorotnikov-Filipenko, USSR 1987 or better 4...a6!? 5 ♗a4 (5 ♗xc6 dxc6 6 ♘xe5 ♕e7 7 d4 cxd4 8 cxd4 f6 9 ♘f3 ♕xe4+ 10 ♗e3 ♗b4+ 11 ♘c3 ♘e7 = Ardeleanu-Sandu, Romanian Ch 1992) 5...b5 6 ♗c2 ♕c7 7 0-0 d6 8 ♖e1 g6 9 a4 ♖b8 10 d3 ♗g7 11 ♗b3 ♘ge7 = Smagin-Lorenz, Næstved 1988.

Instead 4 d4!? can be very sharp: 4...exd4 (Filipenko prefers this to 4...cxd4 when he feels 5 ♗c4!? is more dangerous – *although this contradicts his view that after 4 ♗c4, 4...♕c7 discourages 5 d4 on account of 5...cxd4 – editor's note*) 5 cxd4 (after 5 ♗c4 ♘f6, 6 ♘g5 can be met by 6...♘e5) 5...cxd4 and here:

a) 6 ♘xd4 ♘f6 7 ♘c3 (7 ♘xc6 dxc6 8 ♕xd8+ ♔xd8 = has also been seen a few times) 7...♗b4 8 ♘xc6 (8 ♗c4!? 0-0 9 0-0 ♗xc3 10 bxc3 ♘xe4 11 ♗a3 d6 12 ♖e1 ∞ was an interesting pawn offer in D.Lawson-C.Duncan, Dublin Z 1993) 8...dxc6 (8...bxc6 9 ♗d3 0-0 10 0-0 is less clear) 9 ♕xd8+ ♔xd8 10 ♗g5 h6 11 0-0-0+ (11 ♗xf6+ gxf6 is nothing) 11...♔e7 12 ♗h4 (12 ♗d2 ♗e6 with an equal position, Trabert-Galliamova, Adelaide wom jr Wch 1988) 12...g5 13 ♗g3 ♗e6 with equality in the game Nemirovski-Chevallier, Val Thorens 1989.

b) 6 ♗c4 ♘f6 (7...♗b4+!?) 7 0-0 ♗c5 (this line is very similar to the Max Lange Attack of the Two Knight's Defence, with the difference being that here the pawns on c2 and c7 are absent; it is not clear that this necessarily favours Black – whilst his d-pawn is passed his king is more exposed if he castles queenside) 8 e5 d5 9 exf6 dxc4 10 ♖e1+ (10 fxg7 ♖g8 and now 11 ♕c2!? ♖xg7 12 ♕xc4 was an original idea in Lobianidze-Nadanian, Erevan 1996, but it fell just short after 12...♗d6 13 ♖e1+ ♗e6 14 ♗g5 ♕a5 15 ♘bd2 ♖xg5 16 ♖xe6+ fxe6 17 ♕xe6+ ♗e7; instead after 11 ♗g5 ♗e7 12 ♗xe7, 12...♕xe7? 13 ♘xd4 ♘xd4 14 ♕xd4, as in Šibarević-Pavlović, Yugoslav Ch 1992, is obviously good for White, but 12...♔xe7! is the right move by analogy with the Max Lange) 10...♗e6 11 ♘g5 ♕d5 12 ♘c3 ♕f5 13 ♘ce4 0-0-0 14 fxg7 (14 ♘xe6 fxe6 15 g4 ♕d5 16 fxg7 ♖hg8 17 ♘f6 ♕d6 18 ♗h6 d3 19

♘xg8 ♖xg8 20 ♕f3 with a distinct advantage for White, Sivokho-Ono-prienko, USSR Cht 1988 but again 15...♕e5 is correct by analogy with the Max Lange) 14...♖hg8 15 ♘xc5 ♕xc5 16 ♖xe6? (16 ♘xe6 fxe6 17 ♕g4 ♕f5 18 ♕xf5 exf5 favours Black, In.Meyer-Elsen, Germany 1989) 16...fxe6 17 ♘xe6 ♕d5 18 ♘xd8 ♖xg7! 19 f3 ♔xd8 ∓ Vorot-nikov-Filipenko, USSR 1987. More tests are needed.

4...♕c7!?

This is Alexander Filipenko's invention to discourage White from an early d4 (as the c4 bishop will come under potential attack from Black's queen). In addition the d8-square is freed for Black's knight to defend in case White should begin an assault on f7. Instead 4...♗e7 is too passive, and Black is asking for trouble after 4...♕b6?! 5 0-0 ♘f6 6 d4 (Sresh-nikov-Khenkin, Moscow 1989) or 4...♕f6?! 5 d4! (V.L.Ivanov-Iva-nets, Moscow 1995).

After the old move 4...♘f6 Black faces sacrificial dangers similar to some variations of the Two Knight's Defence: 5 ♘g5! d5 6 exd5 ♘xd5 (6...♘a5 7 ♗b5+ ♗d7 8 ♕e2 and then 8...♗xb5 9 ♕xb5+ ♘d7 10 d3 a6 11 ♕a4 b5 12 ♕e4 ± was Wolff-Andonov, St John 1988; Black can try 8...♗d6, as in Martinenko-Luk-ovnikov, Belovechensk 1988, but White is better) 7 d4 (7 ♕f3 ♕xg5 8 ♗xd5 ♕g6!? is possible for Black, but simplest for White is the finesse 7 ♕h5! g6 8 ♕f3 ♗e6 9 ♘xe6 fxe6 10 d3 ♗e7 11 ♘d2 ± Okhotnik-Kapetanović, Romania 1988 and 11

♗h6 ± Dolgov-Podbolotov, Corr 1991) 7...cxd4 (7...♗e7!?) 8 ♘xf7!? (or 8 ♕b3 ∞ when Black must choose between 8...f6 and 8...♗e6 9 ♘xe6 fxe6 10 ♕xb7 ♖c8) 8...♔xf7 9 ♕f3+ ♔e6 10 0-0 ♘a5 *(D)* and here White can try:

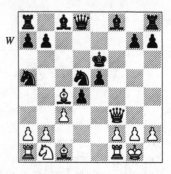

a) 11 ♗d3 ♕f6 12 ♕e4 ♘f4 13 b4 ♘xd3 14 ♕xd3 ♘c6 (14...♔f7!? 15 bxa5 ♗d6?! 16 cxd4 exd4 17 ♘d2 ♗f5 18 ♘e4 ♗xe4 19 ♕xe4 ± Shteinikov-Limarenko, USSR 1988, but 15...♗f5!? ∞) 15 b5 ♘e7 16 ♕c4+ ♔d7 (16...♗f5?! 17 f4 e4 18 g4+! ♔xg4 19 f5 ± and Black's king should not escape White's attack, Shteinikov-Isaev, USSR 1987) 17 cxd4 ♕e6 18 ♕a4 ♘d5 19 ♖e1 e4 20 ♘d2 with a continuing attack for the sacrificed material, Nemtsev-Isaev, USSR 1987.

b) 11 ♗g5!? ♕d6 12 g4 (?! – Burgess; 12 ♗d3 or 12 ♗b5 are alternatives) 12...♕d7? (12...♕c6 and if 13 ♗d3, then 13...♘f4!? Nunn, e.g. 14 ♗e4 ♘h3+!) 13 ♗d3 ♕f7 14 ♗f5+ ♔d6 15 cxd4 ♗xf5 16 dxe5+ ♔xe5 17 gxf5 ♘c6 18 ♖e1+ ♔d6 19 ♖e6+ ♔c5 20 ♗e3+ ♘xe3 21 ♕xe3+ ♔b5 22 ♕d3+ ♔b6 23 ♕b3+ ♔c7

24 ♖xc6+ and White wins, Evans-Saint Amant, 1847 (note that the initial move-order was 1 e4 e5 2 c3 c5 3 ♘f3 ♘c6 4 ♗c4 ♘f6 5 d4 cxd4 6 ♘g5 d5, etc.).

Even with the Captain Evans game the sacrifice on f7 looks murky, so 7 ♕h5! is the safest route to a guaranteed edge.

5 0-0

Sharpest. 5 ♘g5 ♘d8 6 ♕b3 ♘e6 is equal, while 5 ♕b3 is also met by 5...♘d8 (and not 5...♘a5?! 6 ♗xf7+ ♔e7 7 ♕d5 ♘f6 8 ♕xe5+ ♕xe5 9 ♘xe5 d6 10 ♘c4! Ivanchuk). The quiet alternative is 5 d3 ♘f6 (D) and here:

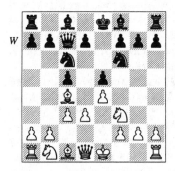

a) 6 ♘g5 ♘d8 7 f4 (inaccurate in this position) 7...exf4 8 0-0 ♗d6 9 ♘a3 a6 10 ♕e1 ♘e6 11 ♘f3 ♗g4 ∓ Karaklajić-Krnić, Yugoslavia 1989. However reasonable was 7 ♕b3 d6 8 f4 h6 9 ♘f3.

b) 6 ♗g5 ♗e7 7 ♘bd2 (7 ♗xf6!? ♗xf6 8 ♘bd2 ♖b8 9 a4 d6 10 ♘f1 ♗e6 11 ♘e3 0-0 12 h4!? ♕d8 13 g4 a6 14 g5 ♗e7 15 ♘h2 b5 16 axb5 axb5 17 ♗d5 ♕d7 18 ♘hg4 gave kingside pressure in Schmittdiel-Lutz, Altensteig 1991 but capturing

on f6 without provocation gives an odd impression) 7...d6 8 ♘f1 ♗e6 9 ♘e3 0-0 10 0-0 ♔h8 11 a3 ♖ab8 12 b4 b5 13 ♗a2 ♖fc8 14 bxc5 dxc5 15 ♘d5 ♕d8 16 ♘xe7 ♕xe7 17 ♗d5 ♕d6 18 ♗xc6 ♖xc6 19 ♗xf6 gxf6 20 d4 cxd4 21 cxd4 exd4 ½-½ Tiviakov-Krasenkov, Polanica Zdroj 1995.

c) 6 0-0 ♗e7 and now:

c1) 7 ♘g5!? (playing for f4) 7...0-0 (after 7...♘d8 8 f4 h6 White does not have to give up the f-pawn: 9 ♘h3 exf4?! 10 ♘xf4 d6 11 ♘h5! ± Sveshnikov-Grosar, Torcy 1990) 8 f4 h6 9 ♘xf7!? ♖xf7 10 ♗xf7+ ♔xf7 11 fxe5 ♕xe5 12 ♗f4 ♕e6 13 ♘a3 ♔g8 14 ♘b5 ∞ as in Sveshnikov-Sherbakov, Cheliabinsk 1989 and P.Stimpson-M.Johnson, Corr 1991.

c2) A better try for an edge is the modest 7 a4, followed by 8 ♘bd2 or 8 ♘a3. Then White plays a standard strategy of manoeuvring his queen's knight round to e3 to control the d5-square.

c3) 7 ♗b3 is also common idea in these types of positions as a prophylactic measure against ...♘a5.

5...♘f6

On 5...♗e7 possible is 6 ♘g5!? ♗xg5 7 ♕h5 d5 8 exd5 ♗f4 9 dxc6 ♘f6 10 ♕e2 0-0 11 cxb7 ♗xb7 12 d3 ± Smagin-Brendel, Dortmund 1993.

6 ♘g5

6 ♖e1 ♗e7 (6...d6 7 h3 ♗e7 8 a4 0-0 9 ♘a3 ♘a5 10 ♗a2 ♗d7 11 d4 a6 12 b4 cxb4 13 cxb4 ♘c6 14 b5 ± Maciejewski-Levin, Polish Cht 1990) 7 d4!? (of course White can continue

slowly with 7 d3 or 7 ♗b3; also 7 ♘a3 a6 8 ♘c2 0-0 9 d4 d6 10 dxe5 dxe5 11 ♘e3 ♘a5 12 ♘d5 ♘xd5 13 ♗xd5 ♗g4 14 h3 ♗h5 15 g4!? ♗g6 16 h4 h5 17 ♘g5 ♗xg5 18 ♗xg5 hxg4 19 ♕xg4 ± Berelovich-Beshukov, Azov 1993) 7...d6 (7...cxd4 8 cxd4 ♘xd4 9 ♘xd4 is risky for Black: 9...♕xc4 10 ♘f5 or 9...exd4 10 e5 ♕xc4 11 exf6 gxf6 12 b3! ♕c6 13 ♗a3 d6 14 ♘d2 ♖g8 15 ♘e4 ♗e6 16 ♕xd4 with an attack, S.Arkell-Thorsson, Reykjavik 1990) 7...d6 8 ♘a3 0-0 9 dxc5?! dxc5 10 ♗d5 ♗g4 11 h3 ♗h5 ∓ Blatny-Filipenko, Katowice 1992.

6 ♘g5 ♘d8 7 f4!? *(D)*

7 ♕b3 ♘e6 8 d4 cxd4 9 cxd4 ♘xd4 10 ♗xf7+ ♔e7 11 ♕b4+ d6 12 ♘c3 h6 13 ♘d5+ ♘xd5 14 ♗xd5 hxg5 15 ♗xg5+ ♔e8 ∓ Ng-Filipenko, Sydney 1988 or 7 d3 h6 8 ♘f3 d6 = Sariego-Guerra, Cuban Ch 1991.

7...exf4

If 7...♘e6 then 8 ♗xe6 dxe6 9 fxe5 ♕xe5 10 d4 ± M.Marić-Arakhamia, Biel 1990. On 7...h6 8 ♘f3 exf4 9 e5 Black landed in trouble after the continuation 9...♘g8 10 ♕e2 ♘e7 11 d4 cxd4 12 cxd4 ♘g6 13 ♘c3 ♘e6 14 ♔h1 ♗b4 15 ♘d5 ± in

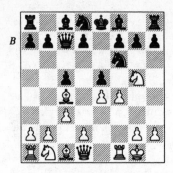

Kiik-Galliamova, St Petersburg 1996 but 9...♘h7 is less clear, for example 10 ♕e2 ♘g5 11 d4 cxd4 12 cxd4 ♘xf3+ 13 ♖xf3 ♘e6 Angelov-Delchev, Bankia 1991.

8 e5 d5 9 ♗b5+

Also dangerous for Black is 9 exf6 dxc4 10 d4 cxd4?! 11 ♗xf4 ♗d6 12 fxg7 ♖g8 13 ♗xd6 ♕xd6 14 ♘e4 1-0 de Armas-T.Hernandez, Cuba 1991.

9...♘d7 10 d4 ♗e7 11 ♗xf4 ♕b6 12 ♗a4 cxd4 13 cxd4 ♕xb2 14 e6 fxe6 15 ♗e5 ♗xg5 16 ♕h5+ ♘f7 17 ♕xf7+ ♔d8 18 ♕xg7 ♗e3+ 19 ♔h1 ♖e8 20 ♗f6+ ♔c7 21 ♕g3+ ♔b6 22 ♕xe3 ♕xa1 23 ♕b3+ 1-0.

Not totally clear by any means, but White has scored several quick victories in this aggressive 6 ♘g5 line.

Index of Variations

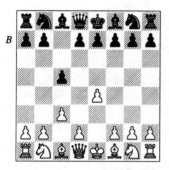

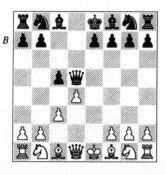

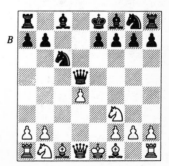

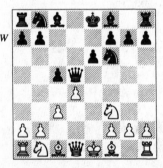

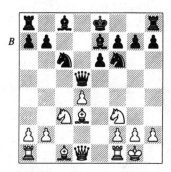

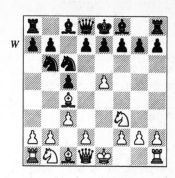

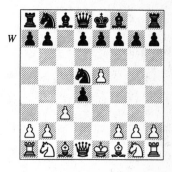

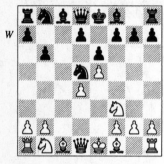